Jesus, Deliver Us

Studies in Peace and Scripture
Institute of Mennonite Studies

Titles in the series

Vol. 1
The Gospel of Peace: A Scriptural Message for Today's World
by Ulrich Mauser; published by W/JK (1992)

Vol. 2
The Meaning of Peace: Biblical Studies
edited by Perry B. Yoder and Willard M. Swartley;
1st ed. published by W/JK (1992)
2nd ed. with expanded bibliography published by IMS (2001)

Vol. 3
The Love of Enemy and Nonretaliation in the New Testament
edited by Willard M. Swartley; published by W/JK (1992)

Vol. 4
Violence Renounced: René Girard, Biblical Studies and Peacemaking
edited by Willard M. Swartley;
published by Pandora Press U.S. and Herald Press (2000)

Vol. 5
Beyond Retribution: A New Testament Vision for Justice, Crime and Punishment
by Christopher D. Marshall; published by Eerdmans (2001)

Vol. 6
Crowned with Glory and Honor: Human Rights in the Biblical Tradition
by Christopher D. Marshall; published by Pandora Press U.S., Herald Press, and Lime Grove House, Auckland, NZ (2002)

Vol. 7
Beautiful upon the Mountains: Biblical Essays on Mission, Peace, and the Reign of God
edited by Mary H. Schertz and Ivan Friesen; published by IMS and Herald Press (2003)
Reprint by Wipf & Stock (2008)

Vol. 8
The Sound of Sheer Silence and the Killing State: The Death Penalty and the Bible
by Millard Lind; published by Cascadia Publishing House and Herald Press (2004)

Vol. 9
Covenant of Peace: The Missing Peace in New Testament Theology and Ethics
by Willard M. Swartley; published by Eerdmans (2006)

Vol. 10
Atonement, Justice, and Peace: The Message of the Cross and the Mission of the Church
by Darrin W. Snyder Belousek; published by Eerdmans (2011)

Vol. 11
A Peaceable Hope: Contesting Violent Eschatology in New Testament Narratives
by David J. Neville;
published by Baker Academic (2013)

Vol. 12
Struggles for Shalom: Peace and Violence across the Testaments
edited by Laura L. Brenneman and Brad D. Schantz; published by Pickwick Publications (2014)

Vol. 13
Rooted and Grounded: Essays on Land and Christian Discipleship, edited by Ryan D. Harker and Janeen Bertsche Johnson, Pickwick (2016)

Vol. 14
The Irony of Power: The Politics of God within Matthew's Narrative, by Dorothy Jean Weaver, Pickwick (2017)

Vol. 15
The Vehement Jesus: Grappling with Troubling Gospel Texts, by David J. Neville, Cascade (2018)

Jesus, Deliver Us

Evil, Exorcism, and *Exousiai*

Willard M. Swartley

 CASCADE *Books* • Eugene, Oregon

JESUS, DELIVER US
Evil, Exorcism, and *Exousiai*

Copyright © 2019 Willard M. Swartley. All rights reserved. Except for brief quotations in critical publications or reviews, no part of this book may be reproduced in any manner without prior written permission from the publisher. Write: Permissions, Wipf and Stock Publishers, 199 W. 8th Ave., Suite 3, Eugene, OR 97401.

Cascade Books
An Imprint of Wipf and Stock Publishers
199 W. 8th Ave., Suite 3
Eugene, OR 97401

www.wipfandstock.com

PAPERBACK ISBN: 978-1-5326-5401-5
HARDCOVER ISBN: 978-1-5326-5402-2
EBOOK ISBN: 978-1-5326-5403-9

Cataloguing-in-Publication data:

Names: Swartley, Willard M.

Title: Jesus, deliver us : evil, exorcism, and *exousiai* / Willard M. Swartley.

Description: Eugene, OR: Cascade Books, 2019 | Includes bibliographical references and index.

Identifiers: ISBN 978-1-5326-5401-5 (paperback) | ISBN 978-1-5326-5402-2 (hardcover) | ISBN 978-1-5326-5403-9 (ebook)

Subjects: LCSH: Spiritual warfare. | Good and evil—Religious aspects—Christianity.

Classification: BS680.G6 .S80 2019 (print) | BS680.G6 (ebook)

Scripture quotations are from the New Revised Standard Version of the Bible, unless otherwise noted.

© 1987 Hope Publishing Company, Carol Stream, IL 60188. All rights reserved. "Praise the One Who Breaks the Darkness." Words: Rusty Edwards. In Chapter 5. Used by permission.

© 1966 Cristo Music. Text by Tom Booth. Here I Am (81036). Stanzas 1 and 3 plus refrain for "Here I am." In Chapter 8. Published by Spirit & Song, a division of OCP. 5536 NE Hassalo, Portland, OR 97213. All rights reserved. Used with permission.

© Lutheran World Federation, Geneva, Switzerland. "Christ has arisen." In Chapter 12. (stephane.gallay@lutheranworld.org). Permission granted.

Baker Publishing Group. Granted "fair use" of the 124 words cited in chapter 1 from Steven Bouma-Prediger, *For the Beauty of the Earth*.

Eerdmans. Granted permission to utilize parts, especially in Chapter 6 on Paul, from *Covenant of Peace*.

Manufactured in the U.S.A. 01/23/20

Dedicated to those
who have been set free
by the Name and Power
of the Lord Jesus Christ.

Prayer
Lord God, Jesus Christ, Holy Spirit,
Keep those who read this book secure in Jesus Christ.
Protect them from all evil and the evil one.
We thank you for your salvation and deliverance.
In the strong name of Jesus, amen.

I love you, O Lord, my strength.
The Lord is my rock, my fortress, and my deliverer,
my God, my rock in whom I take refuge,
my shield, and the horn of my salvation, my stronghold.
I call upon the Lord, who is worthy to be praised,
so I shall be saved from my enemies.

—Psalm 18:1–3

But I say to you,
Love your enemies and pray for those who persecute you,
so that you may be children of your Father in heaven;
for he makes his sun rise on the evil and on the good,
and sends rain on the righteous and on the unrighteous.

—Matthew 5:44–45

Contents

List of Diagrams and Tables | ix
Series Preface | xi
Acknowledgments | xv
Preface | xvii
List of Abbreviations | xix

Introduction | 1

Part I
Progressions in Deliverance from Evil
Crucial Journeys within Scripture

1. Scriptural Portrayal of Evil | 15
2a. From Killing the Enemy to Loving the Enemy | 37
2b. Two Major Transformations: Land and Enemy | 60
3. Evil and Deliverance in Psalms, Proverbs, and Prophets | 78

Part II
Biblical Perspectives on Deliverance
Multi-dimensions of Deliverance from Evil

4. Old Testament to Synoptic Gospels: Mark | 105
5. Matthew and Luke–Acts | 127
6. Paul: Victory over Evil | 148
7. John's Gospel, Letters, and Revelation | 173
8. Hebrews, James, 1–2 Peter, Jude | 198

Part III

Biblical Practices for Deliverance and Witness to the Powers
Toward Faithful Responses

9. The Early (and Later) Church's Responses | 219
10. Christian Witness to Christ's Lordship Over the Powers | 236
11. Deliverance Healing: Theory, Discernment, and Methods | 259
12. Embracing a Holistic Approach to Jesus' Victory Over Evil | 280

Summary and Conclusion | 300

Appendix 1: Resources: Prayers for Healing-Deliverance | 311
Appendix 2: Case Reports of Exorcisms by Dean Hochstetler | 318
Appendix 3: Treatment of Evil in Texts on NT Theology or NT Ethics | 326

Bibliography | 329
Author/Editor Index | 357
Subject Index | 365
Ancient Documents Index | 379

Diagrams and Tables

Diagram 2b.1 Parallels between Deuteronomy and Luke's Central Section | 68

Diagram 3.2 *Evil* and *Deliverance* in the Psalms | 90

Diagram 4.1 YHWH's Politics versus Israel's Politics | 113

Diagram 5.1 Chiasm: Lord's Prayer at Center of the Sermon on the Mount | 130

Diagram 5.2 Luke's Chiasm with Jesus' Emphasis on *Release* | 140

Diagram 6.0 Biblical theological contexts and language for evil in OT and NT | 152

Diagram 6.1 Chiasm of Colossians 2:13–15: Only "b" Components Have Finite Verb | 157

Diagram 7.1 Alternate loyalties: *world* or *God* | 178

Diagram 7.2 Revelation's Mode and Scope of Faith-Proclamation | 186

Diagram 8.1 Psalm 34/Romans 12/1 Peter | 210

Diagram 10.1 Issues for Speaking Truth to Government | 247

Table 7.1 Church, Evil, and Victory in Revelation | 187

Table 10.1 Gushee's Ten Priorities for Witness to Government | 247

Series Preface

VISIONS OF PEACE ABOUND in the Bible, whose pages are also filled with the language of violence. In this respect, the Bible is thoroughly at home in the modern world, whether as a literary classic or as a unique sacred text. This is, perhaps, a part of the Bible's realism: bridging the distance between its world and our own is a history filled with visions of peace accompanying the reality of violence and war. That alone would justify study of peace and war in the Bible. However, for those communities in which the Bible is sacred Scripture, the matter is more urgent. For them, it is crucial to understand what the Bible says about peace—and about war. These issues have often divided Christians, and the way Christians have understood them has had terrible consequences for Jews and, indeed, for the world. A series of scholarly investigations cannot hope to resolve these issues, but it can hope, as this one does, to aid our understanding of them.

Over the past century a substantial body of literature has grown up around the topic of the Bible and war. Numerous studies have been devoted to historical questions about ancient Israel's conception and conduct of war and about the position of the early church on participation in the Roman Empire and its military. It is not surprising that many of these studies have been motivated by theological and ethical concerns, which may themselves be attributed to the Bible's own seemingly disjunctive preoccupation with peace and, at the same time, with war. If not within the Bible itself, then at least from Aqiba and Tertullian, the question has been raised whether—and if so, then on what basis—those who worship God may legitimately participate in war. With the Reformation, the churches divided on this question. The division was unequal, with the majority of Christendom agreeing that, however regrettable war may be, Christians have biblical warrant for participating in it. A minority countered that, however necessary war may appear, Christians have a biblical mandate to avoid it. Modern historical studies have served to bolster one side of this division or the other.

Meanwhile, it has become clear that a narrow focus on participation in war is not the only way, and likely not the best way, to approach the Bible on the topic of peace. War and peace are not simply two sides of the same coin; each is broader than its contrast with the other. Since the twentieth century and refinement of weapons and modes of mass destruction, the violence of war has been an increasingly urgent concern. Peace, on the other hand, is not just the absence of war but the well-being of all people. In spite of this agreement, the number of studies devoted to the Bible and peace is still quite small, especially in English. Consequently, answers to the most basic questions remain to be settled. Among these questions is that of what the Bible means in speaking of *shalom* or *eirēnē*, the Hebrew and the Greek terms usually translated into English as "peace." By the same token, what the Bible has to say about peace is not limited to its use of these two terms. Questions remain about the relation of peace to considerations of justice, integrity, and—in the broadest sense—salvation. And of course there still remains the question of the relation between peace and war. In fact, what the Bible says about peace is often framed in the language of war. The Bible very often uses martial imagery to portray God's own action, whether it be in creation, in judgment against or in defense of Israel, or in the cross and resurrection of Jesus Christ—actions aimed at achieving peace.

This close association of peace and war presents serious problems for the contemporary appropriation of the Bible. Are human freedom, justice, and liberation—and the liberation of creation—furthered or hindered by the martial, frequently royal, and pervasively masculine terms in which the Bible speaks of peace? These questions cannot be answered by the rigorous and critical exegesis of the biblical texts alone; they demand serious moral, theological, and historical reflection of the kind done in this volume.

For some, this book will seem like a departure from the other books in the series with its attention on warfare that is spiritual in nature. Others, however, are invested—through study and action—in deliverance ministries, as this book highlights, and will appreciate Swartley's contention that these are ministries of *shalom*. Indeed, he frames *Deliver Us, Jesus* as a companion volume to his *Covenant of Peace* (2006). Regardless of one's cosmology about evil and its role in the world, in this book you will find careful biblical scholarship and theological reflection in connection with the real world, hallmarks of Swartley's work.

Studies in Peace and Scripture is sponsored by the Institute of Mennonite Studies, the research agency of the Anabaptist Mennonite Biblical Seminary. The seminary and the tradition it represents have a particular interest in peace and, even more so, an abiding interest in the Bible. We hope that this ecumenical series will contribute to a deeper understanding of both.

Laura L. Brenneman, New Testament Editor

Ben C. Ollenburger, Old Testament Editor

Acknowledgments

I GRATEFULLY ACKNOWLEDGE THE help of many readers, most of whom have read portions and given insightful responses: Mark Bredin, Roy Hange, Ted Lewis, Jim and Sally Longley, Bernadine Mast, Pam Short, Darrin Snyder Belousek, Dorothy Jean Weaver, and Drew Strait. I credit Ted Lewis for the alliteration in the titles of the three parts of the book, giving helpful suggestions, and encouraging me to move forward. Roy Hange said, only a few people could combine the two foci of this book; you should do it; it's a timely contribution. Chapters 10 and 11 show portions of his and the Longley's contributions. Dorothy Jean Weaver carefully read the first half of the manuscript in an early draft and made numerous suggestions (some important corrections). At a late stage Bernadine Mast diligently read the entire manuscript with care for details, occasionally improving word choice and correcting infelicities. Her encouragement and appreciation for its content spurred me toward the finish line. Drew Strait pointed me to key sources on Luke-Acts, especially Kavin Rowe's work. Several people helped with title choice, which has gone through several mutations: Willard Roth in the early stage, Leslie Rafaniello toward the end. But Mary gets it right at the very end. Numerous friends encouraged me in the project. For editing of a few parts I thank Willard Roth and Dan Shenk for their help. The series editors, Ben Ollenburger and Laura Brenneman, after seeing the initial chapters and "Contents" accepted the book into the SPS series. I am grateful for their counsel as well.

While the content of this book would have been impossible without the help of these friends, academic and pastoral, the shortcomings of the project—and there are some to be sure—are due to my limitations and infelicities. I am indebted to Mary, my spouse, for her help, and patient endurance through the "long night" of this book's composition. She is a sharp copy-reader, honed by her teaching office skills. She caught various mistakes. I am also grateful to the Wipf & Stock staff, first for accepting the book for publication, and then the cordial help of Rae Harris, Matthew Wimer, Calvin Jaffarian, and editor Rodney Clapp.

Most of all, I thank the Lord, God Almighty and Jesus, for life and health to bring this task to fruition. May God's loving presence and holy power protect and empower us for the ministries to which this book calls us.

Preface

THIS BOOK'S TITLE COMES from the Lord's Prayer. Since the book addresses the complexity of evil and how to live free from its power, the first word, Jesus, is all important. Jesus' name is the power for deliverance from evil. The "deliver" line in the Lord's Prayer has two versions; translations differ. For the OT portion of this book, "deliver us from evil," (KJV, RSV) is more applicable. For the NT, "deliver us from the evil one," (NRSV) is more correct (see chapter 5). Further, "deliver us from the evil one" is linked to the preceding line that implores God to "lead us not into temptation." What follows "deliver us" gives rationale and purpose for freedom from evil: "for yours is the kingdom and the power and the glory." Kingdom recurs often in this book (155x). God's kingdom is the basis of witness to the powers, as in G. F. Handel's *The Messiah*: "the kingdom of this world shall become the kingdom of our Lord and of his Christ."

The subtitle identifies the three foci of the book: evil, exorcism/deliverance, and *exousiai* (the Greek for *powers*). This entails witnessing to Jesus' Lordship over the powers that rule this world. The term, "speaking truth to power," flows out of the Great Commission. It is part of what Jesus taught and did. The Commission calls Jesus' disciples to be and speak a Jesus-witness to all nations.

The content of this book complements my book, *Covenant of Peace* (Eerdmans, 2006). *Evil* is the antonym of *shalom-peace*. Evil exists in this world in many forms and guises. It jeopardizes and short-circuits *shalom-peace*.

For some readers this book will be disturbing, to think that exorcism or "deliverance ministry" should be taken seriously. Or that striving for higher moral values and practices in the *Powers that Be* is really possible, since evil is so systemic in the sociopolitical structures of society. Some may regard this as an exercise in "futility," to think that biblically grounded (Jewish and Christian) moral witness to the powers can make a difference in our world. In our time, both *evil* tentacles pervade our society and merit our attention. We cannot close our eyes to evil's infiltration into our society, Western and worldwide.

The first parts of chapters 4 and 11 are extensive revisions of an article that Tom Finger and I co-authored (see Finger and Swartley in the Bibliography). Also, chapter 6 on Paul draws heavily on chapter 8 in *Covenant of Peace* (Eerdmans), with references to several portions that appear only in *Covenant*. This chapter, however, revises and adds much new content. Other published articles may appear in revised form in other parts of this book.

"Take and eat," as God told Ezekiel (3:1–3). However, it is not sweet as honey! But then, is Ezekiel, really?

Abbreviations

AB	Anchor Bible
ACCS	Ancient Christian Commentary on Scripture
AMBS	Anabaptist Mennonite Biblical Seminary
ANE	Ancient Near East
ANRW	*Aufstieg und Niedergang der römischen Welt*
AT	Author's Translation
BCP	The Book of Common Prayer
BBB	Bonner Biblische Beiträge
BCBC	Believers Church Bible Commentary
BTB	*Biblical Theology Bulletin*
CGR	*Conrad Grebel Review*
ChrCent	*Christian Century*
FS	Festschrift
GNB	*Good News Bible* translation
HWB	Hymnal Worship Book
IMS	Institute for Mennonite Studies
Interp	*Interpretation*
JBL	*Journal of Biblical Literature*
JSNT	*Journal for the Study of the New Testament*
JSNTSS	Journal for the Study of the New Testament: Supplement Series
JSOTSS	Journal for the Study of the Old Testament: Supplement Series
MCC	Mennonite Central Committee
MH	The Mennonite Hymnal

MQR	*Mennonite Quarterly Review*
NICNT	The New International Commentary on the New Testament
NIGTC	New International Greek Testament Commentary
NTS	*New Testament Studies*
OP	*Occasional Papers* (IMS)
RSA	Republic of South Africa
SBL	Society of Biblical Literature
SBLMS	SBL Monograph Series
SBT	Studies in Biblical Theology
SNTSMS	Society for New Testament Studies Monograph Series
SPS	Studies in Peace and Scripture
ST	*Studia theologica*
SBT	Studies in Biblical Theology
TDNT	*Theological Dictionary of the New Testament*
W/JK	Westminster/John Knox
WUNT	Wissenschaftliche Untersuchungen zum Neuen Testament
ZNW	*Zeitschrift für die Neutestamentliche Wisshenshchaft*

Introduction

WHEN WE WERE BORN, we were delivered by a midwife or doctor. When Israel was born God delivered them from Egyptian slavery. When we were born anew as Christian believers, our heavenly Father "delivered us from the dominion of darkness and transferred us into the kingdom of his beloved Son" (Col 1:13). When we are bound or oppressed by the evil one, we can be delivered from bondage by the strong name of Jesus, known through the centuries as exorcism. God wills shalom for us, as Jeremiah declared in the midst of Israel's exile: "For I know the thoughts that I think toward you, says the Lord, thoughts of peace and not of evil, to give you a future and a hope" (NKJV, 29:11).[1] This was addressed to a nation in captivity. The powers (*exousiai*) can be delivered also from captivity and bondages of deception, arrogance, and rancor, even apartheid as one story in chapter 10 illustrates.

This book is a biblical study of *evil* and *deliverance* to free us for *peace*. What hinders *shalom-peace* is *evil*. "Deliver us from (the) evil (one)," is prayed throughout the Christian world in varied circumstances, a prayer for freedom and *shalom*. In *Covenant of Peace*[2] I proposed that the antonym of peace/*shalom* is *evil*.[3] This book is its counterpart. I consider biblical text(s) on *evil*, a term occurring in every biblical book except Ruth, Song of Songs, Obadiah, and Haggai.

Two different types of action to resist and overcome evil dominate the literature and Christian mission. In deliverance ministry, one seeks to *exorcise/*

---

1. This oft-quoted Bible verse was number four in the top ten in 2104 (http://thegrio.com/2014/12/21/worlds-most-popular-bible-verses-2014/). The NIV translation personalizes it to encourage trust in God, "'For I know the plans I have for you,' declares the Lord, 'plans to prosper you and not to harm you, plans to give you hope and a future.'"

2. Swartley, *Covenant*.

3. Plantinga defines sin as "a culpable disturbance of shalom," in *Not*, 18.

deliver a person from demons. In witness to the powers, efforts to confront, subvert, or minimize *systemic structural* evil in economics, politics, and even religion, utilize a variety of means, e.g., from social media signatures to this and that to student walkouts to street protests against gun violence.

This book's contribution addresses this dual approach to deliver us from evil. My own life experiences consist of both dimensions: participating in deliverance ministry and sending many letters and emails to local, state, and federal governments, and signing many online letters attempting to speak truth to power, to make politics and economics serve the common good, protect us against evil, and transform our rancorous sociopolitical culture.

Three types of personal experience shape this book. First, for over thirty years I taught a course on War and Peace in the Bible, often with an OT teaching partner.[4] This classroom experience has influenced my perceptions significantly.[5] I thus view Scripture's teaching on peace within the larger context of God's combat against evil.[6]

Second, for five years I served as a biblical-theological consultant on an Indiana-Michigan Mennonite Conference Oversight committee for Dean Hochstetler, who engaged in exorcism ministry for over thirty-five years.[7] Through the committee's analysis of Hochstetler's reports on specific cases and my participation in deliverance ministry sessions I have come to affirm, despite my rational resistance, the reality of the spirit world and believe deliverance from evil spirits is a part of Christian ministry.

It is one thing to sit around the table with a psychiatrist and other church leaders to discuss "cases" that Dean Hochstetler would bring to the group (see Appendix 2), but quite another experience to participate in a session of exorcism. My first time to do so was revealing. Clinging to my rational resistance, I responded as a compassionate counselor to the woman, so I thought, even though I heard Dean say at one point we will not be addressing "you" (the person), but the evil spirit(s) troubling you. I extended my sympathy to *the woman*, saying you must have had hurtful experiences

---

4. Lind and Ollenburger. Note their books: Lind, *Yahweh*; Ollenburger, *Zion*, as well as his articles on *creation*.

5. My *Covenant* book may be viewed as a twin to this book. Also, my *Health, Healing* book is topically related.

6. For several years we used Boyd's *God at War* as one of the texts.

7. Dean Hochstetler kept records of his deliverance sessions with people who came or, more frequently, were brought to him. Many of these "reports" of what happened in the session, including the names of the cast-out demons, have been compiled and edited by Ben Snyder, fellow member in Dean's church and co-participant in deliverance ministry. The book has 152 pages with the title, "The Ministry of Dean Hochstetler: 1974–2005."

that Jesus can heal. Seconds of silence—maybe fifteen, then a deep guttural voice said, "You must not know who you are talking to!" I was smitten and silent for the rest of the session. The woman was there in body, but another voice had taken control, speaking through her, until the demon left, by "in the name of Jesus commands" by Dean and her pastor.

That experience began a shift in my worldview, even though earlier with my open rational mind, I would not deny that such could be true. Not long after that experience I had a choking feeling before falling off to sleep. Something was choking me, literally. I commanded as strongly as I could in the name of Jesus that "you choking spirit" go to Jesus for your judgment, and instantly the "attack" ended—the spirit left. Satan did not want me in deliverance ministry; only in Jesus' name is there victory over Satan's power.[8]

Third, my pilgrimage has been influenced by the writings of Walter Wink and René Girard, both of whom I learned to know personally. Both take seriously the depth and nature of evil. Wink has done extensive analysis of the New Testament's depiction of the powers, to help us see how pervasive evil is in the systemic, structural dimensions of our culture.[9] Girard unmasks the hidden mechanisms of human behavior: *desire* leads to *imitation* of the other that leads to *conflict* and potential violence. But violence is averted by finding an innocent victim, projecting onto that person the cause of the rivalry, and then killing that person, the innocent victim. This sacrificial ritual makes peace for a time, until the next similar cycle.[10]

My goal is to bridge these two faces of evil: the systemic structural evil in the socio-economic-political spheres *and* evil that oppresses a *person*, for whom exorcism in deliverance is necessary for freedom. I contend that these two faces of evil are *two sides of the same coin*. While bibliography for either face is long, few books and articles address both, especially the practical sphere.[11] In my judgment, both derive from the same biblical canon and theology.

---

8. Within a year later a brother in the church asked me for spiritual help for his sister. Her psychiatrist, who served on the Responsibility Committee for Dean Hochstetler, suggested this approach for her, one of his clients, since symptoms did not match anything he encountered before, like auto-backward handwriting, among others.

9. Especially in vol. 3: *Engaging the Powers*.

10. See the book I edited, *Violence*, with my "Introduction," 19–28, and my contributions at a Conference (in 2000) celebrating Wink's work and engaging with his contributions: in Gingerich and Grimsrud, eds., *Transforming*. Wink's chapter is titled, "The New Worldview," 17–28. My response appears in chapter 12 of this book.

11. MacNutt, in *Deliverance*, deals mostly with exorcizing evil spirits. Briefly, though, he takes up Wagner's mapping of cities, land areas, or other geographical places, 253–58, followed by one short section on "Unmasking," 258–64. Those pages end with a "Both-And: An Example of Social Exorcism," which narrates McClain's exorcist

In "Resistance and Nonresistance in the New Testament," Dorothy Jean Weaver addresses both sides of the coin:

> To read the New Testament is to enter a world caught in the throes of an apocalyptic power struggle between the forces of God the Creator and those of the devil or Satan, that cosmic "adversary" (1 Pet 5:8) who is the agent of death (Heb 2:14), destruction (1 Cor 5:5), and deceit. The outcome of this power struggle in the ultimate triumph of God is never in question, a reality which is confirmed in advance by the resurrection of Jesus from the dead. But in the present moment the New Testament writers know themselves and their readers to be living in that final turbulent era just before "the end" or "the consummation of the age," an era in which Satan's "wrath" is intensified precisely because he "knows that his time is short" (Rev 12:12).[12]

Prior to these paragraphs, Weaver refers to Walter Wink whose trilogy on the powers focuses mostly on the other side of the coin, the systematic structural sociopolitical powers.

Richard Beck's *Reviving Old Scratch: Demons and the Devil for Doubters and the Disenchanted*, also speaks to this dual face of evil, at least to some extent. Beck first heard the term, "Old Scratch," from his prison ministry's partner, who prayed for protection of the inmates from "Old Scratch," a British colloquialism for the *devil*.[13] For "doubters," Beck's book is a good read in tandem with this book. Be alert to, and resist "Old Scratch."[14]

Here, enjoy Beck's description of Thomas Jefferson's snipped-up Bible:

---

approach to getting the Methodist Board of Pensions to divest from South Africa because of its apartheid political practices, and Dr. Peck's analysis of the MyLai massacre (Peck, *People*, 262–64). MacNutt also cites Dr. McAll's study of the demonic in the "Bermuda Triangle"—lost ships and planes—as a result of "the thousands of slaves dumped overboard and drowned in this area of the Atlantic . . . Their souls were crying out . . . for revenge." (267). MacNutt's final chapter (23) is titled "Baptism in the Holy Spirit," the source of power and discernment for deliverance/exorcist ministries (271–77).

12. Weaver, *Irony*, 5.

13. Beck, *Reviving*. While Beck often speaks of the personal face of evil, he cites no account of an exorcism akin to that of Jesus' ministry in the Gospels or stories in this book. Such stories with analysis from several disciplinary perspectives appear in *Even the Demons Submit* edited by Johns and Krabill. Other similar stories and assessments appear in an earlier book I edited, *Essays*.

14. While working in a psychiatric hospital for four years, Beck's faith floundered. Years later, he regained his faith through prison ministry as he came to see that the Christian life involves battle against evil. His prison ministry, with his partner's prayers for the inmates' protection against "Old Scratch," spurred his revived faith.

Too many Christians are playing Thomas Jefferson with Jesus. We wind up following a Swiss Cheese Jesus, a Jesus full of holes, snipped to suit our preferences and prejudices. And when it comes to Jesus' battle with Satan, both conservative and progressive Christians snip out critical parts of the conflict.[15]

Walter Wink, in *Unmasking*, briefly discusses the role of Satan in personal bondage.[16] His view of evil, however, is influenced much by Carl Jung's psychology, which competes with Scripture's worldview of evil,[17] even though Wink speaks much of Jesus' healing and exorcist ministry.[18] Rather than regarding Satan as a power outside us and human institutions, Wink speaks of the inner and outer nature (good and/or evil) of a person or corporate organization. Wink names this worldview *dynamic holism*, i.e., *integral*. For biblical support Wink appeals to the messages to the seven churches in Revelation 2—3. That message is addressed not to the churches, but to the angels of the churches. The angel is the spirit that characterizes and rules the church. Wink's *integral* worldview, however, is problematic. I critique it in chapter 12.

Wink's view thus differs from Beck's, who regards the devil as an evil spiritual power outside and invasive of the material realm, one that tempts individuals to make evil choices. Satan is also at work in corporate structural

---

15. Ibid., 35. Beck continues:

> With their focus on traditional family values, the Protestant work ethic, and "God and Country" patriotism, conservative Christians snip out the Jesus who marginalized the family, who was a friend of sinners, who sided with the poor against the rich, and who was executed by the state for sedition. Snip. Snip. Snip.
>
> Progressive Christians snip out different stuff. We're aware that Jesus was executed by the state but fail [to] notice that Jesus' battle with the Satan didn't look a whole lot like what we'd describe as political activism. . . . Jesus didn't lead a "March on Rome" or carry a sign through downtown Jerusalem protesting Roman oppression. Jesus' one disruptive action, clearing the Temple, was the restoration of a house of worship so that it could be a house of prayer. And most worryingly, Jesus was routinely gracious to the colonial occupier and agents of empire like tax collectors and Roman centurions, to say nothing of telling his oppressed countrymen to "Love your enemies."

Cf. here MacNutt's statement: "Conservative Christians often excoriate social activists as 'bleeding-heart liberals' and call for a stronger military, while social activist Christians scorn conservatives who seem to come down on the side of the wealthy and ignore how unjust structures oppress the poor." (*Deliverance*, 264).

16. Wink, *Unmasking*, 22–64.

17. Wink, *The Powers*. He describes his view in chapter 1, where he rejects the Heaven/Earth polarity which, in my view, undermines God's transcendence.

18. See my quotation from Wink's *Engaging* (134) in chapter 6 below.

dimension of institutions, which can make the evil greater than any of its individual participants.[19] Beck speaks often about "spiritual warfare," though he focuses mostly on institutions, such as warring against evil in prisons, economics, and politics (Nazism and Hitler). But his seven-point conclusion regards spiritual warfare quite broadly: "Spiritual warfare is prayer, worship, holiness, discerning the spirits," et al.[20]

Hendrik Berkhof's *Christ and the Powers* focuses on Christ's victory over the powers *and* the Christian believers' freedom from and witness to the powers. Evil in personal bondage is neglected. Stott expresses this concern regarding J. H. Yoder's contribution,[21] as does Marva Dawn. Representing the long-standing view of the Christian church, Dawn draws on numerous writers (K. Barth, C. Arnold, Schlier, T. Yoder Neufeld, et al.).

While many scholarly contributions on Jesus' victory over the Powers focus on the sociopolitical face of evil, several widely read authors integrate, but only to a limited extent, the personal and sociopolitical faces of evil: Greg Boyd, N. T. Wright, Nigel Wright, and Marva Dawn.[22] None of these, however, do what Scott Peck, Richard Gallagher, and others do (see chapter 11), i.e., cite accounts of exorcism.[23] Boyd most recently develops his contribution in two volumes that focus on God's battle against and victory over evil.[24] N. T. Wright, in *Evil and the Justice of God*, addresses the topic, but lacks the *praxis* stage. In *Simply Jesus*, he describes the "sheer muddle" people get themselves into: "Despite the caricatures, the obsession . . . , there is such a thing as a dark force that seems to take over people, movements, and sometimes whole

---

19. Note here Reinhold Niebuhr's *Moral Man*.

20. Beck, *Reviving*, 184.

21. See Stott, *God's New Society*, 263–74. See also Stott's concern for this in correspondence with John Howard Yoder, to which I refer in *Send Forth*, 121–22, 289n38-39. See my critique of Yoder, *Send Forth*, 124–25.

22. Dawn in turn utilizes Ellul, Stringfellow, and T. Yoder Neufeld copiously.

23. Peck, *People; Glimpses*. Regarding Gallagher's book in progress, I quote a *Washington Post* (July 1, 2016) news release picked up by the *ChrCent* August 3, 2016 issue:

> DEMON POSSESSED: Richard Gallagher, a board-certified psychiatrist and professor of clinical psychiatry at New York Medical College, was skeptical when a priest/exorcist asked his opinion of a woman diagnosed with demonic possession. In time Gallagher's scientific habits of observation led him to believe that in rare cases, the only explanation for bizarre behavior is that it's the work of evil spirits. Over the past 25 years he has consulted with hundreds of ministers, helping them to distinguish between mental illness and demonic possession. Gallagher, a practicing Catholic, is working on a book about demonic possession in the United States.

24. Boyd, *God at War* and *Satan*.

countries, a force or (as it sometimes seems) a set of forces that can make people do things they would never normally do."[25]

Nigel Goering Wright also addresses evil's dual dimensions, personal and systemic.[26] "It is congenial to the modern mind to speak of the demonic in impersonal terms." Yet Jesus in his ministry and in facing the cross addresses evil as "the devil" or "Satan" (Luke 10:18; 22:31–32). We cannot adequately confront *evil* unless we address it in personal terms as Jesus did. A "Power" is at work, and if we don't call it in personal terms "we run the risk of making the power of evil so abstract that we lose its compelling force and clarity."[27]

Many authors in the church's long history address the demonic in personal terms.[28]

Part 1 of this book, "Progressions in Deliverance from Evil," develops a biblical theology that treats the varied faces of evil within Scripture and the varied responses to evil. These chapters trace crucial journeys: from several OT ways of confronting evil to consummation in Messiah Jesus.[29] But these "journeys" do not assume an upward sequential time-line of divine revelation.[30] Abraham's justification by faith connects directly with

---

25. N. T. Wright, *Simply Jesus*, 121. On 110, 220, 226, Wright connects the Christian gospel to evil, but does not present Jesus as exorcist. See also his *Evil*. Wright's *Lord* has an excellent chapter on "Deliver Us from Evil," 64–76.

26. N. G. Wright, *Dark Side*.

27. Ibid., 67 and 68 respectively for the two quoted sentences.

28. A comprehensive treatment would include numerous contributions from the church's long history, especially from the Roman Catholic and Orthodox communions. The recent book by Kreider, *Patient Ferment*, is a case in point. The practice of casting out demons on the one hand (107–14) and witness to the powers in their distinctive lifestyle and suffering martyrdom illustrates this dual dimension. Another significant resource is Warren's tracing the history of battle with demons from the early church through the Reformation, in *Cleansing*, 4–6. Her chapter 1 reviews the variety of more recent contributions to "spiritual warfare," which term she regards as problematic. She seeks a more expansive view and terminology, like *cleansing*. Her review of the literature to the 2012 date is most helpful, citing contributions from the charismatic, Protestant, and Catholic writers. She is a family physician who in practice, like Peck and Gallagher, had to come to terms with demonic reality. This helpful book is an adaptation of her PhD thesis (University of Birmingham, UK).

29. Focusing on twelve selected Scripture texts with two levels of inquiry (text and theme), Lascaris presents a helpful portrait of the progression from Cain and Abel to new creation in the NT, with good explanations, borrowing from Girard, how conflict and scapegoating lead to order and pseudo-peace: *To Do*, 87–95.

30. My approach differs from but is also akin to Fleischer's *Old*. Fleischer cites a long list of actions where God commands horrible violence of many sorts. He explains this in light of the ANE context and speaks of "Incremental Ethical Revelation" (chapter 2) and later "Incremental Revelation," by which he narrates the unfolding biblical story,

Paul's justification by faith; Abraham's treaty with Abimelech, whose servants stole his wells (Gen 21:22–34), is closer to Jesus' teaching in Matthew 5:39–42, than are the later (David's) wars against the Philistines. The notion of an upward progression from "horrid" to "best" is wrong. Prophet Isaiah is closer to Jesus' moral stance than are James and John wanting Jesus to call down fire on the Samaritans (Luke 9:51–56). Isaiah's Servant Songs are the doorstep to Jesus!

This augurs for a Christocentric perspective for understanding God,[31] in the context of varied views of God in OT Scripture. It declares repeatedly God's "steadfast love" and "faithfulness." In contrast, *evil* has no definitive center except opposition to God. In Scripture *evil* is not a (theoretical) problem; the emphasis falls on God's victory over evil.[32]

Nonetheless, *evil* is a dominant theme in Scripture, occurring over 400x in the OT. Numerous "Theologies of the Old Testament" overlook or discuss evil only minimally. For example, *evil* does not occur in the Subject Index of C. J. H. Wright's *Old Testament Ethics*; it does mention evil at the end to answer the students' questions about God's command to exterminate the Canaanites. His answers are helpful, but minimal.

My chapter 1 zeroes in on how *evil* is portrayed in Scripture, with attention to creation out of chaos. How did God's people in their historical and cultural contexts understand and respond to evil? It considers also how recent theologians understand evil.

Chapters 2a and 2b focus on YHWH War that intended to protect against evil, but it did not yield shalom-peace. It did not overcome evil with good. Its *ḥerem* practice, offering up Canaanite peoples—everything that breathes—as holy sacrifice to God presents an unresolvable conundrum. How does it square with the Lord's promise to Abraham that he and his descendants will be a blessing to the nations (Gen 12:3)? This book seeks to understand what was going on, and why. How does *ḥerem* connect to the NT ethic of love of

---

consummating in Jesus' teaching and servant-death on the cross for human salvation.

31. Boyd develops a *cruciform* hermeneutic and theses in two volumes: *Crucifixion* and his more reader-accessible follow-up, *Cross*. Boyd focuses on the "moral problem texts" of the OT, which results in a negative OT portrait, as Cornell contends, "Testament," 32–36. I recommend reading Boyd's books in tandem with OT Theologies (Goldingay; Bruggemann, Ollenburger—especially the Vriezen chapter on "Knowledge of God," 58–74) that present positive views of the OT, the root of the prophetic moral tradition. Snyder Belousek developed the cruciform focus in *Atonement*, with several *cruciform* chapters: "Interpreting the Cross: Guiding Rules of a Cruciform Hermeneutic," 13–23; "Cruciform Realism, Spirituality, and Community," 560–72; and "Cruciform Peacemaking within the Church," 587–604. For earlier similar emphases, see Gorman, *Cruciformity*, and Forsyth, *Cruciality*. Cf. Kim, *Messiah*, especially 106–18.

32. Wink, *Engaging*, 314–24.

enemy and resisting evil, or non-resisting as a means to overcome evil?[33] Answers are not easy, but given the horrible wars of the last century with brutal torture and killing of innocents in terrorist wars of this century (often in God's or Allah's name), we must examine this topic.

In chapter 3, I focus on evil and deliverance in the Psalms, Proverbs, and two Prophets. *Evil* and *deliverance* occur frequently. The Psalms speak often of evil, in the context of worship; Proverbs, in the context of wise living. The Prophets[34] anticipate a Messiah who overcomes evil.

Crucial to the canonical journey is the transformation of how Scripture views and responds to the *enemy*. How do we understand the divinely commanded response to destroy the enemy ("all that breathes") in order to protect the faith community from idolatries that would undermine the faith and worship of the covenant community? The canonical journey is most important in answering this question. How does Scripture move from *ḥerem*, destruction of the enemy as a holy sacrifice to God, to Jesus' command, "love your enemy?" Holiness is an important component of this enigma, as is the transformation of the notion of "conquest" in Israel's taking possession of the land promised to Abraham (Gen 12:1–3) and how that theme, together with discipline in the community, is transformed in the NT.

Part II, under the title, "Biblical Perspectives on Deliverance: Multidimensions of Deliverance from Evil," consists of biblical exposition on both sides of the same coin: taking account of both the personal and systemic faces of evil, together with how people of biblical faith responded. Chapter 4 focuses on how *bondage* and *deliverance* is understood in both Testaments, followed by exposition of Mark's Gospel on this topic. Chapter 5 treats Matthew and Luke–Acts on the same themes, noting how God's covenant people confronted evil spirit realities. It concludes with several present-day stories of deliverance from demon powers.

Chapter 6 focuses on the Pauline contribution, including the Pastorals, with extended attention to what Jesus Christ's victory means for the principalities and powers *vis à vis* structural, systemic evil. Chapter 7 examines the face of *evil* in the Johannine writings, Gospel, Letters, and Revelation.[35] Each

---

33. An article that wrestles with this topic in detail is "Transforming," by Weaver in Swartley, *Love*, 32–71, and in *Irony*, that reflects her 3-M perspective: *Matthew, Middle East,* and *Mennonite*, 137–74.

34. For prophet Jeremiah *evil* is a major theme (see chapter 3).

35. Scholars differ regarding the authorship of these three differing book-types. See my *John* commentary for the range of views regarding the Gospel, 502–4. I lean either toward the proposal for Lazarus as the Beloved Disciple (see my rationale) and the writing of the Gospel within an early Christian community that identified itself with the witness of the Beloved Disciple. For the identity of the Beloved Disciple, see ibid., 505–7. This ideal disciple in the narrative beckons us to be disciples of love for one

is different, but common emphases prevail. John's Gospel presents Jesus' death as a cosmic exorcism (12:31). Both the Gospel and Letters use the term *world* in positive and negative senses. Love for one another is a hallmark in each. Revelation has its distinctive apocalyptic genre and memorable call to patient endurance and faithfulness, with vivid imagery of evil's destruction. A unique slain Lamb theology empowers Christian believers living through persecution by evil Powers (imminent or present). A crucial aspect of survival is worship, holy praise to God and the Lamb, extolling the Lamb's victory over the Powers. Chapter 8 examines 1–2 Peter, Hebrews, James, and Jude. These Letters exhort believers to shun evil, pray for protection against evil, and overcome evil with good.

Part III of the book (chapters 9–12) focuses on "Practices for Deliverance: Faithful Responses" in facing and confronting evil. Chapter 9 focuses on the faithfulness and model of the early Church in both exorcism and a paradoxical resistance/nonresistance relation to evil Powers. Chapter 10 focuses on Christ's Lordship over the Powers, calling believers to witness to the Powers, with stories of exorcism of systemic evil.

Chapter 11 describes different approaches to the healing/deliverance ministry from personal bondage. It identifies key resources for dealing with personal deliverance from evil bondage, and addresses the church's role in this type of ministry. In consideration of pastoral care and ministry, I offer some discernment criteria for recognizing demonic affliction. The goal is healing from evil's infliction of pain, trauma, and suffering, blocking personal shalom.

Chapter 12 extends previous discussion to integrate more explicitly the two faces of evil. I interact with Walter Wink's and Graham Twelftree's extensive contributions as representative of witness to the powers (Wink) and Christian engagement in exorcism (Twelftree—I choose him because of his numerous contributions to the topic from 1985 to 2007, with some shifting in his position). I cite from Sydney Page's conclusion in *Powers* where he identifies five dangers in focusing too much on evil powers and victory or triumph.[36] I utilize also the three-author book, *Power and the Powers*, to describe five scholars' perception and method of dealing with evil.[37]

An excellent counter-balance to this book is Chris Wright's *The Mission of God* (581 pages). *Evil* does not appear in the Subject Index, though the term occurs a few times in the book (144–46, 315). Written likely in

---

another. The matter intrigues. For authorship of 1, 2, 3 John, see McDermond, *Epistles*, 28–31; for Revelation, Yeatts, *Revelation* 442–46. Yeatts opts for a Palestinian Jew as author, but considers other proposals also.

36. Page, *Powers*.
37. Hardy, Whitehouse, and Yarnell, *Power*.

2003 to 2005, it includes a section on "A Paradigm of Evil: HIV-AIDS" in the context of the mission of the church. Wright illustrates the enormity of its evil by comparing HIV-AIDS death-data in Africa to other major losses of lives: 3,000 lives from the attack on the Twin Towers in New York City equals the HIV-AIDS deaths per day in Africa; the 2004 tsunami in the Indian Ocean killing 300,000 people is equivalent to the HIV-AIDS deaths every month in Africa.[38] I hope these statistics have improved enormously by now.

The Summary and Conclusion shows the support of this study for the theses of this book, how and where in Scripture evil contrasts to peace (*shalom*) with both a micro-analysis of different parts of the canon, and then a macro-portrayal of the biblical story.

Appendix 1, "Resources: Prayers for Healing and Deliverance," consists of prayers I developed for various situations in healing/deliverance ministry. Appendix 2 contains two exorcism reports from Dean Hochstetler, excerpted from over 100 similar reports collated and edited by Ben Snyder. Appendix 3 analyzes briefly the extent *evil* figures into text books on NT Theology and/or Ethics.

I am not clear where to draw the line between moral and non-moral evil.[39] This book focuses on moral evil. I do not think sickness (cancer, heart illness, chronic suffering) is of the devil, but indirectly it may be.[40] Disasters such as tsunamis, earthquakes, hurricanes, mudslides, and tornadoes, are not *moral* evils, but they may be the results of human choices as stewards of creation, i.e., ecological factors. The topic is complex.[41] For

---

38. C. J. H. Wright, *Mission*. See 435–39. The book rejoices in God's mission of love and salvation throughout the biblical canon. Fourteen of Wright's fifteen chapters have OT sub-headings relating to God's salvation purpose. It's a good read in tandem with this one, and with Boyd's 2017 two-volume *magnum opus*.

39. Greenway's recent book *Challenge*, in dialogue with Emmanuel Levinas, Dostoevsky, and Iris Murdoch, is helpful for the philosophical and biblical perspectives on suffering: even the most brutal evil, as Auschwitz survivors attest: there is a way for Joy and Love to stare down evil in its face and be its answer. I also discuss biblical-theological perspectives on suffering in *Health*, 88–104.

40. Thomas's thorough study of the origin of illness in the NT indicates God and/or Satan may be causative in certain illnesses (e.g., Paul's "thorn in the flesh" in 2 Cor 12:7–10): "The affliction inflicted by the angel of Satan proved to be so painful that Paul sought to have the Lord remove it"—so he prayed three times—but then he affirms God's grace is sufficient for him to bear his weakness (69–71). Instruction for healing in James 5:14–17 regards sin as a causative factor, which, unless confessed, is prohibitive to healing (32–37). In Jesus' healing miracles, causation is not specified. Regarding Jesus' exorcisms, no "why" for origin, or "how" for demonic entrance, is given. See Thomas, *Devil*. He cites five OT texts where God is regarded as responsible for illness (32–33).

41. This study does not address *evil* philosophically, as Meister's contributions do

an overview of scholars seeking to understand the "why" of evil I recommend *Five Views*.⁴² John Swinton's excellent book *(Raging with Compassion)* guides readers to face evil with cruciform compassion. He holds that suffering in itself is not evil. However, depending upon one's response, it may become evil. Suffering for the gospel is intertwined with Jesus' call to discipleship, as Cardinal Bernardin states:

> *As Christians, if we are to love as Jesus loved,*
> *we must first come to terms with suffering.*
> *Like Jesus, we simply cannot be cool and detached*
> *from our fellow human beings.*
> *Our years of living as Christians*
> *will be years of suffering for and with other people.*
> *Like Jesus, we will love others only*
> *If we walk with them in the valley of darkness—*
> *the dark valley of moral dilemmas,*
> *the dark valley of oppressive structures*
> *and diminished rights.*
>
> —Joseph Cardinal Bernardin⁴³

(see bibliography). I cite the blurb for *Guide*:

> *Evil: A Guide* . . . is a lively examination of the philosophical and theological problems raised by the existence of widespread evil. It explores classic debates . . . and also engages . . . new challenges posed by scientific advances in evolutionary theory, neuroscience, and cosmology, to concerns of climate change and environmental degradation, to questions raised by increasing religious and secular violence. This second edition also contains new chapters and topics such as Jewish, Christian, and Islamic responses to evil and skeptical theism. The result is an even-handed guide to . . . issues raised by the reality and ubiquity of evil.

A helpful theological-philosophical book is Adams's *Horrendous*.

42. Meister and Dew, eds., *Five*. Nelson's "Facing" offers a fine biblical and pastoral complement.

43. *Gift*, 49.

Part I

Progressions in Deliverance from Evil

Crucial Journeys within Scripture

1

Scriptural Portrayal of Evil

*To deny evil is to lose the freedom of the spirit
and to escape the burden of freedom.
Our present age has witnessed a terrible increase of evil
coupled with the denial of its existence.
But man [sic] is powerless to resist evil
if he fails to recognize it as such.
Human personality deceives itself when,
having made a distinction between good and evil,
it thinks itself competent to delimit evil.
When we abolish such limits and
when man [sic] finds himself in a state of confusion and indifference,
his personality begins to disintegrate,
for the power of conscience is inseparably
connected with the denunciation of evil.*

—Nicholas Berdyaev, Freedom and Spirit

The Lord loves those who hate evil.

—Ps 97:10a; cf. Ps 11:5

WHAT BERDYAEV WROTE IN 1935 has yielded high compound interest these past eighty plus years. The devil is alive and well, and we must come to terms with its reality in its various, and often subtle, manifestations.

Evil in the Old Testament

THE HEBREW WORD FOR evil is *rāʿ*, which in variant forms occurs 433x in the OT.[1] The term occurs often within the lament Psalms, pleading God to save or deliver the psalmist from evildoers (e.g., Ps 27:3). In other Psalms, evil is more generic, such as Psalm 23:4, ". . . I fear no evil" (cf. Ps 34:13, 14, 21). This latter use occurs often in Proverbs (e.g., 12:2, 13, 20; 16:6, 12, 17, 27, 30), though it is often associated with a person who does evil of one sort or another. God's relation to evil is two-sided: in Isaiah 45:7b, God creates evil (RSV; the NRSV reads "creates woe"). But Psalm 97:10 says God hates evil (cf. God's hate of violence in Ps 11:5). Evil is not God's creation, but God is not independent of evil, for *ha sa-tán* in the OT "tests" the righteous, within God's limits—notably in Job 1—2).[2] Whether we seek to understand the origins of evil philosophically or theologically, the quest

---

1 *Young's Analytical Concordance*, 314–15. The most frequent occurrences are in Deuteronomy (24), Psalms (36), Proverbs (44), and Jeremiah (83). Other grammatical forms of *rāʿ* occur also (ca. 30, ibid., 315). *The NRSV Concordance Unabridged*, edited by Kohlenberger III, 422–24, cites 535 occurrences for *evil* in both Testaments including the Apocrypha, with the following usages, including compound words:

> Evil in the sight of the Lord (53)
>
> Good . . . evil (22)
>
> From evil (17)
>
> Evil . . . good (17)
>
> The evil one (12)
>
> Evil spirit (11)
>
> Evil ways (10)
>
> Evil deeds (9)
>
> Evil way (7)
>
> Evil spirits (4)

In addition to these, compound uses occur in both Testaments: evil-hating (1), evildoer (5), evildoers (42, all but 4 in the OT, mostly in Psalms), evildoing (3), and *evils*, pl. (4, all in OT).

2. See N. G. Wright's discussion, *Dark*, 71–73. Garrett develops this point in her discussion of "God and Satan as Partners in Testing?," *Temptations*, 44–49, which draws on non-canonical sources, *The Life of Adam and Eve*, *Testament of Job*, and *Jubilees*. "Job affirms that even satanic afflictions fall under the divine control" (44).

eludes perspicuity.³ Nonetheless, the Psalmist exclaims, "Deliverance belongs to the Lord" (3:7).

Evil has both moral and non-moral connotations.⁴ It often functions in opposition to *good* (*tov*). To illustrate: key contrasts occur in the serpent's words to Eve, promising knowledge of "good and evil" if you eat of the forbidden fruit (Gen 3:5).⁵ Similarly, King Solomon prays for understanding "to discern between good and evil" (1 Kgs 3:9).⁶ Both texts infer that human volition and perception are crucially involved in choosing between *good* and *evil*.⁷ Choosing to violate God's commandments puts one on the path to evil: murder (2 Sam 12:9) and adultery (Deut 22:22). Evil resides in and springs from the human heart (Gen 6:5; Prov 6:14; Eccl 8:11; Jer 17:9).⁸ Throughout the OT, failure in covenant faithfulness abounds (Prov 11:21; 12:13; 2 Kgs 21:9 where Manasseh "misled them [Israel] to do evil"). The phrase, "evil in the sight of the Lord" recurs frequently in Kings and Chronicles. In Deuteronomy the phrase, "so you shall purge the evil from your midst," recurs nine times.⁹ In 2 Kings 21 *evil* occurs numerous times: v. 9 cited above; v. 12, "the Lord . . . says, I am bringing upon Jerusalem and Judah such *evil* that the ears of everyone who hears of it will tingle." Judah's devastation and exile occur "because they have done what is *evil* in my sight and have provoked me to anger, since the day their ancestors came out of Egypt, even to this day" (v. 15); "shedding innocent blood" is *evil* (v. 16).

These textual examples—and there are many more—indicate how *evil* is interwoven with social and religious structures. Idolatry, pervasive in both the northern and southern kingdoms of Israel, ranks as the worst of evils. Worshipping the gods of the nations is infidelity to Israel's covenant God. Evil also takes on corporate dimensions: "The sin of Judah is written with an iron pen, with a diamond point it is engraved on the tablet of their hearts and on the horns of their altars" (Jer 17:1). Persisting in sin is evil: metaphorically, moral *evil* is *sin* on fire, the result of persisting in sin and

---

3. Examples of this effort are summarized by Blocher, *Evil*, 12–83. Chapters 3–5 (84–133) are devoted to biblical perspectives regarding the origin and nature of evil.

4. The non-moral is not the focus of this work. For it, see Fretheim, *Creation*.

5. For analysis of this narrative, with surprising insights, see Bailey, "Who?," 13–18.

6. For a helpful treatment of "good and evil," see Penchansky, "Good," 426–32.

7. Penchansky holds knowledge of good and evil indicates maturity, "Good," 427. It is a merism of all humanity, 428. The Bible views God in charge of both, 427–28.

8. Boyd and Eddy, "Evil," 288–89.

9. Deut 13:5; 17:7, 12; 19:19; 21:21; 22:21, 22, 24; 24:7. Cf. 19:13; 21:9—same idea, but different wording for object. This is the NRSV text. Different Hebrew words occur for the English *purge*.

giving oneself over to its power.[10] Verses 17 and 18 speak of the coming "day of evil (*rāʿ*)," which the NRSV translates as *disaster*. Evil is the antonym of *shalom* (Jer 29:11 and Isa 45:7, translated rightly by NKJV). When *evil* prevails, the well-being of the community and nation is destroyed. As long as evil persists, shalom is compromised and confounded. The prophets link shalom to eschatological hope, when the Lord intervenes in history to perfect shalom. In Revelation the struggle is severe.

Evil is a major theme in Jeremiah, occurring in over 75 percent of its 52 chapters.[11] Many chapters have multiple uses (see chapter 3 below). In most of these *evil* refers either to the sins of the people (especially idolatry) or the certain disaster of the nation's downfall. These uses of *rāʿ* are morally descriptive of human choices or the tragic results of wrong choices. At the same time, however, to the extent that the word in context means "trouble" or "calamity" it carries some degree of the non-moral. Hence the two levels of meaning flow together, especially in Jeremiah.

The occurrence of "evil spirit(s)" is also notable in the OT: Judges 9:23; 1 Samuel 16:14–23 (5x), and again in 18:10 and 19:20—all in reference to Saul. In these verses God/the Lord sends the evil spirit as the result of Saul's disobedience in 15:19, when Saul violated God's orders in the practice of *ḥerem* (see chapter 2a). The OT mention of *evil spirit(s)* is linked likely to the notion of the *jinn*, evil spirits that reside in the uninhabited places.[12] Thus the scapegoat takes the sins of the people back to the desert/wilderness, the abode of the *jinn* (Lev 16:10—here Azazel is head of the evil spirits residing in the desolate places, cf. Matt 12:43). The OT prophets speak of the devastation of Jerusalem or the nation as a deserted place where "animal (evil) spirits" dwell: the hyenas, jackals, and other wild animals (Isa 13:19–22; Jer 49:33; 50:39; see chapter 4 for more on "animal"/evil spirits in the OT).

---

10. See the next chapter for the three Hebrew words for *sin*. A crucial distinction must be made between *sin* and *evil* since evil includes more than sin. The *sin* of idolatry is constituent of evil. For the "Gravity of Sin" in relation to evil, see Rutledge, *Crucifixion*, 167–204.

11. Chapters exempt are 10, 14, 27, 30–31, 33–34, 37–38, 43, 46, 50.

12. *Jinn* or *Jinns* appear in the Qur'an. Their final judgment is: "hellfire is your dwelling-place; you shall live therein forever unless Allah ordains otherwise," Al-Anâm 6:125–127, in Muhammad, *Meaning of AL-QUR'AN*, 220–21. Prior to this judgment is the charge: "You seduced mankind in great numbers," 220. The *jinn* are usually invisible but they appear sometimes in animal form. For an astounding view of the jinn historically—some are granted sainthood—and their relation to the past, present, and future in ethics and ecology, see Taneja, *Jinnealogy*.

Evil as Chaos Versus God's Creation Order

The meaning of the non-moral dimension of evil (*rā'*) is "worthless," "trouble," or "calamity," which may be linked in the OT to *chaos* that resists God's creation order and goodness, a major focus of Jon Levenson's insightful book, *Creation and the Persistence of Evil*.[13] The *chaos* motif is accentuated by Boyd's titles for chapters 3 and 4: "Locking up the Raging Sea: The Hostile Environment of the Earth" and "Slaying Leviathan: Cosmic Warfare and the Preservation and Restoration of Creation."[14] God's power and steadfast covenant love hold back the return to chaos, the pre-creation condition of the dark watery deep (*tehom*) in Genesis 1:2.[15] Bouma-Prediger offers this reflection, in poetic form, upon this narrative of Genesis 1:1–2:4, where God's word shapes creation out of this watery chaos:

> In the beginning was God,
> And over a deep, dark, watery abyss—
> a formless void of nothingness—
> God's creative Spirit swept,
> hovering like an eagle over her brood.
> Like a rushing wind God's Spirit moved
> when it was time to create the heavens and the earth.
>
> And in the midst of this chaotic darkness, God spoke,
> And light, like the pulse of a quasar, came to be,
> And God saw this brilliant light was good,
> and so pushed back the darkness to make room for the light.
> God named the light Day and the darkness Night.
> Evening and morning, the first day.
> God spoke, and it was so.
> Out of chaos, order.
> From what was empty and dark came fullness of light.[16]

---

13. The subtitle is *The Jewish Drama of Divine Omnipotence*. See also Ollenburger, "Peace," and "Creation" in *Struggles*, 26–35. For an excellent article, with additional bibliographic sources see Heiser, "Chaos." Scurlock and Beal have edited numerous essays on this topic in *Creation*. Several essays focus on the presence and function of this motif in ancient cultures.

14. Boyd, *God*, 73–113.

15. N. T. Wright in *Evil* refers to this dimension of evil (13–14, 69–71) but focuses more on human wickedness evident in Gen 4—11 (Cain, Lamech, the Flood, and Tower of Babel). He gives more space to God's response to evil: forming a covenant people in Abraham that leads later to the Servant of YHWH, God's answer to evil (43–74), consummated still later in the Jesus of the Gospels, and the eschatological hope expressed in Revelation's vision of the new heavens and earth.

16. Bouma-Prediger, *Beauty*, 85. In note 15 (198) Bouma-Prediger says he arrived

Each stanza for each day of creation concludes: "God spoke, and it was so/ Out of chaos, order." Compare Haydn's "The Creation." At the end of Day One the Archangel Uriel sings:

> Now vanish before the holy beams
> the gloomy shades of dark;
> the first of days appears.
> Disorder yields to order
> fair the place.
> Affrighted fled hell's spirit,
> black in throngs;
> Down they sink in the deep of abyss
> to endless night.

The choir and orchestra respond in full resound:

> Despairing cursing rage resounds
> attends their rapid fall.
> A new created world springs up
> at God's command.

Perhaps these lyrics overplay the meaning of the formless void (*tohu wabohu*) as fight against chaos. Whatever the depth of the mess, God intervenes and masterfully orchestrates the six-day creation into the order and beauty of the world as humans then and now know it. Later OT texts portray God's intervention as battle against chaos. These appear throughout the Major Prophets and Psalms. An oracle in Isaiah 51:9–11 speaks of "the arm of the Lord" hacking "Rahab in pieces" and piercing "the Dragon," names of the chaos-opponents of God's creation as is evident in the following lines of v. 10:

> It was you that dried up the Sea [*yam*],
> The waters of the great deep [*tehom*],
> That made the abysses of the Sea
> A road the redeemed might walk .

Time wise, these events are located "in the days of old, . . . in former ages" (Isa 51:9b). Verse 10 blends the original creation out of chaos with YHWH's slicing apart the waters of the Red Sea for the redeemed to walk through.

---

at this translation after study of numerous scholars' contributions on the creation story. This list includes Fretheim, Brueggemann, von Rad, Wenham, and Westermann on Genesis, Anderson, *Creation*, and Middleton's "definitive work," *Liberating*.

SCRIPTURAL PORTRAYAL OF EVIL

A similar text appears in Psalm 74:12–17. Here the *ChaosKampf* is joined to God's establishing the ongoing dependability of creation in the natural order of times and seasons.

> Yet God my King is from of old,
> working salvation in the earth.
> You divided the sea by your might;
> you broke the heads of the dragons in the waters.
> You crushed the heads of Leviathan;
> you gave him as food for the creatures of the wilderness.
> You cut openings for springs and torrents;
> you dried up ever-flowing streams.
> Yours is the day, yours also the night;
> you established the luminaries and the sun.
> You have fixed all the bounds of the earth;
> you made summer and winter.

God's answer to Job (chapters 38—41), in the midst of which is Job's penitent response (40:3-5), lifts Job beyond and above his suffering to the power and mystery of the creation in which God "laid the foundation of the earth" (Job 38:4). God racks Job's mind with a long series of questions, some rhetorical (chapters 38—39). In the first half of chapter 41 God's questions focus on Leviathan's mythic mystery and humanly unconquerable strength. God exposes Job's creaturely limits and thus his inability to comprehend the vastness of God's creation-power in conquering the raging chaos-fomenting sea monsters: Behemoth (40:15) and Leviathan (41:1).[17] God in his majestic power slays the monsters and sets the universe in shalom order. This miracle of order, however, continues to depend on God's sustaining power and love. Chaos is ever pounding at the door of the universe-house God built. As in Lewis's Narnia, it takes an Aslan to keep the monsters subdued.

Enemy Nations and Evil

In its life-long struggle against sin and evil, Israel regarded evil as also headquartered in the kings of enemy nations in a sort of semi-historical mythic sense. In Isaiah 14:12–15 the king of Babylon (v. 4) is "fallen from heaven"

---

17. Both mythic huge sea animals symbolize chaos and evil. Note Isaiah 27:1. See Burkholder, *Leviathan*, 62–67, for Leviathan's role in other ANE religions. Burkholder sees a historical development between Leviathan and "Lucifer."

and named "O Day Star, son of Dawn" (KJV, Lucifer!). The Lord God fights against such arrogant "god" powers. Therefore:

> You said in your heart, "I will ascend to heaven;
> I will raise my throne above the stars of God;
> I will sit on the mount of assembly on the heights of Zaphon;
> I will ascend to the tops of the clouds,
> I will make myself like the Most High."
> But you are brought down to Sheol,
> to the depths of the Pit. (Isa 14:13–15)

A similar oracle appears in Ezekiel 28, where the Lord God judges the king of Tyre. The portrayal of this king-god has a more personal descriptor:

> You were in Eden, the garden of God;
> every precious stone was your covering, . . .
> On the day that you were created they were prepared.
> With an anointed cherub as guardian I placed you;
> you were on the holy mountain of God;
> you walked among the stones of fire.
> You were blameless in your ways from the day
> that you were created,
> until iniquity was found in you.
> In the abundance of your trade you were filled
> with violence, and you sinned;
> so I cast you as a profane thing from the mountain of God,
> and the guardian cherub drove you out from
> among the stones of fire.
> Your heart was proud because of your beauty;
> you corrupted your wisdom for the sake of your splendor.
> I cast you to the ground;
> I exposed you before kings, to feast their eyes on you.
> By the multitude of your iniquities, in the
> unrighteousness of your trade,
> you profaned your sanctuaries.
> So I brought out fire from within you; it consumed you,
> and I turned you to ashes on the earth in the sight
> of all who saw you.
> All who know you among the peoples are appalled at you;
> you have come to a dreadful end and shall be no more forever.
> (Ezek 28:13–19)[18]

18. Both of these texts from Isaiah and Ezekiel place the origin of evil before the

In context, this portrayal of the evil king-gods is linked textually to Israel's perennial turn to worshiping idols, and thus doing "evil in the sight of the Lord" (in Kings and Chronicles). Such idolatry is Israel's rank evil. In Ecclesiastes, *hebel* with its general meaning of *vapor*, carries also other levels of meaning. Functioning as a tensive symbol,[19] *hebel* in OT usages within and outside Ecclesiastes has the meaning of *foul, worthless*, or *evil*. This use is frequently associated with "false deities" that Israel/Judah worshiped.[20] The term *rāʿ* occurs 12x in Ecclesiastes, which suggests a close association between *hebel* and *rāʿ*.

The nations' king-gods and their armies take Israel into exile, which in Jeremiah is ordered by God. The Babylonian King Nebuchadressar is even regarded as God's servant (Jer 35:9; Nebuchadnessar in 27:6; cf. King Cyrus, the anointed one, in Isa 44:28–45:1, 13). Israel's and Judah's exiles are foretold in the oracles of Hosea and Amos, Isaiah 1–39 and Jeremiah. Ezekiel shuttles back and forth between the temple in Jerusalem and those already in exile. Isaiah 44 is a parody on the supposed power of the king-gods. If Israel's enemies have triumphed, then what future hope is there? All of these prophets, however, envision a return, a restoration to the land and hope for Israel's future (in Amos, only in the last few verses). The enemy will not triumph. In these prophetic oracles the nations' doom is certain (Jer 46–51).[21]

---

time of these kings, in creation or in the garden of Eden. A much later text (dating from second century BCE or early medieval times) known as the Slavonic Enoch (or 2 Enoch) places the origin of evil during creation, just before the third day in Genesis 1. The following quotation is preceded by a semi-heading, "Here Satanail was hurled from the height, together with his angels":

> But one from the order of the archangels deviated, together with the division that was under his authority. He thought up the impossible idea, that he might place his throne higher than the clouds above the earth, and that he might become equal to my power. And I hurled him out from the height, together with his angels. And he was flying around in the air, ceaselessly, above the Bottomless. And thus I created the entire heavens. And the third day came. (Slavonic Enoch 29:4–5), *Pseudepigrapha*, edited by J. H. Charlesworth, vol. 1, 148.

For a thorough study, see Stuckenbruck, *Myth*. The book includes more than Enoch. E.g., *Jubilees* identifies four stages of sin and rebellion in Genesis 1—11, in addition to the "disobedient angels" to explain the origin of evil (25). See also his article, "Demonic."

19. Miller, *Ecclesiastes*, 41.

20. Miller, *Ecclesiastes*, cites fourteen occurrences, with eight in Jeremiah (2:5, 8; 10:3, 8, 15, 16:19; 51:18; others occur in Deuteronomy 32:21; 1 Kings 16:13, 26; 2 Kings 17:15; Psalm 31:6; Jonah 2:8), 260. These are arranged in tabular form, along with other meanings of *hebel*. See also 263–64. The GNB accentuates this dimension of meaning in Ecclesiastes (ibid., 265).

21. See the commentary on these chapters in Martens, *Jeremiah*, 247–73. Compare Ezekiel's similar oracles against the nations, Lind, *Ezekiel*, 215–59.

Ha sa-tán and Evil

With this more personalized king-portrait of where evil is headquartered and how it shows itself in self-aggrandizement, a *ha sa-tán* role-figure emerges in late OT literature (see Job 1—2; Zech 3:1-2; and 1 Chron 21:1 alongside of 2 Sam 24:1). In Job, *ha sa-tán* is one of the "heavenly beings" who comes with others into the heavenly court (1:6; 2:1) and turns out to be God's "tester" (prosecuting attorney) on assignment to test the righteous Job.[22] This ultimately redounds to God's glory because Job remains faithful to God, even though in his horrible suffering he cursed the day of his birth (Job 3).[23]

In Zechariah 3 *ha sa-tán* appears again in the heavenly court, but he is soon to lose his position because he is the "accuser" of the Lord and servant Joshua. So the Lord rebukes *ha sa-tán*, saying, "'The Lord rebuke you, O *ha sa-tán*" (v. 2). Here *ha sa-tán* becomes more than a "tester," for he oversteps his bounds as an accuser and opponent of the Lord and the Lord's people. In 1 Chronicles 21:1 *ha sa-tán* appears as *sa-tán* (no article). This is the precursor of Satan in the NT. In this text he personifies "the anger of the Lord" (as in the earlier 2 Sam 24:1 text). From here on in Israel's religious conceptions, rebellious Satan subtly seeks in nefarious ways to obstruct, wreck, and destroy God's work of *shalom*, healing, and salvation through Jesus Christ, evident in Jesus' prayer for Simon Peter to protect him from Satan (Luke 22:31–32a). In Wisdom 2:24 Satan is identified as working in and through the Genesis 3 "serpent," strategizing the fall of the first parents, resulting in paradise lost.

In this context eschatological hope emerges in the second century BCE for a Messiah who will defeat evil and mete out judgment upon Satan and his works. The Messiah will come and make war against Beliar, another name of Satan (T. Levi 18:9). Satan will be cast into the fire forever (T. Dan 5:10). In the first century BCE 4 (2) Esdras envisions a messianic kingdom enduring for 400 years (7:28) and the furnace of Hell (*Gehenna*) revealed along with the new Paradise, with nations choosing their destiny (7:36–44). The [evil] spirits that "despised the Law . . . and hated those who fear God" shall "immediately wander about in torments" (7:79). This is followed by a description

---

22. For other instances in which *ha sa-tán* appears as a tester, even an accuser under God's sovereignty see the discussion by Schoonhoven, *Wrath*, 44. For the most comprehensive and well-balanced presentation of *ha sa-tán* as tester and accuser in the OT see Page, *Powers of Evil*, 11–42.

23. For a detailed study of the role of *ha sa-tán* as a celestial figure with a positive role of testing for true piety (Job) and religious purity of Joshua to be high priest (Zech 3), see Rollston, "An Ur–History." Rollston says *Ha sa-tán* is not a bad figure in these texts, but plays a good God-directed role, *tester of* true piety and purity.

of seven ways they will experience torment (7:80–87).²⁴ In the Qumran Community, emerging in this time period, the "Covenanters" expect in the near-future the War of the Sons of Light against the Sons of Darkness.²⁵ The *Zadokite Document* describes the works of Belial (chapter 4) and later in 20:27–34 promises salvation to those who live in accordance with the Law and hearken to the voice of the Teacher (of Righteousness).

In the apotropaic (averting evil) prayers in Qumran and rabbinic Judaism, David Flusser, Jewish NT scholar, identifies three: *Prayer of Levi* (4Q213a 1 i 10–18), *Prayer for Deliverance* (11Q5 xix), and the Syriac Psalm (11Q5 xxiv). In each is a pattern of praying to be distanced from evil, and in the first two from the demonic: "let not (any) satan rule over me" (4Q213a 1 I 17; and 11Q5 xix 15). Rooted in Psalm 119:133b, "let all iniquity not rule over me," Flusser regards these pleas as "a personification of 'iniquity,' attributing it to or identifying it as a demonic being."²⁶

Since the Satan-*persona* is anticipated already in the evil king-gods of Babylon and Tyre, the question arises: who is the enemy? Is it the collective people under the control of these god-kings who oppose God the Creator of the world and Giver of shalom *or* is it the personified Satan power? In the several centuries prior to Jesus-Messiah's coming these two entities, pagan powers under the rule of the king-god powers and the onslaught of Satan and demons, constitute the enemy of Israel's security and hope.

---

24. Charlesworth, *Pseudepigrapha*, 537–39. The 4 Esdras text is here the same as 2 Esdras.

25. For detailed treatment of the perception of evil in Qumran, see Leonhardt-Balzer, "Evil."

26. Morris, in *Warding*, reports on several contributions in his lengthy chapter 2 titled "Anti-Demonic Traditions in Early Judaism" (51–147): David Flusser, on "apotropaic prayers" in the Dead Sea Scrolls (in Morris, 54; in Flusser, "Qumran," 221–22); Esther Eshel, who identifies three Scroll sources (4Q560, 8Q5, 11Q11) where demons are addressed directly (in Morris, 59–60); and Loren Stuckenbruck. Stuckenbruck "arranges the demonologically oriented prayers into three classes: (1) adjurations directed at demonic beings; (2) prayer or songs intended to counteract demonic harm; and (3) petitions that praise the nature and/or works of God in unison with an appeal to God for protection from demons" (in Morris, 62). Stuckenbruck also lists numerous texts from Qumran and Tobit that fall under these three categories (in Morris, 65). Morris summarizes these scholars' contributions and expands on the anti-demonic in Jewish literature, e.g., these citations from *Jubilees*: "*Moses' Intercession* (1:20); the *Prayer of Noah* (10:1–6); *Abram's Prayer* (12:20); and *Abraham's Blessing* (19:28)" (95). Morris's study is detailed and comprehensive; see his "Conclusions" for this section (143–47).

Toward Transformation in Understanding Evil

Crushed by oppression and sustained by hope, the Jewish people expected a Messiah who would fight against and destroy the oppressing powers. Inspired by Davidic precedents and revenging emphases in both apocalyptic and intertestamental writings, they expected the coming Messiah/king to be God's instrument of judgment and liberation. "'Send thy terror upon all nations,' they prayed. 'Lift up thy hand against the foreigners ... Rouse thy anger and pour out thy wrath; destroy the adversary and wipe out the enemy'" (Sir 36:2-3, 7).

One major stream of prophetic literature, however, envisions a transformation, salvation, and inclusion of the "enemy" peoples (see chapter 2b). This stream runs through the OT prophetic literature and intertestamental writings as well, as McKelvey documents in his study of Israel's anticipation of the New Temple to which the nations will come, not as enemies to destroy, but as recipients of God's blessing: "The belief that Jerusalem would one day become the worshipping place of the whole of mankind was . . . something of a theological necessity, arising from the doctrine of Yahweh as creator. The new temple becomes the symbol not only of the unity of Israel but of [hu]mankind."[27] (see Isa 2:1-4 and Mic 4:1-5).

Judah's (Israel's) exile in Babylon resulted in two transformative effects. First, the nation went "cold turkey" on their idolatry addiction. Obedience to Commandments 1 and 2 sinks in. Anti-idolatry becomes one of Judaism's central emphases; now they heed Jeremiah's pre-exilic prophecies and those of other prophets. They now know that their idolatries result in exile, and in exile they converted. The second influence came from Persian dualism that put good and evil in equal eternal combat. Judah (Israel) never accepted this *equal* duality of good and evil because of its firm belief in the Lord God as sovereign. Nonetheless, it had the effect of separating the Lord God from the fallen angel, Lucifer, now personified as Satan who "wars" against God's creation-shalom and God's covenant people.

Lurking within this treatment of *evil* in the OT is the persisting human question of the origin of evil.[28] Is evil part of God's creation, directly

---

27. McKelvey, *New*, 13. Some of the numerous texts describe the rebuilding of the temple and others foresee the inclusion of the peoples into the new sanctuary: Isa 2:1-4; 55:6-7, Mic 4:1-7; Ezek 40-48; Zech 1:16; 4:9f; 6:12, 15; Mal 3:1-4; Tob 13; 14:5; Sir 50 and 36:11-14; 1 Enoch 90:29-30; Pss Sol 17; T Benj 9:2; and Sib Or passim, especially iii.702-808. The theme continues in the rabbinic literature; Rabbi Akiba in Mishnah Pesahim 10:6; the Eighteen Benedictions 10, 14, and 17; Baraitha Megillah 17b-18a; and by Rabbi R. Simon B. Gamaliel (c. 140 CE) in Aboth of R. Nathan 35 (9-24).

28. Rutledge, in short, says, no answer, it *"can only be denounced and resisted,"* *Crucifixion*, 419.

perhaps (Isa 45:7) or indirectly,[29] in light of *ha sa-tán*'s rebellion against God at some point? Nigel Wright identifies four different philosophical-theological options: metaphysical dualism (compare the Persian dualist view noted above); monism: evil must be attributed ultimately to God's will; agnosticism: Scripture doesn't answer the issue or resolve the matter; or the misuse of a *creaturely freedom*, the view generally preferred among Christian thinkers.[30] But "human freedom" is ambiguous. If this alone is the answer, then God as Creator is ultimately responsible (option 2 above). Scripturally, one must fill the gap between God-given human freedom and why humans misused that freedom to disobey their Creator-God. In this drama "the serpent" tempting Eve and Adam to disobey causes "the fall" or "enlightenment," from which sin and evil proceed.

But, underneath this is the next lurking question: why does a created animal, the serpent—the wisest of all the animals—lead humans in this competition with and rebellion against Creator God? The two necessary links are: first, identifying the "serpent" with the devil/Satan, as noted above, and second, the fact that the heavenly *ha sa-tán becomes* the adversarial Satan, a.k.a, the devil, in canonical Scripture.[31]

But then another question: did God create the angels with freedom to rebel? Apparently so, which in turn means God took a risk in granting angels and humans the freedom to choose and rebel against their Creator-God.[32] Angelic rebellion, however, may be the cause of moral evil, but that does not answer how and *why* they rebelled. For this René Girard's massive contribution on the links between *desire, imitation, conflict, and war* illumine to a certain degree.[33] Angels that rebelled *desired* to be as God in his being and sovereignty. Similarly, the serpent's temptation to Eve was such to get her and Adam to *desire* the forbidden fruit and join the attempted coup to displace God and "be like God" (Gen 3:4). That was the *serpent's* segue into human disobedience, thus enticing humans to join with the *wise* serpent to displace God.

---

29. Copan ("Evil," 110–11) lists also Lamentations 3:37–38; Amos 3:6; Proverbs 16:4 with Revelation 17:16–17. Copan cites Tremper Longman's explanation of the latter texts by Genesis 50:20, "You meant evil against me; God meant if for good." Also, God turns Pilate's/Jewish leaders' crucifixion of Jesus into good, redemption for all who believe (Acts 2:22–24).

30. N. G. Wright, *Dark Side*, 68–70.

31. For discussion of the serpent and evil, see Rutledge, *Crucifixion*, 419–22; for Satan, 435–36.

32. This emphasis permeates Boyd's *Satan and the Problem of Evil*.

33. See chapter 11 where I utilize the work of Hardy, Whitehouse, and Yarnell in *Power*. Girard figures into their effort to explain the misuse of *power*.

N. G. Wright discusses Karl Barth's view of evil. Barth speaks of *evil* as *nothingness*, i.e, it has no essence in and of itself. Here Wright quotes C. S. Lewis who appears to mediate between Barth and the more common Christian view: "'Goodness is, so to speak, itself: badness is only spoiled goodness. And there must be something good before it is spoiled. . . . Evil is a parasite, not an original thing."[34] Wright also values Walter Wink's enormous contribution in his "Powers" trilogy, but regards his notion of *spirit-essence* as the interiority of the human being or structural "power" as unsatisfactory, with which I agree.[35]

In sum, as Nigel Wright says "God, in creating the world, made it with the possibility to go astray inherent within it."[36] Thus God included "risk" in creation, granting freedom for angels and humans to freely and lovingly obey or rebel. N. T. Wright, holding that the origin of evil is an insoluble mystery, writes,

> . . . the evil that humans do is integrated with the enslavement of creation. This is seldom a matter of one-on-one cause and effect, but there is a nexus, a web of rippling events that spreads out from human rebellion against the Creator to the out-of-jointness of creation itself. In the same way, when humans are put back to rights the world will be put back to rights. No theory is offered about earthquakes or other natural disasters, though no doubt the prophets would have been happy to identify them as heaven-sent warnings.[37]

While this statement augments human responsibility for evil, it fails to acknowledge the "serpent" source of evil. N. T. Wright's later statement, however, may imply such a source: "Evil is the force of anti-creation, anti-life, the force that seeks to deface and destroy God's good world of space, time, and matter, and above all God's image-bearing human creatures."[38]

Much of this chapter focused biblically on *chaos* as a foundational aspect of evil. Janet Warren rightly regards chaos as crucial to any discussion of evil. In her chapter titled, "Chaos: Evil in Opposition to God," she surveys and critiques dominant scholarly views, including the Augustinian view, perpetuated by Aquinas, that "evil is ordained by God and exists under his control . . . to serve a greater good and contributes to the perfection of

---

34. Lewis, *Mere*, 46–47; in N. G. Wright, *Dark*, 74.
35. N. G. Wright, ibid., 53–58.
36. N. G. Wright, ibid., 74–75.
37. N. T. Wright, *Evil*, 72.
38. Ibid., 89.

creation."[39] She considers Boyd's more dualistic view that requires spiritual resistance to evil; Barth's "nothingness" view that regards evil as absence of the good, thus with no *being* in and of itself;[40] and the views of Claude Lévi-Strauss, Mircea Eliade, and Mary Douglas.[41] She then develops her own view, which takes its metaphorical dimension from science's "dark matter." Her quote from Robert Cook states, "'Black Noise reverberates around the universe as the legacy of Primordial Chaos.'" Thus: "Dark matter as a model for evil accords with biblical views of darkness, theological views of nothingness, and anthropological metaphors of unreality."[42] In this context she develops her chaos-complexity view that regards "boundaries" as crucial to managing and resisting evil.[43]

The New Testament

As we enter the world of the NT the supra forces of evil (Satan, demons, unclean spirits) appear as common and crucial as daily bread. Note the "frames" of the "forgiveness center" of the Lord's Prayer: "give us our daily bread . . . save us in the hour of temptation, and deliver us from the evil one" (my translation). Early Christians regularly tangled with the *powers* of this world, foundationally evident in Jesus' earthly ministry culminating in the cross (chapter 5).[44] Early Christian witness collides with the "powers" in Acts and Revelation; Paul's letters develop a "theology" of the powers (see chapter 6).

Jesus' advent, mission, and ministry must be seen against the OT background of Israel's expected destruction of the enemy and hope for enemy transformation. In Jesus' day, however, it is not Assyria or Babylon, but Rome, whose popularly acclaimed divinized emperors threatened both the Jewish and Christian communities. Rome's divinized emperors are the covenant

---

39. Warren, *Cleansing*, 60. Her chapter titled: "Chaos: Evil in Opposition to God," 55–79, considers numerous views. For a sterling treatment of evil, what it is and is not, see Rutledge, *Crucifixion*, 422–34.

40. Ibid., 61–66.

41. Ibid., 66–69.

42. Ibid., 78.

43. The title for her next major chapter is: "Creation: A Circle on the Face of the Deep," 80–126, in which spatial metaphors are important. See chapter 11 for further discussion of her contribution applied to healing from evil.

44. This point is at the heart of Boyd's recent two-volume *Crucifixion*. While it is generally recognized that biblical interpretation must be christocentric (116–25), Boyd pinpoints the criterion: *cruciform*! All Scripture interpretation is through the lens of the *cross*. Hays regards *cross* as one of three "focal images" unifying NT literature (*Moral*, 197).

peoples' "enemy," thwarting obedience to and worship of the one true God. To maintain freedom to worship God, the covenant people revolt from the oppressor's occupation under gargantuan Roman Empire. The revolt by the Maccabees (168 BCE) and numerous similar attempts during the first century BCE testify to Israel's striving to be free from Rome's control: its taxation, suppression of Jewish freedom to worship the Lord God in the Jerusalem temple, and most of all to refuse Emperor worship at the cost of their lives. As with Israel, the engrafted Jesus-people collided with the *powers*. They resolved: we must obey God above human authority (Acts 5:29).

Two Words for Evil

The primary word for *evil* in the Greek NT is *ponēros*. It is most often descriptive of human choices: by nature doing sinful actions arising from sinful desires. Over one-third of the occurrences of *evil* (*ponēros*) appear in Jesus' Sermon on the Mount in Matthew ("on the Plain," in Luke). Nine of Matthew's twenty-five uses occur in chapters 5—7; five uses of Luke's twelve occur in 6:22–45. As a paradigm for the variety of types of use, I focus on Luke, noting parallels (//) in Matthew. The first occurrence in Luke refers to Herod's *evil* deeds (3:19). Within Jesus' Sermon on the Plain, two uses refer to opponents speaking of you as *evil* (6:22,[45] 35, *wicked* in NRSV//Matt 5:11). Another three, all in Luke 6:45, correlate "evil one" with "evil treasure" and "evil deeds" (//Matt 12:35; cf. 15:19). Two more are references to "evil spirits" (7:21; 8:2; both texts lack //s in Matt, but cf. 12:49, Matthew's parallel to Mark 7:22). The remaining three uses speak of "you who are evil" (11:13// Matt 7:11); "an evil generation" (11:29//Matt 12:39, 45); and the relation between the "evil eye" and "your body is full of darkness" (11:34//Matt 6:23). One remaining use occurs in the parable of the ten pounds where the one who buried his treasure is called "evil servant" (19:22//Matt 18:32, *wicked* in NRSV; 25:26). A related noun *ponērias* (translated *wickedness* in the NRSV) occurs in Luke 11:49.

To summarize the semantic field in Luke: one use is of a king (Herod) doing evil (3:19); two denote opponents maligning believers; two designate evil spirits; five more uses relate to the human disposition, one of which describes "this generation" refusing Jesus' words; and one last use identifies in parable form one who is *evil* because of his imprudent deed. Doing the math, two-thirds (eight out of twelve) refer to human disposition or action. Mark uses *ponēros* only once (7:22, denoting human choice and action),

---

45. Here I include the variant in the Greek text: "cast out your name as evil"—in NRSV, see note *w*.

compared to Matthew's twenty-five and Luke's twelve; it appears that the emphasis on human *evil* is concentrated in the so-called Q document,[46] Jesus' teachings that appear only in Luke and Matthew. Some distinctive uses in Matthew merit notice: 5:37, 39, 45; 6:13 in the Lord's Prayer; 7:17, 18 (4x, a nonmoral use referring to a tree and its fruit, where the NRSV translates *ponēros* as *bad*). Two uses in Matthew's long parable chapter refer to *the evil one* (13:19, 38), another to *evildoers* (12:41) and a fourth use to *evil [people]* (v. 49; cf. 25:26, NRSV, *wicked*). Three of Matthew's occurrences refer to final judgment, when *evildoers* get their due.

Jesus' many exorcisms, dominant in Mark and Luke, use other language to designate this face of *evil*: unclean spirit, demon(s), Satan (see Mark 1:23, 39; 3:11; 15, 21–26; 5:8; 6:7, 13). In the rest of the New Testament, *ponēros* seldom occurs, one or two uses per book, with some exceptions: in 1 John (6x, 2:13, 14; 3:12a, 12b; 5:18, 19); John (3x, 3:19; 7:7; 17:15 "protect them from the evil one"); Acts (7x, with concentration in chapter 19: vv. 12, 13, 16, 19; otherwise 17:5; 18:14; 28:21); Ephesians (3x, 5:16; 6:13, 19)—all these uses except 1 John 3:12a [ref. Cain] refer to "the evil one," i.e., Satan, as is in the Lord's Prayer in Matthew 6:13). What do we learn from analysis?

1. Human nature and desire is often characterized as *evil*.
2. Demons are referred to as *evil* spirits.
3. Opponents of the gospel that malign Jesus-believers are *evil*.
4. Satan is designated "the evil one."
5. Virtually all NT uses of *ponēros* belong to the moral category. Since Satan's "fall" from the heavenly court happened in his rebellion, this too is within the moral category of choice.[47]

In light of this, Christian believers must fight against the inner impulses and outer "powers" that obstruct them/us from walking in the truth and living the new life in Christ. Because of the "opposing evil power at work in the powers" realities, believers will in some situations, usually religious-political, give their lives for the gospel.

Another New Testament term for *evil* is *kakos* (51x, and less frequently *kakia*, 11x). Either word may at times be translated *bad* (Rom 12:3) or sometimes *wrong* (Rom 14:20). While the term *ponēros* occurs often in the Synoptic Gospels, *kakos* predominates in the Epistles, especially

---

46. This refers to the German word, *Quelle*, meaning *Source*. Such does not exist as an extant document and I doubt that it ever did. But it is a shorthand reference to what Matthew and Luke share in common that is not in Mark.

47. Boyd, *Satan*, 47–49.

Romans (16x) and 1 Peter (5x). Many of these occurrences are found in the contrast: "do good; do evil," in Romans 12–13 (6x) and 1 Peter 3 (5x). This concentration arises from Christians facing persecution from political authorities. Of the 51 occurrences of *kakos* in the New Testament 16 are in Romans and 5 in 1 Peter.

Wider Analysis

In Romans 7 Paul struggles with his conflicted desires in the face of the law's demands; he wants to do good but instead he does evil (vv. 19, 21). In Romans 2:9, "those who do evil" are judged severely in the final judgment. The only occurrence of *kakia* in Ephesians is translated *malice* (4:31). While *sin* and *evil* are bedfellows, both words together are hard to find, even though both carry personal culpability. It appears as though *sin* (*hamartia*) denotes personal choice and action, whereas the terms for *evil*—more descriptive of the result of choice—describe the substance of a thing or person. *Sin* may be known only to oneself, whereas evil is transparent for others to see.

Concurring with the second-century church father Athenagoras's view of evil, Boyd says "evil is not due to God's absence but to Satan's presence."[48] Arguing for freedom of choice by the angels and humans, Boyd regards the revolt of rebellious angels, headed by Satan, as their choice, and likewise the "fall" of humanity (Gen 3; Rom 5:12).[49] Thus the

> earth is afflicted by "a ruling prince" and "the demons his followers" who are, of their own free volition, incessantly working against the good administration of the Creator. The world *looks like a war zone* because it is *a war zone*. The will of the Supreme Adminstrator is not the only will that affects things.[50]

---

48. Boyd, *Satan*, 48.

49. In her book *Cleansing*, Warren has a helpful discussion of the fall of rebellious angels, a precursor to the fall of humanity (Adam and Eve). She cites many biblical texts regarding the role of angels in accord with God's will in creating them (106). But some rebelled and "fell" from their divinely mandated mission. She then identifies "four primary clusters of biblical texts . . . used in support of an angelic fall: the serpent of Genesis 3, the sons of god in Genesis 6, the fall of an exalted one (Lucifer) in Isaiah and Ezekiel, and apocalyptic expulsion of the dragon/devil from heaven" (107). She devotes the next five pages to discussion of each, acknowledging ambiguity on this matter. She regards Jesus' declaration in Luke 10:18, "I saw Satan falling from heaven" as "a prophetic statement or continuous action, but not necessarily a 'defeat,'" citing Page, *Powers*, 110; Twelftree, *Name*, 140. See chapter 5 below for my discussion.

50. Boyd, *Satan*, 48.

Though Boyd does not endorse all the particulars of Athenagoras's views he does regard them as "essentially biblical." In Boyd's next two paragraphs he blends the two "homes" of evil: Satan and the "Powers." This is the task of this book: to show from biblical study that the spate of books on the devil/evil spirits/deliverance ministry and the spate of books on the principalities and powers need to be "incorporated" to grasp fully the Christian call to vigilance against evil in this world. Boyd interweaves these several streams of thought mentioned above:

> ... God fights against cosmic threatening waters and powerful chaotic monsters such as Leviathan and Rahab. It constitutes another way of saying that Satan is "the ruler of the power of the air" (Eph 2:2), "the ruler [*archōn*] of this world" (Jn 12:31; 14:30; 16:11), and the "god of this world" (2 Cor 4:4). It is another way of explaining why Christians must fight against spiritual "rulers," "authorities," "powers of this present darkness," and "forces of evil in heavenly places" (Eph 6:12).
>
> [Further] ... something other than God's will and design is at work in creation. From mudslides that bury children alive to diseases that kill multitudes of people [I add tsunamis, floods, and forest fires] it is clear—at least it was clear to Athenagoras and the early church—that God's good will is not being uniformly carried out in history. Atheists argue on this basis that there is no Creator. Early church fathers rather argued on this basis and from God's Word, that there is a Creator God but that he must battle a formidable opponent who has of his own volition made himself evil.[51]

As the first paragraph of this quotation from Boyd's book on evil indicates, another major dimension of evil in the New Testament is associated with the "powers." Whether these powers are under God's control to promote human good or are under Satan's control to wreak evil upon the earth is a dicey issue in NT writings. Romans 13 is witness to the former; Revelation 13, to the latter. While *evil* (*ponēros*) occurs only once in Revelation

---

51. Ibid. Boyd's purpose differs from mine, though it is complementary. In his words, "my entire project attempts to make philosophical sense of the warfare worldview of Scripture" (23). Freedom of decision for humans and angels is the important emphasis throughout the book. Six principles or theses are developed in the first half of the book. These are summarized on p. 205: "*love entails freedom . . . , freedom entails risk . . . , risk entails moral responsibility . . . , moral responsibility is proportionate to the power to influence . . . , the power to influence is irrevocable . . . , and . . . the power to influence is finite.*" The second half of his book turns then to what this warfare entails for humans, nature, and future hope, all grounded in Jesus' ministry and the understandings of the early church, which stretches into the church fathers of the first four centuries.

(16:2) and *kakia* only twice (2:2; 15:2), the reality of evil, both moral and non-moral, dominates the book. Revelation 12:7–11 blends several personified identities of evil and the evil one: dragon, ancient serpent, Devil, Satan, deceiver. These are thrown down from heaven.

The "Messiah" in Revelation is the "slain Lamb." Only the Lamb-Messiah through his death and resurrection conquers evil, and thus is able to open the scroll that unveils the manifold evils together with the Lamb's triumph over evil (see Rev 5:1–6:1; 8:1; 17:14; 19:6–9).[52] Moral evil shows itself in the *beast* and the *false prophet* as well as in those who worship these "powers" (Rev 13). See chapter 7 for the Lamb's triumph over evil in the seven "trumpets," "plagues," and "bowls of wrath," orchestrated by God's judgment of the Empire's evil.

Three other NT texts refer specifically to Satan's downfall. First, in 2 Thessalonians 2:8 the Lord Jesus will slay the lawless one "with the breath of his mouth, annihilating him by the manifestation of his coming." Verse 9 declares "the lawless one is apparent in the working of Satan." Second, Jude 6 speaks of angels who lost their position in heaven (echo of Ezek 28) and are now "kept in eternal chains in deepest darkness for the judgment of the great Day. Jude 10 speaks of "the archangel Michael" who "contended with the devil" over the body of Moses, with a final blow against the devil in Michael's command, "'The Lord rebuke you.'" Third, in Luke 10:18 Jesus sees Satan falling from heaven[53] when the seventy apostles return from their mission proclaiming the advent of the gospel of peace, curing the sick, and casting out demons.[54]

Other texts also portray Jesus' mission as attack and defeat of the devil. These will be discussed in chapters 4 and 5 below. The meta-narrative of the Synoptic Gospels (and with a different decisive "strike" in John's Gospel

---

52. For exposition of the crucial role of Jesus Christ as the Lamb in Revelation, see Johns, *Lamb Christology*.

53. There are two stages in Satan's downfall. The first is Satan getting kicked out of heaven, declared here and in Revelation 12:7–10; Jude 6, and numerous texts in the Enoch literature. The second stage is his defeat through Jesus Christ's death and resurrection, which assures ultimate defeat of Satan's wily work on earth. Victory will be consummated in Jesus' *parousia* as Judge. We thus live in the eschatological "now/not yet" tension, between Jesus Christ's decisive victory over evil in his death/resurrection and evil's final cosmic defeat. This defeat of Satan applies also to the "Powers" (1 Cor 15:24–26; Col 1: 18–20; Rev 20). See Schoonhoven, *Wrath*, for extended discussion, 44–68. God's wrath is directed against Satan and his works; Christ's victory through the cross and resurrection "constitutes the turning point of heavenly wrath" (Rom 1:16–18; 8:35–39; Eph 6:10–18; see Schoonhoven, *Wrath*, 138–48).

54. For extended exposition of this text in Luke see chapter 5 below and Swartley, *Covenant*, 124–26: "The peace gospel is God's way in Jesus and his followers to subdue evil" (126).

also)⁵⁵ is that of Jesus battling and triumphing over Satan by announcing the kingdom of God come and coming through exorcisms, parables, healings, suffering, death, and resurrection. Jesus' suffering-death as means to victory matches the "slain Lamb" of Revelation.

Jesus' victory over Satan, sin, and death has direct impact upon the "powers." Christ reigns over the powers (Col 2:10–15; 1 Pet 3:22; Phil 2:9–11). Schoonhoven writes, " . . . *the death and ascension of Jesus Christ was not just incidentally or peripherally related by the early Christians to heaven and the powers therein, but that on the contrary it formed a middle point of early Christian confession* [with the *Parousia* and final judgment the end point]."⁵⁶ Christ's Lordship means: victory now and final victory in the consummation of all things (Rev 19—22).

So the Journey

The purpose of this chapter and the next two—and consequently the entire book—is to examine the "journey" from the OT to the NT in their respective conceptions of and responses to evil. Some elements of "creation out of chaos" appear in the NT, but these are not as explicit as in the OT. When Jesus stills the stormy sea in Mark 4:35–41 he rebukes the chaos (*epitimaō*), which echoes Yahweh's rebuke of the watery chaos of darkness in Psalm 18:4–15. The word for *rebuke* in Psalm 18:15c (LXX, 17:16) is the same as in Mark 4:39. Jesus' rebuke occurs in Mark's larger "liberation" section, which I develop elsewhere.⁵⁷ A similar text is Psalm 104:7 (LXX, 103:7), with *epitimaō* occurring in the LXX as in Mark 4:39.

A more explicit continuity/discontinuity lies in divine intervention to overcome evil. What is narrated above is summed up well in Hebrews 2:14c–15: "so that through death he might destroy the one who has the power of death, that is, the devil, and free those who all their lives were held in slavery by the fear of death." Jesus' many exorcisms and Paul's "flesh/spirit" dialectic point to the same victory: "the old is gone, the new has come" (2 Cor 5:17, NIV).

---

55. John 12:31b declares, "Now the ruler of this world is cast out" (AT). Though John's Gospel has no individual exorcisms, Jesus' ministry culminating in "my hour" (Jesus' passion, cross, death, and resurrection) is one grand exorcism stripping Satan of his power. This is Jesus' cosmic exorcism in John. Boyd's discussion of Satan's kingdom divided against itself suggests YHWH may "use one group of [evil] spirit-agents to overthrow another" (*Crucifixion*, vol. 2, 1273–75). In deliverance ministry, one demon is often at the head, with others under his power.

56. *Wrath*, 146.

57. Swartley, *Israel's*, 55–57.

The NT speaks clearly of evil and the need for protection against it. In Ephesians 6:10–18 we mindfully clothe ourselves with the armor that resists and counters evil, whether personal or systemic (cf. 1 Pet 4:8–9). In the Lord's Prayer we ask our heavenly Father to protect us from the evil one.[58] The Pauline "put off" and "put on" admonitions exemplify the vigilance needed to resist evil with new clothing: faith, perseverance, and deeds of love and mercy.

Paul's eschatological hope in Romans 8:17–23 envisions redemption from creation's groaning, inferring that creation continues to struggle against chaos. Similarly, Paul's emphasis on the "new creation" in 2 Corinthians 5:17 means the first creation has gone awry, and is "standing in need" of full redemption. This hope flowers in Revelation where the sequential chaos (plagues and bowls of wrath) yearn for a turn-about, which comes in the vision of the New Jerusalem, where all of creation's tumult and chaos is overcome: no more tears, no more sea (chaos?), no more night (the chaotic watery darkness), and "no more dying there"!!

---

58. The Greek has the definite article: *tō ponērou*. The NRSV translates it thus: *evil one*. Matthew 5:39 reads the same, but refers there not to Satan, but to a person who has evil intent.

2a

From Killing the Enemy to Loving the Enemy

Once when Joshua was by Jericho,
he looked up and saw a man standing before him
with a drawn sword in his hand.
Joshua went to him and said to him,
"Are you one of us, or one of our adversaries?"
He replied, "Neither; but as commander of the army
of the Lord I have now come."
And Joshua fell on his face to the earth and worshiped,
and he said to him,
"What do you command your servant, my lord?"
The commander of the army of the Lord said to Joshua,
"Remove the sandals from your feet,
for the place where you stand is holy."
And Joshua did so.

—Josh 5:13–15

Israel's life as a nation begins with God's miracle: delivering the Israelites from bondage in Egypt. Just as Jesus' death and resurrection is the founding event of the Christian church, so Israel's founding event is God's deliverance from slavery in Egypt. Exodus 14:14 describes God's action and the people's role, "The Lord will fight for you, and you have only to keep still." As Lind emphasizes, by this means God fulfills the Abrahamic promise of a "land" and "nation" for Abraham's descendants (Gen 12:1–3). Later under kingship, Israel adopts a standing military army. But God's benchmark is the Exodus 14—15 model, which judges latter wars.[1] Israel's "founding" *deliverance* helps us understand why the Psalms repeatedly speak of deliverance, personally and corporately (chapter 3).

Even though the Lord promises to deliver miraculously, we are confronted with an agonizing moral dilemma: God's command to slaughter and offer all human life as sacrifice to the true owner of the land, the Lord God Almighty. How do we who read Scripture through the eyes of Jesus live with and understand *ḥerem*?

Israel's Warfare *Ḥerem*

A shocking means of Israel's combating evil is *ḥerem*, a God-ordered slaughter of the Canaanite nations in order to save Israel from idolatrous influences upon Israel's worship of the Lord God (the Shema, Deut 6:4–5). Sadly, this type of response to evil has perpetrated similar actions throughout history, a.k.a. ethnic cleansing.[2]

The overall emphasis of the OT, however, reveals God as loving and forgiving (Exod 34:6–7a; Pss 57:10; 108:4; 136; 138:2, et al.), despite Israel's recurring sins prompting God's judgment. The OT is replete with ethical admonitions that anticipate NT teaching.[3] This chapter and the next pursue a canonical trajectory that enables us to see God's unfolding revelation. Thus certain OT practices as Holy War must be assessed in the ANE historical context, while not too readily dismissing OT portraits of God that offend us. Jesus' command to love enemies contrasts sharply, however, to this confounding *ḥerem* practice.

Greg Boyd, in a chapter titled "The True Face of God," writes:

---

1. Lind, *Yahweh*, 23, 48–50, 160–74.

2. This practice and other offensive events in the OT tend to generate unbelief (even atheism). It is not only the "bad things" ascribed to God's commands in the OT that might generate an atheistic response, but also the history of Christian people doing "evil" in God's name. Addressing this difficult matter are: Lamb, *God*, and Zaleski, "Love." Lamb answers the critiques of atheists Dawkins and Hitchens. Zaleski's one-page article leaves us pondering, possibly crying, and reaching for love, even when hope and faith are zonked. Copan, *Is God?* is helpful, as well as C. J. H. Wright's *Old Testament Ethics*. Both utilize NT portraits (as well as other OT portraits) of God to present a fuller canonical view of God. Copan develops his contribution against the claims of the "New Atheists." Copan and Flannagan wrestle with this issue in relation to God's justice, in *Did God?* For a popular read, see Tada and Estes, *When*, 77–93.

3. See e.g. C. J. H. Wright, *Mission*; Leiter, *Neglected*; and Fleischer, *Old*.

It seems apparent that by replacing the *lex talionis* with his instruction to 'not resist an evil person,' to 'turn the other cheek,' and to 'love your enemies' (Matt 5:38, 44), Jesus was calling on people to respond to wrongdoers in a way that is 'the direct opposite' of the OT.[4]

Boyd's voluminous publication (1,400 pages, two volumes) addresses this issue at length. How do we regard Scripture as authoritative, including the OT, and make sense of this contrast between what appears to be a Warrior God in the OT and the model of Jesus Christ's *cross*-response to evil in the NT?[5] In this chapter's epigraph the God-man visitor who appears to Joshua says neither *yes* nor *no* to Joshua's question of "sides." Rather, it confounds Joshua's assumption that the Lord is on Israel's side, for "the army of the Lord" transcends earthly military might. The Lord later becomes enemy to Israel, punishing Israel for its idolatries.

We cannot "jump over" this horrific practice of *ḥerem* in the history of God's people. We must trace the canonical journeys of the rationale for *ḥerem*. The earlier Exodus traditions (composed likely during the Solomonic monarchy) do not prescribe *ḥerem*, whereas the later Deuteronomic traditions (final form written likely during Josiah's reign) and Joshua (written closer in time to Deuteronomy) do prescribe *ḥerem*.[6] This has led numerous scholars, notably von Rad,[7] to regard "holy war" a later idealization, not a historical practice.

---

4. Boyd, *Crucifixion*, vol. 1: *Cruciform Hermeneutic*, 72, see 72–79.

5. Boyd's subtitle for vol. 2 is "The Cruciform Thesis," which extends his "Cruciform Hermeneutic" in vol.1. Boyd employs four "principles" to "defend the Cruciform Thesis:" (1) "Cruciform Accommodation," (2) "Redemptive Withdrawal," (3) "Cosmic Conflict," and (4) "Semiautonomous Power." His third principle, 1005–86, correlates well with my chapters 1, 2a, and 2b. Boyd, however, does not focus on "deliverance from evil," but on a "cruciform hermeneutic and thesis." He contributes more than I do to *atonement*, with the *cross* the center of all interpretation. He appeals to Moltmann's *Crucified God*: "the death of Jesus on the cross is the centre of all Christian theology" . . . "'the crucified Christ' is nothing less than 'the key that unlocks all the divine secrets of Christian theology,'" Boyd, 1.159; Moltmann, 114. Jesus' resurrection and Pentecost enable the birth, survival, and growth of the Christian church with its mission to overcome evil with good by the authority of Jesus' name.

6. Moules, in *Fingerprints*, says archaeology has not confirmed the *ḥerem* conquest as historical. Judges shows a different picture. The *ḥerem* portrait together with the Psalms that recite these events (e.g., 136) are liturgical renderings. This liturgy celebrates God's holiness, not destruction of enemies. Further, Jesus, not Joshua, is the model for response to enemies (138–39 and n27). Moules's proposal draws from various notable scholars in biblical theology, especially von Rad.

7. See Ollenburger's "Introduction" to von Rad's *Holy War*, 1–33, which describes also von Rad's predecessors and more recent scholars who have advanced divergent views from von Rad's. See also Sanderson's extensive bibliography on "War, Peace, and

We begin with the key Exodus narrative: Exodus 23:20—24:1. Yahweh promises to send *an angel* (vv. 20, 23), *my terror* (v. 27), and *"pestilence"* (v. 28) before the Israelites to drive out the enemy nations from the land God promised to Israel. YHWH is the Holy Warrior (Exod 14:14; 15:3). The people *stand still* and see the Lord's deliverance.[8] This text, compared to the next two, does not command Israel *to destroy all that breathes*. God eradicates the enemy by miracle. It does not command Israel to kill the peoples in the land. Rather, it concurs with Exodus 14:14: "the Lord will fight for you, and you have only to keep still." The early Exodus 15 song celebrates God's victory; Israel did not fight. Yahweh is the Warrior.[9]

The next two later texts, in composition, command *Israel* to destroy the people in the land God promised to Abraham. They authorize *ḥerem*:

> When the Lord your God brings you into the land that you are about to enter and occupy, and *he clears away many nations before you* . . . and when the Lord your God gives them over to you and you defeat them, then *you must utterly destroy them. Make no covenant with them and show them no mercy. Do not intermarry with them,* . . . [T]his is how you must deal with them: break down their altars, smash their pillars, hew down their sacred poles, *and burn their idols with fire*. For you are a *people holy to the Lord your God*; the Lord your God has chosen you out of all the peoples on earth to be his people, *his treasured possession*. (Deut 7:1–6)

> When you go out to war against your enemies, and see horses and chariots, an army larger than your own, you shall not be afraid of them; for the Lord your God is with you . . . . Before you engage in battle, the *priest* shall . . . say to [the troops]: "Hear, O Israel! Today you are drawing near to do battle against your enemies. Do not lose heart, or be afraid, or panic, or be in dread of them; for it is the Lord your God who goes with you, to fight for you against your enemies, to give you victory." (Deut 20:1–4).

Justice" in von Rad, 135–66. She lists three basic views of Israel's origin in Canaan: conquest, peaceful penetration, and peasant revolt, naming scholars who hold these differing views (150). Wood, in *Perspectives*, 19, lists eleven elements in Holy War, derived from von Rad's *Holy War*. He makes an important point, citing Fischer, "'war is not holy because God commanded it; it is holy only in the sense that the victory is totally ascribed to God'" (Wood, 18; Fischer, "War and Peace," 28).

8. See Lind's seminal contribution: *Yahweh*; cf. Longman and Reid, *God*, which includes also Jesus and NT teaching.

9. The LXX boldly translates this text to say, "The Lord crushes/destroys (*suntribōn*) wars."

Three points are crucial. First, the rationale is God's election of Israel: "the Lord your God has chosen you out of all the peoples on earth to be his people, *his treasured possession*." The land God will give you is God's, not Israel's. This is the foundational rationale for *ḥerem*. Second, the battle is under the authority and blessing of the priest. This is not *military* warfare. Third, 20:4 carries forward Exodus 14:14. The people do not fight to win the battle. God fights and wins the battle.[10]

Deuteronomy 20:10–18 contains a new policy concerning towns far away, not in the God-promised land. Here the rules differ, for they are commanded to first offer "terms of peace." If they accept, then do not destroy them, but utilize them for forced labor. If they do not accept the "terms of peace" then kill all the males and take all the rest as booty.[11] But "the towns of these peoples that the Lord your God is giving you as an inheritance, you must not let anything that breathes remain alive. You shall annihilate . . . [the inhabitants] just as the Lord your God has commanded, so that they may *not teach you to do all the abhorrent things* that they do for their gods, and you thus sin against the Lord your God." The rationale for killing the males in towns far away that refused a peace treaty is to guard against their military power overtaking Israel in the God-promised land.

Another text, however, while preserving *ḥerem* portrays conquest as a parade: seven priests and seven trumpets go ahead of the ark of the

10. This point is at the heart of Lind's contribution, in *Yahweh*, with Exodus 14:14 as paradigm.

11. YHWH as Warrior is one of many OT portraits of divine judgment, generally regarded as *violence*; see Seibert, *Disturbing*. Seibert describes a wide range of God's "violent" actions, with commendable scope of interpretive efforts to explain and resolve the problem to some degree of satisfaction from a Christian point of view. He judges all such portraits against the Jesus of the Gospels as our normative moral guide (he slights Pauline literature). His is a vast undertaking, but not altogether satisfying. What Seibert fails to do is trace the *trajectory* of similar thought within the OT and between the Testaments. Seibert has a section on "Progressive Revelation" (*Disturbing*, 89–92), but this needs an intra-canonical trajectory that shows transformation. This chapter and the next contribute to this task, but more needs to be done. Seibert's more recent book, *Disarming the Church*, assumes this trajectory that leads to Jesus Christ, and masterfully calls Christians to "*Forsake Violence*" (from subtitle) in order to "*Follow Jesus*." What is not clear is that the OT is stitched into the NT and the NT cannot be understood apart from the OT. See my *Israel's*: "the OT is a precondition for the Synoptics' story of Jesus," 282, and Hays, *Reading Backwards*. The book of essays, *Wrestling*, edited by Carroll and Wilgus, contributes to this ongoing task; see especially the essays by Dallaire, "Taking," and Martens, "Toward an End." Dallaire presents in vivid language the horror of *ḥerem* in its *Wirkungsgeschichte* in later history when similar violent destruction of enemy peoples occurred. She includes Heimbach's summary of von Rad's contribution to Holy War; fifteen related proscriptions with citation of supportive biblical references, 62–63. She also describes briefly the history of interpretation, including renown Jewish scholars, Maimonides and Rashi, 66–67.

covenant, symbol of God's presence. But ahead of them are *warriors, armed men* (Josh 6:3–14), a clear shift toward synergistic action.[12] The rationale for *ḥerem*, however, is clearly stated: no idol worship! If *ḥerem* is not done, the idolatrous peoples in the land will lead Israel into idolatry and intermarriage. Israel will not remain holy unto the Lord. Israel must destroy everything, taking no booty in towns in the land.

Israel's battle against Ai (a city *within* the God-promised land) shows the seriousness of disobedience. God could not win the battle because Achan coveted booty and "took a beautiful mantle from Shinar and a bar of silver weighing 200 shekels, and a bar of gold weighing fifty shekels"—all now hidden in the ground (Josh 7:21). Not until this violation of *ḥerem* was punished by all Israel stoning Achan and burning him to death did the Lord turn "from his burning anger" (7:22–26). Then YHWH commanded Joshua to take all the fighting men to war against Ai again for victory. Matties makes an arresting point. After the Ai narrative the phrase, "*the word of the Lord* spoken to Joshua" *ends* (8:1, 18, 27)."[13] Joshua 24:12–13, however, in a summary statement, indicates the Lord continued to fight the battles.

All prescriptions for entering the land, nonetheless, call for trust in miracles, e.g., Jericho's walls falling from trumpet blasts after the seventh walk around the city (Josh 6), or Gideon's use of torch-lights inside jars that when smashed scare off the people (Judg 7).[14]

---

12. From today's perspective we regard these "conquest" actions as *violent*. However, *violence* (*hamas*, occurring in the OT 66x) describes *human conduct, which God hates*. See Swartley, *Covenant*, 393–98. Leithart, in "Violence," explicates this more fully. The term *nonviolence* occurs nowhere in Jewish-Christian Scripture. Psalm 99:8 voices the two poles of God's character: "O Lord our God, you answered them; you were a forgiving God to them, but an avenger of their wrongdoings," or, "You answered them, O Lord our God; You were to them God-Who-Forgives, though You took vengeance on their [evil] deeds" (NKJV). Focusing on "nonviolence" may be "an ethical decoy that lures us from speaking what is most important about atonement: through the cross God *and* Jesus Christ in self-donation make peace between humans and God and between humans and humans" (*Covenant*, 183n13). God has the divine prerogative and necessity to execute *judgment* of evil—would we want it otherwise?—and for Jesus' followers to be peacemakers. Cf. Z. Klassen, "(Non)Violent."

13. Matties, *Joshua*, 171, 184, 187.

14. The variations, however, indicate that YHWH War does not assume practice of *ḥerem*. Dunham argues for a clean distinction, noting that the exodus deliverance was YHWH War but not *ḥerem* and the Flood Destruction in Noah's time was a form of *ḥerem* but not YHWH War. YHWH War is also not strictly limited to Israel's possession of the promised land of Canaan, for the Prophets employ it as God's form of judgment of the nations and also of Israel. The destruction of the earth by fire, envisioned in 2 Peter 3 is *ḥerem*, but not YHWH War. See Dunham's lengthy and detailed analysis of this in "Yahweh War." His sources are extensive, beyond the limits of this study.

Even though YHWH war practices end, and military battles begin, *ḥerem* appears in OT Scripture as rationale for other practices. Douglas Earl identifies three contexts in which the term *ḥerem* appears in the OT. First, to receive the God-promised land of Canaan, God commands Israel to destroy the people and the animals ("all that breathes") as well as their belongings, as noted above. Second, *ḥerem* occurs in prophetic literature as annihilation, but "in an eschatological/apocalyptic sense to describe the fate of the nations (Jer 50:21, 26; 51:3), including Israel (Isa 43:28)." A third use appears in the priestly literature where people and possessions are "irrevocably dedicated to Yhwh (e.g. Lev 27:21–29)."[15] What is here "devoted to the Lord" is harvest firstfruits and tithes. Jubilee is based on the same: the land is devoted to the Lord. Here *ḥerem* is applied internally, ensuring all belongs to God.[16] In its primary meaning *ḥerem* is the basis for Israel's sabbatical and Jubilee practices; they attest to YHWH's ownership of the land.

The YHWH war practices of *ḥerem*, however, did not rid the land of idolatry. For the prophets castigate Israel for its idolatries, worshipping the gods of peoples in Canaan! So *ḥerem* practice, killing all that breathes in the land, did not accomplish its goal—which lends support for von Rad's view: later idealization!

Interpretations of this abhorrent practice fall generally into two categories: literal and symbolic, though literal has many variants, presented in *Show Them No Mercy*.[17] Merrill, who holds a dispensational, premillennial view, contends the God-commanded *ḥerem* is expressive of God's character in establishing a covenant people:

> [I]t was only after Israel had been constituted as a nation . . . that Yahweh war became not just a display of God's redemptive power and grace on behalf of his people but a constituent part of the covenant relation itself. Israel from then on would not just witness God's mighty deeds as heavenly warrior but would be engaged in bringing them to pass.[18]

---

15. Earl, "Holy War." See also Earl's earlier contributions in *Reading Joshua*.

16. Matties, *Joshua*; Gerbrandt, *Deuteronomy*, 552–53; Earl, "Holy War," 152–75. In comparing these texts with the ANE myths of creation, Trudinger emphasizes the vast difference. The ANE are *really violent* ("Friend," 32–33). Analyzing Psalms 74, 24, 93—*ChaosKampf* renditions of creation—Trudinger shows that these Psalms pair *earth* and *temple* (Zion), which accentuates their function for worship. Earth is not "the corpse of a dead enemy of God," as in some ANE texts, but joins in praise-worship of God, Creator of earth and sea (40).

17. Cowles, Merrill, Gard, and Longman, *Show*.

18. Merrill, "The Case," in *Show*, 66; note also Longman III's approving response to this citation from Merrill's essay, 107–8. *Show* presents four views on the thorny topic. Cowles persuasively contends for radical discontinuity, in which these commands

The literal interpretation regards this practice necessary for Israel to remain faithful to their covenant God.[19] YHWH war testifies to a *holy* God of Israel who requires separation from the unholy, i.e., pagan idolatry.[20] While holiness is to be valued throughout Scripture, Holy War as a means of achieving it is not. Holy War reflects ANE warfare patterns; in this respect God did not yet fully convert Israel. As Johnson has contended, and Allman has summarized,[21] Holy War contrasts to Jesus' life and teachings. Holiness in all strands of NT teaching *contrasts* to, even repudiates YHWH War *killing* enemies.

The symbolic interpretation, beginning with Origen, holds these texts emphasize for Christians the seriousness of sin. The significance of *ḥerem*

must be attributed to human perspective projected onto God; the God *represented by* the commands of *ḥerem* cannot be correlated with Jesus' definitive revelation of God who loves enemies. They represent the human Moses. Holy War and *ḥerem* are to be thoroughly rejected as divine revelation. Since Jesus' "love of enemies" command is the definitive revelation of God all else that does not conform to this norm is thereby judged un-Godlike. The second view, Merrill's, argues for moderate discontinuity, viewing all Scripture as the word of God but also relegating *ḥerem* as God's word to the covenant people to a historical time and place, for four reasons: 1) Israel's hardness of heart; 2) to protect Israel from spiritual corruption; 3) destruction of idolatry; and 4) "the education of Israel and the nations as to the character and intentions of the one true God" (85). The third view, Gard's, holds to continuity, but within an eschatological purpose to achieve God's ultimate purposes in history. The fourth view, Longman's, holds to continuity, but with a spiritualizing of the actual events to correlate with the spiritual conflict between Jesus and Satan (and demons) and the Christian believers' battle against the principalities and powers in the NT. Longman contends Revelation portrays Jesus as Warrior with devastation on a worldwide scale, in the face of which the destruction of the Canaanites does not begin to compare (the slain Lamb, in his view, apparently turns back into a Lion!). My own view embraces elements of each: discontinuity, but also continuity; the ANE historical context; eschatological purpose; and for Jesus vs. Satan, the OT portrayal of pagan kings depicted in Isaiah 14:12–21 and Ezekiel 28:11–19.

19. In discussing "The Ban," Niditch cites parallels from contemporary ANE cultures, specifically Moab, from the Mesha Inscription: *War*, 31. Lind cites the parallel also; the difference is the "concept of political power—the unilateral rule of Yahweh" in Israel: *Yahweh*, 82.

20. Earl's explanation confuses: first, that holy war shaped Israel's identity in their separation from the surrounding nations, but then later the Joshua model liberalizes the Deuteronomic model of separation by making torah-obedience central to Israel's identity, thus "seeking to reshape perceptions of others and boundaries" (*Reading*, 203). Hence, "life with YHWH" is broader and fuller than "life in the land" (202). Earl's Christian eyes *bend* Joshua to fit his Christian reading (is that his book's purpose?).

21. Johnson, *Holy*, 37–42; Allman, *Who?*, 153–54. Regarding Allman's ten types of Holy War I demur on #3: God defends the Hebrews in the Red Sea miracle. I question also his #8, "the soldier of Christ," i.e. spiritually struggling against sins of the flesh (Eph 6:10). If that is a type of Holy War, then *this* entire book is Holy War! His ten types stretch Holy War and thus confuse. "Humans *killing* enemies" characterizes Holy War.

for the Christian church is through metaphor, a point Gerbrandt develops when examining scholarly views. He quotes Moberly:[22] "Deuteronomy is using the ritual of *ḥerem* as a metaphor for God's demand of absolute loyalty or fidelity as stated in the Shema." Further, "'... The practice of *ḥerem* as a metaphor for religious fidelity, is that which demonstrates and enables Israel's unreserved love for YHWH' ... Absolute devotion to God requires absolute separation."[23]

Holiness motivating *ḥerem* is basic in Nelson's contribution.[24] His theses correlate the noun *ḥerem* with *holiness* or the *state of holiness* (קָדוֹשׁ); the meaning of the word is broader than its function in "Holy War." Its primary meaning is "sacred to the Lord," *not* "devoting to destruction." It is used for "a penalty inspired by YHWH (Exod 22:19; Lev 24:29), a private act of religious dedication (Lev 27:28), the jubilee law on an unredeemed field (Lev 27:20-21), and punishment by the community (Jdg 1:11; Ezra 10:8)."[25]

When applied to warfare it means the city or land is already the Lord's. Israel does not own it. Taking booty jeopardizes divine ownership. It violates the *Shema:* worship and serve only the Lord our God, who is one. And because Israel, once in the land, worshipped other gods, the Prophets announce to Israel God's certain judgment upon Israel and their imminent captivity!

The notion of clean/unclean is also part of *ḥerem*. The people that lived on YHWH's land worshiped idols that would contaminate Israel's covenant fidelity to YHWH. Nelson thus argues that *ḥerem* is God's restoring to Godself the land that belongs to God, to ensure Israel's holiness in worship and covenant loyalty. Israel itself became the object of *ḥerem* (Isa 43:28; 63:10).

---

22. Moberly, "Toward." Moberly holds *ḥerem* must be viewed metaphorically. Properly used, it gives "content to love of God," 144. *Killing* the Canaanites, horrible as it is, relates to "the stark contrast between worship of YHWH and worship of other gods," 136. C. J. H. Wright's "Appendix: What About the Canaanites?" in his OT *Ethics* addresses the underlying ethical problem of the *ḥerem* destruction of the Canaanites vis à vis God's promise to Israel to be a blessing to all nations. While not claiming a "solution" to the problem, he contends that God's judgment of evil historically is consistent in biblical thought. Our sense of "fairness" may not tally with God's (474-79). The relation between divine judgment and mission (Gen 12:3 and Matt 28:17-20) merits its own chapter. Chris Wright's 2008 book, *God,* addresses at length the moral dilemma of YHWH war and the Canaanite extermination, 73-110, and joins it to two other moral dilemmas, the violence of the cross and the violence forecast in the end times, 111-92. This is a notable contribution to this moral enigma.

23. Gerbrandt, *Deuteronomy,* 552-53; the quotations from Moberly are from "Toward," 135 and 136.

24. See Earl's many articles on this topic, in Matties, *Joshua,* 487.

25. R. D. Nelson, "Ḥerem." I changed Nelson's punctuation between chapter and verse from comma to colon, the style of this book.

Failure to keep the covenant, worship of other gods, and presuming *to own* the land is cause for Israel's exile.

While our response to Israel's *ḥerem* practice is revulsion (analogous to genocide today), we must temper that judgment, since the original intention in Exodus 14:14; 23:20–30 was: God gives the land by miracle, as Lind emphasizes.[26] It thus remains God's land, not Israel's. In contrast to political warfare including genocide, *ḥerem* yields no profit: no gold nor silver, no cattle nor other livestock, no slaves, women, nor children. Hence, *ḥerem* shares the rationale that governs the Sabbath, the sabbatical, and care for the widow, orphan, and alien. The land is the Lord's.

Given this view of the land, *ḥerem* is less problematic, Nevertheless, this portrait of God differs radically from Jesus' command to love enemies (Matt 5:45//Luke 6:27, 35). In light of Nelson's perspectives regarding *ḥerem*, we must distinguish, as he does, between *ḥerem* and mass genocide such as Hitler's holocaust of the Jews (the *Shoah*) and modern genocides that occurred in Cambodia (Kymer Rouge: two million killed), Uganda, the Balkans, and Myanmar today. Nonetheless, the Christian crusades of the twelfth century and the Muslim practice of *jihad* share some, but not all, the elements of *ḥerem*. Infringing on God's or Allah's holiness is, in this conception, the catalyst for killing ruthlessly (ethnic or religious cleansing) so that God's or Allah's community is protected from idolatry.[27]

---

26. Lind, *Yahweh*, 58–60. I address at length how the divine warrior motif is reshaped in the NT in *Israel's*, 95–153, and more minimally in *Covenant*, 92–100, 112–17, 119.

27. Whatever rationale for *ḥerem* we might propose, such ruthless killing falls far short of the character of God revealed in Jesus Christ. The *jihad* mentality that fanned the ISIS slaughter in northern Iraq and Syria and the killing and kidnapping of many people [Muslims and Christians] by the Boko Haram in northern Nigeria (cf. the terrorism in Mali as well) cannot be reconciled with the God revealed in Jesus Christ. Merrill ("Case") treats this topic briefly, citing the Qur'an that legitimates *jihad*, and in certain cases commands it (Sura 2:16, 191, 217, 9:5, 29; 9:5 is the most explicit). Other texts, however, advocate a pacifist response to controversy or difference (i.e., Sura 15:94–95). See Merrill, 93–94. Merrill's follow-up to this reality is commendable:

> In light of full biblical teaching, one thing is clear. Whether Christian or Muslim, "holy war" has no justification and for that reason must be condemned. Only a flawed theology that fails to distinguish Yahweh war in its unique setting from any other kind of conflict can possibly defend its continuing, devastating consequences . . . One must quickly affirm . . . that the genocide sanctioned by Scripture was unique to its time, place, and circumstances. It is not to be carried over to the age of the church (94).

Merrill, as well as Gard, envisions Christ's return in judgment to be violent, based on their reading—but not mine—of Revelation. Dispensational theology, when applied to "holy war," shows both its strength and weakness.

As the title of Nelson's article indicates, his overall thesis contends that *ḥerem* does not negate Deuteronomy's strong "social conscience," i.e., the ethic of care for the poor, the widow, the stranger (outsider) and all that the sabbatical and Jubilee represent. Nelson acknowledges that the humane ethic of Deuteronomy is an "internal ethic, one that applied also to only those few foreigners (slaves and resident aliens) who shared Israel's canonical experience of servitude and oppression."[28] It has no application outside that circle. Deuteronomy's directive for *ḥerem* was not an end in itself, but a means to an end, part of its larger program of inspiring loyalty and fidelity to YHWH.[29]

Since Israel was exiled later for its idolatries is cause to question the *ḥerem* practice. It did not accomplish its intended goal. In light of the accounts in Judges, was *ḥerem* truly practiced? The *ḥerem* chapter in Israel's history was dubiously God's will; it reflects the practice of other ANE nations. Though its rationale was God's and Israel's holiness, it didn't keep Israel from idolatry. So its practice, if it did occur historically, is pointless in the end, and offensive to the Christian mind shaped by Jesus' command to "love your enemies."

Further, the Joshua 5 epigraph for this chapter jeopardizes the *ḥerem* practice, since YHWH with a drawn sword, the commander of the armies of the Lord, refuses to take sides. What is all important is that Joshua recognizes he stands on holy ground. This text contests the *ḥerem* tradition, for it establishes God's openness to both sides with divine holiness as supreme. When the commander of the armies of the Lord is neither *for* nor *against* Joshua (thus Israel's) "side," the horizon opens to something greater to unfold, in the Prophets and NT. The confessional recital in Joshua 24:12, "it was not by your sword or by your bow," but by "hornets" et al. that I gave you this land, further qualifies *ḥerem*, even though such commands by God continued in Joshua's "conquest" narrative.[30]

The failure of *ḥerem* to ensure God's holiness gives way in the prophetic literature to a grander and more encompassing vision of God and God's holiness. In Isaiah we learn that Israel's God is "the Holy One of Israel," a title occurring twenty-six times, as B. Anderson notes.[31] The

---

28. For fuller treatment of social justice in Deuteronomy, see Hamilton, *Social Justice*.

29. Nelson, *Ḥerem*, 54.

30. See here Matties's exposition of this section, *Joshua*, 126–40.

31. B. Anderson, "Holy One." The title occurs only nine times in the rest of the OT: statistical data, p. 3. For an extensive study of holiness in the OT, see Gammie, *Holiness*. For Isaiah specifically, see Oswalt, *Holy*. See the helpful article "Holiness" by Brower, with choice bibliography, in *Dictionary*.

term occurs in the "historical particular" portions of Isaiah and also in the eschatological, apocalyptic genre portions. The title is associated with Israel's cult (Ps 71:22), royal covenant theology (Pss 78:41; 89:18), prophetic literature (Hab 3:13; Jer 50:50; 51:5; Hos 11:9), and God as the "Divine Warrior who is extolled for going forth to rescue 'your people' and 'your Anointed' (Hab 3:13)."[32]

The Lord God's Sinai theophany discloses God's definitive character: "The Lord, the Lord, a God merciful and gracious, slow to anger, and abounding in steadfast love and faithfulness" (34:6). "Holy, holy, holy" is Isaiah's response to the Lord God when called to be a prophet (6:8). "Yahweh alone is holy, and things and people become holy by being drawn into relationship with the Holy One. Yahweh's name is *qannā* ('jealous/zealous') which means Yahweh claims exclusive devotion people (Exod 34:34)."[33] In Isaiah "the Holy One of Israel" is viewed as the "universal God [who] is manifest in the historical particular" (8:8; cf. 18:7; 24:3) . . . [and] will become 'a fire,' 'a flame' that consumes an arrogant Assyrian empire (10:17)." The Holy One of Israel is "the Creator of the ends of the earth, who calls the stars by name (40:25–26, 28), and is Israel's Maker and King (43:15; 45:11)."[34] The particular becomes universal vision:

> Living in the presence of the holy God means to be exposed to God's judgment from which there is no escape, but more than that: to be embraced by divine concern and purpose. Indeed, it is no divine judgment first and divine mercy beyond, rather God's saving purpose is operative through the judgment, in order that there may appear a new Jerusalem, a new humanity, a new creation . . . what was given in the historical particular . . . thus invites all peoples to join in praising Yahweh, the Holy One of Israel.[35]

Another important assessment of *ḥerem* is the word of the Lord to Jeremiah, which he speaks to exiled Israel in Babylon: "seek the *welfare* [*shalom*] of the city where I have sent you into exile, and pray to the Lord on its behalf, for in its *welfare* you will find your welfare" (Jer 29:7). Bourne draws on J. H. Yoder's work to make the case that this exilic counsel becomes normative for the church in relation to nation and "enemy" in the older narratives governed by *ḥerem* commands:

---

32. Anderson, "Holy One," 3.
33. Ibid., 9. See Anderson's fuller discussion.
34. Ibid., 7.
35. Ibid., 19. See Isa 25:6; 52:7–10; 55:9–10; 65:17–19.

Yoder begins by insisting that it would be anachronistic to read contemporary understandings of the morality of killing into texts like those of Joshuanic war or the planned [painful] sacrifice of Isaac. One can no more equate this early tradition of "YHWH war" with the Crusades, for example, than one would view the story of Sarah giving her servant Hagar to her husband Abraham "as a wife" (Genesis 16) as equivalent with the modern notion of so-called "open marriage." Differences of context, intention, and reception of such narratives preclude such a method. What would have struck the first readers or hearers, and what the author is likely to have intended in these stories of war and sacrifice, is the importance of utter dependence on God.

Nevertheless, it is difficult not to read as misplaced hyperbole the [Yoder's] assertion that "[f]ar from constituting an embarrassment for those who follow Jesus' nonviolence, Hebrew holy war is the historical foundation for the same."[36]

For this and other problematic texts depicting divine violence (or better, *judgment*) in the OT, the historical situation is crucial. Moving from that context and depiction of God's character in Holy War to the revelation of God's character in Jesus Christ is possible only by holding to some form of "unfolding revelation" within the biblical canon.[37] As Martens argues, Jeremiah's word of the Lord to landless Israel is the definitive prelude of Jesus' ethic of nonviolence,[38] or better, active peacemaking rather than nonviolence, as I contend in *Covenant of Peace*.[39] It is essential, therefore, to understand *ḥerem* in its cultural, historical context, with its similarities to warfare among the nations of that time.

---

36. R. Bourne, *Seek*, 95–96. Bourne's citation of Yoder is from Yoder's *For the Nations*, 85n11. Though "holy war" is not the focus of Yoder's chapter, the practice of *ḥerem* assumes such a context. Nugent's summary of Yoder's view of "Yahweh war" is helpful, outlined in six points, here abbreviated: 1) trumpet alert—no military arsenal and no soldier skills; 2) all booty devoted to the true Owner of the land—a ceremonial consecration; 3) all warriors must trust Yahweh, confident that the Lord "will give over the enemy into your hand"; 4) God gives the victory, the Israelites mop up, devoting the bloody mess to Yahweh; 5) the battle is consummated by destroying "the lives and goods of the enemy"; 6) the divine demobilization consists of "To Thy Tents, O Israel": Nugent, *Politics*, 53–54. For this summary of Yoder's approach to this difficult topic Nugent draws on five of Yoder's publications (Nugent, 53n29).

37. Anderson, *Unfolding*.

38. E. Martens, "Toward." Martens's last two sections rightly declare exilic theology means a new "Divine Modus Operandi," as J. H. Yoder argues in *Jewish-Christian*; also Christopher-Smith, *Biblical*, and Christopher-Smith and Southwood, *Religion*, chapters 2 and 5.

39. Swartley, *Covenant*, 6–7, 420–21.

The Holiness Journey, Consummating in the New Testament

Already in the "Latter Prophets" of the Hebrew Bible (Isaiah, Jeremiah, Ezekiel, and The Twelve) *holiness* is dissociated from any practice of *ḥerem*. In Isaiah's call to be a prophet he saw the Lord sitting on a throne and then heard the seraphim choir calling, "Holy, Holy, Holy, Lord God Almighty." Isaiah was humbled, felt lost and guilty, saying "I have seen the Lord" (6:1–5). This prompts a seraph to touch Isaiah's mouth with a live coal from the altar, and proclaim cleansing from his sin and guilt. Then the Lord calls him "to go for us" as a prophet to proclaim God's word(s) to the people, even though they will not listen (6:6–11). God's holiness empowers Isaiah to be a prophet. Hear Hosea's agony and ecstasy on God as holy:

> How can I give you up, Ephraim? How can I hand you over, O Israel? . . . My heart recoils within me; my compassion grows warm and tender. I will not execute my fierce anger; I will not again destroy Ephraim; for I am God and no mortal, the Holy One in your midst, and I will not come in wrath. (11:8–9)

This text, reflective of Hosea's marital imagery, taking back an unfaithful wife (chapters 1—3), accentuates God's forgiving character. Similar emphases appear in other prophetic books. A twin emphasis to holiness is God's glory, which comes to full expression in John's Gospel.[40] God's holiness is also partner to God's love and mercy, which outlast God's wrath (Pss 23:6; 30:5; 118:3–4; 136:1–26; Sir 5:6; 16:11; 51:12, 14; et al.).[41]

Alan Kreider's contribution on "social holiness" is pertinent.[42] Holiness is often viewed as personal, not social. But Kreider rightly perceives Scripture's universal vision: God calls Abraham to be a blessing to the nations (Gen 12:3). The whole world is the scope of God's salvation and victory over evil. Psalm 67 calls the peoples of the nations to praise of God: "let all the ends of the earth revere him" (v. 7). Psalm 98:1–3 ends with, "All the ends of the earth have seen the victory of our God." The wondrous text of Isaiah

---

40. Swartley, "Glory," in *John*, 516–18, 64–65, 309. See 518 for reference to essays on *glory* in the *Exodus*, *Isaiah*, and *Ezekiel* commentaries (BCBC). For more, see Swartley: www.heraldpress.com/bcbc/John, 146.

41. Boyd says rightly, "God's 'wrath' can only be understood as a contingent expression of this [God's] love." He quotes Eichrodt, "*wrath never forms one of the permanent attributes of the God of Israel*," unlike holiness and righteousness. This point has direct bearing on Boyd's view of atonement—not penal, but the ultimate manifestation of God's love in the giving of his only Son for our salvation. See *Crucifixion*, vol. 2, 769.

42. A. Kreider, *Journey*, depicts holiness on the march, advancing throughout Scripture to bring all peoples into saving relationship to God. Holiness is not static, but forward bound until the kingdom fully comes.

52:7-10—"beautiful upon the mountains are the feet of the messenger who announces peace"—ends with "all the ends of the earth shall see the salvation of our God." Habakkuk, in the context of violence and evil engulfing God's people (chapter 1) declares hope: "But the earth will be filled with the knowledge of the glory of the Lord, as the waters cover the sea" (2:14).

The New Testament

The closest NT parallel to the OT *ḥerem* is the rare occurrence of *anáthema*, which makes one the object of a curse. "It denotes something dedicated or consecrated to deity"—but this can involve "destruction" as part of consecration.[43] Its NT uses appear in Paul's writings. No one who curses Jesus can say "Jesus is Lord" (1 Cor 12:3); cursing Jesus would mean "delivering Jesus to destruction by God."[44] Paul uses this curse formula three times. The first is for anyone who does not love the Lord (1 Cor 16:22; *anáthema* is followed by "*Maranatha*: Our Lord, come"); the second, for those who preach another gospel other than that of Jesus Christ (Gal 1:8); and the third is self-applied: "For I could wish that I myself were accursed and cut off from Christ for the sake of my own people, my kindred according to the flesh" (Rom 9:3).[45]

These uses of *anáthema* do not mesh with the NT purposes and practices of discipline, which seeks restoration of one who sins. It indicates, however, that Paul took "boundaries" seriously and why the early church practiced *discipline*, linked to *holiness*.

Holiness as noun or adjective (*hagios*) is a dominant theme in the NT, occurring 229x, with the verb (*hagiadzō*), 29x. Most of the noun-uses are in Luke–Acts and Revelation, both oriented to outbursts of prayer-worship that punctuates the narrative.[46] The concentration in Acts (54x), however, refers often to the *Holy* Spirit. In Revelation *holy* occurs in the seven worship songs of praise (e.g. 4:8 [three absolute uses] and in 21:2,

---

43. The LXX translates *ḥerem* with *anáthema* in Lev 27:28-29; Deut 7:26; 13:17; Josh 6:17f.; 7:11ff.; Zech 14:11. Behm, "ἀνάθεμα (*anáthema*)," *TDNT*, 1.354.

44. Ibid.

45. Käsemann refers to these as "Sentences of Holy Law." For a perceptive discussion, including how various NT scholars interpret these Pauline "curses," see R. Yoder [Neufeld], "*Cherem*."

46. J. B. Smith, *Greek-English*, 3. This source shows in tabular format the various English translations (in the KJV), which for *hagios* is *holy* (161x), *saints* (61x), *Holy One* (4x), plus three more English words under Misc. (3x). See also Kohlenberger, ed., *NRSV Concordance*, 617-19 (with OT and NT together, the occurrences of "holy" number ca. 680, plus 150 in the Apocrypha).

10; 22:19 [adjectival, in "holy city"]). An important verbal use is in the Lord's Prayer, "Hallowed be your name" (Matt 6:9). As in Psalm 99 (vv. 5 and 9) this is the foremost aspect of God's Godness for humans to grasp, own, and applaud (cf. Hos 11:9).[47]

A pertinent oft-cited NT text is 1 Peter 2:9: "But you are a chosen race, a royal priesthood, a holy nation." Another is: ". . . as he who has called you is holy, be holy yourselves in all your conduct; for it is written, 'You shall be holy, for I am holy'"(1 Pet 1:15–16; the phrase here is a quotation of Lev 19:2, indicating continuity between the Testaments). In 1 Corinthians, Paul calls believers to be a holy temple, "God's temple is holy, and you are that temple" (3:17). Here holiness describes the church body corporately, matching Peter's *holy nation*. Later, in addressing sexual purity, Paul says, ". . . do you not know that your body is a temple of the Holy Spirit within you, which you have from God, and that you are not your own" (1 Cor 6:19). Paul calls believers to be a "holy and acceptable" living sacrifice to God (Rom 12:1). In the context of these last two citations, killing "fleshly desires," prominent in Paul's Epistles, is the path to holiness. This is continuity-in-transformation between the Testaments. A more explicit "transformation" of killing enemies occurs in Paul's "killing the enmity in him" (AT).[48] Christ, our peace (Eph 2:14), *kills* the long-held *enmity* between Jews and Gentiles. The two become one (4x in vv. 14–18), and this new *one* "grows into a holy temple in the Lord" (Eph 2:21).

In John, Jesus addresses God as *Holy Father* when petitioning his Father to protect his disciples from *the evil one* (17:11–12, 15), *for they do not belong to the world* (v. 16). In Revelation, God is worshiped as the Holy One, "*Holy, holy, holy is the Lord God Almighty*" (4:8b).[49] One might view the driving energy of Revelation as God establishing *holiness* through judgment of the Empire's evils: its war-making and emperor worship colliding with believers' devotion to the Lord God Almighty. Thus the evil beast, false prophet, and Satan are destroyed, a mutation of *ḥerem*. Only then can God Almighty in and through the Lamb's victory over evil establish the new heavens and new earth, in which there will be no more killing *ḥerem*-practice, for *all* (the whole earth and its peoples, including the kings who go in and out of the gates of the New Jerusalem) belong eternally to the *holy* Lord.

The early church received the same vision from Jesus before his ascension, "But you will receive power when the Holy Spirit has come upon

---

47. As the KJV reads, describing true worship in Psalm 96:9a: "Worship the Lord in the beauty of holiness." I love it!

48. See here, above all, T. R. Yoder Neufeld, *Killing*, 90–92.

49. Worship and praise of Almighty God, the Holy One, is an important window into Revelation. See Swartley, *Covenant*, 324–49, and Ruiz, "Politics."

you; and you will be my witnesses in Jerusalem, in all Judea and Samaria, and to the ends of the earth" (Acts 1:8). The global vision of God's holiness continues in Ephesians and Revelation:

> With all wisdom and insight he has made known to us the mystery of his will, according to his good pleasure that he set forth in Christ, as a plan for the fullness of time, to gather up all things in him, things in heaven and things on earth (Eph 1:8b–10).

> I saw no temple in the city, for its temple is the Lord God the Almighty and the Lamb. And the city has no need of sun or moon to shine on it, for the glory of God is its light, and its lamp is the Lamb. The nations will walk by its light, and the kings of the earth will bring their glory into it. Its gates will never be shut by day—and there will be no night there. People will bring into it the glory and the honor of the nations. (Rev 21:22–26)[50]

With over 250 occurrences of the noun *holy* and the verbs, *hallowed* or *make holy*, plus another four uses of *holiness*, this dominant NT emphasis may be grouped under these headings:

<u>God as *holy*</u>

1. *Holiness* is descriptive of God's essence (Matt, 1 Pet, and the Rev texts above).
2. God is worshipped as *holy* (Revelation's hymns of praise—seven of them)
3. Prayer petitions to God rightly address God as the *holy* One.
4. The covenant people's holiness is derivative from God's holiness.
5. Holiness is God's command for God's corporate people (1 Pet; implied in Rom 12; 1 Cor 3).
6. God's people are called to be holy personally (1 Pet 1:15; 1 Cor 6).
7. God's people are called to keep their bodies holy (1 Cor 5 and 6).

All these points are true of holiness in the OT also. *But never in any of the NT texts does God command the new covenant people to kill or slaughter enemy peoples (as a sacrifice) to ensure the holiness of the people, or to protect God's holiness.* In this is a vast difference between the Testaments.[51] How-

---

50. For how *social holiness* blends with global mission, see Krabill and Murray, *Forming*, 67–77 in context of 53–66.

51. This point could be used to support Bultmann's term *miscarriage* to describe the relation between the Testaments. See Lind's critique of Bultmann on this point in

ever, the *separation* of God's faithful people from *evil* or the *world* (in its negative sense) is an important aspect of holiness in the NT. In this respect continuity between the Testaments is significant.[52] How do we explain the difference that we find continuity and sharp discontinuity? The answer lies, partly, in the next point: how does "possessing land" play out in the NT and how are God's people instructed to relate to the enemy.

Discipline (Discipling) in the New Testament (Holiness Continued)

NT texts on discipline in the Christian body transform the OT *ḥerem* into redemptive actions that protect the faith community's holiness. Hebrews correlates discipline with holiness: "For they [human parents] disciplined us for a short time as seemed best to them, but he [the Lord] disciplines us for our good, in order that we may share his holiness" (12:10).

The primary goal of discipline in the church is the restoration of errant brothers and sisters into full fellowship within the church. Discipline presumes discipleship; without discipleship, discipline lacks integrity.[53] The context for effective church discipline is communal commitment to follow Jesus and seek to live a holy life.[54] The pertinent texts are Matthew 18, which

---

"Bibliographical," 230.

52. One might view God's "holy nation" in both Testaments as a "body politic," as Gombis, in "Political Vision," describes the continuity via holiness:

> ... the church as a body politic takes its orientation from Israel as a political entity. Israel's identity and mission shape the church's identity and mission. This is signaled by Paul's language for the church, which he borrows from Scripture's language about Israel. Paul uses holiness language quite often to speak of his churches' identity with reference to God, referring to believers as "holy ones." This does not merely point to a moral purity before God, though it may include this. It points to Israel's politically oriented vocation. God called them as a radically different sort of people who were to embody a radically different domestic set of social practices and a completely unique set of relationships with the surrounding nations. When Paul uses holiness language for the church, he's getting at how the *polis* of Jesus is supposed to be this sort of people among the various peoples of the world. (81)

53. Swartley, *Covenant*, 92–112; *Israel's*, 95–115. Discipleship is a widely recognized theme in Mark's central section: Stock, *Call*; Sweetland, *Journey*, 51–69; Best, *Following*, 165–225; Swartley, *Mark*, 135–47.

54. On discipleship that entails self-discipline, see Foster, *Money*. This book is right on for what Christian believers face almost daily in today's world. To strengthen us against these temptations I recommend also Bonhoeffer's *Cost*; T. Kelly, *Testament*; and Camp, *Mere*. Faithful discipleship and joyous worship insure for protection against evil entering into our thoughts and actions.

outlines a process for discipline, and 1 Corinthians 5—7, which speaks of a particular case of discipline (5:1-3; see also 2 Cor 2:1-11).

Matthew 18:15-18 prescribes a procedure for discipline that seeks redemptive restoration of the one who has sinned (against you).[55] The meaning of "bind" and "loose" is not clear.[56] Does "bind" mean "bind the power of Satan" and "loose" mean "set the person free?" This fits with "the gates of hell shall not prevail" against the church and with giving to Peter "the keys of the kingdom" in 16:18-19, which states: "whatever you bind on earth will be [literally, will have already been] bound in heaven and whatever you loose on earth will be [ditto to above] loosed in heaven." Or, are *bind* and *loose* here referring to moral discernment of what is permissible and what is not as in the Jewish halakic tradition, thus *forbidding* or *approving* certain actions? Or, does "bind" mean "no" to the person's standing in the church and "loose" to forgive sins and reaffirm the person's standing in the church? If the first option is correct, then discipline is an integral part of exorcism and deliverance, and merits considerable space here.

As White and Blue note, utilizing J. H. Yoder's contribution, the purpose of this action is not protecting the reputation of the church or safeguarding against moral laxity,[57] though these concerns count significantly for church's witness to the world. Love for the offending person motivates the process. In speaking one-to-one with the person it may become clear that "the offense" was misunderstood. Clearing it up at this stage ends the process. But if the offender resists the inquiry—refusing to listen or making excuses for it—then the second stage of going to him or her with another brother or sister in the church is mandated. This hopefully will lead to restoring the offender. If this does not clear up the offense, then the matter is to be taken to the church, i.e., local congregation. If step three does not resolve the matter, then the offender is to be put out of the assembly, and regarded as "a Gentile and a tax collector."[58]

---

55. Some ancient manuscripts lack *against you*. While a difficult variant to decide [C], the USB Greek text Committee decided to put it in the text, but put it in square brackets (Metzger, *Textual*, 45).

56. For extended discussion of these terms in Matthew, see Swartley, *Israel's*, 120-22. For discussion of similar terms (John's parallel to "bind" in Matthew is "retain sin"), see Swartley, *John*, 460-62. The order of the two terms in John, and also the meaning of each, differs from Matthew's. A recent article, given the cultural context, supports option 1: Kim, "Ancient."

57. White and Blue, *Healing the Wounded*, 52. Yoder's article, which White and Blue print as an Appendix, was first published in *Concern* 18: 2-32. A briefer version is in Yoder's *Body Politics*, 1-13.

58. The larger context of this disciplinary procedure is crucial. Earlier in chapter 18 Jesus extols the *child*—in the culture where children had lowest societal rank: unless

Crosby, noting its cultural context, says, "Just as the Jews had 'insiders' and 'outsiders' based on the Law, so now, 'outsiders' will be those refusing to be reconciled as disciples within the community."[59] Forgiveness and reconciliation are the goals of this disciplinary process. While protecting the community's holiness is not a stated reason for discipline, it is the result when the process succeeds. The holiness of believers is derived from God as holy.[60]

A quite different situation and process for discipline from Matthew 18:15–18[61] appears in 1 Corinthians 5:1–3, where Paul directs the church to "hand this man [guilty of incest] over to Satan for the destruction of the flesh, so that his spirit may be saved in the day of the Lord."

It appears that the congregation resolved the issue either before Paul wrote 1 Corinthians or right after they received it. Whichever, the process was painful, assuming his second letter refers to this same incident and its resolution (2 Cor 2:1–11). Most puzzling is the distinction between the man's *flesh* and *spirit*: Does this mean consignment of his flesh/body to death, while at the same time assuring salvation of his spirit because through the death of the flesh/body his spirit is cleansed and saved for eternal life? Most commentators hold that *flesh* here denotes his *fleshly desires*, causative of his sexual immorality.[62] The rationale for this severe discipline is protecting the holiness of the community, so that a little leaven will not leaven the whole lump, imagery that immediately follows (1 Cor 5:6–8; cf. Gal 5:9). Then Paul gives "principled" instruction to separate oneself from the immoral

---

one humbles oneself like a child one cannot enter the kingdom of heaven (vv. 1–5). Causing one of these "little ones" to stumble is sin worthy of death (vv. 6–7); the point is resumed briefly in vv. 10–11, "do not despise one of these little ones," and reinforced by the example of the shepherd who leaves ninety-nine sheep to find the lost one (vv. 12–13). Conclusion: "So it is not the will of your Father in heaven that one of these little ones should be lost" (v. 14). That's the setting for Jesus' teaching on "binding and loosing"—the procedure of discipline of an offending brother or sister. The end-frame focuses on forgiveness, without limits: responding to Peter's question, "how often—seven times?" Jesus answers, "seventy times seven."

59. Crosby, *House*, 51.

60. Other NT texts that carry the same goal for the offender are Luke 17:3 and Galatians 6:1–2.

61. But it is not so different, if the first meaning of "bind and loose" in Matthew 18 is accepted. When in the process of writing I saw this connection between the Matthew and 1 Corinthian texts, "the lights went on." The first step in discipline is to "bind" the powers of evil. See Foster, with King, *Binding and Loosing*, especially 139–78.

62. Barrett, *Corinthians*, 127–28; Hays, *Corinthians*, 85. Hays rightly says: "Probably Paul did not expect the community to perform a ceremony explicitly cursing the man; rather, delivering him to Satan is a vivid metaphor for the *effect* of expulsion from the church." Hays cites other references: 1 Tim 1:20; 2 Thess 2:9–10, and 1 Cor 1:18.

practices of worldly conduct (1 Cor 5:9–13), ending with: "'Drive out the wicked person from among you.'"

What does "delivering over to Satan" mean? Laura Brenneman, in her dissertation, sheds light. Brenneman narrates the developmental history of Satan: from the *sa-tán* role as God's deputy to test/or accuse the righteous (e.g., in Job) to Satan in the NT as a personal adversary to God's people. Satan's demotion from heaven is the result of his revolt: Satan is a fallen angel who took other angels with him (Jude 6, 9, and also the "Watchers" myth in 1 Enoch). However, it appears that Satan's role as "tester," as well as "tempter," continues. Both are present in Jesus' temptations. This perspective helps us understand Paul's counsel to the Corinthian church when he speaks of "turning the man over to Satan," as Brenneman says:

> I have argued that Satan was originally conceptualized within the OT traditions as an agent of God. . . . although most of the other occurrences of Satan/the devil in the NT display a view of Satan as God's opponent, Paul actually continued to espouse the notion that Satan's action could fall within the parameters of God's will. In 1 Corinthians 5 Paul reveals that his only hope that the offender will be saved and the community purified is in handing 'such a one' over to Satan.
>
> In this way, Satan's destructive power may have a positive effect.[63]
>
> I have already proposed that separation from the presence of God is equivalent to destruction; thus permanent separation is eternal punishment. If Satan is successful in his attempts to sever the connection between humans and God, then the process of destruction begins. This is why being 'merely human' is particularly troubling to Paul. Humans, because of fleshly weakness, are susceptible to the lures of sin. Temptation is laid as a snare by Satan and if humans get caught in it, then Satan has grounds for a case against them. The offender in 1 Corinthians 5 has fallen into the trap and has not curtailed his sinning. Hence, Paul recommends that the Corinthian fellowship hand him over to Satan.
>
> Although destruction of 'the flesh' will occur when the offender is handed over to Satan, Paul believes that such a thing can actually result in the sinner's salvation in the day of the Lord. Therefore, while separation from God is a consequence of being handed over to Satan, it is Paul's understanding that this may be a temporary situation. He hopes that the punishment,

---

63. Brenneman, "Corporate Discipline," 139 (used with author's permission).

i.e. 'destruction' will excise the man's fleshly weakness and lead him to salvation. (139)[64]

The closest parallel in the NT to this text is 1 Timothy 1:20. Hymenaeus and Alexander are to be turned over to Satan so they may learn not to blaspheme. The verb for *learn* is a form of the Greek *paideuō*, meaning "to educate" through instruction or "to practice discipline" to give guidance, often with an aspect of punishment. It "refers to an activity that seeks to instill proper conduct or belief in spiritually immature people."[65] Although this text does not speak of restoration or salvation of these offenders, "the author has not abandoned them to their sin—he hopes that they will learn not to blaspheme."[66]

Taking a brother or sister to court in 6:1-8 is likely related to the *incest* transgression in 5:1-5, since such is illegal in both Roman and Jewish law.[67] Chapter 6:9-20, then, is a matching unit that first celebrates deliverance of some from immorality and wicked deeds and then again moves to "principled" admonition not to flirt with prostitution but keep your body holy, for do you "not know that your body is a temple of the Holy Spirit within you, which you have from God, and that you are not your own?" 1 Corinthians 5—6 is oriented to discipline that protects the holiness of the community. Elias, in "No Flirting with Idolatry," demonstrates the intertextuality of Paul's admonitions on protecting the holiness of God's new covenant people, through discipline and obedience.[68] Elias cites parallels from the OT and NT on temptations to idolatry:

> This recognition of the spiritual peril of flirting with demons leads Paul to plead tenderly with the believers in Corinth, *Therefore, my dear friends* (Greek: *my beloved*), *flee from the worship of idols* (10:14). Referring to the Lord's Supper (10:16-17) and sacrificial meals in the Jewish temple (10:18) and pagan ritual meals (10:20) Paul drives his point home. During all of these occasions of eating and drinking in the presence of a deity, a partnership is formed between the worshiper and the god being worshiped. In 11:25, with reference to the Lord's Supper, Paul uses the language of covenant. For Paul the upshot of the

---

64. Ibid, 134-35.
65. Ibid., 152.
66. Ibid., 153.
67. Roman: Cicero, *Pro Cluentia* 6:15; Gaius, *Institutes* 1.63. Jewish: Leviticus 18:8; Deuteronomy 27:20 (cited by Quast, *Reading*, 44). In chapter 6 "Paul has not really changed the subject from the topic of chapter 5" (Hays, *First Corinthians*, 93).
68. Elias, *Remember*, 114. See Elias's parallels between Paul on discipline and Israel's offenses, with location.

argument is clear: *You cannot drink the cup of the Lord and the cup of demons. You cannot partake of the table of the Lord and the table of demons* (10:21).[69]

This admonition echoes the OT *ḥerem* in concern to maintain Israel's Shema loyalty (Deut 6:4–5), no flirting with idolatry and sexual sins (2 Cor 10:6–11; cf. 1 Cor 5—6). While these NT emphases on holiness and discipline show continuity with the OT, vast differences exist. For holiness and discipline in the NT arises not from "land" or "enemy" rationales but the shalom of a new covenant community for which Jesus gave his life while we were "weak, sinners, enemies" in our standing before God (Rom 6:6–9). Jesus as "holy warrior" dies *for* enemies to birth a new creation. NT holiness thus subverts the OT holiness motive behind *ḥerem*. Jesus' death kills the enmity, not the enemy. He reconciles enemies (Eph 2:14–17; 2 Cor 5:17–20), creating one new body in Christ!

---

69. Ibid., 115–16.

2b

Two Major Transformations: Land and Enemy

> *Holy Land has to do with welcoming refugees and immigrants*
> *and trying to remove the causes*
> *and alleviate the problems of . . . population dislocations. . . .*
> *Where land is sanctified,*
> *it engenders contentment and stability and fosters love of home. . . .*
> *Unholy land produces refugees,*
> *sanctified land performs a redemptive function.*
>
> —Marlin Jeschke, *Rethinking Holy Land*

This chapter develops further the title of chapter 2a and focuses on *possessing the land* and/or *killing enemies*. The call to trust in God pervades both Testaments and is emphasized in this chapter. The "land-conquest" motif, often causative of war, ancient and modern, undergoes major transformation in the Latter Prophets and NT.

From Possessing the Land to Entering the Kingdom (Trust in God)

Three interrelated themes bear on "possessing the land." First, how is the promise of land construed in later OT thought when Israel is landless, in exile, and how is it understood in the NT? Also, how is God's promise to David, "I will establish the throne of his kingdom forever. I will be a father to him and he shall be a son to me" (2 Sam 7:13b–14a; see also v. 29) to be understood? This motif will be traced in Matthew's Gospel and other NT writings.

Second, a remarkable linguistic feature occurs in correlating "entering the promised land" in the OT with "entering the kingdom of God" in the NT. For this, Mark's Gospel will guide us.

Third, Jesus' teachings in Luke's Journey narrative (9:51–19:46) appear to be modelled on Deuteronomy, shaped significantly by a "journey-destiny." Through these three Gospel-lenses, and other NT texts we journey from *land* to *world*. First, however, we discuss OT covenants.

The Promise of Land

To grasp the scope of this trajectory we must take into account God's promises to Abraham: that his descendants will inherit the promised land of Canaan, will become a great nation, and will be a blessing to the entire world (Gen 12:1–3).[1] In the canonical unfolding of this promise we learn that two OT covenant promises are *conditional* and two are *unconditional*.

God's covenant with Moses promises Israel to become *a nation* (Exod 19:5–6). Later, God's covenant with Solomon promises God's presence in the *temple* Solomon built (1 Kgs 9:4–9; 2 Chron 7:19–22). Both covenants are *conditional*, dependent on Israel's obedience to God's commandments, notably the Ten Commandments: no making of and worshiping idols, keeping the Sabbath holy, honoring parents, no killing,[2] no committing adultery, no stealing, no bearing false witness, and no coveting. The Israelite people, however, repeatedly broke these commandments (Samuel, Kings, and Chronicles), thus voiding the covenant promises. The *prophets* declare that Israel *broke the covenant* (Hos 1; 8:1; Isa 1–5; Jer 7:1–15; 26:1–6; 31:32;) and that Israel first, and later Judah, will go into exile (721 and 586 BCE respectively). God, however, renews the promise of nationhood and temple for a second chance beyond exile (Hos 1:10–11; 3:1–5; Ezek 36—37, 40—48). During this second temple period Israel's transgressions are less blatant (no idol images) but are transgressions nonetheless, as witnessed in Ezra, Nehemiah, and

---

1. God's covenant with Noah is universal, for all humankind. It promises to never again destroy the earth by water-chaos, with a covenant-promise sign: the rainbow in the sky (Gen 9:8–16).

2. Though the NRSV translates Exodus 20:13 with the verb *murder*, W. Bailey has questioned this translation in, "*You Shall Not.*" Bailey contends that the Hebrew word (*tirtsakh*) more likely means *kill*, not *murder*. Her conclusion is based on a contextual study of the thirteen uses of the word in OT. The change from the RSV *kill* to *murder* in the NRSV is unwarranted. The KJV and JB render *tirtsakh* as *kill* also; the NEB, NLT, TNIV render it *murder*.

Malachi. The fall of Jerusalem and the dispersion of the Jewish people (70 CE) signifies and manifests the conditional nature of the promise of *nation* and the promise of divine presence in the *temple*.

Israel's leaders, i.e., "chief priests and Pharisees" and Sadducees prominent in the Council (with some notable exceptions), rejected Jesus as Messiah and condemned Jesus, though God did disown his election of Israel (witness Rom 9—11). Nationhood and temple imagery, however, are now applied to "the Way" people (Acts 22:3; 24:14, cf. 26:10-11), which later became known as Christian believers, saints, or church (Paul's salutations in his letters, 1 Cor 3:9; Eph 2:19-22; 1 Pet 2:4-10). Further, the promise of a "great nation" made to Abraham (Rom 4:16-17) is now viewed as fulfilled by Jewish believers accepting Gentile believers (the word *ethnē* also means *nations*). Some early church fathers regarded the fall of Jerusalem in 70 CE as God's judgment, but the NT literature does not *explicitly* say this, though some texts may be cited to *implicitly* support this view (Matt 21:33-46// Mark 12:1-12; Luke 20:9-19).

But how are we to understand God's promise to give a specific land to Abraham's descendants? Through "transformation" of the promise, the *meek/faithful* will inherit not only the land (as in Ps 37) but the *earth-world* (Matt 5:5, earth/*gēn*; Rom 4:13, *world/kosmou*; 1 Cor 3:22-23, *world/kosmos*; and Rev 21:1-4, *new heaven and earth*). *Land* is no longer a territorial claim, but has become global, wherever *nations* are. Jesus' Great Commission (Matt 28:17-20) embraces all the nations of the earth.[3] The singular *nation* becomes plural, *nations*. Inheriting *land* (repeated 5x in Psalm 37) now becomes inheriting the *earth/world*. Jesus' commission has "gone geographically viral" (fulfilling Acts 1:8).

The promise of land is transmuted and universalized in the NT to denote the entire earth or world. As Munther Isaac writes, the land in the

---

3. This is a debated issue among scholars, e.g., Brueggemann says *land* permeates biblical thought, including the New Testament: *Land*, 157–72, especially p. 157 where he dissents from Davies. Brueggemann does acknowledge that "kingdom of God," not *land* as such, is at the center of Jesus' proclamation, but nonetheless "the coming of Jesus is understood with reference to new land arrangements" (161). Davies, in *Gospel* contends rightly, I believe, that *land* is not a factor in NT literature. Jesus' Beatitude that promises "the meek" will inherit the earth does not mean Jesus' followers will possess territorial land. Davies holds that the promise of land is universalized, thus "deterritorializing" the promise to Abraham (179). Davies also sees *land* in the OT linked to *temple* and this too is transformed into a new trope: "the Christian community as the new temple of God" (193; see McKelvey on "temple" in chapter 1, n27). March's contribution is helpful. He contends that land belongs to God; humans are stewards and caretakers of land: *Israel*, and an updated citation of sources in *God's*. See also Habel, *Land*. None of his six ideologies ably developed for *land* in the OT readily carries over to the NT. See below, however, my discussion of *land*-affiliated themes that do appear in the NT.

TWO MAJOR TRANSFORMATIONS: LAND AND ENEMY

OT becomes lands in the NT (and Eden becomes the Renewed Earth).[4] Nowhere in the NT does it say Israel shall return to the land. The lack of NT texts on the "return" theme verifies the point that the OT texts speaking of Israel's return to the land refer primarily to their return from the exile in 538 BCE.[5]

This profound truth has eluded some scholarly contributions and many lay Christians, especially those who appeal to Scripture to support the contemporary nation of Israel and its claim to the land (Zionism) at the expense of Palestinians, razing their houses and leaving them more and more landless in the West Bank.[6] An anonymous early Church Father expressed the Christian view of land in the *Letter to Diognetus*, "*Every foreign land* is their *fatherland*, and yet for them *every fatherland* is a *foreign land*" (5:5; italics mine).[7]

The transformation of the *land* promise, however, began in Jeremiah's exilic theology, long before the New Testament. In *diaspora (Galut)* theology, covenant faithfulness flourishes apart from land, and provides the norm for Christian living, in any land, not as owner but as steward. This shift in thinking appears already in the Septuagint translation (250 BCE) of the Hebrew Masoretic text. James's decisive role at the Jerusalem Conference (Acts 15) demonstrates this turn from *land* to the inheritance of *earth* for all people as the fulfillment of God's promise to Abraham. The first part of 15:17 reads, "that the rest of mankind [*adam*] may seek the Lord" ("so that all other peoples may seek the Lord," NRSV, quoting a Greek translation close to the LXX) whereas the Hebrew text reads: "that they may possess the land of Edom."[8] F. F. Bruce comments on this remarkable transformation:

> The reinterpretation conveys a promise like that of Isa. 55:3f., where the fulfillment of the covenant mercies to David brings

---

4. Isaac develops this point in detail, working through relevant OT and NT texts: *From Land to Lands*. This book came to my attention too late to work its theses into my discussion, but his conclusions match mine.

5. Almost all the OT texts were written before and/or in reference to Israel's exile into Babylon (586–539 BC) and therefore refer to the homecoming in 538 BCE. Ezekiel 37 refers to Israel's return home in 538 BCE. Ezekiel 39:23-25 explicitly mentions return from captivity. See also Jeremiah 27:22; 29:10–11; 30:3. The exile deeply influenced much of the OT literature, notably the laments in Psalms 74; 79; 80; 137; and Lamentations. For further study of how God's promises to Abraham are fulfilled or not fulfilled canonically, see Swartley, "Bible."

6. Among the many good resources on this topic, I recommend Sizer, *Zionism*; Burge, *Jesus*; and Barclift, "Zionism." A good complementary source is M. Barth, *Jesus*.

7. Richardson, ed. and trans., *Early*, 217.

8. For fuller analysis of this difference in quotations (Greek trans. and Hebrew text) see Bruce, *Peter*, 93–95.

hope for the world at large, in keeping with Israel's mission to impart the knowledge of the true God to her neighbors. Whereas "the remnant of Edom" was the object of the verb "may possess" in the Hebrew text, "the remnant of mankind" becomes the subject of the verb "may seek" in the Greek version, where the unexpressed object of the verb is to be understood as "me" (i.e. the Lord, as the quotation in Acts explicitly says) ... The Son of David [Jesus] is extending his sovereignty over a wider empire that David himself ever controlled, and extending it by the persuasion of divine grace, not by force of arms. This and similar Old Testament oracles are now [in Acts 15] receiving a more comprehensive and detailed fulfillment than either the Hebrew prophets or even their Greek interpreters could have envisaged.[9]

The Hebrew text envisions restoration of David's past land-glories, comprising Edom, but the Greek text (LXX) foresees the land-promise extending to all humankind; all peoples "inherit the earth." The textual change is only a shift in vowels, from ' ēdōm to ' ādām, Further, the Hebrew "may possess" (yir su) was changed in the translation to "may seek" (yidr su)—a remarkable example of scribal liberty, responding to the changing reality of the Hebrew people in 250 BCE.

This dramatic reinterpretation of the land-promise testifies to its conditional nature. Now a specific territorial *land* is transformed and universalized. Israel becomes a worldwide blessing as Abraham's descendants were promised to become. The promise of land is linked also to messianic hope and kingship. That promise is fulfilled in and through the gospel of Jesus Messiah as it is proclaimed throughout the *world* (see the confessional summary in 1 Tim 3:16).

In contrast to the conditional nature of God's covenants with Moses and Solomon, the Abrahamic covenant (Gen 12:1–3; 17:4–8) and the Davidic covenant (2 Sam 7:12–16) are God's covenants with Israel *as a people*. Both are unconditional. The NT sees both covenants fulfilled in Jesus and his messianic community, beginning with the first disciples. Christian believers (Jew and Gentile) are now viewed as also the descendants of Abraham and heirs of the promise to Abraham (Rom 4:13–16; Gal 3:6–9, 14; 4:21–31). Paul calls the church the "Israel of God" (Gal 6:16). Paul speaks also of God's continuing covenant with the Jewish people (Rom 11).[10]

---

9. Ibid., 95–96.

10. This is a conundrum, which has spurred much research and a vast spate of literature. The topic as such lies outside my scope of consideration here, though it does bear on the judgments made above.

The reign of Jesus as King, begun at his resurrection, fulfills God's promise to David (Rom 1:3; Acts 2:22–36; 15:15–18; 1 Cor 15:24–26; Rev 4–5; 11:17–18; 17:14; 19:11–16). God's covenant-promises to Abraham and David are fulfilled and universalized in Jesus Christ and his followers, both Jews and Gentiles. Jeremiah 31:31–34 is fulfilled in the new covenant, sealed by the blood of the crucified Messiah (Matt 26:26–30; Heb 8:8–13).

Matthew's Gospel accentuates Jesus as the Davidic king. David emerges in OT literature as the ideal king. This occurs not because of moral superiority but for his confession of his sin and God's blessing upon him to conquer the marauding "enemies" round about, especially the Philistines. God's promises to David (2 Sam 7:13–14, 29) and the motif of David as the ideal king permeates messianic hope, and appears as a significant trope in Matthew. Deirdre Good, in her insightful study, *Jesus the Meek King*,[11] holds that Matthew's description of Jesus in his triumphal entry as *meek (präus)* is most significant. Linked to and interpreted in light of 5:5, "Blessed are the meek,..." Jesus describes himself in 11:29, "I am meek and humble of heart..."[12] Good contributes a thorough lexical study of *meek*, concluding that it belongs to "the category of positive moral qualities: what is good, kind, just, holy, perfect, humble, gentle, blessed, merciful."[13] She investigates the political portrait of "the ideal king" in Hellenistic writings. In these, the ideal king *learns* meekness through discipline in control and rejection of anger, which enables him to become a gentle, benevolent king. Further, meekness is a virtue that generally belonged to the female and slave roles in both Judaic and Hellenistic societies.

Good proposes that Matthew's presentation shares elements of the ideal king, but differs crucially in that Jesus declares his meekness in a "revelational" context (11:25–27), linking meekness to Jesus' dependence on and obedience to his Father. This in turn harks back to the temptations where Jesus rejects Satan's enticements to achieve power: to make stones into bread, to jump off the temple, and to rule over the kingdoms of this world. Jesus' filial obedience to his Father resists Satan's offers that appeal to his status and power as Son of God. Rather, Jesus lives the model he sets forth for his followers, to be meek and humble to enter the kingdom

---

11. Good, *Meek*. See 18, 26–27, 35, 70, 82, 92–93, 104–5. In further support, Good cites the *Didache*, Ignatius, and the Desert Fathers. See also Mauser, *Gospel*, 52, for his excellent treatment of this emphasis.

12. Translations that use *gentle* for *präus* in Matthew 11:29 and 21:5 obscure the significance of Matthew's emphasis on meekness. Here see W. Carter's excellent comparison of Jesus' word about his *yoke* as "easy and light" to imperial uses of *yoke* in the Jewish literature of the time and the Roman world as well: *Matthew*, 122–23.

13 Good, *Meek*, 13.

(18:4). Jesus' meekness contrasts to the Gentiles' tyrant-lords who abuse their subjects (20:24–28), the context for Jesus' triumphal entry as a *meek* king riding on a donkey.

Good's contribution, however, must be supplemented by understanding humility and meekness in the OT-Jewish traditions presented by Klaus Wengst. Based upon numerous Scriptures and later Jewish texts,[14] Wengst argues that humility in the Gospels is not a virtue attributed to a noble king but a condition of humiliation in which one stands in solidarity with the poor and oppressed. Numerous texts contrast the humble person to the oppressing rulers and wealthy, prosperous people. Those humble and meek, often associated with the poor (*anawim*), do not strive to become rich and powerful, but cast their lot with the poor, trusting in God for vindication. Wengst treats Matthew 11:28–30 in parallel to Jesus' blessing of the poor in the first Beatitude. Jesus identifies with those who know the burden of slave-like toil, those who are exhausted from life's demands upon the poor. The "yoke" is not so much contrasted to Pharisaic legalism, but to economic oppression under Roman occupation and its oppression. Mark Bredin concurs with Wengst, saying Jesus in Matthew calls us to identify with the poorest of the poor, and to act to alleviate their suffering.[15]

One need not choose between Wengst's/Bredin's and Good's contributions, for both support a thoroughly transformed understanding of what kingship means in Matthew. In Good's view, the character of the "ideal king" is not achieved by self-exertion or rivalry but by divine character and status that God grants to Jesus at his baptism: "This is my Son, the beloved one" (3:17), reaffirmed at Jesus' transfiguration (17:5). Jesus' triumphal entry in Matthew also transforms "power" views of kingship into that of a humble king, in which *children* sing praises to King Jesus. Matthew then quotes Psalm 8:2: "infants and nursing babies" model the innocent, loving, and fitting response to humble King Jesus!

Entering the land and entering the kingdom (Mark)

Two features in Mark's Gospel indicate an authorial strategy to transform Israel's entrance into and possession of the land. First, Mark uses the motif *on the way* (*en tē hodō*) twice in his opening verses and seven times in Mark's central section (8:27—10:52): Jesus' journey from Galilee to Jerusalem.

---

14. Wengst, *Humility*. Wengst bases his view on numerous texts: Amos 2:6f.; Isa 11:3b–5; Zeph 3:1b–13; Ps 37; *Eth Enoch* 94:6—104:13; Prov 15:33; *Sir* 2:4f.; 3:17–20; 7:11; 4:8; 4:1–10; 12:7, and several Qumran texts (1QH 5:20–22; 1QS 11).

15. Bredin, *Jesus . . . Poor*, 6–7; 125–28.

After his title verse (1:1), Mark introduces his Gospel by citing in sequence two key OT "way" texts in 1:2–3, as follows.

> "See, I am sending my messenger before you,
> who shall prepare your *way*" (Malachi 3:1, reflecting Exod 23:20)
> the voice of one crying in the wilderness:
> "Prepare the *way* of the Lord,
> Make his paths straight" (Isa 40:3; italics mine)

This distinctive opening together with his central section framed by "on the way" marks Mark the "Gospel of the Way." This emphasis contributes also to Mark's uniquely disclosed Christology, with Mark 8:27–30 the pivot in his narrative "play" with the messianic secret. The phrase "on the way" (*en tē hodō*), occurs in the first and last verses of the journey section, and in structurally strategic "self-disclosures" in Jesus' teaching his disciples the *way* of discipleship (double entré intended). In 8:27 *en tē hodō* precedes his first passion-resurrection announcement. In 9:33–34 (2x) it immediately follows his second passion announcement. The phrase occurs again in 10:32, preceding Jesus' third passion-resurrection declaration.[16] The last two uses frame the Bartimaeus story (10:46, 52). The very last words of the journey section are "on the way" (*en tē hodō*) in the NRSV and Greek Testament. In the OT the *way* journey anticipated inheritance of the land of promise.

Within this section the phrase, "enter the kingdom of God," occurs five times: 9:47; 10:15, 23, 24, 25; add to this the twice recurring *eternal life* in 10:17, 30. The destiny of those who follow Jesus *on the way* is not "entering into the land" (Deut 1:8; 4:1; 6:18; 16:20) but "entering into the kingdom of God," which connects also to inheriting eternal life.[17] The interweaving of *en tē hodō* and "entering into the kingdom" in this section is most significant, for it joins the two OT motifs crucial to the transformation of Israel's *way-land* texts (Exod 23:20) and entrance-into-the-land formula. Mark's uses of these two tropes occur within the *way* narrative and function as frames for Jesus' passion and resurrection predictions in

---

16. The phrase occurs also in 10:17 introducing Jesus' encounter with the man who asks Jesus: "what must I do to inherit eternal life?" Mark connects *the way* (*en tē hodō*) here with inheriting eternal life (cf. John 14:6).

17. For extended discussion see Swartley, *Israel's*, 102–6. See numerous footnotes where other writers on Mark observe similar points, though not put together to show the interconnections of various points above.

8:31; 9:31; 10:32. In Mark these motifs anticipate the cross, and shape the Christians' unique political response to evil.[18]

Living in the land and living in the kingdom (Luke)

Luke's journey narrative (9:51—19:44) differs strikingly from Mark's and Matthew's. It is three times longer than Mark's. Scholars, with few exceptions, have been baffled by its structure. A breakthrough, in my judgment, is C. F. Evans's proposal that it parallels Deuteronomy. Unit by unit the parallel is insightful, persuasive, and significant. I cite only a few of the parallels, using numbers from my full twenty-two listings elsewhere:[19]

Diagram 2b.1 Parallels Between Deuteronomy and Luke's Central Section

Deut 2–3:22 // Luke 10:4–16	4. Messengers sent to Sihon and Og with word of peace // Seventy sent out with word of peace
	5. If rejected, destroy people, etc. // If rejected wipe off your feet and leave.

Deut 5–6 //
Luke 10:29–37
	8. Shema and "inherit the land…in order to live //
	    lawyer asks about inheriting eternal life;
	    Jesus answers with Shema

Deut 7 // Luke 10:29–37	9. Destroy the foreigner; show no mercy // parable of Good Samaritan; show mercy

Deut 9:1–10:11 //
Luke 11:14–26
	10. Lord drives out strong nations //
	    Jesus drives out strong demons;
	    Phrase "finger of God" occurs in both!

Deut 20 // Luke 14:15–35	19. Excused from Lord's battle for new wife, house, vineyard // similar excuses of invited guests to the Great Banquet who miss the Feast

---

18. For extended discussion of this in relation to peacemaking and non-retaliation, see Swartley, *Covenant*, 107–17.

19. Swartley, *Israel's*, 151–53. For Evans's proposal, see "Central."

TWO MAJOR TRANSFORMATIONS: LAND AND ENEMY   69

Deut 21:15–22:4 //   20. How father handles rebellious son
Luke 15   —stone him //

  father seeks prodigal son—celebrates
  his return

Deut 24:6–25:3 //   22. Injunctions against oppressing the poor
Luke 16:19–18:8   and needy //

  Lord judges those who oppress the poor

These parallels between Luke's Journey narrative and Deuteronomy's prescriptions stun. They not only demonstrate Evans' thesis, but testify also to the transforming of Israel's mandates for living in the land to the moral mandates of Jesus' followers who enter into the kingdom of God and inherit eternal life.[20] This transformation presents contrasting responses to evil.

Numerous motifs associated with *land* in the OT appear in the NT with new meaning. Elmer Martens, in his excellent article in the Festschrift for him published in 2009, introduces the genre of *metaphor* and major *motifs* in the NT that form the unity of the Testaments and, at the same time, show the transformative dimensions of these metaphors and motifs. For each of these metaphors and motifs I summarize or quote a key sentence or two, an inadequate substitute for the richness and breadth of his article.[21] Martens examines the metaphorical use of *land* in Romans, in which "the groaning of all creation" (Rom 8:22) functions in a totally new context as "salvation/ redemption language." Hebrews contains the OT linkage between *land* and *rest*, which overflows in meaning to embrace the promise of a new reality: "not only the environment of peace in a physical land but part of the larger salvation" reality established in Jesus Christ as fulfillment of God's promise.[22] These metaphors and motifs then follow.

---

20. Some parallels are *contrasts*; others, *similar*; and others show *transformation* of similar topical thought. In my fuller analysis of the parallels in *Israel's Scripture*, I use letter-symbols to denote type of relationship between Deuteronomy's and Luke's units: (P) for parallel; (C) for contrast; (T) for transformation.

21. Martens, "'Land.'" Martens notes that the Hebrew word *erets*, translated in the LXX as *gē*, can mean *land* in a specific territorial sense and *earth* in a wider sense, designating the entire, global earth, 225–27.

22. Ibid., 229–31.

Hermeneutic metaphors

Land as New Habitat, Home, Security, and Rest. Phrases as "in Christ," abiding in Jesus as the true Vine, and "in the kingdom" signify relational places where Christian believers find *home, security, and rest.*[23]

Land as Abundance, and Satiation. The *land* "flowing with milk and honey" is transposed into motifs such as abundant life in John 10:10, Jesus' feeding of the multitudes with loaves left over—everyone satiated—and Jesus promising "the bread of life" to those who believe and, I add, in John 14:2 plentiful rooms where Jesus' followers abide with him eternally.[24] Martens points to Ephesians where *in the heavenlies* in 1:3, 7, *lavished* in 1:8, and *riches of his glorious inheritance* in 1:18 satiate believers with security and abundance.[25]

Land as promise. This motif permeates the OT. In the NT *fulfillment* is a key word, e.g., Matthew 1:23; 2:5–6; 4:15–16, as Martens notes.[26] Mark's keynote for Jesus' ministry is: "The time is fulfilled, the kingdom of God has come near; repent and believe the gospel" (1:15).

Land as gift. The Hebrew *nātan/gift* occurs more than thirty times in Deuteronomy, and permeates the OT. Note Joshua 24:12, in the context of covenant renewal and Israel's pledge to worship the Lord God only. "Yahweh gave the land, not to an individual, but a community. Land was not a commodity, the coinage of power, but instead, it was a gift over which stewardship was to be exercised."[27] In the NT, "God's kingdom, Jesus, or salvation—all are gifts."[28]

Land as Place of God's Presence. Martens writes, "Yahweh's primary relationship was to a people and then, only secondarily, to land. The NT incorporates both: in the Word become flesh; living (tenting) among us in John

---

23. Ibid., 233. In n34 Martens quotes C. J. H. Wright's *God's*: "'In Christ', answering to 'in the land', denotes a status and a relationship, a position of inclusion and security," 111.

24. See an exegesis of this text in Swartley, *John,* 340–42.

25. Martens, "Land," 234–35. See also the role of *Land* in Martens's *God's Design,* 98–118. While he regards *land* important to Israel (God's covenant to Abraham), with the word occurring over 500 times in Hebrew Scripture, yet he sees movement away from *land* as central in Israel's later history. His topical headings differ from those in his "'O Land'" article. His chart on 239–40 puts *land* into a variable category, with shift in emphasis from the pre-monarchy ("Land, et al., Abraham"), to the monarchy ("royal dynasty"), to the post-monarchy periods ("interior law").

26. Martens, "Land," 236–37.

27. Ibid., 237.

28. Ibid.

1:14; and God was in Christ. Christ also 'abides in them' (1 John 3:24), and for all eternity God 'will dwell *skēnōsei* with them'" (Rev 21:3).[29]

Land as Place of Righteousness. In the (OT) land of promise and in the NT, God's kingdom inaugurated by Jesus Christ's righteousness (*tzedeqah/ dikiaosunē*), occurs in numerous exhortations and declarations. Martens cites many texts from both Testaments, including Matthew 5:20–48 and Romans 15:17.[30]

To this list might be added one motif from Brueggemann: "Land as Temptation."[31] Here the link to the NT includes Jesus' refusal of Satan's temptations to acquire rule over the kingdoms of the world "if you will fall down and worship me" (Matt 4:9–10; cf. Luke 4:6–7)

In summary, these interrelated forays into the relationship between *land* and its associate themes in the OT and fulfillment motifs in the NT—at the center of which is God's kingdom (in the Gospels) and righteousness (Paul's Epistles)—demonstrates *transformation* that is rich and abundant, testifying to both the unity and diversity of Scripture. Kingdom-living, which Jesus came to inaugurate and make possible, means going the journey from a territorial land-based claim to a pilgrimage-based faith with Jesus Christ and the Holy Spirit as our guide until our exile (borrowing N. T. Wright's trope[32]) is consummated in the New Jerusalem, impinging itself upon us now for living the Christian life.[33] For followers of Jesus Christ and even many Jews, territorial land is not a "marker" for the people of God.[34]

---

29. Ibid, 238–39.

30. Ibid, 239–41. Martens's citations of many sources related to his article's theses stimulate further research.

31. Brueggemann, *Land*, 50–56.

32. N. T. Wright, *Jesus*. If Wright is correct that *exile* is the contextual *Leitmotif* of Jesus' proclamation, this contradicts Brueggemann's strong emphasis on *land* that carries through into the New Testament under different arrangements. *Land* does not appear in *Restoration*, edited by Newman. In this work C. Evans assesses N. T. Wright's view in his essay, "Jesus." Evans cites many extra-biblical Jewish texts written during or shortly after the Second Temple period that reflect *exile* consciousness (82–91). He also identifies events or teachings in the Gospels that may reflect the end or consummation of *exile* in Jesus' actions and teachings (91–100). Hays, however, in Newman, "Victory," says, "It seems to me that Wright has overstated his case on this [exile] point" (147). But "for 'Victory over Violence,' Wright makes an important contribution" (ibid.).

33. See Harker's provocative article, "Intertexuality," which contends that the New Jerusalem is not a "by and by" hope, but a hope-muscle exerting power to live now its moral excellence and beauty. Harker exemplifies "intertextuality" at the evocative level between the OT promised covenant relationship, especially in Ezekiel, and the New Jerusalem as fulfillment. The image of "New Jerusalem" in Revelation thus entails not *place* but *relationship*—what *covenant* signifies. This *relational* emphasis bears upon moral vision and living *now*.

34. Zionist-oriented Jews (and Christians), however, see the present nation of

The Journey of *Enemy* between Old and New Testaments

The Old Testament (this section anticipates chapter 3)

In journeying from the OT to the NT we focus first on how *enemy* functions in the Psalms and the Prophets before treating Jesus and the NT on this topic. Many Psalms speak of "enemies" with the psalmist's cry to God to save or deliver from the enemy (e.g., Ps 18). Many Lament Psalms cry for "healing" and/or "deliverance."[35] The Psalms, intended for worship across time, transcend their original settings, generalizing their description of the enemy who causes anguish of spirit, pain, and outright oppression that obstruct worship of the Lord God. Thus the Lament Psalms portray the enemy in a more generalized mode, so that "foes," "adversaries," and "enemies" take on new meaning in various times and settings of use.

Some Psalms, such as 82 (cf. 58), accuse the king-gods of the nations of inflicting injustice, and therefore deserving doom. Other Psalms conceptualize evil as oppressing personally (Pss 3, 5, 12, 18, 22, 25, 55, 68, 69, 118:5–8). For the psalmist God is rock, refuge, shelter, fortress, shield, protector, (horn of my) salvation, and deliverer (chapter 3).

Psalm 89, a royal Psalm extolling God's eternal covenant with David, mentions *enemy(ies)* four times (vv. 10, 22, 42, 51). The Psalm first extols the "Lord of hosts" for victory over the enemies but then becomes increasingly desperate to remind the Lord that enemies are now taunting the Lord; they are a threat to the fulfillment of Lord God's covenant promise.

Many uses of *enemy* reflect an original warfare context, but that context is no longer specific; enemies are generalized. What matters is that in the midst of threats—whatever they are, including sickness[36]—the psalmist struggles toward freedom to worship and praise God (Ps 71 exemplifies this beautifully). In a few imprecatory Psalms,[37] however, the Psalm ends by crying to God to destroy the *enemy* (Pss 7:6; 44:23–25). In these Psalms destruction of the enemy is followed by a loud cry for, or affirmation of, deliverance.[38] Ollenburger describes the enemies in the Psalms:

Israel a fulfillment of God's land-promise to Abraham. This view, however, overlooks or downplays the major transformations within the canonical journeys, within the OT and into the NT.

35. Swartley, *Health*, 50–51. See also the next chapter for documentation and assessment.

36. Ibid, 50–61.

37. Holladay, in *Psalms,* points out that numerous Psalms or parts thereof have been omitted in the Roman Catholic Liturgy for the Hours (e.g., 5:10; 54:7; 55:16). Psalms 58, 83, 109, plus nineteen others.

38. Psalm 137 has no breakthrough, only weeping for the loss of home and land—the

Often in the Psalms, the innocent are portrayed as suffering illness, poverty, and abandonment—making them easy prey for the wicked. In Ps 35, the speaker—again portrayed as David—contrasts his behavior with that of his enemies. When they were sick, he was grieved; he fasted and prayed for them. But now, in his affliction, his enemies mock him, slander him, declaring that he deserves his fate, and that God has abandoned him. The enemies seize upon the weakness and sickness of the innocent as their own vindication. If those who rely on God are poor and sick, then their enemies are vindicated in their wickedness and injustice.... The arrogance of the wicked, the enemies, is not only a threat to the innocent—the poor, the weak, and the sick; it is also a threat to God's own righteousness. Those who call on God suffer at the hands of their enemies who deny God. Yet God remains the only hope of the innocent.... The innocent have no recourse, no one to turn to, no strength of their own in the face of their enemies; their only weapon is prayer. Prayer is an act of faith, and an appeal to God's own righteousness.[39]

On the cross Jesus quotes from the Psalms: 22:1 in Mark 15:34; 22:19 in John 19:24; and 31:5 in Luke 23:46. Psalms 22:12, 16 and 31:8, 15 speak either of bulls attacking, evildoers, enemies, adversaries, and/or persecutors.[40] Both Psalms include hope or praise at the end. Psalm 69:4d, 13e, and 18b complain of enemies; 69:4 is quoted in John 15:25, "they hated me without a cause," and 69:9 in 2:17, "Zeal for your house will consume me." The disciples *remember* this when Jesus cleanses the temple, transforming its function and meaning from a physical structure to *his body*, through which, crucified and resurrected, disciples worship God. The Gospel's citations from Psalms 22, 31, and 69 accentuate Christology.[41] Psalm 118 guides interpretation of Jesus' triumphal entry and his vineyard parable: "Hosanna ..." in Mark 11:9 (with Matt/Luke parallels), and John 12:13 citing 118: 25–26 (with variations); Mark 12:10-11 quotes 118:22.[42]

---

plight of many in our world today. Psalms 83 (national) and 88 (personal) also have no breakthrough to praise or affirmation. Psalm 58 cites how horrible it is for life under "the gods" (v.1) and ends with assurance that "there is a God who judges the earth."

39. Ollenburger, "Enemy," 2.

40. For fuller treatment of the Gospel's depiction of Jesus fulfilling key verses in Psalms 22, 31 (LXX, 30), and 69 (LXX, 68), see Hays, *Echoes...Gospels*, 83–85, 140–41, 161–62, 235, 286, 297, 311–12, 326, 416n86, 433n68.

41. Cf. also Mark 14:33–34 with Psalm 42:6, 12; 43:5 and Mark 14:62 with Psalm 110:1. See chapter 3 for "deliverance from evil/enemies" in the Psalms.

42. See Hays, 476, for numerous page references in *Echoes . . . Gospels* that cite Psalm 118.

While the *enemy* in the OT is often pagan nations, Israel also is God's enemy (Amos 2:6; 5:20; 8:2; Isa 10:5-27; 43:28; 63:10; Jer 21:4-6).[43] Isaiah 63:10 is blunt:

> But they [the people of Israel] rebelled
> and grieved his holy spirit;
> therefore he became their enemy;
> he himself fought against them.

Israel/Judah is God's enemy; the Lord fights against Israel/Judah and even uses kings of *enemy* nations as *servant, shepherd,* or *anointed* to accomplish exilic punishment of Israel for its idolatries and post-exilic restoration to the homeland (Jer 25:9; 27:6; Isa 44:28–45:1).

Enemy in the New Testament

In the New Testament enemy *(echthros)* is used in the singular to denote the devil or Satan, explicitly in Matt 13:28, 39; Luke 10:17-19; Acts 13:10; inferentially in Mark 3:23-27//Matt 12:22-30//Luke 11:14-21; and wherever Jesus confronts demons. In the plural it can denote individual foes (e.g. Matt 10:36) or the Jews' military enemy.[44] Zechariah's song exults in the Messiah's advent who brings liberation "from our *enemies,* from the hand of all who hate us" (Luke 1:71, 74). Jesus, weeping over Jerusalem blind to "the things that make for peace" (Luke 19:41-42), forecasts imminent judgment: *your enemies* will erect siege-works around the city, demolish its buildings, and "crush you to the ground, you and your children within you" (19:44a).

Certainly Zechariah, Jesus, and the Gospel writers had in mind the Romans as the *enemy.*[45] As the occupying power ruling Palestine by force

---

43. Among the many sources on Holy War in the OT, in addition to those cited in chapter 2a are: P. Miller, Jr., "God," and essays in *Holy,* edited by Thomas et al. Earl's fine essay, however, fails to show the trajectory of transformation within the biblical canon, with Jesus as God's definitive revelation for human conduct.

44. Furnish, *Love,* 47. In Luke 19:27 the term denotes *enemies* of God. See also Foerster, ἐχθρός *(echthrós), TDNT* II, 813-14. W. Klassen discusses the wider biblical use and meaning of *enemy* in "Love,"158-59.

45 Whether Zechariah had the Romans in mind is uncertain, but probable. The phrase might reflect the Psalms, pleading God to deliver from the enemy. The Samaritans were also Israel's enemies, reflected in the parable of the Good Samaritan (Luke 10:30-37). See Donahue, "Who," in Swartley, *Love,* 137-56. Donahue narrates the history of enmity between the Jews and Samaritans. He shows how Jesus' "love of enemy" in the Good Samaritan parable and Jesus' journey into Samaria (John 4) overcame the enmity relationship. The phrase "hate your enemy" describes the attitude of the Qumran Essene community toward the Romans (1QS i,1-4). The Covenanters were enjoined "to love the sons of light" but "to hate all the sons of darkness" (vv. 3-4), which, as O. J. F. Seitz says, referred mostly to the Romans (the Kittim). See Seitz, "Love," 50-51.

since 63 BCE, they offended Jewish religious sensibilities.[46] Pontius Pilate not only "mingled the blood of the Galileans with their sacrifices" (Luke 13:1, RSV), but also caused outrage by diverting the sacred treasure *(corban)* to build an aqueduct and erecting Caesar's images in Jerusalem.[47] The Romans imposed heavy financial burdens on the Jews, impoverishing the people through tax-collectors. Imposing military force, the Romans retaliated against a major revolt headed by Judas the Galilean in 6 CE in Sepphoris (three miles north of Jesus' hometown Nazareth), crucifying 2,000 people.[48] Hengel aptly describes Palestine in Jesus' time "a politico-religious tinderbox."[49]

Into this situation Jesus comes with his new command, "'Love your enemies!'" This, together with Jesus' proclamation that the kingdom of God now come near,[50] was shockingly radical amidst this messianic expectancy and endemic insurrection. Its location in Jesus' first extended sermon shows its importance in Jesus' ministry. In Luke "love your enemies" is Jesus' very first ethical teaching (6:27). In Matthew, it is the climax to six antitheses in the Sermon on the Mount, in which Jesus establishes a "pattern of life in the kingdom of God."[51] Three of the six antitheses address situations of potential violence: murder and anger (5:21-26); response to evildoers (5:38-42); and love your enemies (5:43-48).

"Love your enemies" (Matt 5:44; Luke 6:27, 35) marks one's identity as "children of the Father." The same "identity feature" is declared for *peacemakers* in 5:9.[52] Jesus commanded his disciples to love their enemies because God, who sends the rain on the just and the unjust, loves all people, regardless of their good or evil deeds. In Luke the accent falls on God's mercy toward us. Because God has shown mercy to us, as recipients of that mercy we are commanded and thereby empowered to love our enemies. When disciples love their enemies, they extend the heavenly Father's mercy

---

46. For the history of these offenses and resultant conflicts, see Brandon, *Jesus*, 65-135, who identifies Jesus with the Zealot cause. Jesus' command to love enemies, however, diverges sharply from the Zealot response to the Romans. For the structure and method of Roman government, see Cassidy, *Jesus*, App.1; 87-97.

47. Josephus, *Wars*, Book II, ix.4, in *Works*, 609, col. 1.

48. Josephus, *Ant.*, XVII, x.5, 10, in *Works*, xvii, 9.5, 10, 469-71.

49. Hengel, *Victory*, 56.

50. Hengel, *Was Jesus?*, 26. This command, however, is not unique to Jesus. W. Klassen cites numerous pre-Christian parallels in "Novel." See also his survey of the history of research on the love command in "Some Reflections." Stendahl observes that Jewish parallels to Jesus' teaching on non-retaliation, especially in Qumran literature, are motivated by storing up wrath for God's final judgment. But Jesus' love command seeks the welfare and friendship of the enemy; it *reflects the attitude of God*: in "Hate."

51. Jeremias, *Sermon*, 34-35. See also Hunter's exposition in *Design*.

52. For extended discussion, see Swartley, *Covenant*, 56-59 and 130-32 for Luke, and *Send*, 45-53.

and live out their identity as God's children. Peacemakers and enemy-lovers are *children* of God (Matt 5:9, 45). If we as Jesus' disciples behave in this way, we will reflect the Father's mercy and love toward us, for while we were ungodly, sinners, indeed enemies (Rom 5:6–10) we were reconciled to, and have peace with God. We are called to take up the ministry of reconciliation (Rom 5:1, 11). Ollenburger speaks our Christian confession:

> We are communities of the ungodly, enemies of God, who know God's mercy and forgiveness and reconciliation. On this basis we can be, as we are called to be, ambassadors and agents and communities of reconciliation . . . We cannot separate the love command, or any other command, from the cross, and thus from God's grace—or from the resurrection, and thus from God's power. The church exists to proclaim the gospel, and in nothing is that proclamation so powerful and eloquent, or so authentic, as in our love for our enemies.[53]

Jesus calls his disciples to go beyond retaliation. The command, "Do not resist one who is evil" (Matt 5:39), is congruent with and serves the positive command to love the enemy;[54] it accords with standard apostolic teaching, "Do not be overcome by evil, but overcome evil with good" (Rom 12:21; cf. 1 Thess 5:15; 1 Pet 3:9).[55] This radical challenge to be reconciled with our enemies through loving them, and doing good instead of evil, accords with God's response to us (Rom 5:8–10). Ronald Sider sums it well: "One fundamental aspect of the holiness and perfection of God is that God loves His enemies. Those who by His grace seek to reflect His holiness will likewise love their enemies—even when it involves a cross."[56] Love of

---

53. Ollenburger, "The Enemy," 10.

54. This has been argued well by Schottroff in "Non-Violence," 9–28, and in her article "Give." Matthew 5:39 might be translated "Do not resist by evil means," with the third inflection (*tō ponērō*) an instrument of means: Ferguson, *Politics*, 4–5. The five examples of non-resistance are effective expressions of the radical nature of Jesus' teaching; they make our mouths fall open, exclaiming, according to Tannehill: "We should do even that?" They "attack . . . our natural tendency to put self-protection first," 71. See Tannehill's literary study of Jesus' teachings, in *Sword*. The referent of *tō ponērō* has been debated (John Chrysostom: Satan; Luther and Calvin: neuter form, injustice) though most agree it refers to evil actions by those who would do violence. This is congruent with the example of one who strikes (*rhapizei*) on the cheek. The striker is a person, not Satan (though Satan may incite the person) nor a composite force (Robitaille, "Sermon," 40).

55. Piper has ably documented the fundamental unity between Jesus' command to 'love the enemy' and this "fixed rule . . . in the [early] Christian paraenetic tradition," in "*Love*," 17, 171, 174.

56. R. Sider, *Christ*, 26.

TWO MAJOR TRANSFORMATIONS: LAND AND ENEMY 77

enemies requires readiness to forgive, which enables reconciliation (Rom 5:11; 2 Cor 5:18–20).

A stunning story of forgiveness, an authentic demonstration of these Jesus-type actions—forgiveness, suffering, sharing, service, love—is the Amish community's response to the tragic shooting of ten Amish schoolgirls, by a neighbor, Charles Carl Roberts, October 2, 2006, in Lancaster County, Pennsylvania (four died and several live with disabilities).[57] Columnist Diana Butler Bass details how the Amish practice of forgiveness leads to peacemaking, refusing enemy relations.

> [It] unfolded in four public acts over the course of a week. First, some elders visited Marie Roberts, the wife of the murderer, to offer forgiveness. Then, the families of the slain girls invited the widow to their own children's funerals. Next, they requested that all relief monies intended for Amish families be shared with Roberts and her children. And, finally, in an astonishing act of reconciliation, more than 30 members of the Amish community attended the funeral of the killer. As my husband and I talked about the spiritual power of these actions, I commented in an offhanded way, "It is an amazing witness to the peace tradition." He looked at me and said passionately, "a witness? I don't think so. This went well past witnessing. They weren't witnessing to anything. They were actively *making* peace."[58]

---

57. See D. Kraybill, Nolt, and Weaver-Zercher, *Amish*. On love of enemy, see Vanderhaar, *Enemies*. The book develops "method" and discusses "attitude," citing illustrations where nonviolence subverted enemy encounter or challenge. See also Podimattam, "Love." This article addresses "How? Why? What?" It concludes with seven pastoral reflections—excellent.

58. http://www.beliefnet.com/columnists/godspolitics/2006/10/diana-butler-bass-what-if-the.html Also, paragraphs 11 and 12 in "Amish forgiveness is about 'actively making peace.'" *Cochrane Eagle*, October 18, 2006. http://www.harbeck.ca/cww/cww_061018.html.

3

Evil and Deliverance in Psalms, Proverbs, and Prophets

Deliver me, O Lord, from evildoers;
protect me from those who are violent,
who plan evil things in their minds
and stir up wars continually.

—Ps 140:1–2

"Keep your tongue from evil,
and your lips from speaking deceit.
Depart from evil, and do good [repeated in 37:22];
seek peace, and pursue it."

—Ps 34:13–14

Deceit is in the mind of those who plan evil,
but those who counsel peace have joy.

—Prov 12:20

"They are skilled in doing evil
but do not know how to do good."

—Jer 4:22c

"they proceed from evil to evil."

—Jer 9:3c

Psalms

MANY PSALMS CONTAIN CRIES for deliverance from *evil* or *enemies*. Jesus and the NT writers often heard variations of "deliver us from evil, evildoers, or enemies" in their worship. The focus is on these key terms: *evil, evildoers,* and *enemy(ies)* and *deliver/deliverance* as they appear in the NRSV. *Wickedness/wicked* often occur (sometimes *sin/sinned*) in texts that speak about *evil, evildoers, enemy(ies)*; I comment on these only if the key terms appear also. Words denoting *deliverance* (e.g., *rebuke, save, depart, crush, judgment,* or *bring them to an end*) qualify. These are my criteria for choosing which Psalms are included for comment. I italicize key words in Scripture quotations to alert the reader.

Books introducing Psalms neglect the correlation I pursue here, where both *evil/evildoers* and *deliver/deliverance* occur. Brueggemann, with over a hundred articles, books, and reviews on the Psalms, culminates his extensive contribution in his recent captivating introduction to the Psalms.[1] While he mentions *deliver/deliverance* and *evil/evildoers* a few times,[2] he does not correlate them. He rightly emphasizes covenantal relationship between God and the people as context for the candor in the verbal exchanges between God and the psalmist. Millar's section on the Psalms complements mine, noting that *Calling on the Name of the Lord* accords with God's messianic promise to *deliver* his people.[3]

While the terms *evil, evildoers, enemy(ies)*, and *deliver/deliverance* appear in different types of Psalms, most occur in Lament Psalms. Waltner counts 61 Lament Psalms, over two-fifths of the 150. Of these he lists 45 as individual laments and 16 as communal laments.[4] In these Psalms the psalmist pleads God to protect from or despoil the *enemy* or *evildoers*.

Deliverance and Healing Psalms sometimes overlap since both illness and threats from malevolent powers are presented in generalized terms.[5] In many of these Psalms the psalmist cries out for deliverance from the enemy,

---

1. Brueggemann, *From Whom*. For his Psalms bibliography, see 178–88.

2. Ibid., 19, 118 for *evil/evildoers*; 23, 90–91 for *deliverance*. Enemies and the wicked occur a few times also.

3. Millar, *Calling*, 132–66.

4. Waltner, *Psalms*, 787. See his "Genre" discussion, 762–67 and his "type" identification, 789–91. In his titles for the Psalms (7–11) and his Outline (719–44) the word *evil* never occurs, though he cites *wicked, enemies,* and *judgment* quite often. For titles of Psalms 14 and 53 he uses *deliverance* and *deliverer*, but the term *evildoers* (14:4; 53:4) never appears in a title. It does appear in his commentary, to which I refer below. His title for Psalm 59 begins with *Deliver* me (9); the noun form occurs in the outline (726); and *enemies* in the commentary.

5. See the "Table on Healing and Deliverance Psalms" in Swartley, *Health*, 51.

portrayed as personal oppression (Pss 3, 5, 12, 18, 68, 118:5–18). Mbon notes that the enemies are not usually identified; they transcend the original historical situation and often refer to the godless, or the wicked. He cites S. Mowinckel, who suggests these are "'supernatural beings, demons, or evil spirits,' which he prefers to classify under the general term 'sorcery' (*awen*), and which, he further suggests, may have been responsible for the psalmists' physical condition in some of the 'psalms of illness.'"[6]

Who are the *workers of evil* (41: 8), *enemies* (41:10), or *evildoers* (10:15) in these Psalms? Scholars have made several suggestions: they arose from party strife within Israel; they were prayers of the accused, perhaps fugitives who fled to the temple for asylum from some act of injustice; or the *evildoers* were magicians or witches who put curses on the sufferer or demons who attacked the person.[7] In Psalms where *deliverance* (*deliver*) occurs, a national enemy threatening Israel's people or land concurrent with David's reign is sometimes in view.[8]

To clarify the *evil/deliverance* feature in the Psalms, I utilize four categories. In the first group (total 30) the *enemies/evildoers*, *foes*, or *wicked* people are *internal*. If the Psalm *title* denotes the situation as internal or external, the classification follows suit. In the second (total 5) the adversaries appear to be *external*, outside Israel. In the third (total 3), the identity of the *enemy* or *evil/evildoer* is unclear. In the fourth (total 22) one of the crucial terms is lacking.

Since the descriptions of *evil/enemy* and *deliver/deliverance* are often similar, I have put my brief discussion of about half of these Psalms in the footnotes to make the text reader-friendly. I omit Psalm titles; most are "of David" or "David to the leader" (sometimes named). Some (i.e., 3, 7, 18, 22, 34, 59) have specific situational titles; a few are "Of Asaph." For topical titles, see *The Harper Collins Study Bible*. The Summary/Conclusion identifies the key topics, citing supporting references. In quoted Scripture, *italics* are mine.

Group 1: Adversaries are internal

Psalm

3 *Deliver*, *deliverance*, and *enemies* occur in vv. 7–8:

> Rise up, O Lord! *Deliver* me, O my God! For you strike all *my enemies* on the cheek; you break the teeth of the *wicked*.

6. Mbon, "Deliverance," 9.

7. This is Mbon's view, held by Mowinckel whom Mbon quotes.

8. In the first two (of the five) books of Psalms (Pss 1—41 and 42—72), David's name occurs in most titles. The second book concludes with "The Prayers of David son of Jesse are ended" (Ps 72:20).

> *Deliverance* belongs to the Lord; may your blessing be on your people! Selah.

The Psalm's conclusion exalts the Lord: "*deliverance* belongs to the Lord." The phrase, "ten thousands of people" (v. 6), might suggest the nations, but the Psalm's title (when fleeing from Absalom) indicates the *enemies/wicked* are internal, but of national consequence.[9]

8 A unique strategy! "Out of the mouths of babes and infants you have founded a bulwark because of your foes, to silence the enemy and the avenger" (v. 2). Jesus quotes from the Psalm (Matt 21:16) to counter the chief priests' and scribes' anger at Jesus' reception and blessing of the children! Babes and infants model trust: God defends and judges. Not hate, but love for enemies subverts evil's power.

10[10] *Wicked* appears numerous times: vv. 2, 3, 4, 13, 15, "Break the arm of the wicked and *evildoers*; seek out their wickedness until you find none (15)." The *evils* are persecuting the poor (vv. 2, 9b–c), cursing, deceit, and oppression, as well as mischief and iniquity (vv. 7–11).

Deliver does not occur, but *judgment*, when executed, is *deliverance*. The Psalm begins with a downcast mood, questioning whether the Lord attends to such *evils*. It ends with assurance: you, the Lord "will hear the desire of the meek; you will strengthen their heart, you will incline your ear to do justice for the orphan and the oppressed" (vv. 17–18).

The evils named here and in other Psalms remind us of today's crimes, where the rich oppress the poor. Too often the policies of a country and

---

9. Psalms 5—6: These Psalms cry for deliverance from *evil, evil workers*, or *enemies*. Topically these could be one: 5:4-6 "For you are not a God who delights in *wickedness*; *evil* will not sojourn with you. . . . ; you hate all *evildoers*. You destroy those who speak lies; the Lord abhors the bloodthirsty and deceitful." The *evil* is murder and deceit. *Enemies* appears in v. 8. Rather than *deliver*, the Lord is refuge, protection, and shield (vv. 11–12), the source of deliverance. Cf. Psalm 18:1-3, 6:8, and 10 "*Depart* from me, all you *workers of evil*, for the Lord has heard the sound of my weeping . . . All my *enemies* shall be ashamed and struck with terror; they shall turn back, and in a moment be put to shame." The imperative, *depart*, carries exorcist/*deliverance* effect. This Psalm supports Mowinckel's view that the psalmist cries for freedom from some sort of sorcery (*awen*).

Psalm 7:6, 9, 14 "Rise up, O Lord, in your anger; lift yourself up against the fury of my *enemies*; awake, O my God; you have appointed a judgment . . . O let the *evil of the wicked* come to an end, but establish the righteous . . . O righteous God . . . See how they *conceive evil*, and are pregnant with mischief, and bring forth lies." In v. 10 God is David's shield "who *saves* [*delivers*] the upright." God will severely punish *evil* (here, lies). God judges the *evil* of the *wicked*, implying *deliver*, for the *enemies* conceiving *evil* will be vanquished (in vv. 8, 11 the Lord is judge).

10. In the LXX Psalm 10 is part of Psalm 9. From here on the English text is advanced one number ahead of the LXX.

city are made to the advantage of the rich: allocating money for military weapons and defense with tax cuts for the rich. Education and health care for all are slighted. The rich receive lenience for crime, while the poor, especially African Americans, are sent to prison for felonies. *Evil* is done to both humans *and God*. God is *judge* of such policies.

18 This Psalm is classic. Though it lacks *evil*,[11] *enemies/enemy* recur in vv. 3, 4, 17, 40, and 48 (2x). One of my favorites, it protects against evil!

> I love you, O Lord, my strength. The Lord is my rock, my fortress, and *my deliverer*, my God, my rock in whom I take refuge, my shield, and the horn of my salvation, my stronghold. I call upon the Lord, who is worthy to be praised, so I shall be saved from *my enemies* (vv. 1–3); . . . *He delivered me from my strong enemy*, and from those who hated me; for they were too mighty for me. They confronted me in the day of my calamity; but the Lord was my support (vv. 17–18).

Delivered/deliver recurs in vv. 2, 4, 19, 27, 43, 48. *Rebuke* in v.15 (*ga' ar*) puts the entire Psalm under the umbrella of God's sovereignty in creation, *delivering* the world from chaos by God's creation (a different view than the peaceful *commands* in Gen 1, or God as artist making *adam* from the *adamah* in Gen 2):

> Then the channels of the sea were seen, and the foundations of the world were laid bare at your *rebuke*, O Lord, at the blast of the breath of your nostrils. He reached down from on high, he took me; he drew me out of mighty waters. He *delivered* me from my strong enemy . . . (18:15–17)[12]

22 Jesus on the cross quotes verse 1, "My God, my God, why have you forsaken me" (Mark 15:34//Matt 27:46). While *evil* or *enemies* does not occur, the psalmist feels *evil* around him (vv. 12–19) and *enemies* accusing him (vv. 6–8). The key term *deliver* occurs twice (vv. 8 and 20) and then as a noun in a different mode: "Posterity will . . . proclaim his *deliverance* to people yet unborn" (vv. 30–31). The contrast between vv. 1 and 3 surprises! Verse 3 declares, "Yet you are holy, enthroned on the praises of Israel." In his despair, faith, hope, and worship extol the Holy One, "enthroned on the praises of

---

11. Here I make an exception to my "Group" criteria: the preponderance of *enemies/enemy* substitutes for *evildoers*.

12. This Psalm is sometimes read (in part) in a "deliverance session." It makes demons tremble, defiantly saying, "he/she belongs to us." Only by command in the name of Jesus will those demons leave, going to Jesus for judgment.

Israel" (cf. Heb 13:15: "the fruit of [human] lips" is "praise to God;" "confessing his name" *enthrones* God).

23 This precious Psalm speaks of both *evil* (v. 4) and *enemies* (v. 5), complementing *deliver* in Psalm 22. But Psalm 23 has a different tone. It is not *lament*. It assures us that our Shepherd-Lord enables us to "fear no *evil*" in dark times and will host us at table "in the presence of my [our] enemies." Reciting this Psalm keeps demons away; it is *deliverance*.

25 This Psalm is framed by *enemies* (v. 2) and *deliver* (v. 20). The context of *deliver me* describes the *enemies*: "Consider how many are my *foes*, and with what *violent hatred* they *hate* me" (v. 19). From this *evil* (*hatred*) the psalmist cries for *deliverance*.[13]

26—27 *Evildoers* occurs in both Psalms (26:5; 27:3) and *evil* in 26:10a. *Enemies* recurs twice (27: 6a, 11), with *adversaries* "who breathe out *violence*" as a parallel in 27:12. Rather than *deliver*, the psalmist's *integrity* (26:1, 11) is armor against *evil* together with memorable 27:1, "The Lord is my light and my salvation; whom shall I fear? The Lord is the stronghold of my life; of whom shall I be afraid?" Both Psalms speak of "the house of the Lord" (26:8; 27:4), a safety net (preventive *deliverance*) from *evil/evildoers*.[14]

34 Though this psalm is oriented to blessing and magnifying the Lord, it also affirms *goodness* in the *fear the Lord* (vv. 7, 9 [2x], 11), and *deliverance* "from all my foes" (v. 4b) and *evil* (13, 14, 21)/*evildoers* (v.16). It includes these key admonitions: "Keep your tongue from *evil*, and your lips from speaking deceit. *Depart* from *evil*, and do good [repeated in 37:22]; seek *peace*, and pursue it" (vv. 13–14). Note the antonym: *evil* versus *peace*. The longer structural parallel equates *deceit* with *evil*. These admonitions are applicable to life in every sphere: vocation, relationships, politics, financial

---

13. Menno Simons (mid-sixteenth century) wrote commentary on Psalm 25, from the standpoint of being hated by *enemies*. He connects *evil* and *evildoers* to Satan and the Devil. Viewed as a heretic by the state church, he writes: "Once I was a friend, now I pass for an enemy. Then I was considered wise, now a fool, then pious, now wicked; then Christian, now a heretic, yes, an abomination and an evildoer to all." Simons, "Meditation," 63–86, quotation on 71.

14 Similar to 18, Psalm 31 has *deliver* from *enemies* twice, but first in a positive-negative: "I will exult and rejoice in your steadfast love, because . . . you have not *delivered* me into the hand of the *enemy*" (vv. 7–8). The second is a direct plea to the Lord, "My times are in your hand; *deliver* me from the hand of my *enemies* and persecutors" (v. 15). Like 26 and 27 the Psalm shifts to extolling the Lord. It concludes with confidence of protection: "Be strong, and let your heart take courage, all you who wait for the Lord" (v. 24).

matters, and cultural values. "*Evil* brings death to the *wicked . . .*" (21a).¹⁵ USA's priorities, its culture and politics, fall short.¹⁶

37 This Psalm is a gem. Numerous verses refer to the *wicked, evil devices,* and *enemies* (vv. 1, 7c, 10, 14, 20–22, 27–28; 32, 34c, 35, 38b, 40). These contrast to the recurring emphasis on "the meek will inherit the earth" (11, 22, 29, 34; cf. 3a, 9,). Hear Jesus' third Beatitude, "Blessed are the meek, for they shall inherit the earth." Another gem is: "Depart from *evil*, and do *good*; so you shall abide forever" (v. 27). The final verse assures the righteous of *deliverance*: The Lord "*rescues* them from the wicked, and *saves* them, because they take refuge in him" (v. 40).

40 The psalmist knows both despair and the Lord's *deliverance* (vv. 1–4) and 9a: "I have told the glad news of *deliverance*." He has known *evils* (v.12) and calls upon the Lord to *deliver* him (v.13). He pleads the Lord to bring those who foment evil against him to shame, confusion, and dishonor (vv. 14–15), and ends with testimony of the Lord as his *deliverer*: "As for me, I am poor and needy, but the Lord takes thought for me. You are my help and my *deliverer*; do not delay, O my God" (v. 17).

50 In vv. 16 and 19 *wicked* occurs. Also in 19: "You give your mouth free rein for *evil*, and your tongue frames *deceit*. *Deliver* occurs in v. 15 and "I *rebuke* you" in v. 21.

51 David confesses his sin of adultery with Bathsheba and murder of her husband Uriah: "Against you, you alone, have I sinned, and done what is *evil* in your sight" (v.4b). Note v. 14: "*Deliver* me from bloodshed, O God, O God of my salvation, and my tongue will sing aloud of your *deliverance*." *Deliverance* is from *evil, sin,* and guilt.¹⁷ ¹⁸

---

15. Psalm 35: This Psalm breathes *deliverance* from those who do *evil* against David (v. 9b); it also mentions "the weak" (10b), for those who seek the Lord face *evil* (4c, 12); "treacherous *enemies rejoice over me* . . . and *conceive deceitful words* (19–20). Verse 26 pleads for vindication against *evildoers*, while in vv. 27–28 a choir affirms the Lord's vindication, praising the Lord's judgment and "tell[ing] of your righteousness and of your praise all day long."

16. For an insightful, critical analysis, listen to Rod Dreher and a panel discussing his book, *The Benedict Option*, at: http://www.plough.com/en/events/2017/benedict-option?source=pwo31617.

17. A Jewish choir under the direction of Abraham Kaplan sings a beautiful rendition of this psalm.

18. Psalm 52: Note the phrase, "you love *evil* more than good" and "deceitful tongue" (vv. 3–4) words directed to *Doeg the Edomite who "ratted" to Saul that David was with* Ahimelech. Judgment is sure (v. 5).

56 Though this Psalm involves national security, it is David's personal cry for deliverance (v. 13) from his *enemies* (vv. 2 and 9) and his *foes* whose "thoughts are against me for *evil*." Vv. 3-4 is a memory-gem: "when I am afraid, I put my trust in you. In God, whose word I praise, in God I trust; I am not afraid; what can flesh do to me?" Verse 8b is precious as we live in a world of mounting socio-economic-political evils and natural catastrophes: "Put my tears in your bottle."

64 "Hear my voice, O God, in my complaint; "preserve my life from the dread *enemy*. Hide me from the secret plots of the *wicked*, from the scheming of *evildoers* (1b-2). After describing the *enemy's* tactics (sword-tongues, bitter words like arrows, and shooting from ambush in vv. 3-4), and persistence, "They hold fast to their *evil* purposes" (5a), they are assured God will do to them what they do: "God will shoot his arrow at them" (v. 7). Finally: "Let the righteous rejoice in the Lord and take refuge in him." (v.10). *God* punishes *evildoers*.

94 *Evildoers* are mentioned twice (vv. 4 and 16), also *wicked rulers* (v.17; cf. *wicked* in v. 3). Verse 22a implies *deliverance* from *wicked rulers*. God will mete out vengeance and "wipe out" such rulers for their *wickedness* (v. 23): national leaders *with whom God cannot ally* (v. 20).[19]

71 *Deliver/rescue* is strong (in vv. 2, 4a,11b, 23b); *enemies* occurs in 10a and *wicked* in 4a. These infer *evil*. Praise/ing (7x) is the dominant genre—a most lovely Psalm.

109 The first verses detail how the *wicked* oppress the Psalmist (*deceitful mouths . . . lying tongues; attack me without cause*). "So they reward me *evil for good* and *hatred* for my love" (v. 5). Verses 6-19 voice the accuser's retort against the righteous one. But, in v. 20 the accused one pleads that all this evil happen to the sarcastic accuser, "But you, O Lord, act on my behalf for your name's sake, because your steadfast love is good, *deliver* me" (v. 21). He lists reasons he merits deliverance from his accusers (vv. 22-27) and

---

Psalm 61—62: These Psalms are mostly testimonial: God is "a strong tower against the *enemy* (61:3) and "On God rests my *deliverance* and honor" (62:7)—an important testimonial. *Enemy* here substitutes for *evil*.

Psalm 66—67: Verse 66:3b references *enemies*. These Psalms are praise genre, with 66 more personal and 67 more corporate. Both, but especially 67, have the *nations* in view.

19. Psalm 97: "The Lord loves those who hate *evil*; he guards the lives of his faithful; he *rescues* them from the hand of the *wicked*" (v. 10). This praise Psalm reminds us that the Lord hates *evil* (cf. 11:5) and will *rescue* the faithful.

requests God's severe judgment upon them (vv. 28b–29). Then he thanks and praises the Lord, assured that the Lord will side with the needy; otherwise his accusers will condemn him to death (vv. 30–31).

140–141 These Psalms resume the Complaint form of *deliverance* from *evildoers* or the *wicked*. **140** begins, "*Deliver* me, O Lord, from *evildoers*; protect me from those who are *violent*, who plan *evil things* in their minds and stir up wars continually" (vv. 1–2). The *wicked* and *violent* are linked to *evil* plotting (vv. 4–8), with v. 7 calling upon the Lord, "my strong *deliverer*." The psalmist pleads God to help and deal harshly with those bent on mischief and harm: "Let burning coals fall on them . . . let *evil* speedily hunt down the violent!" (vv. 10–11; cf. Prov 25:21–22). **141** more moderately requests the Lord to keep him from those people: "Do not turn my heart to any *evil*, to busy myself with *wicked* deeds in company with those who work iniquity; do not let me eat of their delicacies" (v. 4; cf. *wicked* in 5c, 10), but bring judgment-doom on them (7). The Psalm ends, pleading: "Keep me from the trap that they have laid for me, and from the snares of *evildoers*. Let the *wicked* fall into their own nets, while I alone escape."[20]

Group 2: Adversaries are External, the Nations

9 *Nations* appears four times: vv. 5, 15, 17, 20. *World* occurs in v. 8; *peoples*, in vv. 8 and 11, and also in v. 15. The *rebuke* (**ga'ar**; cf. 76:6) against the *nations* in v. 5 approximates *exorcism* against the wickedness of the nations, twice denoted here as *my enemies*, in vv. 3 and 6:

> When *my enemies* turned back, they stumbled and perished before you. . . . You have *rebuked the nations*, you have destroyed the *wicked*; you have blotted out their name forever and ever. The *enemies* have vanished in everlasting ruins; their cities you have rooted out; the very memory of them has perished . . . (vv. 3–6). "The *wicked* shall depart to Sheol, all the *nations* that forget God. For the needy shall not always be forgotten, nor the hope of the poor perish forever. Rise up, O Lord! Do not let mortals prevail; let *the nations* be judged before you. Put them

---

20. Psalms 143, 144: These Psalms complement each other. The first speaks of *enemy/enemies* (vv. 2, 8, 13) with *adversaries* as parallel to *enemies* (v. 13). The second is a cry for *deliverance*. It affirms, You are "my *deliverer*" in v. 2 (cf. to 118 for the other armor imagery). Cries to "free and *rescue*" (vv. 7, 10, 11) end the "complaining"; the Psalm then turns to expectant blessing with material abundance: sons and daughters, filled barns, increase of sheep, fields in tens of thousands, and cattle heavy with young.

in fear, O Lord; let *the nations* know that they are only human. Selah" (vv. 17–20).

This Psalm reminds us of the "Oracles against the Nations" in Isaiah and Jeremiah, in which God *judges* the nations, rebuking their haughtiness and power. They will be destroyed.

68 This song celebrates God's victory over the *enemies*, progressing from cry to God to rise up and *scatter* the *enemies* (v. 1) to assurance that "God will *shatter* the heads of his *enemies*" (v. 21)—*from scatter to shatter*! It is national (vv. 11–17); *enemies* substitute for *evil*.

74 Israel's laments because enemies have desecrated Mount Zion and "your congregation" (v. 2). *Enemy* occurs 3x: vv. 3, 10, 18, and *adversaries* in v. 23. *Dragons* and *Leviathan* appear in vv. 13–14, thus connecting Israel's devastation to pre-creation chaos, which the following verses attest in recounting God's creation acts to assure Israel of *deliverance* from present tragedy. Thus: "Do not *deliver* the soul of your dove to the wild animals; do not forget the life of your poor forever" (74:19). They plead God *not to deliver* Israel to the *enemy*.

Group 3: Psalms in which the
internal or *external* is not clear.

14/53 These are almost identical except for the end of 53:5. Both *evildoers* and *deliverance for Israel* occur. They fit the "nation" category, since v. 7 speaks of restoring Israel's fortunes:

> Have they no knowledge, *all the evildoers* who eat up my people as they eat bread, and do not call upon the Lord? There they shall be in great terror, for God is with the company of the righteous. You would confound the plans of the poor, but the Lord is their refuge. O that *deliverance for Israel* would come from Zion! When the Lord restores the fortunes of his people, Jacob will rejoice; Israel will be glad. (14:4–7)

Waltner, however, locates the *evildoers* within Israel (vv. 4–6); he may be correct. He says a possible identity of the *evildoers* is that they "made use of magical acts, the enemy swallowing a piece of bread on which was written the name of the one to be harassed" (cf. 14:4b).[21] This conforms to

---

21. Waltner, *Psalms*, 85, citing Kraus, 1986: 135.

Mowinckel's view. Paul alludes to these Psalms in Romans 3:10–11 to make the point that there is none righteous.[22]

59 While this Psalm is personal, it has a national component. It begins with two key words (2x): "*Deliver* me from my *enemies*, O my God . . . " (1a); "*Deliver* me from those who *work evil* (2a). Verse 5 contains both *nation* and *evil*: "You, Lord God of hosts, are God of Israel. Awake to punish all the nations; spare none of those who treacherously plot *evil*. Selah." Each night *they* "come back howling like dogs and prowling about the city" (vv. 6, 14). Verses 11–15 fascinate, first the plea not to kill them, "or my people may forget" (v. 11). Wow!

118 National oppression (*enemies*?) appears in the middle verses; cf. v. 6c, "those who hate me" with this strong deliverance accent: from *enemies/evil*:

> All nations surrounded me; in the name of the Lord I cut them off! [11]They surrounded me, surrounded me on every side; in the name of the Lord I cut them off! [12]They surrounded me like bees; they blazed like a fire of thorns; in the name of the Lord I cut them off! [13]I was pushed hard, so that I was falling, but the Lord helped me. [14]The Lord is my strength and my might; he has become my salvation. [15]There are glad songs of victory in the tents of the righteous: "The right hand of the Lord does valiantly; [16] the right hand of the Lord is exalted; the right hand of the Lord does valiantly." [17]I shall not die, but I shall live, and recount the deeds of the Lord. [18]The Lord has punished me severely, but he did not give me over to death. (Ps 118:10–18)

The Psalm's tone shifts in v. 19 to a more corporate, triumphant strand.

---

22. Psalm 21: This Psalm extols the king, assuring that the Lord will search out the *enemies* (v. 8) and any *evil* devised against him and the nation will not succeed. *Deliver* does not occur; *destroy* and related images appear.

Psalm 44 In the first part of the Psalm God's people reminisce on the good times, when God was protector and deliverer: "your own hand drove out the nations" (v. 3a). But now God appears to be sleeping, not responding:

> You have made us the taunt of our neighbors, the derision and scorn of those around us. You have made us a byword among the nations, a laughingstock among the peoples. All day long my disgrace is before me, and shame has covered my face at the words of the taunters and revilers, at the sight of the *enemy* and the avenger. All this has come upon us, yet we have not forgotten you, or been false to your covenant. (13–17).

This Psalm is unique in that it mostly complains about what God has not done for them, with sharp accusations against God (vv. 9–22). Hence the final verses are "Rouse yourself"—do something about our predicament.

Group 4: Psalms in which one of the key term-referents is lacking.

11–13 *Wicked* appears in 11:2, 5, 6; 12:8; *enemy* occurs in 13:2c and 4a; and *foes* in 13:4b. These Psalms contain neither *evil* nor *deliver*, though these three terms could be considered *evil*.[23]

32 "You surround me with glad cries of *deliverance*" (7c) is linked with personal sin and guilt (similar to 51 below) but not to *evil or enemies*. Nonetheless, it is important for a theology of *deliverance*. Demonic oppression may occur from unconfessed sin of the person or ancestor(s). This Psalm is public confession, which has great power to heal![24]

92 This Psalm begins with thanksgiving and praise. But vv. 7 and 9 speak of *evildoers* twice and *enemies* thrice (9, 9, 11); v. 11b refers to *evil assailants*. Rather than *deliverance*, the assurance of God's faithfulness (v. 2) and the righteous flourishing (vv. 12–15) negate need for *deliverance*.

116 *Deliverance* is dominant (v. 8) with the recurring phrase, "I called on the name of the Lord" (vv. 4, 17) for deliverance and healing: "The snares of death encompassed me; the pangs of Sheol laid hold on me; I suffered

---

23. Psalms 15—16: Both Psalms use terminology of *wrongdoing*, but affirm those "who abide in your tent" and don't do the *wicked* deeds named in the Complaint Psalms.

Psalm 28: Similar to 26 and 27, this Psalm speaks of *workers of evil* (v. 3, // with *wicked*) and "the *evil* of their deeds" (v. 4). It pleads, "Hear the voice of my supplication, as I cry to you for help" (v.2); *deliver* does not appear.

24. Psalm 36: The heart of this Psalm affirms God's steadfast love (vv. 5–10). But this is framed by lament of those who "do not reject *evil*" (10) and final judgment of *evildoers*: they will "lie prostrate" (v. 12). The Psalm begins with "Transgression speaks to the *wicked*." *Enemies* and *deliver* do not occur. The Psalm is significant, but a bit marginal.

Psalms 42—43: These Psalms are continuous with a repeated threefold structure. Only in 42:9c is there reference to the oppression of the *enemy*. While the downcast mood appears in all three strophes, yet the conclusion is "Hope in God; for I shall again praise him, my help and my God" (42:5, 11; 43:5). This hope and praise substitutes for the cry for deliverance—and is, in fact, power for deliverance!

Psalm 45: *Enemies* are mentioned in v. 5, but adoration of the king is the main theme of this love song.

Psalm 54: This Psalm has *enemies* twice (vv. 5 and 7b); *evil* occurs in v. 5, but it lacks *deliver*.

Psalm 69: This is an "I" complaint psalm. Though *evil* does not appear, *enemies* recurs thrice (4c, 14b, 18; akin to *evil*), with *delivered* in v. 14 and *set me free* in v. 18. The final portion (vv. 30–36) moves to praise genre.

Psalm 70: Only *deliver* occurs at beginning and end; in 5b, "You are my . . . *deliverer*." Other key terms are lacking.

distress and anguish" (v. 3) The phrase, "You have loosed my bonds," (v. 16) "rings" *deliverance*. *Evil/enemies* do not appear.[25]

125 Two terms, *wickedness* (v. 3a) and *crooked ways* (5a) anticipate the assurance that "the Lord will lead away with *evildoers* (5b)." Hear the final line: "Peace be upon Israel" (5c). *Evil* contrasts to *peace*, a key point in this book in relation to *Covenant of Peace*.

Summary and Conclusion

Evil in these *deliverance* Psalms is essentially:

Diagram 3.2 *Evil* and *Deliverance* Psalms

  a No knowledge of God (Ps 10:4, 13 and 14/53, esp. v. 4 in both)

    b Strife/magic/cursing within the community (14:4–6 [see Waltner, *Psalms*];18:43; 56:6)

      c Taking advantage of/persecuting the weak and needy (35:10b,c; 70:5; 109:22, 31)

        d Murder (5:6; 94:6)

          e Deceit/lies (5:6; 7:14; 10:7; 12:2; 34:13; 35:20b; 109:2)

        d' Scoffing God and the righteous (10:3-4; 94:4-7)

      c' Oppressing the poor, widows, and orphans (10:2, 9; 11:5; 14:5; 94:4–6, cf. 20–21)

    b' Arrogating power and prosperity to oneself (10:5–6; the contexts of texts in c and c')

  a' Worship of other gods (78:57–58; 106:36–39; these, however, lack either *evil* and/or *deliver*)

The means of dealing with these evils are:

1. Affirming God as Protector: shield, refuge, stronghold, bulwark, etc. (5:8; 7:10; 8:2; 9:9; 18:1–3 [exemplar!], 18:35; 31:1–3).
2. Crying/pleading to God/the Lord for deliverance (6:8; 14:7/53:6; 18:16–19; 31:14–18; 40:12–13; 44:23–26; 69:13, 18; 141—142).

---

25. Psalm 121 might also be included with its assuring declaration: "The Lord will keep you from all *evil*; he will keep your life. The Lord will keep your going out and your coming in from this time on and forevermore" (Vv. 7–8).

EVIL AND DELIVERANCE IN PSALMS, PROVERBS, AND PROPHETS

3. Rebuking[26] the enemy/evil/evildoer or evil deeds (9:3, 5; 50:19–21).
4. Declaring God will intervene and shame, confuse, or dishonor the enemies (6:10; 35:26; 40:14–15).
5. Pleading with God to take vengeance on the enemies (7:11–13; 94:23).
6. Affirming God will vindicate the righteous and punish evil (9:15–20; 18:20–24; 35:27–28).
    a. Let the evil self-destruct; it will be the doom of the evildoers (7:15–16; 9:15–17).
    b. Countering evil through praise, thanksgiving, and worship of God (7:17; 8:1, 3–8; 9:11–12: 18: 27–33, 46–50; 22:3, 22–31; 23:4–6; 31:19–24).[27]
    c. Reaffirming one's trust and faith in God who saves me/us from evil/evildoers/enemies (Pss 25—27; 34—36; 41—43; 56; 61—62; 66; 91; 92; 94:16–19, 24; 97; 116; 141; 118).
    d. Assurance that God will intervene and vindicate the righteous (7:9; 9:7–8; 22:8–21; 23:4–6; 37 *passim*; 68:1–20; 92:7–9; 97:3, 10; 109:21–31; 141).
7. Destroy the evildoers: bring them to an imminent end (9:6; 10:15; 21:8–12; 54:5, 7; 64:7–8; 70:2; 94:1–2, 23; 143:12).
    a. Let their punishment be severe/harsh (11:6; 36:12; 59:4b–7; 68:2, 21; 69:22–28; 140:10–11; implicit in 118:10–12).
    b. Let their little ones be dashed against the rock (Ps 137:9—this Ps does not fit "deliverance").

Psalms 44 and 74 do not fit fully the criteria of these categories. They complain to God of enemy devastation. They implicitly view God as Israel's (potential) enemy. In neither case do those who cry out to God/the Lord for deliverance take vengeance into their own hands. God/the Lord is trusted and affirmed to deliver and punish the enemy(ies). In neither Psalm is there forgiveness of these evildoers or a blind eye to evil. Nor is there much hope for reconciliation with the enemy(ies).[28] This is an important difference

---

26. Rebuke (*ga'ar*) is a form of exorcist command, often used in a deliverance ministry encounter. Cf. 18:15, its use against chaos.

27. Crews, in, "Praise," develops this excellently, noting that liturgy of worship is an alternative to theodicy. It may "accuse God" but transcends the evil through exalting and praising God, e.g., Psalm 22:1-3. "Praise exalts the God who *is* the transcendent source of life, who 'grounds our existence' even when evil seeks to undermine it" (45).

28. Some exceptions occur in the OT historical narratives, e.g., Genesis 26:17-33;

between the OT and NT, even though the OT frequently declares God is merciful and forgiving. God also seeks reconciliation with Israel, despite Israel's multitude of sins, especially deceit, lies, and idolatry.

Most significant, in Psalms 34:14 and 125 *evil* and *peace* occur as antonyms. The contrast between the two is often implied (e.g. 35:20 in context; cf. 37:27, 37; 109:5). Where *evil* is, *shalom* is not. When one has enemies, shalom is fractured.

Is this Psalm analysis related to current practice of exorcism or deliverance? Yes, in that the Lord's Prayer petition, "Deliver us from evil," is a recurring cry in the Psalms, Israel's worship manual. Second, worship of other gods denies worship of the God who delivered and formed Israel as a people. The "worst" sin is sacrificing sons and daughters to demons (Ps 106:37 in context). The Psalm cries for deliverance from these wicked practices: "Save us, O Lord our God" (v. 47a). Third, Psalm 91:5–6 references demonic affliction, and assures deliverance from evil (vv. 3, 10).[29] Fourth, these Psalms' strong affirmations of the Lord God's protection from evil (18:1–3 e.g.) aggravate demons, when read in a deliverance session. A Spirit-inspired quotation affirming God's protection puts demons to flight. They cannot stand against God's Holy Word.

Numerous Psalms speak truth to power (note Group 2). Psalm 94:20–23 is similar. Prophet Nathan speaks truth to King David (Ps 51), which wrought change of heart and public confession of sin, God's forgiveness, and freedom to continue in his God-appointed role.

Proverbs

The fear of the Lord is hatred of evil

—Prov 8:13a

Unlike Psalms, *deliver/deliverance* does not occur in Proverbs. Rather, *fear of the Lord* is crucial; wisdom, prudence, and uprightness/righteousness protect from, and contrast to *evil*. While many of the Psalms are King David's, the Proverbs are King Solomon's fount of wisdom. Most themes in Proverbs parallel Egyptian wisdom texts.[30] Seven emphases in Proverbs contribute to

---

2 Kings 6:8–23

29. Notably, the devil tempted Jesus by quoting in part vv. 11 and 12, bending it his way (Matt 4:5–6//Luke 4:9–10). The devil omitted "to guard you in all your ways." Jesus' response, "Do not put the Lord your God to the test" (Deut 6:16) confounded and stunned the devil with implied Christology: do you know *whom* you are tempting?

30. This point appears in most commentaries on Proverbs. In grad school I wrote a

avoidance from, protection against, or means to subvert evil. I list these and cite pertinent verses.

1. Fear of the Lord bears the fruit of wisdom. Hear two powerful texts:

> It [wisdom, prudence] will save you from the way of *evil*, from those who speak perversely, who forsake the paths of uprightness to walk in the ways of darkness, who rejoice in doing *evil* and delight in the perverseness of *evil*. (2:12-14)

> The fear of the Lord is hatred of *evil*. Pride and arrogance and the way of *evil* and perverted speech I hate. (8:13).

This catalogue of *evil* (5x with intensity) affirms *wisdom* as a fence that protects from evil. Wisdom comes from reflection on life—a key characteristic of wisdom. "The fear of the Lord is the beginning of knowledge; fools despise wisdom and instruction" (Prov 1:7). The fear of the Lord is the foundation of wisdom; it enables one to say emphatically, "The fear of the Lord is hatred of *evil*." This hatred is not directed toward a person (or people) but to evil actions.

2. Covetousness and deceit are opposed to wisdom and righteous living. These sins are *evil*:

> Whoever is steadfast in righteousness will live, but whoever pursues *evil* will die . . . Whoever diligently seeks good seeks favor, but *evil* comes to the one who searches for it. Those who trust in their riches will wither, but the righteous will flourish like green leaves. (11:19, 27-28)

> The *wicked* covet the proceeds of *wickedness*, but the root of the righteous bears fruit . . . The *evil* are ensnared by the transgression of their lips, but the righteous escape from trouble . . . Deceit is in the mind of those who plan *evil*, but those who counsel peace have joy. No harm happens to the righteous, but the *wicked* are filled with trouble. (12:13, 20-22)

---

paper on the themes that appear in ten Egyptian *Wisdom* texts (mostly, the *Wisdom of Amenemopet*) and in Proverbs. Comparing Proverbs 22:17—23:11 with *Amenemopet*, only three verses lack parallels (Prov 22:23, 26, 27). There are basic differences also. In Egyptian *Wisdom* a foremost duty is to please the gods. "Immortality" is stressed: thus "make your grave preparations early in life." Egyptian *Wisdom* texts lack a most important emphasis of Proverbs: "The fear of the Lord." *Wisdom* was the Zeitgeist of the time; in Babylonian and other ANE texts as well. Who borrowed from whom? Did King Solomon discuss *wisdom* during the Queen of Sheba's visit?

In these texts *righteousness* contrasts to *evil* and protects from evil. The righteous "will live . . . bear fruit . . . [and] escape from trouble" because those who "counsel peace have joy." In contrast, deceit and lying lips are the bedfellows of *evil* and *wickedness*. In the blending of these texts *evil* or *wickedness* is the antonym of *peace and joy!* A related point regards the *righteous*: "One who justifies the *wicked* and one who condemns the *righteous* are both alike an abomination to the Lord" (17:15). Siding with the *wicked* or the *righteous* is an important life decision; it determines one's moral behavior.

3. Those who oppress the poor are the *wicked* whose behavior contrasts to the *righteous*:

> Those who oppress the poor insult their Maker, but those who are kind to the needy honor him. The *wicked* are overthrown by their *evildoing*, but the righteous find a refuge in their integrity. (14:31–32)

> An *evildoer* listens to *wicked* lips; and a liar gives heed to a mischievous tongue. Those who mock the poor insult their Maker; those who are glad at calamity will not go unpunished . . . *Evil* people seek only rebellion, but a cruel messenger will be sent against them . . . *Evil* will not depart from the house of one who returns *evil* for good. (17:4–5, 11, 13, 15)

Listening to the wicked, oppressing and mocking the poor, and returning evil for good are an abomination to the Lord. God is on the side of the poor. Evil intentions make the poor suffer.

4. Desiring to do *evil* is at the heart of the matter. This point is made directly and indirectly in the following catenae of verses (see above verses also):

> Whoever is steadfast in righteousness will live, but whoever pursues *evil* will die . . . Whoever diligently seeks good seeks favor, but *evil* comes to the one who searches for it. (11:19, 27)

Searching for *evil!* Explicit and revealing! One whose heart is set on doing *evil* searches it out, *seeking* to harm others. Today's analogies are sexual assault, stealing in homes or on streets, setting houses or forests afire, pushing drugs, gang-killings, mass shootings, and fomenting riots for varied reasons. Indeed:

> There are six things that the Lord hates, seven that are an abomination to him: haughty eyes, a lying tongue, and hands that shed innocent blood, a heart that devises *wicked* plans, feet that hurry

to run to *evil*, a lying witness who testifies falsely, and one who sows discord in a family (6:16–19).

This action, "feet that hurry to run to *evil*," blended with the other six, constitutes the semantic and moral field of *evil* "that the Lord hates."[31]

5. *Evil*, as opposition to justice. This point is related to #3 above, mocking the poor and insulting their Maker, God. Evil cannot understand justice: "The *evil* do not understand justice, but those who seek the Lord understand it completely... Those who mislead the upright into *evil* ways will fall into pits of their own making, but the blameless will have a goodly inheritance." (28:5, 10) *Evil* is the converse of justice; misleading the righteous into *evil* has its own built-in consequence.[32]

6. Evil will end in judgment. Many texts imply there will be judgment against evil. Explicit is 24:20, "the *evil* have no future; the lamp of the *wicked* will go out." Preceding verses anticipate judgment, "Whoever plans to do *evil* will be called a mischief-maker" (v. 8); "Do not fret because of *evildoers*. Do not envy the *wicked*" (v. 19). Why, because the Lord will judge against *evil* and *evildoers*. In 24:16b, "the wicked are overthrown by calamity." Later verses weigh against the wicked, "Whoever says to the *wicked*, 'You are innocent,' will be cursed by peoples, abhorred by nations; but those who rebuke the *wicked* will have delight, and a good blessing will come upon them" (vv. 24–25). In short, do not allow evil in any form to rule your minds and hearts (cf. the NT insurance against evil contaminating the mind: "Set your minds on things above..." (Col 3:1–4) and direct your minds to whatever nourishes morally and spiritually (Phil 4:7–9).

7. Withstanding, countering, and overcoming evil. Proverbs 25:21–22 are key verses, "If your *enemies* are hungry, give them bread to eat; and if they are thirsty, give them water to drink; for you will heap coals of fire on their heads, and the Lord will reward you" (cited in Rom 12:19–21). These verses describe the means of overcoming *evil*. For interpretation of "heap coals of fire on their heads," see chapter 6 with my comments on Romans 12:18–21.

---

31. These "things" correlate well with my summary for the Psalms. "Sowing family discord" is not explicit in the deliverance Psalms, but it is likely evident in Psalm 55.

32. Two proverbs speak of the king's role in "winnowing" out evil: "A king who sits on the throne of judgment winnows all *evil* with his eyes..." (20:8) and "A wise king winnows the *wicked*" (20:26).

Summary and Conclusion

These seven points sum up Proverbs' wisdom on *evil*. Indeed, the "fear of the Lord" is the beginning of wisdom (this occurs also in Psalm 111:10; cf. Prov 19:9; 22:23; 25:14; 33:8, 18; et al.). In light of this recurring motif, "fear of the Lord" is the common foundation of both wisdom and praise of God. The Hebrew word for fear (*yr'*) may mean in certain forms and situations being afraid or frightened. Hence a theophany (God appearing to humans) often begins with God saying, "Do not be afraid" (Isa 41:10; Luke 1:30). In the Psalms and wisdom literature it conveys acknowledgment of the numinous mystery of God as God, who overwhelms and makes us feel our smallness (Rudolph Otto's *mysterium tremendum*). God is not one among humans ("I am God and no mortal," Hos 11:9). The otherness of God elicits worship, contrition, and praise of God (Isa 6:1–8 is a classic). The "fear of God/the Lord" is linked to keeping the commandments (in Deut 4:10; 5:29; 6:2, 13, 24; 10:12, 20; 14:23; 17:19; 31:12–13; and in some Psalms, e.g., Ps 119:63, 72–74, 79, 118–20). The fear of the Lord/God is closely related to *knowledge* (*da' at*) of God. "Fear of God" occurs often in parallel to *righteousness/upright* (15:28).[33]

How often today do we even mention the "fear of the Lord"? Arnold Snyder says this was a prime factor in early Anabaptism, enabling followers to endure death, even praising God when executed. Snyder cites lines from an early Swiss Brethren hymn on the Holy Spirit:

> The first gift . . .
> Is called the Fear of God,
> It is the beginning of wisdom
> Which prepares the path of life to us.
>
> It trembles at the Word of God
> And enters through the narrow gate,
> It drives out sin and a godless life,
> Diligently watches and protects the house.[34]

While the Psalms are cries for help, to be delivered from evil, Proverbs exhorts against doing evil from the perspective of wisdom, justice, righteous

---

33. For these emphases see Stähli's article, "*yr'*/Fear," in Jenni and Westermann, *Theological*, 2.573–77.

34. C. A. Snyder, *Following*, 33. Snyder cites from the 1564 *Ausbund*, which had several later editions, and appears in English in *Songs of the Ausbund* 1.100 (Snyder 191n7).

living, and care for the poor (14:16; 16:17; 22:2, 22–23). *Evil* contrasts to the *good* (14:19; 15:3). As in the Psalms, deceit and lying are partners to evil (12:19–20). Riches and wealth are potential pitfalls that ensnare one in evil, though they may also be the blessing of the Lord (8:18–21; 10:22). So the dictum: No fear of the Lord; no wisdom; thus no moral discernment between good and evil; and no *shalom*.

Prophets

This analysis is limited to Isaiah and Jeremiah.[35] The term *deliver/deliverance* rarely correlates with *evil/evildoers* and *enemies*. This brief section identifies key texts and treats others in groups.

Isaiah

Three key texts occur early in Isaiah: 1:16–17; 3:9; and 5:20. They expose Israel's *evils*:

> Wash yourselves; make yourselves clean; remove the *evil* of your *doings* from before my eyes; cease to do *evil*, learn to do good; seek justice, rescue the oppressed, defend the orphan, plead for the widow. (1:16–17)

The core of Israel/Judah's *evil* is: failing to *do good* and to *seek justice*: i.e., *rescuing* the oppressed, defending the orphan, and pleading for the widow. This failure in justice, Isaiah's major critique, pervades the entire book (5:7; 11:3b–5; 32:7; 58:6–8; cf. v. 9c–d; 61:8).

The context of the second text (3:9) speaks memorably of beating swords into plowshares (2:1–5) and then lambasts Israel for its *evils*: the land is: "full of diviners and soothsayers," "filled with silver and gold," "filled with horses, ... [with] no end to their chariots," and "Their land is filled with idols" (2:6b–8). The Lord God judges these evils, with focus on idols:

> The idols shall utterly pass away. Enter the caves of the rocks and the holes of the ground, from the terror of the Lord, and from the glory of his majesty, when he rises to terrify the earth. On that day people will throw away to the moles and to the bats their idols of silver and their idols of gold, which they made for themselves to worship, to enter caverns of the rocks and the clefts in the crags, from the terror of the Lord, and

---

35. For Hosea, see chapters 4—5, 8—10, 13, and *evil/evildoers* in 6:8; 7:15; 9:15.

from the glory of his majesty, when he rises to terrify the earth. (Isa 2:18–21)

The judgment of "the Sovereign, the Lord of hosts" will take away "warrior and soldier, judge and prophet, diviner and elder, captain of fifty and dignitary, counselor and skillful magician and expert enchanter" (3:2–3). In this context, hear 3:9:

> The look on their faces bears witness against them; they proclaim their sin like Sodom, they do not hide it. Woe to them! For they have brought *evil* on themselves. (3:9)

The *evil* in v. 9 denotes numerous practices that repudiate God's sovereignty and violate God's covenant law with Israel/Judah. Israel's persistence in *evildoing* leads to captivity and exile. Judah will not escape God's cleansing the earth of evil: "I will punish the world for its *evil*, and the wicked for their iniquity; I will put an end to the pride of the arrogant, and lay low the insolence of tyrants" (13:11; cf. 2:17; 3:9 in the context of v. 8).[36] The second part of Isaiah (40—55, as well as the third part, 56—66) foresees a new world for Israel with a servant-leader who brings forth justice (42:1 and the four servant songs), and a new covenant of peace (54:10; cf. Ezek 34:25–31; 37:26–28).

The third text exposes Israel/Judah's obstinacy: calling *evil* good, and good *evil*: "Ah, you who call evil good and good evil, who put darkness for light and light for darkness, who put bitter for sweet and sweet for bitter" (5:20). The promised cleansing for their "sins as scarlet" (1:18) will not "wash" in light of this obstinacy, as indicated in 6:9–13 where the prophesied response to the Lord's calling of Isaiah to be a prophet will be stopped ears to his prophetic word and closed eyes to his prophetic deeds. Rather than listen to the prophet, the people will call *evil* good, and good *evil*. What deception? Little wonder, then, the exile, and the rebirth of God's chosen people who through exile learn their core *evil* is idolatry, a mocking of the Shema. While justice is important for God's covenant people, *anti-idolatry* is even more important, indeed primary (so the first two commandments: Exod 20:1–3).[37]

Several later texts are relevant also. One set is Isaiah's oracles against the nations (13—19). God's judgment of evil is not confined to Israel, but to

---

36. Also Babylon, which is "the glory of the kingdoms, and splendor and pride of the Chaldeans, will be like Sodom and Gomorrah when God overthrew them" (13:19), because God will stir up the Medes against them (v. 17).

37. My Jewish scholar-friend, Sandor Goodhart, made this point at a Colloquium on René Girard at the Anabaptist Mennonite Biblical Seminary in 1994.

its enemy nations as well: "I will punish the world for its *evil*, and the wicked for their iniquity" (13:11). That might well be the heading for the next seven chapters, with judgment against Babylon, Moab, Damascus, Ethiopia, Egypt, Tyre-Sidon-Tarshish in chapter 23. The next chapter (24) returns to global judgment of "the earth." *Earth* recurs numerous times, with concentration in vv. 3–6 and again in 17 merging into 18d–21 (seven occurrences!):

> . . . the foundations of the *earth* tremble. The *earth* is utterly broken, the *earth* is torn asunder, the *earth* is violently shaken. The *earth* staggers like a drunkard, it sways like a hut; its transgression lies heavy upon it, and it falls, and will not rise again. On that day the Lord will punish the host of heaven in heaven, and on *earth* the kings of the *earth*.

Another judgment against *evildoers* is in 31:2 when God lampoons the people for allying with Egypt for military protection: relying on their horses and chariots and not looking "to the Holy One of Israel" (31:1). "The Egyptians are human, and not God; their horses are flesh, and not spirit" (31:3). The righteous "shut their eyes from looking on evil" (33:15c; cf. v. 20b).

Jeremiah

Evil occurs more often in Jeremiah than in Isaiah, most likely because Jeremiah is the prophet of inner anguish. He bares his soul, so his "confessions" (18:19–23; 20:7–12, 14–18 ["Cursed be the day . . ."]). Jeremiah laments Israel's *evils*: "for my people have committed *two evils*: they have forsaken me, the fountain of living water, and dug out cisterns for themselves, cracked cisterns that can hold no water" (2:13); "you have done all the *evil* that you could" (3:5d). They forgot the Lord who redeemed them and pursued their stubborn *evil* ways. Four dominant emphases occur. The first two are similar to Isaiah's critique of Israel's failure to do justice. God judges against injustice (*evil* occurs only in the second set, but the actions of the first verses fit what Isaiah calls *evil*), with sarcastic bite:

> ⁴Do not trust in these deceptive words: "This is the temple of the Lord, the temple of the Lord, the temple of the Lord." ⁵For if you truly amend your ways and your doings, if you truly *act justly* one with another, ⁶if you do not oppress the alien, the orphan, and the widow, or shed innocent blood in this place, and if you do not go after other gods to your own hurt, ⁷then I will dwell with you in this place, in the land that I gave of old to your ancestors forever and ever. ⁸Here you are, trusting in deceptive

> words to no avail. ⁹Will you steal, murder, commit adultery, swear falsely, make offerings to Baal, and go after other gods that you have not known, ¹⁰and then come and stand before me in this house, which is called by my name, and say, "We are safe!"—only to go on doing all these abominations? ¹¹Has this house, which is called by my name, become a den of robbers in your sight? (7:4–11; cf. 22:3)

> But this command I gave them, "Obey my voice, and I will be your God, and you shall be my people; and walk only in the way that I command you, so that it may be well with you." ²⁴Yet they did not obey or incline their ear, but, in the stubbornness of their *evil will*, they walked in their own counsels, and looked backward rather than forward. (7:23–24)

The second *evil* is stubbornness, despite God's covenant love: "Yet they did not obey or incline their ear, but everyone walked in the stubbornness of an *evil will*. So I brought upon them all the words of this covenant, which I commanded them to do, but they did not" (11:8; cf. 13:10). Or, more sharply, "They are skilled in doing *evil*, but do not know how to do good" (4:22c); "they proceed from *evil* to *evil*" (9:3c). Thus the caustic rhetorical question: "Can Ethiopians change their skin or leopards their spots? Then also you can do good who are accustomed to do *evil*" (13:23)! This emphasis permeates chapter 23 that begins with, "Woe to the shepherds of Israel . . ." *Evil doing* or *evildoers* appears in vv. 2e, 14c, 22cd (cf. v. 10d). Israel is not only stubborn in wanting to do evil, but is persistent in it also: "For the people of Israel and the people of Judah have done nothing but *evil* in my sight from their youth; the people of Israel have done nothing but provoke me to anger by the work of their hands, says the Lord" (32:30).

A third type of *evil* occurs some verses later: "The Lord of hosts, who planted you, has pronounced *evil* against you, because of the *evil* that the house of Israel and the house of Judah have done, provoking me to anger by making offerings to Baal" (11:17). The *evil* God will bring is certain captivity, a recurring warning throughout the book (4:6; 6:1): "For I have set my face against this city for *evil* and not for good, says the Lord: it shall be given into the hands of the king of Babylon, and he shall burn it with fire" (21:10; cf. 39:16).

If the people would repent God would change his mind and not bring disaster upon them:

> It may be that they will listen . . ., and will turn from their *evil* way, that I may change my mind about the disaster that I intend to bring on them because of their *evil* doings (26:3; cf. 36:3).

> At one moment I may declare concerning a nation or a kingdom, that I will pluck up and break down and destroy it, ⁸but if that nation, concerning which I have spoken, turns from its *evil*, I will change my mind about the disaster that I intended to bring on it. ⁹And at another moment I may declare concerning a nation or a kingdom that I will build and plant it, ¹⁰but if it does *evil* in my sight, not listening to my voice, then I will change my mind about the good that I had intended to do to it. ¹¹Now, therefore, say to the people of Judah and the inhabitants of Jerusalem: Thus says the Lord: "Look, I am a potter *shaping evil against you* and devising a plan against you. Turn now, all of you from your *evil* way, and amend your ways and your doings." ¹²But they say, "It is no use! We will follow our own plans, and each of us will act according to the *stubbornness of our evil will*." (18:7–12)

> And when you tell this people all these words, and they say to you, "Why has the Lord pronounced all this great *evil* against us? What is our iniquity? What is the sin that we have committed against the Lord our God?" ¹¹then you shall say to them: It is because your ancestors have forsaken me, says the Lord, and have gone after other gods and have served and worshiped them, and have forsaken me and have not kept my law; ¹²and because you have behaved worse than your ancestors, for here you are, every one of you, following your *stubborn evil will*, refusing to listen to me. ¹³Therefore I will hurl you out of this land into a land that neither you nor your ancestors have known, and there you shall serve other gods day and night, for I will show you no favor. (16:10–13)

Jeremiah laments Israel's *evil* as agony of his heart. He takes it personally: "Is *evil* a recompense for good? Yet they have dug a pit for my life" (18:20).

A fourth use of *evil* with *deliverance* echoes the Psalms (*wicked* occurs in the first citation). Here is God's promise to Jeremiah, who needs assurance that God will uphold him and the needy; the exile of the nation appears certain:

> And I will make you to this people a fortified wall of bronze; they will fight against you, but they shall not prevail over you, for I am with you to *save* you and *deliver* you, says the Lord. I will *deliver* you out of the hand of the *wicked*, and redeem you from the grasp of the ruthless. (15:20–21; cf. 1:8) Sing to the

Lord; praise the Lord! For he has *delivered* the life of the needy from the hands of *evildoers*. (20:13)

The last chapters of Jeremiah (37—52) narrate the historical outworking of God's punishments upon Israel, as Jeremiah prophesied. Judah goes into Babylonian exile, and Nebuchadrezzar appoints Zedekiah king over those left in Israel, the poor to work the land for Babylon's benefit. Even those who went down to Egypt to escape destruction by Babylon, taking Jeremiah along, fall under God's judgment: captivity, pestilence, and sword (43:17), meted out by Babylonian King Nebuchadrezzar as agent. God's wrath was poured out not upon Israel alone (see 48:2 regarding Moab). Zedekiah's fortuitous reign is summed up predictably: "He did what was *evil* in the sight of the Lord, just as Jehoiakim had done" (52:2).

Summary and Conclusion

Both Isaiah and Jeremiah regard Israel (here Judah) as stubborn in heart to do *evil*, refusing to do good and seek justice. The people do not care for the poor, the widow, and the orphan. They amass wealth and military power; they seek out diviners and enchanters. And worst, they make for themselves idols of silver and gold, and worship them. Their worship of idols witnesses to *evil* corrupting their hearts and minds (cf. Ps 96:5 [LXX 95:5]; Deut 32:17). Exile is their doom.

Worship of idols/demons is a serious affront to the Lord God who called Israel into covenant relationship, commanding in the Shema worship of the Lord God alone, and expecting faithful obedience in caring for the needy. It is thus no surprise that the Messiah will call Israel anew to worship the Lord God alone, inaugurate God's kingdom, care for the needy, welcome outsiders, and bring help and hope to "the least" in society. But Healer of the sick and Deliverer from demonic oppression surpass common hopes, even though the Psalms cry out for healing and deliverance. The Psalms are Israel's song book. Singing protects and delivers!

> The Lord lives,
> and blessed be his name.
> Exalted be the God of my salvation (3x).
> (cf. Pss. 18:46; 72:18–19; Isa 12:2-6)

Part II

Biblical Perspectives on Deliverance

Multi-dimensions of Deliverance from Evil

4

Old Testament to Synoptic Gospels
Mark

Evil confronts every person with the stark, horrific truth
—it is both within us and "out there."
Scripture renders a complex profile of evil
and of a God who judges, saves,
and forges a pathway toward reconciliation.[1]

O come, thou Rod of Jesse, free
thine own from Satan's tyranny.
From depths of hell thy people save,
and give them vict'ry o'er the grave.
Rejoice, rejoice, Immanuel
shall come to thee, O Israel.

—Verse 2, "O Come, O Come, Immanuel"
Anonymous, 6–7th century

Introduction

THE FOCUS OF THIS chapter is on the broader reality of evil in both Testaments and deliverance from evil through Jesus Christ, with focus on the earliest canonical Gospel, Mark. Examining the biblical data raises

---

1. Cover Introduction to *Interpretation* issue 57:1 (2003) on *"Evil,"* likely by editor Brashler.

broader theological questions: its significance for us in our "modern" world, its implications for exorcism[2] and whole person health and healing.

The First Century Worldview

Greco-Roman Perspectives

In the centuries before and after Jesus' ministry, belief in the spirit world was assumed. In the ninth to fourth centuries BCE the word *daimon* could refer to either a good or evil spirit. Plato conceived it primarily as good. Later, however, the word was associated more with evil spirits. Philosophers often associated pagan religious rites with demons. Demons were linked to the souls of the dead who would avenge wrongs done against the deceased person. Common belief held that demons in the intermediary regions between heaven and earth assisted or thwarted communication between humans and gods. But they believed also in personal guardian spirits as deputies of the gods. They could possess human beings, cause madness, or afflict the body. Many magical formulas and rites developed for their exorcism.[3]

Jewish Perspectives

Jewish literature, like the Greek, does not have a consistent doctrine of demons. It does speculate about their origins.[4] YHWH governs the universe through numerous spiritual beings; some govern natural forces.[5] Long ago, YHWH placed such spirits in authority over all nations—except for Israel, whom he rules directly.[6] These beings were to teach humans the arts, crafts, and just government. Some spirits, however, conspired to rule humankind rather than serve them. One-third of the angel spirits rebelled and lost their

---

2. The word *deliverance* is preferred by those engaging in this ministry. However, *exorcism* (cast out) is used in the Bible as well as in anthropological studies more generally.

3. Betz describes magical formula that the Greeks used to ward off demon powers. In his phenomenological study of demonic beliefs, Smith, "Interpreting," compares beliefs in the Greco-Roman world with those in the Orient and more primitive animistic religions. In all, the intermediary world between heaven and earth is important: people do not relate directly to God but indirectly through intermediary spirits and powers. This concurs with Ferguson, *Demonology*, 58–59.

4. For what follows, see Finger, *Christian Theology*, vol. II, ch. 7, and Ferguson, *Demonology*, 94–95.

5. Jub 2:2; 1 Enoch 60:11–24; 82:7–20.

6. Jub 15:31–32.

standing in the heavenly court. They were headed by several "satans," or by a "Satanal" who had previously sought equality with YHWH.[7]

Under their rule, justice was perverted and crafts intended for peaceful purposes, such as metallurgy, were used for war.[8] These beings were also called "sons of God," who produced giants through unions with human daughters (Gen 6:1-4). Drawing humans into their wars, the giants began killing each other off; when they were slain, evil spirits emerged from their bodies. These demons incited people to warfare and worship of idols.[9] Since the nations—including Israel—willingly followed these spirits, YHWH allowed them to afflict humankind. These satan-spirits had access to "the Lord of Spirits"; they tempted humans to do evil and then denounced them before the heavenly court.[10] Although in pagan nations magic was often employed to ward off the power of these beings, Israel disapproved it. Proper antidotes were meditating on God's word, obeying God's commandments, and praying. Quite strikingly, Enoch asserts against the rebellious Watchers and their followers, "there is no peace for you" (1 En 12:5; 16:4); the same is pronounced against Azaz'el in 13:1. It occurs also in Qumran texts.[11] Here is strong evidence for this book's thesis: *evil in its very origin is pitted against peace, its antonym!*

Early Jewish thought gave only marginal space to *spirits;* even the evil spirit that tormented Saul *was sent from/by the Lord* (1 Sam 16:14; cf. 1 Kgs 22:23; Judg 9:23). During Israel's wilderness period, the Destroyer Angel (Exod 12:24; 1 Cor 10:10 explaining Num 25), executed judgment within God's providence. In Israel's early history *the Lord's* anger incited David to take a military census (2 Sam 24:1). In a later post-exilic account, with the influence of Persian dualism, *Satan* incited David to take the census (1 Chron 21:1).

Satan appeared first in biblical literature as *ha sa-tán*, one of the ministering spirits, or "sons of God," within the heavenly court (see chapter 1). His role was that of prosecuting attorney or manager of God's wrath

---

7. 1 Enoch 6 and 69 speaks of the "satans" who persuaded some 200 "Watchers" to descend to earth for this purpose. "Satanail" appears in 2 Enoch 29:4-5; 31:30-36: cf. Life of Adam and Eve, 12-17.

8. Jub 4:15; 1 Enoch 8 and 69.

9. 1 Enoch 15, Jub 11:2-7; cf. Gen 6:2-4. Semyaza is the leader of the fallen angels, with Azazel his partner, according to 1 (Eth.) Enoch 6:1—7:9. The giants in 15:8-15 are called "evil spirits," which afflict, oppress, attack, and destroy (Twelftree, *Christ*, 26). For extensive treatment of these texts that connect the giants to evil spirits and war-making see N. Forsyth, Old Enemy, 44-191.

10. 2 Enoch 40:7.

11. Stuckenbruck, "Demonic," 67n23. An error occurs in line 2: one "have" should be "no" or "never."

department. He tested humans to prove goodness, or to execute punishment (1 Chron 21:1; Job 1–2; Zech 3).[12] Walter Wink contends that Satan was first of all a servant of God and only through human sinful choices became and becomes the "Evil One" opposing God's purposes.[13]

A closer study of the biblical record, however, shows other conceptions of evil as well. In his exhaustive study Edward Langton discusses seven forms of demon appearance in the earlier OT literature. These are (1) the "fiery serpents" which God sent to bite the people (Num 21:6)[14] and fiery flying serpents (Deut 8:15, Isa 14:29; 30:6);[15] (2) demons in the shape of hairy he-goats (*Se'irim*; as in Lev 17:7 [RSV, *satyrs*]; 2 Chron 11:15; 2 Kgs 23:8; Isa 13:21; 34:14);[16] (3) other demonic animals, including wild beasts (*Ziyyim*, Isa 34:14), doleful creatures (*'Ochim*, Isa 34:14); ostriches (*Benoth ya'anah*); wolves (*'Iyyim*), and jackals (*Tannim* also in 34:14);[17] (4) Azazel, the goat driven out into the wilderness to take evil back to its headquarters as part of the atonement ritual (Lev 16:8);[18] (5) *Lilith* (in Isa 34:14c), a female demon, translated quite differently by English versions: screech owl (AV); night monster (RV); night hag (RSV); Lil'ith (NRSV); (6) the darkness-pestilence (*Opel*) and the noonday-destruction (*Shud*) demons of Psalm 91:6; both *Opel* and *Shud* are translated *daimonia* in the Septuagint (the KJV translates these as *evil thing* and *evil spirit*),[19] and (7) the *Shedim*,

---

12. For an insightful and quite comprehensive treatment of these texts see Page, *Powers*, 23–36. A much earlier, even more quite thorough study of the OT is Schärf Kluger's *Satan*.

13. Wink, *Unmasking*, 30–33.

14. It is striking that the Hebrew consonants for the word *serpent* in Genesis 3 may also mean "to divine." This would indicate that the serpent is here already playing the role of counterfeit; hence Eve's deception may have involved the difficult issue of discerning whether the voice was really the voice of God or the voice of a counterfeit.

15. Langton thinks that the seraphim (Isa 6:2–7) were originally also connected to the same notion although in Isaiah they are angelic spirits. He bolsters this association citing 1 Enoch 20:7, where both the seraphim and cherubim are under the rule of Gabriel in paradise (30:8).

16. The Greek Septuagint (LXX) regularly translates this word with *daimonia*.

17. The LXX translates almost all these with *daimonia*. Cf. these with other possible, but improbable "demon-animal" references, cited by Page, *Powers*, 85.

18. Langton believes that Azazel may have first been a Semitic god of the flocks and was later "degraded to the level of demon under the influence of Yahwism" (46). Twelftree, in *Christ*, confirms this in citing Ethiopic Enoch 6:7; 9:16; 10:46 where Azazel is regarded as a demon (23). See, however, Page, *Powers*, 83–85, who doubts this meaning of Azazel and suggests other meanings of the word, which are just as doubtful.

19. With this Langton, *Essentials*, mentions also the *'Alukah* demon of Proverbs 30:15, translated *leech* (RSV and NRSV), but which, Langton argues, might be better translated *vampire*. This is a bloodsucking demon, parallel to Babylonian texts that

translated as demons (Deut 32:17; Ps 106:37 in the RSV and NRSV), the recipients of the sacrifices of pagan neighbors.[20]

While this study of demonic-type animals is significant—and the Septuagint regards these as demons—the OT gives slim evidence of a worldview where demons played significant roles. Hence the question: does the conceptualization of demons as entities independent from God represent a psychological projection of the people's fears arising from the uncertainties and turbulence of the intertestamental times?[21] Certainly, the political crises of the intertestamental period with the influence of Zoroastrian Persian dualism contributed to the NT view of good and evil spirits, in which Satan heads the evil spirits. We now examine these OT views of evil within a broader OT theological perspective.

Old Testament Theological Perspectives

In this section we examine OT thought regarding:
- the heavenly court,
- the relation between pagan kings, gods, and Satan or the devil,
- the relationship between idols and demons,
- the OT view of sin and its relation to the demonic,
- the relationship between Israel's political infidelity and cultic adultery, and
- Israel's holy warfare practices.

---

speak of "demons that spill the blood of men, devour their flesh, and suck their veins" (50).

20. This may be, in part, the rationale for Israel's sacrifices to the Lord God in the OT. Origen comments on pagan and Israelite sacrifice in regard to Balaam's fortune-telling powers: "Balaam was accustomed by these sacrifices to invoke daemons. Indeed, in this way sacrifices are offered in the daemon world. Thus, God instituted from the first the offering of sacrifices for the people, so that, they in offering to God, would cease offering to daemons," cited by Berchman, "Arcana Mundi," 126, drawing on Migne, *Selecta in Num.*

21. Böcher cites numerous passive means of resistance to demons, such as ascetic living styles in clothing, hygiene, fasting, sexual continence, sleeping regulations, covering of eyes, or silence: *Neue*, 42–50.

The Heavenly Court

In Psalm 82:1–2 God (*Elohim*) is surrounded by heavenly hosts. God takes his place in the divine council, where God holds judgment among the gods, accusing the pagan gods—and the kings they controlled—of oppressive rule. In Psalm 89:5–18, YHWH is again surrounded by heavenly beings, an image of warfare denoted by the phrase *YHWH Sebaoth* (v. 8), which means "Lord of hosts" or "Lord of the Heavenly Armies." Battle imagery also occurs in the phrase, "Thou didst crush Rahab," which stands in parallel to "thou didst scatter thy enemies with thy mighty arm" (v. 10). The ancient sea-chaos monster is referred to as Rahab (Ps 87:4; Isa 51:9) and Leviathan (Job 41:1; Ps 74:14; 106:26; Isa 27:1). YHWH's triumph over this monster highlights God's power to create order out of chaos (Gen 1 and Ps 33:6). These allusions to ancient primeval chaos affirm God's creative power over the forces of chaos. God is creator and sustainer of the universe. Psalm 89 attributes to God: righteousness and justice, steadfast love and faithfulness (v. 14). These attributes maintain order and harmonious relationships among humans.

This prevailing OT theological conviction of the Lord God's transcendence over creation as Creator and moral governor of the universe contrasts to both Mesopotamian and Egyptian mythologies on creation, in which the tired gods created humans to do their work, fight among themselves, and live luxuriously off the people's tribute. In turn, the people's security depends on rightly discerning the capricious will of the gods, who oppressed their subjects.

The Relation between Pagan Kings/their Gods and Satan or the Devil or Demons

As noted in chapter 1, two important texts are Isaiah 14 and Ezekiel 28, oracles of doom against the kings of Babylon and Tyre respectively. [22] The imagery in these texts links the "fall of Lucifer" (Isa 14:12, KJV; "Day-Star, son of Dawn," in the RSV and NRSV)[23] and the prince "in Eden, the garden of God" (Ezek 28:13) to the kings of these two nations. These images appear in later Jewish and Christian history to describe Satan and the devil. In the early Christian fathers these texts also refer to pagan kings, but indicate they

---

22. 1 Enoch 63; 67 connects the fallen angels and evil spirits from the giants to earthly "kings, rulers, and landlords."

23. For wider ANE understandings of Lucifer's relation to a god named Dawn (*Shachar*), see Burkholder, *Leviathan*, 62–63, 66.

are even truer descriptions of the devil.[24] See chapter 9 for citations from Church Fathers Origen, Justin, Tertullian, et al. These texts connect the gods of the pagan nation's kings with the devil, Satan, and/or the demons. Three OT texts put *idols* and *demons* in parallel, regarding them interchangeable:

- They sacrificed to *demons* and not to God, to *gods* . . . they knew (Deut 32:17; LXX, *daimoniois*).
- "For all the *gods* of the people are idols" (Ps 96:5; LXX 95:5, *daimonia*).
- "They sacrificed their sons and daughters to the demons" (Ps 106:37; LXX 105:37, *tois daimoniois*).[25]

Apocryphal Baruch is also instructive on this point:

> . . . you provoked him who made you, by sacrificing to demons and not to God (4:7, RSV) . . . For fire will come upon her from the Everlasting for many days, and for a long time she will be inhabited by demons (4:35, RSV).

Striking here is the connection between paganism and demonic realities. Not only are the kings the prototype of Satan and the devil, but the idol worship of the nations over which these kings rule is ascribed to demon-inspiration. Isaiah (44:9–22, 46–47) and the Psalmist (115:3–8; 135:15–18) boldly declare, however, that the idols cannot speak and give direction for life. Isaiah 44:9–20 is a "put-down satire" [read it aloud!] on the (un)reality of these gods whose functional power, however, was all too real in Israel's idolatries.[26]

---

24. Ferguson, *Demonology*, 108.

25. A most interesting text occurs in Isaiah 65:3 where the LXX adds a phrase not in the Hebrew text (nor the NRSV, RSV, or KJV). The English translation would be: "*burning* incense *upon* the bricks to the demons that are not (do not exist)." This reflects later (ca. 250 BCE) thinking regarding demons functionally and ontologically. The statement both recognizes the reality of demons dominating people's lives and religion and yet denies their ultimate reality.

26. Wisdom of Solomon 12—15 is an extended spoof on the gods of nations. One part of this satire relates to some modern insight on how people get hooked into demonic forces:
For a father, consumed with grief at an untimely bereavement,
made an image of his child, who had been suddenly taken from him;
and he now honored as a god what was once a dead human being
and handed on to his descendants secret rites and initiations.
Then the ungodly custom, grown strong with time, was kept as a law,
and at the command of monarchs graven images were worshiped.
(Wis 14:15–16)

Sin and Its Relation to the Demonic

The OT has three words for sin: *ḥāṭāh,* meaning "to miss the mark"; *asham,* which entails a sense of guilt (thus *asham* and *ashmah* are Hebrew words for guilt offering); and *pesha,* which regards sin as rebellion. These words merely outline some of sin's formal features. To apprehend sin's reality, we must ask: in what circumstances did sin manifest itself? What kind of norms did it transgress, a willful act, a rebellion? In Israel's history, sin manifested itself primarily in turning away from YHWH's covenant, thus idolatry.[27]

This view of Israel's foremost sin is confirmed by the prophetic judgment in Israel's primary history (Deut through 2 Kgs), which repeatedly measures Israel's faithfulness or faithlessness to YHWH by whether or not the kings destroyed or promoted idolatrous pagan practices. Note these contrasting descriptions of Israel's most wicked king, Manasseh, and Israel's ideal righteous king, Josiah:

> Manasseh, evil: And he built altars for all the host of heaven in the two courts of the house of the Lord. And he burned his son as an offering, and practiced soothsaying and augury, and dealt with mediums and with wizards. He did much evil in the sight of the Lord, provoking him to anger. And the graven image of Asherah that he had made he set in the house . . . But they did not listen, and Manasseh seduced them to do more evil than the nations had done whom the Lord destroyed before the people of Israel. (2 Kgs 21:5–7a, 9, RSV)

> Josiah, good: Moreover Josiah put away the mediums and the wizards and the teraphim and the idols and all the abominations that were seen in the land of Judah and in Jerusalem, that he might establish the words of the law, which were written in the book that Hilkiah the priest found in the house of the Lord. Before him there was no king like him, who turned to the Lord with all his heart . . . (2 Kgs 23:24–25, RSV)

In later OT literature Israel was judged faithless because it engaged in sorcery practices by pagan peoples (Isa 47:10–15; 57:3–10, etc.). Paganism, sorcery, and idolatry were part of one package under the power of the demons and Satan. Israel's turning to idols was a paradigm shift affecting all of life:[28]

---

27. To punish Israel for such sin, YHWH often handed Israel over to the enemy. When Israel would repent and cry for help, YHWH would raise up a deliverer (Judg 2:11–18). Or God would punish through a plague (Num 16:41–50; 25:1–13), or famine (2 Sam 21:1–8), or exile (Jer 18:1–17).

28. Gerbrandt's dissertation on kingship substantiates this point: Israel's kings were evaluated according to their record of allowing or destroying pagan worship within Israel: *Kingship,* 264–73.

By turning to other national gods, therefore, Israel turned away not only from the religious commands of YHWH's covenant but from its social ones as well. Idolatry meant not only preference for another religious cult but for the whole way of ethical and cultural behavior which accompanied foreign cults. It meant asking the gods of Egypt, Canaan, and Assyria, etc., for economic prosperity and military protection in exchange for adopting the moral and social way of life, which they represented.[29]

Israel's Political Infidelity and Cultic Adultery

Faithfulness to YHWH affected all of life, both religious and political. Israel's worship of idols (a cultic issue) and Israel's dependence on the politics of power (a political military issue) were inherently interconnected. Religion and politics were never separated in Israel's faith. Of the many texts demonstrating this point, I focus primarily on a well-known text, Isaiah 2:1–22.

Isaiah 2:1–22

This chapter, central to understanding Isaiah's overall theological emphasis, sharply contrasts YHWH's politics of trust and shalom to Israel's idolatries, amassing of wealth and achieving political power. The alternative components look like this:

Diagram 4.1 YHWH's Politics

A Go to YHWH's mountain to learn *the way* of YHWH (v. 2–3b)

  B To walk in YHWH's paths (v. 3c)

    C YHWH's *law* goes out from Zion (v. 3d)

  B' YHWH's Judgment (v. 4a–b)

A' Swords beat into plowshares and people learn war no more (v. 4c–d)

Israel's Politics

A Israel went after diviners and soothsaysers (v. 6)

  B Sought riches and war power (v. 7)

    C Israel's land is filled with idols (v. 8)

---

29. Finger, *Christian Theology*, vol. 1, 328.

  B' False abasement (v. 9) [2:10–19: haughty pride
   which YHWH will punish]

 A' Israel's idols will be cast to the moles and bats (v. 20)

In this concentric structure, the center strophe (C) discloses the heart and accent of the composition. The Torah law, given by the prophet, is God's revelation to Israel (Deut 18:15–22); the idols with various forms of sorcery are the symbolic power center of the pagan world (Deut 18:9–14). The idolatrous ways of the nations produced pride, power, and military terror. Their haughtiness and blasphemous claims, however, reap disaster (Isa 47:8–10).

 YHWH's politics of "learning the way of the Lord and walking in YHWH's paths" lead to economic conversion: war technology is converted into food-production technology. Trust in YHWH's way (2:1–4) contrasts to anxious scheming via diviners and soothsayers. Sorcery is set against YHWH's power (2:6–20). The alternatives are two opposing ways of organizing personal and corporate life. Against YHWH's will, Israel sought a king like that of the nations. This led to the amassing of military power and wealth. Predictably, their history is replete with YHWH's judgment upon their idolatries. God's covenant lawsuit case against Israel cites Israel's unending desire to seek diviners, to worship Baal and the Asherah (with male and female sexually carved tree groves and all the sexual paraphernalia, including cultic prostitution, part of pagan worship). For these sins—messing with the ways of the nations—Israel and Judah went into exile.[30]

 The rationale for Israel's Holy War (chapters 2a and 2b) is the destruction of pagan idolatry that seeks guidance and power from the gods other than the God of Israel. The list of abominations includes sorcerers, wizards, necromancers, augurs, soothsayers—in short anyone who practices divination, i.e., seeking power through evil or the pagan religions (Isa 2:6;

---

 30. A study of Ezekiel 6—7, as well as chapter 16, would document the same points made above in the Isaiah 2 study. In his study of "the knowledge of God," a formula occurring eighty-one times in Ezekiel, Lind points out that "the knowledge of God" is interconnected with Israel's public political policies. The issue is whether they will pursue quiet trust in YHWH's sovereign Lordship or whether they will amass military power and go the way of political pride (*hybris*). Israel's cultic adultery and political infidelity are deeply interconnected. Israel did not trust YHWH but amassed military armaments. Hosea 14:3 sums up this crucial point:

> Assyria shall not save us!
> We will not ride upon horses:
> And we will say no more, "Our God,"
> to the work of our hands.

Lind, *Ezekiel*, 199. Lind adds the next line also, "For in you the fatherless find compassion" (NIV), which implies loss of fathers in war.

Deut 18:10–11; Hos 4:12). Over against this is God's command to listen to the prophet, one who shall be raised up like unto Moses (18:15–18). The prophets call Israel to seek only YHWH for deliverance from enemies. YHWH even uses an ass to safeguard this trust from the divine side: "no divination against Israel" (Num 23:23)!

Summary

Many OT narratives call Israel to trust and obey God's commands and resist pagan practices inspired by rebellious spirits linked with the gods of the nations. The demonic in the OT is interrelated to Israel's failure to worship God faithfully. Religious and political dimensions are intertwined: sin and the demonic (the gods of the nations) are part of the societal fabric. The demonic can overtake an entire people's values, including socio-economic-political structures that become idolatrous.

New Testament Perspectives

God's warfare against evil has elements of both continuity and discontinuity between the Testaments. It is difficult to adequately assess the Gospels' portrait of Jesus' combat both against demons and societal practices that foster oppression. Jesus' call for a revolutionary new order continues elements of OT Holy War, thus a holy warfare interconnection between the testaments.[31] William Brownlee rightly sees both discontinuity and continuity. Unlike the Maccabean warriors (167–130 BCE) whose blood pleaded "for vengeance like the blood of Abel," the warrior Jesus' "blood pleads only for forgiveness and redemption." Brownlee sees continuity, however, in that YHWH's warfare is carried forward by Jesus as the human warrior-martyr who is also the divine warrior defeating demonic forces:

> His exorcisms are the inauguration of a holy war which reaches its climax in His death and resurrection wherein He decisively defeated the Devil and his hordes. In this capacity He is acting as the divine warrior.[32]

Christ has won the war against evil in his "love of enemy" teaching and by bearing the cross, the mysterious power of weakness in which God's

---

31. Bender's Master's thesis, "Holy War," shows this interconnection. Contributions by Eller, *War*, and McCurley, *Ancient* are helpful. Lind, *Yahweh*, and Ollenburger, *Zion*, develop major OT perspectives on YHWH war.

32. Brownlee, "From Holy War," 286. See Stevens, "Divine Warrior."

strength is made perfect.³³ Revelation extols the slain Lamb who conquers evil. The Lamb's followers conquer evil powers through their patient endurance. Brownlee summarizes well this continuity and discontinuity:

> . . . in the area of biblical theology, we often see modifications and enrichments as we move from the earliest to the latest Scriptures; but in the present case we have the most dramatic development and transformation of all, as we move from the institution of Holy War, with its *herem* of total destruction of the enemy, to the divine-human Warrior, Who gives His life for the salvation of the whole world, including His own enemies. Yet, between the *herem* and the Cross there is not simply contrast, a radical break with the substitution of one for the other, but a theological continuity whereby in the history of Holy War the one led to the other.³⁴

Jesus and the Gospels³⁵

Jesus began his ministry within the context of Israel's distinctive OT holy warfare emphases as well as the widespread beliefs about demonic powers in the intertestamental period. We have also seen how God's battle against evil expressed itself in many dimensions: creating order out of primordial chaos, electing Israel as the covenant people to establish an alternate society to pagan idolatry, fighting for Israel against the pagan nations, and calling Israel to a quiet trust in YHWH's defense (chapters 2a and 2b). Moreover, hope emerged in Israel that in the eschatological messianic battle God will overthrow all forces of evil headed up by Beliar or Mastema (alternate names for Satan, the captain of the demons).

In this context Jesus begins his ministry, announcing: the kingdom of God has come near. This proclaims God's sovereignty over creation and conquest over evil powers now dawning into human history.³⁶ Jesus' exorcisms,

---

33. Dawn's second chapter (35–69) in *Powers*, is a rich source on this topic; also Kim, *Messiah*.

34 Brownlee, "From Holy War," 291. The same development of thought is reflected when the Septuagint translates the OT "man of war" in Exodus 15:3 by the phrase "The Lord destroys war" (*kurios suntriben polemous*): W. Klassen, "God of Peace," 127.

35. This abbreviated portion, with more thorough treatment in chapters 5—8 functions as an overview of Jesus' and the NT teaching on the demonic powers, thus introducing the successive chapters.

36. W. Klassen also treats the relationship of Jesus to the OT warfare imagery. Citing texts from intertestamental writings and some contemporary to Jesus, he concludes, "Jesus embraced the Messianic war idea but followed those of his Jewish colleagues who

prominent in all three Synoptic Gospels, have been recognized by various scholars as the depiction of "a cosmic struggle in history to inaugurate the eschatological reign of God."[37] McCurley shows a trajectory of emphasis from God's triumph over the primeval-creation chaos, to God's victory over chaos through YHWH, the Warrior and King in Israel's history, to Jesus as "The Son of God Versus Chaos."[38] To illustrate continuity and transformation, McCurley parallels YHWH's rebuke of Satan in Zechariah 3 to Jesus' rebuke of the sea in Mark 4:35–41 (this rebuke harks back to God's own rebuke of primeval chaos). In rebuking and exorcising the demons Jesus carries forward God's victory over evil.[39]

The Earliest Gospel: Mark

*"The time is fulfilled,
and the kingdom of God has come near;
repent, and believe in the good news."*

—Mark 1:15

In Mark's Gospel Jesus' proclamations of the kingdom of God in word and deed are death-blows to *evil*. In light of its brevity (16 chapters), Mark prioritizes Jesus' exorcisms and conflict with evil: about one-third is devoted to exorcisms.[40] Various scholars have viewed this emphasis in Mark as reflective of YHWH's warfare against chaos and evil in the OT.[41]

Immediately after Jesus' baptism with a voice from heaven that declares Jesus to be God's Son-Servant, Jesus is driven by the Spirit into the wilderness (the *jinn* locale of demonic powers) in order to be tempted by Satan. Mark alone has the phrase "drove him out" (*auton ekballei*). The word for temptation (*peirazō*) may imply Satan's eschatological attack upon the One who

---

saw it as a struggle in which suffering love even to the point of dying for one's enemies could bring liberation." "Jesus," 155–75, quote on 175.

37. Robinson, *Problem*, 38.
38. McCurley, *Ancient*, 12–71.
39. Ibid., 46–52.
40. The extensive Scriptures on this theme in Mark's Gospel are: directly, 1:13, 23–27, 39; 3:11–12, 14–15, 22–30; 5:1–20; 6:7, 13; 7:24–30; 8:31–33; 9:14–29, and indirectly, Jesus' clash with the religious leaders (chapter 12) and Jesus' trial and crucifixion (chapters 14—15).
41. Robinson and McCurley persuasively stress this connection to OT texts with this *rebuke* emphasis (Pss 18:15c; 74:12–17; 104:7; cf. Ps 65:6; 76:6; Isa 50:6e; 51:9–10). See Swartley, *Israel's*, 56–58.

comes to do eschatological warfare against the evil powers. Jesus' encounter with and resistance to Satan's temptations thus begins in the wilderness and continues until Gethsemane. His entire ministry is a clash between the powers of God and the powers of Satan. Garrett develops this point in detail showing that after Mark 1:13, where the Spirit "drives out" (literally, "casts out") Jesus into the wilderness to be tempted by Satan, the entire Gospel has motifs of *testing* and *temptation* pervading the narrative.[42]

Jesus appears in Galilee proclaiming the "gospel of God." This is the first time Jesus speaks in Mark: "The time is fulfilled, and the kingdom of God has come near; repent, and believe in the good news" (1:15). The coming of the kingdom of God sets the tone of the gospel as a whole. Every event and saying in the Gospel is ultimately related to this narrative purpose. Jesus as Teacher "with authority," Healer, and Exorcist are essential components of Jesus' kingdom of God ministry. "Bringing the kingdom" *is* the epigraph for Jesus' ministry, the components of which are teaching, healing, and exorcizing demons. Jesus' kingdom ministry means new mind, body, and spirit. None of these is marginal, but all are essential—and it is these that trigger opposition from the religious leaders that ultimately leads to his death. The entire package is the basis of our salvation and holy wholeness. Western culture and religion (except for the Pentecostal churches) marginalize exorcism since it is problematic for the rational, modern mind. But in so doing we distance ourselves from Jesus and his kingdom ministry.

Jesus' first action after his keynote address is to gather disciples (soldiers?) for the kingdom (1:16-20). Then comes the first event in a synagogue, with his disciples apparently present—wow, what happens means a steep learning curve for them. This first Gospel story blends his authoritative teaching with an exorcism in the synagogue (Mark 1:21–28). Not long into his teaching in the synagogue, an unclean spirit cries out, "'What have you to do with us, Jesus of Nazareth? Have you come to destroy us? I know who you are, the Holy One of God.'" Jesus rebukes the demonic spirit, "'Be silent, and come out of him!'"

Then "the unclean spirit, convulsing and crying with a loud voice, came out of him."[43] The Greek word *rebuke* (v. 25) is a form of *epitimaō*.

---

42. Garrett, *Temptations*, 59 to end. See, e.g., Mark 8:11–13; 10:2; 12:13–17. Here the *temptations* are initiated by Jesus' opponents (his enemies), but his disciples in their failure to understand also test Jesus. The Passion week is filled with tests and temptations of numerous types, from both his disciples and the religious leaders. Garrett shows how each section of Mark's Gospel carries forward this aspect of Jesus' ministry.

43. This exorcism, like Jesus' others, contrasts to exorcisms reported in other contemporary literature that elaborately embellish stories of exorcisms. Jesus' *word* alone is the weapon of victory. For understanding Jesus as Exorcist, see Twelftree, *Jesus*; Witmer, *Jesus*. Twelftree establishes the historicity of Jesus as Exorcist; Witmer sets this feature

The Septuagint usually uses *epitimaō* to translate the Hebrew *ga'ar*. In the Psalms *ga'ar/epitiman* (Hebrew/ LXX) "is used with parallels such as 'destroy' or 'vanquish' in appeals to God as Warrior coming in judgement against foreign nations or imperial regimes that conquer and despoil Israel" (Pss 9:5–6; 18:15c; 28:31; 76:6; 80:16; 104:7). "Zechariah 3:2 is especially striking with regard to the spiritual-political dualism at Qumran and Jesus' exorcisms: 'YHWH subject *ga'ar/epitiman* You, O Satan.' In the Qumran Scrolls *ga'ar* occurs in the struggle between God and Belial."[44]

Mark's Gospel declares a counter-political message. A new vision of divine sovereignty and power emerges in the Gospel. Brownlee suggests the unclean spirit's addressing Jesus as "the Holy One of God" fits with the warfare theophanies in which the Lord goes forth to battle with the "holy ones."[45] Later, Jesus' ministry is defined as plundering Satan's ranks. Horsley and many other NT scholars treat these texts as veiled critique of the Empire, bolstered by Jesus' exorcism of the Gadarene demoniac (Mark 5:1–20) where the demons name themselves *Legion*, the name of a cohort (ca. 5000 to 6000 soldiers) of the Roman army occupying Palestine.[46] Hence Jesus' casting out Satan and plundering the property of the "strong man" are symbolic references to the kingdom of God clashing with and overcoming the kingdom of Satan, a.k.a., the Empire.[47] In my judgment this is a tendentious interpretation.[48] While this may be viewed as an appealing

---

within its contemporary culture and describes its significance.

44. Horsley, "'Finger,'" 65. Horsley refers to the "War Scroll" (1QM 14:9–11 and 4Q491). The Psalms texts between the two quotations are both corrections from Horsley's and additional citations as well. For an extensive discussion on the "Scrolls" treatment of evil, see Leonhardt-Balzer, "Evil at Qumran," in *Evil*, 17–33.

45. The relevant texts are Zechariah 14:3, 5; Deuteronomy 33:2–3; Psalm 89:5–10. See Brownlee, "From Holy War," 286.

46. Horsley, "'Finger,'" 65–66. Horsley draws on an older article by Kee, "Terminology." See also Swartley, *Israel's*, 57–58. In his commentary on Mark (*Binding*, 190–94), Myers was one of the first to popularize the view that this demon named Legion was a code name for the Roman Legion that occupied the Gadarene territory in which this exorcism occurred. Myers' book is laudable in many ways, but I critique this interpretation in my review. As far as I can tell from my experience in deliverance ministry the plight of the demonized has little to do with political oppression, though the person may feel marginalized because of their "secret" demons. In some cases mental health issues are involved (see chapter 11). Trauma is often a causative factor of personal oppression.

47. An article by Horsley and Myers, "Idols, Demons," also illustrates this view, 648–49.

48. Beck, *Reviving* (see Introduction), in his later chapters concurs with Horsley's interpretation, despite the book's earlier indications that we must get beneath the political to the spiritual empowerment behind evil actions in systematic structures. N. T. Wright, in *Jesus*, has an excellent section on this topic in his chapter, "The Questions."

harmonization between Jesus' exorcisms and Paul's proclamation of Jesus' power and authority over the principalities and powers, it fails to point out that Jesus' exorcisms and the victory over Satan are necessary precursors to Paul's theology. One stream of thought does not weaken the other; the two are complementary, as this book's thesis contends. Both are important ministries for the faithful church.[49]

Boyd presents a helpful alternative to a yes/no interpretation of Legion-demon referring to Roman occupation. Boyd describes both realities as analogous to the other. As a Roman Legion oppressed the people under their occupation, so the Legion of demons oppressed this Gadarene demoniac. The demonic oppression does not collapse into political oppression.[50] Rather, they are two manifestations of evil, two sides of a coin or dual faces of evil.

Kallas regards the Synoptic Gospels' exorcisms a major theme of Jesus' ministry.[51]

> The arrival of the Kingdom is simultaneous with, dependent upon, and manifested in the routing of the demons. The Kingdom arrives in a limited localized area as the demon's rule is broken. The Kingdom will arrive on a world-wide basis when the world-wide rule of Satan is broken. The Kingdom's arrival is to be seen ... in the cleansing of the world which has fallen captive to and obeys the will of the God-opposed forces of the evil one.[52]

His heading for part (ii) of his discussion is "The Real Enemy Identified: not Rome, but Satan" (451). He later relocates the battle in part (iii), "The Battle Relocated: Israel and Satan" (459–60). His entire discussion is related to the "kingdom" come and coming. He speaks of the "satanic twisting of Israel's role" (461). Certainly we should not disconnect Satan and demons from politics, but just as surely we cannot collapse demons into the Roman Empire. Satan's work is multifarious, corrupting the politics of any nation, with Hitler's Germany and Stalin's Russia at its worst, with shocking traces in the USA 2017 Charlottesville, Virginia, violence incited by a coalition of white supremacists, neo-Nazis, the Alt-Right, and the KKK. Responding with violence, however, only plays into their ploy.

49. One might critically respond by asking how this can be true, since Paul seems to know little about Jesus' earthly life. Here we must revalue the role of oral tradition, Paul's strong theology of Jesus' victory over the powers assumes Jesus' battles with the devil, culminating in Jesus' crucifixion and resurrection, the heart of Paul's theology.

50. Boyd, *Crucifixion*, vol. 1, 566–70.

51. Kallas, *Significance*. He contends Jesus' triumph over demons is as important as eschatology. Most scholars have emphasized the latter, but have given little attention to the former.

52. Ibid., 78.

Binding the Strong Man

Jesus' authority over the demons in his early ministry led to a clash with crowds, family, and scribes (in Matthew, also Pharisees) from Jerusalem who scorned Jesus' authority:

> Then he went home and the crowd came together again, so that they could not even eat. When his family heard it, they went out to restrain him, for people were saying, "He has gone out of his mind." And the scribes who came down from Jerusalem said, "He has Beelzebul, and by the ruler of the demons he casts out demons." And he called them to him, and spoke to them in parables, "How can Satan cast out Satan? If a kingdom is divided against itself, that kingdom cannot stand. And if a house is divided against itself, that house will not be able to stand. And if Satan has risen up against himself and is divided, he cannot stand, but his end has come. But no one can enter a strong man's house and plunder his property without first tying up the strong man; then indeed the house can be plundered. (Mark 3:19b–27)

Jesus' power and authority to cast out demons clashes with the authority of the scribes (representing Israel's religious leaders) and mystifies his family whose restraint was likely an effort to protect him. The scribes ascribe Jesus' power to Beelzebul, head of demon powers.[53] Only in Mark does Jesus respond in the form of a riddle, a *parabolic question* (v. 23), "How can Satan cast out Satan?" Jesus' extended explanation hinges on the impossibility of evil casting out evil. In such a case, a house (or ministry) divided against itself cannot stand.[54] Jesus' defense of his ministry to the religious leaders

---

53. For the several plausible origins and meanings of *Beelzebul*, see Twelftree, *Jesus the Exorcist*, 104–6. Sorensen presents a helpful description of the exorcisms in the Gospels and Acts, noting which ones, with duplicates, have origin in Mark or the Q source (in Matthew and Luke). He rightly stresses that we learn nothing about the cause of demonization or the character of the one delivered, before or after. The demonized person is often, but not always, a passive figure. Rather, the exorcisms testify to the exorcist, Jesus—who he is or the source of power; the Gospel narrative in some cases also reports on the reactions of the crowds or religious leaders (*Possession*, 122–27).

54. Does the "divided house" of the strong man refer, as Boers suggests, "to the chief priests, scribes and elders disputing among themselves who should be their allies, the demons and impure spirits, and therefore contribute to the downfall of their kingdom? Is what Jesus does in Mark's gospel enter the divided house of the metaphoric strong man [Satan] to bind him and plunder his house?" In "Reflections," 262. This assumes the demons are in collusion with the religious-political leaders. This view does not collapse demons into the political powers, but Satan colludes with the "powers of this world" (cf. Matt 4:8–9; John 12:31b; 14:30, 16:11; 1 John 5:19; 2 Cor 2:8; Eph 2:2). See chapter 12 for Girard's explanation of how Satan does cast out Satan.

and his family rests upon his authority and power to cast out demons (Mark 3:20–28). Jesus appointed the twelve to be with him and commissioned them to proclaim the gospel. He gave them "authority to cast out demons" (Mark 3:14–15) and later when he sent them out, he reiterated granting them authority to cast out demons (Mark 6:7, 13).

Jesus' exorcisms in Mark—the demonized man in the synagogue (1:21–28), the Gadarene demoniac (5:1–20), and the healing of the epileptic boy (9:14–29)—play significant roles in the Gospel's narrative. Jesus' exorcism of the Gadarene demoniac extends the power of the kingdom to the Gentiles—the first in Mark. The exorcism in 9:14–29 contrasts Jesus' kingdom power (manifest in the Transfiguration) with the disciples' lack of faith and prayer.

These numerous exorcisms, together with other miracles such as healing the paralytic in Mark 2:1–12 where Jesus forgives sins (note v. 10), raises a continual run of queries (1:27; 4:41; 6:49-52; 8:27-30), "Who is this man?" Hence, the "messianic secret" in Mark, since Jesus' mighty deeds are followed by commands to "tell no one." *Heaven knows (1:10–11), hell knows (3:11–12), but humans do not know.* Even with Peter's confession in 8:27–30 that Jesus is the Messiah, the "rebuke" exchange between Jesus and Peter in 8:31–33 (Jesus rebukes Peter, "Get behind me, Satan") indicates Peter, and the other disciples, do not comprehend who Jesus is.

Jesus' entry to Jerusalem, especially the temple confrontation, may be seen as God's holy warrior, Jesus, coming to reclaim the nation from its evil and assert God's sovereignty—anticipating a new world, *The Upside-Down Kingdom*, as Donald Kraybill calls it.[55] Riding on a donkey, Jesus fulfills the peacemaking vision of Zechariah 9:9-10, demonstrating that his victory is not by military means but by the long-standing model of quiet trust in God's sovereignty and power. The religious leaders and the political leaders became part of the satanic effort to detour Jesus from the course of his kingdom ministry.[56]

Jesus' ministry, in its entirety, counters demonic power: demon possession of individual persons; temptations from Satan, even of his disciples; the hostility and blindness of religious leaders; and the political powers that crucified Jesus. While the demonic had sabotaged God's shalom upon earth,[57] Jesus confronted and overcame the forces and ravages

---

55. D. Kraybill, *Upside-Down*. Kraybill focuses on Jesus' teachings that turn the world upside-down.

56. Finger, *Christian*, vol. 1, 291–98.

57. Luke's Gospel emphasizes this point by announcing that Jesus' coming is "Peace on earth; good will for humanity" (2:14). Jesus' public ministry consummates with an antiphonal response from Jesus' disciples, "peace in heaven, and glory in the highest"

of Satan's work in the world. Two features of the earlier Exodus deliverance from evil tradition appear: First, God fights on behalf of the people: Jesus as God's Son has authority to carry on this warfare; he also delegates that authority to his disciples, both to cast out demons (Mark 3:15) and to "take up the cross" (8:34–37). Second, as in the OT, the prophetic word is the primary instrument of warfare. The word is God's power that restores peace to the demonized and calmness to the sea, heals the sick, raises the dead, proclaims the kingdom, and announces its coming through Jesus' death and resurrection. Each of Jesus' exorcisms in Mark plays significant narrative and geographical roles:

1. Jesus' first ministry event: in the Capernaum synagogue, his base for ministry (1:21–27).

2. The Beelzebul controversy, in his home town Nazareth: "*who* is this man?" (3:20–27), asked by family and religious leaders.

3. Jesus' exorcism of the Gadarene demoniac (5:1–20), location uncertain but likely on border between Jewish and Gentile world.

4. Jesus casts out an evil spirit in a Syrophoenician woman's little daughter (7:24–30), clearly outside Israel, in the Gentile world.[58] The gospel's gift of deliverance, healing, and salvation is for all!

5. Jesus heals an epileptic boy, casting out a demon (9:14–29), at the foot of a high mountain, location uncertain, possibly Hermon. Significant here is the contrast between the heavenly glory scene of the Transfiguration (9:2–8) and the earthly realm, in which his disciples are confronted with a most difficult task, which only Jesus can do. Jesus says this difficult case requires prayer (in some later manuscripts, also fasting).

Two distinctive features appear in Mark's account of Jesus' healing of the epileptic boy, when compared to Matthew and Luke. First, Mark has an extended exchange between Jesus and the father of the epileptic boy, in which Jesus reprimands the man for saying, "If you can . . . ," which in turns leads to the father's memorable, "I believe, help my unbelief" (v. 24). Second, only in Mark do readers *hear Jesus speak* the rebuke to the demon; Matthew and Luke say, "He rebuked," putting this into the third person. In Mark, Jesus

---

(19:38). Luke uses the word peace (*eirēnē*) 14x, emphasizing God's shalom includes "healing all those who were oppressed" (Acts 10:36, 38).

58. Jesus' feeding the four thousand on the Gentile side of the Sea of Galilee in 8:1–21, climaxing in a boat ride with a final exam for his disciples regarding the two feedings (Mark 8:14–21), also points toward Gentile inclusion.

commands, "'You spirit that keeps this boy from speaking and hearing, I command you, come out of him, and never enter him again!'" (9:25). Mark *portrays* the drama and authority of Jesus' power to cast out the demon.

Jesus' rebuking Peter, "Get behind me Satan!" (Mark 8:33//Matt 16:23) is also exorcism. Peter had already rebuked Jesus for his words regarding his future suffering and rejection, apparently thinking such a notion for the Messiah was off the chart. This is not Peter at his best. It is, however, Satan speaking through Peter, since he opened himself up to Satan in his point of view. Jesus *rebukes* Satan directly. In light of what Jesus says to and about Peter (Matt 16:18–20), this point is essential for us to grasp when following Jesus' command to cast out demons. No matter how devilish the words that come from a person, his/her true self is much different, with great potential for becoming God's servant.

Tempting by the religious leaders is also part of the satanic trap (Mark 8:11; 10:2 [*peirazontes* in both]; 12:15 [Jesus asks, "why do you tempt/*peirazete* me"]): Jesus wins these temptations by clear perception and declaration of God's will. Already in Mark 3:6 the religious leaders seek to kill Jesus. In Mark 12:13–17 they try to trap Jesus with the tax(ing) question, potentially explosive enough to get him crucified (cf. Luke 23:2).

Jesus' entry into Jerusalem fulfills the peacemaking vision of Zechariah 9:9–10. Riding on a donkey, he symbolizes his servant kingship: victory is not by military power but by trust in God's sovereignty and power (Exod 14:14; Isa 30:15). Upon entering the city, he goes to the temple, assesses its situation, and returns in the morning to confront the desecrating economic temple practices, the buying and selling of animals in the Gentile court. As God's holy warrior, Jesus reclaims the temple for God, cleansing it *"for all nations."*[59] The cleansing occurred in the *Gentile* court! His cleansing exorcised its evil practices to make it holy for Jews *and* Gentiles to worship the sovereign God. Hence, the demonic oppresses not only individuals (Mark's exorcisms), but also instigates evil actions in religious and political structures. In Mark 12 these leaders represent Satan's effort to trap Jesus by questions that could stir the crowds against him. But Jesus' answers stun, so that the narrative exposes the evil intent of the questioners.

When Jesus on the cross cries out "My God, my God, why have you forsaken me?" (Mark 15:34//Matt 27:46), it appears that evil has won. But in response to Jesus' dying breath on the cross, the Gentile soldier exclaims, "Truly this man was the Son of God." This confession together with God's dramatic raising of Jesus on the third day testifies that the powers, who thought they had defeated Jesus, were themselves defeated by the Spirit

---

59. Thus my book title, *Mark: The Way for All Nations*.

power of Jesus' ministry, a ministry of prophetic word and love of enemy, even unto death. Jesus' crucifixion confronts, confounds, and conquers the powers of evil. The resurrection proclaims God's sovereign victory through Jesus Christ over all evil.

Story

One type of demonic oppression in the USA occurs when people make secret coven vows that entail some form of witchcraft or Satanic rituals with blood pacts. Such vows, especially for the latter, require exorcism to break the vows and covenants, and thus free the person from bondage. Ponder this case: A woman came to a pastor in the USA northeast who had no experience with deliverance ministry. The woman was not a churchgoer, but as a social worker she attended a funeral at the pastor's church to support her client in grief. She was so impressed with the faith of the church community that she later approached the pastor to ask if he would be willing to help get her out from these binding vows that resulted in voices in her head telling her what to do, headaches, and fear.

The pastor wanted to help, and phoned me for counsel. After several calls for discussion and instruction, and much prayer, he was open to do what he could for the woman. He gathered a small group from the church to meet with the woman and to do what they could by God's power and grace in Jesus' name. The battle was heavy in the second and third sessions, with the demons threatening to kill the woman in session two. Finally in session three, the demons under command in the name of Jesus left. The Lord Jesus triumphed, and the woman, highly pregnant, was freed. To the coven members who threatened curses on anyone who would not come to the annual ritual, she wrote a letter of confidence and joy, expressing her desire that they too come to realize God's great power and love. What a testimony![60] This woman, a wonderful person, was regarded highly in her town. No one would ever have guessed she was part of such a coven. To what extent it was Satanic I don't know. Members were required to meet certain times a year in some mountain area to reaffirm their vows and practice some form of ritual sacrifices. She would not describe these, only to say we would be horrified to know.

About twenty years later this pastor stopped at my house to visit. He asked, "You remember _____ (her first name)?" I said, "Yes, how is she doing?" He said she is doing well and her daughter (the baby in her womb during the exorcism) is engaged to the pastor of another church. I met the

---

60. A copy of the letter, which I treasure, is in my files. "Wonderful Grace of Jesus" is the song that comes to my mind as I write this.

woman last week and she gave me a big hug and said, '___, if you hadn't helped me, I don't know where I'd be in life.'"

In this situation I do not believe the woman could have found freedom except through exorcism that enabled her to renounce the demonic power and practices those vows entailed. Such situations call for the exorcist/deliverance approach, to gain healing and wholeness.

5

Matthew and Luke–Acts

*Praise the One who blessed the children
with a strong yet gentle word;
praise the One who drove out demons
with a piercing two-edged sword.
Praise the One who brings cool water
to the desert's burning sand;
from the well comes living water
quenching thirst in ev-'ry land.*

—"Praise the One Who Breaks the Darkness"
Verse 2 in *Sing the Story*, #1, Rusty Edwards[1]

*He comes the prisoners to release,
in Satan's bondage held.
The gates of brass before him burst,
the iron fetters yield.
He comes the broken heart to bind,
the bleeding soul to cure,
And with the treasures of his grace
to enrich the humble poor.*

—"Hark! The glad sound!" The Savior comes!
Verse 2 in *HWB*, # 184
Philip Doddridge, 1735
Translation and Paraphrases

---

1. Copyright ©1987 Hope Publishing Company, Carol Stream, IL 60188. Used with permission.

MARK'S GOSPEL PORTRAYS JESUS as miracle worker and exorcist.[2] Luke is a close second. As generally thought, Matthew lags behind. Matthew has five long discourses. While true, we must not underestimate Matthew's contribution to this topic.

Immediately after Jesus' baptism certifying him as God's divine son now filled with the Holy Spirit, all three Synoptic Gospels tell us Jesus was led by the Spirit into the wilderness to be tempted by the devil (Matt 4:1; Mark 1:14; Luke 4:1)—"From the Dove to the Devil."[3] Slight variation occurs between Matthew and Luke in naming the evil one. In Matthew "the tempter came . . ."; in Luke "he was tempted by the devil." In each temptation "the devil" is initiator. Only in Matthew, however, does Jesus say at the end of the third temptation, "Away with you, Satan" (4:10). Conflict between Jesus and Satan is accentuated later as well (Matt 9:32; 12:22). Jesus' entire ministry was a clash between the powers of God and the powers of Satan. Jesus' resistance to Satan's temptations began in the wilderness and continued until Gethsemane. Each temptation faced Jesus with an alternative route to Messiahship! These are:

> Turn stones into bread (Matt 4:3–4; Luke 4:3–4)—Jesus feeds the multitudes
>
> > He could be a welfare Messiah
>
> Jumping off the pinnacle of the temple (Matt 4:5–7; Luke 4:3–4)—Palm Sunday entry

---

2. Geddert, in his commentary, *Mark*, contends the use of the term *exorcism* is problematic, since *exorkizō* does not occur in any of the narratives of Jesus casting out demons. Further, he rightly says that this Greek term, from which *exorcism* is derived, means *to put under oath* (238). He demurs also on the term "demon possessed" for demons don't own a person. He also cautions against the use of the terms *deliverance ministry* and *spiritual warfare* since they easily become code words for someone's theory about them (239). He does not rule out, however, the *"need for a deliverance ministry"* (239). He recommends C. Arnold's books on this topic because Arnold is a NT scholar and has trusty insight on this topic (239). Geddert was apparently unaware of Twelftree's 1985 and 1993 books and those of other NT scholars. Twelftree's 2007 book (after Geddert's commentary) is more cautionary than his 1985 book. My response to Geddert's hesitancy to use the term *exorcism* is: yes, it means to adjure by oath and that speaks much for two realities: first, Jesus doesn't need to adjure by oath to another's greater power. That fact witnesses to his divine authority as Son of God. Jesus' exorcisms are deeply christological—thus the confounding questions at the end of his first exorcism in Mark 1:27. Second, believers today have no power to drive out demons except *by command* in the name of Jesus. That "command" is a form of adjuring, but in keeping with Jesus' and James's teaching against oaths, it is not *swearing* by Jesus' or God's name.

3. Mackay's title for Chapter 1, *His Life*.

> He could be a Pope with ecclesiastical authority over temple and people

Bow down to Satan, and worship him (Matt 4:8–10; Luke 4:5–8)—dodge the cross

> He could call twelve legions of angels, dodge the cross, and be political President[4]

Later in Matthew, the religious and political leaders are the mouthpieces of the Tempter. The jeering taunt, "If you are the Son of God, come down from the cross" (Matt 27:40), repeats the wilderness temptations, "If you are the Son of God, . . ."

In Matthew's first summary of Jesus' ministry, healing "demoniacs" is mentioned, among other types of healing. The distinction in Matthew 4:23–25 between driving out demons and healing is important. Note also the geographical extent of his ministry:

> Jesus went throughout Galilee, teaching in their synagogues and proclaiming the good news of the kingdom and curing every disease and every sickness among the people. So his fame spread throughout all Syria, and they brought to him all the sick, those who were afflicted with various diseases and pains, demoniacs, epileptics, and paralytics, and he cured them. And great crowds followed him from Galilee, the Decapolis, Jerusalem, Judea, and from beyond the Jordan.

The Gospel writers distinguished between physical/neural illness and demon affliction that hinders one from being one's true self. See chapter 11 for more on this.

The next crucial witness to Jesus *vis à vis* the demonic is in the Lord's Prayer, which as Ulrich Luz has shown is the chiastic center of the Sermon on the Mount.[5] Here in outline form are the matching chiastic parts (with modified captions):

---

4. For more, see Swartley, *Send Forth*, 77–81. Each of Jesus' temptations (*peirasmoi*) in Matthew and Luke prove Jesus' faithfulness to his baptismal designation as God's Son, Servant, Beloved One. Jesus is tested precisely on whether he will continue to be God's peacemaker (*eirēnopoios*) refusing vengeance against enemies or seeking security through violence (*Send Forth*, 80).

5. Rather than duplicate here Luz's full pictorial diagram of Matthew 5—7 that visually shows the Lord's Prayer at the center, see my book, *Covenant*, 91.

Diagram 5.1 Chiasm. The Lord's Prayer at Center of the Sermon on the Mount

a 5:1–2 Setting/situation

  b 5:3–16 Beatitudes (fitness for kingdom of heaven)

    c 5:17–20 Greater righteousness

      d 5:21–48 Main section: antitheses

        e 6:1–6 Righteousness before God

        The Lord's Prayer (6:7–15)

        e' 6:16–18 Righteousness before God

      d' 6:19–7:11 Main section: possessions, judging, prayer

    c' 7:12 Golden rule

  b' 7:13–27 Call to discernment/faithfulness

a' 7:28–8:1a Reaction of hearers

It is no "stretch" to regard the entire Sermon as God's/Jesus' way to counter and overcome evil. Not resisting evil with evil and loving the enemy are foundational to the Gospel's teaching on resistance to, protection from, and overcoming evil.[6] In the Lord's Prayer three petitions are directly related to evil. First, "forgive us our sin as we forgive the sins of others." One who does not, will not forgive, opens the door to evil's home in their psyches and actions. Second, the petition, "do not lead us into temptation (*peirasmon*)" requests God to guard and guide our thoughts, relationships, and actions so that we do not set ourselves up for situations that entice us to sin or do evil.

Temptation and *test* are different. "Temptation is allurement to what is sinful. It has a negative connotation. A test or trial has positive connotation."[7] The prayer is not to avoid illness or disasters that *test* us, in the sense of refining our faith. Rather we pray that we will not succumb to "the shipwreck of the soul."[8] This is more comprehensive than the render-

---

6. The literature on this is vast: see the twelve essays by diverse authors and extensive bibliography I have prepared on this in *Love of Enemy*. See my treatment in *Covenant*, 58–65.

7. Ayo, *Lord's Prayer*, 92. Ayo's comments excel on this and the next petition. He cites numerous Church Fathers and current scholars. In some instances, e.g., Jesus' facing the cross is a test with a twist toward temptation, to yield to Satan's bypass of suffering and death. Jesus' cry from the cross, "My God, my God, why have you forsaken me?" reflects the *test* of Jesus' obedience unto death, even death on a cross.

8. Ibid., 90.

ing, "Save us in the hour of temptation," derived analogically from Jesus' and his disciples' temptation to yield to the snare of the devil during the Gethsemane experience.

The next petition, "*Deliver us from evil*," or better in my judgment, "evil one," as the Eastern Orthodox Church translates the Greek *tou ponērou*. *Evil one* is parallel to *temptation* in the preceding line, for it is the *evil one* who tempts (cf. James 1:12–15). Further, Matthew has the same term in 13:38, *the evil one* snatches the seed on the path (cf. Mark's *Satan* in 4:15 and Luke's *devil* in 8:15). The case for the translation, "the evil one" is further advanced by Ayo: "From a logical point of view, the translation of deliver us from the *evil one* does seem to distinguish this line from its predecessor more clearly. Temptation suggests an impersonal evil; the evil *one* points to our personal adversary the devil."[9]

The devil, however, is also the Tempter, so both lines may contain the personal dimension; "save us in the time of trial" may seem more impersonal, but not necessarily so. The bottom line in both petitions is praying to be protected from the devil's tactics to "sink us" spiritually. This petition is at the heart of this book, and everything herein is related to these five important Greek words (*rhusai 'ēmas apo tou ponērou*), which Jesus taught us to pray.

Within Jesus' Sermon, however, is an important caution, regarding exorcism:

> "Not everyone who says to me, 'Lord, Lord,' will enter the kingdom of heaven, but only the one who does the will of my Father in heaven. On that day many will say to me, 'Lord, Lord, did we not prophesy in your name, and cast out demons in your name, and do many deeds of power in your name?' Then I will declare to them, 'I never knew you; go away from me, you evildoers.'" (Matt 7:21–23)

What do we make of this text? Given all the biblical testimony of exorcism in Jesus' ministry, Jesus authorizing the apostles to cast out demons, and the early church's (post-150 CE) practice of "casting out demons," this passage cannot be interpreted to denounce this ministry. The context, before and after the text, provides the interpretive clue.

The key is *character* that produces "good fruit" by the one who does these works in Jesus' name, i.e., "consistency" in one's moral life and obedience to Jesus' teaching. This applies not only to exorcism that defeats the devil's dominion in one's life, but also to other types of good works, done in the name of Jesus. Jesus' judgment is harsh: eternal shunning and regarding such as an

---

9. Ibid., 93.

evildoer. This is one of Jesus' most troubling words in Scripture. It is clear that "deeds of power" alone do not prove the authenticity of one's spiritual standing before God. One's character that manifests truth, love, caring for one another, and love for the enemy indicate spiritual authenticity.

We know what Matthew 5—7 is: The Sermon on the Mount! But do we know what immediately follows? In chapters 8—9 Matthew arranges a distinctive sequence of ten healing miracles—a likely NT antitype to the ten plagues in Exodus. *Only Matthew* joins together these ten stories of Jesus' miracles of healing and exorcism, i.e., deliverance from demons, punctuated with two vignettes on discipleship (8:12–22; 9:9–13). Notably, the fifth (8:28–34), and last (9:32–34) are exorcisms! The fourth miracle, Jesus' stilling of the storm (8:23–27) also has exorcist dimensions, since he *rebukes* the chaos.[10] Thus three of the ten miracles are exorcisms.

After the third miracle, Jesus' healing Peter's mother-in-law from a fever, a summary statement informs us that Jesus did many more miracles of healing and exorcism: "That evening they brought to him many who were possessed with demons; and he cast out spirits with a word, and cured all who were sick" (8:16). In Luke this miracle has exorcist overtones: he "stood over her and *rebuked* the fever." The ten miracles with this summary statement indicate that healing *and* "casting out demons" typified Jesus' ministry. Exorcism is a special type of healing (see chapter 11 for contemporary documentation). This section ends with Jesus fulfilling prophet Isaiah's word, "He took our infirmities and bore our diseases" (8:17//Isa 53:4). These chapters (8—9) narrate what the Sermon on the Mount looks like "on the ground" through gospel ministry.

I do not believe in a health and wealth gospel and I also do not believe in a "no healing gospel." Rather, I believe in a healing/deliverance gospel *with* discipleship. Two times, costly "follow me" stories punctuate these healing/deliverance miracles (8:22 and 9:9). This ministry of healing-discipleship belongs not to Jesus alone, but also to his disciples (10:1), named in Matthew 10:2–4 with the beginning *inclusio*: "giving to them authority over unclean spirits, to cast them out, and to cure every disease and every sickness." The end *inclusio* is "preach as you go, saying, 'The kingdom of heaven has come near.' Cure the sick, raise the dead, cleanse the lepers, cast out demons . . ." (10:7–8). In verse 1 "casting out demons" is in first position; in verse 8 is in the last position. "Cast out demons" is the "frame" of the commands.

While this is a twist to our normal way of thinking, might "casting out demons" be expressive of Jesus' "love of enemy command" in 5:45? The

---

10. Numerous writers have noted that Jesus' rebuke (*epetimēsen* in 8:26) carries forward Yahweh's fight against the sea chaos in creation and exodus: McCurley, *Ancient Myths*, 58–61; Mettinger, "Fighting."

person under the power of the demonic is not the enemy. Satan's demons are the "enemy" and, depending on the nature of the demon, those demons impel one to take violent action(s) toward others or to oneself. Here is the dilemma: the person desires and wants freedom, but demonic oppression blocks the person from that desire and experience. My story at the end of this chapter exemplifies this surprising connection between love of enemy and deliverance from violent demons.

Matthew's account of Jesus' clash with Satan, a.k.a. the Beelzebul controversy—the longest of the three (Matt 12:22–32//Mark 3:22–27//Luke 11:14–15, 17–23)—speaks indirectly to this point. Jesus' blunt response: "How can Satan cast out Satan?" (Mark 3:23) infers opposition between his ministry of casting out demons and Satan's work. Augustine comments, "So let the Pharisees choose what they want. If Satan could not cast out Satan, they could find nothing to say against the Lord. But if Satan can cast out Satan, let them look out for themselves all the more and let them abandon his kingdom because it cannot stand divided against itself."[11]

Jesus then says, "But if it is by the Spirit of God that I cast out demons, then the kingdom of God has come to you" (Matt 12:28). In his exorcist ministry Jesus announces "the kingdom of God has come to you"—an astounding claim and beautiful blessing. Chrysostom sees in this response a note of conciliation, since Jesus says not only that the kingdom of God has come but also "to you." That is, "Good things have come specifically to you, so why then do you feel so displeased that you are wonderfully blessed? Why do you make war against your own salvation?"[12] Indeed, Jesus' deeds of deliverance were a potential blessing to all, and continue so today. In his power and redeeming love Jesus casts out the demons, to bring freedom and wholeness—a sign of "your kingdom come." God's Spirit empowers Jesus for this ministry (Matt 3:16–the Spirit descends upon Jesus in his baptism).[13]

The Matthew/Luke parallel states it sharply: "If it is by the Spirit of God ('finger of God' in Luke 11:20; see phrase in Deut 9:10) that I cast out demons, then the kingdom of God has come upon you" (Matt 12:28). This declaration indicates that Jesus' exorcisms were a key sign that the kingdom of God has come and that the Spirit of God was (and is) at work in Jesus Christ. In this confrontation Jesus' kingdom plunders Satan's work and realm: "But no one can enter a strong man's house and plunder his property

---

11. Augustine, Sermon 71.1, *Matthew 1—13*, in Simonetti, ed., ACCS, 246.

12. Chrysostom, *The Gospel of Matthew*, Homily 41.2, *Matthew 1—13*, in Simonetti, editor, ACCS, 248.

13. Luke emphasizes the Holy Spirit throughout his narrative The (Holy) Spirit, while seldom occurring in Mark, is vital to Jesus' ministry and discipleship in Mark (1:8–10; 3:29; 12:36; 13:11; Mansfield, "*Spirit*," 25–69, 134–39).

without first tying up the strong man; then indeed the house can be plundered" (Mark 3:27; cf. Matt 12:29//Luke 11:21–22).

Matthew and Luke share an event Mark lacks. Jesus casts out a demon from a "dumb demoniac" (Matt 12:22–23//Luke 11:14—in Matthew he is also "blind"). Matthew also has a distinctive exorcism, not in either Mark or Luke:

> After they had gone away, a demoniac who was mute was brought to him. And when the demon had been cast out, the one who had been mute spoke; and the crowds were amazed and said, "Never has anything like this been seen in Israel." But the Pharisees said, "By the ruler of the demons he casts out the demons." Then Jesus went about all the cities and villages, teaching in their synagogues, and proclaiming the good news of the kingdom, and curing every disease and every sickness. (9:32–35)

This unique exorcism in Matthew with his grouping together ten miracles, three of which have exorcist components, as well as the longer version of the Beelzebul controversy compared to Mark's, indicates the topic is significant for Matthew.

In the interpretation of the Parable of the Soils (Matt 13), the three Gospels differ in naming the evil that steals the seed sown on the path. Matthew names it *the evil one* (13:19; cf. the Lord's Prayer petition); Mark, *Satan* (4:15); Luke, *the devil* (8:12). Both Matthew and Luke speak of what was sown in the *heart* (Luke, *hearts*). Luke adds, "so that they may not believe and be saved" (cf. Mark 4:11–12). Matthew has then a unique *"enemy"* parable:

> He put before them another parable: "The kingdom of heaven may be compared to someone who sowed good seed in his field; but while everybody was asleep, an *enemy* came and sowed weeds among the wheat, and then went away. So when the plants came up and bore grain, then the weeds appeared as well. (Matt 13:24–26)

When the slaves quiz Jesus about the weeds, he again says, "'An *enemy* has done this'" (13:28). Later the disciples ask for an interpretation of this "enemy" parable.

> He [Jesus] answered, "The one who sows the good seed is the Son of Man; the field is the world, and the good seed are the children of the kingdom; the weeds are the children of *the evil one*, and the enemy who sowed them is *the devil*; the harvest is the end of the age, and the reapers are angels. Just as the weeds

are collected and burned up with fire, so will it be at the end of the age. The Son of Man will send his angels, and they will collect out of his kingdom all causes of sin and *all evildoers*, and they will throw them into the furnace of fire, where there will be weeping and gnashing of teeth. Then the righteous will shine like the sun in the kingdom of their Father. Let anyone with ears listen! (Matt 13:37–43; emphasis mine)

Understanding this parable and its interpretation is not easy. It seems to conflict with Matthew 18:15–18, which calls for discipline to deal with sin entering into the community. But in this parable the *field* is the *world*, not the *church*. The disciplinary text is dealing with temptation and sin. The *world* parable is dealing with *weeds/evil* and the *devil*. In neither case is exorcism in view. The *devil* is at work in the world until the end of the age, and it is impossible to expel him from the world, but it is possible to fence him out (Janet Warren's imagery) or exorcize him from believers and those coming to faith (see chapter 9). Capon's exposition intrigues.[14]

Matthew's distinctive treatment of Satan/devil/evil is not slack compared to Mark and Luke, even though exorcisms are not as prominent proportionally, given the length of his Gospel.[15] Matthew's discourses alert his disciples to Satan's designs. Works are matched by words on the same subject, with care for the disciples not to succumb to the wiles of the devil.

Matthew shares with Mark Jesus' exorcism of the Syrophoenician woman's daughter (Matt 15:21–28//Mark 7:24–30). Both locate the event in Tyre and Sidon. But Matthew has several notable comments not in Mark: (1) the disciples plead with Jesus to send the woman away (they are elect Israelites and protest this woman's plea); (2) in Matthew the woman calls Jesus *Lord* three times compared to Mark's one (7:28); (3) only Matthew

---

14. R. F. Capon, *Parables of the Kingdom*, 97–109. His exposition of "Let it be . . ." is problematic (105–9). True, the verb is the Greek *Aphete*, a verb-form that also means *forgive*, the same verb used in the Lord's Prayer. His exposition scintillates, but a given word can have different meanings in different contexts (cf. the English word *bat*). I doubt that Matthew had in mind that "Let it be . . ." means we should *forgive* the devil for his *weeds*, or even *forgive* the *weeds*. While we ought not use evil means to counter evil, protesting it by the standard of *truth-telling* squares with the larger biblical witness (see chapter 10).

15. Other texts that speak of evil or evildoers are 13:49; 15:4; 16:4 ("evil and adulteress generation/*genea*), which in Matthew appears numerous times as an antonym to *ethnē*/nations or Gentiles. The parables in 21:33–22:14, while not mentioning *evil*, speak of conduct that leads to severe punishment: "throw him into outer darkness, where there will weeping and gnashing of teeth," a phrase occurring several times in Matthew. *Hell* occurs more often in Matthew than in any other NT book. Cf. Matt 23. I devoted a section in *Covenant* to whether "love your enemy" and "non-retaliation" are contradicted by the Matthean Jesus elsewhere (68–72).

names the woman's response as *faith*—Mark implies it; (4) most important, whereas Mark identifies the woman as Syrophoenician, Matthew identifies her as *Canaanite*.[16] Striking! Israel slaughtered the Canaanites in its holy wars. Might this shift reflect Matthew's "love of enemy" command in 5:45? *A Canaanite is now the recipient of Jesus' exorcising power.* The enmity, rather than the enemy, is killed (cf. Eph 2:16[17]). A Canaanite woman receives Jesus' healing-deliverance love.

Jesus' commission to Peter in Matthew 16:16-18 possibly contains an exorcist dimension. Binding and loosing[18] may refer to binding evil spirits and loosing persons from bondage (see the discussion in chapter 2b: how this text connects with forgiving or retaining sins in John 20:23).[19]

Jesus' last exorcism in Matthew, the epileptic boy in 17:14-21, is a sequel to Jesus' transfiguration. The transfiguration prefigures Jesus' resurrection glory and power. In Matthew's final paragraph, Jesus, located on a mountain echoing Mt. Zion's royal traditions, declares, "All authority (*exousia*) in heaven and on earth has been given to me" (28:17). This contrasts to Satan's offer in 4:9, "All these (the kingdoms of this world) I will give you."[20]

Jesus' ministry of healing and exorcism not only restores health and wholeness to individual persons, but is also a counter-power to the imperial powers. Carter, summing up Matthew's many stories of healing and exorcism, with an anti-imperial punch, writes:

> This summary [4:23-24] is touched on eight other times in Matthew, surrounded by 14 individual healing scenes: a leper (8:1-4), a paralyzed slave (8:5-13), Peter's fevered mother-in-law (8:14), two demoniacs (8:28-34), a paralyzed man (9:2-8), a woman with a hemorrhage (9:20-22), a dead girl (9:23-26), two blind men (9:27-31), a deaf man who cannot speak (9:32-34), a man with a withered hand (12:9-14), a demoniac who cannot see or speak (12:22-24), a demon-possessed girl (15:21-28), a "moonstruck" demon-possessed girl (15:21-28), a

---

16. This is not a geographical problem since Syrophoenicia was historically part of the Canaanite population. But Matthew's choice of terms echoes the OT holy war treatment of the Canaanites.

17. See T. Yoder Neufeld, *Killing Enmity*.

18. Foster, with King, *Binding and Loosing*. This book tells numerous stories of miraculous deliverance from demons, interconnecting people and situations.

19. Swartley, *John*, 460-62, with its online Supplement. In this interpretation *retain* (*krateō*) may mean power to prevail over sin that is not forgivable, living with its consequences, as proposed by Oyer, "Interpreting," 330. But that doesn't jibe well with *bind* in Matt 16:19, though *loose* readily parallels *forgive*.

20. See my treatment of this "mountain" scene, *Israel's Scripture*, 228-32.

"moonstruck" demon-possessed boy (17:14–20), and two blind men (20:29–34).[21]

Carter searches for the significance of these actions: what do they contribute to the gospel of Jesus as agent of God's saving reign? Carter stresses Jesus' ministry as a contrast, alternative world to the Empire filled with sickness and poverty, with 80 to 90 percent living below subsistence. In Jesus' kingdom the sick are healed and demoniacs set free, in sharp contrast to the Empire's health care. Carter titles his article, "Imperial Power Is Bad for Your Health."

Satan countered Jesus' ministry by instigating criticism and opposition, to keep people from seeing Jesus' exorcisms as signs of God's reign begun in Jesus and God's Spirit. Gardner comments, ". . . God's reign is . . . overcoming evil. Jesus' critics are . . . opposing God's rule!"[22] Many scholars accept Jesus' exorcisms as historically authentic (see Twelftree).[23]

Matthew begins with a royal Davidic genealogy and ends on the mountain of God's royal reign, with *all authority* to send forth his disciples into worldwide mission (Matt 28:17–20, echoing Isa 52:7), to teach all things Jesus taught and continue his work of healing and exorcism. Jesus as God's Immanuel has overcome the evil one. Glory, hallelujah!

Luke–Acts

Luke: Jesus' Mission Destroys the Evil Powers

Luke's story of Jesus and the early church clearly proclaims Jesus came to destroy the powers of evil oppressing humanity. Luke's narrative turns a wide furrow, showing how the gospel grows in the cradle of Judaism, how Jesus' ministry is empowered by prayer, how Jesus anointed by the Spirit proclaims in word and deed a gospel that "loosens the bonds of wickedness, undoes the bands of the coercing yoke, releases the oppressed into freedom, and breaks apart every unjust contract."[24] Luke's Gospel is toned with forgiveness and joy, peace and praise.[25]

---

21. Carter, "Imperial," 34.
22. Gardner, *Matthew*, 201.
23. Twelftree, *Jesus*. Twelftree's list of crucial texts in his "Contents" (xii) is helpful, both for its comprehensiveness and parallels within the Synoptic Gospels. Some crucial summary statements, however, are missing.
24. Garrett, *Demise*, 71–72.
25. Swartley, *Covenant*, 121–51.

Luke is as strong as Mark on exorcism, and in some ways even more so (see 6:17–19; 7:21; 8:2; 13:10–17, 32; 22:53).[26] The parallel between Luke 7:18–23//Matthew 11:2–6 is striking. When John the Baptist queries whether Jesus is the one to come, or whether we should look for another, Luke mentions deliverance from *evil spirits* as context (7:21) for Jesus' answer in v. 22, inferring for the reader this is also a sign answering John's question.

Luke 8:1–3 has an astounding special:

> Soon afterwards he went on through cities and villages, proclaiming and bringing the good news of the kingdom of God. The twelve were with him, as well as some women who had been cured of evil spirits and infirmities: Mary, called Magdalene, from whom seven demons had gone out, and Joanna, the wife of Herod's steward Chuza, and Susanna, and many others, who provided for them out of their resources.

Women participated in Jesus' itinerant ministry, and helped finance it[27] (cf. Matt 27:55)! Some were demonized, but are now freed. Mary Magdalene was freed from seven demons! She plays a significant role in all four Gospels. In John's Gospel she is *first witness* to Jesus' resurrection (20:1–18). Mary Magdalene amazes. That women accompanied Jesus' itinerant disciples is radical! Perhaps women were among the seventy apostolic missioners announcing the gospel of peace, proclaiming "the kingdom of God has come near" (Luke 10:1–18).

Luke's gospel-mission of the seventy is another *special*.[28] This mission in 10:1–20[29] includes exorcism and concludes with Jesus seeing Satan falling from heaven (vv. 17–20)! Garrett shows how Jesus' gospel mission is the downfall of Satan.[30] The seventy return from their gospel peace-mission (10:5–6) jubilant, saying, "'Lord, in your name even the demons submit to us!'" (v. 17). Jesus then exclaims, reporting his vision, "'I watched [Greek im-

---

26. Klutz's scholarly treatment of exorcism in Luke–Acts, *Exorcism*, substantiates this point well. Note how Luke dramatizes Jesus' first exorcism by including, "When the demon had thrown him down" in 4:35//Mark 1:26. Cserháti notes that Luke omits six of Mark's miracles/exorcisms but adds eight others, "Binding," 113.

27. Joanna, a key financier, is mentioned after Mary Magdalene as resurrection witnesses in Luke 24:10.

28. Each Synoptic Gospel records Jesus sending out the Twelve (Matt 10:1, 7–11// Mark 6:6b–13//Luke 9:1–6). Here only Luke uses the word *demons* (*diamonia*); Matthew and Mark use (the) *unclean* (*spirits*).

29. Much in Luke's "Journey Narrative" (9:51–19:41) does not appear in Matthew and Mark. This raises questions about the origin and purpose of this narrative. See Swartley, *Israel's*, 126–45, for a proposal.

30. Garrett, *Demise*, 46–60. Read this in the context of 34–45.

perfect verb, *was watching*] Satan falling from heaven like a flash of lightning. See, I have given you authority to tread on snakes and scorpions, and over all the power of the enemy; and nothing will hurt you'" (10:18-19).[31] Garrett connects Jesus' vision with his resurrection;[32] Twelftree, with the mission of the seventy. I add to the latter: *peace-announcing* mission.[33]

Significantly, Luke's Gospel narrative connects exorcism with peacemaking (cf. Luke 10:5-6 with vv. 17-18). This connection makes us think more deeply about exorcism and peacemaking,[34] as well as war-making. When I read Nugent's *Masks of Satan*, I cannot help but wish Hitler's hatred of the Jews would have been exorcised. I see on the PBS evening news (July 25, 2017) the Muslim Rohingya fleeing persecution by the Buddhist Myanmar military to Bangladesh where many suffer, starve, and die. Might exorcist prayers have prevented the tragedy, as well as bombed Mosul, with thousands of bodies dead or dying under the rubble? War is a major component of evil. Yes, "War is hell!" (chapter 10); yet war, violence, and terrorism is worldwide—sad and terrifying, amid God's good and beautiful creation.

Luke's Gospel witness on exorcism is anticipated already in his inaugural platform: 4:18-19, which directly follows Jesus' encounter with the devil in three powerful temptations (4:1-13). Jesus' victory over Satan empowers him to announce the Magna Carta of his ministry:

> "The Spirit of the Lord is upon me, because he has anointed me to bring good news to the poor. He has sent me to proclaim release to the captives and recovery of sight to the blind, to let the oppressed go free, to proclaim the year of the Lord's favor."
> (Luke 4:18-19)

In quoting Isaiah 61:1-2a, Jesus modifies it by omitting the second strophe, "to bind up the broken-hearted." He puts in its place his fourth strophe, "to set free the oppressed" (from Isa 58:6). Jesus thus makes *release* (*aphesis*) central to his gospel.

---

31. Warren slights this text in her discussion of fallen angels. By NT times Satan is no longer a prosecuting attorney, *ha sa-tán*, as in OT texts Warren cites. Boyd links fallen angels to demons, which the OT links to idols (*Crucifixion*, 1032; *Satan*, 24-25, 44-49, 171-77). When people accept the peaceable Messiah-Jesus, Satan is defeated. In that sense Satan's fall is continuous with mission.

32. Garrett, *Demise*, 50-55. Theologically, yes, to Garrett. But in Luke 10, it's the *peace-kingdom-gospel* mission. Vollenweider contends that Jesus' vision belongs to Jesus' historical exorcist ministry: "Ich sah," 190-91.

33. Morris insightfully summarizes both Garrett's and Twelftree's contributions: *Warding*, 28-30.

34. Luke uses peace/*eirēnē* 14x: Swartley, *Covenant*, 123-38, 140-48.

Diagram 5.2 Chiasm with Emphasis on Release

a To preach good news to the poor

  b To proclaim release to the captives,

    c And recovery of sight to the blind,

  b' To send forth the oppressed in release,

a' To proclaim the acceptable year of the Lord.

This composition[35] accentuates *release* in matching lines, b and b'. While Luke's Jubilee theme is widely known, his related emphasis on *release from Satan's power* is not, even though it is an essential part of Luke's Jubilee theology.[36]

Special also is Jesus' healing a woman with *a spirit* that crippled her for eighteen years (Luke 13:10–17). Twice the story stresses she is set free (forms of *luō* in vv. 12 and 16) from her ailment and bondage. What better "work" might one do on the Sabbath!

Another Lukan special is Jesus' address to Simon Peter:

> "Simon, Simon, listen! Satan has demanded to sift all of you like wheat, but I have prayed for you that your own faith may not fail; and you, when once you have turned back, strengthen your brothers. (22:31–32)

Jesus' praying for Peter is "preventive demonization." For Judas, it was not to be, however.

Acts: The Power of the Gospel Mission

You know the message he sent to the people of Israel,
preaching peace by Jesus Christ
—he is Lord of all. . . .
God anointed Jesus of Nazareth with the Holy Spirit and with power;
. . . he went about doing good
and healing all who were oppressed by the devil,
for God was with him. Acts 10:38

---

35. Some scholars hold this is Luke's selection, not Jesus' own, just as the entire Gospel reflects Luke's special contribution to the Jesus-gospel. My own judgment is *both*; we cannot "slice" it.

36. See Swartley, *Israel's Scriptures*, 77–78, 85–86; also Garrett; Twelftree; Morris, *Warding*, 26–30; Cserháti; Klutz.

The great Pentecost event climaxes with Peter's affirmation: "Know you therefore that God has made this Jesus both Lord and Christ" (Acts 2:36). Cullmann and others have argued that the title "Jesus is Lord" *(kyrios)*, the earliest Christian confession, proclaims the lordship of Christ. In Acts 10:36 it is "Lord *of all*," which renders the imperial lords ruling the Greco-Roman world subject to Jesus Christ as *Lord*.[37] *Lord* (*kyrios*), occurring strategically in Luke 2:11, is most important in Luke–Acts, occurring "roughly two hundred times."[38] Jesus is Lord over the powers, both political and spiritual. This early Christian confession, powerful and sustaining in the face of political persecution and demonic powers, was and is central to the church's identity and mission (cf. Phil 2:5–11).

Peter, after baptizing Cornelius, summarizes Jesus' ministry as "preaching good news of peace," and "healing all who were oppressed by the devil." As in the shocking Luke 7:1–10 story of a centurion seeking out Jesus to heal his dying servant, so here in Acts a *centurion* is exemplar of the Gentiles' reception of the gospel[39] through Peter, who summarized Jesus' ministry as "proclaiming the gospel of peace" and "healing . . ."! No way is the gospel without political impact in Luke–Acts![40] Later, Luke sums up Paul's mission to the Gentiles as opening their eyes, "that they may turn from darkness to light and from the power of Satan to God, so that they may receive forgiveness of sins and a place among those who are sanctified" (Acts 26:18).

Analysis of Exorcism in Acts

To grasp this emphasis in Acts, I identify three summary exorcist statements, two unique features, and four stories that narrate what happened.

Summary statements

With my italics on crucial parts:

---

37. Rowe's *World* explores the significance of this claim, detailing and laying low widespread emperor worship and its deity pretensions.

38. Rowe, "Luke–Acts," 294. Schneider's *kyrios* list for Luke–Acts has 33 in Luke and 51 in Acts that refer to God, *Lukas*, 214–15. See D. Jones for uses that put Jesus as *kyrios* in competition with Roman Emperors, "Title," 85.

39. Both Rowe and Howell in their *JSNT* articles discuss the issue of Roman centurion-benefactors. In Luke–Acts they are recipients of Jesus' healing power and Peter's gospel proclamation. Amazing!

40. I address this issue in Swartley, "Politics," 18–27. See Rowe, *World*, 105; "Luke–Acts," and Howell's response, "Imperial."

Acts 5:16 A great number of people would also gather from the towns around Jerusalem, bringing the sick and *those tormented by unclean spirits*, and they were all cured (note also vv. 17–20).

Acts 10:38 Epigraph (see vv. 34–39 for context).

Acts 19:11–12 God did extraordinary miracles through Paul, so that when the handkerchiefs or aprons that had touched his skin were brought to the sick, their diseases left them, and *the evil spirits came out of them*.

Unique features

Acts 19:13–16 Then some itinerant Jewish exorcists tried to use the name of the Lord Jesus over *those who had evil spirits*, saying, "I adjure you by the Jesus whom Paul proclaims." Seven sons of a Jewish high priest named Sceva were doing this. But *the evil spirit* said to them in reply, "Jesus I know, and Paul I know; but who are you?" Then the man with *the evil spirit* leaped on them, mastered them all, and *so overpowered* them that they fled out of the house naked and wounded.

Acts 17:18 Also some Epicurean and Stoic philosophers debated with him. Some said, "What does this babbler want to say?" Others said, "He seems to be a proclaimer of *foreign divinities*." (This was because he was telling the good news about Jesus and the resurrection.)

The term for *foreign divinities* is literally *strange demons*.[41] The philosophers believed Paul's preaching had some demonic impulse.

Four Exorcist Stories

Most striking is how Luke accentuates Jesus' gospel as victorious over magic, sorcery, and demonic powers in the Greco-Roman world. The four stories are:

1. Philip's (and the apostles') encounter with Simon Magus in Samaria (Acts 8:8–24).

---

41. The OT, especially the LXX, identifies foreign gods with demons. NT translators use *foreign gods* for the Greek *diamonia*. The word, *deisidaimonia* in 17:22 is translated *extremely religious* (NRSV) and *deisidaimonias* in 25:19 as *superstition* (NRSV). The KJV uses *superstitious/ion* in both cases. The demonic is inherent in all three terms.

2. Paul's encounter with Elymas the magician in Salamis, Cyprus (Acts 13:4–12).
3. Paul's exorcism of a spirit of divination from a slave girl in Macedonia (Acts 16:16–18), and the gospel confronting sorcery and magical arts in Ephesus (Acts 19:11–20). Those who brought charges against Paul and Silas in 16:19–23 "witnessed in Paul's exorcism the inherently destabilizing power of Jesus Christ for their pagan way of life."[42]
4. Paul's rebuke of the demon in the slave-girl had great economic consequence, exposing the connection between demons, idolatry, and economics.

In the last story (19:13–20; see text above under unique features) some Jewish exorcists tried using the name of Jesus to cast out demons from those demonized, but it backfired. They were not believers in Jesus. Their attempt was a form of magic. Later in chapter 19 an even more extensive economic collapse occurs as the result of Paul's exorcism. The result: "many of those who became believers confessed and disclosed their practices. A number of those who practiced magic collected their books and burned them publicly; when the value of these books was calculated, it was found to come to fifty thousand silver coins."

Demetrius, whose successful business had collapsed, attempted a counter-coup against Paul, which, short of the town clerk's shrewd handling of the case, would have landed in the Roman court (vv. 21–40). Paul's Gospel preaching had huge effects: Paul's proclamation of "The Way"/Jesus' gospel undermined both the Artemis religion and Demetrius's business. The economic toll of that power encounter was a huge loss of money for Demetrius's business: "50,000 silver coins [*drachmas*] worth of magic stuff going up in flames" (Acts 19:19). Beck calculates this catastrophic loss to amount to over seven million dollars in US currency.[43] In Acts as the gospel enters a new region, a power encounter with the evils of magic and/or idolatry occurs. Rowe's analysis, specifically on the connection between religion and economics (and culture more broadly), shines.[44]

In Luke's Jubilee, Jesus breaks *every* yoke of oppression, both in the spirit world and in the socio-economic-political structures that oppress humankind. In Paul's words to Elymas, the gospel dares to say to every evil power,

---

42. Rowe, *World*, 26.

43. Beck, *Reviving*, 163.

44. Rowe, *World*, 41–51; cf. his "Luke–Acts" article. While Rowe focuses on the imperial effects of proclaiming Jesus Christ as "Lord *of all*" (Acts 10:36, emphasis mine), he skirts the role exorcisms play in Acts. Acts 10:38 does not appear in his Scripture Index, though he quotes it on 105.

"You son of the devil, you enemy of all righteousness, full of all deceit and villainy, will you not stop making crooked the straight paths of the Lord?" (Acts 13:10). What a powerful denunciation of the devil!

Beck follows this up with the gospel's impact on politics in Paul's "turning the world upside down" in Thessalonica: "political work often fails to get to the spiritual roots of systemic injustice and oppression, the sacred and unquestioned values that justify and perpetuate the political and economic systems of the world. Until the gods of the nation are called into question, radical change is not possible."[45]

The encounter with magicians in Acts 8 and 19 form the inclusio of the spread of the gospel outside Jewish culture. In Luke–Acts the Holy Spirit counters Satan's destructive work.[46] Luke intends to show that the gospel of Jesus Christ is God's power to overcome magic, idolatry, sorcery, and every spirit reality that ruled and oppressed people in the Greco-Roman world.[47]

Borg in his early writings presents Jesus and his mission empowered by his Spirit-filled relationship to God.[48] Jesus was first and foremost a mediator of the world of Spirit-power into the material world. His exorcisms and miracles testify. Borg also says we moderns cannot grasp Jesus and his mission until we come to terms with our own culture. The rationalism of the Enlightenment has defined our reality, effectively excluding the spirit realm. Jesus knew spirit was ultimate reality. He ministered with deep compassion for the sick and those possessed by demons. Only with this portrait of Spirit-power and intense compassion for those broken by sin and Satan can we rightly glimpse the historical Jesus, the One his followers knew as "Deliverer," "Healer," and "Restorer" to God's design for human life.[49]

Exorcisms, like Jesus' other mighty works in the Gospels, disclose who Jesus is. Jesus is not just another person or prophet. He comes as God's Messiah to free not only Israel but all people from evil's power. In rebuking and exorcising the demons Jesus carries forward God's purpose to establish God's sovereignty and victory over evil.[50] He sets the captives free.

Much of the Christian church today outside the West (Latin/South America, Africa, and Asia) knows what our rationalistic-scientific-technological culture does not perceive, though Scott Peck, Richard Gallagher,

---

45. Beck, *Reviving*, 163–68. While Beck speaks often of the personal face of evil, he does not describe an exorcism akin to Jesus' exorcisms or stories in this book.

46. Cserháti, *Binding*, 115.

47. For extended analysis of exorcisms in Acts, see Garrett, *Demise*, 61–109. Note her Conclusion, 101–9.

48. Borg, *Jesus*, especially 39–75.

49. Ibid., 50.

50. Ibid., 46–52.

Tilda Norberg, Janet Warren, and Richard Foster, and the many books on exorcism/deliverance ministry[51] won't let us off the hook (see Introduction; chapters 11 and 12). Our Western culture rakes in billions of dollars from magical practices intended to entertain: computer games, Harry Potter books, and movies filled with devil images. We and our children are not immune to the power that these "fun things" have over their lives. In fact, we are sadly blinded to the toll such entertainment takes from deep-rooted *shalom* in our lives, especially when we yield to it to gain power through sorcery, witchery, and deception. The toll our modern culture takes on adolescents is great: anxiety, depression, eating disorders, suicidal thoughts and attempts (some successful).[52]

Belief systems, such as New Age and Scientology, negate the reality of sin, deception, and evil. They allure, but do not cure. Matthew Fox's books and Shroyer's *Original Blessing* downplay the sin/evil component of reality, but are one-sidedly strong in the Christian tradition.

Jesus, "deliver us from evil—for shalom" is the yearning of our hearts. Give us passion for mission, in your strong name, with love for the gospel of salvation. Your kingdom come!

Story 1

The stories of exorcisms in Acts continue as part of missionary witness. Loren Entz, Mennonite missionary in Burkina Faso, tells the story of how Abou, a Muslim leader who became a Christian, claimed Christ's power in victory against the sorcery power of the village's elders:

> One night elders who were fetishers invited Abou in order to test him. Was the power of his Jesus greater than their fetish occult power? First they tried to poison him with food, but Abou found victory over that as he offered a prayer of thanks before he partook of the food. God showed himself to be Abou's right hand and he suffered no ill effects.
>
> Then the elders took him to their sacred grounds late that night. Abou was placed beside a huge gaping hole. The six elders sat on the other side of the hole. Fire escaped from the hole. A special whistling brought poisonous bees from the pit to do

---

51. Foster, *Prayer*, "Authoritative Prayer," 229–42.

52. See the *Time* article by Schrobsdorff, "Anxiety." While this article focuses mostly on girls, a "Response" in the next issue (November 14, p. 5) points out the "trouble" is wider and greater: "depression and anxiety also exist within the 50% of the U.S. population that is male, and 33% that is not white."

their evil work against Abou, but again with no success. Abou could not be stopped.

They had one test left, a test which no one else had ever escaped. The old men whistled a second time and a huge snake about 18 inches in diameter emerged. It came toward Abou. It tried to push him into the pit as countless others before him had been pushed in and disappeared. But the snake could only brush his leg. The snake itself fell into the pit. There was no doubt whose power was greater, God's power working through Abou or that of the fetishes through the village elders. The rest of the night Abou preached of Jesus to them, until daybreak, when he returned to Orodara.[53]

Story 2

One personal encounter in deliverance ministry exposes the relation between demons and Jesus' love of enemy in a stunning manner.

A co-laborer in deliverance ministry phoned me one afternoon asking me immediately to pray and bind the demon of murder in a man who had just threatened to come to his church and murder the pastor. He, I, and the threatened pastor prayed, binding in the name of Jesus this demonic power that had overtaken this man. While we were each praying in separate locations, the man came into the church parking lot, started toward the church with a gun, suddenly stopped, and then got into his pickup truck, sped out of the church lot, went home, and phoned his pastor pleading, "I need help. I am overcome with this evil compulsion to murder." The pastor requested my co-laborer and me to come and assist him in a deliverance session that evening.

During my twelve-mile drive to the church I struggled with how a nonresistant Mennonite would handle the violence likely to be manifested. The word that kept coming to me was, "Jesus said, 'Love your enemies.'" "How does this figure when one is confronted with violence?" I agonized in mind and speech. It didn't make sense. I couldn't rationally connect that answer, which the Spirit gave me three times, to my ethical dilemma. Not long into the session, I thought I was a "goner." The man, much bigger than me, lunged toward me with his fist aimed at my head. These words, without my thinking, burst out of my mouth, "Jesus said, 'Love your enemies.'" The man collapsed to the floor, with swinging arm gone limp.

---

53. Entz, "Challenges."

Then we learned from the demon, which when under Jesus' authority to speak truth regarding his legal right to defy the exorcist commands in Jesus' name to leave the man, spoke with guttural voice that someone murdered his father when he was twelve, and all these twenty-five plus years he nurtured the desire to find and kill the man who killed his father.

When we bound back the spirits afflicting him and talked directly to the man, telling him what we learned, the man broke down, "How do you know this? I've told no one. It's true. I am overcome by the spirit of murder." He then wept and wept, confessed his sin, and asked for God's forgiveness. From then on we knew what we were dealing with, and expulsion of that demon came quickly in the next round of command-confrontation. The spirit of murder cannot stand when confronted with Jesus' command to love the enemy.

Chapter 6

Paul: Victory over Evil

Principalities and Powers

*He disarmed the rulers and authorities
and made a public example of them,
triumphing over them in it [the cross; RSV, him].*[1]

—Col 2:15

*The root of the [Empires'] problem [with the early Christians]
was their resistance against Satan and sin
as the true rulers of this world,
the resistance that had shaped
Christian practice through and through.*

—Luise Schottroff

*In Paul (and Luke) peace (shalom) and evil
are closely intertwined.
Salvation-shalom is deliverance from the devil.*

---

1. The Greek, *en autō*, could refer back to the cross ("nailing it to the cross," v. 14b) or to the subject "He" of v. 15, which extends back through vv. 9–14, with v. 8 ending with "Christ."

PAUL'S WRITINGS POWERFULLY PROCLAIM God's triumph through Christ over evil powers. He frequently admonishes believers to shun evil and, rather, strive for love and truth. Paul describes how God's victory in Christ Jesus is connected, directly and dynamically, to God's triumph over evil. God's salvation in Jesus Christ is *power* that delivers us from "the dominion/*exousia* of darkness and transfers us into the kingdom of his beloved Son, in whom we have redemption, the forgiveness of sins" (Col 1:13-14; cf. Eph 1:7). By the power of this gospel believers are set free from the bondages of sin, evil, devil, and demons—manifested in many forms: be it personal oppression or structural, systemic manifestations of demonic power. Deliverance from the powers of evil is the precondition and gift of our peace with God and fellow humans.

How Paul Understands Evil

Paul speaks of evil power in five ways.[2] The **first** is Satan or devil, which occurs often.[3]

Many texts speak of the believers' resistance against Satan (1 Cor 7:5; 2 Cor 2:11; 11:14; 12:7; 1 Thess 2:18; Eph 4:26). Satan's ways are deceitful; he masks himself as an "angel of light" (2 Cor 11:14) and with deceitful designs seeks to get an advantage over the believer (2 Cor 2:11). Paul speaks of Satan hindering the missionary team from visiting the Thessalonians (1 Thess 2:18). Believers are to give no place to the devil, by not letting the sun go down on his or her anger (Eph 4:26-27). The incestuous man is to be turned over to Satan for the "destruction of his flesh so that his spirit might be saved in the day of the Lord" (1 Cor 5:5). Paul proclaims God's victory in Jesus Christ as *gift* and *power* that delivers us from the works of Satan, the devil, so we can know and enjoy "the peace of Christ" ruling in our hearts and uniting us in one body in and through Christ (Col 3:15).[4]

A striking text occurs at the end of Romans, where Paul calls believers to be wise about what is good, and *innocent/kerapous* (NIV; KJV, *simple*;

---

2. Compare four in Finger, *Christian*, vol. 1, 322-33.

3. "[T]he main functions of Satan and Satan-like figures Beliar (2 Cor. 6.15), the god of this world (2 Cor. 4.4), the destroyer (1 Cor. 10.10); and the tempter (1 Thess. 3.5) are: temptation (1 Cor. 7.5; 2 Cor. 2.1; 11.3, 14; 1 Thess. 3.5), blinding and disguise (2 Cor. 2.11; 4.4; 11.14), obstruction (1 Thess. 2.18), causing harm and painful experiences (2 Cor. 12.7), and destruction (1 Cor. 12.7). All this is the work of Satan—and of his angels (2 Cor. 12.7)." Becker, "Paul," 136.

4. This hymn text comes to mind: "There is no other hope; there is no other plea. Salvation full, salvation free, must come alone through Thee [Christ]!" "O Lord within My Soul," Elisha Albright Hoffman, 1900, *MH* 590.

NRSV, *guileless*) about what is evil: for "the God of peace will soon crush Satan under your feet" (RSV 16:20). This pronouncement combines "God of peace" with crushing Satan's power. Its jubilant declaration unites two major trajectories in biblical theology: God the Warrior and God the Peacemaker. They also meet in the life of the person and the believing community when Satan's power is "bound" (Rev 20:2) by God's power in Jesus Christ. God triumphs over evil and bestows shalom-peace.

A **second** type of evil power(s) is Paul's fourfold reference to *demons* in one textual admonition, warning believers against idolatry (1 Cor 10:20-21). Echoing the OT connection between idolatry and demons, Paul draws a parallel between Israel's worship of idols (10:6-13) and the Corinthian believers' potential idolatry through participating in cultic meals dedicated to pagan gods (10:14-22). While in 8:4-6 Paul said pagan gods/idols have no real existence,[5] in 10:14-22 he acknowledges that demons, nonetheless, exert functional power. He recognizes their power and calls Christian believers away from their influence: "... I imply that what pagans sacrifice they sacrifice to demons and not to God. I do not want you to be partners with demons. You cannot drink the cup of the Lord and the cup of demons. You cannot partake of the table of the Lord and the table of demons. Or are we provoking the Lord to jealousy? Are we stronger than he?" (10:20-22). Paul's view concurs with the OT understanding (Deut 32:17; Ps 106:36-38). The idols Israelites worshiped were actually demons, anti-God powers.

A **third** way Paul speaks of evil relates to sin, flesh, and death. The evil *flesh* impulse (Rom 7:5-18) opposes God's Spirit (Rom 8:3-9; Gal 5:16-18, 24; 6:8). Paul knows deep despair caused by sin, flesh, and law, from which he is delivered through Jesus Christ (Rom 7). Believers put off the old and put on the new (Gal 5:16-23; Col 3:1-17; Eph 4:25-32).[6]

A **fourth** face of evil is the forces that lie behind pagan religions and philosophies, and the law as means for self-justification. Believers are redeemed from under the law and freed from "the elemental spirits (*stoicheia*) of the universe" (Gal 4:3, 8-9; see also Col 2:8, 18-23). These structures and rituals were powers that dominated life and destroyed freedom. For the Jews it was not the law itself, but doing works of the law as a

---

5. The word *real* occurs rarely in English Bible translations, though the notion is at home in Greek thought. In the NRSV *really* is supplied. The RSV translates the phrase, "an idol has no real existence" and the NRSV translates it, "no idol in the world really exists." The phrase is difficult to translate since it lacks a verb and also has no adjective (*real*) or adverb (*really*). Barrett says, "Paul does not say that they do not exist, only that they are 'no gods,'" (*Paul*, 58). Functionally, yes, people worship "gods," but such have no life, no ultimate existence.

6. Paul nowhere calls any of these sins *demons*; yet his overall theology recognizes that demonic power works through sin and preys upon human weakness.

means of salvation. For Greeks *stoicheia* consisted of astrological fate and fortune, powers governing nature's cycles and imparting secret knowledge about the cosmos.[7]

From these texts and Romans 1:18-32 we gain a basic understanding of idolatry. Structures that are deemed good are turned into ultimate values, ends in themselves, and thus elevated to powers over one's life, and then worshiped as gods.[8] Paul describes this process: through sinful impulses humans fail to see God's revelation in nature and therefore turn to idolatry, worshiping the creation and creature instead of the Creator. Hence, God gave them over—repeated three times (Rom 1:24, 26, 28)—to the course and consequences of their wickedness. Only the liberating power of the gospel frees humans from this chain of sin. Jesus "gave himself for our sins to deliver us from the present evil age" (Gal 1:4, RSV). Released from the power of these elemental forces that govern and oppress, believers claim freedom in Christ.

The **fifth** way evil expresses itself is related to *rulership*: principalities, powers, dominions, thrones (Eph 1:20-21; see Weaver in Introduction). While these powers have a positive function in the world—restraining evil as agents of God's wrath—they readily become demonic. These powers crucified the Lord of Glory (1 Cor 2:6-9).

---

7. Mauser's analysis of "the rudimentary elements of the world" (*stoicheia*) in Colossians is pertinent here. He contends that these likely refer to the four primary elements that the Greek philosopher Epimenides named: fire, water, air, earth (*Gospel*, 143-44). In order not to offend these powers, the Colossian Christians thought it necessary to engage in various ascetic and ritual practices. Honoring these powers as gods undermined the supremacy of Christ.

8. For this process see Patte's exposition of Paul's faith convictions in Romans 1-8, in *Paul's*, 256-87.

Diagram 6.0 Biblical theological contexts and language for evil in OT and NT

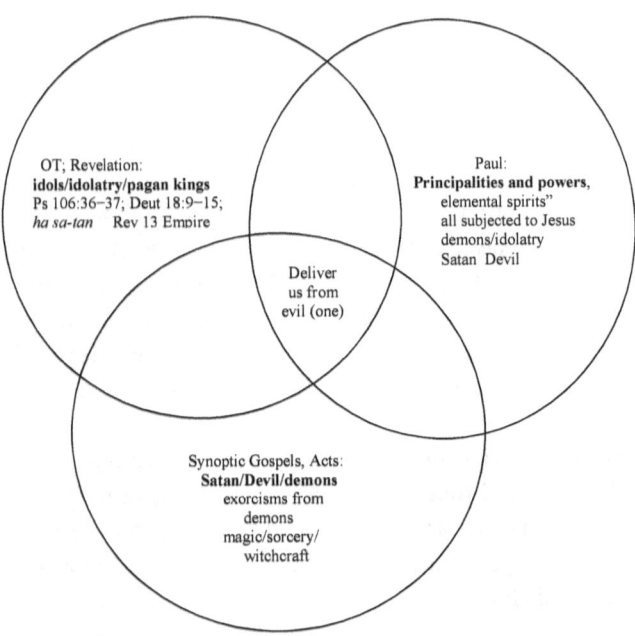

The Principalities and the Powers

The "powers" texts fall into three types. I classify them as negative, positive, and normative.[9] Since some of the negative texts correlate the world powers with evil, I list these here:

- Matthew 4:8–10//Luke 4:6–8. The devil (Satan in Luke) tempts Jesus to bow down, worship me, and I will give you all the kingdoms of this world.

---

9. See my three-column Diagram in *Covenant*, 229. This insight came to me when teaching "Biblical Peacemaking" in Swaziland in 1982 (MCC sponsored) to mostly black and colored pastors from RSA. Local police learned of the ten-day seminar when a RSA person in Lesotho came to teach nonviolent resistance. Public discussion of politics was illegal under apartheid. The group of twenty-five had to decide whether to continue or have police monitor the seminar. Those from RSA said we put up with threats all the time—some had been in prison—and we knew when we registered to come we might suffer reprisal. They voted to continue. So police monitored my teaching. On the first day they came I presented these three views of government. The police entered just after I finished explaining 666 in Revelation 13:18. The story is long, but in short, one policeman at the end wanted to be invited as a person, not a policeman, for later seminars!

- Mark 10:42. The rulers of the world *lord* over their subjects.
- Mark 13:9–13. The rulers persecute and kill believers (James, Acts 12:1–2, et al.).
- Luke 13:1–3. Pilate massacres many in Galilee, mixing their blood with the sacrifices.
- Luke 13:31–33. Jesus calls Herod a *fox*, one conniving to get him.
- 1 Corinthians 2:6–8. The rulers crucified the Lord of glory, Jesus.
- 1 Corinthians 6:4. World's court judges are those least esteemed by believers.
- Ephesians 6:11–12. Believers wrestle against rulers and authorities, "against the cosmic powers of this present darkness, against the spiritual forces of evil in the heavenly places" (perhaps echoing Isa 14:12–15).
- Revelation 13. The *beast* (Roman emperor) allies himself with the *dragon* (in 12:9 equated with the devil/Satan).

The positive texts, though fewer (Rom 13:1–7; 1 Tim 2:1–4; Titus 3:1; 1 Pet 2:13–17), have had the strongest influence on the Christian view of "the powers." I address Romans 13 later.

The normative texts declare Christ's victory over the powers. This is the theological, christological, and ecclesiological basis for Christian witness to the powers. The core claims are:

- 1 Corinthians 15:24–27. Every authority, rule, and power has been put in subjection to Christ; when Jesus hands over the kingdom to the Father, they will be stripped of all power.
- Colossians 1:15–16, 20. The powers, in all their variant expressions, owe their origin to God's creative work through Jesus Christ as agent of creation, and are included in the ultimate reconciliation of all things in Christ.
- Colossians 2:10, 15. Jesus is head over the powers (v. 10). God/Christ disarmed them, making a public exposure of them (they put Jesus on the cross), but Christ triumphed over them (v. 15).
- Ephesians 1:19–23. The exalted Lord Jesus reigns, far above all rule and authority. The powers are subject to Christ for the sake of the church, enabling the church to spread the knowledge of God and radiate God's love to all (3:17–19).

- Ephesians 3:9–10. The church witnesses to the powers by displaying the manifold wisdom of God in uniting formerly hostile parties in Christ.
- Ephesians 6:12–18. Believers take a stand against the strategies of the powers to trick, deceive, and defeat us. The armor of resistance to and battle against evil is God's armor (see below).
- Romans 8:35–39. Nothing in all God's creation, not even the powers, can separate believers from the love of God which is in Christ Jesus our Lord.
- 1 Peter 3:22. All angels, authorities, powers are subject to Jesus Christ who is at God's right hand.
- Revelation 18:2b, 10c. "Fallen, fallen is Babylon the great . . . For in one hour your judgment has come."

The authority of the believers derives from their relationship to the victorious Jesus Christ, seated at God's right hand, with all powers put under his feet (Eph 1:18–22). The vindicated, resurrected Jesus is exalted and given "the name above every name" to which every knee will one day bend and "confess that Jesus Christ is Lord" (Phil 2:9–11; cf. Acts 2:36).

Political powers may be viewed either negatively or positively. The powers are not intrinsically good or evil, but may be *either* good or evil depending upon whether their policies express God's will or Satan's conniving—whether they think and act in accord with God's purpose, or in rebellion against God's purpose, perpetrating evil.

A key question arises: are the powers what people make them to be? Can they in their "fallenness" (ontology) be evil apart from humans' evil choices? My view is *yes*. Their pull toward evil is beyond those at their helm. The powers are prone to systemically *compound* evil. Their fallen state readily links them to Satan.[10]

In light of Paul's five perceptions of evil, I propose: Satan tempts rulers and utilizes systemic structures for evil. Rulers are tempted to operationalize Satan's sinister goals.

Scholars raise numerous interpretive issues (authors cited support that view).[11]

---

10. See chapter 1. My view of Satan differs from Wink's as described in *Unmasking*, 9–40. Wink holds that Satan's power is actualized by "our (human) choices" (32); I contend that while our choices actualize Satan's power within/over us, Satan is also a power prior to these choices. Hence the phrases: "stand against the wiles of the devil" (Eph 6:11) and "take the shield of faith . . . to quench all the flaming arrows of the evil one (6:16). Temptation presupposes an "other" power that through diverse tactics tempts us to choose against God/Christ.

11. For fuller analysis, see Swartley, "War," 2350–54. See also Dawn's excellent and

1. Are the powers benign (Carr),[12] or adversarial to God's purposes (most writers)?

2. Are the powers to be demythologized and relegated to a primitive worldview (Bultmann), or are they to be viewed as spirit powers, super-intelligent demons opposing God's purposes, often associated with idolatry (Arnold, O'Brien)?[13]

3. Are the demonic powers to be understood in terms of and virtually identified with socio-economic-political structures (Berkhof, J. H. Yoder, Tambasco, Wink),[14] and/or should these structures, systems, and institutions be understood in both inner and outer dimensions, invisible and visible, to ascertain their spirit "personality" (Wink. Tambasco)?

4. Does Christ's victory over the powers now benefit believers only, while the scope of its effect extends only eschatologically to the powers? (Morrison)

5. Does Rom 13:1 assume a double dimension, i.e., spiritual powers and human rulers?

---

accessible treatment of the various interpretations of the "powers" in *Powers*, 1-34. Camp has a brief outline of Paul's perspective on the source, nature, and intention of the powers: (1) that the powers are created by God as good; (2) that they are fallen and therefore in rebellion against the original purposes of God — in this fallen state, rather than serving humankind, they enslave it; (3) that the powers are used by God for good even in their state of rebellion; and (4) that the domination of the powers has been broken by the work of Christ. Camp, *Mere*, 89.

12. Carr, *Angels*.

13. C. Arnold, *Ephesians* and *Powers*. O'Brien also sees no need to demythologize, for we confront the same reality today. The faithful church is called to vigilance against these powers, appropriating Christ's victory through prayer and the word of God: "Principalities," 141-47.

14. Berkhof, *Christ*; Yoder, *Politics*, 134-211; Tambasco, "Principalities"; Wink, *Naming* and *Unmasking*. Marva Dawn analyzes Jacques Ellul on this matter. She observes that in his earlier writings (*Ethics of Freedom*, 1976) Ellul said that even after scrutinizing every dimension of political power, "'we have still not apprehended its reality; [rather] *another power intervenes and indwells and uses political power, thus giving it a range and force that it does not have in itself*.'" But she notes that later (in *Subversion of Christianity*, 1986) Ellul identifies six great evil powers that the Bible speaks of — "'Mammon, the prince of this world, the prince of lies, Satan, the devil, and death.'" They are characterized by "'their functions: money, power, deception, accusation, division, and destruction.... There is no infernal world or hierarchy of fallen angels with superimposed eons. There is nothing behind it. We are told about powers that are concretely at work in the human world and have no other reality or mystery.'" Dawn observes that Ellul seems to have shifted his view. See her article, "Biblical"; quotes from 175, 184. In my judgment, both Ellul's earlier and later views need to be seen as one whole, with the earlier informing the latter. Four of the six great powers Ellul speaks of are evil spirit-power, and cannot be exhausted by "their functions," which he rightly identifies!

Or, does one decide in each use: is it spirit powers or governing authorities in view?

The Christus Victor view of the atonement emphasizes Jesus' binding and plundering the demon powers.[15] In Paul's writings, the death and resurrection of Jesus means cosmic victory over evil spiritual powers.[16] How should we understand the powers today? In a sermon at the Anabaptist Mennonite Biblical Seminary, Metropolitan Paulos Mar Gregorios of India spoke on Colossians 1:15–20, titled, "The Comprehensiveness of Christ." Hear his memorable word:

> I think the people of Colossae did not live in our kind of secular world. They could understand many things which we cannot understand—like thrones, powers, principalities, authorities. These are lost to us, but for the Colossians these were important concepts because in the prevailing culture of that time . . . the belief was that there were other beings besides ourselves in this cosmos—visible as well as invisible. We don't believe that. Our secular civilization tries to teach us that whatever is open to our senses is all that there is. . . . But that is not what the Colossian

---

15. Finger proposes that the patristic view of the atonement (Irenaeus and Gregory of Nyssa especially) as the "deception of the devil" was not intentional deception. The "disguise" was Jesus' true servant nature, which the powers could not perceive since such is antithetical to their being; *thus* they were deceived: "Satan and the powers then were deceived by Jesus. But [it was] not because he tricked them by appearing in some deceitful disguise. In Jesus, God came to humankind as he truly was: gracious, forgiving, seeking to win people by love and not by force." *Christian Theology*, vol. 1, 333. Ray's treatment of Anselm's, Abelard's, and patristic views is most instructive in light of feminist and liberationist critiques of the first two. Ray values the patristic view in light of the weaknesses of Anselm's (who too readily underwrites "power over" and legitimizes suffering of the weak, thus playing into patriarchy and oppression) and Abelard's (unrealistic regarding evil's power that despite love and good will continues to manifest itself—in such "Christian" atrocities as the Holocaust and Rwanda massacres). Her contribution is insightful, as this quotation illustrates: "In my retrieval of the patristic model of atonement, what is confronted and overcome by Jesus the Christ is not merely individual sin, as is the case of most construals of atonement; rather, Satan or the devil represents the sum total of evil, and so it includes not only individual sin but the countless ways in which human evil manifests itself interpersonally, communally, and globally": *Deceiving*, 131. Her treatment emphasizes Jesus' refusal to return evil for evil, nonviolence when persecuted and killed, and love [I add, even for the enemy] in the face of evil. She recognizes that we are never free from moral ambiguity, but that "through relationships of love and respect; of tasting the sweetness of freedom from evil" we might know "the satisfaction of being transformed toward fuller life, freedom, and responsibility" (145). Her book is rich. The same theme is picked up by Boyd in his genial "God's Aikido-like strategy to defeat his cosmic foes." This theme begins in *Crucifixion*, vol. 2, 1056, chapter 23, "When Hell Breaks Loose: Redemptive Withdrawal" (1099–1142), and continues through the next 150 pages, with chapter 24 titled, "The Dragon-Swallowing Dragon: Examples of Cosmic-Level Aikido Warfare," 1143–92.

16. Tambasco, "Principalities," 118–19.

people believed. They believed in a whole hierarchy of beings surrounding the human community.[17]

In a later dinner conversation on this subject a pastoral counseling professor said, "Granted there are these various phenomena that we must consider . . ." Gregorios incisively cut into the sentence, "Not phenomena, but *beings*." This incident exemplifies how steeped we are in our scientific worldview, and how prone we are to reduce all reality to the empirical. Even God-talk may point only to function of belief, not to an actual Being, whose Word-Act, in combat against evil, determines the reality of the empirical, as classical Christian faith holds.

The most explicit description of Christ's triumph over the powers is, "He disarmed the principalities and powers, and made a public example of them" (Col 2:15). Ernest Martin illumines the structure of this text, showing a parallel pattern for 2:13–15. In Greek, in each verse, clauses a and c are participial; clause b is declarative, with the finite verb:[18]

6.1 Chiasm of Colossians 2:13–15: Only "b" Strophes Have Finite Verb

13 a. when **you** were dead in your transgressions

and the uncircumcision of your flesh,

b. HE MADE **YOU** ALIVE TOGETHER WITH HIM,

c. having forgiven **us** all our transgressions,

14 a. having canceled out **the certificate of debt**

consisting of decrees against us and which was hostile to us,

b. HE HAS TAKEN IT OUT OF THE WAY,

c. having nailed **it** to the cross.

15 a. When he had disarmed **the rulers and authorities,**

b. HE MADE A PUBLIC DISPLAY OF **THEM**,

c. having triumphed over **them** through him.

The language of v. 15 evokes the scene of Emperor Vespasian and son Titus (army general responsible for Jerusalem's destruction) leading Jewish captors, putting them on display, in the streets of Rome after the fall of Jerusalem (70 CE). Paul memorably utilizes this political imagery, "But thanks be to God, who in Christ always leads us in triumphal procession, and through us spreads in every place the fragrance that comes from knowing him" (2 Cor 2:14). Not Rome, but God in Christ leads a triumphal

---

17 From Mar Gregorios's sermon.
18 E. Martin, *Colossians*, 113.

procession of gospel fragrance (thank you, Paul, knowing you were persecuted). Imperial powers are no longer victor. Christ is victor!

In Ephesians 1:20–23 Christ is the head, the church is his body, and the powers are put under Christ's feet. Paul regards the Christian community, composed of previously hostile parties, as God's witness to the principalities and powers, a demonstration of God's power over all other so-called powers. The frequent use of Psalm 110:1 throughout the NT, speaking of Christ's rule at God's right hand, testifies to his victory over the powers.[19]

What is the eschatological situation for the Powers? Here emerge two divergent emphases. Some texts speak of "destroying [or better, 'rendering powerless'] every rule and authority" (1 Cor 15:24–28; cf. 2 Thess 2:3–11). Other texts speak of reconciling the powers to God (Col 1:19–20; Eph 1:9–10). Revelation (see chapter 7) contains this dual emphasis. What is crystal clear in all texts, however, is Jesus' Lordship over the powers.

Jesus Is Lord and Victor!

Believers' Relationship to the Powers

Pilgrim identifies three stances of Christian believers toward the powers, consisting of three models of relationship: Subordinationist (Pauline), Critical Distancing (Jesus and the Gospels, Acts), and Endurance of Oppression and Persecution (Peter and Revelation). Pilgrim acknowledges that Romans 13:1–7 is Paul's most explicit treatment of the rulers and authorities and that these verses call believers to subordination. But he makes six key points of qualification.

1. Romans 13 does not provide a Christian doctrine of the state, nor a political theory of the state. Paul's primary purpose is to offer ethical instruction on proper conduct toward rulers.

2. Romans 13 and the other loyalty traditions cannot be used to give unqualified status to earthly governments as somehow established by God with a corollary unconditional obedience.

3. Romans 13 is part of a larger picture. Paul is clear: there is only one sovereign Lord: "Jesus Christ is Lord" (1 Cor 12:3; 8:5–6; Rom 10:9; et al.). On coins and inscriptions, the ruling Caesar claimed to be *divi Augustus* (divine Augustus). Earthly rulers are not supreme.

---

19. Hay, *Glory*, 59–64.

4. For Paul and the early church, the Christian's true citizenship is in the kingdom of God (Phil 3:20) . . . Governmental structures pass away.
5. Central to Paul's message is "Christ crucified" (1 Cor 2:2; Gal 3:1). Neither Paul nor his hearers could be naïve or sentimental about the Empire that nailed their Lord to the cross.
6. Finally, consider Paul's view on Christian suffering. He imitates Christ who bears in his body the "sufferings of Christ" (2 Cor 4:7–12; Gal 6:17; Rom 8:17; Phil 3:10).[20]

Stubbs's more recent treatment of Romans 13:1–7 adds much. She describes differing interpretive views:[21] Porter points to the ambiguity in "be subject/*hypotassesthō*," which is either a middle[22] or passive verb in Greek, that means both willing, voluntary subjection and the imposed social order of subjection. Thus Paul does not object to having or not having a sociopolitical order, but rather lives within the order to honor Christ above Caesar.

Stubbs then sums up Johnson's view, which situates this political order within the larger "Household Codes" dominant in Paul's writings. These "orders" in first century Roman society are *natural*, but within those orders Paul calls for transformed thought and behavior—the Romans 12 context. Elliott's contribution falls along the same lines, but extends it to consider the "constraining force of ideology," i.e. the ideology of the Roman imperial cult that managed society within hierarchical structures. Within these orders, Christians lived out their new vision and ethic, facing threats and intimidation, but nonetheless confident of their faith.

For quite another stream of interpretation, Stubbs summarizes T. Carter's view that the text should be read as *irony*: sure, we know what the sociopolitical structures are and we describe them accordingly, but in fact we know also we are freed from those powers. We live by the power of Romans 12 and 13:8–14. Thus: "rather than endorsing the authority structures of the Roman Empire, Paul critiques them. His readers do not accept his words at face value."[23]

---

20. Pilgrim, *Uneasy*, 7–36.

21. Stubbs, *Indebted*, 87–141 (chapters 5 and 6). In 5 she reviews various scholars' interpretations; in 6 she develops her own view, as suggested by her book's title—quite a craft!

22. Building on the meaning of the middle voice of the verb, P. Bender proposes that Jesus *stripped himself off from* the powers, the means of his divine warfare and victory. For more, see Swartley, *Covenant*, 235n26.

23. Stubbs, *Indebted*, on Carter, 104.

Stubbs reviews Botha's contribution under the rubric, "Conformity and Conflict."[24] The imperative, "Then do what is good, and you will receive its approval, for it is God's servant" (vv. 3–4a) is crucial to this view. Following Perdue's sociological model of order, Botha regards the Pauline instruction as conforming to the norms of the existing social order, but living within it as "good" so that the Christian believers subvert the power of the "social structure and provide for the formation of a different one."[25] Change is possible, and Romans 12:1–21 and 13:8–14 point the direction: to the church, an "alternative society" within the world.

Next, Stubbs reviews Neil Elliott's view that Romans 13 is best understood within "Kyriarchal" categories, i.e., who is Lord! He sees a conflict between the non-Judean Christians who trended toward accepting the imperial "lording" of the empire, while the Judean Christians remained more aligned with the sole authority of Jesus as Lord. Since Paul was a non-Judean and by cultural formation aligned with the Empire, he could do no other than counsel the churches he founded to accept and submit to the realities of their sociopolitical world.

Finally, Stubbs considers Nanos's novel contribution, in which he holds that the text calls the "righteous Gentiles to submit themselves, not to Roman state authority but to the institutional requirements of the synagogue."[26] What a novel, strange, but somewhat persuasive reading!

Stubbs then develops her own genial and persuasive interpretation, that Romans 13:1–7 is to be understood through the lens of v. 8, "Owe no one anything but love." How does debt and love fit together—a point Fitzmyer regarded an oxymoron. Stubbs analyzes other texts in Romans where *debt* appears (1:14, Paul's self-assessment; et al.) and discovers it is inherit to Paul's view of gospel, of our salvation-standing before God, and relation to other believers. Thus her title, *Indebted Love*, and her distinctive interpretation of Romans 13! Debt was a familiar Empire word, inherent to its structure. Her work is rich; one might guess her conclusion: "Paul's understanding of indebted love as expressed through the concept of loving one's neighbor as oneself stands in contrast to indebted relationships in the broader Roman world."[27] The difference is *freedom* versus *captivity*! Christian believers constitute a new humanity kindly subversive of the "Powers that Be."

---

24. Stubbs, *Indebted*, 106–11.
25. Ibid., 109.
26. Ibid., 113–18.
27. Ibid., 134.

What stance then ought believers take in their relationship to the governing authorities (13:1–7)? While I and other writers have appealed to the newly imposed special import/export tax that might have prompted the text, which makes its authority situational,[28] Schottroff does not. She argues that Romans 12:2 and 13:2 present a normative pattern. In 12:2 the believer is called to resist: "do not be conformed" to this age/world;[29] and in 13:2, "to not resist" *authority* "God has appointed." The same Greek word for *resist* (*anthistēmi*), noted earlier in Matthew 5:39 and Ephesians 6:13, appears here. The resistance, Schottroff says, is against Satan and the world. In principle, the believer does not resist the powers that God ordained. But living out the nonconformity command often puts Christians in collision with state powers, because in them the very Satan that Christians must resist is at work. Christians did not desire conflict with the Empire, and at times sought to avoid it, but their faithfulness to the command to "resist" evil brought them into conflict. "The root of the problem was their resistance against Satan and sin as the true rulers of this world."[30] Further, she contends that the "resistance of Christians against Satan is not the resistance of the powerless. God's power is on their side."[31] Living through this paradox gave early Christians freedom to serve God, even in a hostile environment.[32]

This unique blend of nonresistance and resistance to evil in NT literature[33] and the early church prior to Constantine confounded the powers, and gave Christians strength against evil. The peace of Jesus Christ was more powerful than the Pax Romana, simply because it not only confronted human sin and the social, structural, and systemic evils of the time, but also because it transformed the sinner and created a contrast community.[34] The blend of resistance and nonresistance is necessary because evil manifests

---

28. See *Covenant* (239n24) for my interpretation, which takes account of a specific situation in Rome.

29. A description of one's former life before salvation through Jesus Christ is: "following the ruler of the power of the air, the spirit that is now at work among those who are disobedient." For commentary, see T. Yoder Neufeld, *Ephesians*, whose title for 2:2 is "Under Control of an Evil Power" (92).

30. Schottroff, "Give to Caesar," 242–43. The full quote, with my inserts, is: The root of the [Empires'] problem [with the early Christians] was their resistance against Satan and sin as the true rulers of this world, the resistance that had shaped Christian practice through and through.

31. Ibid., 244.

32. Stubbs's view meshes well with Schottroff's.

33. Two studies complement this chapter: T. Yoder Neufeld, "Resistance," 56–81; Weaver, "Resistance."

34. See Wengst, *Pax Romana*.

itself in both Satan's personal attacks on Jesus' followers and in the socioeconomic and political powers that "rule" the world.[35]

In *Covenant of Peace* I describe the sharp difference between how the Empire understood *peace* and how the early church understood *peace*.[36] The Empire killed enemies to maintain peace whereas Jesus killed the enmity that makes enemies. Warfare metaphors occur often in the NT. For both Jesus and Paul the war is against evil in all its forms, with Jesus' command to love enemies as the bottom line for winning the war against Satan and his demons. Paul proclaims God's victory over the powers through Jesus' death (cross!) and resurrection. Mauser writes,

> The whole struggle is not against but, without abridgment and reservation, for the benefit of and on behalf of all human life, including the human adversary. The battle against Satan does include the command, "Love your enemies and pray for those who persecute you" (Matt. 5:44); in fact, love to the human enemy is the very battle line at which the victory over God's adversary is decided.[37]

The bottom line in both Pilgrim's and Schottroff's work is: Christian believers take a stand against evil, the work of Satan and his demons. This stand guides discernment to know when to not resist (be subordinate) and when to resist (e.g., conscientious objection to war; refusal to participate) and persevere therein, praising the Lord God Almighty and the Lamb in the face of persecution (the model in Revelation). Resistance, of whatever type, never resorts to violence, military power, or armed revolution (see chapter 10). Paul's own experience with Roman rule and the so-called *pax Romana* was decidedly mixed. Although a Roman citizen by birth, he often experienced the Empire's harsh and cruel face. In 2 Corinthians 11:23–33, Paul enumerates his sufferings, beatings, torture, stoning, imprisonment, banishment, and nocturnal escape over a Damascus wall. Both Jewish and Roman officials were responsible for these actions. Paul was not naïve about Roman injustice and killing enemies.

Luise Schottroff's correlation of Romans 12—13 with Matthew 5:38–48 is most helpful. Her view on the paradoxical and necessary relationship between Christian resistance and nonresistance is theologically and exegetically profound. She identifies a sevenfold paranesis:

> "Do not curse" (12:14).

---

35. Schottroff, "Give," 242–43. Schottroff's epigram for this chapter states the problem well.

36. For description of the Empire's "peace" in contrast to Paul's view, see my *Covenant*, 38–40, 245–51.

37. Mauser, *Gospel*, 174.

"Repay no one evil for evil" (12:17).

"Never avenge yourselves" (12:19).

"Do not be overcome by evil, but overcome evil with good" (12:21).

"Leave it to the wrath of God" (12:19).

"Vengeance is mine" (12:19).

"If your enemy is hungry, feed him, . . . for by so doing you will heap burning coals upon his head" (12:20).[38]

Each of these admonitions protects against evil and the evil one's strategies to tempt us into sin and evil. They are also *peacemaking means to peaceable ends*. As Hays writes, "There is not a syllable in the Pauline letters that can be cited in support of Christians employing violence."[39] The devil loves violence and incites it when he can, even in Christians who confess Jesus as Savior and Lord. Christians have supported wars and participated in them, believing that violence overcomes evil. It does not. Violence begets more violence. The classic case of this century is the toppling of Saddam Hussein to defeat what was perceived to be a chemical threat, now known to be errant. The result was the rise of ISIS and its terror. The horrible, prolonged war in Syria exemplifies the same. Millions have been killed, and peace is still elusive (in 2018).

Some interpreters take the image of heaping burning coals upon the enemy's head as a form of violence or consigning the enemy to God's judgment, but as Fitzmyer, after examining numerous interpretations, writes, this action must concur with the spirit of the other exhortations, i.e., extending a loving response.[40] W. Klassen proposed such an interpretation, appealing to an Egyptian ritual in which coals of fire carried upon one's head (in a pan) symbolized penitence, and thus conversion from wrong to right action.[41]

Toews also regards this image congruent with acts of kindness in this larger exhortation:

> Such action [kindness] Paul explains with the strategic metaphor of *burning coals upon his head*, signifying that it will confuse the opponent. It is not clear whether the metaphor connotes judgment (Zerbe, 1992: 182–84, 196–201) or symbolizes contrition

---

38. Schottroff, "Give," 223–57, with section titled, "Make Room for God's Wrath: Romans 12:14–21."

39. Hays, *Moral*, 331.

40. Fitzmyer, *Romans*, 657–58.

41. W. Klassen, "Coals of Fire," 337–50.

and repentance (Klassen, 1962: 337–350). But the exhortation to act kindly is clear. Responding to evil with hospitality and kindness has a positive effect—it unsettles the enemy. The final counter-action uses the imagery of a Christian standing in the middle of a battle with the evil of the present age. Do not respond to the power of evil by using the means of evil, hostility or retaliation, but with the power of good.[42]

Might the GNB translation hit the nail on the head: "burning with shame"? In that honor and shame culture this image connotes "shamed to repentance."

Does the stance of non-retaliation and kindness toward enemies extend to Paul's exhortations to believers in their relationship to the governing authorities (13:1–7)? Paul exhorts believers to live in peace (*eirēneuontes*; Rom 12:18) and not retaliate. "Nonretaliation is thus both a loving and witness-bearing activity" (Gorman).[43] It resists evil through the power of love and deeds of kindness.

To sum up these insights for understanding Romans 12:9–13:10, I note the recurring emphases (8x: 12:9, 17(2), 21(2); 13:3, 4, 10) on how to respond to evil: either to *ponēron* as in 12:9) or *kakos/evil* in the sense of *bad*. Paul's answer is unmistakably clear:

1. Hate (stay clear of) evil (*to ponēron*)
   but hold fast to the good (*to agathon*) (12:9).

2. Bless those who persecute you,
   bless and do not curse (12:14).

3. Repay no one evil (*kakon*) for evil (*kakou*)
   but focus on good (*kala*)
   and making peace (*eirēneuontes*) (12:17–18).

4. Do not be conquered by evil (*kakou*)
   but conquer evil (*kakon*) with good (*agathon*) (12:21).

5. Be subject to the authority(ies), who is (to be)
   a terror to evil (*kakō*),
     not to good (*agathō*);
   he is God's servant to you (13:3)
     unto the good (*agathō*).
   If you do evil (*kakon*), fear,
   for the servant avenges God's wrath (*orgē*) against evil
     (*kakon*) (13:4).

---

42. Toews, *Romans*, 312.
43. Gorman, *Cruciformity*, 248, and *Becoming*, 96–97, 166, 177, 236n61.

Be subject therefore not only to avoid wrath (*orgē*),
but also for the sake of conscience (13:5).

6. Pay what is owed (*opheilas*);
owe (*opheilete*) no one anything but love (*agapē*) (13:7-8).

7. Whoever loves (*ho agapon*) fulfills the law (!)
whoever loves (*ho agapon*) the neighbor
does no evil (*kakon*) to the neighbor (adultery, killing, stealing, coveting)

Love (*agapē*), therefore, is a fulfillment of the law (13:9, 10).

Note also the contrast between the works of darkness and the armor of light in 13:12.

Peacemaking, doing good, and loving the neighbor (enemy) are the Christian responses to evil; avenging evil is forbidden, for vengeance (*ekdikos* used three times, 12:17, 19; 13:4) belongs to God and the servant of wrath (*orgē*), used three times, 12:19; 13:4, 5).

Believers' "Warfare" Against the "Powers"[44]

When Paul speaks of "warfare," he says, "we do not wage war according to human standards; for the weapons of our warfare are not merely human, but they have divine power to destroy strongholds" (2 Cor 10:3-4). Similarly, the call to resist (*anthistēnai*) evil (Eph 6:13), refers to spiritual warfare, not military warfare. This is *not* the "crusader" image that impelled Christians through the centuries into horrific persecution of its "enemies." Under Theodotian II's reign in the fifth century Christians began persecuting Jews.[45] Such massacres are worlds away from standing clothed with Christian armor against the "principalities and powers," or against the wiles of the devil (Eph 6:11). *Refusing* participation in persecutions was itself "spiritual warfare." Military war violates what Jesus and the NT teaches.[46]

Harnack has described well Paul's "warfare" texts:

> We encounter immediately with Paul a number of warlike-sounding admonitions and images (1 Thess 5:8; 2 Cor 6:7; Rom 6:13-14, 23; 13:12; Eph 6:10-18), and we see that they have their

---

44. See T. Yoder Neufeld's excellent discussion of 6:10-18 (*Ephesians*, 290-316) and his Essay on "Powers" (*Ephesians*, 353-59).

45. For an overview of the horrible attacks on Jewish communities in the fifth century under Theodotion II, see Küng's encyclopedic work, *Religious*, 153-54.

46. Here see my description of the Pacifist/Nonresistant position in *Slavery*, 112-37.

origin in the images of the Old Testament prophets. This is particularly clear with the most extended allegory of this kind (Eph 6:10–18). But even its detailed execution shows at once that virtually everything, the weaponry and the battle, is meant in a spiritual sense. It states expressly that it is concerned with the "gospel of peace." So the whole presentation is given the character of a lofty paradox, and the military element is neutralized.[47]

The use of *warfare language*, however, is problematic, an issue that cannot be glossed over. Miroslav Volf, in his brilliant *Exclusion and Embrace*, points us in the right direction:

> Is not the language of "struggle" and "combat" inappropriate, however? Does it not run at cross-purposes with nonviolence? Consider the fact that Jesus' public ministry—his proclamation and enactment of the reign of God as the reign of God's truth and God's justice—was not a drama played out on an empty stage, vacated by other voices and actors. An empty stage was unavailable to him, as it is unavailable to us. It was there only in the beginning, before the dawn of creation. On the empty stage of nonexistence, God enacted the drama of creation—and the world came into being. Every subsequent drama is performed on an occupied stage: all spectators are performers. Especially in a creation infested with sin, the proclamation and enactment of the kingdom of truth and justice is never an act of pure positing, but always already a transgression into spaces occupied by others. Active opposition to the kingdom of Satan, the kingdom of deception and oppression, is therefore inseparable from the proclamation of the kingdom of God. It is this opposition that brought Jesus Christ to the cross; and it is this opposition that gave meaning to his nonviolence. It takes the struggle against deception and oppression to transform nonviolence from barren negativity into a creative possibility, from a quicksand into a foundation of a new world.[48]

The numerous NT texts employing warfare imagery do not negate the ethic of non-retaliation and love of enemy. Analogous to the theology of God as Warrior in the OT, God's prerogative makes it possible for humans to be nonviolent. Believers are called to trust in God's protection and provision.[49] Standing against evil by putting on God's armor of "truth,

---

47. Harnack, *Militia*, 35–36.
48. Volf, *Exclusion and Embrace*, 293.
49. See Lind, *Yahweh*; Longman and Reid, *God*; and Boyd, *God at War*.

justice, peace, et al." is the best antidote to waging military warfare, as the early church understood.[50]

The martial imagery and conflict between good and evil in Pauline writings is the logical extension of Jesus' confrontation of the demonic power in the Gospels. Wink's study of "power" language in *Naming* and *Unmasking* see this as one whole.[51] The *personal* and *systemic, structural* aspects are present in both the Gospels and the Pauline writings.

Paul regards the Christian gospel as both an assault against and protection from the evil powers. Ephesians 6:10–18 is a call to Christian warfare. This spiritual armor is derived from Isaiah where it earlier described God's battle against chaos and evil. The correlation is:

- girdlebelt around waist   Isa 11:5
- breastplate of righteousness   Isa 59:17
- helmet of salvation   Isa 59:17
- feet shod to proclaim the gospel of peace   Isa 52:7
- shield of faith   Isa 7:9b
- sword of spirit, the word of God   Isa 11:4; 49:2

Finally, prayer is the important means by which we appropriate God's armor for our victorious living (6:18).[52] The OT context of these metaphors is important. This text is prone to misunderstanding, unless set within the larger emphasis of Christ's victory over the powers and informed by the divine warfare theology of the OT culminating in the NT kingdom-peace-gospel combating evil. Only then can we understand rightly what it means to put on the *armor of God*. These are divine attributes mighty in power against all that defies God's sovereignty.

The text begins with emphases that permeate the whole: "Finally, be strong in the Lord and in the strength of *his power*. Put on the whole *armor of God*, so that you may be able to stand the wiles of the devil" (Eph 6:10–11; emphasis mine). Most important in understanding this text and spiritual warfare is that it is *God's* battle; it is God's armor. Believers wear *God's* armor and only then are they/we able to stand firm in the struggle, "not against enemies of blood and flesh, but against the rulers, against the authorities,

---

50. They prayed to bind the spirits that incite war: Tertullian, *Apog.* 32; Origen, *Cels.* 8.68–75; Athanasius, *Inc.* 52.4–6. Their prayers do more for the peace of the empire than the army does.

51. I agree here with Wink, *Naming* and *Unmasking*.

52. The larger context of this passage, Ephesians 4:1–5:20, is important here as well. Using the alliteration of the KJV, it is: walk worthy of your calling (4:1); walk not as the Gentiles (4:17); walk in love (5:2); walk as children of light (5:8); and walk circumspectly (5:15). Newer translations obscure this *walk* that lives God's image.

against the cosmic powers of this present darkness, against the spiritual forces of evil in the heavenly places" (6:12–13). Elsewhere Paul states the nature of the Christian's weapons:

> Indeed, we live as human beings, but we do not wage war according to human standards; for the weapons of our warfare are not merely human, but they have divine power to destroy strongholds. We destroy arguments and every proud obstacle raised up against the knowledge of God, and we take every thought captive to obey Christ. We are ready to punish every disobedience when your obedience is complete. (2 Cor 10:3–6)

Ephesians 6:10–20 is not alone in portraying Christian living as a battle against evil: the powers, Satan, or the devil. Leivestad in *Christ, the Conqueror* makes this point, treating Ephesians 6 together with numerous other "victory" texts (like Eph 4:8–10) and the NT as a whole.[53] He shows a strong stratum of unity in NT thought, and especially between the seven letters of Paul and Ephesians and Colossians.[54] Boyd's portrayal of evil includes: Satan as "Ruler of this World," the "Fallen Powers," "Evil behind Sickness, Sin, and Obstacles to Ministry," "Jesus's Revolt against the Fallen Powers," "Jesus's Lifestyle Warfare," and "Christus Victory: the Defeat of Satan on the Cross." He utilizes much NT Scripture.[55]

Indeed, if peace with God (Rom 5:1–11) and among believers achieved by the cross (Eph 2:1–23) is to be maintained, spiritual warfare must be considered an essential feature of the Christian life. The word *katargeō* in 1 Corinthians 15:26 cannot be translated *abolished*.[56] The powers remain as long as human history continues. It is essential to stand against the evil of the powers, however they manifest themselves.

Clinton Arnold puts this spiritual warfare text into the context of the Ephesian believers' past religious allegiances to the Artemis cult, with its various forms of magic and astrology, and to other mystery cults, in which fear of demonic powers played a major role.[57] Christ's victory defeated the powers; believers are called to stand against them with the divine armor: "Victory over the 'powers' is not assured apart from the appropriation of the power of God. Failure to resist allows the devil to reassert his dominion."[58]

---

53. Leivestad, *Christ*.

54. Kallas has made the same point through his numerous writings (see bibliography), and for Paul, *Satanward*.

55. Boyd, *Crucifixion*, vol. 2, 1041–57.

56. Wink, *Naming*, 52.

57. C. Arnold, *Ephesians*, 14–41.

58. Ibid., 121.

Often commentators note that all parts of the armor, except the sword of the Spirit, are defensive. The point is good to the extent that it guards against misconstruing this text as a call to some sort of Christian crusade. In this view, the sword, the word of God, is offensive, since it is the means of evangelism, of rescuing people from the bondage of evil and gathering them into Christ's kingdom.[59] But while the weapons of armor, except the sword, are primarily defensive, the spiritual actions they denote are defensive and offensive.[60] A tension thus exists between the tenor of the metaphor (belt, breastplate, shoes, etc.) and the spiritual virtue or action to which it connects. Truth, righteousness, salvation, gospel of peace, and faith are powerful in confronting and disarming the enemy.

In Christian living, the offensive and defensive blend together. Empowered with these attributes derived from God's character combating evil, believers synergistically extend the *divine* warfare. They are then stronger in their defense to withstand the evil one. The danger of stressing only the defensive stance lies in its fostering what Yoder Neufeld describes as becoming a church that keeps to itself, rather than confronting evil: "The church's true existence consists of the active and bold actualization of gospel truth, justice, peace, and liberation in human relationships."[61] The call to peacemaking (Eph 2:13-17) is empowered by putting on the divine armor, consisting of virtues that protect against and confront evil.

Further, the church as a body is called to this spiritual vigilance. While individual responsibility should not be pitted against the corporate, it "is much more in keeping with the gist of Ephesians to see this summons to battle directed to the church as a whole, to the body of Christ acting as a unified divine force."[62] Both the systemic evil in institutions and oppression in people's lives must be acknowledged, without one negating the other.[63] This inclusive approach to what believers contend against requires vigilance against "the flaming arrows of the evil one" (v. 16). It is important also in that it bears wit-

---

59. C. Arnold represents well this view: *Powers*, 154-58.

60. See T. Yoder Neufeld, *Ephesians*, for the same point. He criticizes both H. Berkhof and J. H. Yoder, saying they "downplay the offensive nature of the church's struggle much more than does Ephesians," 315.

61. Ibid.

62. Ibid., 292. T. Yoder Neufeld contends that in Ephesians 6 God's work as Divine Warrior is "democratized" so that the church, the saints, participate with God in the battle against evil (see his earlier work, *"Put,"* 111). While the term "democratized" may mislead because of its several connotations, the corporate calling to this divine armor is important; it is *God's* armor, which believers corporately wear.

63. T. Yoder Neufeld, *Ephesians*, 314: as Yoder Neufeld states: ". . . the view of demonic forces affecting persons is vulnerable to underestimating the broad-ranging opposition to God's efforts at peacemaking. Likewise, however, a view of the demonic restricted to influences on institutions in society is just as vulnerable to underestimating how individual persons may be bound (e.g., Luke 13:16)."

ness to the full canonical portrait: exorcising demons in the Synoptic Gospels and boldly proclaiming Jesus' Lordship over all powers (gods and goddesses, rulers and authorities, principalities and powers) in Paul.

Ephesians 6:10–18 set beside 2:11–22 blends spiritual warfare and peacemaking.[64] The metaphor, "feet shod with the preparation of gospel of peace" (KJV) evokes Isaiah 52:7, blending peacemaking and warfare imagery. Indeed, the battle is peacemaking, not some anticipated result (*end*) of literal warfare, but rather "standing against" with the divine armor as the *means* to peace. Believers are enlisted, yes at baptism,[65] in the warfare of peacemaking.

Finally, a promise: ". . . the Lord is faithful; he will strengthen you and guard you against the evil one" (2 Thess 3:3). This echoes the Lord's Prayer petition: "Deliver us from the evil one."

Addendum: The Pastoral Epistles
(likely post-Pauline, with a different focus on this topic)

My treatment of the Pastorals in *Covenant of Peace* focused on the christological titles for Jesus that subverted the use of the same titles ascribing deity to the Emperor. The Letters (1–2 Timothy and Titus) strengthened believers in their stance against the evil imperial cult. Explicit mention of evil, Satan, or devil, however, is not pitted against the imperial cult but in the fight against evil gnawing at the believers' perseverance in the faith and holiness of life. Prominent people are leading believers astray, into the sway of Satan or the devil—both terms are used (1 Tim 1:20; 5:15; 2 Tim 2:26). Thus some have opposed the gospel, and turned or fallen away from the faith and teachings they once affirmed. I consider four different text-groups:

Texts using the terms Satan, Devil, or Evil
(all emphases mine)

The context of these verses is also significant:[66]

---

64. Other texts make the same point: "The God of peace will shortly crush Satan under your feet" (Rom 16:20) exhibits a startling blend of war and peace imagery. Similarly, 2 Corinthians 10:3–6 put alongside Romans 12:17–21 presents a complementary set of images, one of warfare and the other of peacemaking. Both seek to overcome evil with good.

65. T. Yoder Neufeld emphasizes this point: baptism is enlistment in this new creation army of love and peacemaking, *Ephesians*, 311–12, 316.

66. See the larger contextual discussions for each of these texts in Zehr, *1–2 Timothy*,

> By rejecting conscience, certain persons have suffered shipwreck in the faith; among them are Hymenaeus and Alexander, whom I have *turned over to Satan*, so that they may learn not to blaspheme (1 Tim 1:19b–20).
>
> So I would have younger widows marry, bear children, and manage their households, so as to give the adversary no occasion to revile us. For some have already *turned away to follow Satan.* (1 Tim 5:14–15)
>
> Have nothing to do with stupid and senseless controversies; you know that they breed quarrels. And the Lord's servant must not be quarrelsome but kindly to everyone, an apt teacher, patient, correcting opponents with gentleness. God may perhaps grant that they will repent and come to know the truth, and that they *may escape from the snare of the devil*, having been held captive by him to do his will. (2 Tim 2:23–26)

The second set of texts supplement the above (*Satan* or *Devil* do not occur).

> Guard the good treasure entrusted to you, with the help of the Holy Spirit living in us. You are aware that all who are in Asia *have turned away* from me, including Phygelus and Hermogenes. (2 Tim 1:14–15)
>
> Avoid profane chatter, for it will lead people into more and more impiety, and their talk will spread like gangrene. Among them are Hymenaeus and Philetus, who have *swerved from the truth* by claiming that the resurrection has already taken place. They are upsetting the faith of some ... (2 Tim 2:16–18)
>
> Let everyone who calls on the name of the Lord *turn away from wickedness.* (2 Tim 2:19)

All of 2 Timothy 3:1–9 is relevant. I cite vv. 8–9: "As Jannes and Jambres opposed Moses, so these people, of *corrupt mind and counterfeit faith, also oppose the truth*. But they will not make much progress, because ... their folly will become plain to everyone." See also Titus 1:10–12 and 3:8–11 for similar *evils*, though the word is not used.

A third set of texts speak of *evil or the evil one or "attack" by evil*: 1 Tim 6:9–12: "For the *love of money is a root of all kinds of evil*, and in their eagerness to be rich some have wandered away from the faith and pierced

---

Titus, 113, 117, 124, 163, 166, 193, 228, 271, 311. In the same volume, see also Zehr's essay on "Conscience," which is *clear* in four texts, in others *seared* (1 Tim 4:2) or *corrupted* (Titus 1:15), 338–39. When the conscience is not *clear*, evil lurks within.

themselves with many pains" (v. 10). Titus 2:7–8 is similar: "Show yourself in all respects a model of good works, and in your teaching show integrity, gravity, and sound speech that cannot be censured; then any opponent will be put to shame, having *nothing evil to say of us*." Titus 3:1–5a is relevant, with v. 2 identifying *evil* in the context of subjection to rulers and authorities, to be obedient, to be ready for every good work, *speak evil of no one*, to avoid quarreling, to be gentle, and to show every courtesy to everyone. Note also the self-testimony in 2 Timothy 4:17–18: "The Lord will rescue me from *every evil attack* and save me for his heavenly kingdom. To him be the glory forever and ever. Amen."

A fourth set (1 Tim 4:1–2) mentions *demons*: "some will renounce the faith by paying attention to *deceitful spirits and teachings of demons*" and 5:20–21 may imply such in the command: "As for those who persist in sin, *rebuke* them in the presence of all."

Timothy and Titus, highly recommended church leaders, had to deal with the devil's inroads into the life and health of the churches. Satan's wiles manifest in devious ways: turning away from the gospel, indulging in pleasures defiling holy living, and controversies causing divisions and laxity in faith. We might ask why the Epistles did not advise exorcism of those turned over to Satan or those ensnared by the devil's tactics. These Letters focus on maintaining the faith. If evangelism were foremost, the Letters might be different. It is a miracle these churches survived. As alternative communities to the Caesar cult, they stood against Satan's evils to maintain qualified moral leadership whose behaviors would give no reason for nonbelievers to *speak evil of them*. Let this be a siren "alert" for our times!

> *Be careful then how you live,*
> *not as unwise people, but as wise*
> *making the most of your time,*
> *because the days are evil.*
>
> —Eph 5:16

7

John's Gospel, Letters, and Revelation

*Now is the judgment of this world;
now the ruler of this world will be driven out.*

—John 12:31

*Holy Father, protect them in your name that you have given me,
so that they may be one, as we are one . . .
I am not asking you to take them out of the world,
but I ask you to protect them from the evil one.*

—John 17:11b, 15

*We know that those who are born of God do not sin,
but the one who was born of God protects them,
and the evil one does not touch them.
We know that we are God's children,
and that the whole world
lies under the power of the evil one.*

—1 John 5:18–19

*I am writing to you, young people,
because you have conquered the evil one.*

—1 John 2:13b

THIS CATENA OF TEXTS represents a third NT dimension of the Christian believer's understanding of and response to evil. In John we encounter a theology of *cosmic exorcism* in numerous texts. We also encounter another twofold emphasis: *protection* against the evil one and affirmation of those who have *conquered* evil in the face of persecution.[1] John's *cosmic* perspective and *select* miracles are unambiguous *signs* of Jesus' divine identity

John's Gospel and Letters

While the context for Revelation is Empire-persecution of Christian believers, the context for John's Gospel is opposition from Jewish leadership. The Gospel affirms salvation is from the Jews with whom Jesus identified (4:22), but a branch of Jews referred to as "the Jews" (John 8) oppose Jesus, and likely the group of Jews Jesus speaks for.[2]

John's Gospel does not contain individual *exorcisms*, but does speak about evil. Related terms also abound: *light vs. darkness, belief vs. unbelief, truth vs. lies, love vs. hate,* and *life vs. death.* Symbolically, even *day vs. night* signifies positive/negative poles: *And it was night* (13:30), evoking the light-darkness motif lacing the earlier narrative. In her commentary on John, O'Day refers to Satan's entry into Judas (13:27) as *possession*, and Jesus' "battle with the demonic forces and evil is saved until the consummate battle of Jesus' own hour."[3] But there were precursors to this battle (intimations in 11:33–35, the hot dispute of 8:31–59, and Jesus' word about Judas in 6:71). Jesus' *hour* comes in 12:23 (v. 24 is parabolic of Jesus' death) and "explodes," as it were, in 12:27–30. In 12:31 Jesus pronounces that the prince of this world will be *cast out* (12:31)! The culmination of Jesus' battle against

---

1. Neither Paul's letters nor this Johannine corpus narrate exorcisms of individual people, a point influencing Twelftree to modify his earlier view (1985 and 1986) that exorcism is a mandate for the church's practice today. See my discussion of Twelftree in chapters 5 and 12.

2. Jesus was a Jew as were all the NT writers, except Luke. This is a complex issue. I have elsewhere assessed various scholarly interpretations of what "the Jews" means (Swartley, *John*, 216–24, 227–29, 520–25). While scholars hold differing views, I agree with Jewish scholar Daniel Boyarin. The gospel is pro-Jewish and anti-Jewish. Jesus' vendetta against "the Jews" does not refer to all Jews, but to those Jews who opposed Jesus. Numerous scholars contend "the Jews" (the *Ioudaioi*) is better translated *Judeans*. But Boyarin offers a more complex answer with roots in the exile and internal tensions between Jews in the land and those who returned and assumed political leadership. Jesus sided with the former. The Gospel is for all Israel (1:11; 4:22; 19:40) and Samaritans (John 4)! See Lizorkin-Eyzenborg, *Jewish Gospel*, xvi and entire book. We must not use John's Gospel to fuel anti-semitism.

3. O'Day, *Gospel of John*, 730.

evil is begun and will climax in this last week of Jesus' three-year ministry in John. John treats *evil* and the *devil* on a cosmic scale, with a counter-triumphal emphasis: Jesus' *glorification* through death and resurrection, the devil's defeat.

John's Gospel, Epistles, and Revelation present distinctive renditions of Paul's proclamation of Christ's victory over the principalities and powers. The Gospel declares: "now is the prince (ruler) of this world cast out" (12:31). *Satan* occurs only once (13:27) and *devil* occurs three times (6:20; 8:44; 12:2)—all in reference to Judas's betrayal. John's Gospel theology, comparable to Paul's *principalities and powers*, speaks of the *evil one* as *the ruler of this world*. As Skinner observes: this term, *the ruler of this world* appears first in 12:31, "within the ironic context of Satan's defeat: 'Now is the judgment of this world; now the ruler of this world will be driven out.'" In its second occurrence (14:30) Jesus announces: *the ruler of this world* is coming "with the strong implication that he is coming to kill Jesus." But Jesus pronounces "Satan's impotence: 'He has no power over me' (14:31b). The final occurrence is in 16:11: 'the ruler of this world has been condemned' . . . Jesus not only predicts the permanent defeat of Satan but speaks about it in a manner of ongoing effects."[4]

In the context of this threefold disclosure of Satan as *the ruler of this world*, Jesus' and the believers' experiential agony *and* also their faith-hope is accentuated: "Now my soul is troubled. And what should I say—'Father, save me from this hour'? No, it is for this reason that I have come to this hour" (12:27) and "I have said this to you, so that in me you may have peace. In the world you face persecution. But take courage; I have conquered the world!" (16:33)

First John assures the believer: "the evil one does not touch" the one who believes and does not sin (a continuous sense is implied), for "We know that we are God's children, and that the whole world lies under the power of the evil one" (1 John 5:18–19). Culpepper is correct in his concluding discussion of the "dualisms" in Johannine thought ("above and below, true and false, love and hate, good and evil, life and death, light and darkness, Christ and the devil"), when he says, "Christology, not dualism, is the real focus of each of the Johannine writings."[5] Culpepper also presents elements of ecclesial duality in noting that opposition between the Lamb and the powers is intertwined with the conflict between the dragon (Satan) and the

---

4. Skinner, "Overcoming," 118–19.

5. Culpepper, "Introduction," 23–24. In *John* I avoid using "dualisms" or "dualistic." I use the term *dualities*, which implies a functional role in the tension between heaven and earth, between God's goodness and evil.

followers of the Lamb. The latter, refusing to worship the beast, are conquerors through their faithful testimony, even unto death.

In every instance where sharp dualities appear, the purpose is to magnify Jesus as Life- and Light-Giver to all who believe (cf. the role of the *Logos* in 1:2–4, 9–12). Jesus is and brings life versus death, light versus darkness, and love versus hate. On the cross Jesus shows forth God's undying love for the world, that his followers and ultimately the world be saved from the *evil one* (John 3:16–17; 17:6–15).

Warren's imagery of the gospel bringing light that sets boundaries for darkness is especially applicable to John's Gospel. In her chapter, "Christ: A Light in the Darkness," she contrasts two "Figures." In the first square, light is only a white dot within a gray-black block, the darkness of the world, which in her imagery connects to the OT pre-creation chaos. With Christ's coming, the dot becomes a full circle with the darkness pushed to the gray-black corners of the block.[6] While she does not discuss John's Gospel specifically, the imagery in her chapter on "Cult: A Tabernacle in the Wilderness" is most applicable to John:

> Jesus is the new temple—his holiness and light radiate outwards revealing and dispelling the darkness. Jesus is the light, life, and truth, in opposition to darkness, death, and lies. Truth, which connotes reality, confirms the idea that evil, in binary opposition, is unreal, or less real. Jesus represents ultimate reality. Spatial imagery locates evil at the periphery, diminishing its ontological status. Temple imagery does not picture Christ as sneakily establishing a small "beach-head' in a world ruled by Satan; it shows Christ bursting into the world to reestablish and extend the sacred center.[7]

Satan's entrance into Judas at the Last Supper is the narrative pivot that launches the Gospel toward its denouement. Judas's role in the Gospel is complex and sobering:

---

6. These two figures appear on 175 and 189 in her book, *Cleansing*.

7. Warren, *Cleansing*, 186. This imagery fits perfectly the Gospel of John, especially because of its emphasis on light, which in John is linked to glory, the divine presence coming into and abiding in this world. Her imagery regarding the temple connects with John's placing the cleansing of the temple at the beginning of Jesus' public ministry, in John 2, right after the wedding. The temple must be cleansed to enable the light to shine into and through it, i.e., Jesus' resurrected body! Jesus wedding *sign*, water into wine, climaxes with its effect: "[it] revealed his glory: and his disciples believed in him" (2:11). Light and glory drive back the darkness. This imagery of light setting a boundary against darkness-chaos meshes with her chapter, "Creation: A Circle on the Face of the Deep" (80–126). Warren expands our imagery, including metaphors, in speaking about/against evil.

John is more explicit than the Synoptics about Judas's actions done under the power of the devil (already in 6:70–71), but the synoptic Gospels also witness to Satan's entrance into Judas as causative of the outcome (Luke 22:2). Furthermore, the statement "It would have been better for that one not to have been born" (Matt 26:24c//Mark 14:21c echoing 1 Enoch 38:2–3) judges Judas's motives as sinister (Matt 26:15 and par.). We might wish the Gospels had treated Judas more kindly. One might contend that his action was necessary in order for Scripture to be fulfilled (Matt 26:24a; John 13:18b, quoting Ps 41:9; 40:10 LXX) and that Judas is a hapless victim. Even so, the Gospel narratives do not attribute innocence to Judas (even if one accepts the view that he intended to spark Jesus to "strike" his opponents with victorious power and win God's liberation battle). My sympathy for Judas arises when I ask whether he could have resisted Satan's entry. John seems to answer no. My only response, with the help of the Lord's Prayer, James 4:7, and putting on the Christian armor (Eph 6:10–18) is to cry to God: Protect me—protect us—from diabolic power entering me and any in Jesus' disciple band today![8]

John's story of Jesus has a dominant conflict between good and evil, devil and Jesus. Only in John do Jesus' opponents (here, "the Jews") specifically accuse him of having a demon (8:52; a parallel to the Beelzebul controversy in the Synoptic Gospels?). But there Jesus is in Galilee; here he is in Jerusalem at the Feast of Booths [Succoth]). Only in John does it say, "Satan entered into him" immediately *after* Jesus gave Judas the bread dipped in the wine (13:27).[9] Only in John does *light vs. darkness* and *truth vs. lies* pervade long stretches of the narrative. Thus John teaches much about evil, its nature and expressions, without using the term. As light and truth, John's Gospel confronts: calling hearers/readers to decision. Some believe, but many do not, for "people loved darkness rather than light because their deeds were *evil*" (3:19). *True* and *truth* are moral barometers in John's Gospel: in 3:21; 6:55 and John 8:32–46. Truth and life companion the way (14:6) to the heavenly rooms Jesus is preparing for us.

The term *world* in John presents a related, enigmatic matter, as a comparison of John 1:10 ("the world was made through him"); 3:16–17 (God loves the world and seeks to save it); 15:18–19 (the world hates you and "you do not belong to the world"); and 17:23–24 (the unity of believers convinces

---

8. Swartley, *John*, 321.

9. Luke places this earlier, before the meal (22:3); after the meal he deals with the disciples' dispute: which of them is the greatest (22:24).

the world of the trinity of love: that God sent Jesus [love implied] and God loves them as believers love Jesus)! The end result: so that the world might see Jesus' glory, "which you have given me because you loved me *before the foundation of the world*" (17:23–24). And also: "My kingdom is not from *this world*. If my kingdom were from *this world*, my followers would be fighting to keep me from being handed over to the Jews. But as it is, my kingdom is not from here" (John 18:36).

In the Gospel God and Jesus are linked to the *world* as Creator, Savior, and Judge. In both the Gospel and Epistles, the duality between the believers and the world is pervasive. Jesus declares, ". . . in me you may have peace. In the *world* you face persecution. But take courage; I have overcome the *world!*" (16:33). Jesus promises the gift of *peace* to his disciples, in contrast to the tribulation the *world* gives (14:27). The opposition between Jesus and *the world* and between the believers and *the world* occurs in John 5, 7, and 8, and intensifies in the "Farewell" discourse (14:17, 19, 22, 27, 30, 31; 15:17–18, 16:11, 20, 33 [in 16:21 and 28 *world* is used in the neutral sense]; 17:6, 9, 11, 13–19, 21, 25 [however, in v. 23, the Father *loves* the *world*, as in 3:16]). The negative connotation occurs also in 1 John 2:15–17:

> Do not love the world or the things in the world. The love of the Father is not in those who love the world; for all that is in the world—the desire of the flesh, the desire of the eyes, the pride in riches—comes not from the Father but from the world. And the world and its desire are passing away, but those who do the will of God live forever.

The alternate loyalties of the believer between the *world* and *God* continue in 1 John. The polarities are aptly visualized by McDermond:

Diagram 7.1 Alternate Loyalties: world or God

Exhortation and First Reason

Do not love the world
   or the things in the world (v. 15a)

                                   The love of the Father is not in those
                                       who love the world (v. 15b)

Parenthetical Statement

for all that is in the world (v. 16a)—
   the desire of the flesh (v. 16b)
   the desire of the eyes (v. 16c)
   the pride in riches (v. 16d)

> *comes not from the Father*
> *but from the world* (v. 16e).

<u>Second Reason</u>

And the world and its desire
  are passing away (v. 17a),

> *but those who do the will of God*
> *live forever* (v. 17b).[10]

Though *world* in this text has the negative sense, in 1 John 4:14 Jesus is sent to be the Savior of the world—here perhaps a neutral sense. But in 1 John 5:3–5 *world* is clearly negative:

> For the love of God is this, that we obey his commandments. And his commandments are not burdensome, for whatever is born of God conquers the world. And this is the victory that conquers the world, our faith. Who is it that conquers the world but the one who believes that Jesus is the Son of God? (1 John 5:3–5)[11]

Then in 5:18–19, *world* is linked directly to the *evil one*:

> We know that those who are born of God do not sin, but the one who was born of God protects them, and the evil one does not touch them. We know that we are God's children, and that the whole world lies under the power of the evil one.

These verses together with 3:8b, "The Son of God was revealed for this purpose, to destroy the works of the devil," leaves no doubt that in 1 John *world* is mostly negative, linked to the devil whom Jesus Christ came to destroy. At the same time "love for one another" is proof that the believers have been freed from the devil-world power and are protected by God. There is a consistent link between *world* and *devil* in 1 John,[12] on the one hand, and the link between keeping the commandments and loving one another, on the other. Jesus' love casts out evil![13] The Matthew/Luke imperative to love enemies is a theological parallel.

---

10. McDermond, *1, 2, 3 John*, 127–28.

11. Here begins the distinctive Johannine use of *conquer* that permeates John's vision in Revelation.

12. Ibid. See McDermond's helpful diagrammatic visualization of these verses, *1, 2, 3 John*, 166–72

13. See my story of "Jesus said, 'Love your enemies'" at the end of chapter 5 above.

In John's Gospel and 1 John *love vs. world* is a recurring polarity, though *world* also often occurs in the Gospel in a morally neutral or positive sense.[14] The context for this is:

> Apocalyptic thinking . . . dominates John's mind . . . That is why the *devil* (*diabolos*) is used four times in [1 John 3:7–10] verses 8 (3x) and 10 (once). Moreover, he repeatedly notes the theme of sin and siding with either God or the devil. The background to *devil* is Jewish. In the LXX, the devil is God's accuser (Ps. 109:6), opponent (Esther 7:4 and 8:1) or adversary (1 Chr. 21:1 and Job 1:6). (*śaṭan* in Hebrew, or *diabolos* in Greek) appears even more frequently in Hellenistic Jewish thought in the two centuries before Christ (cf. *Apocalypse of Moses* 15-20 [*Life of Adam and Eve* 9-17]; *Jubilees* 1:20; 11:5; 48:15, 18; *1 Enoch* 40:7; *Apocalypse of Zephaniah* 4:2-7; 10:1-5). Within the Gospel traditions, being *of the devil* denotes opposition to Jesus Christ and his work (Matt 16:23/Mark 8:33; Luke 22:3/John 13:2, 27).[15]

Numerous scholars have stressed that in John's Gospel believers are turned in upon themselves; some have used the language of "believers hating the world." Indeed, the "world" is hostile, and it will *hate* believers just as it *hated me (Jesus)* (John 3:20; 15:18, 23–25; 17:14–16; 1 John 3:13). But nowhere do we read that Jesus' followers hate the world or the people of the world. Rather, "God so loved the world . . ." is the prototype for the disciples' mission in the world.[16] The term *world* is used in four different senses, though the positive and negative are most readily discernible. The other two uses are derivatives from or combinations within the four.[17] The positive use of *world* as *cosmos* or *people* is interchanged with a *negative* use, in which *world* signifies *people* who oppose Jesus. This negative use in 12:31 occurs in Jesus' cosmic exorcism: "Now is the judgment of this *world*; now the ruler of this *world* will be driven out." But this negative is overshadowed by birthing a new community, "And I, when I am lifted up from the earth, will draw all people to myself" (v. 32).

---

14. World (*kosmos*) occurs 185 times in the NT. More than half appear in the Johannine literature (78x in the Gospel, 23x in 1 John, once in 2 John, and only 3x in Revelation).

15. McDermond, *1, 2, 3 John*, 173.

16. Although the world hates Jesus and the believers (15:18–25), Johannine believers are not instructed to hate the world (unbelievers), even in 1 John 2:15. Meeks vacillates on whether the Johannine believers hate or love the world: *Origins*, 58–61. Rensberger correctly correlates John's "sectarianism" with the Gospel's strong mission emphasis, so that the *world* ultimately never lies outside God's love for it and God's goal to redeem it: *Johannine Faith*, 138-52.

17. See Swartley, *John*, 538, for extended discussion of these four uses.

The Upper Room discourse (John 13—17) is Jesus' Farewell Speech to his disciples. He teaches and prays for his disciples that they will be protected from the evil one, and stand against the hostile world that persecutes them. Brodie views this "Farewell" as Jesus' taking his disciples through a cleansing/purification/sanctification experience that will fortify the disciples from the devil's induction of them into his power.[18] Jesus' farewell speech is thus spiritual formation. This formation prepares the disciples to live in the hostile world after Jesus leaves them. They comprehend this, though, only after Jesus' resurrection.

Spiritual Formation for the Disciples

Brodie sees unity and development of interrelated emphases, taking the disciples through three stages: cleansing, purification, and sanctification.[19] This pattern charts the changes necessary for the disciples also to face down the world and its prince, Satan, to live victoriously. Brodie's exposition of these chapters sees this process in three stages:

> Stage 1, John 13—14: *cleansing*: the believers are intermingled with the world's evil; Jesus' teaching drives out the evil. Footwashing is cleansing from sin.
>
> Stage 2, John 15—16: *purification*: "when the root of evil has been driven out and God is purifying the believer, there is a certain withdrawal from the world, a painful struggle to be free from all that chains the heart." This contains dual emphases: God's purifying and the hating action of the world:
>
>> a key function of the picture of the world's hatred is to highlight the idea that in following Christ, in drawing close to God, one must go through a stage of letting go of the world, a stage of separation, and one must place one's roots where they truly belong—in God. The world, feeling challenged or spurned, tends to feel resentment, and from this comes an antipathy, a hatred [against the believers].
>
> Stage 3, John 17: *sanctification*: "when one's identity in God has been firmly established, there is a return to the world—not as something to be either exploited or idolized, but as something

---

18. Brodie, *Gospel*.
19. Ibid., 428–29.

in which, despite its evil, one works for faith and understanding (17:11, 15, 21, 23)."[20]

The word *evil* occurs in each stage, but the believer's stance or relationship to evil changes throughout this process. In the second stage (16:4b–33) there is both a deepening of the "Spirit-led discernment of truth" and a change in the image of peace:

> . . . the believer now understands the Father's love directly (16:26–27) . . . the negative does not win; one is not alone and beaten. On the contrary, . . . the distress of the world, though very real, has been overcome, and in the presence of the Father there is a deep peace. Hence the final phrase: "I have defeated the world."[21]

A similar point occurs in 1 John 5:4b–5: "And this is the victory that conquers the world, our faith. Who is it that conquers the world but the one who believes that Jesus is the Son of God?" In John 13—17 there "is a gradual disentangling of the forces of good and evil": first, interwoven (betrayer in the midst); second, a division reasonably clear (Judas gone and Peter's denial foretold); third, clearly separated (14—16); and finally, in chapter 17, "evil has been left aside." The whole discourse is about "Jesus' God-oriented battle against evil and the believer's consequent journey to God."[22]

Jesus' gift of peace is interwoven literarily with four recurring themes in the "Farewell Speech": love one another, Jesus' going away, the promised gift of the Holy Spirit (five times in chapters 14—16), and preparing the disciples to live in a hostile world that will persecute them. *Only through the indwelling and transforming work of the Holy Spirit are we separated from and protected from the evil of this world.*

Jesus' gift of peace flows out of the oneness, the mutual indwelling of the Father and the Son, a pattern shaping the Farewell Prayer and Jesus' prayer: first for himself (17:1-8), then for his disciples on the basis of the Father-Son mutual indwelling (9-19), and then for those who will come to believe on the basis of the disciples' witness (20-27). John 20:19-23 fulfills Jesus' promise of the Holy Spirit's coming and shows the inherent connection between Jesus' bestowal of peace and the gift of the Spirit. Indeed, "Jesus' gift of peace is 'from God,' a gift that the quantifiable and fragile peace

---

20. Ibid., 429–33. I have utilized this quotation also in *Covenant*, 301–2, but in a different context under the heading: "Receiving and Living the Peace of Christ." Victory over the evil one is essential in John, and for us today, to know the peace of Christ and the God of peace. This book complements *Covenant of Peace*.

21. Ibid, 435.

22. Ibid.

produced by the politics of this world can never match."[23] Jesus' peace is rooted in the Gospel's new creation themes of light, life, and love, gifts from God in and through Jesus. This new creation theology is the heart of salvation and ethics in John. John's Gospel also shows how the devil's opposing evils are present: in darkness, death, and hate.

Jesus in his first resurrection appearance greets his disciples twice with "peace be with you" (20:19, 21). He then breathes upon or into his disciples (echo Gen 2:7) and says, "Receive Holy Spirit." Here Jesus extends his role as Agent of Creation or Co-Creator with God (John 1:3–4). Jesus conveys to his disciples *life*, a recurring theme of the Gospel (3:15–16; 5:26–27; 10:10; 11:25–26; 14:6; 17:3). This peace and new creation fulfills the OT royal messianic hope: victory over evil. The eschatological victory comes through *suffering and death on a cross*, with Jesus' triumphant word, "It is finished" (19:30). Jesus' obedience unto death, vindicated by God's resurrecting him to life, enables God's decisive deliverance from evil. Evil's power is broken; Jesus is Victor. All the *life* promises in John's Gospel are consummated. In a helpful article, Nelson regards this *redemptive* face of evil important, "For Christians, redemptive suffering breaks the power of evil and its desire for repetition."[24]

Jesus' suffering and death is not the end. God's vindication of Jesus' obedience unto death is Jesus' resurrection, God's power over sin and evil. This co-creation of the Son and the Father leads to sharing new life with his disciples through the gift of the Spirit. Jesus *breathes* Holy Spirit *life* into his disciples and commissions them: As the Father has sent me, so I send you (20:21; cf. 3:16; 17:3). This is John's great commission (cf. Matt 28:18–20).

---

23. Moloney, *Gospel*, 410.

24. Nelson, "Facing Evil," 398–414; quotation on 412. She quotes from Heim and Ottati. This "Face" of evil expresses well the Johannine view of suffering, both in the Gospel and Revelation. Referring to Ottati's citation that speaks of Jesus' "innocent suffering" on the hill of Calvary, Nelson says, "Through the lens of redemptive suffering, the horror of other hills [in our world] is exposed, and those who see no longer remain the same" (412).

Revelation: Conquer (*nikaō*), Key to the Future

And war broke out in heaven;
Michael and his angels fought against the dragon.
The dragon and his angels fought back, but they were defeated,
and there was no longer any place for them in heaven.
The great dragon was thrown down, that ancient serpent,
who is called the Devil and Satan, the deceiver of the whole world—
he was thrown down to the earth,
and his angels were thrown down with him.
Then I heard a loud voice in heaven, proclaiming,
"Now have come the salvation and the power and the kingdom
of our God and the authority of his Messiah,
for the accuser of our comrades has been thrown down,
who accuses them day and night before our God.
But they have conquered him by the blood of the Lamb
and by the word of their testimony,
for they did not cling to life even in the face of death. (Rev 12:7–11)

He [an angel] seized the dragon, that ancient serpent,
who is the Devil and Satan,
and bound him for a thousand years. (Rev 20:2)

The blood of the martyrs is the seed of the church.

—Tertullian, *Apology* 50

The content of Revelation is a vision received by the exiled author, "John"[25] on the Isle of Patmos "on the Lord's day" (1:10). One therefore expects the vision to be "John's" worship service. This frequently misunderstood book does not disappoint. Worship outshines all else, and much else there is! This Apocalypse portrays *evil* in full dimension with its horrendous effects upon human life and the cosmos.[26] While terminology differs, the same war between good and evil, life and death, and faithful worship of

---

25. I use "John" to denote the final editor; the Apocalypse is rightly associated with the Johannine corpus.

26. While not addressing Revelation as such, Adams's *Horrendous Evils* addresses such in our time in the light of Christian belief in *the goodness of God*.

God versus worship of evil-now-impersonated continues. In apocalyptic genre, Revelation portrays God's judgment of evil, in which God Almighty, Creator of order out of chaos, destroys the "destroyers of the earth" (11:18d), a pertinent emphasis for the twenty-first century, in which we see terrorist killings and drastic effects of climate change. Revelation 18 portrays God's judgment upon the greedy and godless Empire.

The christological title "Son of man" *frames* Revelation (1:13 and 22:17) and echoes its use in the Gospel (1:51; 3:13-14). Revelation 21:6 and 22:17 complement John's *water of life* imagery in 7:37-39. These life-giving images, however, are sharply contested by an opposing conflictive ethos that pervades the entire Johannine corpus: a conflictive moral, ecclesial, and political stance of believers in the hostile world.[27]

Differences between the Gospel (also Letters) and Revelation are significant. The genre of Revelation is apocalyptic; its extended visions have no Gospel parallel. Cosmological dualities differ: in the Gospel "from above" and "from below" are oppositional; in Revelation the alternating heavenly and earthly scenes are both complementary but also potentially as different as heaven and hell—when we see what is unleashed through the breaking of the seals, the blowing of the trumpets, and the pouring out upon the earth God's judgments. The verb *believe* (*pisteuō*) occurs in John's Gospel 100x, but never in Revelation. The adjective (*pistos*) appears only once in the Gospel (20:27), but eight times in Revelation to denote the "faithful" who follow the Lamb.[28]

The "predominant dualities," as Culpepper observes,

> relate to the opposition between the false powers of earthly (Roman) authority and the true power of Christ. Christ is the lamb who was slain (5:6), while the emperor (probably Nero or Domitian) is portrayed as the beast with a mortal wound (13:1-3) . . . In the end, the great harlot (Rome) who received power from the dragon (Satan) is overthrown, and those who worshiped the beast are destroyed by terrible plagues.[29]

As with Paul, Christ is victor over the powers of evil. Theologically, the primary axis of relationship between Christian believers and these world powers is through Christ's victory over the powers. The believers, even when threatened with death, do not regard themselves as victims, but as bearers of Christ's victorious power over all powers. The martyr is saint triumphant.[30]

27. Swartley, *Covenant*, 276-89; cf. Culpepper, "Introduction," 9-27.
28. Perkins, "Apocalyptic," 289.
29. Culpepper, "Introduction," 24.
30. This concurs with the above emphasis that the dualities of ecclesial, moral, and

To grasp Revelation's message, in its scope of theology, Christology, ecclesiology, eschatology, God's sovereignty, and call for worship, I poetically sum its drama:

7.2 Revelation's Mode and Scope of Faith-Proclamation

APOCALYPTIC	Via multimedia projection on
	a cosmic screen
	the book of Revelation
	dramatizes
CHRISTOLOGY	how a bleeding Lamb
ECCLESIOLOGY	aids harmless saints
	to victoriously battle
	against militant horsemen and devouring beasts
	enraged for kill
	by a fierce dragon whose tail
	strikes down a third of the stars.
	In the midst,
	around,
	and above
THEOLOGY—	we see a <u>Throne</u>!
GOD'S	A throne—of God Almighty!
SOVEREIGNTY	The Lamb—with robe dipped in blood!
	The martyrs—those come out of great
ESCHATOLOGY	tribulation—in white robes!
WORSHIP	The Lamb's Bride
	The Lamb Hallelujah!
	The Throne Amen!

The hymns in Revelation end and transcend the respective visions of judgment of evil, including the strategies of Satan to corrupt the churches (chapters 2—3) and the wickedness of the Powers, specifically the Empire with its arrogance in demanding submission and worshiping the Emperor. It exposes Satan and the Powers as grossly evil, making war on Christian believers.

---

political dimensions are rooted in the Christology. The Logos brings the light into the world. Darkness, i.e., unbelief in John, has not, does not, and will not overcome the light. In the City of God there will be no night. Jesus Christ is the light.

Conquer (*nikaō*) over Evil

This word *conquer* (*nikaō*) is distinctive to the Johannine literature. Note its several occurrences in the epigraph texts. Jesus declares, "I have *conquered the world*" (16:33).

The Revelator's (Jesus Christ's, 1:1) message to the *seven* churches each ends with a challenge and blessing to those who *overcome* (*nikaō*) the *evil* that the church has faced, or is facing.[31] The following Table shows both the evil named and the promised reward for *overcoming that evil* for each of the churches:

Table 7.1 Church, Evil, and Victory in Revelation

The Church	The Evil	If you Overcome (*nikaō*),[32] promised Reward,
Ephesus (2:1–7)	evildoers & Nicolaitans[33]	"to eat of the tree of life . . . in the paradise of God" v. 7
Smyrna (2:8–11)	synagogue of Satan;[34] the devil	"shall not be hurt by the second death" v. 11
Pergamum (2:12–17)[35]	Satan's throne/dwells, Nicolaitans	"hidden manna, white stone with new name" v. 17

---

31. The messages to the seven churches and the promised rewards are described well and at length in numerous commentaries. See Yeatts, *Revelation*, 53–93. Yeatts cites excellent sources and offers helpful interpretation to the imagery in these "messages" to the churches then, and in the "Text in the Life of the Church" sections, to churches now.

32. This table does not show God's judgment upon those described in column two. While that's important the purpose here is to show the *evil* or *deficiency* believers had to *overcome*, and their reward. Only then does one enter into the hallelujah triumph of the seven crescendo-songs of praise, and finally, the new Jerusalem of Revelation 21—22.

33. The evils of the Nicolaitans were: eating food offered to idols (cf. 1 Cor 10:14–22) where food offered to idols (demons) was brought to the Lord's table for the Eucharist. Sexual immorality expressed their religious freedom.

34. See here Bredin, "Synagogue," 160–64.

35. Yeatts, *Revelation*, 64, along with other commentators, points out that Pergamum was not only where sacrifices were made to local pagan gods, but also the place of the Roman Emperor judge's bench with titles as "Savior" and "Lord" ascribed to the Emperor. Yeatts describes other similar details of significance for each of the churches.

The Church	The Evil	If you Overcome (*nikaō*),[32] promised Reward,
Thyatira (2:18–29)	Jezebel: teaching fornication/eating demon food [see n.13]] "the deep things of Satan"	"authority over the nations" v. 26 "the morning star" v. 28
Sardis (3:1–6)	in name, alive, but you are dead works not perfect in God's sight	clothed in white robes vv. 4–5 name not blotted out from book of life v. 5 will confess name before Father and angels v. 5
Philadelphia (3:7–13)	little power, but kept word, but some belong to synagogue of Satan	will be a pillar in God's temple, with name of God and name of the city of God on it—new Jerusalem
Laodicea (3:14–21)	lukewarm: neither cold nor hot; wretched, poor, blind, and naked	grant to sit with me on my throne// as Jesus is seated with my Father on throne

The structure of the narrative that follows shifts from heaven to earth, with contrasts; the glory, praise, and power of God contrasting to the horrible calamities that come upon the earth, choreographed with breaking the seven seals, blowing the seven trumpets, and pouring out bowls of divine wrath upon the arrogant evil powers and their devotees. The narrative "see-saw" is not only between heaven and earth as well as glory and destruction, but also between the divine and the demonic. What is "let loose" upon the earth takes away peace (*shalom/eirēnē*): wars,[36] nature-disasters, and the "beast/false prophet" alliance persecuting the saints, the result not only of arrogant kings and economic oppression (Rev 18). Revelation presents the head of evil in personalized form: personified protagonists and systemic political structures that oppress and persecute: see the epigraph above.

36. The red horse of 6:4 takes peace from the earth. I interpret this as predictive of wars, calamities, and idolatry.

As Revelation 12 ends and chapter 13 begins, the "dragon" stands on "the sand of the seashore" and "a beast" rises "out of the sea." The faces of evil converge: dragon, ancient serpent, Devil, Satan, deceiver, the Devil's angels, and the "*beast.*" Revelation 13—20 is preoccupied with the "Beast" who represents the powerful, idolatrous, devilish, economically rich, oppressive, and blasphemous Roman Empire.

Against this background persecution looms large against the followers of the Lamb, but the apocalyptic narrative breathes triumph through the suffering of the Lamb and the patient endurance of the faithful saints. For a chapter on this "conflictive" element in the entire Johannine corpus, see chapter 10 in my *Covenant*, 276-95. The conflict arises from the battle between the Beast and the Lamb-people.[37] In Revelation the conflictive reality has terminology that reflects a particular political conflict between the Empire and the Christian community scattered throughout Asia Minor.[38] The conflict is five-dimensional, and these overlap: christological, ecclesial, moral, political, and economic. Believers must align themselves with the Lamb (christological and ecclesial). They must break with the Empire's moral and religious demands: whom do they worship? This entails political decision, to obey God and not the Emperor. Further, there are economic consequences, for they must refuse the "mark" of the beast's devotees that allows one to buy and sell (13:16-17). Thank God, Revelation celebrates the downfall of this blasphemous power: "Fallen, fallen is Babylon the great. It has become the dwelling place of demons" (18:1-2). Chapter 18 details Rome's economic opulence and religious-political arrogance.[39] The great

---

37. John's Gospel has conflictive portions (people of light and people of darkness; believers and "the Jews") that interface with other dominant themes: incarnation, discipleship, weddings both explicit and implicit, mission, healing, the "I Am" Christology blended with a distinctive Father-Son relationship of oneness and love, much clear teaching on belief and behavior, Jesus' Farewell discourse, both future and realized eschatology, a most distinctive account of Jesus' trials and death as God's faithful servant-Messiah, a glorious resurrection with distinctive post-resurrection appearances. See my commentary's Introduction and Essays that discuss these emphases: in *John*.

38. In Revelation this conflict has already spiraled into persecution, in my judgment. Numerous scholars have argued, however, against this view. They hold that the persecution as such had not yet occurred, but the text presents a "perceived crisis" of threatening persecution fueled by the increasing marginalization of the Christian communities in the Empire. I describe the differing views in *Covenant*, 327, with notes. With an excellent summary of varied views (Yarbro Collins, L. Thompson, Barr, Schüssler Fiorenza, Kraybill, Giesen, and Koester) under the heading, "Social Setting and Purpose," Osborne maintains that severe conflicts, even persecution, had already begun (citing Bredin and Beale in support: *Revelation*, 10-12).

39. For the economic dimension of Rome's oppressive power, see J. N. Kraybill, *Imperial Cult.*

Hallelujah chorus in chapter 19 declares the doom of the beast and its allies. God triumphs over evil. The new heavens and earth appear (chapters 21—22) and the followers of the Lamb enjoy the new Jerusalem with its paradisiacal felicities. The glorious end is: "Worship God" only.[40]

Paul Rainbow in his fine treatment of Johannine theology describes the political situation facing the early Christians and the doom of the beast and his allies. Rainbow details the phases of God's judgment, damnation of all evil's personified faces (he denotes Revelation as Apoc):

> Roman military and political might may be supreme over the nations, unconquerable and irrepressible (Apoc 13:2–4), but God has limited the term of the beast (Apoc 19:20–21). Religious acclamation of the living emperor (Apoc 13:8, 12–15) will lead to punishment in fire and sulfur forever (Apoc 14:9–11). Rome's economic engine, the envy of the kings of the earth (Apoc 17:1–2, 15; 18:9–19), is personified as a besotted whore appointed to drink to her own downfall (Apoc 16:19). Three angels streak across midheaven announcing that the hour of God's judgment, and of his compensating faithful saints, has come (Apoc 14:6–13). Then in serial fashion we see the powers fall: the world-system (bowls [Apoc 15:5–16:21]), Babylon the harlot (Apoc 17:1–19:10), beast and false prophet with the kings and their armies (Apoc 19:11–21), the dragon (Apoc 20:1–10). After the general resurrection and the last assize based on deeds (Apoc 20:11–15), the new creation comes into view (Apoc 21:1–9), in which Lady Jerusalem will be radiant in God's light forever (Apoc 21:9–22:9).
>
> This stout Johannine "no" pronounced over a world that will not repent (Apoc 9:20–21; 16:11) but instead only hardens in the blasphemies (Apoc 13:1, 6; 17:3) and curses the very God who gave it existence (Apoc 16:9, 11), refreshes a theme of the Old Testament prophets (e.g. Is 13–27; 34–35; Jer 46–51; Ezek 25–32). God Almighty will counteract and conquer the evil that has permeated his world. God will resoundingly show himself blameless over against the intractability in wickedness that is the root of human suffering.[41]

When the sixth angel pours out his bowl of wrath on the Euphrates river, the anti-holy trinity (note italics, mine) is named as recipient of the divine judgment:

---

40. Swartley, *Covenant*, 284.
41. Rainbow, *Johannine Theology*, 416–17.

> And I saw three foul spirits like frogs coming
> from the mouth of the *dragon,*
> from the mouth of the *beast,*
> and from the mouth of the *false prophet.*
> These are demonic spirits, performing signs,
> who go abroad to the kings of the whole world,
> to assemble them for battle on the great day
> of God the Almighty.
>
> (Rev 16:13–14)

The battle of Armageddon (16:16) is announced as already won, for the seventh angel "pours his bowl into the air, and a loud voice came out of the temple, from the throne, saying, 'It is done!'" (v. 17; *gegenon*). This exclamation matches John 19:30 when Jesus speaks his last word from the cross: "'It is finished (*telestai*).'" Victory is won by Jesus' death on behalf of sinners, those who crucified him. The slain Lamb wins the battle against the anti-holy trinity of 19:13: *dragon* (is identified as ancient serpent, Devil and Satan in 20:2); *beast*: "Babylon the great, mother of whores and of earth's abominations" (17:5) together with "Fallen, fallen is Babylon the great! It has become a dwelling place of demons" (18:2); and the *false prophet* (19:20). Revelation announces God's judgment that destroys the evil powers and celebrates the Lamb's and his followers' triumph over evil. The doom of the beast and his allies, the kings of the earth and their armies, together with the false prophet is severe: thrown into the lake of fire. Satan is bound for a thousand years and the Lamb's followers come to life (Rev 19:19—20:3). Then, triumph:

> Then I saw thrones, and those seated on them were given authority to judge. I also saw the souls of those who had been beheaded for their testimony to Jesus and for the word of God. They had not worshiped the beast or its image and had not received its mark on their foreheads or their hands. They came to life and reigned with Christ a thousand years. (Rev 20:4)

Beck rightly connects this battle with spiritual warfare (Eph 6):

> Our battle is not against "flesh and blood"—individual human beings—but against *systemic* and *structural* evil. In the Bible, these systems are often identified with the image of Babylon [which in Revelation is Rome], the violent and bloody symbol of empire in the Bible, the city that exploits the poor and the weak.

Spiritual warfare is resistance to empire, to the political and economic manifestations of Babylon in our own time and place.[42]

Through Bible Studies with prisoners Beck tells how *singing* breaks demonic power that inmates feel; it frees them to smile and recover their human identity and relationship to God.[43]

The positive response from the believers includes faithful witness, patient endurance, and resistance. This resistance consists in the community's faithfulness to God Almighty and the Lamb, even though it may involve martyrdom (1:5, "the faithful witness/*ho martys ho pistos*").[44] Antipas, in 2:13, is thus remembered: "I know where you are living, where Satan's throne is. Yet you are holding fast to my name, and you did not deny your faith in me even in the days of Antipas my witness, my faithful one, who was killed among you, where Satan lives" (2:13).[45] Via Christian resistance—not returning evil for evil, but a willingness to suffer for loyalty to Jesus Christ—the Revelator Jesus Christ (1:1) echoes the central testimony of the NT witness to the cross, Jesus' love for us in his suffering and death defeats *evil*, for God vindicates Jesus' faithful obedience by raising him from the

---

42 Beck, *Reviving*, 24. Though Beck speaks often of demons, most of his emphasis and stories connect to the manifestations of evil in the systemic, structural dimensions, which develop from personal choice [possession?], or a set of circumstances that form a "religion" of idolatry, such as economics that are idolatrous (161–67) and the *Zeitgeist* that ruled Germany during Hitler's holocaust, a demonic power that took over the minds of good people through Hitler's demonic political aspirations and Eichmann's role as "the Office Manager and the Paper-Pusher of Death" (103–5). Beck narrates similar manifestations of the demonic, highlighting people who stood against the demons, risking their lives—not because they could change the system but because this was what they had to do in witness to the interruption of Jesus' gospel and God's kingdom into the strongholds of systemic evil (see 179–83).

43 Beck, *Reviving*, 130–32. "In the years I've spent with the Men in White [the prison inmates], we've discovered a potent weapon in our shared battle to hold on to hope. If I were an exorcist this would be my crucifix and holy water. 'Singing'" (130). I (Swartley) recall that during an exorcism service, the demon left the person when the group sang "There's Power in the Blood." Demons don't like praise-singing and worship songs with Jesus or God as recipient. Revelation testifies to the same. Demons do not like Jesus, the Bible, the cross, and God's/Jesus' resurrection power that is the power of song that delivers and frees us.

44. The death of Michael J. Sharp, a UN peacemaker in the Congo, bears witness to just such a death. He arbitrated successfully between warring tribal groups. He and a Swedish woman, together with four Congolese accompanying them in their motorcycle travel to carry forward their peacemaking efforts were killed, however, on one of their journeys. Google Michael J. Sharp for numerous posts: in *Washington Post* and *New York Times*.

45 Yeatts, *Revelation*, 64, calls attention to the past tense used here: (aorist in Greek). Mounce documents, Yeatts says, the legend that Antipas was "roasted in a brazen bull" (64; Mounce, *Book*, 97).

dead. The slain Lamb is also the resurrected Lord, seated with God on the Throne. The paradoxical image of victory through suffering love is the heart of Revelation's Christology. Jesus walked this road for us; we are called to follow. The believers resist *evil* in their identity with the slain Lamb, who suffered for and with us.[46]

The Lamb's War against Evil: Suffering-Triumph over the Powers

The image of Jesus Christ as a *lamb* appears first in Revelation 5 in connection with the opening of a sealed scroll, which no one was worthy to open. A "mighty angel" proclaims "with a loud voice, "'Who is worthy to open the scroll and break its seals?' And no one in heaven or on earth or under the earth was able to open the scroll or to look into it" (Rev 5:2b–3). An elder then says:

> "Do not weep. See, the Lion of the tribe of Judah, the Root of David, has conquered, so that he can open the scroll and its seven seals." Then I saw between the throne and the four living creatures and among the elders *a Lamb standing as if it had been slaughtered*, having seven horns and seven eyes, which are the seven spirits of God sent out into all the earth. He went and took the scroll from the right hand of the one who was seated on the throne. (Rev 5:5–7)

Then follow four scenes of praise to the Lamb for his worthiness to take the scroll, open it, and enact it. First, the four living creatures and twenty-four elders act:

> When he had taken the scroll, the four living creatures and the twenty-four elders *fell before the Lamb*, each holding a harp and golden bowls full of incense, which are the prayers of the saints. They sing a new song: "You are worthy to take the scroll and to open its seals, for you were *slaughtered* and by your blood you ransomed for God saints from every tribe and language and people and nation; you have made them to be a kingdom and priests serving our God, and they will reign on earth." (Rev 5:8–10)

Second, the voice of many angels joins the choir:

---

46 Two books that cut to the heart of Revelation are: J. N. Kraybill, *Apocalypse*; Gorman, *Reading*.

> Then I looked, and I heard the voice of many angels surrounding the throne and the living creatures and the elders; they numbered myriads of myriads and thousands of thousands, singing with full voice, "*Worthy is the Lamb* that was slaughtered to receive power and wealth and wisdom and might and honor and glory and blessing!" (Rev 5:11–12)

Third, the voices of all creation sing:

> Then I heard every creature in heaven and on earth and under the earth and in the sea, and all that is in them, singing, "To the one seated on the throne and *to the Lamb* be blessing and honor and glory and might forever and ever!" (v. 13)

Fourth, "the four living creatures said, 'Amen!' And the elders fell down and worshiped" (v. 14).

The action then begins: the *Lamb* goes forth to fight against and conquer evil:

> Then I saw *the Lamb open one of the seven seals*, and I heard one of the four living creatures call out, as with a voice of thunder, "Come!" I looked, and there was a *white horse*! Its rider had a bow; a *crown* was given to him, and he came out *conquering and to conquer* (5:1–2).

Without the Lamb at the center of Revelation's theology and Christology, the Apocalypse would not be Christian.[47] Loren Johns rightly holds the word for Lamb, *arnion*, in Revelation (28x) fits the martyr tradition.[48] The *Lamb* by dying conquers evil. Johns sums it well:

> Our analysis of chapter 5 led us to conclude that the strategy of the Seer is to introduce the Lamb in chapter 5 in such a way as to underscore a central reversal in his apocalypse—a reversal in the conventional wisdom about the nature and function of power in the world. This reversal is set up with symbols clearly tied to the messiah, symbols like one from the tribe of Judah and the root of David. But there is a redefining of the *nature and method* of the messiah's victory. . . . the power and authority—or worthiness—to unfold God's will for humanity are located in the readiness to die a witness's death. At the heart of this reversal lies an ethical intent; at the surface lies a Lamb Christology.

---

47. Ford, in *Revelation*, proposes Revelation is a Jewish, pre-Christian apocalypse. My response? No, not with the *Lamb* central!

48. In John 1:29, 36 *amnos* occurs, echoing deliverance (and sacrificial) themes.

The Lamb Christology predominates in this vision precisely because it expresses best the author's own understanding of the nature and importance of the death and resurrection of Christ for the question of how believers in the province of Asia are to express *their* resistance to evil. The theology of the Apocalypse can even be characterized as a theology of peace, with peace defined not as absence of conflict, but as an ethic of nonviolent resistance to evil. This ethic requires the assurance that the death of faithful testimony is really a symbol of victory—both for Christ and for believers who follow in his footsteps.[49]

Revelation portrays evil in full dimension in its attempt to destroy Jesus' followers. The Lamb, however, is God's means of triumph over evil. Though persecution threatens, believers who follow the Lamb trust God and endure with patience (*hypomonē*), knowing the Lamb leads the way to victory over the systemic evil. Both Satan and the Powers are destroyed, because the slain Lamb, Jesus, the bright and morning star, conquers (*nikaō*). Believers likewise conquer through the power of the Lamb. The Lamb's war is testimony (*martyria*) to Jesus, "the spirit of prophecy" in 19:10.

This *martyria* (occurring ten times: 1:2, 9; 6:9; 11:7; 12:11, 17; 19:10, 10; 20:4) risks death as *martyr* (*martys*, five uses: 1:5; 2:13; 3:14; 11:3; 17:6). The saints *conquer* (2:7, 11, 17, 26; 3:5, 12, 21; 21:7), just as the Lion/Lamb (5:5) has conquered (17:14) and some believers have already conquered (2:13; 12:11; 15:2), even though the beast makes war to conquer the saints (11:7; 13:7). Though the beast conquers the "testifiers" (11:7), the martyrs conquer the beast (12:11); though the beast conquers the saints (13:7), those singing the "Song of the Lamb" conquer the beasts and its image (15:2–3).[50] To God and the Lamb be the glory!

A key text (19:11–16) celebrates the Lamb's conquest, utilizing OT prophetic imagery (Isa 49:2). The rider on the white horse is named "the Word of God." God in wrath judges and destroys the persecutors of the Lamb and his followers by this Word of God white horse rider (Rev 19:13–21). The weapon of the white horse warrior is a "sharp sword" (Heb 4:12; Eph 6:17), the "Word of God" (19:13) that breaks the enemy's opposition to establish God's reign of justice and peace.[51] The metaphor "sharp (two-edged) sword of his mouth" (1:16; 2:12; 19:15) is crucial to Revelation's theology. The Lamb's and his followers' victory is not by military sword, but by word-sword.[52] He captures the

---

49. Johns, *Lamb*, 202–3. This is the most complete treatment of the Lamb and its role in Revelation.

50. Swartley, *Covenant*, 337.

51. Caird, *Revelation*, 198, 245; Yeatts, *Revelation*, 356–60.

52. McDonald, *God*, 259–74; Swartley, *Covenant*, 332–33; Bredin, *Revolutionary*...

beast, the armies of the kings of the earth, and the *false prophet*. They with those who worshiped the beast were slain by the rider's "sword that came from his mouth" (19:21). The judgment is reiterated in chapter 20:10, 14–15. Evil meets its doom! The devil and his allies are bound a thousand years. On the Lamb's robe and thigh a triumphant name is inscribed, "King of kings and Lord of lords" (19:16). Yes, hallelujah!

Christian believers yearn for a new heaven and a new earth where evil is no more. The Lamb's glory is the light, no more night and dying there (Rev 21:23)! Without these choirs singing praise to God (seven times), I doubt Revelation would be in the canon. These great hymns inspired parts of Handel's *Messiah*—in which we hear "King of kings and Lord of lords." Punctuating this drama of the Lamb's defeat of *evil* and his persevering, faithful followers, these great anthems of praise shine as gospel hope. I utilize these hymns for a worship service in which all seven songs celebrate the Lamb's victory over Satan, Sin, Death, and the Powers. These anthems punctuate the chaos of God's judgment of *evil*. Rome-Babylon falls, but God and the Lamb on the Throne and the worshipers who *faithfully endure*, praise and worship.[53]

Hebrew Scripture's account of creation contrasts to the creation myths of neighboring creation myths with violence endemic to creation. Scripture ends with a peaceable new creation:

> In Revelation 22 we have an image of the river of life flowing from the throne of God. Beside this river grow trees and the leaves of these trees are for the healing of the nations. The image of the river of life flowing from the throne of God . . . [is] culturally and politically contrasted to the river of death and captive slaves that flowed regularly into the seat of power of the Roman Empire. . . . Whereas the death, destruction and captivity of peoples flowed to the thrones of the emperors in Rome . . . , the image of God's throne is of a place where life and healing flow out to all nations.[54]

Revelation is God's *cosmic exorcism of evil* (recall John 12:31). The "choirs" praise God, Creator and Redeemer. Singing fervently, they

---

Peace.

53. I have put together two versions of this Worship Service, one shorter and one longer. For the shorter one (30–35 minutes using the NIV text), see *Covenant*, 345–55. For the longer version (45–50 minutes using the NRSV text), see *Send Forth*, 239–62. This one is better for human-inclusive wording in several texts. For hymns in Hymnal Worship books that might be used to complement this Service, see Yeatts, *Revelation*, 463–65.

54. Hange, "Revelation," 134–35.

worship God Almighty and the Lamb.[55] Through worship believers resist the idolatry of the emperor cult. Praise anthems proclaim God's shalom-triumph, an eschatological promise to those who persevere in faithful endurance. Singing saints from every tribe and nation join in ardent praise to God and the Lamb on the throne![56]

> After this I looked, and there was a great multitude that
> no one could count,
> from every nation, from all tribes and peoples and languages,
> standing before the throne and before the Lamb,
> robed in white, with palm branches in their hands.
> They cried out in a loud voice, saying,
> "Salvation belongs to our God who is seated on the throne,
> and to the Lamb!"
> And all the angels stood around the throne
> and around the elders and the four living creatures,
> and they fell on their faces before the throne
> and worshiped God, singing, "Amen!
> Blessing and glory and wisdom and thanksgiving
> and honor and power and might
> be to our God forever and ever! Amen."
>
> —Rev 7:9–12

Jesus is Lord and Victor. We, with Thomas looking at Jesus' nail-prints, exclaim: "my [our] Lord and my [our] God!" *The Lamb-Lord has conquered evil.*

---

55. See the excellent article, Ruiz, "Politics of Praise."

56. *Throne* occurs 46x in Revelation; *Lamb*, 28x times. It is *the* identity-mark of the Revelator, Jesus Christ.

8

Hebrews, James, 1–2 Peter, Jude

Hebrews

Since, therefore, the children share flesh and blood,
he himself likewise shared the same things,
so that through death he might destroy the one
who has the power of death, that is, the devil,
and free those who all their lives
were held in slavery by the fear of death.

—Heb 2:14–15

This Hebrews text is distinctive. It addresses in one long sentence four aspects of *evil*:

Devil

Death

Slavery by fear of death

Freedom from fear of death

What does it mean to say: "so that through death he might *destroy* the one who has the *power of death*, that is, the *devil*"? Christian believers should thus have no worries about *evil*, and even more, enjoy freedom from the *devil*, as though we live in Paradise restored. But for whom is that really true? Why pray the Lord's Prayer, asking our heavenly Father to "lead us not into temptation, and deliver us from (the) evil (one)"? Victory over sin and freedom from evil's enticements are possible, but only within an eschatological perspective. In the consummation of Jesus' victory over Satan, sin, and devil, however, will we experience fully this marvelous truth. Then our struggle ends.

Jesus died at the hands of the systemic structural demonic collusion between Roman authorities and Jewish leaders. Jesus' willing and sacrificial death, followed by his resurrection (see 1 Peter below) defeated the devil, his power, and his strategies.[1] By destroying (*katargēsē*, rendering powerless) the devil, Jesus' death nullifies death's power, so there is no longer need to fear death. God's victory in Jesus Christ makes possible what Paul says so eloquently:

> . . . in all these things we are more than conquerors through him who loved us. For I am convinced that neither death, nor life, nor angels, nor rulers, nor things present, nor things to come, nor powers, nor height, nor depth, nor anything else in all creation, will be able to separate us from the love of God in Christ Jesus our Lord. (Rom 8:37-39)

Christian believers are freed from both the fear of death and death's power over us. The Hebrews text has affinity to 1 John 3:8, "Jesus came to destroy the works of the devil," and 1 Corinthians 15:24-26: "Then comes the end, when he hands over the kingdom to God the Father, after he has destroyed every ruler and every authority and power. For he must reign until he has put all his enemies under his feet. The last enemy to be destroyed is death."

The impressive part of Hebrews' contribution is how so much is said within one long sentence! Jesus shared our "flesh and blood" and partook of the same nature as ours (*the children/ta paidia*), but did not allow the devil's testing (*peirastheis*) of Jesus (2:18) to succumb to the evil one. Rather, he overcame the devil and his power. The text does not mention the principalities and powers but note its similarity to the text just quoted (1 Cor 15:24-26) and 2 Corinthians 2:6-8 where the powers both crucify Jesus and are defeated by his death. Thus, Jesus is Victor over the powers.

---

1. Among the various atonement theories, the Christus Victor view (note Aulén's *Christus*) has influenced many recent treatments of "atonement": from J. H. Yoder to Denny Weaver to Michael Hardin to Snyder Belousek, with significant differences among these and *many other* contributions. See my Foreword to Jersak and Hardin, eds., *Stricken?* In *Killing*, T. Yoder Neufeld has a helpful overview of the contributions, with a paragraph pertinent to this Hebrews' text: "*Christus Victor* enjoys more favour, especially among those whose theology is centred on liberation. Humanity is not so much 'bad' as 'captive,' not so much perpetrator but victim. Humanity is thus less in need of punishment than of liberation or salvation. Humanity is not saved from God's wrath, but Satan's hold on it" (83-84). To understand the covenantal context of atonement, see Gorman, *Death*, an excellent book.

This text continues with an explicit statement on "atonement," intrinsic to Jesus' temptation/*peirasmos*-victory: "Therefore he had to become like his brothers and sisters in every respect, so that he might be a merciful and faithful high priest in the service of God, to make a sacrifice of atonement for the sins of the people. Because he himself was tested by what he suffered, he is able to help those who are being tested" (Heb 2:17–18; both verbs are forms of *peirazō*). Jesus' victory over the devil bears the fruit of an atoning sacrifice for human sins. It is a sacrifice *once for all*, both in *time* and *for all people*. Thus Christ's finished work on the cross destroys both the devil and human fear of death. The word for destroying (a form of *katargeō*, used here and in 1 Corinthians 15:24) means "to render powerless." Death continues for all humans, but its *fear-sting* is gone (1 Cor 15:55–56).

The Hebrews text affirms two prominent emphases regarding atonement: the defeat of the devil and sacrificial atonement. While atonement views have been widely and vigorously discussed since Aulén's contribution in 1931,[2] the explicit combination of *Christus Victor* and *sacrifice* has not received adequate attention, except now in the excellent work of Fleming Rutledge, where these two motifs and six others, including *deliverance*, are integrated superbly.[3]

The next eight chapters compare the benefits of the new covenant with those of the old in numerous ways. Jesus is a better high priest cleansing the sins of the people, a better sanctuary, and a better sacrifice (chs. 3—10), which is "once for all" (7:27; 9:12, 26; 10:10, 12–13; cf. 7:25, 9:28).[4] At the

---

2. Here a text from Wisdom connects: "for God created us for incorruption, and made us in the image of his own eternity, but through the devil's envy death entered the world, and those who belong to his company experience it" (2:23–24). F. F. Bruce, in *Hebrews*, 50, cites S. W. Gandy's incisive lines (which draw also on two texts in 1 Peter that we will straight-away examine):

> "He hell, in hell laid low,
> Made sin, He sin o'erthrew,
> Bowed to the grave, destroyed it so,
> And death, by dying, slew."

3. Rutledge, *Crucifixion*, 232–83: *Sacrifice* means no "cheap atonement." Rutledge quotes from George Hunsinger to enrich her shining exposition: "Christ's blood is a metaphor that stands primarily for the suffering love of God. It suggests that there is no sorrow God has not known, no grief he had not borne, no price he was unwilling to pay, in order to reconcile the world to himself in Christ . . . [I]t is a love that endured the bitterest realities of suffering and death in order that its purposes might prevail . . . [T]he motif of Christ's blood signifies primarily the depth of the divine commitment to rescue, protect, and sustain those who would be otherwise lost." (Hunsinger, *Disruptive Grace*, 361–62.)

4 While *once for all* is most likely to be understood in a temporal sense, since the former sacrificial procedures were repeated, the priests were replaced periodically (Heb

heart of this comparison is the explicit declaration of Jesus' death enacting the new covenant (Heb 8:6–9:15). Within this exposition the writer quotes Jeremiah's messianic hope—for sometime/somehow to be fulfilled,

> [8]"The days are surely coming, says the Lord, when I will establish a new covenant with the house of Israel and with the house of Judah; [9]not like the covenant that I made with their ancestors, on the day when I took them by the hand to lead them out of the land of Egypt; for they did not continue in my covenant, and so I had no concern for them, says the Lord. [10]This is the covenant that I will make with the house of Israel after those days, says the Lord: I will put my laws in their minds, and write them on their hearts, and I will be their God, and they shall be my people. [11]And they shall not teach one another or say to each other, 'Know the Lord,' for they shall all know me, from the least of them to the greatest. [12]For I will be merciful toward their iniquities, and I will remember their sins no more." [13]In speaking of "a new covenant," he has made the first one obsolete. And what is obsolete and growing old will soon disappear. (Heb 8:8–13/Jer 31:31–34).

The blessings of this "new covenant," bestowed upon us in Hebrews anticipate the marvelous "God of peace . . ." benediction at the end of the Epistle. Four important components of NT theology are streamed sequentially, for theological insight and import for Christian living:

> Destroy the devil/evil → Atonement →
> New Covenant → God of Peace Blessing

> Now may the God of peace, who brought back from the dead our Lord Jesus, the great shepherd of the sheep, by the blood of the eternal covenant, make you complete in everything good so that you may do his will, working among us that which is pleasing in his sight, through Jesus Christ, to whom be the glory forever and ever. Amen. (Heb 13:20–21)

Linking Jesus' defeat of the devil *with* the new covenant *with* the God of peace blessing is the heart of NT theology and ethics, for whatever view of atonement one espouses.

In the latter part of Hebrews, *Satan/devil* is never mentioned, but his broken power is assumed; *evil* occurs three times. The writer warns against jeopardizing Christ's work on our behalf: "Take care, brothers and sisters, that none of you may have an *evil*, unbelieving heart that turns away from

---

7:23), it also can be viewed as *for all people.*

the living God" (3:12). Hebrews is concerned also with the lack of maturity among the believers in 5:11–13 and therefore admonishes them to be "trained by practice to distinguish good from *evil*" (5:14b). His hope for the believers to live triumphantly over evil is expressed later in the Epistle:

> ... since we have a great priest over the house of God, let us approach with a true heart in full assurance of faith, with our hearts sprinkled clean from an *evil* conscience and our bodies washed with pure water. Let us hold fast to the confession of our hope without wavering, for he who has promised is faithful. (Heb 10:21–23)

Hebrews 11 is a recital of OT saints who lived and acted by faith, they conquered temptations and enemy powers.[5] Chapter 12 then is new-life-insurance against sins that could and might beset the believers. Its first three verses reiterate the ground and warrant of this insurance, for it harks back to Jesus' cross-victory over Satan and sin:

> Therefore, since we are surrounded by so great a cloud of witnesses, let us also lay aside every weight and the sin that clings so closely, and let us run with perseverance the race that is set before us, looking to Jesus the pioneer and perfecter of our faith, who for the sake of the joy that was set before him endured the cross, disregarding [or *despising*, KJV][6] its shame, and has

---

5. Faith and trust are basic for God's people in the OT and NT, even in *ḥerem* war, requiring radical trust in the Lord God's initiative to miraculously give victory against the enemy. It is notable, though, that *Joshua* is not mentioned in the Hebrews 11 catalogue of the faithful, though Rahab is! The OT prophets called Israel to trust in the Lord rather than in military defense against Assyria and later Babylon. B. Anderson (*Understanding*, 330) translated v. 9 in Isaiah 7:1–14, a political confrontation between Isaiah and King Ahaz, "if your faith is not sure, you will not be secure!" Jesus called his disciples to *faith*, to "consider the lilies of the field." The Apostle Paul presents a rich theology in which the *faith* of Jesus Christ is the means of our salvation through faith in his redemptive work. Faith is a major trope throughout Scripture, beginning with Abraham, whose *faith* was credited to him as righteousness. It is the basis of Paul's argument for salvation by faith in Galatians and Romans. Faith is a major theme also in the earliest Gospel: see C. D. Marshall, *Faith*. Key texts are Mark 4:35–41; 5:25–43; 11:20–25. Faith and *trust* are important to God's people from Genesis to Revelation. I identify selected texts for reflection, to inspire us toward deeper faith and trust, drawing on both the noun *faith* (*pistis*) and the verb *believe* (*pisteuō*): Gen 15:1–6; Rom 3:21—4:25; Gal 3:6–9; Pss 37:3–6; Prov 3:6; See also Isa 30:15–16; 31:1–3; Matt 6:25–34; 8:5–13//Luke 7:1–10; John 1:12; 3:14–21, 36; 5:39–47; 6:47; 11:24–27; Gal 3–4; Rom 10:1–17; Eph 2:8–10; Phil 3:9–10.

6. I think the KJV is correct, influenced some by Girard but also the above exegesis of Hebrews 2:16–17. Jesus did not disregard (the significance) of the cross, but maintained his honor despite the shame of crucifixion. Jesus *despised* the violence the cross represented. A study of John 18—19 takes this view in the context of the first century

taken his seat at the right hand of the throne of God. Consider him who endured such hostility against himself from sinners, so that you may not grow weary or lose heart. (Heb 12:1–3)

Hebrews 13 warns against sins that could overtake the believers: immorality, adultery, love of money, and strange teachings (vv. 4–5, 9)! But this is prefaced by encouragement to continue the practices of the new life: hospitality to strangers and remembering those in prison. Then follow great promises (vv. 6 and 8), and the important salvation-memory: "Therefore Jesus also suffered outside the city gate in order to sanctify the people by his own blood. Let us then go to him outside the camp and bear the abuse he endured. For here we have no lasting city, but we are looking for the city that is to come" (13:12–14). Further, celebrate, for: "Through him, then, let us continually offer a sacrifice of praise to God, that is, the fruit of lips that confess his name. Do not neglect to do good and to share what you have, for such sacrifices are pleasing to God" (13:15–16). *This "acceptable sacrifice" is worship and living that blocks out the devil.*

The book of Hebrews, offensive to René Girard in his earlier writings for all its *sacrificial* language, transforms sacrifice: from scapegoating an innocent victim to offering oneself, from recurring sacrifices to a once-for-all Redeemer's self-sacrifice. The *new covenant* culminates the old, instituting a new once-for-all sacrifice, noted in the closing benediction:

> Now may the God of peace, who *brought back from the dead our Lord Jesus*, the great shepherd of the sheep, by the *blood of the eternal covenant*, make you complete in everything good so that you may do his will, working among us that which is *pleasing in his sight*, through Jesus Christ, to whom be the glory forever and ever. Amen. (Heb 13:20–21; emphases mine)

James

No one, when tempted, should say,
"I am being tempted by God";
for God cannot be tempted by evil and he himself tempts no one.
But one is tempted by one's own desire, being lured and enticed by it;

---

societal ethos regarding "honor/shame": Neyrey, "Despising." By maintaining his honor in the face of the most dreadful, shameful death, intended for the worst of the criminals, Jesus overcame the power of death—and I add—the demons-at-play in the Jewish and Roman powers that incited such a shameful death.

> then, when that desire has conceived, it gives birth to sin, and that sin,
> when it is fully grown, gives birth to death.
> Do not be deceived, my beloved.
>
> —Jas 1:13–16

> But if you have bitter envy and selfish ambition in your hearts,
> do not be boastful and false to the truth.
> Such wisdom does not come down from above,
> but is earthly, unspiritual, devilish.
> For where there is envy and selfish ambition,
> there will also be disorder and wickedness of every kind.
>
> —Jas 3:14–16

> Submit yourselves therefore to God.
> Resist the devil, and he will flee from you.
> Draw near to God, and he will draw near to you.
> Cleanse your hands, you sinners,
> and purify your hearts, you double-minded . . .
> Humble yourselves before the Lord,
> and he will exalt you.
>
> —Jas 4:7–8, 10

These citations from James treat three interrelated aspects of evil. The first is temptation (*peirasmos*), which is not of God but from the human evil desire (*yetzer*) of the heart (the Jewish understanding that humans are torn between evil and the good desires/*yetzers*). In light of the suffering and possible persecution of the believers, this "testing" may relate to faithful endurance and/or wondering why God's power and love allows such to occur. James' response is that this "testing" produces the refiner's gold or makes faith stronger (Abraham in Gen 22 or Job). But there is also the biblical tradition where temptations (*peirasmoi*) are attributed to Satan (notably 1 Chr 21:1 here *Satan* replaces God's *wrath* in the earlier narrative of 2 Sam

24:1).[7] Jesus' own temptations in the wilderness are from and by Satan, which, however, God allows and deems necessary. And not least, the Lord's Prayer associates *temptation* with the *evil one*. James's text clearly says God *tempts* no one, for "God cannot be tempted by *evil*" (1:13).[8] The text moves in the Jewish vein, which holds that every person struggles against evil impulses, which compete with the good desires, or *yetsers*.[9]

The second cited text is a sin-circle around presumptuous wisdom, which at its core is *devilish*. This sin-circle includes envy, selfish ambition, boasting, and falsifying truth, which lead to "disorder and wickedness of every kind." James loads the verdict against such wisdom: "earthly, unspiritual, *devilish*." The *earthly* in the NT is frequently the inferior, contrasted to the *heavenly* (John 3:12; Phil 3:19; cf. 1 Cor 15:40; 2 Cor 5:1).[10] The "unspiritual" is *worldly* (1 Cor 1:20; 2:6) or *fleshly* (2 Cor 1:12), in contrast to the long Jewish tradition where *wisdom* is viewed as heavenly, from God (Prov 2:6; 8:22-31; Sir 1:1-4; 24:12; Wis 7:24-27; 9:4, 6, 9-18).[11] To clinch his point James calls such wisdom *devilish*. Here Davids paraphrases: "You claim," says James, "to have the Holy Spirit. Impossible! You are inspired, all right—you are inspired by the devil!"[12] This harsh judgment is made on the basis of what I have called the "circle of sin" (four sins named above) and the result of such wisdom, "disorder and wickedness of every kind."

The third citation is unmistakably on target with the key topic of this book. In 4:7 James commands believers to "resist the devil, and he will flee from you." (cf. 1 Pet 5:8-9; Eph 6:13).[13] If James would say only this, we might cry out, yes but, just how are we, in our human frailty often beset by temptation from the evil one, to do this? James guides us:

> Draw near to God, and he will draw near to you.

---

7. The relation between God's *wrath*, *evil*, and *Satan* merits a study of its own. The composition of Chronicles is most likely post-exilic. Chronicles concludes the Hebrew Bible canon, the last book in the *Ketuvim*. In Romans 13 the "authorities" function as meting out God's *wrath* against the *bad*, which may connote *evil*. Thus "the rulers and authorities" ("principalities and powers") would be a fourth factor in this study. Since David is tempted to take the census, he as the "authority" is linked in these two texts to both God's wrath and Satan!

8. The converse (*human* testing of *God*) is in Deuteronomy 6:16, "You shall not put the Lord your God to test as you tested him at Massah," which Jesus quoted against Satan in his temptations (Matt 4:7 and Luke 4:12).

9. Davids, *Epistle*, 79–88.

10. Davids, *Epistle*, cites Hermas, *Man.* 9:11, where earthly/*epigeios* is cited "as from the devil" (*para tou diabolou*), 152.

11. See further citations on *wisdom* linked to the Spirit of God, Davids, *Epistle*, 152.

12. Ibid., 153.

13 Davids, *Epistle*, cites numerous extracanonical references that enjoin the same, 166.

> "To resist the devil is to commit oneself to follow God or to draw near."[14]

Cleanse your hands, you sinners, and purify your hearts, you double-minded.

> Lament and mourn and weep.

Let your laughter be turned into mourning and your joy into dejection.

> Humble yourselves before the Lord, and he will exalt you.

Do not speak *evil* against one another, brothers and sisters.

> Whoever speaks *evil* against another or judges another,
>
> speaks *evil* against the law and judges the law; but if you judge the law,
>
> you are not a doer of the law but a judge. (Jas 4:8–11)

These four spiritual disciplines enable believers (us) to resist the tricky *devil* who uses every means to bash us. Notice that *evil* occurs three times in the last admonition. If we harbor evil thoughts or utter such speech against others (brothers and sisters) we lose; the devil wins. We must repent and practice anew, even again and again, the first three disciplines.

To these three quotations from James I add another:

> Come now, you rich people,
>
> weep and wail for the miseries that are coming to you.
>
> Your riches have rotted, and your clothes are moth-eaten.
>
> Your gold and silver have rusted, and their rust will be evidence against you,
>
> and it will eat your flesh like fire.
>
> You have laid up treasure for the last days.
>
> Listen! The wages of the laborers who mowed your fields,
>
> which you kept back by fraud, cry out, and the cries of the harvesters
>
> have reached the ears of the Lord of hosts.
>
> You have lived on the earth in luxury and in pleasure;
>
> you have fattened your hearts in a day of slaughter.
>
> You have condemned and murdered the righteous one,
>
> who does not resist you. (Jas 5:1–6)

---

14. Ibid.

This text does not mention temptation, devil, or Satan. But it recognizes that riches may harm the spiritual identity and fellowship within the community of faith true to Jesus Christ. It is a deafening alarm against the perversity in thought and action that can come from the arrogance of the rich (the *plousioi*; cf. 2:6–7) toward the poor and mistreatment of the laborer. Does wealth or high social standing bolster one's self-pride *or* evoke a generous spirit to share with the poor within the congregation? Does one lower the wage of the workers who do the hard and messy work or does the employer establish not only a fair wage, but a generous wage? How this plays out in a community of faith will affect the spiritual life of the community, and even worse, make the selfish rich people ally themselves with those who "condemned and murdered the righteous one, who does not resist you" (5:6), likely an echo of Jesus' nonresistance to the wealthy who condemned and killed him (the Jewish Sanhedrin and Rome's well-salaried Pilate).

One might also question whether James's counsel to anoint the sick for healing is related to the demonic, since confession of sin is part of the procedure. The connection is possible, but inconclusive and doubtful since James does not speak of the demonic as such. The anointing is to be "in the name of the Lord" (5:14). The closing, saving one who has "wandered from the truth" by call to repentance, is likewise a doubtful reference to the demonic, though such cannot be altogether negated. For the fallen one likely gave in to some temptation from the evil one.

A song to empower us to resist evil

Here I am[15]

Refrain
Here I am, standing right beside you.
Here I am; do not be afraid.
Here I am, waiting like a lover,
I am here; here I am.

Stanza 1
Do not fear when the tempter calls you.

---

15. Text and Music: Tom Booth. In *Sing the Journey* 100; *HWB* Supplement © 2005 by Faith & Life Resources.
  Music: Tom Booth, arranged by Tom Booth, Ed Bolduc and Nancy Bolduc; accompaniment by Ed Bolduc
  Text and music copyright © 1996 Cristo Music. Published by Spiritandsong.com, 5536 NE Hassaolo, Portland, OR 97213. All rights reserved. Used with permission.

Do not fear even though you fall.
Do not fear, I have conquered evil.
Do not fear, never be afraid.
Refrain

Stanza 3
I am here in the midst of ev'ry trial.
I am here in the face of despair.
I am here when pardoning your brother.
Here I am; I am here.
Refrain

1 Peter

Do not repay evil for evil or abuse for abuse;
but, on the contrary, repay with a blessing.
It is for this that you were called—that you might inherit a blessing.
For "Those who desire life and desire to see good days,
let them keep their tongues from evil and their lips from speaking deceit;
let them turn away from evil and do good;
let them seek peace and pursue it.
For the eyes of the Lord are on the righteous,
and his ears are open to their prayer.
But the face of the Lord is against those who do evil."

—1 Pet 3:9–13

And baptism, which this prefigured, now saves you—
not as a removal of dirt from the body,
but as an appeal to God for a good conscience,
through the resurrection of Jesus Christ,
who has gone into heaven
and is at the right hand of God,
with angels, authorities, and powers made subject to him.

—1 Pet 3:21–22

> *Discipline yourselves, keep alert.*
> *Like a roaring lion your adversary the devil prowls around,*
> *looking for someone to devour.*
> *Resist him, steadfast in your faith,*
> *for you know that your brothers and sisters in all the world*
> *are undergoing the same kinds of suffering.*
>
> —1 Pet 5:8–9

These texts blend the two sides of the coin this book presents. The first text describes Christian behavior within the "Household Codes" (2:13–3:7), which in chiastic form is punctuated at midpoint by Jesus *not returning evil for evil*, thus breaking the cycle of evil by his suffering death and leaving us an example.

Mary Schertz has analyzed the syllabic pattern in the Greek of 1 Peter 2:21–25, which highlights Jesus' new way of responding to evil. She notes that the first and last lines in the Greek are both eight syllables and similarly the mid-line (v. 23b) is also eight:

πάσχων οὐκ ἠπείλει   when he suffered, he did not threaten

Schertz rightly sees this as the heart of Jesus' response to evil done against him, which functions as prototype for our responses to evil that faces us in varied circumstances ("stations") of life.[16]

Doing good and not retaliating evil against evil lies at the heart of 1 Peter. It has its roots in the larger biblical story, as parallel texts arranged by E. Waltner:[17]

---

16. Schertz, "Nonretaliation, 268–69.
17. E. Waltner, *1–2 Peter*, 101.

Diagram 8.1 Psalm 34 // Romans 12 // 1 Peter 3

Psalm 34:12-16 (LXX 33:13-17)	**Romans 12:14-17**	**1 Peter 3:9-12**
Which of you desires life, and covets many days to enjoy good? Keep your tongue from evil, and your lips from speaking deceit. Depart from evil, and do good; seek peace, and pursue it. The eyes of the Lord are on the righteous, and his ears are open to their cry. The face of the LORD is against evildoers, …	Bless those who persecute you; bless and do not curse them. Rejoice with those who rejoice, weep with those who weep. Live in harmony with one another; do not be haughty, but associate with the lowly; do not claim to be wiser than you are. Do not repay anyone evil for evil, but take thought for what is noble in the sight of all.	Do not repay evil for evil or abuse for abuse; but, on the contrary, repay with a blessing. It is for this that you were called—that you might inherit a blessing. For "Those who desire life and desire to see good days, let them keep their tongues from evil and their lips from speaking deceit; let them turn away from evil and do good; let them seek peace and pursue it. For the eyes of the Lord are on the righteous, and his ears are open to their prayer. But the face of the Lord is against those who do evil."

The parallel printing of these three texts shows how crucial and foundational they are to biblical ethics. Peter stands in a biblical tradition rooted in Israel's hymnbook (Psalms). Not returning evil for evil subverts its power over us. We leave the punishment and judgment of evildoers to God.[18] We believe God vindicates believers who "follow in the steps" of Jesus' non-retaliation. This moral exhortation empowers believers to endure mistreatment both in the sphere of the Household Codes or from imperial pressures to recant their beliefs.

First Peter, written to believers suffering for their faith, abounds with moral injunction to shun evil. Significantly, the terms *evil* and *good* (with variants of *doing* evil or *doing* good) occur in partial or complete parallelism a dozen times within the segment.[19] Repetition signifies the author's concern.

1. Maintain *good* conduct ... so that when accused of *evil-doing* they will see your *good works* (2:12)
2. Governors are to punish *evil-doers* and praise *good-doers*; by being subject and *doing good* you put to shame the *ignorance of foolish*

---

18. Revelation uses fiery imagery (cast into the "lake of fire," 19:20; 20:10).
19. Swartley, "Method," 115-16.

humans (same word as in 2:13 to describe the *human* institution of government) (2:14–15)

3. Do not use your freedom as a pretext for *evil* (2:16)
4. God approves enduring suffering for *doing good* but not for *sinning* (2:20)

   Parallel thought, but with the terms *not reviling* when reviled and *not threatening* when suffering (2:23)

5. Wives are to be *good doers* and not be *terrified*, presumably by *evil* treatment (3:6)
6. Do not return *evil for evil*, but rather *bless* (3:9)
7. He who sees *good* days keeps his lips from speaking *evil* (3:10)
8. Turn away from *evil* and do *good* (3:11)
9. The Lord regards the *righteous* . . . but is against those *doing evil* (3:12)
10. Who is there to *do evil* against you if you are zealous for the *good* (3:13)
11. By keeping a clear conscience when *abused* those who *revile* you for *good* in Christ are shamed (3:16)
12. It is better to suffer for doing *good* than for doing *evil* (3:17)

The permeation of *good* (*agathos*) and *evil* (*kakos*) occurring in each of the five sub-units indicates the author's intention, namely, that a particular kind of conduct, i.e., *doing good*, is the Christian way to confront those doing *evil* to us. The text focuses not on sociopolitical institutions *per se*, but the manner in which the institutions and relationships express themselves. Thus believers may experience evil in these varied circumstances: from authorities, slaves from masters, and wives from husbands. The consistent response of *doing good* provides the model for Christian moral response. The last contrast (#12) summarizes the point.

The following text (3:13–22) affirms Jesus' death and resurrection as Christ's victory over evil done by principalities and powers. It addresses rebellious spirits in prison, followed immediately by Jesus' exaltation to the right hand of God, with "angels, authorities, and powers made subject to him" (3:22):

> The moral admonition in 3:9–18 is framed by Christ's own example in 2:21–25 and 3:18a-c: "For Christ also suffered for sins once for all, the righteous for the unrighteous, in order to bring you to God." In the related pericope in 4:13, the believers'

sufferings are to be understood as "sharing Christ's sufferings" (*koinōneite tois tou Christou pathēmasin*; cf. Col 1:24).

While Peter appeals directly to Christ as the moral paradigm, he also punctuates this model with trusting God, the faithful Creator. Jesus' own suffering has similar ultimate warrant: "he entrusted himself to the one who judges justly" (2:23d). In light of the tendency to focus solely on Christ for this pattern of non-retaliation and suffering, it is important also to see its ultimate grounding in God. Erland Waltner points out that "God" (*theos*) occurs 105 times in 1 Peter; it is not a "distant reality" and "not only one to be worshiped (2:5; 4:11) but one who can be trusted (1:21; 4:19; 5:7) and also one to be reckoned with (1:17; 2:23; 4:5, 17) as the final arbiter and creator of justice."[20]

Schertz proposes that 3:18–22 also substantiates the moral teaching of 3:9–17. The apparent digression of "preaching to captive spirits" is exemplary of the non-retaliatory Christ who overcomes evil with good: "In other words, the resistance the believers offer to evil by bonding in baptism and not repaying-in-kind is grounded in a hope that is, in turn, grounded in a cosmic reality. The non-retaliatory Christ, vindicated by God, won over the imprisoned spirits. Therefore the non-retaliatory readers, vindicated by God, will win over their opponents."[21] This elusive text extends the non-retaliatory ethic of 2:21–24 and 3:9–17 to Jesus' victory over the powers of evil. Jesus is again prototype, reinforcing the portrait of 2:21–24.

Another enigmatic verse baffles readers and scholars alike: "For this is the reason the gospel was proclaimed even to the dead, so that, though they had been judged in the flesh as everyone is judged, they might live in the spirit as God does" (4:6). E. Waltner, borrowing from Scot McKnight

---

20. Swartley, *Covenant*, 268, summarizing E. Waltner, "Reign," 237.

21. Schertz, "Radical," 430–41. This interpretation of 3:18–21 differs from most, but it fits best with the theme of its larger context. See Davids for a summary of five different understandings of Jesus' preaching to the spirits in prison and his own argument that it means Jesus proclaimed judgment to "the fallen angels, sealing their doom as he triumphed over sin and death and hell, redeeming human beings" (*1 Peter*, 138–40, citation on 140). For Davids's excellent discussion of Jesus as moral paradigm, see *Epistle*, 108–9. This text, together with 4:6 is the basis for the "Descent into Hell" phrase in the Apostles Creed. For an insightful treatment of this topic, see Rutledge, *Crucifixion*, 395–461. She describes this "harrowing of hell" in iconography as depicting "the image of a rampant Christ treading the padlocks of hell underfoot as he hauls the Old Testament patriarchs and matriarchs bodily out of the inferno by the might of his arm," 410. Her discussion excels since it addresses not only the historical and iconographical depictions, but also the origin of evil, with this memorable sentence, "*Evil is a vast excrescence, a monstrous contradiction that cannot be explained but can only be denounced and resisted wherever it appears,*" 419.

who concurs with J. N. D. Kelly,[22] puts in diagram form three major interpretations (each with different accents) of the five text-components: *in which, spirits, prison, he went,* and *preached.*[23] The crucial point for this book on evil is that Jesus descended into the spirit world and proclaimed salvation-victory over all evil (spirits). What more is said by commentators is tentative and perhaps problematic.

The last epigraph text (5:8–9) speaks to facing evil personally. It commands us to resist the devil, visualized here as a roaring lion seeking to devour us. Scary? Yes! This is not an African safari into lion country, but it is "Old Scratch" chasing us with lion-like intent. This warning occurs in the context of "suffering," which harks back to 2:21–25. For this text, 5:6–7 together with 10–11 are the *alpha* and *omega* inclusion:

Alpha:

Humble yourselves therefore under the mighty hand of God, so that he may exalt you in due time. Cast all your anxiety on him, because he cares for you.

Omega

And after you have suffered for a little while, the God of all grace, who has called you to his eternal glory in Christ, will himself restore, support, strengthen, and establish you. To him be the power forever and ever. Amen.

What rich provision for us to "quench all the flaming arrows of the evil one" (Eph 6:16c)!

2 Peter and Jude

But false prophets also arose among the people,
just as there will be false teachers among you,
who will secretly bring in destructive opinions.
They will even deny the Master who bought them—bringing swift destruction on themselves.
. . . For they speak bombastic nonsense, and with licentious desires of the flesh

---

22. McKnight, *1 Peter,* 216–17; J. N. D. Kelly, *Epistles of Peter and Jude,* 151–56.
23. E. Waltner, *1–2 Peter,* 127.

> they entice people who have just escaped from those who live in error.
> They promise them freedom, but they themselves are slaves of corruption;
> for people are slaves to whatever masters them.
>
> —2 Pet 2:1, 18–19

> But when the archangel Michael contended with the devil
> and disputed about the body of Moses,
> he did not dare to bring a condemnation of slander against him,
> but said, "The Lord rebuke you!"
>
> —Jude 1:9

Second Peter does not mention evil, Satan, or devil, but its chapter 2 is similar to Jude in describing catastrophic judgment upon those "who indulge in the lust of defiling passion and despise authority. Bold and willful, they are not afraid to revile the glorious ones" (2 Pet 2:10).

Their licentious behavior and bombastic speech (1 Peter 1:2, 7, 14, 18; Jude 16) will land them in God's judgment like that of Sodom and Gomorrah (2 Pet 2:6; Jude 7):

> Likewise, Sodom and Gomorrah and the surrounding cities, which, in the same manner as they, indulged in sexual immorality and pursued unnatural lust, serve as an example by undergoing a punishment of eternal fire. Yet in the same way these dreamers also defile the flesh, reject authority, and slander the glorious ones. (Jude 1:7–8)

Verses 12–16 of 2 Peter describe elaborately all manner of sinful attitudes and actions, but do not explicitly ascribe such to Satan or the devil. In stark contrast to these licentious sins is 2 Peter's *gem*: believers become "partakers of the divine nature" (1:4b), which yields a sequence of virtues, in the mode of "practice." This is what believers are and do!

> Thus he has given us . . . his precious and very great promises,
> so that through them you may escape from the corruption
> that is in the world because of lust,
> and may become participants of the divine nature.
> For this very reason, you must make every effort to support
> your faith with goodness,

> and goodness with knowledge, and knowledge
> with self-control,
> and self-control with endurance, and endurance
> with godliness,
> and godliness with mutual affection, and mutual affection
> with love...
> For anyone who lacks these things is nearsighted and blind,
> and is forgetful of the cleansing of past sins.
> Therefore, brothers and sisters,
> be all the more eager to confirm your call and election,
> for if you do this, you will never stumble.
> For in this way, entry into the eternal kingdom
> of our Lord and Savior Jesus Christ
> will be richly provided for you.
>
> 2 Pet 1:4–7, 9–11 (emphasis mine)

This manner of living becomes a strong protective hedge against the plots and deceptions of the evil one. It describes Christian virtues that shun evil and point toward our future destiny: entry into the eternal "kingdom of our Lord and Savior Jesus Christ will be richly provided for you" (v. 11). This is our shield against the strategies of Satan to make us stumble and fall.

Jude, while similar to this, includes the text cited here in the epigraph, which speaks of heavenly warfare of Michael the archangel against the devil, over the body of Moses, which is settled with the Lord's *"rebuke"* against the demonic power.

Lastly the Benediction in Jude (see end of chapter) is one of the few that, on the one hand, speaks of "falling"—presumably from yielding to Satan's temptations—and, on the other hand, declares triumph over Satan's potential attacks on us. The powers, with whatever face they appear, have been subjugated. The praise-phrase, "glory, majesty, power, and authority," ascribes to God and Jesus Christ victory over evil and human dominion as well.

In contrast to this, 2 Peter 3 presents a blatant portrait of human rebellion and sin, and ends with a terrifying portrayal of punishment:[24]

> But the day of the Lord will come like a thief, and then the heavens will pass away with a loud noise, and the elements will be dissolved with fire, and the earth and everything that is done on it will be disclosed. Since all these things are to be dissolved in this way, what sort of persons ought you to be in leading lives

---

24. For more detailed and competent treatment of 2 Peter and Jude, I recommend Charles's commentary, *2 Peter, Jude,* 201–340.

of holiness and godliness, waiting for and hastening the coming of the day of God, because of which the heavens will be set ablaze and dissolved, and the elements will melt with fire? But, in accordance with his promise, we wait for new heavens and a new earth, where righteousness is at home. Therefore, beloved, while you are waiting for these things, strive to be found by him at peace, without spot or blemish. (2 Pet 3:10–14)

Whenever I read or hear this passage, I recall two statements: first, my science professor colleague Kenton Brubaker at Eastern Mennonite University, saying, "We are called to care for the good earth God has made. Why would God destroy his good creation in this way?" Second, at the 2006 conference of the Colloquium on Violence and Religion in Ottawa, René Girard made the statement, while seated, to this effect: "at a time in history when we are literally able to blow up the earth and all its inhabitants with nuclear war [and fire], why is it that preachers no longer speak much about end-time eschatology?" No one answered his question. But the question lingers. I wonder, with Kenton and René, what to do with this text. Yes, it is apocalyptic genre, but what does it mean for us, our children, and our grandchildren? "What does it mean, O Lord?" May our nations repent, and all of us, to avert such a tragic end to civilization as we know it.

Yes, the text, like Revelation, speaks of a new heaven and earth (v. 13), and for that we hope, cry, and deeply yearn! But does the heaven and earth in which we now live and love need to be destroyed? In the context of current enmities among the nations and the development of nuclear war-power within numerous nations, such incineration—at least of millions, maybe billions of humans—is not implausible. "O Lord, have mercy!"

In light of the bombastic evils Jude mentions, his benediction shines!

Now to him who is able to keep you from falling,
and to make you stand without blemish
in the presence of his glory with rejoicing,
to the only God our Savior, through Jesus Christ our Lord,
be glory, majesty, power, and authority,
before all time and now and forever. Amen.

—JUDE 1:24–25

Part III

Biblical Practices for Deliverance and Witness to the Powers

Toward Faithful Responses

9

The Early (and Later) Church's Responses

One of the oldest hymns in our current hymn books is:
"Let all mortal flesh keep silence"
Stanza 3 is especially
relevant to the topic of this chapter.

Rank on rank the host of heaven
spreads its vanguard on the way,
as the light of light descendeth
from the realms of endless day,
that the powers of hell may vanish
as the darkness clears away
HWB 463 vv. 3–4

—St James Liturgy (n.d., but early centuries)

Learning from the Early Church

THE EARLY CHURCH'S (SECOND to fourth centuries) beliefs and practices ubiquitously reflect awareness of the powers of evil and Christians claiming Christ's victory over them. Numerous texts in the writings of the early Church Fathers speak about pagan kings, and describe them with devil imagery.[1] Both Origen and Justin connected the worship of pagan gods with

---

1. Ferguson, *Demonology*, 108. After citing a series of texts from the Fathers (Tertullian, Justin, Theophilus of Antioch, Origen, and Athanasius), Skarsaune and

worship of demons. Origen writes, "the worship which is supposed among the Greeks to be rendered to gods at the altar, and images, and temples is in reality offered to demons."[2] Justin explained this by saying that the pagan people "not knowing that these were demons, called them gods, and gave to each the name which each of the demons chose for himself."[3] Tertullian had similar views. Minucius Felix says that "demons are involved in magic, idolatry, divination, oracles, healing cults, and sacrifice."[4] Clinton Arnold cites seven specific texts from the early Church Fathers (second to third centuries) that emphasize vigilance against the evil one, devil, or demons gaining entrance into the believers' life.[5] These texts associate the devil with false teachings by certain people (Marcion) or the heretical Gnostics, especially those deceived by Valentinus, who mislead people into heresy, which one text identifies with idolatry:

> Tertullian (2nd-3rd centuries A.D.) "no one ought to doubt [that] 'spiritual wickednesses,' from which also heresies come, have been introduced by the devil, or that there is any real difference between heresies and idolatry, seeing that they appertain both to the same author and to the same work that idolatry does." (*Prescription against Heretics*, 40).[6]

Engelsviken, in "Possession," says,

> These texts reveal common themes that occur throughout the teaching of the ancient church. The first theme is the gods of the Gentiles are considered to be demons. The roots of this concept lie in the Old Testament, where the existence of the gods of the Gentiles are not denied. In Psalm 96:5, for example, the gods of the peoples are referred to as *'ĕlilim*. This word often stands in a synonymous parallelism with the word "idol," but also to *shedim*, "demons" (Deut. 32:17; Ps. 106:37), and *se'irim*, "evil spirits" (Lev. 17:7; 2 Chron. 11:15; Isa. 13:21; 32:14). In Deut. 32:17 it is said of apostate Israel: "They sacrificed to demons who were not God, but gods whom they have not known . . ." The second theme is the notion that when people worship demons they risk being possessed by them. (In Moreau et al., eds., *Deliver*, 69–70.)

2. *Against Celsus* VIII.69; cf. VII.65; cited by Ferguson, *Demonology*, 112, 137n27.

3. *1 Apology* 5; cf. 9; Ferguson, ibid.

4. Ferguson, *Demonology*, devotes two pages to Minucius Felix, 112–13 and cites *Octavius* 26–27 as source. Minucius Felix casts a wide swath for demon-influence: including astrology, sooth saying, divination, and necromancy (113).

5. *Epistle of Barnabas* 2.10; *Shepherd of Hermas* (Mandate 11:3–4); Ignatius (*Letter to the Trallians* 6–8); Justin Martyr, two citations from *Apology* 58 and 26; Irenaeus, *Against Heresies* 1.13.1, 3, 4 and 5.26.2; Tertullian, *Prescriptions against Heretics* 40; and Cyprian, *Treatise* 1.3. See C. Arnold, *Three*, 60–61.

6. C. Arnold, *Three*, 61.

The church of the first three centuries did not directly confront or challenge the powers but perceived itself to be a contrast community to the world ruled by the evil powers. The early church witnessed to the power of Jesus Christ's victory on the cross, God's resurrection of Jesus from the dead, and God's exaltation of Jesus Christ to God's right hand, with all powers subject to him (1 Pet 3:22). The church served not the Roman Emperor, but Jesus Christ as Lord and King! The church proclaimed God's triumph over the powers in both political and personal spheres.

In light of this pattern we today do not so much need to confront the political powers directly because Jesus Christ has done that decisively in the cross and resurrection.[7] Rather, by life and word we present another community construct, in which love and care for one another are core virtues. This does not mean we do not witness to the powers (see chapter 10). There is a difference, however, between living in the early centuries under totalitarian Empire rule and living in democratic countries. Democratic citizens have the right and are encouraged to express their views. Christians thus ought to speak against policies that oppress the poor and disadvantaged, and those that foment wars abroad and strife within the country (see point 2 below and chapter 10). Martin Luther King did this memorably in his "How Long? Not Long" speech: "How long will justice be crucified and truth bear it?" King asked the 25,000-strong crowd. "How long? Not long, because the arc of the moral universe is long, but it bends towards justice."[8] Both in the early AD centuries and now, the need to exorcize evil in personal or systemic structures is normative for the life of God's kingdom community.

Exorcisms

Everett Ferguson, a widely respected church historian, has shown in his thorough study, *Demonology of the Early Christian World*,[9] that exorcism of evil spirits from men and women, especially in those coming to Christian faith, was an essential feature of the attraction, power, and growth of early Christianity, even amid a political situation where the political powers oppressed and persecuted Christians. Ferguson regards the early church's

---

7. "[W]e need not, nor should not confront the powers because Jesus Christ has done that. We rather bear witness to Christ's victory over the powers. We bear this witness most faithfully when we are truly the church, with Jesus as Lord, with freedom from the tyranny of the powers." J. H. Yoder, *Politics* 148–49, 157–58.

8. See: https://www.scotsman.com/news/politics/insight-civil-rights-50-years-after-martin-luther-king-1-4716411.

9. Ferguson, *Demonology*, 129–34.

ability to deal with spirit world as an essential part of its missionary success in the first three centuries.

> The most notable mark of the early church was its ability to deal with the spirit world in the Roman Empire. . . . I am persuaded that an important factor in the Christian's success in the Roman world was the promise . . . it made of deliverance from demons.[10]

In the early centuries of the church the Christian mission was shaped by Jesus Christ's victory over demons. The bishop's office was "to tread down Satan under his feet." Membership in the Christian church by baptism was preceded by dramatic exorcisms. This binding of Satan's power enabled the gospel to flourish, with more and more peoples turning from pagan worship to worship of the true God. Christian believers thus gained immunity from sorcery.[11]

Ferguson further observes that the early church fathers regarded Jesus' death and resurrection as the defeat of Satan. For Irenaeus, "Christ's victory over the devil [is] the key motif in developing his doctrine of the atonement!"[12] The preaching of the gospel is a means to defeat the demons. It brings the victory of Christ to bear upon oppression here and now, and releases humans from Satan's tyranny. "By reason of . . . baptism," Irenaeus says, "Christians are delivered from the power of demons and have been identified with Christ . . . They should have every confidence that they can prevail against the demons."[13] People coming to the gospel were under the power of the demons of pagan religions. Since baptism was the climax of expelling the demon powers, candidates entered into a lengthy period of catechism that included exorcist prayers. Baptism was the climax of this decisive break with the powers of darkness.[14]

Catechism and baptism regularly included exorcism in many parts of the early Christian church. Since catechumens were baptized often on Easter morning, the six preceding weeks of Lent were devoted to cleansing the new believer from the defilement of idolatry. The baptizands went to the priest every morning for prayers focusing on the power of the gospel to break every demonic influence, thus transferring the baptizand from darkness into light

10. Kreider, *Change*, 129.
11. Brown, "Sorcery," 136.
12. Ferguson, *Demonology*, 124.
13. Adapted from ibid., 125.
14. See Kreider, *Change*, 17. Kreider describes further the stages of this catechetical process that includes exorcism: Kreider, *Patient*, 107–14; 133–84. *Patient* also addresses the stance of the church to Empire pressures and occasional persecution.

(Col 1:14). Growth of the Christian church promising deliverance from demons confounded the powers. The church, both nonresistant and resistant to the Empire's evils, thus suffered persecution and martyrdom.[15]

In his careful study of why early Christianity flourished, Alan Kreider, concurring with Ramsay McMullen, says exorcism was the chief factor in conversion, attracting people from the pagan world to Christianity because of its power over evil spirits. Kreider cites numerous sources from the Fathers, including a report from Origen: someone attending Origen's instruction of catechumens suddenly cried out under the power of an impure spirit when Origen cited the words of Hannah: "My heart has exulted in the Lord." Origen continued to instruct from Hannah's hymn of praise, while others spoke to the woman, who under the power of Origen's continued exposition of Hannah's hymn of praise to God was eventually set free. Such episodes were not infrequent in early Christianity, and became a key factor in the church's growth. Origen says, "Things like this lead many people to be converted to God . . . to come to the faith."[16]

Kreider describes the early church's preparation of catechumens for baptism. In some parts of the church, especially the Eastern sector and prior to Constantine, the instruction would last for three to five years, and regularly include exorcist prayers for candidates. Not only was the final act of the bishop before baptism an exorcist prayer, but the baptismal vow included a renunciation of Satan as well as confession of faith in God as Father, Son, and Holy Spirit.[17] Upon ascending from baptism by immersion, after years of preparation in teaching and exorcism, the person entered the life of the church as a full member, eligible to partake of the Eucharist.[18] Wink too asserts that for the early Christians, baptism was viewed as *exorcism*,[19] quoting Justin Martyr: the "Son of God became man 'for the destruction of the devil.'"[20]

The early church knew what most modern and postmodern churches have forgotten: that preparation for baptism and baptism itself are practices

---

15. Ibid., 129. See Woolley, *Exorcism*, for extensive study of exorcism and healing of the sick in the early church.

16. Kreider, *Change*, 17.

17. Persons in certain types of work were excluded from baptismal catecheticism. In one part of the church, the catechetical procedure and vows are quite detailed: *Treatise*, edited by Dix and Chadwick, 23–39.

18. Kreider, *Change*, 25; *Patient*, 133–84; regarding Constantine, 253–55, 277.

19. Wink, *Unmasking*, 51. Compare his discussion on "Dying to the Powers" in *Powers*, 95–97.

20. Wink, *Powers*, 89. This reflects the Christus Victor view of the atonement, dominant in the early church.

that include deliverance from evil powers. Evil powers in modern culture allure young and old in a variety of ways, with Satan and his tactics enticing and addicting: forms of sorcery, magic, and violence in the entertainment world of television, social media, computer games, hurtful messaging on smart phones through which one can access all the above addictive evils. Evil often distorts the good potential, and thus becomes a parasite of the good.

However, the older ways of perceiving evil and protecting oneself against it continue, in a variety of ways. Fr. Jeffrey Steffon in a section titled "The Church's Abiding Belief" cites Catholic Church statements through the centuries that reaffirm "belief in the existence of the devil and demonic spirits" and Satan's devious ways to enter and control people's lives. He cites texts from the Lateran Council in AD 1215 to the Second Vatican Council (1962). He cites also Pope Paul VI, "This matter of the Devil and of the influence he can exert on individuals as well as on communities, entire societies or events, is a very important chapter of Catholic doctrine which should be studied again . . . ."[21] Steffon later emphasizes that the battle against Satan is daily, and notes that there are numerous activities that can lead one captive to Satan's control in witchcraft and sorcery: playing Dungeons and Dragons,[22] Tarot cards, and even New Age beliefs and practices, especially Wicca with its goddess worship.[23]

The Syrian Orthodox baptismal rites retain to this day strong exorcist language, addressed directly against Satan: e.g. "I adjure you by God . . . Be uprooted and dispersed. Be vanished from God's creation, O you accursed one, unclean spirit, spirit of deception, and fuel for the unquenchable flames. Make haste and do not resist . . ."[24] A "Short Form" reads:

> In Your name, O Lord God, I seal and cast out from this Your creation the evil and unclean spirit. Depart + + + , perverter

---

21. Steffon, *Satanism*, 32.

22. Dean Hochstetler and I were once called to a nearby college dormitory to exorcize satanic influence in the men's dorm—students seeing ghosts at night and even being harassed physically. Upon commanding unclean spirits to manifest themselves, the problem was traced to some students playing Dungeons and Dragons, with one student willfully giving himself to Satan's powers. This, of course, required exorcism of that Satan power.

23. Steffon, *Satanism*, 45–105. His list of dangerous beliefs and practices goes on. He then describes Satanism, and includes the "Satanic Ritual Calendar" that prescribes sacrifices on certain dates, sometimes human, but more frequently, an animal. Sometimes the sacrifice specifies a *child* of a certain age range (143).

24. These are just a few lines (from Part I, preceded by parts A–H) of the "Exorcism" liturgy on pp. 36–38 (quote from 38). For the full text of the standard (long) "Exorcism" see Samuel, *Sacrament*. In this book the original Syriac text appears on the right page, and the English translation on the left.

and rebellious one, and let Your servant be purified from deceitful spirits. Fear + + + O unclean spirit, the coming judgment. Do not assail this creature of God because he (she) is not the dwelling place of demons. I adjure you + + + in the name of the Father, Son, and Holy Spirit to be uprooted and dispersed, O unclean spirit, make haste and do not resist.[25]

The early eastern Syrian Orthodox and Armenian Churches' preparation for baptism included a special anointing of the baptizand with oil to signify entry into the royal-priestly community (1 Pet 2:9–10). This rite developed from the OT practice of prophets anointing priest-kings and, even more important, Jesus' own baptism, when God speaks from heaven to declare Jesus' royalty identity (Ps 2:7) and servant identity (Isa 42:1–2). The rite welcomes the baptizand into the priestly, royal, servant community of faith (see *Didascalia apostolorum* 9 and 16 as witness to this practice).[26] Syrian Orthodox members say the Lord's Prayer in the Aramaic-Syriac translation, "deliver us from the evil one," renewing the exorcist baptismal rite.

In his book, *From Exorcism to Ecstasy*, Russell Haitch describes eight different understandings of baptism. The chapter on Alexander Schmemann, representing early Orthodoxy (8–16), includes exorcism as part of the baptismal preparation, extending over a period of time. Haitch notes three convictions important to why exorcism is practiced: first "Evil is an irrational power that cannot be understood or overcome by reason alone"; second, "this power of evil is personal"; and third, "exorcism says that evil must be confronted . . . The devil cannot be placated, circumvented, or explained away, but must be dealt with, and the best way to do so is by praying—by speaking words with God-given authority":

> The Lord lays thee under ban, O Devil!
> . . . who also upon the Tree did triumph over adverse powers,
> . . . by death has annihilated Death.
> and overthrew him who exercised the dominion of Death,
>   that is thee, O Devil.

---

25. Ibid., 40–42

26. Winkler "Prebaptismal." This article draws on her larger German monograph, *Das armenische Initiationsrituale*. For a comprehensive treatment of the many baptismal rites that include rejection or renunciation of the devil and all his works, see H. A. Kelly, *Devil*, 161–87 (chapter title: "The Byzantine and West Syrian Liturgies"). Baptismal exorcist prayers are similar to the above (in text), though one also "grants an angel of light to be a companion for his [the baptizand—male or female] life," 186. As Kelly's exhaustive work shows, not all parts of the early church included exorcist rites at baptism. In those parts of the early church they were to be completed *before* baptism. See his chapter 8, 123–57.

> I adjure thee before God.... be thou under ban!...
> Fear, be gone and depart from this creature, and return not again;
> neither hide thyself in him either by day or by night;
> either in the morning or at noonday;
> But depart thence to thine own Tartarus
> until the great day of Judgment which is ordained....
> Begone, and depart from this sealed, this newly enlisted warrior of God;
> ... Begone, and depart from this creature with all thy powers and thine angels.[27]

Of the seven other church-types by representative writers (J. H. Yoder, Thomas Aquinas, Martin Luther, John Calvin, John Wesley, Karl Barth, and Aimee Semple McPherson),[28] only one, Martin Luther, retains the practices of the earlier centuries. The baptismal service enjoins participants to pray seriously, for in this service we confront the devil and "'it is no joke to take sides against the devil.'"[29] My reading of Haitch's description of the service identifies eleven actions (e.g., #1, "the officiant blows three times under the child's eyes, telling any unclean spirit to leave"). Exorcisms begin with action-word #5: "'so hearken now, thou miserable devil, adjured by the name of the eternal God and of our Savior Jesus Christ, and depart trembling and groaning, ... have nothing to do with the servant of God who now seeks that which is heavenly.'"[30] The chapter on Aimee Semple McPherson with its strong emphasis on "anointing of/by the Holy Spirit" implies forsaking the devil, but no exorcist commands occur.[31]

While Haitch has contributed a valuable study, it may be faulted for its choice of sources. For example, in the tradition I know best, Anabaptist Mennonite, the sources Haitch quoted, mostly from J. H. Yoder's article, "The Otherness of the Church"[32] is not representative. Most Ministerial Handbooks of the last century in the Mennonite tradition have included a question to the person to be baptized: "Do you forsake (renounce) Satan and all his works?" Granted, some ministers have glossed over this, but

---

27. Haitch, *Exorcism*, 11. The quote is from Schmemann, *Water*, 64.
28. Haitch, *Exorcism*, 23–173.
29. Ibid., 85–86.
30. Ibid.
31. Ibid., 155–73.
32. In Yoder, *Royal*, 53–64.

many have not. I expect a similar sort of question appears in ministerial handbooks of other denominations Haitch describes.

Webber mentions other features of preparation for baptism. The sign of the cross indicated the sealing of the catechumen to Jesus Christ. Laying on of hands upon the candidate may have been itself an exorcist act, the mediation of divine power against all other power. The priest/minister also gave salt to the candidate, a sign of hospitality welcoming the person into the covenant. A rite of breathing was also used, in which the candidate blew out every evil spirit and inhaled the Holy Spirit.[33] Webber summarizes,

> Rejecting Satan and accepting the tradition is absolutely essential to conversion. The period of purification and enlightenment with its exorcisms and presentations provides the converting person with one more opportunity to deepen his or her commitment to Jesus Christ as Lord and Savior.[34]

That baptism and exorcism were closely linked in the Eastern and Roman Catholic communions through the centuries is well-attested. H. A. Kelly traces this history in *The Devil at Baptism*. At baptism the priest asked the candidates, "Have you renounced Satan?" The candidates answered, "We have renounced him." In some rites, the candidates were then instructed to breathe out Satan and spit upon him.

Another text speaks of breathing out anything of a contrary nature to the gospel. In some rites long exorcist prayers accompanied baptism in which words were addressed directly to the devil, commanding him to leave and never to return. For example:

> Be rebuked and go out, unclean spirit. For I adjure you by him who walked upon the surface of the sea as if upon dry land, and rebuked the storm of winds, whose glance dries up abysses, and whose threat dissolves mountains. For he even now commands you through us. Be afraid, go out, and leave these creatures and do not return or hide in them or encounter any of them or work upon them or attack them either by night or by day or at the hour of noon. But go to your own Tartarus until the determined great day of judgment. Be afraid of God . . . before whom angels tremble. . . . Go out and depart from the sealed, newly chosen soldiers of Christ our God.[35]

---

33. Webber, *Celebrating*, 35–37.
34. Ibid., 82.
35. H. A. Kelly. *Devil*, 164.

As a freed, contrast community to the Empire,[36] the early Christians experienced harassment, ostracism, and sometimes outright persecution from the Empire. The Roman gods and the Christian God had little in common. One could not simultaneously serve the gods of the cultural environment and the God of the Lord Jesus Christ. Changing allegiance and worship required conversion, a retraining and renewal of life that entailed expelling demons from catechumens. In this drama of changing old self to new self, it became crystal clear that Jesus Christ is Victor over Satan, sin, and evil. Unhindered praise of God and the Lord Jesus became the sterling sign that one's life was freed from demonic powers, remade for living in Christian community. This new life, personally and in community, was a testimony to and often against the powers.

> Hear, O Powers: Jesus Christ is Lord and Victor;
> The Name of Jesus Be Praised.

Early Church Ethics Contrasted to Empire Ethics

Living under the powers of the Roman Empire, the early church came into sharp conflict with the Powers. Prior to 171 AD Christians consistently refused service in the military. The Church Fathers taught against participation in the military up to the time of Constantine. Why so? Scholars disagree on the fundamental reason for this refusal. Cadoux and Hornus identify the chief reason as refusal to kill another human being, for Jesus commanded: love the enemy.[37] Helgeland, Daly, and Burns argue, conversely, that Christians refused to participate in the military because military service then involved idolatry.[38] Since idolatry is not involved in contemporary war Christians cannot appeal to these sources for refusal to participate in the military today.[39] Luz, in his commentary on Matthew, however, says, "The problem of killing was likely more important than that of idolatry."[40]

---

36. For "contrast community," see Lohfink's *Jesus*.

37. Cadoux, *Early Christian*, 272–75; Hornus, *Lawful*. Camp draws on this early church tradition of "love of enemy" to shape our attitude today toward Islam: in *Who?*

38. A valuable "Sourcebook" that presents primary texts, with discussion and summary of three related issues is *Killing*, edited by Sider. These primary texts are most helpful. It is striking that while diversity of views occur for non-participation in war as well as the degree of Christian participation in war, the sources concur that abortion is wrong and contrary to Christian belief and practice. This contrasts sharply to the Empire's practice of infanticide (especially of female babies).

39. Helgeland, Daly, and Burns, *Christians*.

40. Luz, *Matthew 1—7*, 331.

My response to this debate is Yes! Why so? Based on OT texts like Isaiah 2:6–22, I conclude: amassing weapons of war and idolatry are bedfellows.[41] Massive war arsenals mean humans no longer trust Lord Yahweh. Other gods co-opt human hearts. Early Christians refused participation in war precisely because it involved both idolatry *and* killing of the enemy, which Jesus forbade when he taught us to trust only in God and to love our enemies.

For a variation to this debate, Wink and Horsley face off on whether it is permissible for Christians to use violence to fight against systemic injustice.[42] Though Horsley grew up as a Quaker pacifist, he argues for a Yes-response, especially for oppressed peoples in developing countries (defending liberation theologies that regard violence as necessary to end oppression and systemic injustice). Wink, who grew up in a military tradition, argues for a No-response because Jesus' teaching on nonviolence is non-negotiable (he is reluctant, however, to identify with pacifism since it tends to be passive). Nonviolent resistance is *the* means to work for justice and truth-telling in this world of evil and violence. It exposes and overcomes violence. It also stands with and for the voiceless.

Important to the early church's refusal of war is the case the Church Fathers made for their positive contribution to the Empire. When pagan philosopher Celsus criticized Christians for shirking their duty to defend the Empire but yet reap its benefits, they gave a threefold defense: (1) They are duty-bound to follow the "law of Christ," which consists of "beating swords into plowshares," refusal of military warfare, and doing good to, even loving, the enemy;[43] (2) Because the army required an oath to the emperor and sometimes emperor worship, they could not participate in war, since Jesus forbade all oaths and all Scripture forbids idolatry. (3) Their warfare was more significant, namely, praying against the demons that incite fighting and war.[44]

The Christians thus contended that they were the true defenders of the peace of the Empire because they prayed against the evil powers that incite war and violence—how pertinent to the topic of this book! Moreover, Christians worshiped the true God who gives earthly kings their power and,

---

41. After writing this, I see Bartley concurs, with explanation, *Faith*, 23–24.

42. Horsley and Wink, in Swartley, editor, *Love*, 72–136.

43. Justin, 1 *Apol*. 39; Irenaeus, *Haer*. 4.34.4; Tertullian, *Iud* 3; Origen, *Cels*. 5.33; 3.7–8; Hippolytus, *Trad. ap*. 17b. and 19. Elster has shown that in many Church Fathers the "law of Christ" referred specifically to beating swords into plowshares and loving the enemy: "New Law," 108–29. In a complementary essay, "Early," Elster argues the point in detail.

44. Tertullian, *Apol*. 32; Origen, *Cels*. 8.68–75; Athanasius, *Inc*. 52.4–6.

further, they said, we pray that the armies will maintain the peace of the land in accord with God's sovereign purpose.[45] The story of Marcellus (died 298 AD), whose martyr bones lie in the Notre Dame Basilica crypt (Notre Dame, IN), illustrates the Christian resistance to war. To the judge he declared: "I threw down (my arms); for it was not seemly that a Christian man, who renders military service to the Lord Christ, should render it (also) by (inflicting) earthly injuries."[46]

Was Marcellus's bold testimony a *confrontation* of the powers? It was, but quite different than we usually think. It was not, e.g., a protest march. Rather, the testimony of one headed for martyrdom confounded the powers because it witnessed to a unique strength and power among Christians, apart from the protection of the Empire. They did not make confrontation their goal. In effect, the Christians said and did what Jesus taught: we are the salt of the earth; we are the light of the world. *Our* existence is *new creation*; the powers are of this passing world. *Our* loyalty is to the sovereign Creator and Redeemer of the world. True, abundant life is in our communities. Our primary allegiance is to the Lord Jesus Christ, Victor over the Powers.

As Luise Schottroff points out, the early Christians promised submission and a degree of allegiance to the Empire, but for the Empire it was never enough.[47] She explains: "The root of the problem was their resistance against Satan and sin as the true rulers of this world, the resistance that had shaped Christian practice through and through."[48] Their unique blend of nonresistance and resistance to evil confounded the powers, and gave Christians strength against evil. The peace of Jesus Christ was more powerful in confronting both human sin and the social structural evils of the time than was the Pax Romana.[49]

> Hear O Powers, Jesus Christ is Lord and Victor.
> Praise to the name of Jesus.

Practice of Charity and Mutual Aid

Early Christianity witnessed to Jesus Christ's victory over the powers by means of the church's incredible practice of charity and mutual aid. The Roman world treated human life with contempt in many instances, allowing

---

45. Tertullian, *Apol.* 30:4.
46. Cadoux, *Early*, 584.
47. Schottroff, "Give," 223–257; 250.
48. Ibid., 242–43.
49. See here the excellent book by Wengst, *Pax*.

infants, especially females, to die, with their bodies decaying in open sewers running down the middle of the city streets. Rodney Stark, from his sociological study of early Christianity, says, "We've unearthed sewers clogged with the bones of newborn girls." The early Christians "had to live with a trench running down the middle of the road, in which you could find dead bodies decomposing."[50] Christians did not put sewer systems in the cities, but they did speak against infanticide; they cared for each other and for the weak in a society that otherwise blinded itself to human need. Though agnostic in his personal stance toward Christianity, Stark is convinced that the early Christians made a striking difference in their world, by standing for life over against death, caring for each other, and valuing women and children, granting them dignity and worth that manifested God's kingdom values amid an immoral, degenerate social order.[51]

The depth of conviction and practice among early Christians to care for each other is amazing. Their commitment enabled the church's manifold wisdom of God to be made known to the principalities and powers (Eph 3:10). To illustrate:

> In AD 251, the church in Rome had a massive program of care for the widows and the poor. The church, consisting of many house fellowships throughout the city, had 1,500 people on its roll for support. Bishop Cornelius was aided by six presbyters, seven deacons, seven more sub-deacons, and ninety-four people in minor roles [aiding the ministry of care for the needy].[52]

Caring for the poor and conferring human dignity upon women and children testified powerfully to Jesus Christ's unmasking the illusions of the powers. When Constantine became emperor under the banner of his Christian conversion, though he was baptized only just before his death, he took over the system of Christian charity already developed, maintaining it as a welfare system. Christian communities that enact the gospel of Jesus Christ in this manner will bear not only a nonviolent testimony to the powers, but demonstrate how Christian faith and life orders society through love and honoring the dignity of each human being.

Hear O Powers, Jesus Christ is Lord and Victor.
Praise the name of Jesus.

---

50. Stark, *Rise*, and the interview with Stark, "Double Take," for quotations.

51. Stark, "Interview," 47. For this paragraph and further discussion of mutual aid in the NT churches and the history of healthcare for one another up to the period of the Reformation, see Swartley, *Health*, 138–53.

52. "Mutual Aid," in Swartley and Kraybill, eds., *Building*, 32.

The Nature of Early Christian Worship

The fourth force that made Christianity an unrivaled power against the powers of the Empire was early Christian worship. As Webber has shown, early Christian worship celebrated Jesus Christ's triumph over the powers of evil. Worship, with celebration of the Eucharist, empowered Christian communities to live freed from the devil's power and the Empire's domination.[53]

Similarly, Alan Kreider and Taylor Burton Edwards, in studying early Christian liturgy, show how basic the celebration of Christ's peace was in the liturgies, including the Eucharist.[54] Kreider describes in detail (over thirty-seven pages) the practices and procedures that were a normal part of Sunday morning worship. "Their encounter with God in worship involved bodily gestures and rites that became habitual, repetitive, reflexive ways of being."[55] His treatment notes some differences between morning and evening worship as well as variations in various geographic sectors of the early church. But sermon instruction, teaching, Eucharist, kiss of peace, and sharing in community needs marked it as new creation. In some areas of practice, deacons stood at the doors to prevent from entering anyone who was not a part of the Christian body. These worship practices created a new habitus, a new society in the midst of the pagan world.

Janet Warren, utilizing spatial imagery to broaden and enrich our view of "spiritual warfare," with diagrams that show light filling the space of a square originally dark, regards worship as important in extending the boundary of light and diminishing the darkness:

> Worship functions to reinforce boundaries on evil by proclaiming and exalting Christ. The sacrament of baptism can be conceived of as cleansing, and in fact was associated with exorcism in ancient and orthodox churches. Soaking in the center and receiving the Spirit dispels evil spirits. The Eucharist can be a reminder of the defeat of evil at Christ's death and resurrection, thus reinforcing boundaries on evil. However, Christians are called out from the center to minister to the periphery.[56]

If we are to be God's witnessing people, it is imperative that we know whom we serve and whom we have renounced. The matter of allegiance is

---

53. Webber, *Worship*, 1–16, in context of *Celebrating* (see above).

54. A. Kreider, "Military" and "Peacemaking"; Burton-Edwards, "Teaching"; E. Kreider, *Communion*, 44–50.

55. A. Kreider, *Patient*, 185. Thirty-seven pages describe various parts of worship, 185–222.

56. Warren, *Cleansing*, 277.

all-important. Prayer in the worship service empowered believers to live in peace and thrive in growth, even though outsiders in many church practices were barred at the door!

> Prayer, Origen was convinced, actually makes a difference . . . Origen viewed prayer as a resource of unimaginable power. Intercessions are more powerful than armies, so Christians contribute most to the common good by their prayers.[57] Indeed, it was the early Christians' practice of prayer that empowered them and gave them buoyancy . . . Scholars have noted in bewilderment that the early Christians did not spend a lot of time praying for the conversion of outsiders.[58] Instead, energized by the power of God that they experienced in worship, many of them lived interesting lives. And the rumors got out. Christian worship was a place of empowerment. "Who," Origen asked, "on hearing these things, will not be summoned to the army of God?" "Who will not be inspired to fight for the church against the enemies of the truth?"[59] The outsiders wanted access to the power center of prayer.[60]

God's People Confronting the Spirit World: The Story Continues

At a seminar in Lancaster, Pennsylvania, a woman who served in a mission in one of the Central American countries told how her life was threatened by a witch doctor who was about to hurl a huge weight upon her. As the man advanced toward her, she and two other Christians, all in their own first (but different) languages, said, "In the name of Jesus, drop it!" The man collapsed and could do no harm. He had no recourse but to acknowledge the power of Jesus over his witchcraft.[61]

So what learnings can we derive from this biblical evidence that can inform ministry today? I would suggest several. First, in our modern time what appears to be demonized behavior may or may not be intertwined

---

57. In addition to Origen believing such regarding prayer (*Cels.* 8.73) A. Kreider cites other writers making the same or similar point: Aristides, *Apol.* 16.6; Hippolytus, *Comm. Dan.* 3.24.7; *Patient*, 211n137

58. Here A. Kreider, in *Patient*, cites numerous early church writers and secondary sources in support, 211n139.

59. Kreider, *Patient*, 211, citing Origen, *Hom. Num.* 25.4.3.

60. Ibid., 211.

61. See here the pertinent stories in Shorter, *Jesus*.

with psychological disorder. Second, discernment is needed for each situation; a clear test is how a person responds to Scripture read authoritatively or praise to Jesus Christ in song or Spirit-empowered spoken word. Holding up a cross is also a good test, for demons regularly react negatively. Third, love for the person must be strong, and resistance against the devil and his work strong as well. Fourth, no demon will ever leave on the basis of someone's human authority. Only in the name of Jesus Christ and by his power and the power of God Almighty are people freed from demonizing oppression. This is possible because Jesus has bound the strong man. His house has and will continue to be plundered by Jesus' followers as they minister in his name. Fifth, those taking up this task of freeing in Jesus' name those oppressed by demonic power must pray for a shield of protection around them and their families, even close friends (see MacNutt's suggested prayer at the end of chapter 11 below). It is best to engage in deliverance ministry with a small group that supports each other in love, prayer, and ongoing relationships.

What can the church do? I suggest five responses:

1. We retain or put back into our baptismal vows the question, "Do you renounce Satan and all his works?" Pre-baptismal catechism might include some exorcist-type liturgy. See Appendix 1. Celebrate with those freed from Satan's bondage; joyfully exclaim, "praise the name of Jesus. To God be the glory!"

2. Wear the whole armor of God so we can withstand Satan's crafty tactics. Catechism might include asking candidates to memorize Scripture: Philippians 2:5–11 or Ephesians 6:10–18.

3. Pray for one another, and seek the Spirit's discernment and empowerment ministries.

4. Consider preaching-teaching that takes evil and temptation seriously. To illustrate, I cite from James Stewart's *A Faith to Proclaim*:[62]

> When Jesus became obedient unto death, even the death of the Cross, He did it in the confidence that in this final act the dark powers would overreach themselves and so be finished forever: had they known that, Paul suggests, they would never have done it [1 Cor 2:8]. But this was the will of Jesus in His death. In the words of P. T. Forsyth: "The holiness of Christ was the one thing damnatory to the Satanic

---

62. From "The Lyman Beecher Lectures of Yale Univeristy," presented also at Princeton, Pittsburgh, and New York in 1952 (footnotes appear here in brackets, adapting the style-form of biblical references).

power. And it was His death which consummated that holiness. It was His death, therefore, that was Satan's fatal doom." [*The Glorious Gospel*, 6]. Hence Paul was entirely right when with magnificent daring he pictured Christ as the one who wielded the hammer at Calvary: the bond was cancelled, . . . nailed to the tree.[63] "He disarmed the principalities and powers, and made a show of them openly, triumphing over them at the Cross" [Col 2:15]. As Calvin puts it, commenting on these words from Colossians, "There is no tribunal so magnificent, no throne so stately, no show of triumph so distinguished, no chariot so elevated, as is the gibbet on which Christ has subdued death and the devil, and trodden them under His feet." . . .

It is here that the Pauline atonement theology requires to be correlated with the basic doctrine of union with Christ . . . Jesus identifies Himself with my trouble and weakness and defeat, must I not now identify myself with His sacrifice, His power, His victory?[64]

5. Make *worship* services a time of rehearsing God's goodness and salvation from sin, evil, and Satan as well as instruction for living the new life in Christ.

---

63. From the context in Colossians 2:14 it is not clear whether "he" in the participle *nailing* refers to God or Christ. The same applies to the "He" that begins v. 15, "He disarmed the principalities and powers . . ." If we hold that the subject here is Christ, as I am inclined to do, then it is also Christ that wielded the hammer, as strange as that appears. Stewart concurs. It is a theological point, and not a historical description, for the Gospels make clear it was the Roman soldiers who nailed Jesus to the cross.

64. Stewart, *Faith*, 84–95.

10

Christian Witness to Christ's Lordship Over the Powers

That is our vocation: to convert . . . the enemy into a guest
and to create the free and fearless space
where brotherhood and sisterhood can be formed and fully experienced.

—Henri Nouwen, Reaching Out

[That we may know] . . . what is the immeasurable greatness
of his power for us who believe, . . .
God put this power to work in Christ when he raised him
[Jesus] from the dead
and seated him at his right hand in the heavenly places,
far above all rule and authority and power and dominion,
and above every name that is named,
not only in this age but also in the age to come.
And he has put all things under his feet
and has made him the head over all things for the church,
which is his body, the fullness of him who fills all in all.

—Eph 1:19–23

Does the church's mission include witness to Christ's lordship over the governing powers on specific policies, locally, state, or national? How does Jesus' lordship affect vocations that directly or indirectly are part of local, state, or national government?

In answering these questions we know *power* is constituent of government. "The language of power pervades the entire New Testament also. No NT book is without the language of power."[1] The breadth of NT vocabulary referring to the powers is extensive: "*dynamis* (power), *exousia* (authority), *archē/archōn* (principality/ruler), *stoicheion* (basic element), *kyrios/kyriotēs* (lord/dominion), *onoma* (name), *Satanas* (Satan), *diabolos* (devil), *daimonion* (demon), *pneuma* (spirit), *angelos* (angel/messenger), *basileia/basileus* (kingdom/king), *christos* (messiah)."[2]

Jesus Christ's lordship over the powers means gospel witness cannot be restricted to only certain areas of life. Nor is Christian witness to the powers mitigated by "separation of church and state," a valued understanding, which H. S. Bender contended had its roots in sixteenth-century Anabaptism.[3] In all life's dimensions gospel witness is acutely needed.

The OT prophets addressed their oracles of judgment to their own people and to the nations. Jeremiah was called to be a prophet to the nations (1:4–10). Numerous oracles are addressed to foreign nations (Isa 13—24; Jer 46—51; Ezek 25—32). This prophetic tradition guides the church's role in relation to the *powers*. Regarding Revelation, Schüssler Fiorenza rightly asserts, "The central question . . . of the whole book is: 'Who is the true Lord of this world?' The answer? The author insists that the 'Lord' of the world is not the emperor but Jesus Christ who has created an alternative reign and community to that of the Roman Empire."[4]

This chapter calls us to be a Jesus-inspired prophetic witness to the powers in our corporate life as Jesus-people and in our verbal witness to the powers.[5]

Biblical Basis for Witness to the Powers

Jesus Christ's victory over the powers is the *theological* basis for Christian witness to the powers and for guidance to Christian believers in government vocations. Four emphases in Scripture undergird this conviction.

First, the OT phrase, "Lord of hosts," helps us understand "power" terms in the NT. "Lord of hosts" (Hebrew, *YHWH Sabaoth*) occurs

---

1. Wink, *Naming the Powers*, 7.
2. Weaver, *Irony*, 3.
3. H. S. Bender, *Anabaptists*.
4. Schüssler Fiorenza, *Book*, 4; and *Invitation*, 72.
5. *Christian Political Witness*, edited by Kalantzis and Lee, contains important articles on this topic.

frequently in the OT.[6] In these texts *Sabaoth* is translated *dunameis* in the Greek (LXX) text, thus "Lord of the powers."[7] The word *tsaba* (sing.) means "military service" (e.g., Isa 40:2, "warfare" (RSV); "served her term," NRSV) or "army (troops)," but also the *host* of heaven (e.g., Dan 8:10). Some scholars suggest *YHWH Sabaoth* means "Lord of the (heavenly) armies."[8] Six dimensions of *Sabaoth* presence are interconnected: (1) the *Lord of hosts* dwells in the temple (at the ark of the covenant) where divine holiness humbles humans, with contrite hearts (Isa 6:1-8; cf. Ps 80; LXX 79); (2) "Lord of hosts" is associated with *Zion* as the temple mount, but even more closely with "Zion" as a theological symbol denoting YHWH's kingship and sovereignty, proffering security and defense for the covenant people who trusted God for defense (Pss 20; 48; 84); (3) the symbolic place from which *YHWH Sabaoth* goes forth to battle, on behalf of Israel (Pss 24:8-10; 89:8-18—in battle against primordial chaos); (4) *YHWH Sabaoth* restores Israel from its devastator-enemies (Ps 80:3, 7, 14, 19—here both *God of hosts* and *Lord of hosts* occur);[9] (5) the *Lord of hosts* judges the nations that devastated Israel: "Assyria, the rod of my anger" (Isa 10:5), which in turn falls to Babylon (Isa 14:24-27), and then haughty Babylon falls, like Lucifer from heaven (Isa 14:3-23, v.12, KJV). (6) the term *hosts* denotes that the *powers* is the divine council: angels (Ps 148:2) or the gods of the nations (Ps 82), scorned to naught (v. 5) because they do not do what they should do: "Judge justly, ... give justice to the weak and the orphan, and maintain the right of the lowly and the destitute" (vv. 2-4). All powers in the heavenly court function as

---

6. Pss 24:7-10; 46:7,11; 80:4, 7, 14, 19; 84:1,3; 89:8; 148:2 (in the LXX Pss 9-10 are one; so all these are one earlier); Isa 5:16; 6:3,5. Isa 24:23c, "for the Lord of hosts will reign," and 31:4e, "so the Lord of hosts will come down," are rendered "the kingdom of God shall be" or "is revealed" in the Aramaic, the language Jesus likely used.

7. In Isaiah 6:3, "Holy, holy, holy, is the Lord of hosts," *Sabaoth* is retained, not translated in the LXX, indicating its importance in relation to the holy.

8. The context for Psalm 46:11 is "He makes wars cease to the end of the earth" (v. 9a). YHWH Sabaoth was clearly connected to the ark (first at Shiloh), then to the temple where YHWH's kingship and sovereignty were denoted by *Zion* as a theological symbol. *Zion*, even in texts where YHWH *Sabaoth* does not appear, symbolized God's security and defense of the covenant people. God coming from Zion to protect and defend permeates numerous Psalms (20; 48; 50:1-6; 76) and Isaiah. Many of the Zion texts emphasize both security and God's/YHWH's defeat of enemies, protecting Israel from chaos. See Ollenburger's treatment of key texts in both Psalms and Isaiah: *Zion*, especially 46-80, 107-29, 144-62. W. F. Albright, 377-81, in a review of a French monograph by Wambacq, associates *YHWH Sabaoth* with the ark of the covenant that leads early Israel's armies into battle.

9. This emphasis in the church's liturgy goes back to the second century. An ancient Greek hymn places the powers (*dunameis*) subservient to the Trinity, Lord of the powers: http://www.amaranthpublishing.com/PapyrusHymn.htm.

servants of God's purpose, including *ha sa-tán*.[10] But he led a rival group to oppose God, and he with the rival group was deposed. Though government powers are *ordained* or *ordered* of God, they, like *ha sa-tán* may refuse, deny, and rebel against God's sovereignty.

Isaiah indicted Israel for forsaking the Lord to go after diviners (magic), wealth (mammon), and chariots and horses (martial might): "Their land is filled with idols" (Isa 2:6–8). Isaiah (5:7b) puns Israel's evils: *bloodshed* (*mishpah*) instead of *justice* (*mishpat*); the *cry* of the poor (*tze'aqah*) instead of *righteousness* (*tzedaqah*). Thus, "the *Lord of hosts* has a day against all that is proud and lofty" (2:12). To illustrate, consider the Nazi Holocaust horrors during Germany's Third Reich and the Allies storm-bombing more than twenty German cities and the atomic bombing of Hiroshima and Nagasaki. The USA with its imperial tentacles is ever on the brink of the demonic, as its role in the Vietnam, Iraq, Syria, and Yemen wars attest.

Roy Hange informs us that the Syrian Orthodox Church of Antioch has an annual Lenten ritual called "Lord of the Hosts." Observed each Sunday evening during Lent, this ritual sets the world in proper Christian perspective. This has had powerful meaning in now nearly two millennia in the liturgy of Christian worship. He says,

> Hearing a thousand persons in a large church chant this in Arabic in Lent is powerful. It is chanted as a repeated refrain sandwiched between the choir singing the Psalms. There is a shimmering beauty in the resonance between the choir and the congregation when this was sung that led me to imagine that it was heavenly ... I weep when imagining a thousand people singing this weekly in the church in Damascus during Lent during this civil war in Syria ... with the sound of an occasional mortar dropping nearby ... This service is a powerful witness to the ruling powers of this age, which from century to century have changed, but the true Ruler of not only Syria, but of the whole world, reigns now and forever.[11]

---

10. Wink, in his treatment of "Satan," has a lengthy section on "Satan as Servant of God" in *Unmasking* (11–22) before his treatment of "Satan as the Evil One." He cites modern-day examples of governing powers (especially the FBI) overstepping mandates, "instigating murders that it ostensibly existed to prevent" (22). Wink's chapter on Satan is important in relation to my discussion of Wink's contribution in chapter 12.

11. For the Arabic rendition of this service, "Oh Lord of Hosts Be with Us," listen to YouTube: https://www.youtube.com/watch?v=2D6Jhm76Oic. For an English and Arabic chant of "Oh Lord of Hosts," hear: https://www.youtube.com/watch?v=uGOiV-8F_D8. For an English version only of "Oh Lord of Hosts" by an European Eastern Orthodox choir, listen to YouTube: https://www.youtube.com/watch?v=2vLQtAxlark.

Second, in Daniel's visions all powers are/will be subservient to the *Son of Man* who will come on the clouds of heaven.

As I watched in the night visions, I saw one

> like a human being (Son of Man, RSV) coming with the clouds of heaven.

And he came to the Ancient One and was presented before him.

To him was given dominion (*archē*) and glory and kingship,

> that all peoples, nations, and languages should serve him.

His dominion (*exousia*) is an everlasting dominion (*exousia*) that shall not pass away,

> and his kingship is one that shall never be destroyed.
> (Dan 7:13–14)

In the Septuagint both *exousia* and *archai* designate temporal domains and governments: "The kingship and dominion (*exousia*) and the greatness of the kingdoms under the whole heaven shall be given to the people of the holy ones of the Most High; their kingdom shall be an everlasting kingdom, and all dominions (*archai*) shall serve and obey them" (Dan 7:27). "[T]he holy ones of the Most High" share in the sovereignty of the Son of Man. This title denotes Jesus' identity and mission: his earthly authority to forgive sins (Mark 2:10,), his suffering (Mark 8:31; 9:31; 10:33–34), and his future sovereign judgment (Mark 8:38; 14:62).

Third, these two OT streams of divine sovereignty culminate in Jesus' lordship in the NT. Acts 10:36 declares Jesus Christ is Lord of all! As noted in chapter 5, *lord* is a pervasive title for Jesus in Luke–Acts. The emphasis on *Lord of all* means that even the kings and the Empire are "dusted" by the truth and power of this new *Way* gospel. *The* connection between *YHWH* as Lord and *Jesus* as Lord is persuasive when the titles, roles, and actions of both are examined.[12] The church knows and affirms Jesus is Lord, begun with Peter's proclamation empowered by the Pentecost-Spirit outpouring (Acts 2:23–36).

Fourth, Paul proclaims Jesus as Lord with authority (*exousia*) over all "principalities and powers" (RSV), "rulers and authorities" (NRSV; Eph 6:12; recall chapter 6). Jesus is Lord over the powers/*archai* (Col 2:10), which one

---

12. Hurtado in *Lord* and Bauckham in *God* rightly contend that God's character and actions are present in Jesus. Thus, NT believers worshiped Jesus. For my treatment, see *Send*, 213–240, with worship in Revelation, 240–62.

day shall "bend their knee" to the Lord's sovereignty (Phil 2:9–11). Christians derive ethics from Jesus Christ's lordship and God's kingdom reality.

Christian Understanding of Government and Response to Evil

Christian believers regard evil in governments with the awareness, hope, and assurance that evil is overcome through Jesus' exaltation and reign. Jesus alone is Lord. State authorities do not have final authority.[13] This truth guides Christian peace witness to and within political power.[14] The most frequently cited text on the powers is Romans 13:1: Every authority or power that exists is ordained (KJV), instituted (RSV, NRSV), or ordered of God (the Greek verb from the root *tagma* provides strong support for *ordered*). The Greek word for "powers" here (Rom 13:1) is *exousiai* (pl.), translated as *governing authorities* (NRSV). This term together with *archai* occurs frequently in the NT, translated as "principalities and powers" (RSV) or "rulers and authorities" (NRSV, recall chapter 6). Ephesians 1:21 has two additional "power" terms: power (*dunamis*) and dominion or lordship (*kuriotētos*).

Jesus' kingdom contrasts to worldly kingdoms for three fundamental reasons, as Boyd points out. First, "while all human governments in this fallen world are premised on rebellion against God, the Kingdom of God is premised on submission to God." Second, "while all human governments in this fallen world are premised on people pledging allegiance to nationalistic ideals and the structures that express and protect them, the Kingdom of God is premised on people pledging allegiance to God alone." And third, "all human governments in this fallen world are under the strong influence of Satan, the 'ruler' of this world and the 'god of this age'" (John 12:31; 14:30; 16:11; 2 Cor 4:4; cf. Luke 4:5–7; Eph 2:2; 1 John 5:19).[15]

Christians are called to a distinctive Christian ethic. They are not to resist evil by using evil means. Christ has shown a new and better means of

---

13. Kalantzis, "A Witness to the Nations," 104–7.
14. Hauerwas, "Church Matters," addresses this point, 30–33.
15. Boyd, "Different," 377–78: "our unique call is to manifest faithfully a Kingdom that does not at all resemble any of these [worldly] kingdoms, precisely because the citizens of this Kingdom have been freed from the rebellion, allegiance, and Powers that undergird these kingdoms. [F]or these same reasons, the citizens of this Kingdom . . . imitate Jesus in self-sacrificial, Calvary-like love for others and against the Powers, rather than a war of violence against others on behalf of the Powers" (379). Boyd draws on his *Myth*, 14, 17–49, where he contrasts "power over" institutions to the "power under" (22).

resistance. Christian believers are not ministers of God's wrath, but ministers of God's reconciling love (2 Cor 5:17-20).[16] Nor did Paul tell the Christians to withdraw from societal evil; they are to stay in society and there demonstrate Christ's way of response to evil. By so doing, they will also witness to the authorities (Eph 3:8-10) that it is *God in Jesus Christ* who reigns supreme. Not Caesar, but *Christ* is Lord. Christ's means of victory over evil, servanthood and suffering, guide Christian belief and action.

This normative NT view of the Christian attitude toward government (chapter 6) bases itself upon Christ's victory and lordship over the principalities and powers (Col 2:10, 15; Eph 1:19-23; 3:10; 1 Pet 3:22; 1 Cor 15:24-26). The powers have been stripped of ultimate power (Col 2:15). Believers who confess Jesus as Lord derive moral values from him, Commander in Chief of God's army of overcoming love.[17] Romans 13 must be viewed against the moral teaching that instructs us in how to respond to evil in Romans 12.[18] In 13:6 the "authorities" are called God's *ministers* (*leitourgoi*) in such service, but then comes a qualification, "when they attend [or, by attending] to this very thing," which qualifies the God-specified actions and here refers to their taking "tribute" (*phorous*).

This means contested authority for government. It may serve and promote either the good or evil. Christian peacemakers can help define in contemporary, specific political options what is "good and bad." This is not because politics is our ultimate hope, but because followers of Christ should know what the terms *good* and *bad* mean for human life and action.[19] Jim Longley, formerly a Member of Parliament and Government Minister in an Australian State, makes the case that the Christian in government office, who is servant for the people and not lord over the people, is able to infuse government policies for the moral good of the people. He gives numerous examples, from bankruptcy laws to community services to gun law reform, as policies where the Christian servant voice is needed and can make a difference. Collegial respect and due process that strives

---

16. See the models of Christian relation to and responsibility for government presented by Moltmann. His view comes close to the Anabaptist model, not the two-person Lutheran view: see, "Following Jesus Christ in a Nuclear Age," 52-56.

17. Snyder Belousek's important book, *Atonement*, 607-42, describes well this mission of the church. It anchors the church's witness in the cruciform model of Jesus' life, death, and triumph over evil.

18. See chapter 6 above for extended discussion of Romans 13 on this point.

19. For current thinking on Christian values in relation to public order and security, see the articles in Friesen and Schlabach, eds.: *At Peace*: Friesen, "In Search," 37-82, especially 68-75; "Appendix to Part I," 153-64 [with diagram on 153]; Enns, "Public Peace," especially paragraphs b, c, and d on 252-53; Schlabach, "Just Policing," 405-21; and the two articles by Byler and Schirch, 179-94, 423-44.

toward consensus is the ideal—and in some cases this may be as important as the issue itself. Servanthood, not Sovereignty, is an essential stance to make politics a mission of peacemaking.[20]

Ideally the government is to command the obedience, respect, and tax support of its subjects and citizens (1 Pet 2:13–17). When the government is a servant-minister for the common good, then citizens should be not only supportive, but rally to support that good. Boyd, however, discerns that the government's very nature is "power over," which means it can and will resort to violence to maintain its interests.[21] Hence, Christian believers may need to disobey government, as USA conscientious objectors did during World War I, costing suffering and even death.

When governments function as perpetrators of evil,[22] rather than restrainers of evil, *and since Christ faced down evil through love, suffering, and*

20. Longley, "Politics," 15–18. Longley used J. H. Yoder's *Body Politics*, with its five practices as the basis for his paper, developing analogies to these practices for the Christian's servant-contribution in politics.

21. This emphasis is explicit in Boyd's *Myth*, 20–22—with "power over" twice on p. 22.

22. Pearse's *Gods of War* is an insightful contribution on the multiple—often interrelated—causes of war. Hedges' stomach-churning book *War* speaks of "mythic war" and "sensory war." Most Americans know only "mythic war," that glorifies both the "rightness" of the war and the heroism of those who fight the war (hear "The Battle Hymn of the Republic"). But those who fight the battle know "sensory war," which is unspeakable; most veterans want to forget and are mute about it. A news reporter on many wars, Hedges knows both the thrall of mythic war and the stench of *sensory* war. The media, he says, regularly fail to convey the *sensory* aspects of war, though Vietnam in its latter years was an exception—and thus finally the USA's exit from Vietnam, even as a "loser." His book describes the "blood and guts" of war, along with the myth of redemptive violence that "blesses" the war. But it also describes *sensory* war, exposing its incredibly *horrid* inhumanity: the putrid, rancid smells of bleeding, dying, and dead bodies, the cries of the wounded, et al. But Hedges is not a pacifist, nor anti-war. Why? Because he knows the depth of evil to which humans succumb. Knowing well war's illusive "just cause" and its ineffable *sensory* reality, he contends that the USA should have intervened in the genocidal Balkan wars earlier than it did—presumably also into any genocidal war: "We in the industrialized world bear responsibility for the world's genocides because we had the power to intervene and did not" (16). This reflects Niebuhr's ethics, the necessity of choice between the lesser of two evils; one must act, and then ask for forgiveness (17). In reading Hedges, I comment, *war* is the devil's worst, most successful joke. War is hell, as William Tecumseh Sherman rightly said. (He hated newspaper reporters with a passion and at one point said: "They come into camp and pick up . . . camp rumors and print them as facts. I regard them as spies, which, in truth, they are. But if I killed them all, there would be news from hell before breakfast.").

T. Yoder Neufeld moves us closer to the reality of *sensory* war—which the parents and grandparents of Russian Mennonite emigrants know well—as he describes the suffering of people who "fall victim to violence and injustice."

 . . . we see the suffering of those enslaved by demons of state [governments]

death, Christians are called *to do the same and bear witness* of Christ's victory to government powers (Eph 3:8–10). In this light, the most important role of Jesus-followers in the face of government that promotes evil is to be a contrast-society, demonstrating the reconciling reality of the gospel (uniting former enemies, Jews and Gentiles, applicable to racism today). We thus proclaim Jesus' victory with integrity.

Christians are called to be in society, in the thick of the fray, resisting evil and working for good. To describe the methods to use, we may point to a theoretical continuum of responses ranging from inactivity (ignoring the evil), on the one hand, to lethal violence (killing people who do evil), on the other hand.[23] Neither option is acceptable for disciples of Jesus, for neither is consistent with love. Abdication does not take evil seriously; lethal violence does not take one's own evil seriously. Neither genuinely considers the possibility of converting the enemy, thus making his repentance and reconciliation impossible. We cannot resist evil either by wishing it away or by countering with evil. We must resist evil with good and resist falsehood with truth. In whatever government roles we choose to serve or purposefully not serve, seeking and speaking truth as servants of Christ must be

---

and spirit in the Bible, calling out for divine deliverance: "How long, O Lord?" (Rev. 6:10). We do not even have to go back far in history. A litany of suffering in our own lifetime could go on for hours: Rwanda, Chechnya, Bosnia, Kosovo, North Korea, Afghanistan, Zimbabwe, Colombia, Palestine, Israel [and now add for sure, Iraq, Syria, and the plight of refugees, migrants, the millions living in tent cities barely human, the victims of suicide bombers, and 9/11] ("Resistance," 64).

Scranton's article "'Star Wars'" is apropos as he recounts spending a Fourth of July thirteen years ago "on the roof of a building in Baghdad that had once belonged to Saddam Hussein's secret police. Our command had suspended missions for the day, set up a grill and organized a 'Star Wars' marathon—the three good ones—in an old auditorium." Looking out over the bombed city he now saw that the "myth of regeneration through violence," which Richard Slotkin traces "from the earliest Indian captivity narratives through the golden age of the western" in *inverted* perspective: "I was the faceless storm trooper, and the scrappy rebels were the Iraqis." He recounts USA's war history and the gap between what American soldiers or marines know and what civilians know. George W. Bush's "We will prevail" is at the expense of what civilians dare not know! "As an American soldier in Iraq, I was both caught up in that myth and released from it: I could see 'what the work of peace' really looked like, what American violence did to Iraqi homes and bodies, yet it remained my job to be an agent of that violence—a violence that neither redeemed nor enlightened."

23. The violent end of the continuum extends still further, to global lethal violence (cosmocide) in which both the people and environment are destroyed. Adherents to "just war" draw their line of acceptable intervention short of the unacceptable extreme of "indiscriminate" and "disproportionate" killing (e.g., O'Donovan, *Pursuit*). Christians, I believe, are to regard *all* killing as sin and evil.

foremost. Not power or wealth, but truth and service for the people's good, must guide our vocational calling.

The Wider NT Witness

Five streams of biblical teaching form the scriptural and theological basis for the position that Christians and the church are to bear witness to Christ's lordship over the powers. Jesus' lordship over all worldly and super-worldly realms of authority is the thesis at stake here.

First, Jesus proclaimed the kingdom of God (a political notion) has come near (or *is come*, Mark 1:14-15). Jesus' deeds of healing, exorcism, and forgiveness of sin witness to the new kingdom power and reality. His kingdom way leads to shalom. Jesus never used his power to destroy enemies; rather he confronted demonic power, as chapter 5 demonstrates. His kingdom mission threatened the powers, both religious and political.[24] Conflicts with the religious leaders led to his crucifixion. Jesus' power confronting political powers lies at the very heart of the gospel. When the church follows Jesus, its leader and Lord, faithfully, it too threatens the powers, even at the risk of suffering.

Second, as noted above, Paul proclaims Christ *head* over the powers; Christ's victory on the cross and resurrection defeats the powers. The most explicit description of Christ's triumph over the powers is: He "disarmed the principalities and powers, and made a public example of them" (Col 2:15b, RSV). Imperial powers are no longer victor. Christ is victor over the powers! In the church's faith and proclamation, Christ is both the *de jure* and the *de facto* head of all principalities and powers (the NT equivalent of governments, rulers, "ologies," and "isms").[25]

Third, Paul declares "that through the church the wisdom of God . . . might now be made known to the rulers and authorities [principalities and powers, RSV] in the heavenly places" (Eph 3:10). The context is Paul's apostolic call and mission, the uniting of Jews and Gentiles in Christ. What the Roman government's Pax Romana could not achieve, Jesus Christ's gospel did.

Jesus' victory over evil renders powerless the principalities and powers (1 Cor 15:24). Note this chapter's epigraph. The church recognizes,

---

24. In Matthew 2, even Jesus' birth (King of the Jews) threatened Herod as ruler of Judea. Hence, Herod's child massacre.

25. The same Greek word for head, *kephalē*, used here in Colossians 2:10 to denote Christ's relationship to the powers, is used also in Ephesians 5:23 to denote Jesus' relationship to the church.

knows, and confesses Jesus' lordship. The "world" in rebellion to God denies it. Because Jesus is Lord, his atonement has both universal and cosmic significance (Rom 8:18–25; Phil 2:11; Col 1:19–20; Rev 5:13). God's purpose in Jesus' life, death, resurrection, and exaltation is to unite all things in Christ (Eph 1:10). Where war persists, people kill others even of the same faith (Christian, Muslim, and even Jew). Killing closes the door for people to hear the gospel, repent, be baptized, and welcomed into the body of Christ. God wills salvation for all. War breaks church unity; it blocks the Great Commission.

Fourth, Jesus' words to government rulers demonstrate his lordship over the powers. In John, Jesus pronounces restriction upon Pilate's power, declaring that Pilate's rightful power is given him from above, implying that Pilate's power is limited, even contested, by God Almighty who empowers Jesus in his life's ministry and death. "Pilate said to him, 'So you are a king?' Jesus responded, 'You say that I am a king. For this I was born, and for this I came into the world, to testify to the truth. Everyone who belongs to the truth listens to my voice . . . You would have no power over me unless it had been given you from above'" (John 18:37; 19:11a).

Fifth, Christ's lordship, based in Jesus' death and resurrection, empowered the apostles to critique and defy government practices, evident in the following texts from Acts:

- 2:22–24, 36: Peter declares the authorities accountable for crucifying Jesus, which also was in accord with God's plan.
- 4:7–29: again, the leaders are accountable for Jesus' crucifixion (v. 8) and the apostles refuse to obey the leaders' commands not to witness to Jesus, appealing to God's authority as greater than that of the leaders (vv. 18–20).
- 5:27–32: in another round before the authorities the apostles say, "We must obey God rather than any human authority."
- 22:25: Paul objects to the Roman centurion's flogging him, saying, "'Is it legal for you to flog a Roman citizen who is uncondemned?'"
- 24:25: In discussion with the procurator Felix, Paul spoke to him about "justice, self-control, and the coming judgment" and "Felix became frightened."[26]

Uncritical obedience to government, i.e., "My country, right or wrong" or "My government deserves my *ultimate* loyalty," is not the teaching of the NT. Rather, as 1 Peter asserts, we are "aliens and exiles" ("pilgrims and strangers," KJV). This means our primary allegiance is to Christ's body

26. I provide a longer critique of government officials in chapter 8, *Covenant*, 228–34.

universal, not to the nation state. The criteria for obedience/disobedience come from Christ's lordship, not from government authority.

The Challenges of Our Times

In *Christian Political Witness* David Gushee laments that evangelicals lack a Social Teaching tradition, which the Roman Catholic Church has had over the centuries. He identifies ten issues evangelicals need to address *vis à vis* the USA government. Influenced by Ron Sider earlier in his life, Gushee lists the following:

Table 10.1 Gushee's Ten Priorities for Witness to Government

1. Abortion	6. Guns
2. Creation care	7. Immigration
3. Death penalty	8. Torture
4. Economic justice	9. USA war-making
5. Gay rights	10. Women's rights

Gushee concludes with a section on "Christian hope and public witness."[27] Published in 2014, with articles written likely a year or two earlier, one might wonder if the list would differ today, given current (2018) USA political leadership.

I suggest a current list include terrorism, mass shootings, tax policies, health care with its exploding costs of pharmaceuticals and health services generally, and economic justice. On the list must be "defense budget and war-making" and consumerism. I put these first in this diagram to show how the USA war-making at the center skews national priorities.

Diagram 10.1 Issues for Speaking Truth to Government

Economic justice/ health care		Creation care/ climate change
	Consumerism[28] *War-making priority*/ nuclear weapons	
Guns/mass shooting		Torture

---

27. Gushee, "Toward an Evangelical Social Tradition."

28. Clapp, ed. *Consuming Passion*. Chapters 2 by Bill McKibben (40–50) and 10 by Rodney Clapp (169–204) are especially important in regard to framing the issue of *consumerism* as a priority in Christian witness to government.

If sanctity of life and Jesus' command to love enemies motivate one's stance against war and its horrible consequences, opposing abortion and the death penalty, and affirming immigrants and rights for minorities (race and gender) follow. Related to this is Jana Bennett's contribution.[29] Post-Enlightenment individualism lies at the heart of the "rights" discussions. The separation of private and public, together with individual free choice, means that church and family are private. This separation "upends Christ"; it is not the Jesus-spirit:

> An Enlightenment focus on individual choices and autonomy turns us away from proclaiming Christ. I am struck again and again how often Christian arguments . . . about the place of the family in relation to the state utilize the idea of the individual's rights to choose, rather than grounding their arguments in Christ himself.[30]

She documents this by noting how liberals keep the church out of their defense for this and that, and how conservatives want to keep the federal and state governments out of their desired actions. Even though either side may appeal to this or that action by government or church, it is the individual "choices that become the bedrock of civilization." Her appeal to see this differently is Jesus Christ: how his birth, life, and ministry were not private, but were involved in government and sociopolitical issues.[31]

Underlying this discussion is failure to address head-on our propensity as fallen humans to witness against *evil*. Recall the summary of the psalmists' laments and the prophets' critiques in chapter 3. Dominant in their critique of the nation is castigation of worshiping anything other than the Lord God, along with their cries for deliverance from lies and evildoers. These two points might head the list of what the church's critique ought to be in these times: idolatry and truth versus lies (deception). As Farley observes, "the classic devices of the demons" are "deception, illusion, and seduction" so that "the most dangerous temptations are present in the guise of something we think of as good."[32]

---

29. Bennett, "Not So Private."

30. Ibid., 120. Mott in "Groups in Society," 42–57, makes a complementary contribution to Bennett's. He notes that the individual naturally groups with those of like mind, hence also "danger."

31 Bennett, "Not So Private," 121–27. This portion of her article is an excellent discussion starter since it subverts much liberal and conservative discussion on the role of the political, with critique of the role of the private.

32. W. Farley, *Wounding*, 75.

Reticence to call evil *evil* reflects our distance from the prophets of the Hebrew Scripture. Is the USA breeding the white supremacy ideology and idolatry that began in the early 1930s in Germany? Jesus' command, "Love your enemy," cries to be tried to combat evil.

For a country that is sometimes termed *Bible Nation*,[33] Christian believers would do well to ponder how Jesus' love command is relevant also for the cultural and political "cultural wars" of our time—in the church as a body politic, in the context of a nation creating enmity relationships, and threatening what had been friendly relations with other nations. Are the recent mass shootings in the USA the dark underside of Pax Americana, as was the violence of the Pax Romana in Jesus' time?[34]

Witnessing to Christ's Lordship against the evils in Gushee's list and my additions are priorities for Christian witness to the powers. But many don't agree. People are free to choose moral priorities, yes! One's *culture* shapes choices and positions, determining what one values, how one thinks, and why some oppose the moral stance taken above. While one might cite the recent emphasis on *habitus* and *character* as formative, I recommend also a life-sample that shows how one couple's influence shaped the moral values of people on social, ethical matters: *Forming Christian Habits in Post-Christendom: The Legacy of Alan and Eleanor Kreider*. The stories of many people, from around the globe, testify.[35] *Character* and *culture* are key to moral priorities.

Moral Norms for Government?

Does God have two ultimate moral codes—one for the church and one for the government? Over the centuries Christians have understood this matter differently. Moltmann presents the views of Martin Luther, Karl Barth, Political Theology, and our present calling, "Following Jesus Christ in an Age of Nuclear War."[36] While Christians cannot expect government to ex-

---

33. See *Bible Nation* by Moss and Baden, reviewed by David Weaver-Zercher in *ChrCent* (October 11, 2017), 41–43.

34. Wengst, *Pax*, 7–51; see my summary in *Covenant*, 38–39. Wengst's incisive analysis echoes the prophetic critique of the OT prophets. Rome's peace and prosperity came at the cost of vast armies and an odious tax system. Revolts and wars at the Empire's peripheries were numerous (in Sepphoris, three miles north of Nazareth, Rome killed 2,000 people to quell a threatening uprising about ten years before Jesus began his public ministry). Amazing that Jesus commanded, "Love your enemies," to launch his ministry against evil!

35. Krabill and Murray, *Forming*.

36. Moltmann, *Politics*, 3–69.

emplify moral norms given for the *church's* obedience, they may, however, expect a higher moral standard for government. Consequently, when the church or covenant believers address government officials, the witness normally speaks to specific alternatives. It identifies alternatives that more closely approximate the moral norms of covenant faith in all three of the Abrahamic religious traditions—and others such as Hinduism and Buddhism. In this context it is important that the proposed alternatives are put in language that the public can understand (e.g., middle axioms). This is a challenging task: there are allies that can help us, i.e., the many letters we receive via online media that approach what we want to say, with space for further comment.

Our mission then in relation to the morality of government is to pray for those in authority and bear witness to Jesus is Lord of all, pointing to the highest moral practices that might be achieved. The Christian imperative is that governments, at every level, may carry on their work in accord with God's purposes for the "powers." Governments and politics are not the medium for achieving the kingdom of God (the Christendom model).[37] Rather, the goal is to seek for political options most amenable to the Christian gospel. The psalmist says, "Seek peace and pursue it" (Ps 34:14b), a good goal to guide Christian witness.

From a NT Christian perspective, war is wrong. It kills enemies, contrary to Jesus' gospel. While war is sometimes necessary for *defense* of a nation, it is not thereby morally justified. Among the nations, there has been war, is war, and will continue to be war. This does not make war right or "just."[38] The "just war" tradition evolved over time.[39] Many ethicists question, however, whether there ever was a just war. The Anabaptist view holds war is always wrong because it fights evil with evil and kills people for whom Christ died.

Many theologians and ethicists contend war is politically necessary to counteract human evil egoisms. Reinhold Niebuhr has made this case, called Christian realism.[40] But even so, some wars may be politically *un-*

---

37. Bartley's key point in *Faith*, 1–69.

38. Swartley, *Slavery*, 112–49; Boyd, *Myth*.

39. Simpson, *War*. The book begins with pre-Augustinian roots, traces its evolving emphases over time, and concludes with Lutherans (and Catholics) taking a "pacific turn" ca. 1992. Nuclear war cannot meet criteria set forth in this tradition. Changes in the nature of warfare are the key factor in the "pacific turn." Bell's *Just*, beginning with Cicero, complements Simpson, recentering the tradition in the church, rather than the state.

40. For critique of Niebuhr's contribution, see Hays, *Moral*, 215–25; J. H. Yoder, *Reinhold*.

necessary and therefore wrong, even in the geopolitical sense. Many ethicists (Christian and non-religious) regarded the Vietnam War to be politically unnecessary and wrong (cf. the Iraq and Syria wars).

What does this mean for Christian witness to the political order? It means Christian peacemakers witness and affirm war to be wrong, yes *evil*. *Peacemaking, not war-making,* ought to be *the* primary duty and goal of political leaders. Christian peacemakers witness against all war, and especially wars that are judged politically unnecessary; it's more difficult to take such a stand, of course, when wars waged by our nation have widespread and nearly unanimous popular support, as occurred in the USA for World War II. The crucial question confronting the church, however, is how to speak on a political level without distorting the quality of our trans-situational gospel witness. Recent work evolving out of a Mennonite Central Committee study on peace theology speaks of a "middle language," developed from the "middle axioms" model.[41]

Lydia Harder draws on the biblical wisdom tradition as a scriptural model that connects the prophetic-covenantal ethic with life in the world.[42] The model is useful and merits further explication. I suggest Proverbs 8:13–21 enumerates moral attributes of wisdom applicable to addressing government leaders, both civic and national:

1. "Fear of the Lord," recognizing that we are human and mortal (1:9).

2. Hatred of evil and love of the truth (8:13; sorely needed these days!).

3. Hatred of perverted, deceitful speech (8:13c).

---

41. A half-century ago Yoder wrote *Christian Witness*, presenting a theological basis for such witness. While the book's title makes the state the (indirect) object of the witness, I prefer to make *the lordship of Christ* that object. The state is one arena of witness to Christ's lordship. Yoder distinguishes between church and state (government) entities. The church does not speak to the state as though it should operate on the same moral standards that guide the life of the church. Rather, the church's witness to the state is via a "spring-tension," which respects one ultimate morality expressing God's will for human life and the fact that "the state" does not function on those standards. Nevertheless, the state has no independent God-given moral code. Influenced by the post-1948 World Council of Churches language of J. H. Oldham, and later John C. Bennett, Yoder used the concept of "middle axioms" as a means of witness to advocate moral values that stand in continuity with what the church holds for its own practice, yet does not ask government to function on the moral standards of the church. The goal of the witness is to assist the state to be more moral than it is, to choose the better of several alternatives, none of which expresses fully God's kingdom vision. The driving force of such witness to government is not that of superior intelligence or better information but dogged commitment to speak the truth of the gospel, often through middle-axiom language.

42. Harder, "Seeking."

4. Looking to wisdom, not folly, for courage and strength (8:14).
5. Wisdom enabling rulers to rule justly, with righteousness (8:15, 20).
6. Wisdom as source of riches, honor, and prosperity *(shalom)* (8:18–19); wisdom valued above jewels (v. 11) and gold, even fine gold (v. 19).
7. Wisdom as source of "creative ordering" of the world with God (8:22–31).

See chapter 3 above for specific evils (Prov 14:31, 34). Psalm 94 castigates the speech and actions of the "arrogant" (vv. 4–6) and poses the piercing question in v. 20: "Can wicked rulers be allied with you, those who contrive mischief by statute?" We might construct a profile of virtues in this "middle language," by which to address rulers to call them to a standard they would recognize as wise, prudent, and efficacious for security and shalom.

The wisdom model also needs case studies to demonstrate how it works. Harder's example of her father involved in co-operatives, a form of community-governed institutions, is helpful. The banquet symbol in the Gospels' appropriation of the wisdom tradition, which Harder describes, disarmed at least one potentially hostile situation nearly two and a half centuries ago, extending kingdom hospitality to hungry soldiers.

This event from my genealogical history illustrates this wisdom approach during the Revolutionary War. A Rosenberger family brought two Swartley brothers to the "New World" as indentured servants, settling in the larger Franconia, Pennsylvania, area. In the course of time both Swartley young men married a Rosenberger daughter. John's wedding to Magdalena took place during the peak of the War, imperiling the celebration of the wedding reception. Hungry soldiers seeking food for the army often would rampage a festival and take the food. The women who prepared the reception meal at deacon Henry Rosenberger's Skippack home feared just such a catastrophe, and not in vain. Sighting soldiers advancing over the rise from Towamencin, the women consulted in consternation and decided on a plan, a fine Christian response. Several women went out to meet the soldiers as they approached and invited them as welcomed guests to the wedding meal. It worked. John Ruth writes: "There is friendship and respect in the midst of the chaos of a war, and the soldiers, having drunk to the health of the newlyweds, leave without taking so much as a chicken."[43]

Wisdom can perhaps help us with the "middle language," and it needs more real-life stories to illustrate its utility at the local, state, and national government levels.[44]

---

43. Ruth, *Seeding*, 40, 138.
44. Friesen and Schlabach, eds., *Peace*, Appendix to Part I, 153–63 (diagram on 153

Our Calling

Christians may participate in all aspects of our society that are consistent with our calling (Eph 4:1-6). Conversely, we ought not to accept positions of responsibility that exclude love as response to evil. The extent of participation in societal structures will and should raise difficult questions for Christian believers. The individual Christian's conscience and the discernment of our communities of faith are essential guiding resources. In no case, however, may Christians take positions that lead us, either personally or by the logical extension of our actions, to take the lives of so-called enemies. This is incompatible with the way of Jesus.[45] To serve in the armed forces, in the military branches of the civil service, or in industries manufacturing armaments, violates the Christian ethic of peacemaking, doing good and loving the neighbor; indeed, God may be calling those who have jobs in these areas to resign and seek other employment.[46] But Christian believers with political expertise are also badly needed in government to bring Christian ethical perspectives to the table and thus be "salt" and "leaven" to make the policies of a state, province, or nation more reflective of biblical prophetic values (e.g., on the issue of immigration). This takes wisdom and Spirit guidance to make the connection, speaking moral values to a given issue at the right time and in a manner that can gain support. Hard to do, yes, but it's not impossible. Nonviolent and nonresistant Christians have discovered that through prayer God has worked miracles of deliverance in seemingly impossible situations.[47] We are exhorted *to pray* for our government leaders *and* our enemies and persecutors, in whatever situation we are in.[48] This includes "national" enemies!

---

by the MCC Peace Theology Project Team). In my judgment the six facets of wisdom-witness in this diagram lack an important seventh: the ongoing relief and development work of Mennonite Central Committee, which is itself a demonstration to the powers that Pax Christi achieves what Pax Americana cannot (cf. Eph 3:9-10)—and in fact does exactly the opposite of imperial power, which causes war, loss of lives, famine, refugees, orphans, and destruction that takes decades for recovery.

45. Hornus, in *It Is*, 158, 163, 243.

46. For the testimony of a former Lockheed missile engineer who left his job for Christian reasons, see Aldridge, "Courage."

47. For such a miracle in our time, see Corson, "Welcoming"; Jackson, *Dial 911*; and J. H. Yoder, *What?*

48. 1 Timothy 2:1-2. Wallis, "Prayer"; Nouwen, "Letting Go." See also Wink, *Engaging*, 314-17. Recall that leaders in the early church contended that they were the true defenders of the peace of the empire because they prayed against the evil powers that incite war and violence.

Christians in positions of public responsibility must recognize that the laws and institutions of most societies often function to protect the self-interest of certain privileged groups of citizens. For this reason, when we as Christians (or Jews and Muslims) seek to advocate policies that express the biblical mandates for justice, peace, and respect for life, we may well lose our jobs.[49] The primary calling for Christians is not to be agents of *state-government* law and justice, but ambassadors of *God's* way of setting things right (justification) through Jesus Christ. Our vocational employment, therefore, is to seek expression of our Christian vocation of bearing witness to *God's* justice and peace. The Spirit's leading and discernment of the faith community ought to guide and empower.[50]

There are many avenues of service and witness open to Christians.[51] Christians contribute much to society by teaching in schools, working in health care of many types, building homes for people, managing and serving in restaurants, holding positions in local governments, and much more that contributes to the welfare of our communities.[52]

As Christians, we are to be vigilant in our witness to Christ in all spheres of life, speaking truth to power in humility and honesty. We are to seek the welfare of not only "our" country's people, but shalom for all peoples. To illustrate, Christians who seek to obey Jesus' command to love enemies[53] and witness to government on the course of action that will least alienate the enemy—and possibly open doors for cooperation and mutual

---

49. Elkhart Circuit Court Judge William Bontrager in Elkhart, IN, resigned over moral conflict with legal writ: *Newsweek*, December 2, 1981, 1259–60.

50. On paying taxes for an ever-spiraling military (war) budget, see my article, "Payment," 57–65.

51. Sugden, *Dream*; Taylor, *Blockade*; Bishop, *Technique*. For the inspiring story of how a French congregation during World War II saved the lives of more than 2,000 Jews, see Hallie, *Innocent*.

52. Two special problems that arise are use of force in the discipline of children and in the restraint of a thief, rapist, or possible killer. For the former, the good of the child and love for the child require clear expression of parental authority; the discipline (which rarely may include spanking, in my judgment) must be guided not by anger or revenge but by genuine love and concern for the child's well-being (Eph 6:1–4). In the latter case, diversionary tactics and the *word*-weapon of reprimand should be our first response. Use of force as an expression of care to whomever it is applied may be used so long as it is motivated by love and no permanent physical harm is done. We must remember that force usually evokes more force, violence evokes more violence. For stories of nonviolent resistance in life-threatening situations, see Bauman, *Coals*; Lehn, *Peace*; Fry, *Victories*; and Egan, *Peace*.

53. True, many Christians do not believe Jesus' love command applies to war, but restrict the sphere of application. See Swartley, *Covenant*, 60–61, and also *Slavery*, 101. For extensive treatment of the scholarly evasion among German theologians over the last several centuries, see Bauman, *Sermon*.

assistance in the future. When the USA (President George W. Bush and others) began voicing intent to invade Iraq (the second time), it was clear to me that this would alienate more than strengthen either country in the long run. Accordingly, I wrote a letter to *People's Forum* of my local newspaper and sent copies to my representative and senators. Several years after invasion, it became clear that warmongering in Afghanistan and Iraq galvanized terrorists hateful of Western imperialism.

John Paul Lederach, a leading voice in conflict resolution, said this regarding Iraq (I paraphrase): If only the leaders of the two nations had gathered around a table to discuss their fears and differences, the horrible consequences of thousands of casualties (American, Allies, Iraqis, and now Syrians and Kurds as well) and the mounting numbers of widows, orphans, and refugees could have been avoided. Alternative actions were not considered.

Faith voices are too often marginalized by government leaders because they assume they do not have adequate information. In the case of Iraq, however, it became clear that government leaders not only had inadequate information, but also false information. Faith communities frequently have useful data about various countries from non-governmental organizations or relief, service and mission personnel in those countries.

Conclusion, with Stories

Two stories illustrate how the theses of this book, "two sides of a coin," are intertwined.

George McClain, in *Claiming All Things for God*, relates how ritual use of exorcism was used to free social, financial, and political systemic power from demonic control. The setting was Louisville, Kentucky, where the Board of the United Methodist Church was to meet. The time was 1987, prior to the formal ending of apartheid in South Africa. For several years strong protests had been lodged against the United Methodist General Board of Pensions for not divesting funds from South African corporations, but the board did not heed the pleas. In the summer before this event McClain had shared his frustration at a spirituality retreat, "Journey Inward, Journey Outward," that he led. A participant at the retreat suggested a service of social exorcism that she prepared on behalf of the blockage. Spirits of fear and intimidation, lust for power, mammon, and patriarchy were named, for these seemed to be the blockers preventing open consideration of the issues. Several weeks after that session, the general secretary of the board, who was firmly against divestment, announced his resignation.

With this background to the Louisville meeting three months after the retreat, McClain called together a small prayer group the night before a larger group was to conduct a public service of social exorcism outside the Seelbach Hotel in Louisville, where the board was to meet the following day. The exorcist words were not against board members but against the "powers" that blocked change. For the first time, the board was open to the pleas of the Methodist Federation for Social Action, which McClain represented. Dialogue in smaller groups continued into the night, and the way opened for change in the board's policies.[54] While McClain demurs on drawing a direct cause-effect relationship, the apparent divine intervention is striking!

The second story, from Leipzig, East Germany, 1989, shows the power of corporate prayer against Communist oppression. In the St. Nicholai church in Leipzig many began to meet on Monday nights for prayer, crying out to God to change the tyranny of their political system. Both believers and unbelievers came together to pray. As one East German-born Christian from Grand Rapids, Michigan, put it, with tears in her eyes, people who had never come to church came and called upon God for help—in simple but powerfully earnest prayers.

At that point the political situation became very tense, and the people thought the troops of the Communist Party would come and crush their hopes by force. But the church beseeched both the government and the people to refrain from violence. This petition was read from every pulpit in the city and over the municipal public-address system. Organizers called those who wanted to do something for their country to come to the church that evening; 70,000 people showed up.[55] Soon the secret police, for reasons never explicitly stated, departed from the scene of the peaceful rally. The people wept with joy and praised God for a new "Red Sea" miracle.

These are two modern stories of triumph. The church honored its Lord and trusted God for victory over the powers of evil. It is all too true, however, that in some cases, perhaps even similar to either of these two manifestations of evil (personal and power structures),[56] groups resort to hellish strategies. ISIS and Boko Haram terrorist groups kidnap and kill Christian

---

54. McClain, *Claiming*, 120–25. See also MacNutt's narrative of this event under the title "Both-And," in *Deliverance*, 262–63.

55. Moltmann reports that 300,000 joined the prayer vigils over the six Monday evenings, with candles and prayers for the reunification of Germany: Moltmann, "Foreword," in *Politics*, xiii–xiv. Snyder Belousek cites Swoboda, Pierard, and Arnold, *Revolution*; see Snyder Belousek, *Atonement*, 628–29.

56. These stories, together with those ending chapters 5 and 6, exemplify the purpose of this book: to show that evil is to be confronted when the demonic appears in personal or sociopolitical forms. We take a stand against policies motivated by evil principles. Nations rise and fall, but the "Lord of Hosts/Powers" endures and will triumph.

believers, in Iraq, Syria, and northern Nigeria. Evil leaves its legacy of martyrs. What will be the outcome of evil's tentacles in the sociopolitical policies of governments worldwide where the powerful rich threaten the welfare of the weak, the marginalized, and those of different racial or religious origins? Borrowing Jon Meacham's recent book's subtitle, consider *The Battle for Our Better Angels*,[57] but let us insert, *God's*, for *Ours*.

When sequential racial attacks, bombings, and shootings of the innocent for whatever reason occur frequently in our society and other countries as well, we need to examine our personal and corporate souls and pray: "Lord, deliver me (and us) from the demonic powers let loose in our culture, politics, and even in our churches. Bring together all peoples divided by hate and enmity." In these times peacemaking across enemy lines beckons covenantal faith communities to witness against the world's tragic conflicts and wars: Syria/Iraq, Yemen, Afghanistan, South Sudan, the Congo, the August 11–12, 2017, Charlottesville violence, the mass shootings from Sandy Hook Elementary School, Newtown, Connecticut, Las Vegas, Nevada, and Buddhist Myanmar's deadly (genocidal?) treatment of Muslim Rohingyas.[58]

A powerful witness in our time was Steve Hartman's story, "On the Road," contrasting people fighting each other at Charlottesville, Virginia (August 12, 2017), with a scene less than three weeks later from Houston, Texas, where a human chain of about fifteen people linked arms while standing in waist-high water to rescue an African American from a car two-thirds covered with water. Hartman said that if you took out of the chain one Muslim, one undocumented person, or one African American, the chain would break and the person in the car would drown.[59]

Sign of Hope

Enemy Love: Derek Black is the son of Don Black, the brains behind Stormfront, a major white-nationalist website. His mother, Chloe, had been married to David Duke, who is Derek's godfather. Some white nationalists consider Derek the heir to

---

57. Meacham, *Soul*.

58. For a moving analysis of the Syrian conflict, as well as the larger Middle East conflict, I recommend a fifty-three-minute interview of Coy Barefoot with Roy Hange, who spent six years in Syria, three in Egypt, and one in Iran at the Qom Islamic seminary. At http://insidecville.com/world/roy-hange-4-17-17/.

59. (September 1, 2017; "CBS Evening News.") Another powerful story comes from the Hutu-Tutsi genocide in Rwanda and Burundi when forty boys in a school in Burundi would not self-identify Tutsi or Hutu, resulting in the shooting of all of them (with many killed). Told by Jodi Mikalachki in *Rejoice* (January 27, 2017).

leadership of the white nationalist movement. After Derek was outed as an anti-Semite on his college campus, Matthew Stevenson, the only Orthodox Jew on campus, invited Derek to a Shabbat meal. Derek then became a regular at Shabbat meals and eventually renounced white nationalist ideas.[60]

"Lord God, forbid that nuclear war ever begin; save us from 2 Peter 3:11–12, but fulfill the hope and reality of 2 Peter 3:13 and Revelation 21:1–4. Let your will be done, as it is in heaven so on earth . . . deliver us from evil/the evil one" (AT).

Prayerful Reflection: A Franciscan Blessing[61]

May God bless you with discomfort at easy answers, half-truths, and superficial relationships, so that you may live deep within your heart.

May God bless you with anger at injustice, oppression, and exploitation of people, so that you may work for God's justice, God's freedom, and God's peace.

May God bless you with tears to shed for those who suffer from pain, rejection, starvation, and war, so that you may reach out your hand to comfort them and to turn their pain into joy.

And may God bless you with enough foolishness to believe that you can make a difference in this world, so that you can do what others claim cannot be done.

And the blessing of God—Father, Son, and Holy Spirit—be upon you, those you love, and those for whom you pray this day and for evermore . . . Amen

---

60. *ChrCent*, Sept 27, 2017, in "Century Marks" (p. 8), quoted from *Foreward*, Aug 24, 2017. This exemplifies what Roy Hange said in his interview with Coy Barefoot the day after the Charlottesville tragedy: the way forward is not on the streets with opposing sides. It is taking someone on the other side out for lunch for face-to-face conversation, listening respectfully to differences in views of right and wrong. If that is too threatening, each might talk about their grandparents, who they were, their struggles, and their views on the issues of their day. The goal is turning enemies into friends. See Friedrich, "Demons." Sobering, but in the last paragraph, a ray of hope.

61. https://carolyncustisjames.com/2017/03/05/franciscan-blessing-for-our-time/ Mar 5, 2017.

11

Deliverance Healing: Theory, Discernment, and Methods

And though this world with devils filled,
should threaten to undo us,
We will not fear for God hath willed
his truth to triumph through us.
The prince of darkness grim,
we tremble not for him;
His rage we can endure, for lo, his doom is sure,
One little word shall fell him.

—Martin Luther, "A Mighty Fortress is Our God," stanza 3

Pope Francis is urging priests who hear confessions of troubled souls
to call on the services of an exorcist.
An exorcist could be useful in dealing with a variety of spiritual disorders . . .
some of which could have a supernatural source.
Pope Francis has mentioned the devil more frequently than his predecessors,
And he refers to the devil as a physical presence in the world.
The pope has likened priests who sexually abuse children
to those participating in a satanic mass.

—Guardian, March 17, 2017; ChrCent, April 12, 2017

This chapter has three parts. Part 1 addresses the relation of biblical thought on demons and deliverance to our modern/postmodern world with its scientific orientation. While affirming differences between the ancient world and today, I propose that biblical teachings and practices on this topic are relevant in the twenty-first century.

Part 2 sets forth basic understandings for engaging in deliverance ministry: the relation of demonic oppression or obsession to mental health; indications of demonic bondage; and other insights and considerations. It calls for discernment in every situation.

Part 3 identifies and describes different approaches and methods used in healing-deliverance ministries, with evaluative comments.

Biblical to Modern/Postmodern World

When we move from Scripture to our modern/postmodern world, key issues are:

1. Since demons were so much a part of the first century world view, shouldn't we as moderns leave them there?[1] We have seen in chapter 5 that exorcisms were not isolated phenomena in Jesus' ministry. They were integral to the gospel's proclamation, the triumph of God's kingdom over Satan's power. Moreover, Graham Twelftree points out that there was already skepticism about demon possession in the first century.[2] The Gospels distinguish between bondage and illness. Hence Christian believers narrated the gospel story in that context. To hold the view that evil spirits were simply first-century superstitions undermines the earliest Christian testimonies in the Synoptic Gospels on a key point in their testimony.[3]

---

1. Acolatse's recent book addresses this issue, comparing and critiquing Christian believers in the West and Africa on responses to the spirit-world. She begins, saying, "While we cannot simply assert that belief in and attention to spirit(s) has led to the numerical growth in the South, while the lack of such belief has caused the decline of faith in the North, the starkly contrasting experience and expression of Christian witness in the two regions of the world at least raises the question." *Powers*, 1.

2. Twelftree, *Christ*, 27.

3. William James said at the turn of the twentieth century, "The refusal of the modern 'enlightenment' to treat 'possession' as an hypothesis to be spoken of as even possible, in spite of the massive human tradition based on concrete experience in its favor, has always seemed to me a curious example of the power of fashion in things scientific. That the demon-theory will have its innings again is to my mind absolutely certain. One has to be 'scientific' indeed, to be blind and ignorant enough to suspect no such possibility." In *Proceedings*, 586.

2. Do the Gospels clearly distinguish between healings and exorcism? Some texts emphasize the healing ministry of Jesus, and include those demonized as a constituent part (Matt 4:24; 15:28; 17:17f; Luke 6:18; 8:2; 9:42; Acts 15:16). Acts 10:38 describes Jesus' entire ministry as "healing those who were oppressed by the devil." Other texts distinguish between sick and demonized persons (Mark 1:32, 39; Matt 4:24; 8:16; 10:1, 8; Luke 6:18; 13:32: Acts 5:16; 8:7). This difference is resolved when we view Jesus' ministry as a conquest over all evil powers and manifestations. In the first-century worldview sickness and demonization were ultimately interconnected with "paradise lost." Since the Gospels distinguish between possession and illness, this raises two cautions: first, that we not rule out demon oppression and obsession (more rarely, possession) in a person, and, second, that we do not attribute all physical, emotional illness, and disabilities to demons.

3. Since Paul's letters and John's Gospel do not report exorcisms, should exorcism be part of the church's ministry today? Hamm cites this point for why exorcism should not be a continuing ministry.[4] Twelftree (2007) raises cautions also,[5] even though earlier (1985) he held exorcism is mandated for the church. Luke's account of Paul's mission in Acts indicates exorcism was practiced in the spread of the gospel. Since the Synoptic Gospels were written in the last third of the first century for pastoral, missional, and catecheticsal functions, their extensive attention to Jesus' exorcisms would present a most perplexing dilemma to believers then (and now) if it was not understood as part of the church's ongoing ministry.

4. Demonic powers may infest individuals and sociopolitical systemic structures. This cautions us against an exclusive focus on only deliverance ministry in spiritual warfare against evil; or, vice versa, focusing on combating evil only in economic and sociopolitical dimensions. Our Christian calling is to resist and counter evil on both sides of the coin, the image in my "Introduction." The Christ-model is not military conquest of human enemies, but disarming demonic powers through the prophetic Word spoken by humble servants who model the way of the cross and love for the person(s) or structures wherever the enemy is at work.

---

4. Hamm cites ten reasons why the church today should not take exorcism as normative for its practice and then seven reasons why it should. After assessing the arguments, he leans toward employing it in the church's ministry today, but with caution and care: "Ministry," 49–52.

5. Twelftree, *Name*.

5. In the Gospel narratives that narrate deliverance for demonized persons, we gain no clue concerning the cause of demonization. The person is not blamed for the situation, though the Pharisees are held culpable for their unbelief. In light of the relationship between demons, idolatry, and paganism, some "opening" to those powers likely lies behind the phenomenon of demonization, whether by the person directly, through ancestral influence,[6] or other means.

6. Is it possible for believers to fall captive to demon oppression or possession?[7] The Calvinist tradition with its emphasis on the security of the believer in Jesus Christ has tended to answer the question negatively. When believers are living victoriously, praising God, and witnessing to the gospel's power, demonization is nigh impossible. However, in nominal Christianity the situation is too often otherwise: laxity in spiritual nurture and flirting with sin may open one to demonic power. The Roman Catholic Church recognizes the need for more trained exorcists with the goal of a trained exorcist in every diocese, because more and more people are dabbling with various magical practices that lead to oppression or obsession.[8] In today's world with computers and smart phones, evils of all sorts (witchcraft and violence on TV shows and computer games, hurtful, hateful text messages on smart phones, and pornography) worm into our minds and hearts, often surreptitiously. Parental guidance and moral conviction against evil is most necessary. Relationship to Jesus Christ through prayer, meditation on Scripture, and corporate worship (with praise to God and Jesus Christ) are the most effective forms of protection from evil. In contrast, computer games oriented to violence, novels filled with violence and/or wizardry, where spells are cast, and heavy

---

6. On ancestral influence, the OT speaks frequently that the effects of one's sins may extend into the third and fourth generation (Deut 23:2; Exod 20:5). See Littrell, "Origin . . . Limit." Littrell explains this by that culture: households consisted of three or four generations living as one extended family. In contrast, however, to the third or fourth generation limit, God's love extends to thousands of generations (Exod 20:6, *passim*). Ezekiel 18 (cf. Jer 31:30), however, objects to using this generational principle to explain the plight of the exiles, i.e., blaming their punishment on the sins of their forebearers (18:2–3). Rather, Ezekiel affirms personal accountability, "the person who sins shall die" (18:20). Psychological insights of family systems attest, however, to the generational principle.

7. One of the best discussions of this is by Appleby, *It's Only*, 54–81.

8. Hear the podcast: http://www.ministrymatters.com/all/entry/8065/more-exorcisms-and-better-health-care.

metal music (some with Satan-voice lines and invitations) open a person to the demonic.[9]

The OT covenant people were tempted by idolatrous influences and all too frequently capitulated. Likewise, believers are warned against fellowship with demons (1 Cor 10:14–22). As Schlier writes, "Even Christians are not immune from the influence of these dumb idols if they venture near them, for though the idols are nothing, the demons control them."[10]

7. The best way to resist temptations is to be rooted and grounded in Scripture, and do as Jesus did: quote a Scripture that repels the demonic thought, such as: "Resist the devil and he will flee from you" . . . or, begone, Satan, in the name of Jesus. Another: "the truth is in Jesus" (Eph 4:21), "get behind me, Satan." Reciting Psalm 18:1–3 is powerful:

> I love you, O Lord, my strength. The Lord is my rock, my fortress, and my deliverer, my God, my rock in whom I take refuge, my shield, and the horn of my salvation, my stronghold. I call upon the Lord, who is worthy to be praised, so I shall be saved from my enemies.

Everyone sins in thought, if not in deed. But, "If we confess our sins, he who is faithful and just will forgive us our sins and cleanse us from all unrighteousness" (1 John 1:9). Thanks be to God and Christ Jesus. Come, Holy Spirit, to anoint us for service in Jesus' name.

Discernment: Theological and Practical

The Relation of the Demonic to Psychological and Sociological Understandings

The demonic seldom appears in isolation, unconnected with larger psychological, sociological, and/or political realities. Scripture depicts demons/Satan as deceptive (Matt 4:1–11; John 8:44; 2 Cor 2:11; 4:3–6; 11:14–15; 2 Thess 2:9; Heb 2:14). Demonic powers seldom appear in the open. Usually they strive to appear as, and work under the guise of something else.

---

9. Amorth describes "Satanic Rock." It is "the most diffuse method of transmitting the principles of Satanism," which consists of three rules: "you may do all that you wish, no one has the right to command you, and you are the god of yourself." *Exorcist*, 54. He describes what Satanism is and "a rite of consecration to Satan." See 32–37.

10. Schlier, *Principalities*, 27. First Corinthians 10 is addressed to believers.

This has profound implications for the church's healing ministry. It means that outward resemblances between alleged cases of bondage and forms of mental illness do not necessarily mean that the former interpretations are fanciful. While they may be in some cases, it is also possible that psychological illness and demonization are intertwined. Demons may enter and take advantage of malfunctioning psychological and social development arising often from deep hurts and disappointments in life (and here the devil does not play fair or show mercy). The demonic distorts and intensifies fears, hostilities, projections, imbalances, etc. that are already there.

Those engaged in scientific forms of healing are encouraged to consider whether the demonic is a factor. Also, those in deliverance ministries must consider psychological illness. Attempts to explain such cases as wholly psychological are as misguided as attempts to explain all of them as demonic. The ideal is for medical and spiritual healers to cooperate. Each needs the diagnostic abilities of the other. Patients undergoing scientific treatment will need the spiritual strength and community that science cannot give. Those freed from demons will often need psychological counseling and social healing, as well as spiritual nurture and pastoral care lest more devils return (Luke 11:24–26).

The Role of Personal Responsibility

Spiritual interpretations of problems are often rejected because those who suffer seem to blame everything on Satan, avoiding responsibility for whatever occurs. But if the demonic works in conjunction with psychic and social processes, the latter dimensions are to some degree under human control. There will be at least a limited area within which an afflicted person can choose, and positive choices are essential to healing. On the other hand, since evil has a binding power, this means that once one has given in to it, even in little ways, one tends to be afflicted by forces far stronger than bargained for. If the demonic—sin, flesh, the world, Satan's hosts, et al.—are corporate supra-personal Powers, curiously exploring them is like stepping into a rushing river. One may wade in only a few steps before being swept away by a current whose force one cannot break. Nevertheless, one can fight the current to some degree or struggle part way back to the shore, and doing so may be essential to coming within reach of help from another.

In healing, it will be necessary to take both truths into account. Troubled persons must be encouraged to take responsibility wherever they can. Yet the magnitude of their bondage must also be recognized. Deliverance in some form may be necessary.

Indications of Bondage

The demonic may be active in personal psycho-social ways as well as in sociocultural structures of economics and politics. Signs of demonic presence in the personal psychosocial realm are:

1. A sense of being *ultimately* overwhelmed, swamped, trapped, victimized and unable to extricate oneself from the morass. Such feelings may occasionally assail anyone as awareness of evil. But when this recurs, so that hope for deliverance through Jesus (Rom 7:25—8:2) seems impossible, the demonic is possibly at work. This is not to be confused with depression, though in some cases depression *may* be the result of the demonic.

2. A fear of *ultimate* condemnation (1 John 4:17–18), conveyed especially through fear of death (Heb 2:14–16), yet with suicidal promptings. This manifests in feeling unworthy, unclean, unlikeable, deserving of punishment. This is deeper than discouragement or remorse over one's faults. The feeling extends to the core, being inherently polluted. Such cannot come from the Creator, but only from the opposing power that feeds upon life traumas. This is not simply the problem of low self-esteem, but rather the persisting crushing feeling of *no* self-worth.

3. Social marginalization. Many whom Jesus exorcised were outcasts from society or on its fringes. Whether their bondage led to marginalization, or marginalization was causative of bondage, is difficult to discern. Whichever is the case, isolation and alienation are often deeply intertwined with bondage. This underscores the importance of community in the healing process.

4. Response to the holy. Based analogically upon the outcries of the demons in the presence of Jesus, negative reaction to Christian symbols such as the Bible, the cross, or praising God in song—expressions of the holy—are strong indicators. Inability to pray or hear the name *Jesus may* also be signals of demon oppression. Reaction to either a cross, Bible, or name of Jesus may involve violence, cursing, or (trying to) escape.[11]

---

11. In one case a psychiatrist asked me to visit a tormented person in a psychiatric ward, where the two of us were placed in a room with no chairs but only counters (ca. three feet high on opposite sides of the room). The moment I opened my Bible and looked down to read it, the Bible was knocked onto the floor. Either the person "flew" to do it, or the demon itself did it. It's still a mystery to me, since the person I was asked to help was seated on the opposite counter and at the opposite end of the room about twelve feet away from me.

5. Unusual power, pre-knowledge, or actions that defy explanation. The first of these was evident in the Gadarene demoniac. One or more of these have been cited frequently in cases of demonic control throughout history and currently as well, such as a boy walking backward up a wall[12] or backward rapid handwriting.[13]

Exorcism and Jesus' Love Command

A practical issue that arises in exorcism is how we apply Jesus' love command, even for the enemy, in violent situations. It is clear we must distinguish between the individual and the demonic powers oppressing the individual. Caring love must be shown to the individual while at the same time we must have a Jesus-type "cleansing of the temple" response to the evil powers. Declaring Jesus' love command (Matt 5:44; 22:37–39) is a powerful antidote to demonic powers (as my story at the end of chapter 5 illustrates). When a person seeks self-destruction under the influence of the demonic, physical restraint is necessary. But in the experiences I have witnessed, a strong command to "no violence" stops the violence. A proposed guideline is: physical restraint may/should be used if necessary when it expresses love to the one applied; the recipient would acknowledge it as an expression of love when he/she is functioning normally.

Swinton, in his excellent book on pastoral responses to evil, focuses on the necessity of compassion in the face of evil.[14] He does not address exorcism as such, but observes that the post-Enlightenment preoccupation with a "theodicy" to explain evil if God is all-powerful and loving was not the preoccupation of the early church. Swinton tells the story of Flores, who walked into the sea one night in an attempt to take his own life, and then analyzes it from a pastoral perspective. Given the factors that led to Flores's pain, psychological misery, and physical suffering, Swinton says that as Christians we are "to look at what Flores' life looks like when seen from the perspective of the open arms of Christ, who died for all and offers the possibility of forgiveness and redemption to all people."[15] This vision of possible newness of life is necessary when engaging in deliverance ministry—and also in witness to the powers (see chapter 10). Our loving God is the context

---

12. This action was witnessed by police and counselors. Cited in the podcast referred to above.

13. For help in discernment, see Q &A on the demonic: http://qideas.org/videos/qa-exorcism-the-spiritual-reality/

14. Swinton, *Raging*.

15. Ibid., 76n8.

for our compassion: "*a primary mode of resistance to evil is the ability to love God and to find ways of continuing to love God even in the midst of evil.*"[16] Swinton quotes Tom Torrance for this perspective in facing evil:

> This movement of God's holy love into the heart of the world's evil and agony is not to be understood as a direct act of sheer almighty power, for it is not God's purpose to shatter and annihilate the agents and embodiments of evil in the world, but rather to pierce into the innermost center of evil power where it is entrenched in the piled-up and self-compounding guilt of humanity in order to vanquish it from within and below, by depriving it of the structures of half-truth or outright lies on which it thrives and of the twisted forms of legality behind which it embattles itself and from which it fraudulently gains its power. Here we have an entirely different kind and quality of power, for which we have no analogies in our experience to help understand it, since it transcends every kind of moral and material power we know.[17]

The latter half of Swinton's book names "practices" for pastoral response to evil:

> Lament as Resistance and Deliverance
> Forgiveness in the Face of Radical Evil
> Thoughtfulness: What are People For?
> Friendship, Strangeness, and Hospitality Community

In confronting demonic powers, Jesus' love command undermines the very basis on which demonic power flourishes. Commanding demons to leave in the name of Jesus Christ is powerful because of the cruciform love of God in Jesus, God's Son, for our sins.[18]

Scripture's Primary Emphasis: God's Protection and Victory

Demonic oppression must be viewed within the entire biblical revelation. While much Scripture is power encounter (Kamps), the accent falls on God's sovereignty, protection, and victory. The image of Zion,[19] central to Isaiah and many Psalms, connotes God's sovereignty and victory, calling

---

16. Ibid., 76.

17. Ibid., 66–67. Torrance, *Divine*, 136. This quote applies directly to chapter 10 and deliverance ministry, since in many cases *deception* heads the demon coalition.

18. Peckham's *Theodicy of Love* promises development of this approach to evil.

19. Ollenburger, *Zion*; Hess and Wenham, eds., *Zion*. These two sources complement each other, since they focus on different parts of the OT.

us to trust in God's care, and repudiate pride and power. The prominence of angels throughout the biblical narrative gives us confidence that God watches over and protects us.[20] God's angels, the Holy Spirit, and our union with Christ Jesus in his exalted position over all evil powers insures us ample security and safety.

The primary emphasis of Scripture, therefore, is on God's triumph over evil, not on evil itself. The appropriate Christian response is worship, praise, and adoration of God and our Lord Jesus Christ. Our first emphasis should be on prevention of demonic oppression through full commitment of our lives to worshipful praise of God. In Revelation each cycle of oppressive persecution by demonic political power ends with the crescendo of worship bursting out in praise, to the power of God and the victory of the Lamb.[21]

> "You are worthy, our Lord and God,
> to receive glory and honor and power,
> for you created all things,
> and by your will they existed and were created."
>
> "Worthy is the Lamb that was slaughtered
> to receive power and wealth
> and wisdom and might and honor
> and glory and blessing!"
>
> Then I heard every creature in heaven
> and on earth and under the earth and in the sea,
> and all that is in them, singing,
> "To the one seated on the throne and to the Lamb
> be blessing and honor
> and glory and might forever and ever!"
>
> [Then]I heard what seemed to be
> the loud voice of a great multitude in heaven, saying,
> **"Hallelujah!**
> Salvation and glory and power to our God.
> **For the Lord our God the Almighty reigns."**
> (Rev 4:11; 5:12–13; 19:1b, 6b)

---

20. On "Guardian Angels," see Garrett, *No Ordinary*, 139–185. We may pray for God's angels to protect us. References to angels appear more often than do devil(s), Satan, and evil spirits in the Bible, according to Young's *Concordance*. In Smith's *Greek-English Concordance*, angel(s) occurs 186 times; devil, 38 times; demon(s) (noun and verb), 78 times; and Satan, 37 times. While "evil spirit," appears 47 times, the (my) Spirit/Holy Spirit/Spirit of God or Spirit of the Lord/Christ/Truth occurs 226 times.

21. Webber's *Celebrating* richly describes how the worship of the believing, praising community is both historically and contemporarily a crucial resource for triumph over demonic powers.

Methods Utilized in Deliverance Ministry

I identify eleven differing but interrelated approaches to or methods in deliverance ministry. But first I describe briefly my own approach. Since my initial exposure was through Dean Hochstetler's ministry (#1 below), elements of that approach mark my own. But I follow a more structured liturgical approach (#4 below). Resources for this appear in Appendix 1. On occasion I have utilized aspects of healing prayer, similar to numerous methods below, as prelude to confronting demons and commanding them to leave. I am not trained as a counselor. When I perceive this is needed instead of deliverance or as follow-up, I urge the person who has come for help to connect with a counselor that fits the situation, often a psychiatrist.

1. Dean Hochstetler. Dean's approach moves from discernment to confession of known sins (includes generational) to confronting and casting out the demons. It includes commanding the demons to speak their names, give grounds for entering, and tell which demon is head. They then may be cast out one by one, or all commanded to be tied to the "head" demon, and as a group commanded in the name of Jesus to leave.

I have witnessed this method by participating in deliverance sessions in Dean Hochstetler's home. Usually a family member or pastor brings the person to ascertain whether the demonic is causative of certain actions, thought patterns, or illness. Sometimes persons were referred to Dean by a psychiatrist or psychologist/counselor. In some cases a person from some distance might first phone and make arrangements to come by air, and stay in Dean and Edna's home (under command of no violence) up to a week or two, for three to five sessions spread out when a small group of people could meet.

Usually six to eight people were present for a given session, some from Dean's congregation and one or two from his Indiana-Michigan Conference Oversight Committee. A typical session might begin with prayer and Scripture. A second longer stage consists of conversation with the person concerning factors relevant to demon entrance into one's life. For the second stage Dean would often give the person a tablet and ask him/her to list all known sins (including generational) and magician-type practices. When completed, Dean would look over the list and then ask the person to repent of these sins. Then Dean would tear up the sheet, and pronounce forgiveness in Jesus' name, putting it all "under the blood" of Jesus. Then demons, when ordered to leave, could not use any of these sins as grounds to stay.[22]

---

22. This list includes willful sins, trauma experiences, magical practices, or generational sins. Sometimes secretive events in the person's family history, such as a suicide that was "silenced" and consequentially operative as generational influence upon the

The confrontation stage begins with Dean saying to the person, "Now I will not be speaking to you, but to the demons directly." As these commands begin, the person often goes into a type of trance, and the encounter ensues directly with and against demon voices. After demanding the demons to give their names, and reason for entry, Dean would decide whether he takes each demon one by one, or group them for commands to them to leave. Most often the demon would first refuse and give a reason (true or not) for his right to be in this person. Almost always, there were numerous demons (some were strong and stubborn, saying "he/she belongs to me"). Demons love to lie, and were often put to the test of truth, "speak the truth, and nothing but the truth. If you don't, I'll command you to a hotter place in hell." At that point violence might almost erupt, but Dean would command, "no violence in the name of Jesus." If generational demons were found, often the result of curses or occult practices (Deut 27:9–26; Exod 20:5–6), the power of that curse on the person was broken in the name of Jesus.

At times in this process, Dean would ask the gathered praying-group to sing "There's Power in the Blood," "When I Survey the Wondrous Cross," or something similar. On one occasion I recall the demon left shortly after hearing "There's Power in the Blood" sung with gusto. Demons don't like praise to God or Jesus.[23] When a demon leaves, the person is immediately *there* as himself or herself, relieved and joyful, but sometimes only partially so, and hence more discernment, and then confrontation would resume. A given session was usually two hours, but occasionally, the "combat" could go to three or four hours. If victory was not complete, Dean would command the demons not to afflict the person, until the group met again. The person would not know what happened in the exorcism process—only freedom at the end.[24]

On more than one occasion, Dean would find no demon (no voice would speak back). Dean would then say, "I found nothing demonic in the person" and refer the person to a pastor counselor, or mental health worker. After an exorcism Dean discussed follow-up, making sure the person's pastor or counselor would assist toward sustaining Christian victory. Dean emphasized "the authority of the believer." He recommended MacMillan's *Authority*.

---

demonized person, would be the root of the oppression.

23. That's why Robert Webber says that when someone would come to him for help, he would ask, "Are you attending church and worshipping?" If not, then go do that for a while and then come back to see me if your problem persists. If you need help then I'll give the time for it.

24. Not all deliverance healers speak to demons. For those who do and don't, see Warren, *Cleansing*, 11n52–53.

Standard policy was not to touch the person in demonic trance. The distinction between the person speaking and a demon speaking was clear. While words spoken to the person were those of encouragement, care, love, and hope, words spoken to the demons were much different—no signals of love and care for them![25]

2. Charles Kraft and Francis McNutt. I put these two together, representing both Protestant Evangelical and Roman Catholic traditions and their writings and ministries.[26] Kraft's approach first deals with healing of memories. When that is completed, he commands demons attached to any hurtful memories to leave in the name of Jesus Christ.

Several years ago I attended his two-day seminar, "*Two Hours to Freedom*,"[27] in Nappanee, Indiana, at the First Brethren Church that ordained Dr. Kraft many years ago. I was struck with the difference and similarity to what I had learned from Hochstetler. Kraft's healing of memories focuses on any trauma the person experienced, beginning with conception (in the womb) until the present. He moves through one's life-journey, several years at a time, inquiring what "hurts" may have occurred. When a "hurt" would surface in memory, he would ask the person, "do (can) you see Jesus there at that experience and what is he saying to you?" Kraft showed a video of a young woman, in her late twenties, who had many "hurts" beginning with pre-birth in her mother's womb. She was conceived before her parents' marriage. While in the womb she felt "unwanted" and "unloved." Her parents confirmed facts that led to her feelings.

Once the "healing of hurtful memories" through all the phases of her life was completed, Kraft would address any demons that had entered in relation to her feelings of hurt and trauma. This part took about one-fourth the time that was spent on "Healing of Memories." Kraft would command any demon that spoke to leave. Most of the demons spoke in

25. Working with SRA (Satanic Ritual Abuse) requires a different approach, which I do not take up in this book. Deliverance from vows is often required but the need is for ongoing, often "draining" care-giving. I recommend two resources: J. Friesen, *Uncovering*, and Knight and Getzinger, "Care-Giving."

26. For description of Evangelical and Catholic views, see Warner, "Evangelical," and Sears, "Catholic." Sears is especially helpful in identifying four areas of bondage, and the types of deliverance needed for each (108–10).

27. Note Kraft's book subtitle. Kraft's widely known *Confronting* book was prompted by experiencing the healing ministries of Peter Wagner and John Wimber. See pp. 12–15 for his "Testimony." The Vineyard Churches are an outgrowth of Wimber's influence. For critique of Wimber, see Coggins and Hiebert, eds., *Wonders*. See also Smedes, ed., *Ministry* with Hubbard's foreword. A twelfth model, Appleby's, *It's Only*, coming to my attention late, integrates power encounter with truth-telling and deliverance with counseling. Stories of deliverance, written by those delivered, combine practice with testimonies.

already defeated tone, and soon left. One or two, as I recall, tried to hold on. But Kraft with a persistent ordinary tone of speech continued commanding until they left. I wished I had learned this approach earlier, but realize that I had been using a similar approach on several occasions for persons who had come to me for help. Kraft and others in this ministry emphasize "getting the garbage out first."

> What I refer to as garbage includes both *spiritual problems*, such as sin, curses, commitments to occult organizations, dedication to *evil spirits* of the gods of other religions, and *emotional* problems, such as unforgiving, hatred, anger, fear, shame, guilt, lust and the like. Demons are attached to these problems. For the person to receive complete healing, then, both the garbage and the rats need to be dealt with.[28]

Francis MacNutt's approach is similar. The circumstance that led him into deliverance ministry was his worldwide healing ministry that attracted many sick people. But sometimes a person who came to be healed would manifest demonization, through facial contortions or change of voice or switching to "*we* claim him or her." MacNutt rightly holds that demon *possession* is rare, but *demonization* (demonic influence), *infestation*, *oppression*, or *obsession*, are more often the situation. Rather than using the term *exorcism*, which implies *possession*, he prefers *deliverance*, as do most people involved in ministry to bring freedom to those oppressed by demons. A practical manual, his book is most helpful in addressing crucial topics such as discernment (is it demonic or some psychological disorder).[29] MacNutt critiques Wagner's approach of taking authority over territories or certain

---

28. Kraft, *Evangelical Guide*, 40.

29. MacNutt, *Deliverance*, 67–88. His book is laced with stories to illustrate various situations and behaviors that surface in deliverance ministry. He also has a "Questionnaire" (thirty-three questions) that he uses for one seeking deliverance (practices that may have opened the door to demons), which I find helpful, though some are less likely than others, in my judgment (161–64). He says he prefers to err on the safe side, to uncover whatever has occurred to make the person vulnerable. If a reader has been involved in any of these, he counsels: immediately repent, and in Jesus' name he commands any such demon afflicting the person to leave and go to Jesus for judgment. In cases where the demonic voice "claims" the person, MacNutt recommends four "renunciation" statements followed by three Christian commitments, which I deem helpful (207; cf. 216). Another writer and practitioner of exorcism, influenced by MacNutt, is clinical psychologist Dr. Ken Olson, *Exorcism*. His involvement in exorcism developed from his clinical counseling, when he, similar to Norberg's experience and others', came up against demonic responses from people who came for psychotherapy. His book contains quite detailed descriptions of cases he encountered, and the process it took to gain victory—one such stretched over two weeks—with description of daily efforts and behaviors of the person finally delivered, 183–201.

areas where demonization prevents gospel witness. He affirms the need for exorcism of systemic evil, and gives examples.[30]

3. Early church catechism. See chapter 9 for detailed description of this process, which is both deliverance and spiritual healing, transferring a person from the kingdom of darkness—in many cases worship of idols—to a new life and worship of God alone. In some cases this may have consisted of physical healing, but more often spiritual and emotional healing as well.[31]

4. Exorcist Liturgies. These were developed over time and used especially for exorcism (in Roman Catholic, Orthodox, and Anglican communions). This approach is ritual-oriented with careful instruction for the preparation and specific prayers spoken against the demons, with commands for them to leave. These liturgies will seem foreign to most readers, but they tell us exorcism belonged to the church's ministry since Jesus. See a lengthy sample text on YouTube.[32]

5. Tilda Norberg's healing contributions: Gestalt Therapy or Gestalt Pastoral Care. Even though her outstanding book focuses on Gestalt therapeutic healing, with many moving stories of healing numerous clients with quite different blockages to spiritual health, her book is rightly titled: *Consenting to Grace*. Excelling throughout, it describes the processes used in a wide variety of pastoral care situations. *Gestalt* connotes the whole, in both process, which takes account of body language and tone of voice, and in enabling a person to move toward *shalom*.

Unlike Fritz Perls, who introduced Gestalt healing as a *secular* therapy, Norberg, an ordained United Methodist minister, courageously combines the process with the spiritual dimension of one's life, thus Gestalt Pastoral Care. In difficult cases, she attends to whatever God-Spirit-urge comes to her. Her approaches are experimental, in which she respects the client's freedom: they may or may not do what she suggests—and the variations in "experiments" are many—from opening oneself to seeing Jesus by

---

30. He speaks of "Both-And: An Example of Social Exorcism," and narrates McClain's exorcist approach to getting the Methodist Board of Pensions to divest from South Africa because of its apartheid political practices, and Dr. Peck's analysis of the MyLai massacre (262–64). MacNutt also cites Dr. McAll's study of the demonic in the "Bermuda Triangle"—lost ships and planes—as a result of "the thousands of slaves dumped overboard and drowned in this area of the Atlantic . . . Their souls were crying out . . . for revenge." (267) MacNutt's final chapter (23) is titled "Baptism in the Holy Spirit," the source of power and discernment for deliverance/exorcist ministries, 271–77.

31. Alan Kreider describes at length the stages of this catechetical process, *Patient*, 107–14; 133–84.

32. For how designated priests prepare themselves for the exorcist rite (revised in 1952) and how to proceed, with the ritual text see: http://orthodoxanglicanism.blogspot.com/2008/04/rituale-romanum-1962-exorcism-rite.html.

"faith imagination" in a hurtful situation (even for an incest victim), to naming "lies" about oneself—and exposing them as such—so that a person can accept those as "lies" and thus free herself from those "lies" of self-condemnation so that they no longer define her self-value, to inviting a person to write their own ritual for healing, to trying foot-washing for prisoners when speaking (teaching/preaching) didn't cut through to them. Surprisingly, all in attendance chose to participate: the "walls" came down, "tears" flowed, and God's holy presence was with them, opening up new relationships among them.

Regarding these Spirit-led experiments, she says,

> Good experiments, always rooted in the present, ideally reflect the whole of a person: behavior, tone of voice, physical positions, gestures, bioenergy, spirituality, verbal sharing, and so on. Remember, there is always discernible evidence of unfinished business pushing for resolution. The Holy Spirit is always nudging us toward wholeness, and quite often evidence of these nudges can be perceived by a Gestalt Pastoral Care Minister even before the person coming for healing is aware of them.[33]

In one case, after counseling a client for years and getting nowhere, she invited the woman to participate in an exorcism, with several others present, in an evening hour. She used the Episcopal exorcist rite. The "dam" broke and healing opened her to God for wholeness. This ritual was followed by anointing and communion. The woman was miraculously made new.[34]

The last chapter of her book contains three examples of social exorcism. Each is different and together they witness to God's power at work to break demonic holds on "evil" structures and obstacles that existed for years among groups.[35]

Tilda has taught courses in seminaries. Here is her Introduction, "Gestalt Pastoral Care":

> [Gestalt healing] is holistic in its procedure and goals, paying attention to body, emotions, spirituality, cognition, social context. Body awareness in particular can reveal hidden emotions, and can guide us toward healing. Prayer, especially faith imagination, undergirds the entire process. Further, GPC is gentle and respectful. We make it clear that each person is in charge of what will happen in a session and can consent to each experiment . . .

---

33. Norberg, *Consenting*, 142. See also 150 for key paragraphs describing experiments.
34. Ibid., 263–70.
35. Ibid., 286–301.

GPC can also be intense. People often choose to plunge deeply into their depths, confronting fear, sorrow, guilt, trauma, Again and again they find God waiting for them there.[36]

6. *Healing of Memories.* David Seamands wrote on this approach in the 1980s; it has flowered in many directions. This approach, combined with healing prayer, is relevant to Leanne Payne's contribution in *Broken Image.* She focuses on healing "hurts" and "trauma" (often early in life) that connect to same-sex desire and practice.

7. Theophostic Healing: Here the focus is on bringing "truth" or "light" (from the Greek, *phōs*) to heal hurtful experiences. This approach is similar to Kraft's method in that it "invites Jesus into the memory trauma to speak the truth." At times this triggers resistance from demons, for they love and live by lies. Chapter 19 of Smith's book (about thirty pages) is devoted to dealing with the demonic. The key emphasis is to get the garbage out, focus on truth (or the light of Christ), confess sin, and then demons leave relatively easily. Focusing on truth (or light of Christ) exposes the lies (and darkness) that people accept about themselves, causing problems in living and "opening" oneself to the demonic.[37]

8. Emmanuel Prayer Ministries. This healing approach uncovers hurts and trauma to restore shalom within and in relation to others. Dr. Karl Lehman at Reba Place Fellowship, Evanston, Illinois, a medical doctor with specialty in brain science, has developed and utilizes this approach.[38] Lehman holds that internally suppressed hurtful experiences af-

---

36. Quoted from Norberg's Introduction to her course at Eastern Mennonite Seminary (1/16/13). Another of Norberg's books is: *Gathered*, which guides one in writing liturgies for personal healing. Roy Hange's experience with Gestalt Therapy leads him to make these comments: "I have found Tilda Norberg's 'Naming Lies and Truth-telling' healing ritual very helpful in pastoral care. It is a kind of slow exorcism of the falsehoods that are a part of the structures of brokenness [Norberg, *Gathered*, 177–80, for a liturgical process for "Naming Lies, Speaking the Truth"]. I have also found 'Rituals for Generational Healing' an essential way to remove and transform emotional and spiritual evil in a family system. Doing these rituals often surfaces the need to work at other emotional and spiritual healing practices." See P. Smith, *From Generation*, 147–50.

37. This approach was used in seminars led by John Lehman and assistant (Bev Wiebe) at Hesston College, Kansas, for students in the curriculum for Pastoral Ministry. Palmer Becker's critique as teacher was: while the student evaluation was overall positive, some said: "it may claim too much; it does not displace counseling in the broader sense." Others, including Becker, expressed concern that it was too closely linked to one person, Ed M. Smith, whose massive text was used for the Seminar: *Beyond Tolerable Recovery.* Smith's more recent book, *Healing Life's Hurts* has *Theophostic Healing* in its title: see www.theophostic.com. But this has now morphed into Transformation Prayer Ministry: http://www.transformationprayer.org/what-is-transformation-prayer-ministry/.

38. See and hear Dr. Karl Lehman on Emmanuel Prayer: https://www.youtube.com/

fect the brain's functioning, which in turn affects self-valuing and actions. Emmanual Prayer combines some aspects of the Theophostic method and Kraft's approaches. Rather than *truth* functioning as the power that exposes lies and disarms evil (indeed, the demonic), Emmanuel Prayer invites *Jesus* into each "hurt" and trauma. This echoes Ephesians 4:21, "truth is in Jesus."[39] This approach also combines healing of memories with exorcism, enabling deliverance/healing. An important difference, however, is that the first part of a session focuses on the positive: identifying an experience in one's life when he/she felt especially close to Jesus or God. Then in the second part, one identifies "hurt" or trauma that comes to mind as one waits for Spirit-direction. If this for whatever reason doesn't go well, the leader returns to the first part, reminding him of Jesus' presence in the experience cited earlier. I attended a half-day seminar on Emmanuel Prayer and later had a personal session with the leader. I found it helpful and was surprised at the "hurt" from many years ago that emerged. This "hurt" had no demonic edge to it, but did need to be identified, leading to healing through prayer. The leader took notes of the session and gave them to me at the end, enabling my later reflection on the process.

9. *The Body Keeps the Score*. This book by Bessel van der Kolk, MD is written in medical language, beyond my comprehension. But its approach to healing is the medical counterpart to Karl Lehman's emphasis on what happens to the brain as a result of hurtful experiences, especially PTSD caused by war shell-shock, incest, or other hurtful experiences that cause dissociation of one kind or another. It is also a medical complement to both "healing of memories," the "theophostic" healing process, and certainly Tilda Norberg's emphasis on "Gestalt Therapy," which focuses on the *body* that holds debilitating memories. The key difference is that Kolk's model is analytical from a brain, mind, and body perspective. It does not include a component of God/Jesus as Healer.

In reading Kolk's engaging narrative of "Marilyn's" story of incest abuse and his method of directing her healing process,[40] I wondered whether healing might have come sooner by encounter with Jesus as Healer in an exorcist-type ministry. In this regard, a similar book from a Christian perspective[41] integrates the healing of body, brain, and memory more holistically.

---

watch?v=Dt5TDjWruFs.

39. Karl Lehman is John Lehman's son. Google "Emmanuel Prayer" for more detailed information on this approach. Hear Jessica Handy's description of this ministry: https://www.youtube.com/watch?v=GkMdh-UQtmvM.

40. van der Kolk, *The Body Keeps Score*, 125–27.

41. McMahon and Campbell, *Rediscovering*.

10. Janet Warren's *Cleansing* model. Dissatisfied with the "warfare" motif, Warren, a family physician, develops another metaphor for countering evil, applicable to both personal bondage and systemic evil, though she says less about the latter. She describes her model as "Chaos Complexity," regarding evil as chaos that needs ordering and boundaries. Her imagery fits chapter 1 above, building on "Creation out of Chaos." In her last chapter, Warren identifies five "ways" this model has "potential specific applications for counseling." In short, these are: (1) helps to focus on the "in Christ" centering of the counselor ("belief, humility, compassion, wisdom, boldness, and dependence on other Christians"); (2) discernment of "multifactorial causation: exorcism, healing, and cleansing are intertwined; sin and demonization are related; illness and demonization are sometimes associated"[42]; (3) "emphasizes humans can choose which zone of metaphorical space they dwell in—they can draw near to God and resist the devil"[43]; (4) clients can "choose to follow the truth of God rather than the lies of the enemy . . . to stay in the light and avoid the darkness"[44]; and (5) this approach "can provide insights regarding techniques of deliverance" that do not elevate the ontology of the demons (a liability of spiritual warfare), but rather utilizes Jesus' simple command, believing that "holiness dissolves impurity" (this recaps her chapter on temple boundaries and holiness). "Rather than using power, humble dependence on God can be encouraged as a way for demons to be expelled."[45] In her more recent *Holy*,[46] Warren makes her contribution more accessible, for laity to grasp. She combines insights from her medical practice with treatment of biblical teaching on evil spirits: how to be freed and stay freed from their power.

11. *SOZO* ministry, known also as *Shabar*. *Sozo*, a Greek word meaning *saved* or *healed* includes *delivered* in their book title. It is described online as:

> Sozo ministry is a unique inner healing and deliverance ministry aimed to get to the root of things hindering your personal connection with the Father, Son and Holy Spirit. With a healed connection, you can walk in the destiny to which you have been called. A Sozo session is a time for the Sozo team to sit down with you and with the help of the Holy Spirit walk you through the process of freedom and wholeness. Sozo is not a counseling

---

42. Warren, *Cleansing*, 281–82.
43. Ibid, 282–83.
44. Ibid. Quotes for 4 and 5 are on 283.
45 Warren has also a section on application to mission; ibid., 277–79.
46. Warren, *Holy*. This is a marvelous, reader-friendly book.

session but a time of interacting with Father, Son and Holy Spirit for wholeness and pursuing of your destiny.[47]

This ministry began by Bill Johnson at Bethel Church, Redding, California, and is now professionally headed by Dawna De Silva and Teresa Liebscher. It has become a worldwide business, with dozens of books for sale.[48] This may raise questions of integrity. The method assists relating to God as Father (the Father Ladder), Son, and Spirit, with "closing the four doors" ("*fear, hatred/bitterness, sexual sin, and the occult*") that open one to the demonic.[49]

These methods and approaches do not exhaust the ways God's delivering/healing power occurs in one's life. Such might occur in one's local church during "Prayers for Healing."[50] Sometimes it occurs by anointing with oil when pastors, elders, or friends pray.[51] Or it might occur unexpectedly when one in engrossed in Scripture meditation, as it did for me one time.[52]

In our fast-paced life we have neglected times of quiet and deep meditation on the Word (Scripture) that has power to heal. We have also neglected daily prayer as preventive power against evil. Memorized Scripture or set prayers are strong to block out and deliver from one evil's tactics.[53] Healing has occurred also in mass worship gatherings led by Oral Roberts, Kathryn Kuhlman, et al. But some people prayed for were not healed, in-

---

47. From http://bethelsozo.com/. Sozo's inner healing methods were originally developed by Carlos Anacondia during the Argentina Revivals. But in some practices today, the wine of the Spirit goes wild, see: https://closingstages.net/2011/01/27/sozo-part-i/.

48. See the bookshop at: https://shop.bethel.com/collections/sozo?ref=10.

49. De Silva and Liebscher, *SOZO*, 83–94; 131–50; quote on 131. *SOZO* has been criticized, however, especially when "false memories" emerge (as online research indicates).

50. See my *Health*, 80–87, 105–17, and also *Iona Abbey Worship* for "A Service of Prayer for Healing," 88–97.

51. Pastor Phyllis Carter (Goshen, Indiana) tells a fascinating story. An old man in a nursing home requested her to come to anoint him with oil to relieve his racking pain. No problem: this is common in the Church of the Brethren. But she had another problem. She would need to take her eight-year-old son along. On the drive there she exhorted him to be quiet and just listen. When she was done anointing and praying, the man asked the boy to pray for him. He prayed, "Lord, do whatever you can for this old man." The man said, "When the boy prayed my pain left!"

52. My A-Fib converted to a strong normal beat. This was a special gift in June 2012 after my *Health* book was released. In later years, however, I needed medical expertise (cardioversion).

53. Taliaferro, "Evil," uses "set prayers" from BCP as weapons in times of trouble. In my morning walk I recite a prayer section also from BCP as both protection and empowerment.

cluding one of my brothers.⁵⁴ For a wider citation of healing through history see my *Healing*.⁵⁵ Ronald Kydd's typological "models" of healing through the church's history are quite striking:

- *confrontational*—exorcism in the early church, with more recent J. C. Blumhardt.
- *intercessory*—saints on high, Brother André, Mary of Medjugorje.
- *reliquirial*—bones of blessing, miracles as St. Médard.
- *incubational*—Männendorf as place of mercy, message of Morija in persevering prayer.
- *revelational*—William Branham, Kathryn Kuhlman.
- *soteriological*—Oral Roberts.⁵⁶

In J. C. Blumhardt's exorcism of a "possessed" woman (Gottlieben Dittus), the breakthrough came only after several years of confrontational prayer. Blumhardt's ministry to the sick as a dedicated competent pastor had a much wider range of healing than exorcism.

I suggest a "protection prayer" by MacNutt, to be prayed before each exorcism session:

> Lord Jesus, I ask You to protect my family [mention by name] from sickness, from all harm and from accidents. If any has been subjected to any curses, hexes, or spells, I declare these curses, hexes, or spells null and void in the name of Jesus Christ. If any evil spirits have been sent against us, I decommission you in the name of Jesus Christ and I send you to Jesus to deal with as He will. Then, Lord, I ask You to send your holy angels to guard and protect all of us.⁵⁷

---

54. He seldom spoke of this. Thankfully it did not ruin his faith in God.

55. Swartley, *Health*, 79–87, 103–17. Note Jamison-Peterson's singing that heals serious illness through laughter. Sid Roth interviews Vicki, whose husband is a psychiatrist: https://www.youtube.com/watch?v=NFyjbdIdS3g.

56. Kydd, *Healing*, 30–45. Karl Barth credits Blumhardt as one of his mentors. The Johann Christoph Blumhardt (1805 to 1880) story is told by Lejeune, *Blumhardt*, 5–37. Much of the book focuses on his son's (Christoph's) ministry (1842 to 1919) in several stages, first like his father's; then political, championing the Social Democrat Party in Germany. After that, his vision for a contrast community of common life birthed the Society of Brothers.

57. MacNutt, *Deliverance*, 279. MacNutt has other useful prayers as well, 279–80.

12

Embracing a Holistic Approach to Jesus' Victory Over Evil

Our Father in heaven,
Hallowed be your name,
Your kingdom come,
Your will be done,
on earth as it is in heaven.
Forgive us our sins,
as we forgive those who sin against us.
And lead us not into temptation,
but deliver us from evil [the evil one].
For yours is the kingdom, and the power, and the glory forever.
Amen.

I clearly saw all was done and to be done in and by Christ
How He conquers and destroys this tempter,
the Devil, and all his works, and is atop them.
—Quaker Psalm 5

Christian Believer's Authority vis à vis Evil

IN THE OLD TESTAMENT the prophet (*nabi*) is witness to the political order. From Nathan to Isaiah, prophets spoke truth to power. While King David heeded Nathan's words, and repented, most OT kings did not heed the prophets' pleadings for justice, care for the widow, the alien, and the poor, Nor did they heed the prophets' protests against trusting in military arms to wage war (Isa 31:1–3). The Psalms are replete with judgment against reliance on military weapons (20:7; 33:16–17; 44:3–6; 46:9–10; 76:3; 147:10). They affirm trust in the Lord to ward off by miracle the military forces of the enemy.

The same biblical theology that supports Christian witness to government authorities also supports Christian deliverance ministry. Both appeal to God's kingdom come and the sovereign Lordship of Christ. "Your kingdom come" and "deliver us from evil" are twin imperatives in the Lord's Prayer (see epigraph). *God's kingdom*, which endures forever, transcends all other kingdoms. Jesus-kingdom power *delivers us from evil* (Satan, fear of death, and the powers).

Numerous texts in chapters 4—10 above portray the dual face of evil: personal demonic oppression and systemic evil in sociopolitical structures (most notably, Jesus' passion and crucifixion in all four Gospels; as well as 1 Corinthians 2:6–8; Ephesians 6:10–18; and Revelation). The systemic evil of the Empire is focused ultimately in the Emperor (Nero, Domitian, et al.). Nugent's *The Masks of Satan* identifies figures and events in history in which personal demonic inspiration was linked with diabolical socio-religious-political evil.[1] Poole's analysis of evil's manifestations in America is sobering: Part 1 examines America's capricious actions and policies in its earlier history; Part 2 is titled "The Satanic Century," during which America's global economic and political domination with its empire-spirit fomented evil's negative consequences in many countries. Its counterpart appears in popular culture so that violence is entertainment: in movies, computer games, TV ads, and social media. Poole's analysis of America's character is "love of violence and failure to come to grips with its national soul. Both allow us to see America as itself a kind of fallen angel who never knew it fell."[2]

To resist the impact of violence upon us personally and our culture, we must utilize the authority we have as Jesus-people to confront evil in the personal and sociopolitical ordering of society, declaring with authority: "Jesus said, 'Love your enemy.'" This is the authority of the believer. MacMillan's emphases on the believer's authority is based largely on Ephesians (1:19–23; 2:4–6; 3:9–11; 4:26–27; 6:10–19), and also Matthew 28:18. The NT portrays

---

1. Nugent, *Masks*. Nugent traces the "faces" of evil, the demonic (Satanic), in history, including Gilles de Rais (executioner of Joan of Arc), Nietzsche, and Hitler.

2. Poole, *Satan*, quote from xxiii. Now in the twenty-first century we see "white supremacy," KKK, and neo-Nazi groups resorting to violence, faces of evil. Movie ads during commercials often show horrible violence—and that's okay!? We entertain ourselves with *violence*! We do? Really? Yes!

Jesus seated on the throne at the right hand of God, denoting his authority over all powers, with all things under his feet (1 Cor 15:24-28; Heb 2:5-9, 14-15; 1 Pet 3:22; cf. Dan 7:22, 27; Eph 1:22; Col 1:13; 2:10 where Christ is the head over all powers). The exaltation of Jesus Christ in Philippians 2:9-10 fulfills Isaiah's prophetic word in 45:22-23.[3]

For Christians in the early centuries AD, and now as well, opening oneself to the spirit world carries danger, as Kelsey observes:

> There was a real danger in this openness. Being so open to the spiritual world, Christians were more open to evil as well as to the Holy Spirit. Indeed, it was expected that the more they were committed to the Christian community and its life and the greater their influence in the world, the more they would be selected as targets by the Evil One. Christians would be tested again and again. As Tertullian remarked with characteristic exaggeration the devil was fully known only to Christians. But they also had the experience of being able to withstand attack from within and attack of persecution and torture from outside.
>
> Through the church's fellowship, sacraments, symbols, practices of private prayer and meditation, healing, and exorcism, Christians were able to meet evil, much of it incredibly destructive, and not be destroyed. From such experiences the doctrine of the atonement developed. Somehow, through the cross and resurrection, they discovered that the forces of evil had been turned back. In his crucifixion and resurrection Jesus seems to have wrought a change in the objective nature of the spiritual world, and those who were close to him were given protection and saved from evil. At present this was partial, but in the last days his Kingdom would fully come and evil would be cast out.
>
> Nonetheless, we must still confront the question of evil and an Evil One in God's world. Christians have no intellectual answer to the problem of evil. We can give no reason for its existence, but we have a solution that works, one that fits the nature of the beast. This solution is the understanding of the human psyche that we present here. When the power of the Holy Spirit comes into a life, the conflicting forces in this psyche are

---

3. MacMillan, *Authority*, 3-23; some editions include *Encounter with Darkness*. The key motif in these texts is *authority*, which the believer receives from Jesus who has all authority in heaven and on earth. Every believer is heir to this authority. Many believers, however, fail to use this authority for victorious living.

brought into harmony and wholeness, and the person is transformed morally, psychologically, and physically.[4]

At the end of *Powers of Evil*, Page expresses concern regarding excessive focus in popular literature on the demonic. He identifies five dangers. First, "the danger of breeding fear and paranoia by exaggerating the power of the devil and evil spirits." Second, "the danger of appealing to Satan and the demons to excuse one's failings." Third, "the danger of accepting beliefs and practices that are superstitious and sub-Christian." Fourth, "the danger of unrestrained speculation." And fifth, "there is the danger of imbalance." Here he is concerned with focusing too much on the victims of Satanism and demon-possession, and "failing to realize that every Christian is engaged in spiritual warfare and the struggles are primarily religious and moral. It would be wrong to focus on the sensational and unusual . . ." but overlook that in our mundane lives "satanic trials and temptations are the lot of all believers." We must put "on the full armor of God" to stand against the devil's schemes (Eph 6:10–17).[5]

Clinton Arnold has stressed similar points. Arnold helpfully reminds us that spiritual warfare is not just for a few, but an essential part of victory in Christ Jesus. In diagram form he addresses both *imbalance and balance* in regard to three "powers" against which Christians struggle: resisting temptations of the *flesh*, standing firm against the subtle pressures of the *world*, and with the Christian armor (Eph 6:10–18) blocking the *devil's* strategies to oppress us and gain a foothold in our lives as Christians.[6]

Understanding the spiritual world is not easy for us moderns or postmoderns. We may live, act, and react to life's circumstances, horrible as they might be, without ever thinking about spiritual realities. Page and many other authors have reminded us of this neglect. When we speak about evil "powers" many people think only of systemic, structural evil.

---

4. M. Kelsey, *Christo-Psychology*, 42–43. However, elsewhere in the same book Kelsey takes a dim or at least a "qualified" view of exorcism; he does acknowledge that on several occasions he "offer[ed] that sacramental action" (55). He contends that too often what is viewed as demonic is "psychological disturbance." I agree in part, but must say also the reverse: that in some cases what is viewed as "psychological disturbance" has demonic affliction behind the "disturbance," and thus the person needs deliverance through command in the name and power of Jesus. As indicated in chapter 11, this may have generational roots or be the result of openness to seductions from the evil one. Women or men who are sexually molested in pre-teen, teen years or even later, live with trauma that needs healing. If that does not happen, demons may enter for they are like rats that feast on "garbage" in one's life (see Kraft and MacNutt in chapter 11).

5. Page, *Powers*, 269–70.

6. C. Arnold, *Three*, 32–56; note especially 33–34, 55–56. In my recitation of this text, I add to "the helmet of salvation": "to block any evil projections into my mind."

But evil powers can and do, if allowed, torment the person, mentally, emotionally, and spiritually.

Witness to the Powers (Walter Wink)

Walter Wink has done a great service in his *Powers* trilogy. In his more recent work he proposes an "integral" or "holistic" view of evil. He describes this as the *inner* and *outer*. Governments and organizations have both an inner and outer character. Only as one comes to know the "inner" can the good or evil be known in regard to institutions, which (I would add) are made up of individuals that have either good or evil intent for the people they serve, and similar consequence for the nations and local governments they serve, and to some extent the peaceful welfare or warfare actions that affect the entire world.

One of Wink's later contributions on the Powers was presented at Eastern Mennonite University in March 2000, at a conference celebrating Wink's valued writings. I gave a response, both a summary and critique, to his stimulating presentation. It follows here, with adaptations.[7]

I welcome this opportunity and challenge to respond to your [Walter's] presentation. It provides a foundational perspective for understanding your rich contribution, in numerous volumes, on the powers as well as Christ's victory over the powers and the Christian's response to them.[8] Some historical perspective on the "powers" will be useful as "introduction" to my response. Over the years a debate has ensued as to whether the principalities and powers, as portrayed in the NT, are one-dimensional or two-dimensional. Scholars who argue for a one-dimensional meaning contend that the interpreter needs to choose in each given text, whether the referent is to human government or to the spiritual demonic or angelic powers.[9] J. H. Yoder, building on Berkhof,[10] argued persuasively that in (almost) all cases both dimensions, human government and the spirit world, are present, so intended by the writers. A classic text is 1 Corinthians 2:6–8. The human rulers crucified Jesus, the Lord of glory, ignorantly. Demonic spiritual powers were at work in the political rulers to execute this.

---

7. Wink's presentation, "The New Worldview: Spirit at the Core of Everything" is chapter 1 in eds. Gingerich and Grimsrud, *Transforming*. My response to Wink's presentation was titled "Your Worldview Determines What You Can Believe."

8. Wink, *Engaging*.

9. The NRSV in choosing to translate *archē* and *exousia* as "rulers and authorities" leans in the direction of the one-dimensional meaning, which is unfortunate in my judgment.

10. Berkhof, *Christ*.

Your presentation, Walter, contributes to this double dimension, but your version of it is distinctive: all institutions or corporate entities have an *inner* spirit-personality and an *outward* manifestation of the same. The spirit-personality may be more or less good or more or less evil. [Now I speak in third person.]

Wink points out that in Revelation 2—3 the prophetic message is addressed not to the churches, but to the angel of each church. The angel is the spirit that characterizes and rules the church. Wink integrates the two dimension view as inner and outer, and both are important. He names his worldview *dynamic holism*, i.e. *integral*, a view that folds the inner and outer into one reality. Further, all reality is interconnected.

On the matter of "double dimension" Wink and Yoder concur, but in different ways. Whereas Yoder echoes Karl Barth's theology, Wink echoes Carl Jung's psychology, which regards conscious thought as reflecting the deep unconscious. For Wink, inner spirit personality and outward manifestation replace the more traditional worldview in which good and evil spirits have autonomous existence, protecting us from or tempting us into evil. Wink rightly believes that prayer can effectively influence the inner spirit power of a given structural reality: government, corporation, or educational institution. All life is interconnected. The efficacy of prayer, even for plants and animals, is no longer a mystery. Or if it is, we should affirm it.

Wink rightly challenges Western, rationalist assumptions regarding reality. His critique of four worldviews is instructive.[11] But I see some liabilities in his proposed *integral* worldview.

I identify these by asking three questions: first, what view of God emerges in this *integral* worldview? Is *panentheism* functional for Judeo-Christian believers?[12] Granted, process theologians and mystics love it, but that does not necessarily make it tenable. I am struck by the contrasting conclusion of sociologist Peter Berger's similar critique of worldviews, especially the materialist. Toward the end of *Rumor of Angels*, he says:

> The God of the biblical tradition is the polar antithesis of the great identity proclaimed by the mystics, and of any possible

---

11. The first four worldviews he described are: the traditional worldview held by all ancient peoples, including the Jews, which thus became the Judeo-Christian worldview; the dualistic worldview of Gnosticism, which challenged the traditional worldview; the materialist worldview; and the super-naturalist worldview. For his discussion of each view, see his "New Worldview," 18–21. For his new Integral Worldview, see 21–24. Then he discusses four implications: the way we think about *Creation, Prayer, Mysticism,* and *Everlasting Life*—most insightful.

12. Wink rejects pantheism, but proposes *panentheism*: "where everything is in God and God is in everything," "New Worldview," 22.

variation on this theme. To reaffirm this discovery of God in our situation might necessitate the formulation of new creeds, though their content would in this case be quite traditional—the reaffirmation of God who is not the world and who was not made by man, who is outside and not within ourselves, who is not a sign of human things but of whom human things are signs, who is symbolized and not a symbol. It is this God, totally other and yet accessible in human experience, in whom faith will see the foundation of order, justice, and compassion in the world. It is this transcendence of which certain human gestures in the world are signals. And it is the faith in this God that (as it did in the religious history of Israel) eventuates in a hope that reaches beyond the confines of death.

These affirmations are Jewish or Muslim as much as they are Christian.[13]

Berger too calls for a *holistic* worldview that embraces all reality. These two creative scholars, Wink and Berger, propose, however, differing views of God. Wink's view jeopardizes the long-standing Christian conviction regarding God's freedom. This notion counts much in Brueggemann's understanding of prophetic imagination. He writes:

> [I]f we gather around a static god of order who only guards the interests of the "haves," oppression cannot be far behind. Conversely, if a God is disclosed who is free to come and go, free from and even against the regime, free to hear and even answer slave cries, free from all proper goodness as defined by the empire, then it will bear decisively upon sociology because the freedom of God will surface in the brickyards and manifest itself as justice and compassion.
>
> The point that prophetic imagination must ponder is that there is no freedom of God without the politics of justice and compassion, and there is no politics of justice and compassion without a religion of the freedom of God . . . [14]

In light of these two considerations, Berger's and Brueggemann's, both of whom call for a clear distinction between Creator and creation, namely the sovereignty of the Creator over the creation, we need clarification on just how Wink's integral worldview handles this issue.

---

13. Berger, *Rumor*, 112.
14. Brueggemann, *Prophetic*, 18.

Second, what happens to the church's missionary enterprise? Here I am appreciative of Paul Hiebert's contribution.[15] While Westerners have conceived reality in two stories, heaven above and earth that runs by laws of physics, which usually excludes miracles, the majority of the world's population thinks in terms of a three-storied universe, with spiritual powers—both good and evil—in that in-between zone. These powers interact with humans in daily life, enabling both miracles in the power of the Spirit and leaving us also vulnerable to malicious intent. For this reason spiritual protection is most important for Christian believers in most Third World countries. Hiebert notes that Western missionaries have often been ineffectual because they could not accept this three-storied view of the universe and could not be critical of their own modern naturalistic worldview. They could not connect in depth with the people to whom they sought to communicate the gospel. They could not comprehend the culture's worldview.

Third, how does the *integral* worldview understand evil, sin, and salvation? How is salvation understood? What are believers saved from, and what *to* or *for*? What view of evil and sin fits best with this "new" *integral* worldview? Or, does this worldview take us in the direction of New Age thought, in which *evil* per se barely registers?

I appreciate Wink's analyses of various worldviews. It helps us understand more clearly how we think about reality: specifically, what plausibility structures guide our faith, worship, and witness to the political powers, and to our resistance to evil powers and our trust in angelic spirit powers as well. Wink's *integral* worldview shifts our thinking from *spatial* above/below to the *psychic* inner/outer. My queries remain, however. Further, Wink says this may be the first time in human history that we have the option of choosing our worldview. Might not the Gnostics or modern rationalists have said the same thing, however, in promoting their alternatives to the traditional worldview?

I affirm Wink's emphasis on prayer. True it is: miles don't matter; prayer has powerful influence on others. I myself have felt and feel now (in spring 2000, four months after a major heart attack when I was close to death's door) that I am carried by the prayers of many people. However, is this true because we are all integrally part of a cosmic whole, or because our Sovereign gracious God, both transcendent and immanent, hears and answers our prayers, even though at times we might wonder if God hears us? In my case, having had a serious heart attack in the mountains of West Virginia in 1999 and not getting medical help for five hours, I laid in the hospital at Morgantown, West Virginia, not knowing if I would live or die.

---

15. Hiebert, "Flaw."

I prayed to God to give me fifteen more years to live, as King Hezekiah did (2 Kgs 20:1–6a).[16] Now after nineteen years later, I say, "God has heard and has been abundantly gracious."

Thank you, Walter, for a provocative paper that will influence our thought and discussion over these next two days, and years beyond.[17]

Marva Dawn's critique of Wink's "integral" worldview concurs with mine. She quotes from Wink's *Unmasking*: "instead of the old dualism of matter and spirit, we can now regard matter and spirit as one indivisible reality, distinguishable in two discrete but interrelated manifestations." She then critiques Wink's view:

> Wink certainly is right to reject the false dualism of matter and spirit that is frequently imposed on biblical texts, but he is wrong thereby to eliminate entirely a different realm of spiritual forces separate from material agents. His conflation of the two reduces the cosmic battle in which we are engaged and thereby reduces the significance of the work of Christ and the Church's gospel proclamation.[18]

Another critique, comparing the West's and Africa's understanding of *spirit* is Acolatse's insight that Wink over-spiritualizes systemic evil. Further, she says evil has varied meanings in Wink's *outer* and *inner* framework. While she concurs with Wink on Satan as a "sifter" under God, she believes Wink has gone too far, in his efforts to "redeem Satan—or at least rehabilitate him—as one of the powers (Rom 8:38)."[19] "At best, his analysis seeks to

---

16. For a fuller account of this incident, see Swartley, *Health*, 16–17.

17. See other responses to Wink's presentation in the Gingerich/Grimsrud edited book noted above. In a luncheon discussion during an SBL meeting I quizzed Wink regarding his astute discussion of "Satan" and "The Demons" in *Unmasking*, 9–68. I commended him for his helpful discussion, especially his contribution on "Outer Personal Possession," 58–64. But, I wondered, why this does not figure into his contribution in lectures and other writings on the topic? His response was surprising, to the effect: I certainly don't deny this as a reality and procedure sometimes needed. I witnessed such a miracle-type exorcism when Tilda Norberg asked me to be present for back-up support when she utilized an Exorcism Liturgy. She did this one evening out of her professional schedule, to help a woman she had counseled for several years, and made no progress. The result was remarkable. Demons left the woman, and the session ended with communion and anointing with oil. I know this is a reality, but the larger issues of *Engaging the* [Political] *Powers* is my contribution.

18. Dawn, *Powers*, 15. Wink presents his view with numerous diagrams in *Powers That Be*, 13–36.

19. Acolatse, *Powers*, 85. Earlier she scores Wink for inconsistency in language, 80–81. Her treatment of Wink overall, 79–91, is helpful. She regards it a minor variation of Bultmann's demythologization project, 91.

minimize the possibility of the powers as personally autonomous beings and thereby the scriptural witness and account of evil."[20]

Warren also critiques Wink's "integral view" of evil as "the inner spirit and outer expression" of institutions. Utilizing the imagery of creation-ordering, which sets boundaries that cleanse the cosmos from chaos, she both affirms and rejects aspects of Wink's contribution:

> Wink is correct to acknowledge the fluidity of the Pauline language, correct in viewing the powers in opposition to God, and is to be commended for emphasizing human responsibility. However, I believe he goes too far in his demythologization of the powers, minimizing or even dismissing experiential accounts of horrific evil, and minimizing the biblical idea of evil as opposition.... Recognizing, as Schlier and others seem to, that the rulers, authorities, principalities, and powers are a cluster of metaphors used to describe evil forces in opposition to God allows for improved conceptual clarity and consistency. Given the overlap, interchangeability, and semantic range of the terms, this approach is consistent with biblical evidence and with other biblical metaphors for evil that are similarly vague, such as "chaos." I agree with Wink that the powers should be conceived of broadly, but would add that, as powerful metaphors, they depict the reality of the evil spiritual realm. Finally, the multitude of terms suggests that the powers are characterized by disorganization, consistent with previous conclusions. They are analogous to uncleanness as a miasmic force. Perhaps, drawing on chaos-complexity theory, the powers can be viewed as self-organized demons.[21]

I find Warren's "chaos-complexity" theory helpful and especially so for pastoral care for one who has gone through a deliverance experience. I do not think her approach replaces *exorcism* as a foundational biblical and church historical mode of dealing with evil, which in some cases at least is needed

---

20. Ibid., 87. I have trouble using the terms *personal* or *being* for evil spirits. They are anti-personal and anti-being; the same applies to Satan or devil. God is Being, life-giving, and personally disclosed in Jesus Christ.

21. Warren, *Cleansing*, 222–23. To fully understand Warren's critique, one must grasp the implications of her "chaos complexity" theory, which she proposes as an alternative to "spiritual warfare." Boundary-setting against evil is a means of countering evil that is more appropriate for her work as a family physician and for counseling people stressed and "broken" by evil. In essence, countering chaos (evil) means establishing boundaries. A prayer phrase, "put a hedge of protection around us and our families," illustrates the point. Boundary-setting for protection is a means of warding off evil. Similar to Peck's and Gallagher's testimony, her book begins by narrating her experience of encountering chaotic evil in one of her medical clients. See Dr. Olson's experience, cited in chapter 11, n22.

to enable a person to continue to counteract evil via the Warren model. To illustrate, I refer to psychotherapist Tilda Norberg's experiences in several cases where counseling didn't help but, despite her reluctance and resistance to deliverance, this procedure was necessary. Her worldview changed, and so did the health and wholeness of those freed from demon-oppression. These stories, as well as those Scott Peck cites, are mind-boggling on the one hand and on the other hand life-renewing, leading to joy-filled praise.[22]

Exorcism/Deliverance (Graham Twelftree)

I value Twelftree's important and relevant contributions to deliverance ministry for several reasons. First, his five books and articles cover a long span of time: 1985 to 2007.[23] Second, Twelftree's work consists of meticulous research, taking account of a range of twentieth-century contributions to the subject. Third, his position for the church's mandate to engage in exorcism shifts between his first and last writings.[24] Twelftree's earlier writings regard Jesus' exorcisms in the Synoptic Gospels and his commissioning his disciples to cast out demons as an authoritative model for Christian practice today. But in his 2007 book he revises his position, appealing to John's Gospel for an alternative approach to exorcism.[25] In John *truth* is the power that sets one free (8:32; cf. "theophostic healing" in chapter 11). His treatment of John versus the Synoptic Gospels on this matter is succinctly and ably presented in his article, "Exorcisms," where he describes seven explanations for the differences between the Synoptic Gospels and John/Paul/early church writings, none of which he regards satisfactory.[26] These differences, in my judgment, require intra-canonical reflection, in which these major NT contributions (Synoptic Gospels, Paul, and John) complement each other, explicating exorcism in multiple dimensions. All three present Jesus (*Lamb* in Rev) overcoming *evil* in personal, cosmic, and politically systemic dimensions.

22. Norberg, *Consenting*, 263–85. Norberg's Gestalt approach to healing, especially body-work that heals, often involves freeing one from binding generational sin. See also her later contributions: *Gathered* and *Chocolate*.

23. Twelftree's 2007 book is *Name*. C. Arnold's three books address foundational issues, the first a close study of Ephesians: *Ephesians: Power and Magic* (PhD dissertation), a wider study of Paul's Letters: *Powers of Darkness*; and third, his practical, *Three Crucial Questions*. I utilized Arnold's work in chapter 6.

24. His last book skirts Ferguson's monumental *Demonology*. Twelftree's bibliography in *Name* mentions only one of Ferguson's edited volumes (131n11).

25. See Twelftree, *Jesus*.

26. Twelftree, "Exorcisms," 135–37.

Twelftree holds that Paul's Letters also reflect a *non*-exorcist ministry in overcoming evil. He notes Paul referenced "evil spiritual beings" in his trope, "principalities and powers." In light of this, Twelftree says we would not be surprised if Paul referenced exorcism in his writings, but he does not.[27] He then takes up the sticky question of what Paul knew about Jesus. After analyzing Paul's use of *powers* (*dunameis*) and its relation to Jesus' miracles as *powers/dunameis*, he concludes Paul concurs with the Synoptics on *powers* (*dunameis*) even though he never refers to Jesus' miracles. Since Paul speaks of *dunamis/dunameis* he may have been aware of Jesus as a miracle worker and exorcist. Paul's ministry was also "miracle-based," evident in his frequent use of "signs and wonders and powers" (2 Cor 12:12; *sēmeiois te kai terasin kai dunamesin*). Twelftree treats four Pauline texts (Rom 15:18–19; 2 Cor 12:12; 1 Thess 1:5; 1 Cor 2:4–5). He believes these indicate Paul knew Jesus conducted miracles and, in modeling Jesus, he performed miracles himself, most likely including exorcism. Paul considered such miracles salvific events, authenticating his ministry of both "word and deed."[28]

Twelftree considers Luke's portrait of Paul in Acts, miracles (healing, in 14:3, 8–10; 15:12; 19:11–12; 28:7–9, even raising a dead man, 20:9–12) and exorcisms (13:9–12; 16:16–18). Acts 19:13–15 also testifies to Paul's exorcisms.[29] He concludes: though Paul often refers to "powers," Satan, and the devil, there is no evidence in his letters that Paul knew himself as an exorcist or that he modeled such for his church believers. He did not include exorcism among the charismatic gifts.

Twelftree's treatment pits some sources against others, giving priority to those that fit his thesis articulated at the end of his book: i.e., Scripture gives no authority to mandate Jesus' exorcist ministry as normative for the gospel's encounter with evil. He bases this on his findings in John, Paul, and early second-century sources before Justin, ca. 150 CE.[30] He acknowledges that after 150 CE exorcism is an important part of early church practice.[31]

---

27. Twelftree, *Name*, 58–60, 76–77.

28. Ibid., 71.

29. Ibid., 71–73 Twelftree's book, *Paul*, concludes Paul affirms the miraculous as significant, with profound effect upon his ministry, even though Paul cites none of Jesus' miracles nor describes miracles in his own ministry. Twelftree considers seven aspects of Paul's teaching and experiences (155–78), all of which attest the "miraculous" (see the book's conclusion, 313–38).

30. Twelftree, *Name*, 285–86. Twelftree's earlier chapter 7 did show, from primary sources, that exorcism was important in the early church's catechism of new believers (cf. my chapter 9 above).

31. Ibid., 88–89.

He thus concludes that despite Jesus' bestowal of exorcist power upon his followers in the Synoptic Gospels,[32] in light of these major non-exorcist Scriptures and early second century sources, exorcism is *not mandated* for the church today. In his analysis he slights John 12:31 and John 8, which testify to alternate patterns of exorcist power (he does acknowledge that in John 8:32, *truth* sets us free).[33]

After summarizing his findings in what he calls his "narrowly focused study," Twelftree moves to "Contemporary Coda," in which he departs from his earlier position in *Christ Triumphant*, in which he affirmed exorcism as an important mandate for the church.[34] He now holds (in 2007) that Paul, John, and early second-century Christian literature show alternative ways to confront evil: "I am obliged to recognize that it [the whole New Testament canon] has provided the church with a range of options for understanding and dealing with the demonic."[35]

However, Twelftree also says, "I concede that the church may confront the demonic in the form of an exorcism *or* in the form of Truth."[36] In a footnote he calls attention to Neil Anderson's approach, "which encourages encounters with the truth instead of any form of exorcistic power-encounter."[37] Twelftree's final concern is that the demonic not become the focus of our ministry, but that *Jesus* is always the focus.[38] I agree! We have no power of our own to cast out demons or heal afflicted persons. Jesus is the miracle worker and the *divine* power over the demonic. Twelftree's book is titled rightly, *In the Name of Jesus*.[39]

While I affirm Twelftree's important contributions, I think we need to assess the balance between the Synoptic Gospels and Acts (written in

---

32. Twelftree acknowledges that Q (the hypothetical document behind Matthew's and Luke's longer texts not in Mark) includes exorcism (Luke 11:14–26), but Twelftree says that Q plays down exorcist emphasis, 79–99.

33. Ibid., 282.

34. Twelftree, *Christ*. See his chapter 6, "Exorcism Now?" See 191 for his statement: "exorcism has its rightful place as part of the whole ministry given to the church to push back the frontiers of evil."

35. Twelftree, *Name*, 293.

36. Ibid., 293n15.

37. Anderson, *Victory*. Theophostic Healing emphasizes encounter with *truth* (see chapter 11). In Hochstetler's and my ministry *truth* was key to expulsion, since in numerous cases *deception* headed the list of demons present.

38. See also Kraft's and Emmanuel Prayer's approaches in chapter 11.

39. Compare Thurston's excellent treatment of the *name of Jesus* in the early chapters of Acts and Ephesians: *Spiritual*. As I picked up this book from my shelf it was between *Power and the Powers* (topic coming up) and Dawn's *Power*. What treasure in these three books!

different church locales) and Paul's writings. New Testament scholars generally agree that *Paul's writings predated the Synoptic Gospels*. Paul did not write a *bios* or *euangelion* (gospel) of Jesus, but Luke wrote a *bios* of Paul *that included exorcism* as a vital part of the church's growth. Paul wrote to churches to address specific church situations and he presented a summary of the gospel's message (in Romans and Ephesians—the latter possibly post-Pauline). Written in the last third of the first century, the Synoptic Gospels and Acts would have been viewed as foundational to the church's ongoing mission and ministry.[40] Jesus commanded his disciples to continue this ministry. If Paul's letters were the norm for the church on exorcism, I doubt the church would have accepted the Synoptic Gospels.

While it is true that the early second century church's extant writings do not speak of exorcism, the nature of those writings, except for the *Didache*, are of a type that doesn't call for exorcism. Written to the seven churches while taken to Rome as prisoner, Ignatius' letters are concerned with whether or not his imminent death will be a *true* martyrdom, which in turn depends upon the unity of the churches over which he was bishop.[41]

The differences and selective content show the need for intra-canonical reflection in which the three NT corpuses (Synoptic Gospels, Paul, and John) complement each other. Exorcism is explicated canonically in multiple dimensions. All three present Jesus (*Lamb* in Rev) overcoming *evil* in personal, cosmic, and politically systemic dimensions. In light of these considerations and the prominence of exorcism in the early church writings after 150 CE, I suggest that exorcism in some form (see the varied approaches in chapter 11 above) be a normative part of the church's healing ministry.

Praise Jesus, God's Son, Savior-Deliverer, who sets us free.

Power and the Powers
(Hardy, Whitehouse, and Yarnell)

The church's mission to the powers is variously understood. Thomas McAlpine identifies four approaches:[42] Reformed, which seeks to transform the powers to be more accountable to Christian moral standards; Anabaptist,

---

40. Witmer, in *Galilean*, 22–60, presents the cultural context for Jesus' exorcism. Jewish-Christian exorcist rites (48–49) use *Jesus* in one, and *Jesus Chrestus* in another. She cites from the *Greek Magical Papyri* (see Betz, ed.).

41. Swartley, "Imitatio," 81–103. For the topics addressed by the later NT literature and Apostolic Fathers, see Swartley, "Intertextuality," 536–42. The concerns of this literature do not call for exorcism.

42. McAlpine, *Facing*.

which emphasizes the church as a contrast community to the powers; and the Third Wave (Peter Wagner), where missionary strategy confronts and exorcizes evil spirit-powers exerting territorial control.[43] McAlpine's fourth approach is the descriptive sociological-anthropological: evil is understood within worldview contexts.

These differences in approach center on whether Christian mission witnesses to the gospel by confronting evil in the spiritual realm through casting out demons, or whether one confronts evil in the structural systems that dominate and oppress people, or whether one does both. I contend this is not an either-or matter but a both-and mandate.

Power and the Powers[44] discusses five different late twentieth and early twenty-first century views of evil. The book is written from a Christian missional perspective. It considers varied understandings of the origins and expressions of evil in relation to mission. E. Brunner is noted for: "the Church exists by mission as fire exists by burning!" The proponents of the five views of evil that in turn shape the churches' responses, are (briefly):

1. Berkhof and J. H. Yoder (in Hardy, Whitehouse, Yarnell, 22–24). Evil resides primarily in the sociopolitical systemic structures, and expresses itself in varied forms of violence: street shootings, war, systemic evil in sociopolitical structures interconnected with economic oppression. The church directs its witness to the structures: cultural, ecclesial, economic, and political to influence such toward peacemaking.

2. Bellinger (in Hardy, Whitehouse, Yarnell, 25–26). While generally affirming the Berkhof/Yoder contribution, Bellinger critiques their views for their lack of explanation as to *why* it is this way. Is it Satan, human perversity, or the inherent nature of structures? This question raises a broader query for the church's missional response to evil. To answer this *why* question, Bellinger turns to:

3. Girard (in Hardy, Whitehouse, Yarnell, 25–26). Girard contributes an encompassing theory of the origin and nature of violence: violence is rooted in mimetic desire inherent to human behavior. *Desire* and *imitation* inevitably lead two people or groups of people desiring the same thing (toys, success, power, land, wealth, et al.) into competition,

---

43. McAlpine's description (ibid.) of this category is too restrictive. It should include a broader use of exorcism in the ministry of the church. Peter Wagner's theory and strategy regarding territorial powers is only one emphasis, and a disputed one among scholars and practitioners of deliverance ministry. See both Rommen, editor of *Spiritual Power*, and C. Arnold, *Three* and *Powers*. See also McClain, *Claiming*, for use of exorcism to free social and political systemic power from demonic control.

44. Hardy, Whitehouse, and Yarnell, eds., *Power*.

and invariably to conflict. Unless laws, rules, moral convictions, or some external power interrupts and mediates the conflict, the rivalrous conflict is resolved by a scapegoat, one similar to the parties involved, but different enough to be expendable. The scapegoat is killed as the reputed cause of the trouble, but is in fact an innocent victim. The death of the scapegoat, a type of religious ritual, generates a pseudo-peace until the next wave of imitative desire results in another conflict, for which the violent scapegoat mechanism is repeated to achieve a pseudo-peace.

This, Girard asserts, is the metanarrative of virtually all novels. It occurs in all cultures: primitive, medieval, and modern. But in this world literature, the power-side wins. The Gospels, however, side with Jesus, the truly innocent one. That *revelation*, which it *truly is*, *exposes* the mechanism that foments violence. In the Gospels we hear the voice of the victim, which is silenced in the literary myths of the ages, including much of the Old Testament, though the OT prophets anticipate the Gospels' revelation (e.g. Isa 53).[45]

For Girard this violence-scapegoating mechanism is explanatory of the origin of religion. Since the scapegoated person is the means to restore peace, that person may then be regarded worthy of worship, hence deified. The Gospels not only disclose Jesus as the innocent victim of violence, but also side with the innocent victim, not with the Jewish chief priests and Roman rulers. In this respect, the Gospels are unique among the world's literature. Through Jesus, the innocent scapegoat, peace is achieved, and Jesus himself is revered, even deified, and rightly so. Because God is on the side of Jesus, the victim, who commands love of enemies, God raises him to life. This breaks the cycle of violence. The resurrected Jesus breathes into his disciples (the) Holy Spirit (John 20:22), birthing a new creation that lives Jesus'

---

45. In addition to the Hardy, Whitehouse, Yarnell description, see the essays in my edited volume, *Violence Renounced*. Numerous articles in this book of fourteen chapters, the last of which is René Girard's response to the essays, are informative of Girard's impact on biblical studies. Especially helpful to understand his theory in addition to my "Introduction" (19–28) are: Miller, "Girardian Perspectives and the Atonement" (49–69); Collins, "Girard and Atonement: An Incarnational Theory of Mimetic Participation" (132–53); Sandor Goodhart, "René Girard and the Innocent Victim" (200–217); and Swartley, "Discipleship and Imitation of Jesus/Suffering Servant/The Mimesis of New Creation" (218–45). All the essays (by Grimsrud, Mabee, Matties, Hardin, Johns, Keim, Williams, Fodor, and Adams, and the Foreword by Culbertson) contribute to a fuller understanding of the significance of Girard for biblical study. Adams builds upon, but goes beyond Girard to regard God's creation (Gen 1–2) as prior to the founding murder of Gen 4, on which Girard bases his views. Divine Love and *Shalom* precede human murder.

way. The Gospels thus expose the mimetic-conflict-violence-religion mechanism, and thus transform the generative mechanism of mimetic violence into a new model of mimesis. If as readers of the Gospels we identify with the rejected, suffering, and crucified Jesus, the narrative as gospel converts our mimetic desire.

Girard equates Satan with violence, which the *scandal* of mimetic rivalry generates.[46] For Girard, clever Satan does cast out Satan. He first generates the rivalry and division that heats into hatred so that the community is about to explode or war threatens between two communities or nations. The crisis is averted (also Satan's work) by a selected, targeted scapegoat, whose death restores a pseudo-peace to the community, until the next cycle. The Gospels, exposing this generative mechanism of violence, reveal the truth: Jesus is not guilty; God sides with the victim.

My own contribution accentuates transformation of mimetic desire, i.e., the *imitation* of Jesus, in which *scapegoating* is transformed into *self-sacrifice* (a term Girard came to honor as distinct from *scapegoating* in his later writings). Sacrifice is no longer the slaughter of another, but a voluntary giving of one's life for the salvation of others. This costly mimetic discipleship is the "engine" of true mission, which subverts evil by love-confrontation, in the footsteps of Jesus. We learn then to do as Ephesians 4:15 instructs: "truthing [in Greek, a participle] in love" (*alētheuontes en agapē*).

4. Kraft (in Hardy, Whitehouse, Yarnell, 27–29). The authors turn next to Charles Kraft because he grapples with how the worldview of given cultures shapes understanding of and response to spiritual warfare against evil. Cultural analysis is necessary for mission to be effective. For Kraft, spiritual warfare entails power encounter. The spiritual armor of Ephesians 6:10–18 is both defensive and offensive. Exorcism and deliverance/healing ministry effectively disarms Satan and destroys his works. Western missionaries, with an Enlightenment worldview, didn't comprehend the necessity of exorcism/deliverance as part of their spiritual warfare for the gospel to be fully effective in proclaiming Jesus as Savior and Lord.[47]

5. Paul Hiebert (in Hardy, Whitehouse, Yarnell, 29–35). Hiebert excels in perceiving the importance of respecting differing worldviews, and

---

46. When I asked Girard personally at a conference whether demons under Satan's headship instigate the violence, he equivocated. Perhaps so, he said, but that we cannot know. Girard's contribution is at the phenomenological level. Though not a biblical scholar, his theological insights on biblical passages often shine.

47. This indictment of mission is at the heart of Kraft's *Confronting* and editor Rommen's *Spiritual*.

how this perception affects the church's gospel mission in global cultures, especially in regard to "spiritual warfare." Rather than focusing on "power encounter" (Peter Wagner) Hiebert contends that missionaries are to carry forward their mission in terms of "truth encounter." Cross-cultural mission must take into account cross-cultural understandings at the cognitive and affective levels (hampered often by ethnocentrism). Allow the Bible to speak and keep the cross at the center of spiritual warfare within the context of witnessing to the good news of God's kingdom come and coming.

In the modern West this dimension of Jesus' ministry is problematic because many Christians cannot grasp the reality of the spirit world. With the exception of those who have some experience in deliverance ministries, a gap exists between our reality and the reality of our Christian brothers and sisters in many parts of the Two-Thirds (majority) world.[48]

Three different types of rational explanations appear in literature as to why modern "Western" minds cannot come to grips with this reality. First, what was formerly thought to be demonic oppression is mental illness. Hence psychiatric treatment is needed. Psychiatrists thus become or replace exorcists.[49] Second, social science explains demonization as the result of social ostracism and marginalization. Some social science commentaries on Scripture explain Jesus' exorcisms as bold actions of "inclusion," reintegrating outcasts into society. Third, political ideology has regarded demonization symbolic of political oppression, so that the Gadarene's "legion" of demons represents the Roman army legion (see chapter 5 on this).

While these explanations fascinate, none adequately exposits the biblical text. E.g., did Jesus consider himself a victim (Girard's thesis)? No, Jesus was master of the situations that arose, and with his Father's help remained so "to the point of death, even death on a cross" (Phil 2:8). God vindicated his obedience in resurrecting him from the dead and seating him at his right hand with all powers subject to him (chapters 6 and 10).

---

48. This issue lies at the heart of Acolatse's *Powers*.

49. Numerous articles address this viewpoint, e.g. Barker, "Possession," and Pattison, "Psychosocial." This is a provocative analysis of the relationship between the role of the exorcist and the psychiatrist. See Peck, *Glimpses*. This is a fascinating and insightful account of two exorcisms, with three chapters on each exorcism, consisting of: Diagnosis, Exorcism, Follow-up; and an extensive Commentary in the middle. In Part III Peck writes on his "Perspectives" and "What is Possession?" This is especially helpful for those who doubt the existence of the devil and demonic infestation. See also Peck's *People*, which describes his integration of psychiatric practice with his relatively new Christian commitment. The book includes case studies and the methods employed to bring healing, i.e., citing accounts of exorcism. See also psychiatrist Gallagher's book soon to appear on the same subject.

These analyses deal only with symptoms or attendant circumstances of demonic oppression and thus present only partial truth. It is my hope and prayer that this book will take us a step further, both in perceiving evil and gaining through Jesus' name and power the freedom Jesus calls us to experience, with hope and joy. Recall the stories at the end of chapters 4 and 5, where I narrate deliverance from personal oppression manifest in the human persons and the two stories at the end of chapter 10 where corporate prayers, which contained elements of exorcism, brought about a huge political change, freedom. The biblical, theological affirmation of Christ's Lordship over the powers is the basis for all these instances of deliverance from evil/the evil one. These stories and many more testify to the resurrection power that defeated the power of Satan's manifestations. Jesus is Lord of All.[50] Not all the redemptive pay-off comes in this life, however, for evil continues in structures and personal experience.

Nonetheless, the faithful church is called to exercise spiritual authority against evil in the name and power of Jesus Christ, whether it is in exorcism of evil in personal or sociopolitical systemic manifestations. The task is huge in these second and third decades of twenty-first–century realities, with evil exploding in all spheres of life: in entertainment media with its violence, witches,[51] and sometimes explicitly demonic face, popular "TV programs that have some sort of occult or magical theme . . . *Medium, Psychic Sally, Most Haunted, Supernatural, Buffy the Vampire Slayer, The X Files, Paranormal,* to name a few."[52] Add to this our hypersexualized

---

50. A moving story is Chuck Colson's deliverance from personal and systematic evil as a crucial player in the Watergate scandal under Richard Nixon in mid-1970. Read it in the Appendix to Boa's book, *Rewriting*, 193–206.

51. E.g., the film *The Blair Witch Project* and its effect in a fourth grade school room as this January 2001 Associated Press release indicates: "A *substitute teacher* in Greenwood, on her first day on the job, was *fired* after she followed up a discussion of The Blair Witch Project by giving six fourth-graders sheets of instructions [Elkhart Truth says, 'a quarter-page summary'] on how to *become a witch*." Reported in local *Elkhart Truth* and other newspapers. See *Indianapolis Monthly*, vol. 24, No. 6 (January 2001), 119. https://books.google.com/books?id=0-kCAAAAMBAJ.

52. Hardy, Whitehouse, Yarnell, *Power*, 72. These authors add: "The success of the *Harry Potter* novels and films as well as *Lord of the Rings* must not be neglected, or more recently *Game of Thrones*" (72). The series puts readers (children) into the realm of magic and wizardry, including vampires who suck human blood. The demonic "runs" beneath the surface, and could open children to demonic entry. See C. Jacobs's *Deliver*. Jacobs discusses various means of entry and manifestations of evil spirit influence from both Pokemon and the Harry Potter novels. For me, this is difficult to discern. The article by Jenkins, "Speak of the devil," is helpful but it does not take into account the Wiccan factors that contribute to the need for more priests/pastors trained to perform exorcism. A week before this article appeared, as I was driving I saw that the man riding on a motorcycle in front of me had on his jacket the emblazoned identity, "Devil's Disciples."

culture,⁵³ horrible wars dotting the globe and killing so many, (terrorist) kidnappings, mass shootings, political views and policies that marginalize immigrants from certain countries, and the increasing wealth of the rich at the expense of the poor.

The task of Christian witness to the powers is huge, overwhelming, and it is difficult to know how to proceed—maybe it requires absurd symbolism of the Jeremiah or Ezekiel type. More must be done, without closing our eyes to the need for deliverance from demonic powers that oppress individual people, whether from personal sin, generational sin, or trauma that needs healing in the name of Jesus. Remembering the early church, we are challenged today to be an alternative society to the dominant national (empire) priorities, and its religious, social values. Employing Paul's language, there is much to "put off" and to "put on" in order to be God's new creation (2 Cor 5:17), which Jesus called us to be.

> So help us, Almighty God our Creator and Redeemer,
> revealed as Creator-Father, Son, and Holy Spirit!

To conclude, hear this Easter hymn (stanza 5):

> Christ has arisen to set us free.
>
> Alleluia, to him praises be!
> The power of Satan no longer binds,
> nor can enslave the thoughts of our minds
> Jesus is living, let the earth sing.
> He reigns triumphant, eternal king,
> and he has promised those who believe
> into his kingdom he will receive
> Refrain
> Let us sing praise to him with endless joy.
> Death's fearful sting he has come to destroy,
> our sins forgiving, alleluia.
> Christ has arisen, allelulia.
>
> Swahili text, translated by Howard S. Olson, 1969
> Haya melody (Tanzania) 99.99 with refrain.
> Text and music ©1977 Lutheran World Federation⁵⁴
> HWB 267

For this we yearn and pray that it be so in both the personal and systemic faces of evil:

"The kingdom of this world has become the kingdom of our Lord and of his Christ, and he will reign forever and ever" (Rev 11:15).

---

53. On this I recommend Grant, *Divine*.
54. Used with permission.

Summary and Conclusion

In the Introduction I proposed that the antonym of peace/*shalom* is *evil*. In the preceding chapters this point is confirmed at both the *micro* and *macro* dimensions of Scripture. The *micro* sections refer to specific portions of Scripture this study examined regarding *evil*. The *macro* utilizes the micro but narrates more broadly the biblical narrative on how humanity and/or Israel's doing *evil* moves the story forward with new beginnings in light of God's faithfulness But first, we attend to certain topical treatments that pervade the book.

Chapter 1 seeks to understand *evil* in the context of creation out of chaos, citing Scripture throughout the canon. It highlights God's majesty and power to create the world in which we live, and to sustain it from forces that threaten its shalom-order. This extensive OT trope continues into the NT with Jesus as Healer and Deliverer, Savior and Lord, promising a new heaven and new earth, in which shalom is no longer contested by evil and chaos.

Chapters 2a and 2b are focused on the difficult topic of YHWH war, YHWH's command to protect Israel, the elected community, with the mission to be a blessing to the nations! How can they be a blessing when they drive other nations out of the land of promise, killing those peoples to enable Israel to live in the land God promised to them? This for me is an irresolvable conundrum. How can God's chosen people be a blessing to the nations when, while, and by exterminating them—the picture we have in Joshua? This problem is further exacerbated by Israel's later worshiping the gods of the nations they presumably drove out.

Judges gives a different picture of Israel's settlement in the land. Here Israel is living in the land and only occasionally routing enemies that threaten Israel's peaceful existence. There is no adequate historical solution to this dilemma: the difference between Joshua and Judges, though the Holy War portrayal of Jericho's destruction has not been verified by archaeology (see notes 6–7 in chapter 2a). It is tempting to go with one of the scholarly positions that Sanderson describes, e.g., the model of peaceful penetration advanced by three scholars (Alt, Noth, and Weippert) mentioned in n7 in chapter 2a. This resolves the ethical dilemma, but it is difficult to correlate that view with the texts in Deuteronomy, Joshua, and even Judges. Boyd's contribution resolves the conundrum by utilizing four hermeneutic principles (see n.5 in chapter 2a). His "Accommodation" principle, namely God accommodates to Israel's ANE culture in which Israel's neighbor nations undertook warfare with similar loyalty to their gods though there the warfare was synergistic—the people too fought the battle (as in the Maccabean wars).

Lind accentuates this difference, appealing to Exodus 14:14 as *the* God-authorized model: God alone fights; the people do not. Holy War reduces the human role to ludicrous actions (trumpets; torches). This model requires *trust* in YHWH God. Israel "mops up."

At the theological level, Holy War is YHWH's fight against the gods of the nations, thus destroying the idols for the sake of Israel's worship of God alone. Nonetheless, this means killing people, destroying their belongings, and wiping out populations and its cultures. But here, an irony! The same Deuteronomy that authorized Holy War has also a most welcoming acceptance and generous treatments of the alien, the stranger, the outsider. These are fully included in the community and sacred lineage (witness Ruth the Moabite in David's lineage in Matthew 1:5). Hence, Nelson's conclusion: Holy War does not appear to jeopardize the "social conscience" of Deuteronomy. At the moral level, however, Holy War falls far short of Jesus' teaching, which sets forth a radically different response to enemies: "Love your enemies and pray for those who persecute you" (Matt 5:44). Hence, YHWH war remains problematic; it requires us to trace the journey from its practice to the later moral vision of the OT prophets (Isa 52:7, 10; 52:13—53:12) and Israel's messianic hope (Isa 2:1–4; Mic 4:1–5), with its fulfillment in Messiah Jesus, whose life and death is the basis for a cruciform hermeneutic (Boyd, et al). Hay's *Reading Backwards* reverses this method, concurring with Boyd.

This, however, raises a crucial question: does the authority of OT Scripture stand or fall only through its NT interpretation? Many Christians would readily concur, or toss the OT out completely (Marcion fashion). But let us not forget that the exact opposite is also abundantly evident in the NT: much of the NT *is supported by appeal* to OT Scripture; further, much in the NT makes sense only in light of the OT, as my *Israel's Scripture Traditions* documents. Richard Hays' two *Echoes* books demonstrate the same, as does Le Peau's commentary on *Mark*. Listing books on this point would take a page or two. If the Torah (Law) and the Prophets and the Psalms were not already the scriptural canon of early Christian believers, I doubt that the

NT would exist, for Jesus expounds about himself precisely by reference to those Scriptures (Luke 24:27, 44). No OT, no NT! Jesus Messiah has broken the Gordian knot of Holy War in the OT.[1]

The Micro Analysis: Specific Text Portions

1. Psalms. In respect to *"deliverance* from evil" *per se*, the Psalms head the list. Several Psalms connect deliverance from *evil* with peace (*shalom*). Psalms 34 (v. 14) and 125 are explicit, while several others imply the connection (35:20 in context; cf. 37:27, 37; 109:5). Where *evil is*, *shalom* is not. Two terms in Psalm 125, *wickedness* (v. 3a) and *crooked ways* (5a), anticipate the assurance that "the Lord will lead away with *evildoers*" (5b), followed by: "Peace be upon Israel" (5c). In these Psalms *evil* contrasts to *peace*, a key point as this book is a counterpart to my *Covenant of Peace*. In many other Psalms deliverance from evil infers *shalom* as the result.

    Psalm 120 (not included in chapter 3) is quite applicable. It begins, "In my distress I cry to the Lord . . . *Deliver* me, O Lord, from lying lips and deceitful tongues," and then ends with "I am for peace, but when I speak they are for war." While *evil*, the antonym of *shalom* does not occur, *war* is here viewed as evil, contrasting sharply to *peace*. While *war* as such is not an antonym to *shalom* (in light of 2 Samuel 11:7 where David asks Uriah about the *shalom* of the war), *war* is a major component of *evil*, especially in the prophets where war and exile are forecast repeatedly as God's punishment of the nations' (Israel's and Judah's) idolatries and covenantal adultery (read, e.g., Isa 1 and 7—10). While *war* and *shalom* may not be antonyms, nonetheless, war *wars* against shalom; it is a major sub-category of *evil*. Think of the many killed and the many paralyzed veterans! Further, when wars end, we may speak of peace, but war never effects shalom. This is true because the Hebrew *shalom* is more than the English *peace*. Shalom is the well-being (health) of the person and the society. War maims, cripples, and kills. Post-war construction reminds us of shalom lost; it takes years, even decades, to regain shalom.

---

1. To continue and enrich this study, see Peckham, *Theodicy of Love*. Covenant love is the context in which evil is defined and condemned. See Peckham's rules of God's engagement with evil: 153, in the context of his discussion on 55, 112, and 155. Note his quotation from C. S. Lewis on 170.

2. Proverbs. In at least one text *shalom*-peace ("peace and joy)" contrasts to *evil* and *wickedness* (12:13, 20–22). Similarly, a contrast emerged between *peace* and *justice*.

3. Isaiah. The *evils* of the nation's idolatries lace chapters 1—39, although the word *evil* is used sparingly. When it is used, the prophetic trope is sharp, as in 1:16–17; 3:9; and 5:20, with 5:20a judging Judah's perversity sarcastically: "you who call *evil good* and *good evil*." Another text globalizes God's judgment: "I will punish the world for its *evil*, and the wicked for their iniquity" (13:11). Note also the judgment of the nations (10:12—23:18).

In contrast to *evil*, Isaiah's *peace* theology rings loud and clear in 9:1–7; 11:1–10; 54:10; 59:7–15. Beating "swords into plowshares" in 2:1–5 (even though *shalom* and *evil* do not occur), affirms eschatological hope, then and now. Other passages replete with similar theology are 52:7—53:12 (*shalom* occurs in 52:7); 61:1—62:12; 65:17–25; 66:10–22. In chapters 40—66 future *shalom* shines in numerous portions, but in others, lament dims (chapter 64). Hence, return from exile holds hope, yes, but also despair. Hope for deliverance from exile continues into the NT, for fulfillment in the Messiah, as N. T. Wright stresses in *Jesus and the Victory of God*.[2]

4. Jeremiah. Jeremiah speaks often of *evil*. He announces a new covenant in which, implicitly, peace will reign (31:31–34). He calls exiled Israel to seek the welfare (*shalom*) of the city/nation in which they are captive (29:7) with warning not to let "the prophets and diviners who are among you deceive you" (29:8–9—i.e. *evil*). In 29:11 *shalom* is used explicitly as the antonym of *evil* (*rāʿ* : "My thoughts for you are *peace*, and not *evil*" (NKJV).

5. Matthew. Matthew's signature Sermon on the Mount contains both themes. Chapter 5 is the paradigm, with its memorable "Blessed are the peacemakers, for they will be called children of God" and the concluding two paragraphs: "Do not resist an evildoer" together with "Love your enemies and pray for those who persecute you so that you may be children of your Father in heaven." The identity of God's children is at stake.

6. Luke–Acts. Luke's Gospel is most explicit on deliverance/exorcism from evil in tandem with a theology of peace and peacemaking. Read again the Lukan portion of chapter 5 above and chapter 5 in *Covenant of Peace*. While all of Luke is relevant to this thesis, 10:1–18 is the

---

2. N. T. Wright, *Jesus*, 126–29, 428–30, 632–42.

paradigm: the kingdom of God's *peace* greeting leads to healing and exorcism, which is the basis for Jesus' memorable exclamation, "I was seeing Satan falling like lightning from heaven" (AT, 10:18). This text is for the church in all ages: the gospel of peace includes healing and deliverance from evil. Or, put differently, the good news of God's salvation in Jesus Christ, empowered by "peace be with you," collapses the powers of evil. *Satan falls.*[3]

7. Paul and Pauline. On the one hand, Paul's contribution to *evil* is most explicit and full-orbed, from warnings against Satan's temptations and attacks to his frequent references to the powers (principalities and powers) or the elemental spirits of the universe. These powers are fluid, either agents that affirm the good and punish the evil (Rom 13:3–4), to those that enslave us (Col 2:8, 20–23)—therefore we must resist them (Eph 6:10–17)—to ignorantly crucifying "the Lord of glory" (1 Cor 2:8).

On the other hand, these same writings are explicit regarding *peace*, *peacemaking* by *killing enmity*, and *reconciliation*. Romans 5:1–11; Ephesians 2:11–22; and 2 Corinthians 5:17–20 are gems. Put succinctly, ". . . the God of peace will soon crush Satan under your feet" (Rom 16:20). This is the Magna Carta on how *evil* and *peace* are interrelated. God's peacemaking through the death and resurrection of Jesus Christ is the path to and power for overcoming *evil* with good (Rom 12:21), yielding the fruit of *shalom-peace.*

8. John's Gospel and Epistles have two strands that demonstrate how God's *peace* confronts evil. First, since "We know that we are God's children, and that the whole world lies under the power of the evil one" (1 John 5:18–19), the peace Jesus promises his followers is a precious promise: "Peace I leave with you; my peace I give to you. I do not give to you as the world gives. Do not let your hearts be troubled, and do not let them be afraid." (14:27) Further, "I have said this to you, so that in me you may have peace. In the world you face persecution. But take courage; I have conquered the world!" (16:33) Since *world* in its negative meaning is closely linked to *evil*, these promises represent *peace* as the antonym to *evil*.

Second, John is clear about Satan and the devil as *the ruler of this world* whom he has come to *cast out*, i.e, *exorcize*. Because Jesus has

---

3. In this book I have often referred to fallen angels as the basis for Satan and his power. I like Garrett's wider emphasis on angels (*No Ordinary Angel*) as context for "Falling Angels." Her other chapters describe "Angels as Messengers of Truth," "Angels at the Throne of God," and "Guardian Angels."

done this (John 12:31), he can later say, "I will no longer talk much with you, for the ruler of this world is coming. He has no power over me." (14:30) This context enables understanding Jesus' glorification through his death: victory over the evil one is by Jesus' death and resurrection overcoming the powers of evil.

Third, John's Gospel portrays Jesus speaking truth to power in the passion account. Jesus' words to Pilate are theologically and politically pungent, implicitly facing down the evil that consummates in Jesus' crucifixion (18:33–37; 19:9–11, 21–22).[4] Amazingly, both Pilate and the chief priests are "undone" by this exchange, causing the chief priests to commit the ultimate sin in answering Pilate's "trap" question, "Shall I crucify your King?" The chief priests answer, "We have no king but the emperor" (19:15), violates both the Shema and the eleventh of the Jewish *Eighteen Benedictions*.[5]

After the *evil* of Jesus' crucifixion *peace* comes with Jesus' resurrection: Jesus greets his sorrowing disciples, "Peace be with you" (20:19, 26). Then Jesus inaugurates worldwide mission: "'As the Father has sent me, even so I send you'" (20:21), breathing into his disciples the Holy Spirit and empowering them for mission: "'Receive the Holy Spirit. If you forgive the sins of any, they are forgiven; if you retain the sins of any, they are retained.'"[6] The good news of Jesus' victory over sin, Satan, and evil goes forth into the entire world.

9. Revelation. Revelation uses the term *peace only when it is taken away* (6:4). The book's apocalyptic genre vividly portrays the fury of *evil* on the one hand and, on the other, the slain Lamb's triumph over *evil*, in the face of the Empire's persecutions, already experienced or at the doorstep. Its final chapters announce a new heaven and earth, a peaceable kingdom, where the slain Lamb through his suffering obedience and death wins the battle against *evil*.

The Macro Story

In chapters 1 and 4 *evil* prevents, even fights against God's shalom for human well-being. The contrast between God's good creation (Gen 1—2) and

---

4. John's passion account consists of seven scenes, alternating between Pilate and Jesus inside the palace, and Pilate and "the Jews" outside. In this dramatic narrative Pilate and "the Jews" are subservient to divine power, in Jesus.

5. See Talbert, *Reading*, 241, for the drama and sarcasm of this denial of God's sovereignty.

6. See exposition in chapter 7.

human disobedience in Genesis 3 is sharp: the serpent (later a.k.a. Satan or devil) incites the first humans to want to be as God. Then the older son (Cain) becomes jealous of his younger brother (Abel), which culminates in strife and murder (Gen 4). God punishes Cain severely (a curse on the blood-crying out-ground), resulting in Cain's toil and self-identity as a fugitive and wanderer. When Cain complains, God puts a mark on him to protect him from violence and assures him God will avenge: whoever murders you will receive sevenfold vengeance (4:10–16). A generation or two later Lamech kills a man for wounding him, and tells his two wives: "If Cain is avenged sevenfold, truly Lamech seventy-sevenfold" (4:24), apparently with the intonation: "who cares?"

Humans later become so wicked "that every inclination of the thoughts of their hearts was only evil continually" (6:5b). God says, "I am sorry that I have made them" (7d). Twice then the text says, "the earth was filled with violence" (8:11, 13).[7] God then sends a great flood to destroy humankind but saves one family, Noah's, in an ark with two or seven of each kind of animals, to make a new start for humans to live in shalom, under the covenant-love of rainbow-promise. But human pride leads humans to build a great tower to reach to the heavens, which implies that humans are not content with their limits as humans. The effort fails with God scattering the people by giving different languages.

God nonetheless begins a new start, a special relationship with an elect people known as "salvation-history" or story.[8] God calls Abraham and Sarah to birth a new nation. But even in this new era of threefold promise (Gen 12:1–3), evil emerges in numerous forms. As the decades and centuries pass, despite evil showing its head in many forms, God's elective purposes in choosing this new community to be agents of salvific hope for all nations continues. Jealousy among Jacob's sons makes their father's favorite son, Joseph, in Egypt, a captive. God intervenes, however, to transform the situation so that captive Joseph in prison rises to power as Pharaoh's right hand executive. In that role Joseph saves his family from famine and gives them the desirable land of Goshen, where they prospered and multiplied.

---

7. Shroyer's *Original Blessing* conveniently glosses over these texts in her endeavor to debunk "original sin" and focus on *blessing*. It's nice to put "original" with God's blessing rather than with human sin, but Genesis 1 begins with original chaos, and the struggle against cosmic chaos (recall Warren's *Cleansing*). Human evil laces the biblical text. Shroyer's focus on *blessing* and its role in the biblical story is important. It is a "corrective" to negative thinking about the human plight, but her contribution would be stronger if she integrated it in some way with chaos and evil. Indeed, God does bless and is faithful despite human evil.

8. For a treatment of the entire biblical history as story (*Geschichte*) see *Bible*, edited by Bontrager, Hershberger, and Sharp.

SUMMARY AND CONCLUSION

Over time Egyptian rulers forget Joseph and make the Israelites work as tortured slaves, placing upon them unbearable burdens to support Egypt's national economic and political supremacy.

Israel's deliverance from this horrible slave-bondage in Egypt comes 400 years after living in Goshen, when God calls Moses to deliver them, successful only after ten plagues decimate the Egyptian's shalom to the point they are glad to get rid of these foreign pests. Through God's blessing of miracle in the parting of the Red Sea for Israel's escape, under Moses's leadership, a new shalom era lies on the distant horizon. But the next forty years of wandering in the wilderness tells a different story, in which God's faithfulness and human unfaithfulness interact (note Ps 78). Repeatedly, the freed people complain against and *test* God. God heeds their cries, and sends from heaven morning manna and evening quail.

Once in the land of God's promise, the idolatrous evils of the Canaanites repeatedly threaten Israel's shalom. "YHWH War" (chapters 2a and 2b) deals deathblows to numerous Canaanite nations in order to protect Israel from idolatry that erodes Israel's worship of God alone, which the daily recitation of the Shema (Deut 6:4–5) confesses. After a period of leadership under charismatic judges whom God raises up for deliverance from a particular enemy nation, the people want a king to be like the very nations from which God saves them. But wickedness of all sorts, with idolatries paramount, become Israel's and Judah's downfall. Again and again, the idolatries of the people, promoted by evil kings, cut short Israel's and Judah's shalom. These centuries of evil thwarting shalom result in God's judgment: exile for both Israel (to Assyria) and Judah (to Babylon). God's moral judgment, "did evil in the sight of the Lord," is how Israel's and Judah's history is remembered, but yes, God hangs in with them, so exile is not the *last* word of the biblical story! God sends Messiah Jesus to deliver from exile.

God's "sticks with" the chosen people and raises up prophets to call Israel back to shalom for their own sake and beyond (Gen 12:3). But the evils of divination, soothsaying, wealth, and an ever-increasing war arsenal persisted, with idolatry permeating all these evils (Isa 5:6–20). So also "they trample the head of the poor," violate God's sexual ethics, and in all this engage in sham worship (Amos 2:7; 5:21–25). Justice is scorned, so that Amos cries out, "Seek good and not evil, that you may live; and so the Lord, the God of hosts, will be with you, . . . Hate evil and love good, and establish justice in the gate; it may be that the Lord, the God of hosts, will be gracious to the remnant of Joseph" (5:14–15).

In light of this inglorious history, evil threatens shalom. The prophets continually call Israel back to God's shalom purposes, but repeatedly Israel mocks and persecutes the prophets. Hence the prophets look to the future for shalom; the covenant people live by eschatological hope (e.g., Isa 2:1–5; 9:6–7; 11:1–10; 35; 40—55). Similarly, Jeremiah, depressed by Israel's evils, promises a new covenant (Jer 31:31–34), for "I have loved you with an everlasting love" (31:3b).[9] Ezekiel's vision of bringing life to dry bones (chapter 37), and a new temple whose waters flow to bless the nations (Ezek 40—48 and Zech 11—14) are eschatological visions of the elect people's shalom. The new covenant will be a covenant of peace/shalom (Isa 54:10; Ezek 34:25; 37:26; cf. Mal 2:5; Nah 1:15). Ezekiel foresees the dawning of a new creation:

> I will make with them a *covenant of peace* and banish wild animals from the land, so that they may live in the wild and sleep in the woods securely. I will make them and the region around my hill a blessing; and I will send down the showers in their season; they shall be showers of blessing. (34:25–26)

> I will make a *covenant of peace* with them; it shall be an everlasting covenant with them; and I will bless them and multiply them, and will set my sanctuary among them forevermore. My dwelling place shall be with them; and I will be their God, and they shall be my people. Then the nations shall know that I the Lord sanctify Israel, when my sanctuary is among them forevermore. (37:26–28)

In the new covenant, Jesus proclaims the dawning of the kingdom of God, a major emphasis in the Synoptic Gospels, and the co-line to this book's title: "Deliver us from evil, for yours is the kingdom." As this kingdom come and coming is announced people are healed, demons are cast out, and Jesus is affirmed "Lord of all" (Acts 10:36), a challenge to all imperial lord-claims. The heralding of this kingdom's shalom confronts evil in a radically new manner, so much so that Jesus says, "I saw Satan falling like lightning from heaven" (Luke 10:18). Jesus' ministry— his life and teachings, death and resurrection—inaugurates God's kingdom-shalom. The new covenant of peace *is*: "on earth peace"[10] (Luke 2:14). Though evil continues, its doom is sure (Luke 2:14; 10:1–18; Rom 8:30–39; Rev 19—22).

In this entire story God's kingdom shalom includes love for God and love for the neighbor, and love overcoming evil. Shalom-love is God's gift, manifest fully in Jesus Christ, who makes peace (shalom) between former enemies (Eph 2:14–17), the paradigm and power for peacemaking in today's world.

---

9. Oh, that you could hear the memorable song rendition on the CD, *Songs for Our Spirit: Peace and Comfort* (Takestone Music; Nashville, TN).

10. On this, see Gorman, *Death*; Swartley, *Covenant*.

Prayer

Almighty God, Lover of all Your Creation,
Deliver us from evil and the evil one.
Grant us freedom and wholeness of life
through Jesus Christ, our Risen Lord,
to whom is the kingdom,
the power and the glory forever.

Benediction

The Lord keep you from all evil.
    The Lord keep your life.
The Lord keep your going out and your coming in
    from this time on and forevermore. Amen.
    (Ps 121:5–6)

Appendix 1

Resources: Prayers for Healing-Deliverance[1]

THIS "DELIVERANCE" PRAYER MAY be used as liturgy for naming and casting out each named demon or it could be used generically, "for all evil spirits." But naming may be helpful for sense of full relief.

> Lord God Almighty, we praise your holy name,
>> we give you thanks for your great love and power.
> You alone are the Sovereign One,
>> Creator and Ruler of heaven and earth.
>
> Lord Jesus Christ, You are the Savior of the world;
>> by your cross and resurrection you have set us free.
> Deliver us, Lord, from every evil;
>> and grant us peace and wholeness of life.
>
> Lord Jesus, we rejoice in your victory over Satan and sin,
>> and we rejoice that you share your victory with us.
> Lord Jesus, in your name and with your authority,
>> we bind and rebuke every evil spirit
> We claim the power of the Lord Jesus Christ
>> over all demonic oppression.
>
> *In the name and power of Jesus we rebuke and command you,
>> spirit of _____ to leave _____
> Go to Jesus for your judgment.
> Lord Jesus, we bless you
>> that you have overcome the world;
> we praise you, Lord, that you have set us free,

1. These deliverance-healing prayers I have written or modified from other sources, especially McManus, *Healing*, 94–95.

and are now setting _____ free.

Come, Holy Spirit, fill _____.
   with your divine power and love.
May, your holy angels, O God, protect and keep _____.

*Alternate Form (By person)
In the name and power of Jesus I call to you, Lord Jesus Christ
To free me from the oppression of _____.
   Go to Jesus for your judgment.
I praise and magnify the name of Jesus.

A short word of command may be used as follow-up, if spirits seek reentry, as they desire to do:

"Be gone, Satan and every demon, in the strong name of Jesus."

Prayer for Deliverance and Healing

(shortened form)

Lord, by your cross and resurrection
   you have set us free.
You are the Savior of the world.

Deliver us, Lord, from every evil.
   and grant us peace and wholeness of life.

Lord Jesus, we rejoice in your victory over Satan and sin,
   and we rejoice that you share your victory with us.
In your name and with your authority,
   we bind and rebuke this evil spirit-power of _____.

In the name of Jesus Christ we expel the demon-power of _____
   afflicting _____ (person)
   Lord Jesus, free _____ from the bondage
   and oppression of _____.

Lord, we bless you that you have overcome the world;
   we praise you, Lord, that you set us free.
Heal us, O Lord, deliver us, and protect us,
   through the power and love of our Lord Jesus Christ.

The use of either of these prayers assumes prior conversation with the oppressed person, to the point where he or she has named the oppressors and/or source in some life-experience: e.g., trauma like sudden death of loved one, suicide in family background (hushed and not acknowledged), rape, coven witchcraft vows, forms of destructive magic, fear, marriage infidelity, same-sex practices (in certain cases[2]), generational curses, and deception which often instigates and/or functions as cover-up for any of the above. There are occasions when conversation is not possible, in which case one must begin with confrontation, as in my story (at the end of chapter 5).

Before one begins with the above Prayer or at some point in the process—even at the end, one might want to use a statement of renunciation and affirmation to get clarity on the desired commitment of the person needing deliverance. For such, see "THE RENUNCIATION AND AFFIRMATION" by Mark Winslow.[3]

The above Prayer may also be used as a Prayer for Protection, with several modifications. See such in Johns and Kraybill.[4]

Prayer for House Cleansing

Lord God Almighty, we praise your holy name.
    We thank you for your love and salvation.
Lord Jesus Christ, by your cross and resurrection
    you set us free. We thank and praise you.

Lord Jesus, deliver us, from every evil.
    grant us peace and wholeness of life.
In your name and with your authority,
    we rebuke any evil spirit-power in this house.

We renounce any evil power that has come into our lives,
    whether known: _____, _____, or unknown.

We renounce all magical powers over us,
    whether through games, cards, hard metal music, etc.

---

2. This is not to say *all* same-sex attraction is from demonic oppression. In some cases, however, it may be true, as showed up in a few of the over 100 cases in the B. Snyder compilation of Dean Hochstetler's ministry.
3. Winslow, 204, in Swartley, ed. *Essays*.
4. *Even the Demons Submit*, 177.

We renew our pledge to live for Jesus, the Son of God.
    And renounce all other powers that compete with
        You, our living and loving God.

In the strong name of Jesus,
    we break the effects of any evil power
        that may have come upon any of us,
    Parents and children (may name each person)
    we break in Jesus Christ's name any evil influence or curse
that has come upon us,
    Parents or children (may name anything the Spirit brings
to mind of any evil spirit here)
        _____, yes, in Jesus' name and power
        _____, yes, in Jesus' name and power
        _____, yes, in Jesus' name and power

Let the mighty power of the Holy Lord God Almighty
    be present in this home
    to banish from it every unclean spirit,
    to cleanse it from every residue of evil,
    to make it a secure house and loving home for all,
        for every member of this family.
In the strong Name of Jesus Christ our Lord. Amen.

House Blessing

Family, friends, and pastor, or lay leader come together in house

Leader opens with prayer

> *O God of kindness and mercy, enter this home and grant it the grace of your presence. (Banish from this house every unclean spirit and cleanse it from every residue of evil). Inhabit this dwelling, defend it against all evil and be Lord of all in this household.*
>
> *In the name of Jesus we pray. Amen.*

Leader makes the sign of the cross on the front door.

> **Leader:** May this door always open in hospitality, may it always beckon to serve.

We move to the dining room. Person of house lights a candle.

> **All:** May the light of Christ shine in this home.

Person of House or Leader places a Bible on the table.

> All: May the word of God be read and heeded in this home.
>
> **Leader:** May Jesus Christ be head of this home.
> May the Holy Spirit abide here.
>
> All: Lord God, may your blessing be upon all who live here. Extended to both friend and stranger; both neighbor and guest.

Person or people who live there, pray:

> *Bless us, O God, that we may find here shelter, peace, and health.*
>
> *Make our/this house to be our home and a haven for all who enter it.*
>
> *May we receive all guests as we would receive Jesus Christ.*
>
> All: May the Lord and his guardian angels surround this dwelling. The Lord keep your going out and your coming in from this time on and forevermore.

Leader closes with a prayer of blessing

Personal Prayers[5]

Spiritual Reflection (in context of John 8 and 9)

Lord Jesus,

Light of the world
   I come, I come
      To You, to You
   You are Light for all people.

Dispel the darkness
     so I can see
   Bind and loose the evil
     so I am free.

Your Son sets me free
   and I am free indeed.

Touch my eyes
   with your healing light
     so I see all things clearly.

Thank you, Jesus.
Thank you, Jesus.

---

5. This Prayer and the next one are adapted and modified from my book, *Living Gift*, 50 and 122.

Spiritual Reflection (in context of John 17)

Lord Jesus,

Thank you for your prayer for me,
   protect me from the evil one
      and the power(s) of the world
   so that I might be one with
      my brothers and sisters in love.

As the Father was in you,
   so I desire that you, Jesus,
      be in me.
         I in you, you in me.

Make me holy by your Word and Truth.
   Fill me with your love, *agapē* love,
      empower me to do the works of righteousness.
      Do not forsake me,
         but send to me your Spirit
            Counselor, Advocate,
               Helper, Comforter.

Give to me your peace,
   not as the world gives,
      but a lasting, soothing peace
         that brings love, courage, and joy.

Thank you for conquering the evil one.
   Free me from sin and its power,
      lead me in your way
         the Way to the Father.

You are the Way, the Truth and the Life.

      Love (*agapē?*),

Appendix 2

Two Samples of ca. 100 Summaries of Dean Hochstetler's Exorcist Sessions[1]

Most of these persons were referred to him locally by pastors, family members, or counselors and psychiatrists. Some came from a distance.

Case 1 February 22, 2000

A Thirty-Four-Year-Old Fearful Man

A Christian pastor, who is a counselor, and his wife came here a few months ago. They were asking for help with a person in their community who, they said, had insurmountable problems. They went home and did a lot of good preparatory work with their neighbor.

The man's history and personal life follows:

1. He was sexually molested by his older brother. Because of this, he suffered from shame and had only recently begun to address the issue.

2. The father was aloof from his children. He compared them to the neighbor's children and told them, "You don't measure up." As a result, Mr. H. suffered from rejection, fear, hopelessness, worthlessness, and uselessness.

---

1. Citing selected cases from a 178-page booklet consisting of Dean Hochstetler's summaries of each session. Dean sent these summaries to members of his Oversight Committee, a few selected leaders in Indiana-Michigan Mennonite Conference, and Seminary Presidents and Deans at AMBS and Eastern Mennonite Seminary. This unpublished booklet, "The Ministry of Dean Hochstetler 1974–2005" was compiled and edited by Ben Snyder, January 2010, a fellow member at Dean's home church, Yellow Creek Mennonite Church. Several members continue the ministry.

3. He had suffered migraine headaches for years, was afraid of crowds of people, like in church for example, and recently had become suicidal. His fears and anxiety were very irrational.

4. He said, "I feel that I am driven by some internal force."

5. He complained of pressures in his chest and groin area. He said, "I am constantly tired and can't work much of the time. Of late, panic attacks have set in on me. Recently, I have been in bed eighteen hours a day."

Ancestral Occult History

Healing magic (powwow, casting spells—see Deuteronomy 18:11), was present for at least three generations. Applied kinesiology, foot reflexology, and divining rod use were common. Horoscope use was a standard practice.

Personal Occult History

Dr. Abraham's black box for healing purposes was used. The box is a "fetish." Applied kinesiology for muscle testing was used. He was involved in therapeutic touch healings and he used a pendulum to tell if cows were pregnant.

Counseling Procedures

The counselor had helped this man and wife to receive Jesus as their Savior. Prior to this, they "hoped" they might get to heaven (a false understanding of Romans 8:23–24). They had helped them to confess their personal sins including all occult and sexual sins. He had also forgiven his father. The ancestral sins were brought to the cross of Jesus. One does not carry guilt for the forefather's sins, only the consequences (see Daniel 9:3–19).

As progress was made with emotional and spiritual healing, the pains and pressures became greater and more intolerable. He could not work. He either stayed in bed or tried to run away. He got sick every time the counselor came near him. Fears, panic, and anxiety overwhelmed him. The pastor called on Friday, February 4, 2000, saying, "We need help now." They came the next day. The closer they came, the more the voices in his head urged him to exit the van they were in. When they got in my house, he said, "Something is telling me to run away from here."

After hearing the man and hearing what the counselor pastor had done, I came to the conclusion that the problem was demonization. After the preliminary work was finished, I asked permission of him to address the demons. He understood that I would be speaking to "them," not him. I would speak to the spirits that were afflicting him. One of four things will happen:

1. Nothing.
2. Bodily manifestations may occur.
3. Messages or pictures may come to your mind and you need to report them immediately.
4. They may become verbal.

Numbers "3" and "4" occurred. We used Philippians 2:5–11 and Psalms 18 against the spirits. They hated it. He fell into his wife's lap in a trance and his eyes bulged out and became "glassy."

The Spirit List

1. Fear (the chief demon)—with seven helpers; answered to Satan in regard to rank
2. Panic—with one helper
3. Anxiety—with one helper
4. Fear of man—had no helper

These were cast out in Jesus' name, a group at a time. Fear doubled him all up and he fell into his wife's lap. The demons cried pitifully. In rechecking, a "Pain" demon had hidden itself. He left also. I suspect more intervention will be needed later until he gets rebuilt emotionally.

Mr. H. praised the Lord Jesus and said, "I'm very tired." He recovered rapidly. Spirits can be forced to tell truth that stands in judgment before the living God.

The counselor pastor, not of his church group, will see him daily for a while for continuing healing and spiritual care. Mr. H.'s church would not believe any such problem could befall one of their members because they view "Noah's Ark" as a type of "church." If you are in the "ark" (the church) and keep the rules, you are secure. To them you hope you have salvation at the end of life, which is a wrong understanding of Romans 8:23–24.

Observations

1. Emotional brokenness, parental neglect, and programming that belittles a child are dangerous. Wicked spirits can enter thereby.
2. Occult practices violate the second commandment (Deuteronomy 5:9) and open the family system to satanic afflictions and curses (Deuteronomy 28).
3. The Lord Jesus Christ has become a curse for us (Galatians 3:13). He also came to destroy Satan's work (1 John 3:8)
4. Luke 9:1 and 10:17-19 are part of the Gospel and still in force.
5. Ancestral sins of occultism, personal occultism, and emotional brokenness are a deadly combination.
6. Why should it be necessary for these people to drive four hours oneway to secure help with this problem? Why isn't the nearest church group available for this work? Pastors and Christian educators, please pay attention to these truths.

I checked four days later as to how Mr. H. was doing. He was much improved. He needed pastoral care twice a day for a week and then daily for two weeks, as he was very shattered emotionally and physically. Another group of pain spirits were encountered and cast out by the counselor and his wife in Jesus' name. Pastoral care has been a very important part of this man's life. He worked a full week for the first time in many months as of February 18. Spiritual care has been *very* necessary on a daily basis.

I received a report from the pastor in October 2000, telling me his neighbor is doing well, works daily, is supporting his family, and his problems are gone. He rejoices in his freedom in Christ. He is now in his right mind and functioning very well socially and physically (see Mark 5:14b and Luke 8: 35b). The church group that he is a part of, however, scoffed at all this but they could not deny his recovery.

Case 2 December 14, 2001

Pastor's Wife—Age 45

On the first phone call, I needed to answer a lot of questions about my doctrinal beliefs. They needed to be sure that my beliefs were close enough to theirs or they could not come. They thought my beliefs were acceptable.

This couple asked for help with their three youngest children who had been sexually abused by an adopted son of a close relative of the father.

Both the father and mother came from extremely dysfunctional home themselves. Drunkenness, verbal abuse, violence, and sexual depravity were the norm and much more that went with such a life-style. Neither of them had opposite sex relationships before marriage.

It soon came to light that the pastor needed help with unresolved issues, which he received. Next, it became obvious the wife needed help as well as her hurt and pain of past history *was not* resolved, perpetrators not forgiven, nor the pain healed.

This healing work required six lengthy sessions. Next, she called saying, "I'm still harassed by something," and began to divulge the problems. Much of this had not been told to me before. These were her comments:

1. She had no recollection of things under age five.
2. From ages 5–12, she was frequently molested by an uncle, and others, up to age 19 [in] unconscious state.
3. Her brother frequently threw her against a wall, which knocked her into an unconscious state. Her parents ignored it.
4. There was much verbal abuse from her parents.
5. Punishment was *always* done in anger.
6. Her mother saw her own mother crash a chair over her husband's head to avoid bodily harm to herself. It knocked him out.
7. She *never* heard a tender word from her father. Her mother ended her life. It was suicide.

There was much more of a similar nature in the family systems, ancestors on both sides. Several years ago she got involved in iridology and applied kinesiology, which are occult practices, for a skin rash. When she confessed this as sin, the rash returned! Her problems had intensified with these two occult involvements.

She stated some major complaints:

1. Lack of real peace with God
2. Lack of compassion for others
3. Life is always a constant crisis
4. Difficulty in motivation to do anything
5. Can't pray or read Scripture and retain anything I read
6. Sexually "cold" to my husband

7. Thirty-five soul ties (emotional, sexual fantasies as well as the molestation ones)
8. Can't lose weight (obese ancestry)

These soul ties were broken by confession of lust. (As she got older, she had liked it to a degree.) All of these sexual soul ties or emotional contracts were broken verbally and the parts of her that others had were retrieved and the parts she had of them returned. This was done with regard to the several "molesters" as well.

In light of the dysfunctional ancestry, her own horribly painful past and occult involvement, I suspected demonic afflictions and ordered them in Jesus' name to tell truth that stood true in judgment before the living Lord Jesus.

Demonic Spirits in Rank and Number of Helpers:

1. Hate—we are legion
2. Obesity—5 (three generations of this in the ancestry)
3. Sex sins/Perversion—1 (five generations of immorality; the demon said so)
4. Molester—8
5. Worry—Legion
6. Fear—20 (these declared themselves as ancestral spirits)
7. Mind and Body Twister—800
8. Sexual feeler—30
9. Hatefulness—8
10. Mind blocker—40
11. Strangler (death)—90
12. Rage—3
13. Selfish—40
14. Accuser—70

Hate was the ruling spirit declaring he had gained entrance to the family line five generations back with an illegitimate birth (Deuteronomy 23:2). The rest were subordinate except for accuser with 70 helpers. He declared himself a "control" spirit in charge of her bodily hormones.

Some will certainly say that most of this list shows human emotions, which is true. Demons, however, capitalize on broken emotional structures and intensify the problems. Therefore, spirits can have the same names as well as other names. Some years ago I met up with an "Intensifier" demon, who said his task was to intensify every problem the person had!

Hate and Accuser tried to lie but were caught at it and their punishment in the abyss doubled (The believer has authority to bind and loose, Matthew 16:13–19.) Demons are liars by nature, but can be bound to truth that stands in the judgment before the living God. I repeat for emphasis.

"Mind blocker" said, "I'm a personality split" (false). "Molestation," "Sexual feeler," and "Sex-sins" used horribly foul and explicit sexual language. At this point I began to reach for my pocket where I carry a cross. She had no way of knowing what I was about to do. The demon protested, "No not that! No not that!" He was offended by the symbolism. The spirits said that their legal right to stay was gone. The reason there was no legal right to stay and control her was that she had thoroughly confessed [her] sins one by one, brought the whole "core" of generational evil to the cross of Jesus and its blood, broke the curses (Galatians 3:13), and forgave all who had hurt her. She stayed lucid. There was no trance and was later appalled that such language could have come from her mouth.

Method of Deliverance

In this case I was moved to tie them all to "Control," although "Hate" answered to Satan. (This does not always work. Sometimes you have to deal with each one as a separate entity.) I ordered them altogether into one unit to go to the abyss and ordering warrior angels to carry them there. There was a furious protest. They said, "This is our home of many generations in this family and her in particular. We will *never* leave. We will kill both you and her." They were tenacious. After I made the sign of the cross on her forehead, commanding in Jesus' name to go to the abyss, we sang "There's Power in the Blood." We read Psalm 18, Matthew 10:1, Luke 9:1, Luke 10:17–19, Ephesians 3:10, Philippians 2:5–11, and began to read in Colossians 2. On hearing Colossians 2:9–10, the spirits left en masse suddenly and quietly. We continued reading Colossians 2:11–15 and rechecked. No more spirits could be found and she expressed a peace she had not experienced in her life before. The pastor husband agreed to see to his wife's spiritual care.

A crucial part of this event was a book I gave her to read entitled *The Deliverance Ministry* by George Birch, Horizon Books, Camp Hill, PA.

I called several days later and found her enjoying her new found freedom and she was praising the Lord and told others what had happened. She said, "I listened to the complete *Messiah* by G. F. Handel and for the first time it warmed my heart. I had heard it many times before but it was an unprofitable experience."

Many are the captives whom Satan has bound that need release from demonization if only our North American churches could see it (Isaiah 61:1 and Luke 4:18). Many church leaders scoff at this approach to *some people's problems* and seminaries refuse to teach leadership about its reality, recognition, and treatment. It is a rejection of a major part of Matthew 28:18–20.

The ancestral sin "consequence" is a large part of this case study. If this were recognized, there would be sound answers to the statement, "We were born with this tendency." I am referring to same-sex living arrangements, either promiscuous or "covenant."

Several weeks ago, a program on TV called *Dateline* had the president of the American Psychiatric Association speaking to the reality of an exorcism that was presented. (I saw the presentation and have it on video. It was authentic.) His comment was, "This is what some people need. Some need psychological or psychiatric help and some need both the psychological and exorcistic type of help."

Jesus saw the validity of freeing Satan's captives; so did the disciples. The early church, for the first 300 years, affirmed it to be so and acted accordingly. Current church leadership, for the most part laughs, mocks, and says it does not exist. They believe it is not important, nor do they want to learn or be involved. They may suggest, "Please go 'prophesy' elsewhere. Our minds are already made up!"

Nonetheless, occult practices (Deuteronomy 18:9–15, Isaiah 47:9–15 and Acts 16:16), dysfunctional family systems, and the resultant demonization are a vital part of some people's problems. Therefore, the problems need to be addressed in confession, and the use of power and authority in Jesus' name against the intruding spirits. The current Harry Potter craze will intensify the herein mentioned problems. The church pulpit, for the most part, is silent about its evil connections and sees nothing wrong with the books or movies. They are tied to Deuteronomy 18:9–15.

Appendix 3

Treatment of Evil in Texts on NT Theology or NT Ethics

IN THIS BOOK WITH its focus of evil and the Lord's Prayer petition to "deliver us from evil," I examine about a half dozen textbooks on NT theology in regard to the degree that *evil* figures into their discussion.[1] Some textbooks have no listing of *evil* in their Subject Index or, if they do, they cite only a few references. A surprising exception is Rudolf Bultmann's *Theology of the New Testament*. Bultmann's Subject Index has fourteen references, occurring throughout his two-volume book (one-volume paperback). Along with *evil* are other related terms: *demonic* and *demons* (fifteen citations) plus eight for *Devil* and nine for *Satan*. In each of these listings there are some two- or three-page runs. *Exorcism* has five listings, with 128–39 a choice read, since he discusses exorcism and deliverance from demons in connection with the baptismal liturgies of the church, in its witness to Jesus. "In the name of Jesus" is important, and the phrase appears often, especially when he treats second-century Justin. Bultmann understands baptism as a sacrament that "drives out demons . . . by its exorcistic power" (138). This concurs with Kreider's treatment of exorcism in *Patient Ferment* (see chapter 9 above).

Bultmann has seven listings for *Powers*; two more for *cosmic*, six more for *demonic powers*; and three for *principalities*. While beyond the scope of this study, his work attracts on this point, especially in light of its 1951 (volume 1) and 1952 (volume 2) setting, with the realization he was developing and writing this *Theology* during World War II, and all the while keeping his teaching post at Marburg. Many of his citations are related to the personal realm, connected to Jesus Christ's death as defeat and conquest over the Devil and the demonic. His application of all this to the personal *existential* experience of encounter with Jesus explains,

---

1. I do not undertake an extensive study of this matter as I did for *peace* in *Covenant*, 433–71

for the most part, why his theology did not result in conflict with the demonic *powers* in the political reality of Nazi Germany![2] To what extent his program of demythologizing undermines his excellent treatment of these topics is not clear in reading his *Theology*.

Regarding "Theologies" and or "Ethics" texts that have no Index references, I raise these questions in critique. How and why have we glossed over or slighted this major emphasis in Scripture, as has been the case for *peace* also? Especially in the twentieth and twenty-first centuries when war and other evils dominate the realities of our times, why and how do we miss or downplay the canonical contribution on these topics? Boyd's works cited in the bibliography are a welcomed exception. To miss or marginalize this emphasis in OT or NT *Theology* and *Ethics* textbooks is inexcusable. In light of this deficiency, an unnecessary gap exists between biblical study and its power to address the pressing issues we face in today's world.

In contrast to Bultmann's extensive treatment of evil, Leonhard Goppelt's two-volume *Theology of the New Testament* does not list *evil* in his Subject Index, though he might have since it occurs in volume I (75) in connection with exorcism and when he speaks of "conquer evil with good" (156). Writing in Germany three decades later than Bultmann, Goppelt has six references to *Exorcism* and five to *Satan*. His references to exorcism are for the most part inconsequential, often compared with similar practices by others than Jesus. One of his references to Satan implies exorcism in this excellent sentence: "According to Mark . . . Jesus' *dynameis* did not manifest merely divine power, but the delivering power of the promised reign of God (Mk. 3:27) that shattered Satan's power."[3] Virtually all of Goppelt's references to exorcism and Satan are historically descriptive. They do not function as urgent "summons to decision," as in Bultmann. Goppelt's references to Satan in volume II are in relation to Revelation 12, with three arresting comments: (1) "the beast was a reproduction of the dragon described in 12:3, of Satan"; (2) "The attack of political ideology upon the church was not the product of a pre-Christian paganism but of the post-Christian world-situation. It was the reaction of the world—represented by Satan (12:9; 20:2, 7)—that denied God at the appearance of Christ and the establishment of the end-time community of salvation"; and (3) referring to the millennial passage

---

2. In my teaching NT theology and ethics I would often compare Bultmann to Billy Graham. Bultmann's existential encounter is analogous to Graham's emphasis on "the hour of decision." Both are life-transforming, but neither *necessarily* has impact upon one's political perspectives and values, though in my way of thinking, it should!

3. Goppelt, *Theology*, I.156. In note 27 Goppelt refers to other texts where Jesus drives out demons, as well as to Luke 10:18, "'I saw Satan fall like lightning from heaven.'"

in Revelation 20: "After Satan, who according to 12:7–12 had already fallen from power in heaven through the exaltation of Jesus, was also eliminated on earth and thereby temptation and the struggle with doubt were at an end (20:1–3), there dawned the millennial kingdom of Christ (20:4–6)."[4]

How different: Bultmann and Goppelt! A similar comparison could be made between Udo Schnelle's *Theology of the New Testament*, who in his Subject Index has three (two are three-page runs) listings for *evil*, another three (two with two-page runs) for *exorcisms* and nine for *Satan* with three having two-page runs, and Thielman's *New Testament Theology* that has only one listing for *evil* (this is a heading for a short one-page section, "The Triumph of God's Purpose over Cosmic Evil Forces," 126–27). Here he also speaks of demons (which occurs also on 191 and 398, Satan [on 634–35], and devil [on 396]).

Another fascinating comparison is two selected books on NT Ethics: Brian Blount's contribution with subtitle, *Ethics in an African American Context*, and Robert Daly's *Christian Biblical Ethics*.[5] For Blount, *evil* is significant with a ten-page discussion and other mentions as well; for Daly, *evil* does not appear in the Subject Index, nor does *devil* or *Satan*.

This analysis could continue for other volumes on NT Theology and NT Ethics. Such might be taken up by others for more thorough examination, not only of frequency of terms appearing in Indices but the extent to which *evil* (including *exorcism*, *devil*, and *Satan*) is a significant aspect of the whole. The same might be done for OT *Theologies* and *Ethics* as well, though here *evil* would be the crucial term.

---

4. Ibid., 189, 191, 193 respectively.
5. Note Daly's long subtitle. Five other scholars also contributed to the book.

Bibliography

Acolatse, Esther E. *Powers, Principalities, and the Spirit: Biblical Realism in Africa and the West*. Grand Rapids: Eerdmans, 2018.
Adams, Marilyn McCord. *Horrendous Evils and the Goodness of God*. Ithaca, NY: Cornell University Press, 1999.
Albright, W. F. Review of major French monograph on Yahweh Sabaoth. *JBL* 67 (1948) 377–81.
Aldridge, Robert C. "The Courage to Start." In *The Risk of the Cross: Christian Discipleship in the Nuclear Age*, edited by Christopher Grannis, Arthur Laffin, and Elin Schade, 46–50. New York: Seabury, 1981.
Alexander, Patrick H., et al., eds. *The SBL Handbook of Style: For Ancient Near Eastern, Biblical, and Early Christian Studies*. Peabody, MA: Hendrickson, 1999.
Allman, Mark J. *Who Would Jesus Kill? War, Peace, and the Christian Tradition*. Winona, MN: Anselm Academic, 2008.
Amorth, Gabriele, with Stefano Stimamiglio. *An Exorcist Explains the Demonic: The Antics of Satan and His Army of Fallen Angels*. Translated by Charlotte J. Fasi. Manchester, NH: Sophia Institute, 2016.
Anderson, Bernhard W. *From Creation to New Creation*. Minneapolis : Fortress, 1994.
———. "The Holy One of Israel." In *Justice and the Holy: Essays in Honor of Walter Harrelson*, edited by Douglas A. Knight and Peter J. Paris, 3–19. Atlanta: Scholars, 1989.
———. *Understanding the Old Testament*. 4th ed. Englewood Cliffs, NJ: Prentice-Hall, 1986.
———. *The Unfolding Drama of the Bible*. New York: Association, 1970.
Anderson, Neil. *Victory over the Darkness*. Ventura, CA: Regal, 1990.
Appleby, David W. *It's Only A Demon: A Model of Christian Deliverance*. Revised 2d edition. Goode, VA: Spiritual Interventions, 2017.
Arnold, Clinton. *Ephesians: Power and Magic: The Concept of Power in Ephesians in Light of its Historical Setting*. SNTSMS 63. Cambridge: Cambridge University Press, 1989.
———. *Powers of Darkness: Principalities and Powers in Paul's Letters*. Downers Grove, IL: InterVarsity. 1992.
———. *Three Crucial Questions*. Grand Rapids: Baker, 1997.
Augustine. Sermon 71.1, *Matthew 1–13*, vol. 1a. In ACCS, edited by Manlio Simonetti. Downers Grove, IL: InterVarsity, 2001.

Aulén, Gustav. *Christus Victor: An Historical Study of the Three Main Types of the Idea of Atonement.* Eugene, OR: Wipf & Stock [1931] 2003.

Ayo, Nickolas. *The Lord's Prayer: A Survey Theological and Literary.* Notre Dame, IN: University of Notre Dame Press, 1992.

Bailey, Wilma. "Who Gets to Eat in the Garden of Eden?" In *Rooted and Grounded: Essays on Land and Christian Discipleship*, 13–18. Eugene, OR: Pickwick, 2016.

———. *"You Shall Not Kill" or "You Shall not Murder: The Assault on a Biblical Text."* Collegeville, MN: Liturgical, 2005.

Barclift, Philip L. "Zionism, Justice, and the 'Promised Land.'" *Lexington Theological Quarterly* 34 (Winter 2004) 195–224.

Barker, M. J. "Possession and the Occult—a Psychiatrist's View." *Churchman* 94.3 (1980) 246–53.

Barrett, C. K. *The First Epistle to the Corinthians.* New York: Harper and Row, 1966.

———. *Paul: An Introduction to His Thought.* London: Chapman, 1994.

Barth, Markus. *Jesus the Jew: What Does It Mean That Jesus Is a Jew?* [Part 1] and *Israel and the Palestinians* [Part 2]. Translated by Frederick Prussner. Atlanta: John Knox, 1978.

Bartley, Jonathan. *Faith and Politics after Christendom: The Church as a Movement for Anarchy.* Waynesboro, GA: Paternoster, 2006.

Bauckham, Richard. *God Crucified: Monotheism and Christology in the New Testament.* Grand Rapids: Eerdmans, 1998.

———. *The Theology of the Book of Revelation.* Cambridge: Cambridge University Press, 1993.

Bauman, Clarence. *The Sermon on the Mount: The Modern Quest for Its Meaning.* Macon, GA: Mercer University Press, 1985.

Bauman, Elizabeth Hershberger. *Coals of Fire.* Scottdale, PA: Herald, 1954.

Beck, Richard. *Reviving Old Scratch: Demons and the Devil for Doubters and the Disenchanted.* Minneapolis: Fortress, 2016.

Becker, Michael. "Paul and the Evil One." In *Evil and the Devil*, edited by Ida Fröhlich and Erkki Koskenniemi, 127–41. New York: Bloomsbury/T & T Clark, 2013.

Behm, Johannes. ἀνάθεμα (*anáthema*). In *TDNT*, edited by Gerhard Kittel (German); translated and edited by Geoffrey Bromiley (English). Vol. 1. Grand Rapids: Eerdmans, 1964.

Bell, Daniel M., Jr. *Just War as Christian Discipleship: Recentering the Tradition in the Church Rather than the State.* Grand Rapids: Brazos, 2009.

Bellinger, Charles K. *The Genealogy of Violence: Reflections on Creation, Freedom, and Evil.* New York: Oxford University Press, 2001.

Bender, Harold S. *The Anabaptists and Religious Liberty in the 16th Century.* Facet Book: Historical Series. Philadelphia: Fortress, 1970.

Bender, Philip D. "The Holy War Trajectory in the Synoptic Gospels and the Pauline Writings." MA Thesis, AMBS, Elkhart, IN, 1987.

Bennett, Jana Marguerite. "Not So Private: A Political Theology of Church and Family." In *Christian Political Witness*, edited by George Kalantzis and Gregory W. Lee, 112–27. Downers Grove, IL: InterVarsity Academic, 2014.

Berchman, Robert M. "Arcana Mundi between Balaam and Hecate: Prophecy, Divination, and Magic in Later Platonism." In *SBL Seminar Papers 1989*, 107–85. Atlanta: Scholars, 1989.

Berdyaev, Nikolai. *Freedom and Spirit.* London: G. Bles, 1948.

Berger, Peter. *A Rumor of Angels: Modern Society and the Rediscovery of the Supernatural.* Garden City, NY: Doubleday, 1969.

Berkhof, Hendrik. *Christ and the Powers.* Translated by John H. Yoder. Scottdale, PA: Herald, 1962.

Best, Ernest. *Following Jesus: Discipleship in the Gospel of Mark.* JSOTSS 4. Sheffield, UK: Sheffield, 1981.

Betz, Hans Dieter, ed. *The Greek Magical Papyri in Translation, including the Demotic Spells.* Chicago: University of Chicago Press, 1986.

Bishop, Peter D. *A Technique for Loving: Non-Violence in Indian and Christian Traditions.* London: SCM, 1981.

Blocher, Henri. *Evil and the Cross.* Translated by David G. Preston. Downers Grove, IL: InterVarsity, 1994.

Blount, Brian K. *Then the Whisper Put on Flesh: New Testament Ethics in an African American Context.* Nashville: Abingdon, 2001.

Boa, Kenneth. *Rewriting your Broken Story: The Power of an Eternal Perspective.* Downers Grove, IL: InterVarsity, 2016.

Böcher, Otto. *Das Neue Testament und die damonischen Mächte.* Stuttgarten Bibel-Studien 58. Stuttgart: Katholisches Bibelwerk, 1972.

Boers, Hendrikus. "Reflections on Mark's Gospel: A Structural Investigation." In *SBL Seminar Papers 1987*, 255–67. Atlanta: Scholars, 1987.

Bonhoeffer, Dietrich. *Cost of Discipleship.* New York: Simon and Schuster, 1995.

Bontrager, Marion G., Michele Hershberger, and John E. Sharp. *The Bible as Story: An Introduction to Biblical Literature.* 2d ed. Hesston, KS: Workplay Publishing in Cooperation with Hesston College, 2017.

Bontrager, William. "Special Report: [Elkhart] Indiana Justice: Retribution or Reconciliation." *ChrCent* (December 2, 1981) 1259–60.

Borg, Marcus J. *Jesus, A New Vision: Spirit, Culture, and the Life of Discipleship.* San Francisco: Harper and Row, 1987.

Bouma-Prediger, Steven. *For the Beauty of the Earth: A Christian Vision for Creation Care.* 2d ed. Grand Rapids: Baker Academic, 2010.

Bourne, Richard. *Seek the Peace of the City: Christian Political Criticism as Public, Realist, and Transformative.* Theopolitical Visions 5. Eugene, OR: Cascade, 2009.

Boyd, Gregory A. *Cross Vision: How the Crucifixion of Jesus Makes Sense of Old Testament Violence.* Minneapolis: Fortress, 2017.

———. *Crucifixion of the Warrior God: Interpreting the Old Testament's Violent Portraits of God in Light of the Cross.* Vols. 1 and 2. Minneapolis: Fortress, 2017.

———. "A Different Kind of Kingdom." In *Servant God: The Cosmic Conflict over God's Trustworthiness*, edited by Larry Ashcraft et al., 369–82. Loma Linda, CA: Loma Linda University Press, 2013.

———. *God at War: The Bible and Spiritual Conflict.* Downers Grove, IL: InterVarsity, 1997.

———. *The Myth of a Christian Nation: How the Quest for Political Power Is Destroying the Church.* Grand Rapids: Zondervan, 2005.

———. *Satan and the Problem of Evil: Constructing a Trinitarian Warfare Theodicy.* Downers Grove, IL: InterVarsity, 2001.

Boyd, Gregory, and Paul R. Eddy. "Evil." In *Dictionary of Scripture and Ethics*, edited by Joel Green, 288–89. Grand Rapids: Baker Academic, 2011.

Brandon, S. G. F. *Jesus and the Zealots.* Manchester: Manchester University Press, 1967.

Brashler, James A., ed. "Evil." *Interp* 57.1 (October 2003). Front cover.
Bredin, Mark. *Jesus: Revolutionary of Peace: A Nonviolent Christology in the Book of Revelation*. London: Paternoster, 2003.
———. *Jesus: Revolutionary of the Poor: Matthew's Subversive Jesus*. Eugene, OR: Cascade, 2017.
———. "The Synagogue of Satan Accusation in Revelation 2:9." *BTB* 28: 160–64.
Brenneman, Laura. "Corporate Discipline and the People of God: A Study of 1 Corinthians 5.3–5." PhD diss., Durham University, UK, 2005.
Brodie, Thomas L. *The Gospel According to John: A Literary and Theological Commentary*. Oxford: Oxford University Press, 1993.
Brower, Kent. "Holiness." In *Dictionary of Scripture and Ethics*, edited by Joel Green, 361–64. Grand Rapids: Baker Academic, 2011.
Brown, Peter. "Sorcery, Demons and the Rise of Christianity: From Late Antiquity into the Middle Ages." In *Religion and Society in the Age of St. Augustine*, 119–46. New York: Harper and Row, 1972.
Brownlee, William H. "From Holy War to Holy Martyrdom." In *The Quest for the Kingdom of God*, edited by H. B. Huffman, F. A. Spina, and A. R. W. Green, 281–92. Winona Lake, IN: Eisenbrauns, 1983.
Bruce, F. F. *The Epistle to the Hebrews*. NICNT. Grand Rapids: Eerdmans, 1964.
———. *Peter, Stephen, James & John: Studies in Non-Pauline Christianity*. Grand Rapids: Eerdmans, 1979.
Brueggemann, Walter. *From Whom No Secrets Are Hid: Introducing the Psalms*. Edited by Brent A. Strawn. Louisville: Westminster John Knox, 2014.
———. *The Land: Place as Gift, Promise, and Challenge in Biblical Faith*. 2d ed. Overtures to Biblical Theology. Minneapolis: Augsburg Fortress, 2002.
———. *The Prophetic Imagination*. Philadelphia: Fortress, 1978.
Bultmann, Rudolf. *Theology of the New Testament*. Vols. 1 & 2. New York: Scribner, 1951.
Burge, Gary M. *Jesus and the Land: The New Testament Challenge to "Holy Land" Theology*. Grand Rapids: Baker Academic, 2010.
Burkholder, Lawrence E. *The Leviathan Factor*. Eugene, OR: Wipf & Stock, 2017.
Burton-Edwards, Taylor. "The Teaching of Peace in Early Christian Liturgies." MA Thesis, AMBS, 1997.
Cadoux, C. J. *The Early Christian Attitude toward War*. New York: C. Scribners, 1919 [reprint 1982].
Caird, George B. *A Commentary on the Revelation of St John the Divine*. New York: Harper & Row, 1966.
Camp, Lee C. *Mere Discipleship: Radical Christianity in a Rebellious World*. 2d ed. Grand Rapids: Brazos, 2003.
———. *Who Is My Enemy? Questions American Christians Must Face About Islam—and Themselves*. Grand Rapids: Brazos, 2011.
Campenhausen, H. von. "Zur Auslegung von Röm. 13: Die dämonische Deutung des ἐξουσία-Begriffs," in FS A. Bertholet zum 80. Geburtstag, edited by W. Baumgartner, 97–113. Tübingen: J. C. B. Mohr, 1950.
Capon, Robert Farrar. *The Parables of the Kingdom*. Grand Rapids: Zondervan, 1985.
Cardinal Bernardin, Joseph. *The Gift of Peace: Personal Reflections*. Chicago: Loyola, 1997.

Carr, Wesley. *Angels and Principalities: The Background, Meaning and Development of the Pauline Phrase hai archai kai hai exousia.* SNTSMS 42. Cambridge: Cambridge Univiversity Press, 1981.

Carroll, M. Daniel R., and J. Blair Wilgus, eds. *Wrestling with the Violence of God: Soundings in the Old Testament.* Bulletin for Biblical Research Supplement 10; Winona Lake, IN: Eisenbrauns, 2015.

Carter, Warren. "Imperial Power Is Bad for Your Health." *Sojourners* (February 2018) 32–35, 43.

———. *Matthew and Empire: Initial Explorations.* Harrisburg, PA: Trinity, 2001.

Cassidy, Richard J. *Jesus, Politics, and Society: A Study of Luke's Gospel.* Maryknoll, NY: Orbis, 1978.

Celtic Night Prayer. Compiled by members of the Northumbrian Community. London: Marshall Pickering, 1996.

Charles, J. Daryl. *2 Peter, Jude.* BCBC. Scottdale, PA: Herald, 1999.

Charlesworth, James H., ed. *The Old Testament Pseudepigrapha: Apocalyptic Literature & Testaments.* Vol. 1. Garden City, New York: Doubleday, 1983.

Christopher-Smith, Daniel. *A Biblical Theology of Exile.* Overtures to Biblical Theology. Minneapolis: Fortress, 2002.

Christopher-Smith, Daniel, and Katherine Southwood. *The Religion of the Landless: The Social Context of the Babylonian Exile.* Bloomington, IN: Meyer-Stone, 1989.

Chrysostom. *The Gospel of Matthew,* Homily 41.2, *Matthew 1–13,* ACCS, edited by Mario Simonetti, 248. Downers Grove, IL: InterVarsity, 2001.

Clapp, Rodney, ed. *The Consuming Passion: Christianity and Consumer Culture.* Downers Grove, IL: InterVarsity, 1998.

Coggins, James R., and Paul G. Hiebert, eds. *Wonders and the Word: An Examination of Issues Raised by John Wimber and the Vineyard Movement.* Hillsboro, KS: Kindred, 1989.

Copan, Paul. "Evil and Primeval Sin." In *God and Evil: The Case for God in a World Filled with Pain,* edited by Chad Meister and James K. Dew, Jr., 109–23. Downers Grove, IL: InterVarsity, 2013.

———. *Is God a Moral Monster? Making Sense of the Old Testament God.* Grand Rapids: Baker, 2011.

Copan, Paul, and Matt Flannagan. *Did God Really Command Genocide?: Coming to Terms with the Justice of God.* Grand Rapids: Baker, 2015.

Cornell, Collin. "A Testament of Violence." *ChrCent* (November 8, 2017) 32–36.

Corson, Sarah. "Welcoming the Enemy: A Missionary Fights Violence with Love." *Sojourners* 12 (April 1983) 29–31.

Cowles, C. S., Eugene H. Merrill, Daniel L. Gard, and Tremper Longman III. *Show Them No Mercy: 4 Views on God and Canaanite Genocide.* Grand Rapids: Zondervan, 2003.

Crews, Rowan. "The Praise of God and the Problem of Evil: The Problem of Evil from a Liturgical Perspective." *Quarterly Review* 16 (1996) 39–54.

Crosby, Michael H. *House of Disciples: Church, Economics, & Justice in Matthew.* Maryknoll, NY: Orbis, 1988.

Cserháti, Márta. "Binding the Strong Man: Demon-Possession and Liberation in the Gospel of Luke." In *Evil and the Devil,* edited by Ida Fröhlich and Erkki Koskenniemi, 108–15. New York: Bloomsbury/T & T Clark, 2013.

Cullmann, Oscar. *The State in the New Testament.* New York: Scribners, 1956.

Culpepper, Alan. "An Introduction to the Johannine Writings." In *The Johannine Literature*, edited by R. Alan Culpepper, Barnabas Lindars, Ruth B. Edwards, and John M. Court, 9–39. Sheffield: Sheffield Academic, 2000.

Dallaire, Hélène M. "Taking the Land by Force: Divine Violence in Joshua." In *Wrestling with the Violence of God: Soundings in the Old Testament*, edited by M. Daniel R. Carroll and J. Blair Wilgus, 51–73. Bulletin for Biblical Research Supplement 10; Winona Lake, IN: Eisenbrauns, 2015.

Daly, Robert J. *Christian Biblical Ethics: From Biblical Revelation to Contemporary Christian Praxis: Method and Content*. New York: Paulist, 1984.

Davids, Peter H. *The Epistle of James*. NIGTC. Grand Rapids: Eerdmans, 1982.

Davies, W. D. *The Gospel and the Land: Early Christianity and Jewish Territorial Doctrine*. Berkeley, CA: University of California Press, 1974.

Dawn, Marva J. "The Biblical Concept of 'the Principalities and Powers': John Yoder Points to Jacques Ellul." In *The Wisdom of the Cross: Essays in Honor of John Howard Yoder*, edited by Stanley Hauerwas, Chris K. Huebner, Harry J. Huebner, and Mark Thiessen Nation, 168–86. Grand Rapids: Eerdmans, 1999.

———. *Powers, Weakness, and the Tabernacling of God*. Grand Rapids: Eerdmans, 2001.

Defoe, Daniel. *The Political History of the Devil*. Mineola, NY: Dover Publications, Inc., 2016 (reprint of 1726 book).

Dibelius, Martin. *Die Geisterwelt im Glauben des Paulus*. Göttingen: Vandenhoeck & Ruprecht, 1909.

De Silva, Dawna, and Teresa Liebscher. *SOZO Saved Healed Delivered: A Journey into Freedom with the Father, Son, and Holy Spirit*. Shippensburg, PA: Destiny Image, 2016.

Dix, Gregory, and Henry Chadwick, eds. *The Treatise on The Apostolic Tradition of St Hippolytus of Rome: Bishop and Martyr*. Ridgefield, CT: Morehouse, 1937; revised 1968; reissued with corrections, 1992.

Donahue, John R. "Who Is My Enemy: The Parable of the Good Samaritan and the Love of Enemies." In *The Love of Enemy and Nonretaliation in the New Testament*, edited my Willard M. Swartley, 137–56. Louisville: Westminster John Knox, 1992.

Dreher, Rod. *The Benedict Option: A Strategy for Christians in a Post-Christian Nation*. New York: Sentinel, 2017. For interview on book: http://www.plough.com/en/events/2017/benedict-option?source=pw031617.

Dunham, Kyle C. "Yahweh War and Ḥerem: The Role of Covenant, Land, and Purity in the Conquest of Canaan." *Detroit Baptist Seminary Journal* 21 (2016) 7–30.

Dunn, James D. G., and Graham H. Twelftree. "Demon-Possession and Exorcism in the New Testament." *Churchman* 94 (1980) 210–25.

Earl, Douglas S. "Holy War and חרם [ḥerem]: A Biblical Theology of חרם." In *Holy War in the Bible: Christian Morality and an Old Testament Problem*, edited by Heath A. Thomas, Jeremy Evans, and Paul Copan, 152–78. Downers Grove, IL: InterVarsity, 2013.

———. *The Joshua Delusion? Rethinking Genocide in the Bible*. Eugene, OR: Cascade, 2010.

———. *Reading Joshua as Christian Scripture. Journal of Theological Interpretation*: Supplement 2. Winona Lake, IN: Eisenbrauns, 2010.

Egan, Eileen. *Peace Be with You: Justified Warfare or the Way of Nonviolence*. Maryknoll, NY: Orbis, 1999.

Elias, Jacob. *Remember the Future: the Pastoral Theology of Paul the Apostle.* Scottdale, PA: Herald, 2006.

Eller, Vernard. *War and Peace from Genesis to Revelation.* Scottdale, PA: Herald, 1981.

Elster, William. "The Early Christian Doctrine of Pacifism." Unpublished, 1998.

———. "The New Law of Christ and Early Christian Pacifism." In *Essays on War and Peace: Bible and Early Church,* edited by Willard M. Swartley, 108–29. OP 9. Elkhart, IN: IMS, 1986.

Enns, Fernando. "Public Peace, Justice and Order in Ecumenical Perspective." In *At Peace and Unafraid,* edited by Duane K. Friesen and Gerald Schlabach, 252–53. Scottdale, PA: Herald, 2005.

Entz, Loren. "Challenges to Abou's Jesus." *Evangelical Missions Quarterly* (January 1986) 48–50.

Epp Weaver, Alain. *States of Exile.* Scottdale, PA: Herald, 2008.

Evans, C. F. "The Central Section of Luke's Gospel." In *Studies in the Gospels,* edited by D. E. Nineham, 37–53. Oxford: Blackwell, 1955/1967.

Evans, Craig A. "Jesus & the Continuing Exile of Israel." In *Jesus & the Restoration of Israel: A Critical Assessment of N. T. Wright's Jesus and the Victory of God,* edited by Carey C. Newman, 77–100. Downers Grove, IL: InterVarsity, 1999.

Evil: A Guide website blurb. https://www.bloomsbury.com/uk/evil-a-guide-for-the-perplexed-9781501324291/.

Farley, Wendy. *The Wounding and Healing of Desire: Weaving Heaven and Earth.* Louisville, KY: Westminster John Knox, 2005.

Ferguson, John. *The Politics of Love: The New Testament & Non-Violent Revolution.* Greenwood, SC: The Attic, n.d.

Ferguson, Everett. *Demonology of the Early Christian World.* New York: Edwin Mellen, 1984.

Fiddes, Paul S. "Christianity, Atonement and Evil." In *The Cambridge Companion to the Problem of Evil,* edited by Chad Meister and Paul K. Moser, 210–29. Cambridge: Cambridge University Press, 2017.

Finger, Thomas. *Christian Theology: An Eschatological Approach.* Vol. 1. Scottdale, PA: Herald, 1987.

———. *Christian Theology: An Eschatological Approach.* Vol. 2. Scottdale, PA: Herald, 1989.

Finger, Thomas, and Willard M. Swartley. "Bondage and Deliverance: Biblical and Theological Perspectives." In *Essays on Spiritual Bondage and Deliverance,* edited by Willard M. Swartley, 10–38. OP 11. Elkhart, IN: IMS, 1988.

Fischer, James A. "War and Peace: A Methodological Consideration." In *Blessed Are the Peacemakers,* edited by Anthony Tambasco, 17–39. New York: Paulist, 1989.

Fitzmyer, Joseph A. *Romans: A New Translation with Introduction and Commentary,* AB 33. New York: Doubleday, 1993.

Fleischer, Matthew Curtis. *The Old Testament Case for Nonviolence.* Oklahoma City: Epic Octavius the Triumphant, 2018.

Flusser, David. "Qumran and Jewish 'Apotropaic' Prayer." In *Judaism and the Origins of Christianity,* 214–25. Jerusalem: Magnes, 1988.

Foerster, Werner. ἐχθρός (*echthrós*). In *TDNT,* edited by Gerhard Kittel (German); translated and edited by Geoffrey Bromiley (English), vol. II, 813–14. Grand Rapids: Eerdmans, 1964.

Ford, Josephine Massynbaerde. "Response to Thomas Finger and Willard Swartley." In *Essays on Spiritual Bondage and Deliverance,* edited by Willard M. Swartley, 41–42. OP 11. Elkhart, IN: IMS, 1988.

———. *Revelation.* AB. Garden City, NY: Doubleday, 1975.

Forsyth, Neil. *The Old Enemy: Satan and the Combat Myth.* Princeton, NJ: Princeton University Press, 1987.

Forsyth, P. T. *The Cruciality of the Cross.* 2d ed. London: Hodder and Stoughton, 1910.

Foster, K. Neill, with Paul L. King. *Binding and Loosing: Exercising Authority over the Dark Powers.* Camp Hill, PA: Christian, 1998.

Foster, Richard. *Money, Sex, and Power: The Challenge of a Disciplined Life.* San Francisco, CA: Harper and Row, 1985/2009.

———. *Prayer: Finding the Heart's True Home.* San Francisco: HarperSanFrancisco, CA: 1992.

Fretheim, Terrence E. *Creation Untamed: The Bible, God, and Natural Disasters.* Grand Rapids: Baker Academic, 2010.

Friedrich, Jim. "The Demons have come out." *ChrCent* (September 13, 2017) 10–11.

Friesen, Duane K. "In Search of Security: A Theology and Ethic of Peace and Public Order." In *At Peace and Unafraid: Public Order, Security, and the Wisdom of the Cross,* edited by Duane K. Friesen and Gerald Schlabach, 37–82. Scottdale, PA: Herald, 2005.

Friesen, Duane K. and Gerald W. Schlabach, eds. *At Peace and Unafraid: Public Order, Security, and the Wisdom of the Cross.* Scottdale, PA: Herald, 2005.

Friesen, James G. *Uncovering the Mystery of MPD.* San Bernardo, CA: Here's Life, 1991.

Fry, Ruth A. *Victories Without Violence.* Santa Fe, NM: Ocean Tree, 1986.

Fröhlich, Ida, and Erkki Koskenniemi, eds. *Evil and the Devil.* New York: Bloomsbury/T & T Clark, 2013.

Furnish, Victor Paul. *The Love Command in the New Testament.* Nashville: Abingdon, 1972.

Gallagher, Richard (book in progress). *Washington Post* (July 1, 2016), news release appearing in *ChrCent* (Aug. 3, 2016) 9. See: http://www.ncregister.com/blog/armstrong/christs-power-shines-even-in-creepiest-case-of-demonic-possession-says-psyc.

Gammie, John G. *Holiness in Israel.* Overtures to Biblical Theology. Minneapolis: Fortress, 1989.

Gardner, Richard B. *Matthew.* BCBC. Scottdale, PA: Herald, 1991.

Garrett, Susan R. "*Christ and the Present Evil Age.*" *Interp* 57 (October 2003) 370–383.

———. *The Demise of the Devil: Magic and the Demonic in Luke–Acts.* Minneapolis: Augsburg Fortress, 1989.

———. *No Ordinary Angel: Celestial Spirits and Christian Claims about Jesus.* New Haven, CT: Yale University Press, 2008.

———. *The Temptations of Jesus in Mark's Gospel.* Grand Rapids: Eerdmans, 1998.

Geddert, Timothy. *Mark.* BCBC. Scottdale, PA: Herald, 2001.

Gerbrandt, Gerald E. *Deuteronomy.* BCBC. Herald, 2015.

———. *Kingship According to the Deuteronomistic History.* SBL Dissertation Series 87. Atlanta: Scholars, 1986.

Gingerich, Ray, and Ted Grimsrud, eds. *Transforming the Powers: Peace, Justice, and the Domination System.* Minneapolis: Fortress, 2006.

Gombis, Timothy G. "The Political Vision of the Apostle to the Nations." In *Christian Political Witness*, edited by George Kalantzis and Gregory W. Lee, 74–89. Downers Grove, IL: InterVarsity Academic, 2014.

Good, Deirdre J. *The Meek King*. Harrisburg, PA: Trinity International, 1999.

Goppelt, Leonhard. *A Theology of the New Testament*. Vols. 1 and 2. Translated by John E. Alsup. Grand Rapids: Eerdmans, 1981.

Gorman, Michael J. *Becoming the Gospel: Paul, Participation, and Mission*. Grand Rapids: Eerdmans, 2015.

———. *Cruciformity: Paul's Narrative Spirituality of the Cross*. Grand Rapids: Eerdmans, 2001.

———. *The Death of the Messiah and the Birth of the New Covenant: A (Not So) New Model of the Atonement*. Eugene, OR: Cascade, 2014.

———. *Reading Revelation Responsibly: Uncivil Worship and Witness, Following the Lamb into the New Creation*. Eugene, OR: Cascade, 2011.

Gottwald, Norman. *The Tribes of Israel: A Sociology of the Religion of Liberated Israel, 1250–1050 B.C.E.* Sheffield, England: Sheffield Academic, 1999.

Grant, Jonathan. *Divine Sex: A Compelling Vision for Christian Relationships in a Hypersexualized Age*. Grand Rapids: Brazos, 2015.

Greenway, William. *The Challenge of Evil: Grace and the Problem of Suffering*. Louisville: Westminster John Knox, 2016.

Gushee, David P. "Toward an Evangelical Social Tradition: Key Current Debates." In *Christian Political Witness*, edited by George Kalantzis and Gregory W. Lee, 196–213. Downers Grove, IL: InterVarsity Academic, 2014.

Habel, Norman C. *The Land Is Mine: Six Biblical Land Ideologies*. Minneapolis: Fortress, 1995.

Haitch, Russell. *From Exorcism to Ecstasy: Eight Views of Baptism*. Louisville: Westminster John Knox, 2007.

Hallie, Philip. *Lest Innocent Blood Be Shed*. New York: Harper & Row, 1979.

Hamilton, Jeffries M. *Social Justice and Deuteronomy: The Case of Deuteronomy 15*. SBL Dissertation Series 136. Atlanta: Scholars, 1992.

Hamm, Dennis. "The Ministry of Deliverance and the Biblical Data: A Preliminary Report." In *Deliverance Prayer: Experiential, Psychological and Theological Approaches*, edited by Matthew Linn and Dennis Linn, 49–52. Ramsey, NJ: Paulist, 1981.

Hange, Roy. "Revelation and Reconciliation: The Vision of Concord in Abrahamic Traditions." In *Anabaptists Meeting Muslims: A Calling for Presence in the Way of Christ*, edited by James R. Krabill, David W. Shenk, and Linford Stutzman, 128–40. Scottdale, PA: Herald, 2005.

Harder, Lydia. "Seeking Wisdom in the Face of Foolishness: Toward a Robust Peace Theology." In *At Peace and Unafraid: Public Order, Security, and the Wisdom of the Cross*, edited by Duane K. Friesen and Gerald W. Schlabach, 117–52. Scottdale, PA: Herald, 2005.

Hardy, Andrew, Richard Whitehouse, and Dan Yarnell. *The Power and the Powers: The Use and Misuse of Power in its Missional Context*. Eugene, OR: Cascade, 2015.

Harker, Ryan D. "Intertexuality, Apocalypticism, and Covenant: The Rhetorical Force of the New Jerusalem in Rev 21:9–22:5." *Horizons in Biblical Theology* 38 (2016) 45–73.

Harnack, Adolf. *Militia Christi: The Christian Religion and the Military in the First Three Centuries.* Translated by D. M. Gracie. Philadelphia: Fortress, 1981.

Hauerwas, Stanley. "Church Matters." In *Christian Political Witness*, edited by George Kalantzis and Gregory W. Lee, 17–34. Downers Grove, IL: InterVarsity Academic, 2014.

Hay, David M. *Glory at the Right Hand: Psalm 110 in Early Christianity.* SBLMS 18. Nashville: Abingdon, 1973.

Hays, Richard B. *Echoes of Scripture in the Gospels.* Waco, TX: Baylor University Press, 2017.

———. *Echoes of Scripture in the Letters of Paul.* New Haven, CT: Yale University Press, 1989.

———. *First Corinthians.* Interpretation. Louisville: Westminster John Knox, 1997.

———. *The Moral Vision of the New Testament: Community, Cross, New Creation; A Contemporary Introduction to New Testament Ethics.* HarperSanFrancisco, 1996.

———. *Reading Backwards.* Waco, TX: Baylor University Press, 2014/2015.

———. "Victory over Violence: The Significance for N. T. Wright's Jesus for New Testament Ethics." In *Jesus & the Restoration of Israel: A Critical Assessment of N. T. Wright's Jesus and the Victory of God*, edited by Carey C. Newman, 77–100. Downers Grove, IL: InterVarsity, 1999.

Hedges, Chris. *War Is a Force that Gives Us Meaning.* New York: Anchor/Random House, 1996.

Heiser, M. S. "Chaos." In *Dictionary of the Old Testament Prophets*, edited by Mark J. Boda and J. Gordon McConville, 83–86. Downers Grove, IL: InterVarsity, 2012.

Helgeland, J., R. J. Daly, and J. P. Burns. *Christians and the Military: The Early Experience.* Philadelphia: Fortress, 1985.

Hengel, Martin. *Was Jesus a Revolutionist?* Translated by William Klassen. Philadelphia: Fortress, 1971

———. *Victory over Violence.* Translated by David E. Green. London: SPCK, 1975.

Hess, Richard S., and Gordon J. Wenham, eds. *Zion, City of Our God.* Grand Rapids: Eerdmans, 1999.

Hiebert, Paul. "The Flaw of the Excluded Middle." *Missiology* 10, no. 1 (January 1982) 35–47.

Holladay, William L. *The Psalms through Three Thousand Years: Prayer Book of a Cloud of Witnesses.* Minneapolis: Augsburg Fortress, 1992.

Hornus, J.-M. *It Is Not Lawful for Me to Fight.* Translated by Alan Kreider. Scottdale, PA: Herald, 1980 [Orig. French, 1960].

Horsley, Richard A. "'By the Finger of God': Jesus and Imperial Violence." In *Violence in the New Testament*, edited by Shelly Matthews and E. Leigh Gibson, 51–80. New York: T & T Clark, 2005.

———. *Paul and Empire: Religion and Power in Roman Imperial Society.* Harrisburg, PA: Trinity International, 1997.

Horsley, Richard, and Max Myers. "Idols, Demons, and the Hermeneutics of Suspicion: Biblical Traditions Informing Ethics." *SBL Seminar Papers 1989*, 634–55. Atlanta: Scholars, 1989.

Hovey, Craig. *To Share the Body: A Theology of Martyrdom for Today's Church.* Grand Rapids: Brazos, 2008.

Howell, Justin. "The Imperial Authority and Benefaction of Centurions and Acts 10.34–43: A Response to C. Kavin Rowe." *JSNT* 31 (2008) 25–51.

Hunsinger, George. *Disruptive Grace: Studies in the Theology of Karl Barth*. Grand Rapids: Eerdmans, 2000.
Hunter, A. M. *Design for Life*. Rev. ed. London: SCM, 1965.
Hurtado, Larry W. *Lord Jesus Christ: Devotion to Jesus in Earliest Christianity*. Grand Rapids: Eerdmans, 2003.
Iona. *Iona Abbey Worship Book*. Glasgow: Wild Goose, 2003.
Isaac, Munther. *From Land to Lands, from Eden to the Renewed Earth: A Christ-Centered Biblical Theology of the Promised Land*. Langham Monographs. Carlisle, UK: Cumbria, 2015.
Jackson, David. *Dial 911: Peaceful Christians and Urban Violence*. Scottdale, PA: Herald, 1981.
Jacobs, Cindy. *Deliver Us from Evil*. Ventura, CA: Regal, 2001.
James, Williams. *Proceedings of the American Society for Psychical Research*. New York: American Society of Psychical Research, 1909.
Jenkins, Philip. "Speak of the devil." *ChrCent* (September 7, 2017) 44–45
———. "The travels of Psalm 91." *ChrCent* (January 17, 2018) 36–37.
Jeremias, Joachim. *The Sermon on the Mount*. Philadelphia: Fortress, 1963.
Jersak, Brad, and Michael Hardin, eds. *Stricken by God?* Grand Rapids: Eerdmans, 2007.
Jeschke, Marlin. *Rethinking Holy Land: A Study in Salvation Geography*. Scottdale, PA: Herald, 2005.
Johns, Loren. *The Lamb Christology of the Book of Revelation*. Eugene, OR: Wipf & Stock, 2015. Orig.: Tübingen: Mohr Siebeck, 2003.
Johns, Loren L., and James R. Krabill, eds. *Even the Demons Submit: Continuing Jesus' Ministry of Deliverance*. Elkhart, IN: IMS, and Harrisonburg, VA: Herald, 2006.
Johnson, James Turner. *The Holy War Idea in Western and Islamic Traditions*. University Park, PA: Pennsylvania State University Press, 1997.
Jones, D. L. "The Title κύριος in Luke–Acts." In *SBL 1974 Seminar Papers*, vol. 2, edited by G. MacRae, 85–101. Missoula, MT: Scholars, 1974.
Josephus. *The Works of Josephus: Complete and Unabridged*. New updated version. Translated by William Whiston. Peabody, MA: Hendrickson, 1987.
Käsemann, Ernst. "Sentences of Holy Law in the New Testament." In *New Testament Questions of Today*, 66–81. Philadelphia: Fortress Press, 1969.
Kalantzis, George. "A Witness to the Nations: Early Christianity and the Narratives of Power." In *Christian Political Witness*, edited by George Kalantzis and Gregory W. Lee, 90–111. Downers Grove, IL: InterVarsity Academic, 2014.
Kalantzis, George, and Gregory W. Lee, eds. *Christian Political Witness*. Downers Grove, IL: InterVarsity Academic, 2014.
Kallas, James. *The Satanward View: A Study in Pauline Theology*. Philadelphia: Westminster, 1966.
———. *The Significance of the Synoptic Miracles*. Philadelphia: Westminster, 1961.
Kee, Howard. "The Terminology of Mark's Exorcism Stories." *NTS* 14 (1968) 232–46.
Keith, Chris, and Loren T. Stuckenbruck. *Evil in Second Temple Judaism and Early Christianity*. WUNT 2 Reihe. Tübingen: Mohr Siebeck, 2016.
Kelly, Henry Ansgar. *The Devil at Baptism: Ritual, Theology, and Drama*. Ithaca, NY: Cornell University Press, 1985.
Kelly, J. N. D. *A Commentary on the Epistles of Peter and Jude*. Thornapple Commentaries. Grand Rapids: Baker, 1969; 1981 reprint.
Kelly, Thomas A. *The Testament of Devotion*. New York: Harper & Brothers, 1941.

Kelsey, Morton T. *Christo-Psychology*. New York: Crossroad, 1982.

Kim, Yung Suk. *Messiah in Weakness: A Portrait of Jesus from the Perspective of the Dispossessed*. Eugene, OR: Cascade, 2016.

Kim, Seon Yong. "Ancient Binding Spells, Amulets and Matt 16.18–19: Revisiting August Dell's Proposal a Century Later." *NTS* 62 (July 2016) 378–97.

Klassen, William. "Coals of Fire: Sign of Repentance or Revenge?" *NTS* 9 (1962) 337–50.

———. "The God of Peace: New Testament Perspectives on God." In *Towards a Theology of Peace*, edited by S. Tunnicliffe, 121–31. London: European Nuclear Disarmament, 1989.

———. "Jesus and the Messianic War." In *Early Jewish and Christian Exegesis: Studies in Memory of William Hugh Brownlee*, edited by Craig A. Evans and William F. Stinespring, 155–75. Atlanta: Scholars, 1987.

———. "'Love of Enemies': Some Reflections on the Current State of Research." In *The Love of Enemy and Nonretaliation in the New Testament*, edited by Willard M. Swartley, 1–31. Louisville: Westminster John Knox, 1992.

———. "Love Your Enemy: A Study of New Testament Teaching on Coping with an Enemy." In *Biblical Realism Confronts the Nations*, edited by Paul Peachey, 153–83. Scottdale, PA: Herald and Fellowship, 1963.

———. "The Novel Element in the Love Commandment of Jesus." In *The New Way of Jesus*, edited by William Klassen, 106–110. Newton, KS: Faith and Life, 1980.

Klassen, Zacharie. "The (Non)Violent Reign of God: Rethinking Christocentrism in the Light of the Ascension." *CGR* 33, no. 3 (Fall 2015) 296–315.

Klutz, Todd. *The Exorcism Stories in Luke–Acts: A Sociolinguistic Reading*. SNTSMS 129. Cambridge: Cambridge University Press, 2004.

Knight, Cheryl, and Jo M. Getzinger. "Care-Giving: The Cornerstone of Healing. A Manual for Supporting and Caring for Satanic Ritual Abuse Survivors." Baldwin, MI: C.A.R.E., 2001.

Kohlenberger, John R. III, ed. *The NRSV Concordance Unabridged: Including the Apocryphal/Deuterocanonical Books*. Grand Rapids: Zondervan, 1991.

Krabill, James R., and Stuart Murray. *Forming Christian Habits in Post-Christendom: The Legacy of Alan and Eleanor Kreider*. Harrisonburg, VA: Herald, with IMS: Elkhart, IN, 2011.

Kraft, Charles. *Confronting Powerless Christianity: Evangelicals and the Missing Dimension*. Grand Rapids: Chosen, 2002.

———. *The Evangelical Guide to Spiritual Warfare: Scriptural Insights and Practical Instruction on Facing the Enemy*. Grand Rapids: Chosen, 2015.

———. *Two Hours to Freedom: A Simple and Effective Model for Healing and Deliverance*. Grand Rapids: Chosen, 2010.

Kraybill, Donald B. *The Upside-Down Kingdom*. 30 year anniversary ed. Harrisonburg, VA: Herald, 2018.

Kraybill, Donald B., Steven M. Nolt, and David L. Weaver-Zercher. *Amish Grace: How Forgiveness Transcends Tragedy*. San Francisco, CA: John Wiley & Sons, 2007.

Kraybill, J. Nelson. *Apocalypse and Allegiance: Worship, Politics, and Devotion in the Book of Revelation*. Grand Rapids: Brazos, 2010.

———. *Imperial Cult and Commerce in John's Apocalypse*. JSNTSS 132. Sheffield: Sheffield Academic, 1996.

Kreider, Alan. *The Change of Conversion and the Origin of Christendom*. Harrisburg, PA: Trinity International, 1999.

———. *Journey Towards Holiness: A Way of Living for God's Nation*. Scottdale, PA: Herald, 1987.

———. "Military Service in the Church Orders." *Journal of Religious Ethics* 31, vol. 3 (2003) 415–42.

———. *The Patient Ferment of the Early Church: The Improbable Rise of Christianity in the Roman Empire*. Grand Rapids: Baker Academic, 2016.

———. "Peacemaking in Worship in the Syrian Church Orders." *Studia Liturgica* 34.2 (2004) 177–90.

Kreider, Eleanor. *Communion Shapes Character*. Scottdale, PA: Herald, 1997.

Küng, Hans. *The Religious Situation of Our Time: Judaism*. Translated by John Bowden. London: SCM, 1992.

Kydd, Ronald A. N. *Healing Through the Centuries: Models for Understanding*. Peabody, MA: Hendrickson, 1998.

Lamb, David T. *God Behaving Badly: Is the God of the Old Testament Angry, Sexist and Racist?* Downers Grove, IL: InterVarsity, 2011.

Langton, Edward. *Essentials in Demonology: A Study of Jewish and Christian Doctrine. Its Origin and Development*. London: Epworth, 1949.

Lascaris, André. *To Do the Unexpected: Reading Scripture in Northern Ireland*. Belfast: Corrymeela Community, 1993.

Lehn, Cornelia. *Peace Be With You*. Newton, KS: Faith and Life, 1980.

Leiter, David. *Neglected Voices: Peace in the Old Testament*. Scottdale, PA: Herald, 2007.

Leithart, Peter J. "Violence." In *Christian Political Witness*, edited by George Kalantzis and Gregory W. Lee, 147–62. Downers Grove, IL: InterVarsity Academic, 2014.

Leivestad, Ragnar. *Christ, the Conqueror: Ideas of Conflict and Victory in the New Testament*. London: SPCK, 1954.

Lejeune, R. *Christoph Blumhardt and His Message*. Translated by Hela Ehrlich and Nicoline Mass. Rifton, NY: Society of Brothers, Plough, 1963.

Leonhardt-Balzer, Jutta. "Evil at Qumran." In *Evil in Second Temple Judaism and Early Christianity*, edited by Chris Keith and Loren T. Stuckenbruck, 17–33. WUNT 2 Reihe. Tübingen: Mohr Siebeck, 2016.

Levenson, Jon. *Creation and the Persistence of Evil: The Jewish Drama of Divine Omnipotence*. San Francisco: Harper and Row, 1988.

Lewis, C. S. *Mere Christianity*. New York: Collier/MacMillan, 1943.

Le Peau, Andrew T. *Mark Through Old Testament Eyes: A Background and Application Commentary*. New Testament Commentaries. Grand Rapids: Kregel, 2017.

Lind, Millard C. "Bibliographical and Research Notes: The Hermeneutics of the Old Testament." *MQR* 40 (1966) 227–37.

———. *Ezekiel*. BCBC. Scottdale, PA: Herald, 1996.

———. *Yahweh Is A Warrior*. Scottdale, PA: Herald, 1980.

Littrell, Amie D. "The Origin of Divine Punishment Limit to the Third and Fourth Generation Exod 34:6–7." In *Biblical Research* LX (2015) 15–32.

Lizorkin-Eyzenborg, Eli. *The Jewish Gospel of John: Discovering Jesus, King of All Israel*. Tel Mond, Israel: Israel Study Center, 2015.

Lohfink, Gerhard. *Jesus and Community: The Social Dimension of Christian Faith*. Translated by John P. Galvin. Philadelphia: Fortress and Ramsey, NJ: Paulist, 1984.

Longley, Jim. "Politics as a Mission of Peace." AMBS student paper, unpublished, Elkhart, IN, 2006.

Longman, Tremper, and Daniel Reid. *God Is A Warrior*. Grand Rapids: Zondervan, 1995.

Luz, Ulrich. *Matthew 1–7*. Minneapolis: Augsburg, 1989.

Mackay, John A. *His Life and Our Life: The Life of Christ and the Life in Christ*. Philadelphia: Westminster, 1964.

MacMillan, John A. *The Authority of the Believer*. Camp Hill, PA: Christian, 1997.

MacNutt, Francis. *Deliverance from Evil Spirits: A Practical Manual*. Grand Rapids: Chosen, 1995.

Mansfield, M. Robert. *"Spirit and Gospel" in Mark*. Peabody, MA: Hendrickson, 1987.

March, W. Eugene. *God's Land on Loan: Israel and the People of God*. Louisville: Westminster John Knox, 2007.

———. *Israel and the Politics of Land: A Theological Case Study*. Louisville: Westminster John Knox, 1994.

Marshall, Christopher D. *Faith as a Theme in Mark's Narrative*. Cambridge: Cambridge University Press, 1989.

Martens, Elmer A. *God's Design: A Focus on Old Testament Theology*. 4th ed. Eugene, OR: Wipf & Stock, 2015.

———. *Jeremiah*. BCBC. Scottdale, PA: Herald, 1986.

———. "'O Land, Land, Land': Reading the Earth Story in both Testaments." In *The Old Testament in the Life of God's People*," edited by Jon Isaak, 225–244. Winona Lake, IN: Eisenbrauns, 2009.

———. "Toward an End to Violence: Hearing Jeremiah." In *Wrestling with the Violence of God: Soundings in the Old Testament*, edited by M. Daniel R. Carroll and J. Blair Wilgus, 133–50. Bulletin for Biblical Research Supplement 10; Winona Lake, IN: Eisenbrauns, 2015.

Martin, Ernest D. *Colossians and Philemon*. BCBC. Scottdale, PA: Herald, 1993.

Matties, Gordon H. *Joshua*. BCBC. Harrisonburg, VA: Herald, 2012.

Mauser, Ulrich. *The Gospel of Peace: A Scriptural Message for Today's World*. Louisville: Westminster John Knox, 1992.

Mbon, Friday M. "Deliverance in the Complaint Psalms: Religious Claim or Religious Experience." *Studia Biblica et Theologica* 12 (1982) 3–15.

McAlpine, Thomas H. *Facing the Powers: What Are the Options?* Monrovia, CA: MARC, 1991.

McCall, Kenneth. *Healing the Family Tree*. London: Sheldon, 1982.

McClain, George D. *Claiming All Things for God: Prayer, Discernment, and Ritual for Social Change*. Nashville: Abingdon, 1998.

McCurley, Foster R. *Ancient Myths and Biblical Faith: Scriptural Transformations*. Philadelphia: Fortress, 1983.

McDermond, J. E. *Epistles of 1, 2, 3 John*. BCBC. Harrisonburg, VA: Herald, 2012.

McDonald, Patricia. *God and Violence: Biblical Resources for Living in a Small World*. Scottdale, PA: Herald, 2004.

McKelvey, R. J. *The New Temple: The Church in the New Testament*. London: Oxford University Press, 1969.

McKnight, Scot. *1 Peter*. The NIV Application Commentary. Grand Rapids: Zondervan, 1996.

McMahon, Edwin M., and Peter A. Campbell. *Rediscovering the Lost Body-Connection within Christian Spirituality: The Missing Link for Experiencing Yourself in the God of the Whole Christ is a Changing Relationship to Your Own Body*. Minneapolis: Tasora, 2010.

McManus, Richard. *The Healing Power of the Sacrament*. Notre Dame, IN: Ave Maria, 1984.

McMullen, Ramsay. *Christianizing the Roman Empire (A.D. 100–400)*. New Haven, CT: Yale University Press, 1974.

Meacham, Jon. *The Soul of America: The Battle for Our Better Angels*. New York: Random, 2018.

Meeks, Wayne. *The Origins of Christian Morality: The First Two Centuries*. New Haven, CT: Yale University Press, 1993.

Meister, Chad. *Evil: A Guide for the Perplexed*. 2d ed. London: Bloomsbury, 2018.

———. "The Problem of Evil." In *The Cambridge Companion to Christian Philosophical Theology*, edited by Charles Taliaferro and Chad Meister, 214–39. Cambridge: Cambridge University Press, 2010.

Meister, Chad, and Charles Taliaferro, general eds. *The History of Evil*. Six volumes with different volume editors. London: Routledge. Vols. 1–3, 2017; Vols. 4–6, 2018.

Meister, Chad, and James K. Dew, Jr., eds. *God and Evil: The Case for God in a World Filled with Pain*. Downers Grove, IL: InterVarsity, 2013.

———. *God and the Problem of Evil: Five Views*. Downers Grove, IL: InterVarsity, 2017.

Meister, Chad, and Paul K. Moser, eds. *The Cambridge Companion to the Problem of Evil*. Cambridge: Cambridge University Press, 2017.

Merrill, Eugene H. "The Case for Moderate Discontinuity." In *Show Them No Mercy: 4 Views on God and Canaanite Genocide*, by C. S. Cowles, Eugene H. Merrill, Daniel L. Gard, and Tremper Longman III, 61–96. Grand Rapids: Zondervan, 2003.

Mettinger, T. N. D. "Fighting the Powers of Chaos and Hell—Towards a Biblical Portrait of God." *ST* 39 (1985) 21–38.

Metzger, Bruce M. *A Textual Commentary on the Greek New Testament*. New York: United Bible Societies, 1971.

Middleton, J. Richard. *The Liberating Image: The Imago Dei in Genesis 1*. Grand Rapids: Brazos, 2005.

Migne, J.-P., ed. *Selecta in Num*: Patrolia graeca. Paris, 1857–1886.

Mikalachki, Jodi. "The Message of the Cross." In *Rejoice*, 66: for January 27, 2017. In December 2016–February 2017 Issue. Winnipeg, MB: Kindred Productions, and Harrisonburg, VA: MennoMedia, 2016.

Millar, J. Gary. *Calling on the Name of the Lord: A Biblical Theology of Prayer*. Downers Grove, IL: InterVarsity, 2016.

Miller, Douglas B. *Ecclesiastes*. BCBC. Scottdale, PA: Herald, 2010.

Miller, Patrick D., Jr. "God the Warrior." *Interp* 19 (1965) 27–46.

Moberly, R. W. L. "Toward an interpretation of the Shema." In *Theological Exegesis: Essays in Honor of Brevard S. Child*, edited by Christopher Seitz and Kathryn Greene-McCreight, 124–44. Grand Rapids: Eerdmans, 1999.

Moloney, Francis J. *The Gospel of John*. Sacra Pagina. Collegeville, MN: Liturgical, 1998.

Moltmann, Jürgen. *The Crucified God: The Cross of Christ as the Foundation and Criticism of Christian Theology*. Translated by R. A. Wilson and John Bowden. New York: Harper and Row, 1974.

———. "Following Jesus Christ in a Nuclear Age." In *Politics of Discipleship and Discipleship in Politics: Jürgen Moltmann Lectures in Dialogue with Mennonite Scholars*, edited by Willard M. Swartley, 46–69. Eugene, OR: Cascade, 2006.

———. "Foreword." In *Politics of Discipleship and Discipleship in Politics: Jürgen Moltmann Lectures in Dialogue with Mennonite Scholars*, edited by Willard M. Swartley, xiii–xv. Eugene, OR: Cascade, 2006.

Moreau, A. Scott, et al., eds. *Deliver Us from Evil: An Uneasy Frontier in Christian Mission: Consultation on "Deliver Us from Evil."* Nairobi, Kenya, 2000, and Monrovia, CA: MARC, 2002.

Morris, Michael J. *Warding Off Evil: Apotropaic Tradition in the Dead Sea Scrolls and the Synoptic Gospels*. WUNT 2 Reihe 451. Tübingen: Mohr Siebeck, 2017.

Morrison, Clinton D. *The Powers That Be: Earthly Rulers and Demonic Powers in Romans 13:1–7*. SBT 29. London: SCM, 1960.

Moss, Candida R., and Joel S. Baden. *Bible Nation: The United States of Hobby Lobby*. Princeton, NJ: Princeton University Press, 2017.

Mott, Stephen C. "Groups in Society: Danger and Deliverance." In *A Christian Perspective on Political Thought*, 42–57. Oxford: Oxford University Press, 1993.

Moules, Noel. *Fingerprints of Fire . . . Footprints of Peace*. Winchester, UK: Circle, 2012.

Mounce, Robert H. *The Book of Revelation*. NICNT. Grand Rapids: Eerdmans, 1977.

Muhammad. "Jinn(s)." Al-Anâm 6:125–127, in the *English Translation of the Meaning of AL-QUR'AN: The Guidance for Mankind*. Houston, TX: The Institute of Islamic Knowledge, 1997.

Myers, Ched. *Binding The Strong Man: A Political Reading of Mark's Story of Jesus*. Maryknoll, NY: Orbis, 1988.

Nelson, Richard D. "Ḥerem and the Deuteronomic Social Conscience." In *Deuteronomy and Deuteronomic Literature*. Bibliherca ephermeridum theologicarum lovaniensium 113, edited by M. Vervenne and J. Lust, 39–54. Leuven, Belgium: Leuven University Press, 1977.

Nelson, Susan L. "Facing Evil: Evil's Many Faces." *Interp* 57.4 (October 2003) 398–413.

Newman, Carey C., ed. *Jesus & the Restoration of Israel: A Critical Assessment of N. T. Wright's Jesus and the Victory of God*. Downers Grove, IL: InterVarsity, 1999.

Neyrey, Jerome H. "Despising the Shame of the Cross: Honor and Shame in the Johannine Passion." *Semeia* 68, edited by Victor H. Matthews and Don C. Benjamin, 113–37. Atlanta: Scholars, 1996.

Niditch, Susan. *War in the Hebrew Bible: A Study in the Ethics of Violence*. New York: Oxford University Press, 1993.

Niebuhr, Reinhold. *Moral Man and Immoral Society: A Study in Ethics and Politics*. New York: Scribners, 1960.

Norberg, Tilda. *The Chocolate-Covered Umbrella: Discovering Your Dreamcode*. Nashville: Fresh Air, 2008.

———. *Consenting to Grace: An Introduction to Gestalt Pastoral Care*. 1st rev. ed. Staten Island, NY: Penn House, 2006.

———. *Gathered Together: Creating Personal Liturgies for Healing and Transformation*. Nashville: Upper Room, 2007.

Nouwen, Henri J. M. *Reaching Out: The Three Movements of the Spiritual Life*. Garden City, NY: Doubleday, 1975; Image, 1986.

———. "Letting Go of All Things." *Sojourners* 8 (March 1979) 5–6.

Nugent, Christopher. *Masks of Satan: The Demonic in History*. London: Sheed and Ward, 1983.
Nugent, John C. *The Politics of Yahweh: John Howard Yoder, the Old Testament, and the People of God*. Eugene, OR: Cascade: 2011.
O'Brien, P. T. "Principalities and Powers: Opponents of the Church." In *Biblical Interpretation and the Church*, edited by D. A. Carson, 110–50. Nashville: Thomas Nelson, 1984.
O'Day, Gail. *The Gospel of John*. The New Interpreter's Bible. Nashville: Abingdon, 1995.
O'Donovan, Oliver. *In Pursuit of a Christian View on War*. Bramcote, Notts: Grove, 1977.
Ollenburger, Ben C. "Creation and Violence." In *Struggles for Peace: Peace and Violence across the Testaments*, edited by Laura L. Brenneman and Brad D. Schantz, 26–35. Eugene, OR: Pickwick, 2014.
———. "The Enemy in the Bible." Unpublished article, 1990.
———. "Introduction: Gerhard von Rad's Theory of Holy War." In von Rad, *Holy War in Ancient Israel*, translated and edited by Marva Dawn, 1–33. Grand Rapids: Eerdmans, 1992.
———. "Peace and God's Action against Chaos in the Old Testament." In *The Church's Peace Witness*, edited by Marlin E. Miller and Barbara Nelson Gingerich, 70–78. Grand Rapids: Eerdmans, 1994.
———. *Theology of the Old Testament: The Flowering and Future of Biblical Theology*. Winona Lake, IN: Eisenbrauns, 2004.
———. *Zion the City of the Great King: A Theological Symbol of the Jerusalem Cult*. JSOTSS 41. Sheffield: Sheffield Academic, 1987.
Olson, Ken. *Exorcism: Fact or Fiction*. Nashville: Thomas Nelson, 1992.
Osborne, Grant R. *Revelation*. Baker Exegetical Commentary on the New Testament. Grand Rapids: Baker Academic, 2002.
Oswalt, John N. *The Holy One of Israel: Studies in the Book of Isaiah*. Eugene, OR: Cascade, 2014.
Oyer, Linda. "Interpreting the New in Light of the Old: A Comparative Study of the Post-Resurrection Commissioning Stories in Matthew and John." ThD diss.; Faculté de Théologie et de Sciences Religieuses, Institut Catholique de Paris, 1997.
Page, Sydney H. T. *Powers of Evil: A Biblical Study of Satan & Demons*. Grand Rapids: Baker, 1995.
Patte, Daniel. *Paul's Faith and the Power of the Gospel: A Structural Introduction to the Pauline Letters*. Philadelphia: Fortress, 1983.
Pattison, Mansell. "Psychosocial Interpretations of Exorcism." *Journal of Operational Psychiatry* 8 (1977) 5–19.
Payne, Leanne. *The Broken Image: Restoring Personal Wholeness through Healing Prayer*. Grand Rapids: Baker, 1996.
Pearse, Meic. *The Gods of War: Is Religion the Primary Cause of Violent Conflict?* Downers Grove, IL: InterVarsity, 2007.
Peck, M. Scott. *Glimpses of the Devil: A Psychiatrist's Personal Accounts of Possession, Exorcism, and Redemption*. New York: Free, 2005.
———. *People of the Lie: The Hope for Healing Human Evil*. New York: Simon & Schuster, 1982.
Peckham, John C. *Theodicy of Love: Cosmic Conflict and the Problem of Evil*. Grand Rapids: Baker Academic, 2018.

Penchansky, David. "Good and Evil." In *The Oxford Encyclopedia of Bible and Theology*, 426–32. Oxford: Oxford University Press, 2015.

Perkins, Pheme. "Apocalyptic Sectarianism and Love Commands in the Johannine Epistles." In *The Love of Enemy and Nonretaliation in the New Testament*, edited by Willard M. Swartley, 287–96. Louisville: Westminster John Knox, 1992.

Pilgrim, Walter. *Uneasy Neighbors: Church and State in the New Testament*. Minneapolis: Fortress, 1999.

Piper, John. *"Love Your Enemies": Jesus' Love Command in the Synoptic Gospels and in the Early Christian Paraeneis*. Cambridge: Cambridge University Press, 1979.

Plantinga, Cornelius, Jr. *Not the Way It's Supposed to Be*. Grand Rapids: Eerdmans, 1995.

Podimattam, F. "Love for Enemies." *India Theological Studies* 50.2 (2013) 153–78.

Poole, W. Scott. *Satan in America: The Devil We Know*. Lanham, MD: Rowman & Littlefield, 2009.

Quast, Kevin. *Reading Corinthian Correspondence: An Introduction*. Mahweh, NJ: Paulist, 1994.

Rainbow, Paul S. *Johannine Theology: The Gospel, the Epistles and the Apocalypse*. Downers Grove, IL: InterVarsity, 2014.

Ray, Darby Kathleen. *Deceiving the Devil: Atonement, Abuse, and Ransom*. Cleveland, OH: Pilgrim, 1998.

Rensberger, David. *Johannine Faith and Liberating Community*. Philadelphia: Westminster, 1988.

Richardson, Cyril C., ed. and trans. *Early Church Fathers*. Vol. 1. In Library of Christian Classics. Philadelphia: Westminster, 1953.

Robinson, James M. *The Problem of History in Mark*. London: SCM, 1957.

Robitaille, Glenn A. "The Sermon on the Mount and the Doctrine of Nonresistance." In *A Peace Reader*, edited by E. Morris Sider and Luke Keefer, Jr., 38–48. Nappanee, IN: Evangel, 2002.

Rollston, Christopher A. "An Ur-History of the New Testament Devil: The Celestial עָשָׂטָן (śā)-ṭān in Zechariah and Job." In *Evil in Second Temple Judaism and Early Christianity*, edited by Chris Keith and Loren T. Stuckenbruck, 1–16. WUNT 2 Reihe. Tübingen: Mohr Siebeck, 2016.

Rommen, Edward, ed. *Spiritual Power and Missions: Raising the Issues*. Evangelical Missiological Society Series Number 3. Pasadena, CA: William Carey, 1995.

Rowe, C. Kavin. "Luke–Acts and the Imperial Cult: A Way through the Conundrum?" *JSNT* 31 (2005) 279–300.

———. *World Upside Down: Reading Acts in the Graeco-Roman Age*. Oxford: Oxford University Press, 2009.

Ruiz, Jean-Pierre. "The Politics of Praise: A Reading of Revelation 19:1–10." In *SBL Seminar Papers 1997*, 374–93. Atlanta: Scholars, 1997.

Ruth, John L. *'Twas Seeding Time: A Mennonite View of the American Revolution*. Scottdale, PA: Herald, 1976.

Rutledge, Fleming. *The Crucifixion: Understanding the Death of Jesus Christ*. Grand Rapids: Eerdmans, 2015.

Samuel, Metropolitan Mar Athanasius Yeshue (Archbishop of The Syrian Orthodox Church in the United States of America and Canada), editor and publisher. *The Sacrament of Holy Baptism according to the Ancient Rite of the Syrian Orthodox Church of Antioch*. Translated by Deacon Murad Saliba Barsom. 1974.

Schärf Kluger, Rivkah. *Satan in the Old Testament*. Translated by Hildegard Nagel. Evanston, IL: Northwestern University Press, 1967.

Schertz, Mary H. "'Likewise You Wives . . . ': Another Look at 1 Peter 2:11—5:11." In *Perspectives on Feminist Hermeneutics*, edited by Gayle Gerber Koontz and Willard M. Swartley, 75–82. OP 10. Elkhart, IN: IMS, 1987.

———. "Nonretaliation and the Haustafeln in 1 Peter." In *The Love of Enemy and Nonretaliation in the New Testament*, edited by Willard M. Swartley, 258-86. Louisville: Westminster John Knox, 1992.

———. "Radical Trust in the Just Judge: The Easter Texts of 1 Peter." *Word and World* 24 (2004) 430–41.

Schlabach, Gerald. "Just Policing and the Christian Call to Nonviolence." In *At Peace and Unafraid: Public Order, Security, and the Wisdom of the Cross*, edited by Duane K. Friesen and Gerald Schlabach, 405–21. Scottdale, PA: Herald, 2005.

Schlier, H. *Principalities and Powers in the New Testament*. QD 3. Freiberg: Herder/New York: Nelson, 1961.

Schmemann, Alexander. *Of Water and Spirit*. Crestwood, NJ: St. Vladimir's Seminary Press, 1974.

Schneider, G. *Lukas, Theologie der Heilsgeschichte: Aufsätze zum lukanischen Doppelwerk*. BBB 59. Bonn: Peter Hanstein, 1985.

Schnelle, Udo. *Theology of the New Testament*. Translated by M. Eugene Boring. Grand Rapids: Baker Academic, 2007.

Schoonhoven, Calvin R. *The Wrath of Heaven*. Grand Rapids, Eerdmans, 1966.

Schottroff, Luise. "Give to Caesar What is Caesar's and to God What is God's: The Theological Answer of the Early Church to Its Social and Political Situation." In *The Love of Enemy and Nonretaliation in the New Testament*, edited by Willard M. Swartley, 223–57. Louisville: Westminster John Knox, 1992.

———. "Non-Violence and the Love of One's Enemies." Translated by Reginald H. and Ilse Fuller. In *Essays on the Love Commandment*, 9–28. Philadelphia: Fortress, 1978.

Schrobsdorff, Susanna. "Anxiety, Depression, and the American Adolescent." *Time* (November 7, 2016) 42–51.

Schüssler Fiorenza, Elisabeth. *The Book of Revelation: Justice and Judgment*. Philadelphia: Fortress, 1985.

———. *Invitation to the Book of Revelation: A Commentary on the Apocalypse with Complete Text from the Jerusalem Bible*. Garden City, NY: Doubleday, 1985.

Scranton, Roy. "'Star Wars' and the Fantasy of American Violence." *New York Times* (July 3, 2016).

Scurlock, JoAnn, and Richard L. Beal, eds. *Creation and Chaos: A Reconsideration of Herman Gunkel's Chaoskampf Hypothesis*. Winona Lake, IN: Eisenbrauns, 2013.

Sears, Robert T. "A Catholic View of Exorcism and Deliverance." In Swartley, ed., *Essays*, 100–114.

Seibert, Eric A. *Disarming the Church: Why Christians Must Forsake Violence to Follow Jesus and Change the World*. Eugene, OR: Cascade, 2018.

———. *Disturbing Divine Behavior: Troubling Old Testament Images of God*. Minneapolis: Fortress, 2009.

———. *The Violence of Scripture: Overcoming the Old Testament's Troubling Legacy*. Minneapolis: Fortress, 2012.

Seitz, O. J. F. "Love Your Enemies: the Historical Setting of Matthew V.43f.; Luke VI.27f." *NTS* 16 (1969/70) 39–54.

Shorter, Aylward. *Jesus and the Witchdoctor: An Approach to Healing and Wholeness.* Maryknoll, NY: Orbis, 1985.

Shroyer, Danielle. *Original Blessing: Putting Sin in Its Rightful Place.* Minneapolis: Fortress, 2016.

Sider, Ronald J., ed. *The Early Church on Killing: A Sourcebook on Early Christian Views on War, Abortion, and Capital Punishment.* Downers Grove, IL: InterVarsity, 2012.

Sider, Ronald J. *Christ and Violence.* Scottdale, PA: Herald, 1979.

Simonetti, Manlio, ed. *Matthew 1—13.* ACCS. Downers Grove. InterVarsity, 2001.

Simons, Menno. "Meditation on the Twenty-Fifth Psalm." In *The Complete Writings of Menno Simons*, translated by Leonard Verduin, edited by John C. Wenger, 63–86. Scottdale, PA: Herald, 1956.

Simpson, Gary M. *War, Peace, and God: Rethinking the Just War Tradition.* Minneapolis: Augsburg Fortress, 2007.

Sizer, Stephen. *Christian Zionism: Road Map to Armageddon?* Downers Grove, IL: InterVarsity, 2004/2006.

Skarsaune, Oskar, and Tormod Engelsviken. "Possession and Exorcism in the History of the Church." In *Deliver Us from Evil: An Uneasy Frontier in Christian Mission: Consultation on "Deliver Us from Evil,"* edited by Scott A. Moreau, et al., 65–87. Nairobi, Kenya, 2000, and Monrovia, CA: MARC, 2002.

Skinner, Christopher. "Overcoming Satan, Overcoming the World: Exploring the Cosmologies of Mark and John." In *Evil in Second Temple Judaism and Early Christianity*, edited by Chris Keith and Loren T. Stuckenbruck, 101–21. WUNT 2 Reihe. Tübingen: Mohr Siebeck, 2016.

Smedes, Lewis B., ed. *Ministry and the Miraculous: A Case Study at Fuller Theological Seminary.* Foreword by David Allan Hubbard. Pasadena, CA: Fuller Theological Seminary, 1987.

Smith, Edward M. *Beyond Tolerable Recovery: Moving beyond Tolerable Existence into Biblical Maintenance Free Victory.* 4th ed. Campbellsville, KY: Family Care, 2000.

———. *Healing Life's Hurts through Theophostic Prayer: Let the Light of Christ Set You Free from Lifelong Fears, Shame, False Guilt, Anxiety and Emotional Pain.* Ventura, CA: Regal, 2004.

Smith, J. B. *The Greek-English to the NT: A Tabular and Statistical Greek-English Concordance Based on the King James Version with an English-To-Greek Index.* Scottdale, PA: Herald, 1955.

Smith, Jonathan. "Towards Interpreting Demonic Powers in Hellenistic and Roman Antiquity." In *ANRW* II.16.1, edited by W. Haase, 425–39. Berlin: W. de Gruyter, 1978.

Smith, Patricia A. *From Generation to Generation: A Manual for Healing.* Jacksonville, FL: Jehovah Rapha, 1996.

Snyder, Ben, compiler/editor. "The Ministry of Dean Hochstetler: 1974–2005." Unpublished, 2010.

Snyder, C. Arnold. *Following in the Footsteps of Christ: The Anabaptist Tradition.* Maryknoll, NY: Orbis, 2004.

Snyder Belousek, Darrin. *Atonement, Justice and Peace: The Message of the Cross and the Mission of the Church.* Grand Rapids: Eerdmans, 2012.

Sorensen, Eric. *Possession and Exorcism in the New Testament and Early Christianity.* WUNT 2. Reihe 157. Tübingen: Mohr Siebeck, 2002.

Stark, Rodney. *The Rise of Christianity: A Sociologist Reconsiders History.* Princeton, NJ: Princeton University Press, 1996.

———. Interview with Rodney Stark. "A Double Take on Early Christianity." *Touchstone* 13.1 (January–February 2000) 44–47.

Stähli, H.-P. "*yr*'/Fear." In *Theological Lexicon of the Old Testament*, edited by Ernst Jenni and Claus Westermann, translated by Mark E. Biddle, vol. 2, 568–78. Peabody, MA: Hendrickson, 1997.

Steffon, Fr. Jeffrey J. *Satanism: Is It Real?* Ann Arbor, MI: Servant, 1992.

Stendahl, Krister. "Hate, Non-Retaliation, and Love: 1QS x, 17–20 and Romans 12:19–21." *Harvard Theological Review* 55 (1962) 343–55.

Stevens, Bruce A. "The Divine Warrior in the Gospel of Mark." *Biblische Zeitschrift* 31 (1987) 101–9.

Stewart, James S. *A Faith to Proclaim.* London: Hodder and Stroughton, 1953.

Stock, Augustine. *Call to Discipleship: A Literary Study of Mark's Gospel.* Good News Studies 1. Wilmington, DE: Michael Glazier, 1982.

Stott, John R. W. *God's New Society: The Message of Ephesians.* Downers Grove, IL: InterVarsity, 1979.

Stubbs, Monya S. *Indebted Love: Paul's Subjection Language in Romans.* Eugene, OR: Pickwick, 2013.

Stuckenbruck, Loren T. *The Myth of Rebellious Angels: Studies in Second Temple Judaism and New Testament Texts.* Tübingen: Mohr Siebeck, 2014.

———. "The Demonic World and the Dead Sea Scrolls." In *Evil and the Devil*, edited by Ida Fröhlich and Erkki Koskenniemi, 51–70. New York: Bloomsbury/T & T Clark, 2013.

Sugden, Chris. *A Different Dream: Non-violence as Practical Politics.* Bramcote, Notts: Grove, 1976.

Swartley, Willard M. "The Bible and Israel." In *Send Forth Your Light*, 155–82 (see below).

———. *Covenant of Peace: The Missing Peace in New Testament Theology and Ethics.* SPS 9. Grand Rapids: Eerdmans, 2006.

———. "Foreword." In *Stricken by God?*, edited by Brad Jersak and Michael Hardin, 10–12. Grand Rapids: Eerdmans, 2007.

———. *Health, Healing and the Church's Mission: Biblical Perspectives and Moral Priorities.* Downers Grove, IL: InterVarsity, 2012.

———. "The Imitatio Christi in the Ignatian Letters." *Vigiliae Christianae* 27 (1973) 81–103.

———. "Intertextuality in Early Christian Literature." In *Dictionary of Later New Testament and Its Developments*, edited by Ralph P. Martin and Peter H. Davids, 536–42. Downers Grove, IL: InterVarsity, 1997.

———. *Israel's Scripture Traditions and the Synoptic Gospels: Story Shaping Story.* Peabody, MA: Hendrickson, 1994.

———. *John.* BCBC. Harrisonburg, VA: Herald, 2013.

———. *Living Gift: John's Jesus in Meditation and Poetry, Art and Song.* Nappanee, IN: Evangel, 2013.

———. *Mark: The Way for All Nations.* Scottdale, PA: Herald, 1979, rev. ed. 1981. Wipf & Stock, 1999.

———. "Method and Understanding for Texts and Disciples." In *Perspectives on Feminist Hermeneutics*, edited by Gayle Gerber Koontz and Willard M. Swartley, 113–21. *OP* 11. Elkhart, IN: IMS, 1987.

———. "Mutual Aid Based in Jesus and Early Christianity." In *Building Communities of Compassion: Mennonite Mutual Aid in Theory and Practice*, edited by Willard M. Swartley and Donald B. Kraybill, 21–39. Scottdale, PA: Herald, 1998.

———. "Payment of Taxes Used for War." In *A Persistent Voice: Marian Franz and Conscientious Objection to Military Taxation*, edited by David R. Bassett, Steve Ratzlaff, and Tim Godshall, 57–65. Telford, PA: Cascadia, Peace Tax Foundation, and Scottdale, PA: Herald, 2009.

———. "Peacemaking and Mission Empowered by Worship," in *Send Forth Your Light: A Vision for Peace, Mission, and Worship*, 213–240. Harrisonburg, VA: Herald, 2007.

———. "Politics and Peace (*Eirēnē*) in Luke's Gospel." In *Political Issues in Luke–Acts*, edited by Richard Cassidy and Philip Scharper, 18–37. Maryknoll, NY: Orbis, 1983.

———. Review of *Binding the Strong Man*, by Ched Myers, 227–30. In *Critical Review of Books in Religion*. Atlanta: Scholars, 1990.

———. *Send Forth Your Light: A Vision for Peace and Mission, and Worship*. Harrisonburg, VA: Herald, 2007.

———. *Slavery, Sabbath, War and Women: Case Issues in Biblical Interpretation*. Scottdale, PA: Herald, 1983.

———. "War and Peace in the New Testament." *ANRW* II.26.3, edited by W. Haase and H. Temporini, 2298–2408. Berlin and New York: W. de Gruyter, 1996.

Swartley, Willard M., ed. *Essays on Spiritual Bondage and Deliverance*. *OP* 11. Elkhart, IN: IMS, 1988.

———. *The Love of Enemy and Nonretaliation in the New Testament*. Louisville: Westminster John Knox, 1992.

———. *Politics of Discipleship and Discipleship in Politics: Jürgen Moltmann Lectures in Dialogue with Mennonite Scholars*. Eugene, OR: Cascade, 2006.

———. *Violence Renounced: René Girard, Biblical Studies and Peacemaking*. Telford, PA: Pandora U.S. (now Cascadia) and Harrisonburg, VA: Herald, 2000.

Swartley, Willard M. and Donald B. Kraybill, eds. *Building Communities of Compassion: Mennonite Mutual Aid in Theory and Practice*. Scottdale, PA: Herald, 1998.

Swartley, Willard M. and Thomas Finger. "Bondage and Deliverance: Biblical and Theological Perspectives." In *Essays on Spiritual Bondage and Deliverance*, edited by Willard M. Swartley, 10–38. *OP* 11. Elkhart, IN: IMS, 1988.

Sweetland, Dennis M. *Our Journey with Jesus: Discipleship according to Mark*. Good News Studies 22. Wilmington, DE: Michael Glazier, 1987.

Swinton, John. *Raging with Compassion: Pastoral Responses to the Problem of Evil*. Grand Rapids: Eerdmans, 2007.

Swoboda, Jörg, Richard V. Pierard, and Edwin Arnold. *The Revolution of the Candles: Christians in the Revolution of the East German Republic*. Edited by Richard V. Pierard, translated by Edwin P. Arnold. Macon, GA: Mercer University Press, 1996.

Tada, Joni Eareckson, and Steven Estes. *When God Weeps: Why Our Sufferings Matter to the Almighty*. Grand Rapids: Zondervan, 1997.

Talbert, Charles H. *Reading John: A Literary and Theological Commentary on the Fourth Gospel.* New York: Crossroad, 1992.

Taliaferro, Charles. "Evil and Prayer: Set Prayers and Other Special Weapons and Tactics in Times of Trouble." In *God and Evil: The Case for God in a World Filled with Pain,* edited by Chad Meister and James K. Dew, Jr., 152–62. Downers Grove, IL: InterVarsity, 2013.

Tambasco, A. J. "Principalities, Powers and Peace." In *Blessed Are the Peacemakers,* edited by Anthony J. Tambasco, 116–133. New York: Paulist Press, 1989.

Taneja, Anand Vivek. *Jinnealogy: Time, Islam, and Ecological Thought in the Medieval Ruins of Delhi.* Stanford, CA: Stanford University Press, 2017.

Tannehill, Robert C. *The Sword of His Mouth.* Philadelphia: Fortress, 1975.

Taylor, Richard K. *Blockade: A Guide to Non-Violent Intervention.* Maryknoll, NY: Orbis, 1977.

Thielman, Frank S. *Theology of the New Testament: A Critical and Synthetic Approach.* Grand Rapids: Zondervan, 2005.

Thomas, Heath A., Jeremy Evans, and Paul Copan, eds. *Holy War in the Bible: Christian Morality and an Old Testament Problem.* Downers Grove, IL: InterVarsity, 2013.

Thomas, John Christopher. *The Devil, Disease and Deliverance: Origins of Illness in New Testament Thought.* Journal of Pentecostal Theology Supplement Series 13. Sheffield: Sheffield Academic, 1998.

———. "Spiritual Conflict in Illness and Affliction." In *Deliver Us from Evil: An Uneasy Frontier in Christian Mission: Consultation on "Deliver Us from Evil,"* edited by A. Scott Moreau, et al., 28–36. Nairobi, Kenya, 2000, and Monrovia, CA: MARC, 2002.

Thurston, Bonnie. *Spiritual Life in the Early Church: The Witness of Acts and Ephesians.* Minneapolis: Fortress, 1993.

Toews, John E. *Romans.* BCBC. Scottdale, PA: Herald, 2004.

Torrance, Tom. *Divine and Contingent Order.* New York: Oxford University Press, 1981.

Trudinger, Peter L. "Friend or Foe? Earth, Sea and *Chaoskampf* in the Psalms." In *The Earth Story in the Psalms and the Prophets,* edited by Norman C. Habel, 29–41. Sheffield: Sheffield Academic, 2001.

Twelftree, Graham H. *Christ Triumphant: Exorcism Then and Now.* London: Hodder & Stoughton, 1985.

———. "Exorcisms in the Fourth Gospel and the Synoptics." In *Jesus in the Johannine Tradition,* edited by Robert T. Fortna and Tom Thatcher, 145–53. Louisville: Westminster John Knox, 2001.

———. *Jesus the Exorcist: A Contribution to the Study of the Historical Jesus.* Peabody, MA: Hendrickson, 1993.

———. *In the Name of Jesus: Exorcism among Early Christians.* Grand Rapids: Baker Academic, 2007.

———. *Paul and the Miraculous: A Historical Reconstruction.* Grand Rapids: Baker Academic, 2013.

———. "The Place of Exorcism in Contemporary Ministry." *St. Mark's Review* 127 (September 1986) 25–39.

Vanderhaar, Gerard A. *Enemies and How to Love Them.* Mystic, CT: Twenty-Third, 1985.

van der Kolk, Bessel. *The Body Keeps the Score: Brain, Mind, and Body in the Healing of Trauma.* New York: Penguin, 2014.

Volf, Miroslav. *Exclusion and Embrace: A Theological Explanation of Identity, Otherness, and Reconciliation*. Nashville: Abingdon, 1996.

Vollenweider, Samuel. "Ich sah den Satan wie einen Blitz vom Himmel fallen (Lk 10:18)." *ZNW* 79 (1988) 187–203.

von Rad, Gerhard. *Holy War in Ancient Israel*. Translated and edited by Marva Dawn. Grand Rapids: Eerdmans, 1992.

Wallace, T. H. S., compiler. *QuakerPsalms: A Book of Devotions*. Camp Hill, PA: Foundation, 2002.

Wallis, Jim. "The Work of Prayer." *Sojourners* 8 (March 1979) 3–5.

Waltner, Erland. *1–2 Peter*. BCBC. Scottdale, PA: Herald, 1999.

———. "Reign of God, Mission, and Peace in 1 Peter." In *Beautiful upon the Mountains: Biblical Essays on Mission, Peace, and the Reign of God*, edited by Mary Schertz and Ivan Friesen, 235–48. Elkhart, IN: IMS and Scottdale, PA: Herald, 2004.

Waltner, James H. *Psalms*. BCBC. Scottdale, PA: Herald, 2006.

Warner, Timothy M. "An Evangelical Position on Bondage and Exorcism." In Swartley, ed., *Essays*, 77–88.

Warren, E. Janet. *Cleansing the Cosmos: A Biblical Model for Conceptualizing and Counteracting Evil*. Eugene, OR: Pickwick, 2012.

———. *Holy Housekeeping: Understanding Evil and Living Godly Lives*. Belleville, ON: Essence, 2017.

Weaver, Dorothy Jean. *The Irony of Power: The Politics of God within Matthew's Narrative*. Eugene, OR: Pickwick, 2017.

———. "Resistance and Nonresistance: New Testament Perspectives on Confronting the Powers." In *The Irony of Power: The Politics of God within Matthew's Narrative*, 2–23. Eugene, OR: Pickwick, 2017.

———. "Transforming Nonresistance from *Lex Talionis* to 'Do Not Resist the Evil One.'" In *The Irony of Power: The Politics of God within Matthew's Narrative*, 137–74. Eugene, OR: Pickwick, 2017.

Weaver-Zercher, David. Review of *Bible Nation*, Moss and Baden. In *ChrCent* (October 11, 2017) 41–43.

Webber, Robert E. *Celebrating Our Faith: Evangelism through Worship*. San Francisco, CA: Harper and Row, 1986.

———. *Worship is a Verb: Eight Principles for Transforming Worship*. Peabody, MA: Hendrickson, 1992.

Wengst, Klaus K. *Pax Romana and the Peace of Jesus Christ*. Translated by John Bowden. Philadelphia: Fortress, 1987.

———. *Humility: Solidarity of the Humiliated: The Transformation of an Attitude and its Social Relevance in Graeco-Roman, Old Testament-Jewish and Early Christian Tradition*. Philadelphia: Fortress, 1988.

White, John, and Ken Blue. *Healing the Wounded: The Costly Love of Church Discipline*. Downers Grove, IL: InterVarsity, 1985.

Wink, Walter. *Engaging the Powers: Discernment and Resistance in a World of Domination*. Minneapolis: Fortress, 1992.

———. *Naming the Powers: The Language of Power in the New Testament*. Philadelphia: Fortress, 1984.

———. "Neither Passivity nor Violence: Jesus' Third Way (Matt. 5:38–42 par.)." In *The Love of Enemy and Nonretaliation in the New Testament*, edited by Willard M. Swartley, 102–25. Louisville: Westminster John Knox, 1992.

———. "The New Worldview: Spirit at the Core of Everything." In *Transforming the Powers: Peace, Justice, and the Domination System*, edited by Ray Gingerich and Ted Grimsrud, 7–28. Minneapolis: Fortress, 2006.

———. *The Powers That Be: Theology for a New Millennium*. New York: Doubleday, 1998.

———. *Unmasking the Powers: The Invisible Forces that Determine Human Existence*. Philadelphia: Fortress, 1986.

———. *When the Powers Fall: Reconciliation in the Healing of the Nations*. Minneapolis: Fortress, 1998.

Winkler, Gabrielle. "The Origin and Meaning of the Prebaptismal Anointing and its Implications." *Worship* 52 (January 1978) 30–37.

Winslow, Mark H. "Pastoral Care of the Demonized Person." In *Essays on Spiritual Bondage and Deliverance*, edited by Willard M. Swartley, 192–204. Elkhart, IN: IMS, 1988.

Witmer, Amanda. *Jesus, the Galilean Exorcist: His Exorcisms in Social and Political Context*. The Library of New Testament Studies 429. New York: Bloomsbury, 2012.

Wood, John A. *Perspectives on War in the Bible*. Macon, GA: Mercer University Press, 1998.

Woolley, Reginald Maxwell. *Exorcism and the Healing of the Sick*. London: SPCK, 1932.

Wright, Christopher J. H. *The God I Don't Understand: Reflections on Tough Questions of Faith*. Grand Rapids: Zondervan, 2008.

———. *God's People in God's Land: Family, Land, and Property in the Old Testament*. Grand Rapids: Eerdmans, 1990.

———. *The Mission of God: Unlocking the Bible's Grand Narrative*. Downers Grove, IL: InterVarsity, 2006.

———. *Old Testament Ethics for the People of God*. Downers Grove, IL: InterVarsity, 2004.

Wright, Nigel Goring. *A Theology of the Dark Side: Putting the Power of Evil in its Place*. Rev. ed. Downers Grove, IL: InterVarsity, 2003.

Wright, N. T. *Evil and the Justice of God*. Downers Grove, IL: InterVarsity, 2006.

———. *Jesus and the Victory of God*. Minneapolis: Fortress, 1996.

———. *The Lord and His Prayer*. Grand Rapids: Eerdmans, 1997.

———. *Simply Jesus: Who He Was, What He Did, Why It Matters*. New York: Harper One, 2011.

Yeatts, John R. *Revelation*. BCBC. Harrisonburg, VA: Herald, 2003.

Yoder [Neufeld], Rebecca. "The Old Testament *Cherem* and New Testament Sentences of Holy Law." In *OP* 1, edited by Willard Swartley, 19–34. Elkhart, IN: IMS, 1981.

Yoder Neufeld, Thomas R. *Ephesians*. BCBC. Scottdale, PA: Herald, 2002.

———. *Killing Enmity: Violence and the New Testament*. Grand Rapids: Baker Academic, 2011.

———. "*Put on the Armour of God*": *The Divine Warrior from Isaiah to Ephesians*. JSNTSS. Sheffield, UK: Sheffield Academic, 1997.

———. "Resistance and Nonresistance: The Two Legs of a Biblical Peace Stance." *CGR* 21 (2003) 56–81.

Yoder, John H. *Body Politics: Five Practices of the Christian Community before the Watching World*. Scottdale, PA: Herald, 1992/2001.

———. *The Christian Witness to the State*. Newton, KS: Faith and Life, 1977.

———. *For the Nations: Essays Public and Evangelical*. Grand Rapids: Eerdmans, 1997.

———. *The Jewish-Christian Schism Revisited*. Edited by Michael G. Cartwright and Peter Ochs. Grand Rapids: Eerdmans, 2003.

———. *Politics of Jesus*. Rev. ed. Grand Rapids: Eerdmans, 1994.

———. *Reinhold Niebuhr and Christian Pacifism*. Zeist, Netherlands: Heerewegen Pamphlet No. One, 1954.

———. *The Royal Priesthood: Essays Ecclesiological and Ecumenical*. Edited by Michael Cartwright. Grand Rapids: Eerdmans, 1994.

———. *What Would You Do? A Serious Answer to a Standard Question* (expanded ed. with Joan Baez, Tom Skinner, Leo Tolstoy, and others). Scottdale, PA: Herald, 1992.

Yoder, John H., Glen H. Stassen, Mark Nation, and Matthew Hamsher. *The War of the Lamb: the Ethics of Nonviolence and Peacemaking*. Grand Rapids: Brazos, 2009.

Young, Robert. *Young's Analytical Concordance to the Bible*. 22d American ed. Grand Rapids: Eerdmans, n.d.

Zaleski, Carol. "Love in the Time of Evil." *ChrCent* (June 8, 2016) 35.

Zehr, Paul M. *1 & 2 Timothy, Titus*. BCBC. Scottdale, PA: Herald, 1999.

YouTube Videos/Podcasts (not in above entries)

http://thegrio.com/2014/12/21/worlds-most-popular-bible-verses-2014/

http://www.harbeck.ca/cww/cww_061018.html

https://www.scotsman.com/news/politics/insight-civil-rights-50-years-after-martin-luther-king-1-4716411

For the Arabic rendition of, "Oh Lord of Hosts Be with Us," https://www.youtube.com/watch?v=2D6Jhm76Oic

For an English and Arabic chant of "Oh Lord of Hosts": https://www.youtube.com/watch?v=uGOiV-8F_D8

For an English version only of "Oh Lord of Hosts" by an European Eastern Orthodox choir, https://www.youtube.com/watch?v=2vLQtAxlark

Library of Social Science: *Dying and Killing for Nations: Warfare as Sacrifice*: https://mail.google.com/mail/u/0/?shva=1#inbox/15d14bd2704fe7c9

https://www.azquotes.com/author/13493-William_Tecumseh_Sherman

http://insidecville.com/world/roy-hange-4-17-17/

http://orthodoxanglicanism.blogspot.com/2008/04/rituale-romanum-1962-exorcism-rite.html

Podcast: http://www.ministrymatters.com/all/entry/8065/more-exorcisms-and-better-health-care

Q &A on the demonic: http://qideas.org/videos/qa-exorcism-the-spiritual-reality/ *www.theophostic.com*

http://www.transformationprayer.org/what-is-transformation-prayer-ministry/

Dr. Karl Lehman on Emmanuel Prayer: https://www.youtube.com/watch?v=Dt5TDjWruFs

Jessica Handy on Emmanuel Prayer: https://www.youtube.com/watch?v=GkMdh-UQtmvM

http://bethelsozo.com/ and https://shop.bethel.com/collections/sozo?ref=10
https://closingstages.net/2011/01/27/sozo-part-i/
http://www.amaranthpublishing.com/PapyrusHymn.htm
https://www.youtube.com/watch?v=NFyjbdIdS3g
https://carolyncustisjames.com/2017/03/05/franciscan-blessing-for-our-time/ Mar 5, 2017.
http://www.beliefnet.com/columnists/godspolitics/2006/10/diana-butler-bass-what-if-the.html
https://books.google.com/books?id=0-kCAAAAMBAJ

Author/Editor Index

Acolatse, Esther M., 260n1, 288, 297n48
Adams, Rebecca, 295n45
Adams, Marilyn McCord, 12n41, 184n26, 295n45
Albright, W. F., 238n8
Aldridge, Robert C., 253n46
Alexander, Patrick H., 329
Allman, Mark J., 44
Amorth, Gabriele, 263n9
Anderson, Bernhard W., 20n16, 47-48nn31-33, 49n37, 202n5
Anderson, Neil, 292
Appleby, David W. 262n7, 271n27
Arnold, Clinton, 6, 128n2, 155n13, 168-69nn57, 59, 220, 220nn5-6, 283, 283n6, 290n23
Arnold, Edwin. 256n55
Augustine, 133, 133n11
Aulén, Gustav, 199n1, 200

Baden, Joel S., 344
Baez, Joan, 354
Barth, Karl, 6, 28, 226, 249, 279n56
Barth, Marcus, 63n6
Bassett, David R., 350
Baumgartner, W., 332
Beal, Richard L., 19n13, 347
Bell, Daniel M., Jr., 250n39
Bellinger, Charles K., 294
Benjamin, Don C., 344
Berger, Peter, 286
Berkhof, Hendrik. 6, 155, 169, 284, 294
Best, Ernest, 54n53
Betz, Hans Dieter, 106n3, 293n40

Bishop, Peter D., 254n51
Blocher, Henri, 17n3
Blount, Brian K., 328
Blue, Ken, 352
Boa, Kenneth, 290n50
Bocher, Otto, 109n21
Boers, Hendrikus, 121n54
Bonhoeffer, Dietrich, 54n54
Bontrager, Marion G., 306
Bontrager, William, 254n49
Borg, Marcus J., 144
Bouma-Prediger, Steven, 19n16
Boyd, Gregory A., 2n6, 6, 8n31, 11n38, 17n8, 19, 27n32, 29, 31n47, 32-33, 35n55, 38-39, 50n41, 120, 139n31, 150n41, 156n15, 166n49, 168, 241, 243, 250n38, 301, 327
Brandon, S. G. F., 75n46
Brashler, James A., 105n1
Bredin, Mark, xv, 66, 187n34, 189n38, 195n52
Brenneman, Laura, xiii, xv, 57, 345
Brodie, Thomas L., 181
Brower, Kent, 47n31
Brown, Peter, 222n11
Brownlee, William H., 119n45
Bruce, F. F., 63, 63n8, 200n2
Brueggemann, Walter, 20, 62n3, 71n32, 79n1, 286n14
Bultmann, Rudolf, 53n51, 155, 288n19, 326-28
Burge, Gary M., 63n6
Burns, J. P., 338

Burkholder, Lawrence E., 21n17, 110n23
Burton-Edwards, Taylor, 232n54
Butler Bass, Diana, 77

Cadoux, C. J., 228n37, 230n46
Caird, George B., 195n51
Camp, Lee C., 54n54, 155n11
Campbell, Peter A., 276n41
Campenhausen, H. von, 332
Capon, Robert Farrar, 155n14
Cardinal Bernardin, Joseph, 12n43
Carrol, M. Daniel R., 41n11
Carr, Wesley, 155n12
Carter, Warren, 65n12, 137-38, 159
Cartwright. Michael G., 354
Cassidy, Richard J., 75n46, 350
Charles, J. Daryl, 215n24
Charlesworth, James H., 23n18, 25n24
Christopher-Smith, Daniel, 48n38
Chrysostom, 133n12, 76n54, 133
Clapp, Rodney, xvi, 247
Coggins, James R., 271n27
Collins, Robin, 295n45
Copan, Paul, 27n39, 38n2, 334
Cornell, Collin, 8n31
Corson, Sarah, 253n47
Cowles, C. S., 43n17-18
Crews, Rowan, 91n27
Crosby, Michael H., 56
Cserháti, Márta, 138n26m, 140n36, 144n46
Culbertson, Diane M., 295n45
Cullmann, Oscar, 141
Culpepper, R. Alan, 175n5

Dallaire, Hélène M., 41n11
Daly, Robert J., 228n39, 328n5, 338
Davids, Peter H., 205nn9-10, 349
Davies, W. D., 62n3
Dawn, Marva J. 6n22, 116n33, 154n11, 155n14, 288n18, 292n39, 345
Dibelius, Martin, 334
De Silva, Dawna, 278
Dew, James K., Jr., 12n42, 333
Dix, Gregory, 223n17
Donahue, John R., 74n45
Dreher, Rod, 84n16

Dunham, Kyle C., 42n14
Dunn, James D. G., 334

Earl, Douglas S., 43
Edwards, Ruth B., 334
Eddy, Paul R., 17n8
Egan, Eileen, 254n52
Elias, Jacob, 58-59
Eller, Vernard, 115n31
Elster, William, 229n43
Engelsviken, Tormod, 220n1
Enns, Fernando, 242n19
Entz, Loren, 145, 146n53
Epp Weaver, Alain, 335
Estes, Steven, 38n2
Evans, C. F., 68-69, 71n32
Evans, Craig A., 335, 340
Evans. Jeremy, 334, 351

Farley, Wendy, 248n32
Ferguson, John, 76n54
Ferguson, Everett, 106nn3-4, 111n24, 219n1, 220nn2-4, 221-22
Fiddes, Paul S., 242n17
Finger, Thomas, xviii, 106n4, 113n29, 122n56, 149n2, 156n15
Fischer, James A., 40n7
Fitzmyer, Joseph A., 160, 163n40
Flannagan, Matt, 7n30
Fleischer, Matthew Curtis, 38n3, 7n30
Flusser, David, 25n26
Fodor, Jim, 295n45
Foerster, Werner, 74n44
Ford, Josephine Massynbaerde, 194n47
Forsyth, Neil, 107n9
Forsyth, P. T., 234
Fortna, Robert T., 351
Foster, K. Neill, 54n54, 56n61, 136n18
Foster, Richard, 145n51
Fretheim, Terrence E., 17n4, 20n16
Friedrich, Jim, 258n60, 271n25
Friesen, Duane K., 242n19, 252n44, 335, 337
Friesen, Ivan, 352
Friesen, James G., 271n25, 336
Fry, Ruth A., 254n52
Fröhlich, Ida. 330, 334, 349
Furnish, Victor Paul, 74n44

AUTHOR/EDITOR INDEX

Gammie, John G., 47n31
Gallagher, Richard, 6n23, 7n28, 144
Gard, Daniel L. 43n17, 46n27
Gardner, Richard B., 137n22
Garrett, Susan R., 16n2, 118n42, 137n24, 138, 139n32, 140n36, 144n47, 268n20
Geddert, Timothy, 128n2
Gerbrandt, Gerald E., 43n16. 45
Getzinger, Jo M., 271n25
Gingerich, Ray, 3n10, 284n7, 288n17
Girard, René, 3, 7n29, 27n33, 98n37, 202n6, 203, 216, 294-96, 350
Godshall, Tim, 350
Gombis, Timothy G., 54n52
Good, Deirdre J., 65
Goodhart, Sandor, 98n37, 295n45
Goppelt, Leonhard, 327, 328
Gorman, Michael J., 8n31, 103n46, 164n43, 199n1, 308n10
Gottwald, Norman, 40n7, 337
Grannis, Christopher, 329
Grant, Jonathan, 299n53
Green, A. R. W., 332
Green, Joel, 331, 332
Greene-McCreight, Kathryn, 343
Greenway, William, 11n19
Grimsrud, Ted, 3n10, 284n7, 288n17, 295n45
Gushee, David P., 247

Habel, Norman C., 62n3, 351
Haitch, Russell, 225-26
Hallie, Philip, 254n51
Hamilton, Jeffries M., 47n28, 237
Hamm, Dennis, 261
Hamsher, Matthew, 354
Handy, Jessica, 276n39
Hange, Roy, xv, 196n54, 239, 257n58, 258n60
Harder, Lydia, 251-52
Hardin, Michael, 199n1, 295n45, 339
Hardy, Andrew, 10n37, 27n33, 293, 294, 295n45, 296, 298n52
Harker, Ryan D., 71
Harnack, Adolf, 165, 166n47
Haase, W., 349-50
Hauerwas, Stanley, 234, 241n14, 334

Hay, David M., 158n19
Hays, Richard B., 29n44, 41n12, 56n62, 58n67, 71n32, 73nn40, 42, 163
Heath, A. Thomas, 334, 351
Hedges, Chris, 243n22
Heiser, M. S., 19n13
Helgeland, J., 228, 228n39
Hengel, Martin, 75nn49-50
Hershberger, Michele, 306n8, 331
Hess, Richard S., 267n19
Hiebert, Paul G., 271n27, 287, 296-97, 333
Hochstetler, Dean, 2n7, 3n8, 11, 224n22, 269, 271, 318n1
Holladay, William L., 72n37
Hornus, J.-M., 228n37, 253n45
Horsley, Richard A., 119nn44, 46-7, 229n42
Hovey, Craig, 339
Howell, Justin, 141n39
Huebner, Chris K., 334
Huebner, Harry, 334
Huffman, H. B., 332
Hunsinger, George, 200n3
Hunter, A. M., 339
Hurtado, Larry W., 240n12

Isaak, Jon, 342
Isaac, Munther, 62

Jackson, David, 253n47
Jacobs, Cindy, 298n32
James, Williams. 260n3
Jenkins, Philip, 298n52
Jeremias, Joachim, 75n52
Jersak, Brad, 199n1
Jeschke, Marlin, 60
Johns, Loren L., 34n52, 194, 195n49, 295n45
Johnson, James Turner, 44
Jones, D. L., 141n38
Josephus, 75n47-48

Käsemann, Ernst, 54n45
Kalantzis, George, 237n5, 241n13, 330, 337, 338, 341
Kallas, James, 120, 120n51, 168n54
Kee, Howard, 119n46

Keefer, Luke, Jr., 346
Keim, Paul, 295n45
Keith, Chris, 341, 346, 348
Kelly, Henry Ansgar, 225n26, 227
Kelly, J. N. D., 213
Kelly, Thomas A., 54n54
Kelsey, Morton T., 282, 283n4
Kim, Yung Suk, 8n31, 116n33
Kim, Seon Yong, 55n56
King, Paul L., 56n61, 136n18
Klassen, William, 74n44, 75n50, 116nn34, 36, 163–64
Klassen, Zacharie, 42n12
Klutz, Todd, 140n36
Knight, Cheryl, 271n25
Knight, Douglas A., 329
Kohlenberger, John R. III, 51n46
Koontz, Gayle Gerber, 347, 350
Koskenniemi, Erkki, 220, 334, 349
Krabill, James R., 4, 53, 249n45, 337
Kraft, Charles, 272n28, 283n4, 296
Kraybill, Donald B., 77n57, 222, 231n52, 313
Kraybill, J. Nelson, 189nn38–39, 192n46
Kreider, Alan, 7n28, 50, 222nn10, 14, 223, 232, 233nn57–60, 249, 273n31, 338, 340
Kreider, Eleanor, 232n54, 249, 340
Küng, Hans, 165n45
Kydd, Ronald A. N., 279

Laffin, Arthur, 329
Lamb, David T., 38n2
Langton, Edward, 108–9
Lascaris, André, 7n29
Lee, Gregory W., 237n5, 330, 337–39, 341
Lehman, Karl, 275, 355
Lehn, Cornelia, 254n52
Leiter, David, 38n6
Leithart, Peter J., 42n12
Leivestad, Ragnar, 168
Lejeune, R., 279n56
Leonhardt-Balzer, Jutta, 25n25, 119n44
Levenson, Jon, 19
Lewis, C. S., 21, 28, 302n1
Le Peau, Andrew T., 301
Liebscher, Teresa, 278

Lind, Millard C., 2n4, 23n21, 37, 38n1, 40n10, 44n19, 46, 53n21, 114n30, 115n31, 166n49, 301
Lindars, Barnabas, 334
Linn, Dennis, 337
Linn, Matthew, 337
Littrell, Amie D. 262n6
Lizorkin-Eyzenborg, Eli, 174n2
Lohfink, Gerhard, 228n36
Longley, Jim, xv, 242–43
Longman, Tremper, III, 27n29, 40n8, 43–44nn17–18, 166n49, 333, 343
Lust, J., 344
Luz, Ulrich, 129, 228

Mabee, Charles, 295n45
Mackay, John A., 128n3
MacMillan, John A. 270, 281, 282n3
MacNutt, Francis, 3–4n11, 5n15, 234, 256n54, 272n29, 273n30, 279, 283n4
MacRae, G. 339
Mansfield, M., 133n13
March, W. Eugene, 62n3
Marshall, Christopher D., 202n5
Martens, Elmer A., 23n21, 41n11, 49, 69–71
Martin, Ernest D., 157
Martin, Ralph P., 349
Matthews, Shelly, 338
Matthews, Victor H., 344
Matties, Gordon H., 42, 43n16, 45n24, 47n30, 295n45
Mauser, Ulrich, 65n11, 151n7, 162
Mbon, Friday M., 80
McAlpine, Thomas H., 294n43, 299
McCall, Kenneth, 342
McClain, George D., 3n11, 255–56, 273n30, 294n43
McConville, J. Gordon, 338
McCurley, Foster R., 115n31, 117, 132n10
McDermond, J. E., 10n35, 178, 179nn10, 12, 180n15
McDonald, Patricia, 195n52
McKelvey, R. J., 26, 62n3
McKnight, Scot, 212, 213n22

McMahon, Edwin M., 276n41
McManus, Richard, 311n1
McMullen, Ramsay, 223
Meacham, Jon, 237, 257n57
Meeks, Wayne, 180n16, 343
Meister, Chad, 11n41, 12n42, 333, 335, 351
Merrill, Eugene H., 43, 44n18, 46n27
Mettinger, T. N. D. 132n10
Metzger, Bruce M. 55n55
Middleton, J. Richard, 20n16
Migne, J.-P., 109n30
Mikalachki, Jodi, 257n59
Millar, J. Gary. 79
Miller, Douglas B., 23nn19–20
Miller, Marlin E, 295n45, 345
Miller, Patrick D., Jr., 74n43m
Moberly, R. W. L. 45
Moloney, Francis J. 183n23
Moltmann, Jürgen, 39n5, 242n16, 249, 256n55
Moreau, A. Scott, 220n1, 348
Morris, Michael J. 25n26, 139n33, 140n36
Morrison, Clinton D. 155n44
Moser, Paul K., 335, 343
Moss, Candida R., 249n33
Mott, Stephen C., 248n30
Moules, Noel, 39n6
Mounce, Robert H., 192n45
Muhammad, 18n12, 344
Murray, Stuart, 53n50, 249n35
Myers, Ched, 119nn46
Myers, Max, 119n47

Nation, Mark Thiessen, 334, 354
Nelson Gingerich, Barbara, 345
Nelson, Richard D., 45–47
Nelson, Susan L. 12n42, 183
Newman, Carey C., 71n32, 335, 338
Neyrey, Jerome H., 202–03n6
Niditch, Susan, 44n19
Niebuhr, Reinhold, 6n19, 243n22, 250n40
Nolt, Steven M., 77n57
Norberg, Tilda, 145, 272n29, 273, 274n33, 275n36, 276, 288n19, 290

Nouwen, Henri J. M., 236, 253n48
Nugent, Christopher, 139, 281
Nugent, John C., 49n36

O'Brien, P. T., 155
O'Day, Gail, 174
O'Donovan, Oliver, 244n33
Ochs, Peter, 354
Ollenburger, Ben C., xiii, xv, 2n4, 8n31, 19n13, 39n7, 72–73, 76, 115n31, 238n8, 267n19
Olson, Ken, 272n29, 289n21
Osborne, Grant R., 189n38
Oswalt, John N., 42n31
Oyer, Linda, 136n19

Page, Sydney H. T., 10n36, 24n22, 32n49, 108nn12, 17–18, 283
Paris, Peter J., 329
Patte, Daniel, 151n8
Pattison, Mansell, 297n49
Payne, Leanne, 275
Peachey, Paul, 340
Pearse, Meic, 243n22
Peck, M. Scott, 4n11, 6, 7n28, 144, 273n30, 289n21, 290, 297n49
Peckham, John C. 267n18, 302n1
Penchansky, David, 17nn6–7
Perkins, Pheme, 185n28
Pierard, Richard V. 256n55, 351
Pilgrim, Walter, 158–59, 162
Piper, John, 76n55
Plantinga, Cornelius, Jr., 1n3
Podimattam, F., 77n57
Poole, W. Scott, 281n2

Quast, Kevin, 58n67

Rainbow, Paul S., 190
Ratzlaff, Steve, 350
Ray, Darby Kathleen, 156n15
Reid, Daniel, 40n8, 166n49
Rensberger, David, 180n16
Richardson, Cyril C., 63n7
Roberts, Charles Carl, 77
Robinson, James M, 117nn37, 41
Robitaille, Glenn A., 76n54
Rollston, Christopher A., 24n23

Rommen, Edward, 294n43, 296n47
Rowe, C. Kavin, 141nn37-40, 143nn42, 44, 339
Ruiz, Jean-Pierre, 52n49, 197n55
Ruth, John L., 252n43
Rutledge, Fleming, 18n10, 26n28, 27n31, 29n39, 200, 212n21

Samuel, Mar Athanasius Yeshue, 224–25, 347
Schade, Elin, 329
Schantz, Brad D., 345
Schärf Kluger, Rivkah, 108n12
Scharper, Philip, 350
Schertz, Mary H., 209, 212
Schlabach, Gerald, 242n19, 252n44, 335, 336
Schlier, H., 6, 263, 289
Schmemann, Alexander, 225, 226n27
Schneider, G., 141n38
Schnelle, Udo, 328
Schoonhoven, Calvin R., 24n22, 34n53, 35
Schottroff, Luise, 76n54, 148, 161, 161n30, 161n32, 162n35, 163n38, 230n47
Schrobsdorff, Susanna, 145n52
Schüssler Fiorenza, Elisabeth, 189n38, 237
Scranton, Roy, 244n22
Scurlock, JoAnn, 19n13
Sears, Robert T., 271n26
Seibert, Eric A., 41n11
Seitz, Christopher, 343
Seitz, O. J. F., 74n45
Sharp, John E., 331
Sharp, Michael, 192n44
Sherman, William Tecumseh, 243n22
Shorter, Aylward, 233n61
Shroyer, Danielle, 145, 306n7
Sider, E. Morris, 346
Sider, Ronald J., 76, 228n38, 247
Simonetti, Manlio, 133nn11–12
Simons, Menno, 83n13
Simpson, Gary M, 250n39

Sizer, Stephen, 63n6
Skarsaune, Oskar, 219–20n1
Shenk, David W., 337
Skinner, Christopher, 175
Skinner, Tom, 354
Smedes, Lewis B., 271n27
Smith, Edward M., 275
Smith, J. B., 51n46, 268n20
Smith, Jonathan, 106n3
Smith, Patricia A., 275n36
Snyder, Ben, 2n7, 11, 313n2, 318n1
Snyder, C. Arnold, 96
Snyder Belousek, Darrin, xv, 8n31, 199n1, 242n17, 256n55
Sorensen, Eric, 121n53
Southwood, Katherine, 49n38, 333
Spina, F. A., 332
Stähli, H.-P., 96n33
Stark, Rodney, 231
Stassen, Glen H., 354
Steffon, Fr. Jeffrey J., 224
Stendahl, Krister, 75n50
Stevens, Bruce A., 115n32
Stewart, James S., 234
Stinespring, William F., 340
Stimamiglio, Stefano, 263n9, 329
Stock, Augustine, 54n53
Stott, John R. W., 6
Stubbs, Monya S., 159–61
Stuckenbruck, Loren T., 23, 25n26, 339
Stutsman, Linford, 337
Sugden, Chris, 254n51
Swartley, Willard M., xii–xviii, 1n2, 9n33, 34n54, 35n57, 42n12, 50n40, 52n49, 54n53, 55n56, 63n5, 67n17, 68nn18,19, 70n24, 74n45, 75n52, 79n5, 117n41, 119n46, 129n4, 136–40nn19,25,29,34,36, 154n11, 174n2, 177n8, 185n27, 190n40, 192n43, 195nn50,52, 210n19, 229n42, 231n51, 250n38, 252, 254n53, 259n55, 288n16, 293n41, 295n45, 308n10, 313n3
Sweetland, Dennis M., 54n53
Swinton, John, 12, 266–67
Swoboda, Jorg, 256n55

Tada, Joni Eareckson, 38
Talbert, Charles H., 305n5
Taliaferro, Charles, 278n53, 343
Tambasco, A. J., 155, 156n16
Taneja, Anand Vivek, 18n12
Tannehill, Robert C., 76n54
Taylor, Richard K., 254n51
Temporini, H., 350
Thatcher, Tom, 351
Thielman, Frank S., 328
Thomas, Heath A., 74n43, 334
Thomas, John Christopher, 11n40
Thurston, Bonnie, 292n39
Toews, John E. 163, 164n42
Tolstoy, Leo, 354
Torrance, Tom, 267n17
Trudinger, Peter L., 43n16
Tunnicliffe, S., 340
Twelftree, Graham H., 10, 32n49, 107n9, 108n18, 118n43, 121n53, 128n2, 137n23, 139, 140n36, 174n1, 260–61, 290–92, 334

Vanderhaar, Gerard A., 77n57
van der Kolk, Bessel, 276
Vervenne, M., 344
Volf, Miroslav, 166
Vollenweider, Samuel, 139n32
von Rad, Gerhard, 20,39, 40n7

Wallace, T. H. S., 352
Wallis, Jim, 253n48
Waltner, Erland, 209, 212, 213n23
Waltner, James H., 79, 87, 90
Warner, Timothy M., 272n26
Warren, E. Janet, 28, 29n39, 32n49, 139n31, 145, 176n7, 232, 270n24, 277, 289–90
Weaver, Dorothy Jean, xv, 4, 9n33, 151, 161n33, 237n2,
Weaver, Denny, 199n1
Weaver-Zercher, David L., 77n57, 249n33
Webber, Robert E., 227, 232, 268n21, 270n23

Wenger, John C., 348
Wengst, Klaus K., 66, 161n34, 230n49, 249n34
Wenham, Gordon J. 20n16, 267n19, 338
White, John, 55
Whitehouse, Richard, 10n37, 27n33, 293–96, 298n52
Wilgus, J. Blair , 41n11, 333, 334, 342
Williams, James G., 295n45
Wilson, R. A., 334
Wimber, John, 271n27, 333
Wink, Walter, 3–5, 8n32, 10, 28, 108, 154n10, 155, 167, 168n56, 223, 229, 237n1, 239n10, 253n48, 284–89
Winkler, Gabrielle, 225n26
Winslow, Mark H., 313
Witmer, Amanda, 118n43, 293n40
Wood, John A., 40n7
Woolley, Reginald Maxwell, 223n15
Wright, Christopher J. H., 8, 10–11, 28n2, 44n22, 70n23
Wright, Nigel Goring, 6–7, 16n2, 27–28, 353
Wright, N. T., 6, 7n25, 19n15, 28, 71, 119n48, 303, 335, 338, 344

Yarnell, Dan, 10n27, 27n33, 293–94, 295n43, 296
Yeatts, John R., 10n35, 187n31, 187n35, 192n45, 195n51, 196n53
Yoder, John H., 6, 48, 49n38, 55, 155, 169n60, 199n1, 221n7, 226, 243n20, 250n40k, 253n47, 284, 294
Yoder [Neufeld], Rebecca, 51n45
Yoder Neufeld, Thomas R., 6, 52n48, 136n17, 161nn29, 33, 165n44, 169nn60–63, 170n65, 199n1, 243, 244n22
Young, Robert, 16n1, 268n30

Zaleski, Carol, 38n2
Zehr, Paul M., 170–71n66

Subject Index

(the selected word may appear multiple times
—in notes as well—on listed pages)

Abel, 7n29, 115, 306
Amish, 77
adultery, 17, 61, 84, 100, 109,
    113–14n30, 165, 203, 302
adversary(ies)(ial), 4, 26–27, 37, 57,
    72–73, 80, 83, 86–87, 131, 155,
    162, 171, 180, 209
alternate(ive)(ing), ix, 91n27, 113–14,
    116(2x), 120, 128, 137, 160,
    172, 178, 185, 237, 250, 251n41,
    255, 287, 289n21, 290, 292, 299,
    305n4, 312
Anabaptist, xii, xix, 98n37, 156, 226,
    237n3, 242n16, 250, 293, 330,
    337, 349
angel(s)/archangel(s), 5, 11n40, 20,
    23n18, 26–28, 32, 33n51, 34,
    40, 57, 106, 107–10nn9,15,22,
    129, 134–35, 139n31, 149, 154,
    155nn12,14, 184, 188–94, 197,
    199, 208, 211, 212n21, 214–15,
    225n26, 226–27, 237–38, 257,
    268, 268n19, 279, 281, 284–85,
    287, 304n3, 312, 315, 324, 329,
    331, 333, 336, 343, 349
anoint(ed), 22–23, 48, 74, 137, 139–40,
    207, 225–26, 263, 274, 278,
    288n17, 353
apartheid, 1, 4n11, 152n9, 255, 273n30

apocalyptic(icism), 4, 10, 26, 32n49, 43,
    48, 180, 185, 185n28, 186, 189,
    216, 305, 333, 338, 346
Apocalypse, 180, 184, 184n25, 193n46,
    194–95, 341, 346
attack(s)(ed)(ing), 3, 11, 34, 73, 76n54,
    80, 85, 107n9, 117, 162, 165n45,
    171–72, 215, 227, 257, 282, 304,
    319, 327
atone(ing)(ment), 8n31, 39n5, 42n12,
    50n41, 108, 156, 199n1,
    200–201, 222, 223n20, 235,
    242n17, 246, 256n55, 282,
    295n45, 330, 335, 337, 346, 349
    Christus Victor, 156, 168, 199n1,
        200, 223n20, 330
    deliverance, 200
    penal, 59n41
    self-donation, 42n12
    substitution(ary), 116
authority(ative)(ize), 23n18, 30,
    39–41, 56, 106, 118, 120–24,
    128n2, 129, 131–32, 136–39,
    145n51, 147, 152–61, 164, 157,
    170, 184–85, 188, 191, 194,
    199, 214–16, 225, 234, 240,
    245, 254n52, 270, 272, 279,
    281–82n3, 290–91, 298, 301,
    311–13, 324–25, 336, 342

SUBJECT INDEX

authorities, 32–33, 148, 153–54, 156–158, 161, 164, 167, 170, 172, 199, 205n7, 208, 211, 236–37, 240–42, 245–47, 250, 280, 284n9, 289, 339
Azazel/Azaz'el, 18, 107–08nn9,18

Babel, 19n15
Babylon(ian), 21, 23, 25, 26, 29, 48, 63n5, 93n30, 98n36, 99–100, 102, 108n19, 110, 154, 189–92, 196, 202n5, 238, 307, 333
bad(ly)(ness), 24n23, 28, 31, 38n2, 137, 164, 199n1, 205n7, 242, 253, 333, 341
baptism(al)/baptisand, 4n11, 66, 117, 128, 129n4, 133, 170, 208, 212, 222, 223, 223–27nn17,26, 232, 234, 273n30, 326, 337, 340, 347, 353
Barth, Karl, 6, 28–29, 226, 249, 279n56, 285, 339
beast(s), 34, 52, 108, 153, 176, 185–191, 195–96, 282, 327
Beatitude(s), 62n3, 66, 84, 130
belong(s)(ing[s]), 17, 31, 43, 45, 52, 62n3, 65, 81–82n12, 132, 139n32, 165, 177, 181, 188, 197, 200n2, 244n22, 246, 270, 273, 301
beloved disciple, 9n35
benediction(s), 26n27, 201, 203, 215–16, 305, 309
betray(er)(al), 175, 182,
body, 3, 30, 34, 52, 56, 58, 73, 106, 118, 159, 176n7, 208, 214–15, 273–274, 276, 290n22, 323, 343, 352, 354
    church/Christian body, 52, 54–55n57, 59, 149, 158, 169, 232, 236, 243n20, 246, 249, 339
bomb(s)(ing), 139, 239, 244n22, 257
bondage, 1, 5–6, 9–10, 37, 125, 127, 136, 140, 149, 169, 234, 260, 264–65, 271n26, 277, 307, 312, 335, 336, 350, 352, 353

Cain, 7n29, 19n15, 31, 306

canon(ical), 3, 9, 11, 16n2, 27, 38–41nn2,11, 48–50, 61, 63n5, 72n34, 74n43, 105, 170, 196, 205nn7,13, 290, 292–293, 300–01, 327
centurion(s), 5n15, 141, 246, 339
character(izes)(ized), 5, 31, 42n12, 43–46nn18,21, 27, 48–49, 66, 93, 121n53, 131–32, 155n14, 166, 169, 195, 240n12, 249, 281, 284–85, 289, 341
chiasm(astic), ix, 129–30, 140, 157, 209
charismatic, 7n28, 291, 307
child(ren), vi, 33, 46, 55–56n58, 66, 74–77, 81, 111n26, 127, 134, 137, 145, 167n52, 171, 173, 175, 179, 198–99, 216, 224n23, 226, 231, 245n24, 254n52, 259, 298n52, 303–04n8, 314, 318, 321
Jesus/Christ or Jesus Christ, *passim*. See Christology
community(ies), xi, 8n31, 9, 18, 25, 29, 45–46, 54, 56–59, 62n3, 64, 70, 74n45, 76–77, 90, 125, 135, 150, 157, 158, 162, 165n45, 172, 180, 189, 192, 207, 221, 224, 225, 228, 230–32, 237, 242, 252–55, 257, 264–65, 267–68n20, 279n55, 282, 293, 296, 300–01, 306, 318, 327, 333, 338, 341, 346, 349–50, 353
chaos, 8, 19–21, 28–29, 35–36, 45, 61n1, 82, 87, 91n26, 110, 116–17, 132, 167, 176, 185, 196, 238, 252, 277, 289, 300, 306n7, 338, 343, 345, 347
Christology(ical), 34n52, 67, 72, 92n29, 128n2, 153, 179, 175, 185–86n30, 189, 193–95, 330, 332, 339
    Lamb, 10–11, 33–34n52, 35, 38n2, 44n18, 52–53, 115–16, 162, 175, 184–86, 189, 190–97, 268, 290, 293, 305, 337, 339, 353
    Lord/Lord Jesus, passim. See Lordship

SUBJECT INDEX

Messiah(ship), xvii, 7, 8n31, 9,
    24–26, 33, 62, 64–65, 74, 102,
    115n33, 122, 124, 128, 139n31,
    145, 184, 189n38, 194–96, 237,
    301–03, 307, 325, 337, 340
Son of David, 64
Son of God, 65, 117, 124, 128n2,
    129, 179, 182, 223, 314
Son of Man, 134–35, 185, 240
Shepherd, 56n58, 100, 203

church(es), viii, ix,xi, 2, 3n8, 5–8n31,
    10–11, 32–33, 37, 39n5, 41n11,
    45–46, 48, 51–52, 54n52, 55–57,
    62, 64, 76, 83n13, 118, 120,
    125, 131, 135, 137, 141, 144,
    146, 153–55, 158, 159–62, 167,
    169, 172, 174n1, 184, 186–87,
    219, 221–40, 241n14, 242n17,
    245–51, 256–57, 261, 264, 266,
    270n23, 271, 273, 278–79, 282,
    285, 287–94, 297–99, 304,
    318n1–321, 325–27, 330–35,
    338, 339, 341, 343, 345–52
Church Father(s), 32, 33, 62, 63, 111,
    130n7, 219–20, 222, 228–29,
    233, 346
cleanse(s)(ed)(ing), 7n28, 29n39, 32n49,
    38, 46, 50, 56, 73, 98, 120, 124,
    132, 176nn6–7, 181, 200, 204,
    206, 215, 222, 232, 232n56, 263,
    266, 279n24, 277, 289, 306n7,
    313–15, 352
command(s)(ed)(ing)(ment[s]), 3,
    7n30, 8–9, 17, 20, 26, 34,
    37–38, 40–44, 46–48, 53, 61,
    75nn46,50, 76n55, 82n12,
    91n26, 96, 98, 100, 102, 107,
    111n26, 113, 115, 122, 124–25,
    128n2, 132, 136, 147, 161–62,
    172, 179, 205, 213, 224n22,
    226–28, 242–43, 244n22, 246,
    248, 249n34, 254n55, 263n9,
    266–67, 269–72n29, 273, 277,
    283n4, 293, 295, 300, 311
communion(s)/Eucharist, 7, 187n33,
    223, 227, 232, 273, 274, 288n17,
    341

community(ies), xi, 8n31, 9, 18, 25, 29,
    45–46, 54, 56–59, 62, 64, 70,
    74n45, 76–77, 90, 125, 135, 150,
    157–58, 162, 165n45, 172, 180,
    189n39, 192, 207, 221, 224–25,
    228, 230–32, 237, 242, 252–55,
    257, 264–65, 267, 268n20,
    279n55, 282, 293, 296, 300–01,
    306, 318, 327, 333, 338, 341,
    346, 349, 350, 353
compassion(ate), 2, 12, 50, 114n30, 144,
    266–67, 277, 286, 322, 350
conflict(ed)(ive), 3, 5, 7, 27, 32, 39n5,
    44n18, 46n27, 75n46, 117, 128,
    135, 160–61, 167, 175, 177, 185,
    188–89, 195, 228, 245, 255n49,
    257n58, 282, 295–296, 327, 331,
    341, 345, 346, 351
conform(ity), 44n18, 87, 160–61
conquest, 9, 39n6, 40–42nn7,12, 47, 60,
    116, 195, 261, 334
consumer(ism), 247, 333
contextual(ize), 61n2, 71n32, 170n66
convert(ed)/conversion, 26, 44, 114,
    157, 163, 189, 223, 227–28, 231,
    233, 236, 244, 296, 341
counselor(s)(ing), 2, 98, 266n12,
    269–70, 277, 317, 318, 319
covenant(s)(al) (excludes *passim*
    references to my *Covenant*
    book), 9, 17, 19, 26, 29–30,
    40, 43–46, 48, 53, 58–59, 61,
    63–65, 67, 79, 71n33, 72, 79,
    88, 98, 100, 102, 112–14, 116,
    125, 199n1, 200–03, 227, 238,
    250–01, 257, 263, 302–03, 306,
    308, 337, 338
creation, xii, 2n4, 7n26, 8, 11, 16, 17n4,
    19–23, 26, 28–29, 33, 35–36,
    43n16, 48, 59, 69, 82, 87, 110,
    116–17, 132n10, 139, 151,
    153–54, 166, 170n65, 176, 183,
    190, 194, 196, 199, 216, 224,
    230, 232, 247, 277, 285n11, 286,
    289, 295, 299–300, 305, 308–09,
    329–31, 336–38, 341, 345, 347

cross, xii, 7, 8nn30-31, 29, 34-35, 39, 42n12, 45n22, 68, 73, 76, 82, 115-16, 123-24, 129, 130n7, 148, 153, 157, 159, 162, 166, 168, 176, 183, 191-92, 200, 202, 221, 227, 234-35, 245, 261, 265, 270, 282, 297, 311-15, 319, 324, 329, 331, 334, 336-38, 343-44, 347, 349

cruciform(ity), 8n31, 12, 29n44, 39nn4-5, 164n43, 242n17, 257, 301, 337

cult(s)(ic), 45, 109, 113, 145, 150, 159, 168, 170, 172, 176, 189n39, 197, 220, 341, 345, 346

culture(al), 2, 3, 8, 19n13, 44n19, 49, 55nn56&58, 56, 84, 113, 118, 139n43, 143-45, 156, 160, 164, 196, 224, 228, 249, 257, 262n6, 281, 287, 293-301, 331, 333

curse(s)(ed)(ing)/accursed, 20, 24, 51, 56n62, 80-81, 90, 95, 99, 125, 162, 164, 190, 210, 224, 265, 270, 272, 279, 306, 313-14, 321, 324

deceive(ed)(er)/deceit(ful)/deception(s), 1, 4, 15, 34, 78, 81, 83-85, 90, 92-94, 97-98, 108n14, 144-45, 149, 154, 155-56nn14-15, 166, 172, 184, 189, 204, 208, 210, 215, 220, 224-25, 248, 251, 267n17, 274, 292n37, 302-03, 313

deliver(ed)(ance), *passim*

demon(s)(ic)(ized)(ization)/ demonology, 2-4, 6n13, 7, 9-10, 11n40, 23, 25, 29-35n55, 44, 58-59, 68, 74, 82n12, 83, 89, 92, 102, 106-27, 128n2, 129, 131-34, 136-44, 146-47, 149-52, 155-56, 162, 167-74, 177, 187n33, 188-92, 199, 203, 207, 215-25, 228-29, 233-44, 237, 239, 242-43, 268, 255-58, 260-78, 281-84, 288-94, 296n46, 297-99, 308, 311-13, 319-20, 323-36, 344-45, 348-49, 353-54

devil(ish), 4-5, 7, 11, 16, 27, 32n49, 33-35, 57, 74, 83n13, 92n29, 109-11, 115, 120n49, 124, 128, 131, 134-35, 139-41, 144-45, 148-49, 152-56, 163, 165, 167-68, 170-72, 175, 177, 179, 180-81, 183-84, 187, 189-91, 196, 198-201, 203-09, 213-15, 219-27, 232-37, 243n22, 259-64, 268, 277, 280-83, 289-91, 297n49, 298n52, 304-06, 326-30, 334-36, 339-40, 345-46, 349-51

disciple(s)(ing)(ship), xvii, 9n35, 12, 52-56, 64, 67, 73-76, 118, 122-23, 131-38, 176-83, 189, 202n5, 244, 290, 293-96, 298n53, 305, 325, 329-34, 349-50

divination/to divine (see also sorcery), 108n14, 114-15, 143, 220, 305n4, 307

dragon(s), 20-21, 32n49, 34, 87n23, 153, 156n15, 175, 184-86, 189-91, (Dungeons and, 224), 327

dual (theses of book), 2, 4, 7, 120, 158, 181, 281

dualism(ity), 26-29, 107, 109, 119, 175-78, 185, 285n11, 288

earth(ly), 5n17, 19-22, 28, 32-34, 37-44, 48, 50-55, 61n1, 62-64, 69n21, 73, 84, 97-99, 106-07, 110n22, 120n49, 122-23, 136, 151n7, 158, 178n5, 180, 184-85, 188, 190-96, 204-06, 215-16, 229-30, 238n8, 240, 258, 268, 280, 282n2, 287, 299-300, 305-08, 311, 328, 331, 335, 339, 342, 344, 351

Emperor(s)/emperor(s), 29-30, 52, 141nn37-38, 153,157, 170, 185-86, 187n35, 189,190,196-97, 221, 229, 231, 237, 281, 305

SUBJECT INDEX

E(e)mpire/imperial(ism), xi, 5, 30, 34,
48, 52, 64, 65n12, 119, 120n48,
136–37, 141, 143n44, 148, 152,
158, 159–62, 167n50, 174, 179,
185–86, 189, 191–92, 196,
210, 221–23, 228–30, 232,
237, 239–40, 245, 249n34,
253nn44,48, 255, 281, 286, 299,
305, 308, 333, 338–39, 341, 343,
346
enemy(ies), vi–vii, 5, 9, 21–26, 29–30,
37–55, 59–60, 65, 70–92, 95–99,
107n9, 110, 112n27, 215–16,
117n36, 118n43, 120n48, 125,
129n4, 130–36, 139, 144–47,
156n15, 162–69, 79, 195, 202,
228–29, 233, 236–38, 244–45,
248–50, 253–54, 257–58,
261–63, 266, 277, 281, 295,
300–03, 307–08, 332–36, 340,
345–53
eschatology(gical), ii, 18, 19n15, 24,
34n53, 36, 43, 44n18, 48,
116–18, 120n51, 155, 158, 183,
186, 189n37, 197–18, 216, 303,
308, 335
ethic(s)(al)/ethicists, viii, xi, 5n15,
7n30, 8, 11, 18n12, 38, 38n2,
42n12, 45n22, 47–49, 75, 113,
146, 155n14, 158–59, 166, 183,
194–95, 201, 210–12, 228,
241, 243n22, 249–53, 301, 307,
326–28
evangelism(istic), 169, 172, 352
evangelical(s), 247, 271, 335, 337, 340,
346, 352, 354
evil, *passim*
evildoer(s), 16, 31, 73, 75, 78–87,
89–91, 94–95, 97, 99–100, 102,
131–32, 135, 187, 219, 248,
302–03
evil one(s), v, xvii, 116, 29–31, 34, 36,
52, 108, 120, 128, 131, 134, 137,
154n10, 163, 169–71, 173–76,
179, 181, 182n20, 199, 205, 297,
213, 215, 220, 225, 239n10, 258,
280, 282, 283n4, 298, 304–05,
309, 317, 330, 352

evil spirit(s)(ual), 2–3, 5, 6n23, 9, 16,
18, 24, 30–31, 33, 35n55, 80,
106–10, 123, 136–38, 142,
155n14, 156, 220n1, 221–23,
227, 232, 260, 268n20, 272, 277,
279, 283, 285, 289–91, 294,
298n52, 311–14, 342
exalt(s)(ed)(ing)(tation), 32n49, 81, 88,
91n27, 102, 153–54, 204, 206,
211, 213, 221, 232, 241, 246,
268, 282, 328
enthrone(d)(ment), 82–83
exclude(ing)(sive)(sivism), 48, 144, 166,
223n17, 253, 261, 287, 338, 352
exodus/Exodus, 37–38, 39–41, 42n14,
46, 40n50, 61n2, 116n34, 123,
132n10
exorcism(orcize[ed]), *passim*

faith/faithful(ly)(ness), viii, ix, 4n14,
7–10, 17, 24, 36, 38n2, 44, 48,
54, 62–63, 71, 73, 82, 85n19, 89,
91, 102, 110, 112–13, 115, 120,
122, 125, 129n4, 130–31, 140,
151n8, 154n10, 155n13, 157,
159, 161, 167, 169–72, 175–76,
179, 180n16, 182, 184–86, 189,
189n37, 190, 192, 195–97, 200,
202+n5(!), 204, 207, 209–10,
212, 214, 217, 221, 223, 225,
231, 234, 241n15, 245–46, 250,
253–55, 257, 260n1, 263, 274,
279n54, 286–87, 298, 300,
306n7, 307, 330, 332, 340–42,
345–46, 349, 352–53
fear(s)(ed)(ful)(less), 16, 24, 35, 83, 87,
96, 109, 125. 164, 168, 198–200,
207–08, 226, 236, 252, 255, 259,
264–65, 272, 275, 278, 281, 283,
299, 313, 318–20, 323, 348–49
fear of the Lord, 83, 92–93, 96–97,
251
fire(s)(iery), 8, 17, 22, 24, 33, 40, 42n14,
48, 88, 94, 95, 100, 108, 111,
135, 143, 144, 151n7, 163,
190–91, 206, 210n18, 214,
215–17, 294, 330, 340, 344

SUBJECT INDEX

forgive(ing)(ness), 29, 42n12, 55–56, 76–77, 91–92, 115, 122, 130, 135n14, 136n19, 137, 141, 145, 149, 157, 240, 243n22, 245, 263, 266–67, 269, 280, 305, 319, 322, 340

foreign(er[s]), 26, 47, 63, 68, 113, 119, 142, 237, 273, 307

fruit, 17, 27, 31, 83, 93–94, 131, 200, 203, 304

fulfill(s)(ed)(ing)(ment), 37, 62–65, 69, 70–73, 117–18, 122, 124, 132, 165, 177, 182–83, 201, 258, 282, 301, 303

Galilee(ans), 66, 75, 118, 123n58, 129, 153, 177, 353

generous, 207, 301

Gentile(s), 52, 55, 62, 64–66, 122–24, 135n15, 141, 160, 167n52, 220n1, 244–45

gift(s), 12, 70, 96, 123, 149, 178, 182–83, 278n52, 291, 308, 316n5, 332, 350

Girard, René, 3, 7n29, 27, 98n37, 121n54, 202n6, 203, 216, 294–96nn45–46, 297, 350

glory(ify[ies])(ious)(ification), xvii, 24, 50–53, 64, 70, 97–98n36, 122n57, 123, 136–37, 151–53, 158n19, 172, 175–76n7, 178, 188–90, 194–97, 201–03, 213–16, 234–35, 240, 243n22, 268, 280, 284, 304–05, 309, 338

good(ness), in moral or gospel sense, iv, vi, 2, 5, 8, 10, 15–19, 24n23, 26–29, 32–33, 39n5, 49n36, 53–54, 65, 68, 74n45, 75–78, 83–85, 88n22, 93–98, 100–02, 106, 108–09, 112, 117–18, 122n57, 129–34, 138–42, 149–51, 154–55nn11,15, 160, 163–64, 167, 170n64, 171–72, 175–77, 182–84, 192n42, 201–05, 208–14, 216–18, 224, 229, 233, 235, 242–45, 248, 253, 284–87, 297, 303–06, 307, 327, 329, 334, 346

go to Jesus, 3, 272n29, 311–12

Gospel(s)(excluding page titles)/ gospel, ii, vii, 4n13, 7n25, 9–12, 19n15, 73–76, 105, 115–23, 125, 128–45, 149, 151–52, 158, 160–61, 166–85, 189n37, 192n42, 196, 202n5, 212, 222, 227, 231, 235n63, 237, 240, 244–46, 250–52, 260–62, 273, 281, 287–97, 303–05, 308, 321, 330–38, 342–46, 349–51

grace, 11n40, 43, 64, 76, 125, 127, 200n3, 213, 273, 315, 337, 339–40, 344

Hate(ed)(ful)/hatred, 73–75n50, 81–85, 88, 92–95, 139, 164, 174–77, 179–81, 183, 201, 243, 251, 255, 257, 262, 272, 278, 296, 307, 320, 322–24, 349

heal(ed)(ing)(ings)/health, viii, xvi, 2n5, 3, 5, 10–11, 24, 29n43, 35, 55n57, 72, 79, 82, 89, 102, 106, 118–19, 122–23, 126, 129, 132, 136–37, 140–41, 144, 172, 189n37, 196, 207, 220, 223n15, 231n51, 245, 247, 252–54, 259–65, 269–79, 282–283n4, 290–93, 296–97n4, 299–304, 308, 311–12, 315–16, 319–20, 322, 333–35, 340–49, 352–54

heaven(s)(ly)(lies), vi, 1, 5n17, 19, 21–22, 23n18, 24, 27–28, 31, 32n49, 33–36, 43, 52–57, 62, 70, 75, 99, 106–10, 112, 117, 122–23, 130–39, 153, 168, 172, 175n5, 177, 184–85, 188, 190, 193–96, 198, 205, 208, 215–16, 219, 225–26, 236–40, 245, 258, 268, 280, 282n3, 287, 300, 303–08, 311, 319, 327–28, 335, 347

ḥerem, 8–9, 18, 38–52, 54, 59, 116, 202n5, 334, 344, 353

hermeneutic(s)(ical), 8n31, 39nn4–5, 70, 301, 338, 341, 347, 350

Holy Spirit/(the) Spirit, v, 4n11, 19, 51–52, 58, 71, 74, 96, 117–18,

SUBJECT INDEX

124, 128, 133, 137, 140, 144, 146, 169, 171, 182–83, 205, 223, 225–27, 232–34, 258, 263, 268, 273n30, 274, 277–78, 282, 287, 295, 299, 305, 312, 314–15, 329, 334

Holy War(fare), 38–45, 49, 74n43, 114–16, 119, 300–02, 330, 332, 334, 329, 345, 351–52

Hope(s)(d)(ful), xi, xiii, 1, 11, 18, 19n15, 23–26, 29, 33n51, 36, 38n2, 51, 57–58, 64–65, 71n33, 73, 82, 86, 89n24, 91, 102, 116, 149n4, 175, 183, 192n43, 196, 201–02, 212, 216, 241–42, 247, 256–58, 265, 271, 286, 298, 391, 303, 306, 308, 319–20, 346

hostile(ity)(ies), 19, 122, 154, 157–58, 161, 164, 180–02, 185, 203, 252, 264

house(hold), 5n15, 21, 68, 73, 83, 94, 96, 100, 112, 121, 115, 133–34, 142, 159, 209–10, 291–92, 231, 234, 313–15, 319, 333

humble/humility, 65–66, 127, 204, 206, 213, 254, 261, 277, 352

identity(ies), 9n35, 34, 44n20, 54n52, 75–76, 80, 87, 141, 174, 181, 192–93, 197n56, 207, 225, 240, 285, 298n52, 303, 306, 352

idol(s)(atry[ies][rous]), 9, 17–18n10, 23, 26, 38–47, 58–61, 74, 92, 97–98, 102, 107, 109, 111–16, 119n47, 139, 143–44, 150–52, 155, 181, 187n33, 188n36, 189, 192n42, 197, 220–22, 228–29, 239, 248–49, 262–63, 273, 301–03, 307, 338

imitation/imitate, 3, 27, 241n15, 294–95n45, 296

include(s)(ing)(list is selective), 18n10, 28, 30n45, 43, 46, 52, 73, 107, 114, 116, 123n57, 138, 153, 162, 168, 186, 192, 200, 205, 220n4, 222–24n23, 225, 234, 247, 253, 269n22, 272, 281n1, 293, 301, 304, 308

individual(ism), 5–6, 35n55, 70, 74, 76, 122, 124, 136, 156n15, 169, 174, 191, 224, 248, 253, 261, 266, 284, 299

Israel('s), *passim* to 140, 144, 150, 174n2, 201–02, 210, 220n1, 238n8, 239, 244n22, 286, 300–03, 307–08, 329–30, 335–39, 342, 344–45, 349–50, 353

Jerusalem, 5n15, 17–18, 23, 26, 30, 36, 48, 52–53, 62–63, 66, 71, 74–75, 101, 112, 121–22, 124, 129, 142, 157, 177, 187n32, 187, 190, 338, 345, 347

Jesus, *passim*. See Christology

Jewish, xvii, 12n41, 19n13, 25–27n29, 29–30, 41n11, 42n12, 49n38, 55, 58, 62, 64, 65n12, 66, 71n32, 75, 84n17, 98n37, 106–07, 110, 116n36, 123, 142–44, 157, 162, 165n45, 174n2, 180, 194n47, 199, 202–03n6, 204–05, 207, 286, 293n40, 295, 305, 334–35, 340–42, 352, 354

Jinn, 18, 117, 344

joy(ous)(ful)(fully), 11n39, 54, 78, 93–94, 125, 138, 202, 206, 234, 256, 317

Jubilee, 43, 45, 47, 140, 143

Judea(n)(ns), 53, 129, 160, 174n2, 245n24

judge(s)(es)(ment)/Judge (excludes Book title), 22, 32, 34n53, 38, 41–42n11, 69, 73n38, 81–82, 86–87, 95–99, 105, 112, 119, 153, 177–78, 187n35, 191, 206, 212, 230, 238, 251, 307, 347

just war, 244n23, 250, 330, 348

justice/injustice/justify, xii, 6, 38n2, 40n7, 47n28, 72–73, 76, 80–81, 95–99, 102, 197, 110, 144, 162, 166–69, 195, 212, 221, 229, 238–39, 243n22, 246–47, 254, 258, 281, 286, 303, 307, 329–31, 333, 335, 337, 347, 349, 353

SUBJECT INDEX

kill(s)(ed)(ing[s]), vii, 3, 9, 11, 33, 37–55, 59–61n2, 77, 88, 94, 107, 124–25, 136, 147, 153, 156n15, 162–65, 175, 185–86, 192, 199n1, 207, 228–29, 243n22, 244–46, 250, 254n52, 256–257n59, 295, 299–302, 304, 306, 324, 329–30, 348, 353, 354

kind(ness), 65, 94, 112, 163–64, 212, 315

King/king(ship), 17, 22–26, 30, 38, 64–66, 72, 88n22, 89n24, 92–93, 95n2, 100, 102, 112, 114, 202n5, 240, 280, 288, 305, 307
   God/Jesus as King/Kingship, 21, 48, 65–66, 117, 124, 196, 221, 237–40, 245n24, 246, 299, 305, 337, 342, 345

kingdom, *passim* (155x, xvii)
   of God/or Jesus, xvii, 1, 24, 35, 50n42, 55, 60–61, 62n3, 65–71, 75, 102, 116–20, 122–23, 129–35, 137–39n32, 145, 149, 153, 159, 166–67, 169, 178, 184, 192n42, 199, 215, 221, 231, 238n6, 240–41, 245, 250, 260, 280–82, 297, 299, 304–05, 308–09, 328, 332
   of heaven, 56n58, 172
   of this world/or Satan's, 35n55, 120–21, 133, 166, 178

knowledge of God, 8n31, 90, 114n30, 153, 168

land, vii, 3n11, 9, 23, 38, 40–49n36, 54, 59–72, 80, 97, 99, 101–02, 112–13, 127, 174n2, 201, 214, 227, 230, 239, 294, 306–08, 330, 332, 334, 337, 339, 342, 353

laughter, 206, 279n55

Law/law, 24–25, 45, 51n45, 56, 58, 70n25, 98, 101, 111n26, 112–14, 136, 150, 165, 206, 229, 242, 254, 301, 335, 339, 353

Leviathan, 19, 21, 33, 87, 110, 332

liberate(d)(ion), xii, 20n16, 26, 35, 74, 117, 151, 156n15, 169, 177, 199n1, 229, 334, 337, 343, 346

lie(s)/lying, 81n9, 85, 90, 92, 94–95, 97, 155n14, 174, 176–77, 248, 267, 270, 274–75, 277, 302, 324, 346

light (excludes "in light of"), 19, 25, 53, 57, 65n12, 74n45, 83, 98, 141, 149, 165, 167n52, 174–77, 183, 186n30, 189n37, 190, 196, 219, 222, 225n26, 230, 232, 275, 277, 315–16, 322, 340, 348–49

liturgy(ical)(ies), 39n6, 72n37, 91n27, 219, 224n24, 225n26, 232, 234, 238n9, 239, 269, 273, 275n36, 288n17, 311, 326, 332

Lordship, viii, xvii, 10, 35, 114n30, 141, 158, 170, 236–258 chapter, 281, 298

Lord's Prayer, ix, xvii, 29, 31, 36, 52, 92, 129–30, 134, 135n14, 170, 177, 198, 205, 225, 281, 326, 330

love(d)(ing), vii, xvi, 8, 11nn38–39, 12, 15, 19, 21, 33n51, 36, 38n2, 44n18, 48, 50, 52, 55, 66, 74nn44–45, 75–76, 83n14, 85n19, 132, 160, 163, 177–80, 183, 189n37, 199, 243, 258, 266, 271, 308, 314, 317, 331 (many above denote God's love)
   love command, 9, 165
   love of/for God/YHWH, 45, 51, 165, 314
   love one another (for neighbor), 9n35–10, 160, 165, 179, 234, 253, 313
   love(ing) of (the) enemy, 5, 37–39, 46–47, 76, 130, 163–65, 229

monster, 198, 110, 333

Magic(al)(ian[s]), 80, 87, 90, 98, 106–07, 142–45, 152, 168, 220, 224, 239, 262, 269, 290, 293n40, 298, 313, 319, 329, 331, 336

marry (ied)(iage), 49, 171, 252, 257, 271, 313, 322

martyr(s)(dom), 7n28, 115, 184, 185–86, 192, 194–95, 223, 230, 257, 293, 332, 334, 339
   martyria, 195

Mary Magdalene, 138

meek(ness), 62, 65–66, 81, 84, 337

SUBJECT INDEX

Mennonite, xix–xx, 2, 9n33, 98n37, 145, 146, 156, 216, 226, 243n22, 251, 253n44, 275, 284, 318n1, 344, 346, 350
Messiah (see Christology)
messianic, 24, 64–65, 67, 75, 79, 116, 122, 183, 201, 301, 349
metaphor(ically), 17, 29, 45, 56n62, 69–70, 121n54, 162–63, 167, 169–70, 176n7, 195, 200n3, 277, 289
military/militant, xi, 5, 38–39, 41, 43, 49n36, 74–75, 82, 99, 102, 107, 113–14, 122, 124, 139, 162, 165–67, 186, 190, 195, 202n5, 228–30, 232n54, 238, 253, 254n50, 261, 281, 338, 341, 350
mimesis/mimetic, 294, 295n5, 296
miracle(s)(ous), 11n40, 21, 37–38, 40, 42, 44n21, 46, 122, 128, 132, 134, 136n18, 138n26, 142, 144, 172, 174, 202n5, 253, 256, 274, 279, 281, 287, 288n17, 291–92n29, 307, 339, 348
mission, 1, 10–11, 29, 32n49, 34, 38n3, 39n5, 45n22, 53n50, 54n52, 64, 137–41, 144–45, 180, 180n16, 189n37, 222, 233, 236, 240, 242n17, 243–45, 250, 255, 261, 277n45, 293–97, 300, 305, 337, 342, 344, 348–53
moral/immoral(ly)(ity), xii, xvii, 6n19, 8, 11–12, 17–19, 27, 29n44, 31, 33n51, 34, 38, 41n11, 45n22, 49, 54n52, 55–58, 65, 69, 71n33, 94–97, 110, 113, 131, 157n15, 163n39, 172, 177, 180, 185, 187n33, 189, 203, 210–12, 214, 221, 231, 242, 249–51, 253, 254n49, 262, 267, 283, 293, 295, 301, 307, 323, 333–34, 243–44, 349, 351
Moses, 25n26, 34, 44n18, 61, 64, 115, 171, 180, 214–15, 397
mountain(s), 22, 51, 123, 125, 136, 136n20, 137, 277, 352
murder(er), 17, 61n2, 75, 77, 81n9, 84, 90, 100, 146–47, 206–07, 239n10, 295n45, 306, 330

mutual aid, 230–31nn51–52, 350

name of Jesus, v, 1, 3, 82, 125, 128, 131, 143, 146, 228, 230–34, 263–71, 279, 292, 299, 312–15, 326, 351
nation(s), xvii, 1, 8, 17–18, 21–26, 37–40, 42n14–44nn18,20, 45n22, 47–54n52, 61–63, 68, 71n34–72, 74, 81, 85n18–88, 95, 98–101, 106–07, 110–16, 119–20n48, 122–24, 135n15, 144, 188–90, 193, 196–97, 216, 237–41n13, 247–51, 253–56n56, 284, 295, 300–03, 306–08, 331, 334, 337–41, 344, 350, 352–54
Nero, 185, 281
new creation, 7n29, 36, 48, 59, 170, 183, 190, 196, 230, 232, 295, 299, 308, 329, 337–38
nonresistance, 4, 10, 161–62, 207, 230, 346, 352
nonretaliation, 164, 209n16, 212, 334, 340, 346–47, 350, 353
nonviolence, 42n12, 49, 77n57, 152n9, 156n15, 166, 195, 229–31, 253–54n52, 332, 335, 347, 354
nuclear(war)(age), 216, 242n16, 247, 249–50n39, 258, 329, 340, 344

obedience(ient)/disobedience(ient), 18, 23n18, 26–27, 30, 42, 44n20, 58, 61, 65, 102, 130n7, 131, 158, 161n29, 168, 172, 183, 192, 234, 243, 246–47, 250, 297, 305–06
occult(ism), 270, 272, 278, 298, 319, 321–23, 325, 330
oppress(or)(ed)(es)(ion)(ing)(ive), 1, 3, 5, 12, 26, 30, 47, 66, 69, 72, 80–81, 85, 88–90, 94, 97, 99, 102, 107n9, 110, 115, 119n46, 120, 123–25, 133, 137, 139–44, 149, 151, 156n15, 158, 166, 169, 188–89, 221–22, 229, 234, 256, 258, 260–02, 265–72, 281, 283, 286, 290, 294, 297–99, 311–13
outsider(s), 47, 56, 102, 233, 301

pacifist(m), 46n27, 165n46, 229,
    243n22, 335, 354
pagan(ism), 25, 44, 58, 74, 106--12,
    114–16, 143 , 150–52, 187n35,
    219–20, 222–23, 229, 232, 262,
    327
parable(s)(olic), 30–31, 35, 68,
    73–74n45, 121, 134–35, 174,
    332, 334
passion (Jesus'), 35n55, 67, 118n42, 281,
    305, 344
patience(ient), xv, 7n28, 10, 116, 171,
    189, 192, 195, 222n14, 223n18,
    232n55, 233nn57–60, 273n31,
    326, 341
Pax Romana, 161–62, 230, 245, 249, 352
peace(able)(makers)(ful), xi–xiii, xvii,
    xx, 1–3, 7n29, 8, 11, 19n13,
    34, 39–42n12, 49–52, 68–69,
    74–78, 82–83, 90–94, 98, 107,
    116n34, 122–24, 129n4, 137–41,
    148–50, 152n9, 161–70, 175,
    178, 182–83, 188, 192n44,
    195–96, 201–03, 208–10, 216,
    229–33, 241–244n22, 249n34,
    250–58, 284, 294–96, 300–05,
    308, 311–17, 322–27, *passim* in
    Bibliography
persecute(s)(ed)(ing)(or)(ion), vi,
    10, 32, 73, 81, 83n14, 90, 139,
    141, 153, 156n15, 158, 162,
    164–65, 174–75, 178, 181–82,
    188–89n38, 195, 204, 210,
    221–23, 228, 253, 268, 282, 301,
    303–05, 307
Pilate, 27n29, 75, 153, 207, 246, 305
plague(s), 34, 36, 112n27, 132, 185, 307
police(man), 152n9, 244n22, 256,
    266n12
politics(cal)/sociopolitical, ix, xvii,
    2–5n15, 6, 31–32, 44n19, 46,
    49n36, 52n49, 54n52, 55n57,
    65, 68, 75, 76n54, 83–85,
    109, 113–15, 119–24, 129,
    141–44, 152n9, 154–62, 174n2,
    183, 185–186n30, 188–92,
    196–97n55, 202n5, 211, 221,
    237n5, 241–57, 261–65, 268,
    273n30, 279n56, 280–81, 284,
    286–88n17, 290, 293–94,
    297–99, 305–07, 327, 330–54
power(s)/Powers, *passim*
praise(s)(ed)(ing), iv, vi, 10, 25n26,
    43n16, 48, 50–52n49, 53, 66,
    72–73, 82–86, 89, 91, 96, 102,
    127, 137, 162, 187n32, 188,
    192n43, 193, 196–97, 203, 210,
    215, 223, 228, 230–31, 234, 256,
    262–65, 268, 270, 290, 293, 299,
    311–13, 320, 325, 333, 346
Pray(ed)(er[s])(ing), v, vi, viii, ix, xvii,
    1, 4–5n15, 6, 10–11, 17, 24–26,
    29, 31, 36, 48, 51–53, 73, 80,
    92, 107, 122–25, 129–31,
    134–35n14, 137–40, 145–46,
    155n13, 162, 167, 170, 177,
    181–82, 193, 198, 205, 208, 210,
    222–23, 225–30, 233–24, 250,
    253, 256–58, 262, 265, 268–70,
    273–76, 278–82, 285–89n21,
    292n38, 298–303, 309, 311–17,
    322, 326, 330, 333, 335–38,
    342–45, 348, 351–55
principalities and powers/rulers and
    authorities (NRSV), 9, 33, 44,
    120, 148, 152, 157–58, 165, 179,
    185, 199, 205n7, 211, 231, 235,
    249–51, 255 , 284, 289, 291,
    304, 329, 334–45, 347 / 148,
    153, 157–58, 179, 172, 205n7,
    240–41, 245, 284n9
prophet(s)(ic), vii, 8n31, 9, 18, 20, 23,
    26, 28, 32n49, 34, 42n14, 43–52,
    60–61, 64, 72, 78–79, 92, 97–99,
    101, 112, 114–15,123–25, 132,
    144, 166, 188, 190–92, 195–96,
    202, 213, 225, 237, 248–53, 261,
    280–82, 285–86, 296, 301–03,
    307, 332, 338, 351
protect(ed)(ion), v, xvi, 2, 4, 8–10,
    24–25n26, 31, 36, 44n18, 46,
    52–58, 72, 76n54, 78–81n9,
    82–83n14, 86, 88n22, 90–96,
    99, 102, 113, 121, 130–31,
    163, 166–69, 173–74, 177,
    179, 181–82, 200n3, 215, 224,

SUBJECT INDEX

230, 234, 238n8, 241, 254, 262, 267–68, 278n53, 279, 282, 285, 287, 289n21, 300, 306–07, 312–13, 317
purity(s)(pure)/purify(ication), 24n23, 52, 54n52, 166, 181, 202, 204, 206–07, 334

Qumran, 25, 66n14, 74n45, 75n50, 107, 119, 341

Rahab, 20, 33, 110, 202n5
ransom(ed), 193, 346
Rebel(s)/rebellion(ious), 23n18, 24, 27–28, 31–32, 69, 74, 94, 106–07, 112, 115, 154–55n10, 211, 215, 225, 239, 241, 244n22, 246, 332, 349
Redeem(ed)(er)/redemption, 20, 27n29, 36, 69, 99, 101, 115, 133, 149–50, 180n16, 196, 203, 212n21, 230, 244n22, 266, 288, 299, 345
Reconcile(d)(ing)(iation), 46n27, 56, 59, 76–77, 91–92, 105, 153, 158, 200n3, 242–44, 304, 331, 337, 352–53
reign(s)(ed), 35, 39, 65, 80, 102, 117, 137, 153, 165–66, 191–195, 199, 212n20, 237–38n6, 239, 241–42, 268, 299, 303, 327, 340, 352
relation(al)(ship/s), xii, 10, 16, 18nn10,12, 30, 38n2, 43, 45n22, 48, 50n42, 53n51, 54n52, 68n18, 69n20, 70–71, 74n45, 77, 79, 83, 90, 102, 109–10, 112, 116n36, 130, 144, 146, 154, 156n15, 158, 160–62, 164, 169, 182, 185, 189n37, 192, 205n7, 211, 234, 237, 238n7, 239n10, 242nn16,19, 245n25, 248–50, 256–63, 271, 274–75, 291, 294, 297n49, 306, 322, 327, 337, 343
rescue(d), 48, 84–86, 97, 172, 200n5, 257
resurrect(ion)(ing), xii, 4, 34–37, 39n5, 65, 67, 73, 76, 115, 120n49, 123, 125, 136, 138–39, 142, 154–56,

162, 171, 175, 176n7, 181, 183, 189n37, 190, 192n43, 193, 195, 199, 208, 211, 221–22, 232, 245–46, 282, 295, 297–98, 304, 305, 308, 311–13, 345
reveal(s)(ed)(ing)/revelation(al) (excludes book of Revelation), 2, 7, 24, 38, 41n11, 44n18, 46n27, 49, 57, 65, 74n43, 94, 114, 151, 176, 179, 196, 220n1, 238n6, 267, 274, 279, 295–96, 299, 337
revenge(ing)(ful), 4n11, 26, 254n52, 273n30, 340. See vengeance
revolution(ary)(ist), 115, 162, 195n52, 252, 256n55, 332, 335, 338, 346, 351
righteous(ness), vi, 16, 24–25, 50n41, 57, 71, 73, 81n9, 84–85, 87, 88–96, 99, 110, 112, 130, 135, 144, 160, 167, 169, 202n5, 206–11, 216, 239, 252, 263, 317
Rome(an), xi, 5n15, 29–30, 58, 65n12, 66, 75n46, 106, 119–20, 129n48, 141–44, 153, 157–62, 185, 187n35, 189–91, 196, 199, 203n6, 221–22, 228, 230–31, 235n63, 237, 245–46, 249n34, 293–97, 324, 338, 341, 343, 346, 348, 352
royal(ty), xii, 48, 52, 70n25, 72, 136–37, 183, 225, 354

Sabbath/sabbatical, 43, 46–47, 61, 140, 350
Sacrifice(s)(ial)(ed)(ing), 3, 8–9, 38, 49, 52–53, 58, 75, 92, 109, 111, 125, 150, 153, 187n35, 194n48, 199–200, 203, 220, 224, 235, 241n15, 296, 354
salvation(vific), v, vi, xii, 7–8n30, 11n38, 21, 24–26, 50–51, 56–58, 69–72, 82–84, 88, 102, 116, 118, 123, 133, 145, 148–51, 160–61n29, 167, 169, 174, 183–84, 197, 199n1, 202n5, 203, 213, 235, 246, 263, 268, 283n6, 287, 291, 296, 304, 306, 313, 320, 327, 339

save(d)(ing), vi, 16, 29, 38, 48, 50n42, 56–57, 72, 79, 81n9, 82, 84, 91–93, 101, 105, 114n30, 131, 134, 137, 149, 172–77, 199, 207–08, 254n51, 258, 263, 277, 282, 287, 306–07, 334
Samaritan, 8, 68, 74n45, 174n2, 324
Sanctify(ied)(ication), 60, 141, 181, 203, 308
Satan('s)(ic)(ism), 3–7, 11n40, 16n2, 24–37, 44n18, 52, 55–58, 65, 71, 74, 76, 83, 105, 107–12, 116–25, 127–41, 144, 148–56, 161–62, 166–77, 180–81, 184–92, 195–99n1, 201–07, 214–15, 222–30, 234–39n10, 241, 259–60, 263–64, 268n20, 271n25, 281, 283, 288–89, 291, 294–99, 304–08, 311–12, 320–21, 324, 325–31, 336, 339–40, 345–49, 352
   ha sa-tan, 16, 24, 27, 107
   Beelzebub(l), 121, 123, 133–34, 177
   Belial(r), 24–25, 116, 119, 149
   Mastema, 116
   Satanail, 23n18, 197n7
scandal(ize), 296, 298n50
scapegoat(ing), 7n29, 18, 203, 295–296
Scripture/scriptural, *passim*
Sea/sea, 19–21, 25n26, 35–36, 43, 44n21, 51, 82, 110, 117, 123, 132n10, 189, 194, 227, 256, 266, 268, 307, 344, 349, 351
separation, 44–45, 54, 56–57, 76, 113, 146, 154, 181–83, 199, 237, 248, 288, 324
Septuagint / LXX, 63, 108–09, 116n34, 119, 240 / 35, 40n9, 51n43, 63–64, 69n21, 73n40, 81n10, 102, 108nn16–17, 111, 119, 142n41, 177, 180, 210, 238
Sermon on the Mount, ix, 39, 75, 129, 130, 132, 303, 330, 339, 346
serpent, 17, 24, 27–28, 32n49, 34, 108n14, 184, 189, 191, 306
servant(hood), 8, 19n15, 23–24, 30, 37, 49, 74, 98, 108, 117, 124, 129n4, 141, 156n15, 160, 164–65, 171, 189n37, 225–26, 239, 242–44, 252, 261, 295n45, 331
shame(d)(ful)/ashamed, 81n9, 84, 88n22, 91, 164, 172, 202–03n6, 210–11, 272, 318, 344, 348
sick(ness), 11, 34, 72–73, 102, 123, 129, 132, 134, 137, 142, 144, 168, 207, 223n15, 261, 272, 279, 319, 353
   epileptic(s), 122–23, 129, 136
   paralytic(s), 122, 129
sin(s), 1n3, 11n40, 17–18n10, 21, 23n18, 27, 32, 35, 38, 41, 44, 50–51, 55–56n56, 57–59, 65, 79, 84, 89, 92–93, 96, 98, 101, 109, 112–15, 122, 130, 135–36, 141, 144, 145–51, 156n15, 161, 163, 166, 168, 172–, 175–79, 180–83, 196–207, 211–212n21, 214–15, 228, 230, 235, 244n23, 245, 250, 262–64, 267, 269, 272, 275–80, 287, 290n22, 299, 305–06n7, 311–12, 317, 319, 321–235, 333, 348
slave(s)(ry)(like)/enslave(d)(ment), 1, 4n11, 28, 35, 37, 46–47, 65–66, 134, 136, 143, 155n11, 165n46, 196, 198, 211, 214, 243, 250n38, 254n53, 273n30, 286, 209, 304, 307, 350
slaughter, 38, 46n27, 53, 136, 193–94, 206, 268, 296
Son of Man (see Christology)
sorcery (see also divination), 80–81n9, 112, 114, 142–45, 152, 222, 224, 332
   soothsaying(ers), 97, 112–14, 307
   medium(s), 112, 298
   wizards(ry), 112, 114, 262, 298n52
sovereign(ty), 24n22, 26–27, 64, 82, 98, 114, 116, 119, 122–25, 144, 158, 167, 186, 230, 238–43, 267, 281, 286–87, 305n5, 311
spirit(s) (good connotation), 5, 6, 15, 28, 106, 109, 118, 149, 167, 193, 195, 212, 248, 285, 287, 330, 331, 347

SUBJECT INDEX

spirit world, 2, 106, 143–44, 150, 152, 213, 222, 233, 237, 255, 260n1, 266n13, 282, 284–85, 288-89, 297, 304, 329, 336, 353

evil(unclean) spirit[s]), 2–3, 6n23, 9, 16, 18, 20, 24, 29–31, 33, 35n55, 80, 106–10n22, 115, 118–19, 121n54, 123–24, 132, 136, 138, 140, 142–43, 147, 155–56, 161n29, 167n50, 172, 191, 211–13, 220n1, 221, 223-27, 232, 243–44n22, 260, 268n20, 272, 277, 279, 281, 283, 285, 289n20, 294, 298n52, 311–15, 320–21, 323–25, 342

flesh vs. spirit, 35, 99

human spirit, 56, 72, 149, 207. See also Holy Spirit and spiritual

spiritual(ality)(ized), xii, 3n8, 5–7n28, 8n31, 29, 33, 44nn18,21, 58, 77, 95, 106, 119, 119n48, 128n2, 131–32, 141, 153–56, 165–70, 181, 191–92, 204–07, 220, 232, 255, 259, 261–62, 264, 273–75n36, 282–84, 287–89, 291, 294, 296, 316–21, 324, 331, 335–37, 340, 343, 345–46, 350–51, 353

strife, 80, 90, 221, 306

structure(s)(al)(d)
  literary, 67–68, 83, 89n24, 114, 157, 188, 331, 245
  political/societal/economic/ religious, xvii, 2–5, 9, 12, 17, 28, 75n46, 115, 119n48, 124, 143, 149, 150–51, 154–55, 159–61, 167, 188, 191–92n42, 199, 221, 230, 241, 253, 256, 261, 265, 267, 274, 281, 283, 285, 294, 298
  personal(theological/ethical), 275n36, 287, 298, 324

subordinate(d), 162, 323

suffer(ed)(ing), 7n28, 10–12, 21, 24, 35, 66, 73, 77, 80, 89, 94, 117n36, 124, 130n7, 139, 145, 152n9, 156n15, 159, 162, 171, 183, 189, 190, 192–94, 200, 203–04, 209–13, 223, 240–45, 258, 264, 266, 295n45, 296, 305, 318–19, 337, 351

Symbol(es)(ic)(ism)(ize), 21n17, 23, 26, 42–44, 69n20, 114, 119, 124, 163, 174, 191, 194–95, 238, 252, 265, 282, 286, 297, 299, 324, 345

temple, 5n15, 23, 26, 30, 43n16, 52–53, 58, 61–62, 65, 71n32, 73, 80, 99, 122, 124, 128–29, 176, 188, 191, 220, 238, 266, 277, 308, 339, 341, 343, 346, 348, 349

tempt(s)(ed)(ing)(er)/temptation, xvii, 5, 16n2, 27, 29, 54n54, 57-58, 65, 71, 92n29, 107, 117–18, 122, 124, 128–31, 139, 149n3, 152, 154, 163, 198, 200, 202–05, 207, 215, 217, 234, 248, 263, 280, 283, 285, 304, 328, 336

terror(ism)(ist), 9, 26, 40, 46n27, 81n9, 87, 97, 114, 139, 163–64, 185, 247, 255, 256, 299

thank(s)(ed)(ing)(ful)(sgiving), v, xv–xvi, 86, 89, 91, 145, 157–58, 189, 197, 263, 279n54, 288, 311, 313, 316–317

Torah, 44n20, 114, 301

tradition(s)(al), xii, 5n15, 8n31, 25n26, 39, 47, 49, 55, 57, 66, 76, 77, 120n49, 123, 136, 145, 158, 180, 194, 204–05, 210, 226–29, 237, 247, 250–52, 260n3, 262, 271, 285–87, 301, 329–31, 334, 337–39, 344, 348–49, 351–52

transform(ed)(ing)(ation), vii, 2, 3n10, 9, 26, 29, 41n11, 52, 54, 60–75, 116–17, 156n15, 159, 162, 166, 182, 203, 275nn36–37, 283–84, 293, 296, 306, 327n2, 331, 336, 342, 344, 352, 354

Trinity/itarian, 178, 190–91, 238n9, 331

triumph(al)(ant)(ed), 4, 10, 23, 34–35, 65–66, 73, 88, 110, 117, 120n51, 125, 148–150, 153, 157, 175, 183, 185, 187n32, 189–91, 193, 195–97, 202, 212, 215, 221, 225, 232, 235, 242n17, 245, 256, 259–60, 268, 292, 299, 305, 328, 335, 351 truth(ful)(ing), ix, xvii, 2, 31, 63, 92, 105, 132, 135n14, 147, 149, 166, 169, 171, 174–77, 182, 199, 204–05, 207, 221, 229, 233, 240–48, 251, 258, 259, 263–64, 267–68n20, 270, 275–78, 292, 296–98, 305, 317, 320–21, 323–24

Unity(unified), 26, 69, 71, 76n55, 168–69, 177, 181, 246, 293, 333

vengeance, 42n12, 85, 91, 115, 129n4, 163, 165, 306
victim(s), 3, 177,185, 199n1, 203, 243–44n22, 265, 274, 283, 295–97
violence(violent[ly]), xi–xii, 2–3, 7n30, 12n41, 16, 22, 41n11, 42n12, 43n16, 45–46nn22,27, 49, 51, 71n32, 75, 78, 83, 86, 99, 120n48, 129n4, 133, 139, 146, 162–63, 191, 196, 202n6, 216, 224, 229, 241n15, 243–44n22, 249, 253n48–54n52, 256–57, 262, 265–67, 269–70, 281, 294–96, 298, 306, 322, 330–31, 333–42, 345, 347, 348, 350, 353. See Non-Violence/nonviolent
virtue, 65–66, 169, 214–15, 221, 252

war, xi–xii, 2, 6n24, 8, 24–25, 27, 39n7, 40, 42, 44n19, 49, 52, 60, 107, 113–16nn34,36, 119nn44–45, 133, 139, 154n11, 162–63, 165, 167n50, 168, 170n64, 184, 186, 193, 195, 202n5, 216, 228–30, 239, 241n15, 243–44nn22–23, 246–53n44, 254nn50–51, 258, 276, 281, 294, 296, 302, 307, 326–32, 335, 338, 340, 344–45, 348, 350, 253, 354. See Holy War/ YHWH War
Watcher's myth, 57, 107

Way, 62, 67, 124n59, 143, 240, 317, 335, 337, 340–41, 350, 353
wholeness, 118, 126, 133, 136, 274, 277–78, 283, 290, 309, 311–13, 345, 348
wealth(y)/riches, 5, 66, 81–82, 97, 102, 113–14, 132, 171, 189, 194, 206–07, 239, 245, 257, 268, 294, 299, 307
wilderness, as abode of demons, 18, 108, 117–18, 128, 205; as time of testing or preparation, 21, 67, 107, 117–18, 128–29, 176, 205, 307
wisdom, 22, 53, 92–93, 96–97, 154, 194, 197, 204–05, 231, 245, 251–53, 268, 277, 334, 336–37
worship(ing)(ped), xi, 5n15, 6, 9–10, 17, 23, 26, 30, 34, 37–38, 42–46, 51–54n54, 58, 61, 70–73, 79, 82, 90–92, 96–97, 101–02, 107, 111–112n28, 113–15, 124, 129, 141n37, 150–52, 176, 184–86, 189–92, 194–97, 203, 212, 219–22, 224, 228–30, 232–35, 239–40n12, 248, 262, 268, 270n23, 273, 278, 287, 295, 300–01, 307, 337, 339, 341, 350, 352
wrath(ful), 4, 24n22, 26, 34, 35n26, 36, 50, 75, 102, 107, 151, 163–65, 188, 190, 195, 199n1, 204–05n7, 242, 347

YHWH(Yahweh), ix, 8, 2n4, 19n15, 20, 26, 35, 38n1, 40–49, 70, 106–07, 110, 112–17, 119, 132n10, 166n49, 229, 237–38, 240, 300–02, 307, 329, 334–45

Zeal(ous), 48, 73, 75n46, 211
Zealot, 75n46
Zion, 2n4, 43n16, 63, 87, 113, 115n31, 136, 238, 267, 338, 345
Zionism, 63n6, 71n34, 330, 348

Ancient Documents Index

ANCIENT NEAR EASTERN SOURCES

Amenomopet	92–93n30	Babylonian texts	108–9n19
ANE	101n23	Mesha Inscription	44n19

OLD TESTAMENT

Genesis

1–11	23n18
1–2	295n46, 305
1:1–2:4	19
1	20, 110, 306n7
1:2	19
1:7	20
2:7	183
3–4	306
3	24, 32, 32n49, 307
4–11	19n15
4	295n46
6	32n49
6:1–4	107
6:5–7	306
6:5	17
8:11–13	306
9:8–16	61n1
12:1–3	9, 38, 61, 64, 306
12:3	45n22, 50
15:1–6	202n5
16	49
17:4–8	64
20:2–6	26
21:22–34	8
22	204
26:17–33	91n28
37–50	306–7
50:20	27n29

Exodus

	39, 307
6:2–4	107n9
12:24	107
14–15	38
14:14	37, 40–41, 41n10, 46, 124, 301
15	40, 40n9
15:3	40, 116n34
19:5–6	61
20:1–3	98
20:4	41
20:5–6	262n6, 270
20:13	61n2
22:19	45
23:20–24:1	40
23:20–30	46
23:20	67
34:6–7	38

Exodus (continued)

34:6	48
34:34	48

Leviticus

16:8	108
16:10	18
17:7	108, 219n1
18:8	58n67
27:28–29	51n43
27:28	45
24:29	45
27:21–29	43

Numbers

3:5	17
3:7	17
16:41–50	112n27
21:6	108
25	107
25:1–13	112n27
27:20–21	45

Deuteronomy

	16n1, 39, 44n20, 46n28, 47, 61, 69n20, 112, 301
1:8	67
2:1–3:22	68
4:1	67
4:10	96
5–6	68
5:9	321
5:29	96
6:2	96
6:4–5	38, 59, 307
6:4	45, 305
6:13	96
6:16	92n29, 205n8
6:18	67
6:24	96
7	68
7:1–6	40
7:26	51n43
8:15	108
9:1–10:11	68
9:10	133
10:12	96
10:20	96
13:5	17n9
13:17	51n43
14:23	96
16:20	67
17:7	17n9
17:12	17n9
17:19	96
18:9–22	114
18:9–15	152, 325
18:10–11	115
18:11	319
18:15–18	115
19:13	17n9
19:19	17n9
20	68
20:1–4	40
20:10–18	41
21:9	17n9
21:15–22:4	69
22:21–22	17n9
21:21	17n9
22:22	17
22:24	17n9
23:2	262n6
24:6–25:3	69
24:7	17n9
27:9–26	270
27:20	58n67
28	321
31:12–13	96
32:17	102, 109, 111, 150, 219n1
32:21	23n20
33:2–3	119n45

Joshua

	39, 300–301
5	47
5:13–15	37
6–7	42
6:3–14	42

6:17–18	51n43	22:23	107
7:11–26	51n43		
7:21–26	42	## 2 Kings	
8:1	42		
8:18	42	6:8–23	92n28
8:27	42	17:15	23n20
24:12–13	42	20:1–6	288
24:12	47, 70	21:5–9	112
		21:9	17
## Judges		21:12	17
		21:15–16	17
	300–301	23:24–25	112
1.11	45	23:8	108
2.11–18	112n27		
9.23	18, 107	## 1 Chronicles	
			205n7
## Ruth		21:1	24, 107–8, 180, 204
	1		
		## 2 Chronicles	
## 1 Samuel			205n7
11:19	93	7:19–22	61
15:19	18	11:15	108, 219n1
16:14–23	18		
16:14	107	## Ezra	
18:10	18		61
19:20	18	10:8	45
24:1	24		
		## Nehemiah	
## 2 Samuel			61
7:13–14	60–61, 65		
7:29	61	## Esther	
11:7	302		
12:1	280	7:4	180
12:9	17	8:1	180
21:1–8	112n27		
24:1	107, 204–5	## Job	
			57, 204
## 1 Kings		1–2	24, 108
1:13	23n20	1:6	24
3:9	17	1:7	180
7:29	65	2:1	24
9:4–9	61		
16:26	23n20		

Job (continued)

3	24
14:4	21
38–41	21
38–39	21
38:4	21
40:3–5	21
40:15	21
41	21
41:1	21, 110

Psalms

	16n1, 79n5
1–41	80n8
2:7	225
3	72, 80
3:6	81
3:7–8	80–81
5–6	81n9
5	72, 80
5:1–20	119
5:6	90
5:8	90
5:10	72n37
6:8	81n9, 90
6:10	81n9, 91
7	80, 81n9
7:6	72
7:9	91
7:10	15, 90
7:11–13	91
7:14	90
7:15–16	91
7:17	91
8:1	91
8:2	81, 90
8:3–8	91
8:27–10:52	66
9	81n10, 86–87
9:3	91
9:5–6	119
9:5	91
9:6	91
9:7–8	91
9:9	90
9:11–12	91
9:15–20	91
9:15–17	91
10	81
10:2	90
10:3–4	90
10:4	90
10:5–6	90
10:7	90
10:9	90
10:13	90
10:15	80, 91
11:5	15–16, 85n19, 90
11:6	91
11–13	89
12	72, 80
12:2	90
14	87–88
14:4–6	90
14:4	79n4, 90
14:5	90
14:7	90
15–16	89n23
15:28	96
17:17–18	18
18	72, 80, 18, 82, 82nn11–12, 324
18:1–3	vi, 81n9, 90, 92, 263
18:4–15	35
18:15	91n26, 117n41, 119
18:16–19	90
18:20–24	91
18:27–33	91
18:35	90
18:43	90
18:46	102
18:46–50	91
20	238, 238n8
20:7	281
21	88n22
21:8–12	91
22	72, 73, 73n40, 80, 82–83
22:1–3	91n27
22:1	73
22:3	91
22:8–21	91

22:16	73	41–43	91
22:19	73	41:9	177
22:22–31	91	41:10	80
23	83	42–72	80n8
23:4–6	91	42–43	89n24
23:4	16	42:6	73n41
23:6	50	42:12	73n41
24	43n16	43:5	73n41
24:7–10	238n6	44	88n22, 91
24:8–10	238	44:3–6	281
25	72, 83, 83n13	44:23–26	90
26–28	89n23	44:23–25	72
26–27	83, 83n14, 91	45	89n24
27:3	16	46:7	238n6
28:31	119	46:9	238n8
30:5	50	46:9–10	281
31	73, 73n40, 83n14	46:11	238n6, 238n8
31:1–3	90	48	238
31:5	73	50	84
31:6	23n20	50:1–6	238n8
31:8	73	50:19–21	91
31:14–18	90	51	84, 84n17, 92
31:15	73	52:3–5	84n18
31:19–24	91	53	87–88
32	89	53:4	79n4, 90
33:6	110	53:6	90
33:16–17	281	54	89n24
34–36	91	54:5	91
34	80, 83–84, 84n16	54:7	72n37, 91
34:12–16	210	55	72, 95n31
34:13–14	78	55:16	72n37
34:13	16, 90	56	85, 91
34:14	16, 92, 250, 302	56:6	90
34:21	16	57:10	38
35	73, 84n15	58	72, 72n37, 73n38
35:10	90	59	80, 88
35:20	90, 92, 302	59:1	79n4
35:26	91	59:4–7	91
35:27–28	91	61–62	85n18, 91
36	89n24	64	85
36:12	91	64:7–8	91
37	62, 66n14, 84, 91	65:6	117n41
37:3–6	202n5	66	91
37:27	92, 302	66–67	85n18
37:37	92, 302	67:7	50
40	84, 238n8	68	72, 80, 87
40:12–13	90	68:1–20	91
40:14–15	91	68:2	91

Psalms (continued)

68:21	91
69	72–73, 73n40, 89n24
69:4	73
69:9	73
69:13	73, 90
69:18	73, 90
69:22–28	91
70	89n24
70:2	91
70:5	90
71	72, 85
71:22	48
72:18–19	102
72:20	80n8
74	43n16, 63n5, 87, 91
74:12–17	21, 117n41
74:14	110
76	238n8
76:3	281
76:6	86, 117n41, 119
78	307
78:41	48
78:57–58	90
79	63n5
80	63n5, 238
80:3	238
80:4	238n6
80:7	238, 238n6
80:14	238, 238n6
80:16	119
80:19	238, 238n6
82	72, 238
82:1–2	110
83	72n37, 73n38
84	238
84:1	238n6
84:3	238n6
87:4	110
88	73n38
89	72
89:5–18	110
89:5–10	119n45
89:8–18	238
89:8	238n6
89:14	110
89:18	48
91	91
91:3	92
91:5–6	92
91:6	108
91:10	92
92	89, 91
92:7–9	91
93	43n16
94	85, 252
94:1–2	91
94:4–7	90
94:4–6	90
94:6	90
94:16–19	91
94:20–23	92
94:20–21	90
94:23	91
94:24	91
96:5	102, 111
96:9	52n47
97	85n19, 91
97:3	91
97:10	16, 91
98:1–3	50
99:5	52
99:8	42n12
99:9	52
104:7	35, 117n41, 119
106:26	110
106:36–39	90
106:36–38	150
106:36–37	152
106:37	92, 109, 111, 219n1
106:47	92
108:4	38
109	72n37, 85–86
109:2	90
109:5	92, 302
109:6	180
109:21–31	91
109:22	90
109:31	90
110:1	158, 73n41
111:10	96
115:3–8	111

116	89–91	10:22	97
118	73, 73n42, 88, 91	11:19	94
118:3–4	50	11:27–28	93
118:5–18	80	11:27	94
118:5–8	72	12:2	16
118:10–12	91	12:13	16–17, 93, 303
118:22	73	12:19–20	97
118:25–26	73	12:20–22	93, 303
119:63	96	12:20	16, 78
119:72–74	96	14:16	97
119:79	96	14:19	97
119:118–20	96	14:31–32	94
119:133	25	14:31	252
120	302	14:34	252
121:5–6	309	15:3	97
121:7–8	90n25	15:33	66n14
125	90, 92, 302	16:4	27n29
135:15–18	111	16:6	16
136	38	16:12	16
136:1–26	50	16:17	16, 97
137	63n5, 72n38	16:27	16
137:9	91	16:30	16
138:2	38	17	94
140–41	86	17:14	94
140:1–2	78	19:9	96
140:10–11	91	20:8	95n32
141–142	90	20:26	95n32
141	91	22:2	97
143–44	86n20	22:17–23:11	92–93n30
143:12	91	22:22–23	97
147:10	281	22:23	92–93n30, 96
148:2	238, 238n6	22:26–27	92–93n30
		24	95
		24:21–22	95
		25:14	96
		25:21–22	86
		28:5	95
		28:10	95
		30:15	108–9n19
		33:8	96
		33:18	96

Proverbs

	16n1
1:7	93
1:21	17
2:6	205
2:12–14	93
3:6	202n5
6:14	17
6:16–19	95
8:13–31	251–52
8:13	92–93
8:18–21	97
8:22–31	205

Ecclesiastes

1–2	16
8:11	17

Song of Songs

1

Isaiah

	50, 280
1–5	61
1	302
1:16–17	97, 303
1:18	98
2	114n30
2:1–22	113–14
2:1–8	97
2:1–5	303, 308
2:1–4	26, 26n27, 114, 301
2:6–22	229
2:6–20	114
2:6–8	239
2:6	114
2:12	239
2:18–21	98
3:2–3	98
3:8–9	98
3:9	97, 303
3:21—4:25	202n5
5:6–20	307
5:7	97
5:16	238n6
5:20	97–98, 303
6:1–8	96, 238
6:1–5	50
6:2–7	108n15
6:3	238nm6–7
6:5	238n6
6:6–11	50
6:8	48
6:9–13	98
7–10	302
7:1–14	202n5
7:9	167
8:8	48
9:1–7	303
9:6–7	308
10:5–27	74
10:5	238
10:12–23:18	303
10:17	48
10:36	308
11:1–10	303, 308
11:3–5	97
11:4	167
11:5	167
12:2–6	102
13–27	190
13–24	237
13–19	98
13:11	99, 303
13:17–19	98
13:19–22	18
13:21	108, 219n1
14	110
14:3–23	238
14:12–15	21, 153
14:12	110
14:13–15	22, 22–23n18
14:24–27	238
14:29	108
18:7	48
23–24	99
24:3	48
24:23	238n6
25:6	48n35
27:1	21n17, 110
30:6	108
30:15–16	202n5
30:15	124
31:1–3	99, 202n5, 281
31:4	238n6
32:7	97
32:14	219n1
33:15	99
33:20	99
34–35	190
34:14	108
35	308
40–66	303
40–55	98, 308
40:2	238
40:25–26	48
40:28	48
41:10	96
42–53	8, 98
42:1–2	225
43:3	67
43:15	48
43:28	43, 45, 74

44:9–22	111
44:9–20	111
44:28–45:1	74
44:46–47	111
45:7	16, 18, 27
45:11	48
45:22–23	282
47:8–10	114
47:9–15	325
47:10–15	112
49:2	167, 195
50:6	117n41
50:21	43
51:9–11	20
51:9–10	117n41
51:9	110
52	295
52:7–53:12	303
52:7–10	48n35, 51
52:7	137, 167, 170, 301, 303
52:10	301
52:13—53:12	301
55:3–4	63–64
53:4	132
54:10	98, 303, 308
56–66	98
55:6–7	26n27
55:9–10	48n35
57:3–10	112
58:6–9	97
58:6	139
59:7–15	303
59:17	167
61:1–62:12	303
61:1–2	139
61:1	325
61:8	97
63:10	45, 74
64	303
65:3	111n25
65:17–25	303
65:17–19	48n35
66:10–22	303

Jeremiah

	9n34, 18n11, 50
1:8	101
2:5	23n20
2:8	23n20
2:13	99
3:5	99
4:6	100
4:22	78, 100
6:1	100
7:1–15	61
7:4–11	99–100
7:20	101
7:23–24	100, 100
9:3	78
10:3	23n20
10:8	23n20
10:15	23n20
11:8	100
11:17	100
13:10	100
13:23	100
14	18n11
15:20–21	101
16:10–13	101
16:19	23n20
17:1	17
17:9	17
18:1–17	112n27
18:7–12	101
18:19–23	99
20:7–18	99
20:13	102
21:4–6	74
21:10	100
22:3	100
23	100
25:9	74
26:1–6	61
26:3	100
27	18n11
27:6	74
27:22	63n5
29:7–11	303
29:7	48
29:10–11	63n5
29:11	1, 1n1, 18

Jeremiah (continued)

30–31	18n11
30:3	63n5
31:3	61, 308
31:30	262n6
31:31–34	65, 201, 303, 308
32:30	100
33–34	18n11
36:3	100
37–52	102
39:16	100
43	18n11
43:17	102
46	18n11
46–51	190, 237
48:2	102
49:33	18
50	18n11, 48
50:26	43
50:39	18
51:3	43
51:5	48
51:18	23n20
52:2	102

Lamentations

	63n5
3:37–38	27n29

Ezekiel

	50
3:1–3	xviii
6–7	114n30
16	114n30
18	262n6
18:2–3	262n6
18:20	262n6
23:23	115
25–32	190, 237
28	110
28:11–19	44n18
28:13–19	22, 22–23n18
28:13	110
34:25–31	98
34:25–26	308
34:25	308
36–37	61
37	63n5
37:26–28	98, 308
37:26	308
39:23–25	63n5
40–48	26n27, 61, 308

Daniel

7:13–14	240
8:10	238
7:22	282
7:27	240, 282
9:3–19	319

Hosea

	50
1–3	50
1	61
1:10–11	61
3:1–5	61
4–5	97n35
4:13	115
6:8	97n35
7:15	97n35
8–10	97n35
8:1	61
9:15	97n35
11:9	48, 52, 96
13	97n35
14:3	114n30

Joel

16n1

Amos

2:6–7	66n14
2:6	74
2:7	307
3:6	27n29
5:20	74
8:2	74
5:14–15	307
5:21–25	307

Obadiah

1

Jonah

2:8	23n20

Micah

4:1–7	26n27
4:1–5	26

Nahum

1:15	308

Habakkuk

1	51
2.14	51
3:13	48

Zephaniah

3:1–13	66n14

Haggai

1

Zechariah

	74, 74n45
1:16	26n27
3	24, 24n23, 108, 117
3:1–2	24
3:2	119
4:9–10	26n27
9:9–10	122, 124
14:3–5	119n45
14:11	51n43
6:12	26n27
6:15	26n27
11–14	308

Malachi

	62
2:5	308
3:1–4	26n27
3:1	67

APOCRYPHA

Tobit

13	26n27
14:5	26n27

Wisdom

2:23–24	200n2
2:24	24
7:24–27	205
9:4	205
9:6	205
9:9–18	205
12–15	111n26
14:15–16	111n26

Sirach

1:1–4	205
2:4–5	66n14
3:17–20	66n14
4:1–10	66n14
5:6	50
7:11	66n14
12:7	66n14
16:11	50
24:12	205
36:2–3	26
36:7	26
36:11–14	26n27
50	26n27
51:12	50
51:14	50

Baruch

4:7	111
4:35	111

PSEUDEPIGRAPHA

2 Esdras (here = 4 Ezra)

7:28	24
7:36–44	24
7:79	24
7:80–87	25

Apocalypse of Moses

15–17	180

Apocalypse of Zephaniah

4:2–7	180
10:1–5	180

1 Enoch

	34n53
1–36	57
6:1–7:9	107n9
6	107n7
6:7	108n18
8	107n8
9:16	108n18
10:46	108n18
12:5	107
13:1	107
15	107n9
15:8–15	107n9
16:4	107
20:7	108n15
30:8	108n15
40:7	180
60:11–24	106n5
63	101n22
67	101n22
69	107nn7–8
82:7–20	106n5
90:29–30	26n27
94:6–104:13	66n14

2 Enoch

	34n53
29:4–5	23n18, 107n7
31:30–36	107n7
40:7	107n10

4 Ezra (see 2 Esdras)

	25n24

Jubilees

	16n2, 23n18
1:20	24n26, 180
2:2	106n5
4:15	107n8
10:1–6	24n26
11:2–7	107n9
11:5	180
12:20	24n26
12:28	24n26
15:31–32	106n6
48:15	180
48:18	180

Life of Adam and Eve

	16n2
9–17	180
12–17	107n7

Sibylline Oracles

3:702–808	26n27

Testament of Benjamin

9:2	26n27

Testament of Dan 5:10

Testament of Job 16n2

Testament of Levi

18:9	24

Psalms of Solomon

17	26n27

NEW TESTAMENT

Matthew

	9, 9n33, 31n46, 34–35, 41n11, 53, 55n56, 121, 121n53, 158, 293
1:5	301
1:23	70
1:27	128n2
2	245n24
2:5–6	70
3:17	66
4:1–11	263
4:1	128
4:3–10	128–29, 129n4
4:5–6	92n29
4:7	205n8
4:8–10	152
4:8–9	121n54
4:9–10	71
4:9	136
4:10	128
4:15–16	70
4:23–25	129
4:23–24	136
4:24	261
5–7	30, 129, 129n4
5	303
5:1–8:1	130
5:5	62, 65
5:9	75–76
5:11	30
5:13	xvii
5:20–48	71
5:21–26	75
5:37	31
5:38–48	162
5:38–42	75
5:38	39
5:39–42	8
5:39	31, 36n58, 76, 76n54, 161
5:43–48	75
5:44–45	vi
5:44	5n15, 39, 75, 162, 179n13, 266, 301
5:45	31, 46, 76, 132, 136
6:9–13	29, 130–32, 280
6:9	52
6:13	7n25, 31, 225
6:22	30n45
6:23	30
6:25–34	202n5
6:27	75
7:11	30
7:17–18	31
7:21–23	131
8–9	132
8:1–14	136
8:5–13	202n5
8:16	261
8:22	132
8:26	132n10
8:28–34	136
9:9	132
9:23–31	136
9:32–35	134
9:32	128
10:1–8	132
10:1	138n28, 261, 324
10:7–11	138n28
10:8	261
10:36	74
11:2–6	138
11:25–27	65
11:28–30	66
11:29	65, 65n11
12:3	8
12:9–14	136
12:22–32	133

Matthew (continued)

12:22–30	74
12:22	128
12:29	134
12:35	30
12:39	30
12:41	31
12:45	30
12:49	30–31
13	134–35
13:19	31
13:28	74
13:30	135n14
12:43	18
13:28	74
13:38	31, 131
13:39	74
13:49	135n15
15:4	135n15
15:19	30
15:21–28	135–36
15:21	136n16
15:28	261
16:4	135n15
16:13–19	324
16:13	124
16:16–18	136
16:18–20	124
16:18–19	55
16:19	136n19
16:23	180
17:5	66
17:14–21	136
17:14–20	137
17:17–18	261
18	54, 55–56n58
18:4	66
18:15–18	55, 55n55, 135
18:15–16	56
18:32	30
20:24–28	66
20:29–34	137
21:5	65n11
21:16	81
21:33–22:14	135n15
22:24	136
22:33–46	62
22:37–39	266
23	135n15
25:26	31
26–27	281
26:15	177
26:24	177
25:26–30	65
25:26	30
27:40	129
27:46	82, 124, 130n7
27:55	138
28:16	136n20
28:17–20	45n22, 62, 137
28:17	136
28:18–20	325
28:18	281, 282n3

Mark

	34–35, 31n46, 41n11, 54n53, 67n17, 121n53, 293
1:1–3	67
1:10–11	122
1:13	117–18, 117n40
1:14–15	245
1:14	128
1:15	70, 117–18
1:16–20	118
1:21–28	118, 122
1:23–27	117n40
1:23	31
1:27	122
1:39	31, 117n40
2:1–12	122
2:10	240
3:6	124
3:11–15	117n40
3:11–12	122
3:11	31
3:14–15	117n40, 122
3:15	31, 123
3:20–28	122
3:20–27	123
3:21–26	31
3:22–30	117n40

3:22–28	133	12:10–11	73
3:23–27	74	12:13–17	118n42, 124
3:27	134, 327	12:15	124
4:11–12	134	13:9–13	153
4:14	134	14–15	281
4:15	131	14:21	177
4:35–41	35, 117, 202n5	14:33–34	73n41
4:39	35	14:62	73n41, 240
4:41	122	15:34	73, 82, 124
5:1–20	117n40, 122–23		
5:8	31		
5:14	321		

Luke

9, 31n46, 34–35, 41n11, 51, 69n20, 121n53, 139n34, 141, 141nn38–39, 293

5:25–43	202n5		
6:6–13	138n28		
6:7	31, 117n40, 122		
6:13	31, 117n40, 122		
6:49–52	122		
7:22	30	1:8–10	133n13
7:24–30	117n40, 123, 135	1:30	96
7:26	136n16	1:71	74
8:1–21	123n58	1:74	74
8:11	124	2:11	140
8:11–13	118n42	2:14	122n57, 308
8:27–33	122	3:19	30
8:27–30	67, 122	3:29	133n13
8:31–33	117n40	4:1–13	139
8:31	68, 240	4:1	128
8:33	124, 180	4:3–12	128–29, 129n4
8:38	240	4:5–7	241
9:2–8	123	4:6–8	152
9:14–29	117n40, 122–24	4:6–7	71
9:31	68, 240	4:9–10	92n29
9:33–34	67	4:12	205n8
9:47	67	4:18–19	139–40, 140n35
10:2	118n42, 124	4:18	325
10:15	67	4:35	138n26
10:17	67, 67n16	6:17–19	138
10:23–25	67	6:18	261
10:30	67	6:22–45	30
10:32	67–68	6:22	30
10:33–34	240	6:27	46, 75
10:42	153	6:35	30, 46, 75
10:46	67	6:45	30
10:52	67	7:1–10	141, 202n5
11:9	73	7:18–23	138
11:20–25	202n5	7:21	30, 138
12	117n40, 124	8:1–3	138
12:1–12	62		

Luke (continued)

8:2	30, 138, 261
8:12	134
8:15	131
8:35	321
9:1	321, 324
9:42	261
9:51–19:46	61
9:51–19:44	68
9:51–56	8
10	139n32
10:1–20	138–39
10:1–18	138, 303–4, 308
10:4–16	68
10:5–6	139
10:17–19	74
10:17–18	139
10:18	7, 32n49
10:29–37	68
10:30–37	74n45
10:18–19	139
10:18	308, 327n3
10:17–19	321, 324
11:13	30
11:14–26	68, 292n32
11:14–23	133
11:14–21	74
11:21–22	134
11:24–26	264
11:29	30
11:34	30
11:49	30
12:1–3	153
12:36	133n13
13:1	75
13:11	133n13
13:10–17	138, 140
13:16	169n63
13:31–33	153
13:32	138, 261
14:15–35	68
15	69
16:19–18:8	69
17:3	56n60
19:22	30
19:27	74n43
19:38	123n57
19:41–42	74
19:44	74
20:9–19	62
22–23	281
22:2	177
22:3	177n9, 180
22:24	177n9
22:31–32	7, 24, 140
22:53	138
23:2	124
23:46	73
24:10	138n27
24:27	301–2
24:44	301–2

John

	9, 9n35, 34–35, 55n56, 80n14, 180, 189n37, 291n29, 293
1:1–18	185–86n30
1:2–4	176
1:3–4	183
1:9–12	176
1:11	173n2
1:12	202n5
1:14	70–71
1:29	194n48
1:32	261
1:36	194n48
1:39	261
1:51	185
2:11	176n7
2:17	73
3:12	205
3:13–14	185
3:14–21	202n5
3:15–16	183
3:16–17	176–77
3:16	178, 180, 183
3:19	31, 177
3:20	180
3:21	177
3:36	202n5
4	74n45, 173n2
4:22	173, 173n2

5	178	15:18	180
5:26–27	183	15:23–25	180
5:39–47	202n5	15:25	73
6:20	175	16:1	241
6:47	202n5	16:4–33	182
6:55	177	16:11	33, 121n54, 175, 178
6:70–71	177		
6:71	173	16:20	178
7	178	16:21	178
7:7	31	16:26–27	182
8–9	316	16:28	178
8	173, 178, 292	16:33	175, 178, 187, 304
8:31–59	173	17	317
8:32–46	177	17:3	183
8:32	290, 292	17:6–15	176
8:44	175, 263	17:6	178
8:52	177	17:9	178
10:10	70, 183	17:11–12	52
11:24–27	202n5	17:11	173, 178, 182
11:25–26	183	17:13–19	178
11:33–35	173	17:14–16	180
12:2–3	175	17:15–16	52
12:3	304–5	17:15	31, 173, 182
12:13	73	17:21	178, 182
12:23–24	173	17:23–24	177–78
12:27	175	17:23	178, 182
12:27–31	173	17:25	178
12:31–32	180	18–19	202n6, 281
12:31	10, 33, 35n55, 121n54, 173, 175, 196, 241, 292	18:33–37	305
		18:36	178
		18:37	246
13–17	181–82	19:9–11	305
13:2	180	19:11	246
13:18	177	19:15	305
13:27	173, 175, 177, 180	19:21–22	305
13:30	173	19:24	73
14:2	70	19:30	183, 191
14:6	67n16, 177, 183	19:40	173n2
14:17	178	20:1–18	138
14:19	178	20:19–21	183
14:22	178	20:19–23	182
14:27	178, 304	20:19	305
14:30–31	175, 178	20:21	183, 305
14:30	33, 121n54, 241, 305	20:22	295
		20:23	136
15:17–18	178	20:26	305
15:18–25	180n16	20:27	185
15:18–19	177		

Acts

	9, 29, 51, 121n53, 141nn38–39, 158, 293
1:8–10	53
1:8	62
2:22–36	65
2:22–24	27n29, 246
2:23–36	240
2:36	141, 154, 246
4:7–29	246
5:16	142, 261
5:27–32	246
5:29	30
8	144
8:7	261
8:8–24	142
10:34–39	142
10:36–38	123n57
10:36	141, 143n44, 240
10:38	140, 143n44, 261
12:1–2	153
13:4–12	143
13:9–12	291
13:10	74, 144
14:3	291
14:8–10	291
15:12	291
15:15–18	65
16:16–23	143
16:16–18	291
15	63–64
15:16	261, 325
15:17	63
17:5	31
17:18	142
17:22	142n41
18:14	31
19	144
19:11–16	142
19:11–12	291
19:12–13	31
19:13–40	143
19:13–15	291
19:16	31
19:19	31
20:9–12	291
22:3	62
22:25	246
24:14	62
24:25	246
25:19	142n41
26:10–11	62
26:18	141
28:7–9	291
28:21	31

Romans

	29, 32, 168, 290n23, 291n29, 293
1:3	65
1:14	160
1:16–18	34n53
1:18–32	151
2:9	32
3:10–11	88
4:13–16	64
4:13	62
4:16–17	62
5:1–11	168, 304
5:1	76
5:6–10	76
5:8–10	76
5:11	76–77
5:12	32
6:6–9	59
6:13–14	165
6:23	165
7:5–18	150
7:19	32
7:21	32
7:25–8:2	265
8:3–9	150
8:17–23	36
8:17	159
8:18–25	246
8:22	69
8:23–24	319–20
8:30–39	308
8:35–39	34n53, 154
8:37–39	199
8:38	288

9–11	62	5	57
9:3	51	5:1–3	55–56
10:1–17	202n5	5:5	4, 149
10:9	158	5:6–8	56
11	64	6:9–20	58
11:3–5	66n14	5:9–13	57
12–13	32, 162–63, 242	6:1–8	58
12	53, 159–60	6:1–5	58
12:1	52	6:4	153
12:2	161	6:19	52
12:9–13:10	164–65	7:5	149
12:14–17	210	8:4–6	150
12:17–21	170n64	8:5–6	158
12:18–21	95	10	263n10
12:18	164	10:6–13	150
12:21	76, 304	10:10	107, 149n3
13	33, 153, 205n7	10:14–22	150, 187n33, 263
13:1–7	153, 158–61, 164	10:14	58
13:1	155, 241	10:16–17	58
13:2	161	10:18	58
13:3–4	304	10:20–21	150
13:6	242	10:20	58
13:8–14	159–60	10:21	59
13:12	165	11:25	58
14:12–21	44n18	12:3	51, 158
14:20	31, 150, 170n64, 304	15:24–28	158, 282
		15:24–27	153
15:17	71	15:24–26	34n53, 65, 199, 242
15:18–19	291	15:24	200, 245
		15:26	168
		15:40	205
		15:55–56	200

1 Corinthians

1:18	56n62	16:22	51
1:20	205		

2 Corinthians

2:2	159
2:4–5	291
2:6–9	151	1:12	205
2:6–8	153, 281, 284	2:1–11	55–56
2:6	205	2:6–8	199
2:8	234, 304	2:8	121n54
3	53	2:11	149, 149n3, 263
3:1–4	95	2:14	157
3:9	62	4:3–6	263
3:17	52	4:4	33, 149n3, 241
3:22–23	62	4:7–12	159
5–7	55	5:1	205
5–6	53, 58, 58n67, 59		

2 Corinthians (continued)

5:17–20	59, 242, 304
5:17	35–36, 299
5:18–20	77
6:7	165
6:15	149n3
10:3–6	168, 170n64
10:3–4	165
10:6–11	59
11:14–15	263
11:14	149, 149n3
11:23–33	162
12:7–10	11n40
12:7	149, 149n3
12:12	291

Galatians

	71n33
1:4	151
1:8	51
3–4	202n5
3:1	159
3:6–9	64, 202n5
3:13	321, 324
3:14	64
4:3	150
4:8–9	150
4:21–31	64
5:9	56
5:16–23	150
5:16–18	150
5:24	150
6:1–2	56n60
6:2	229n43
6:8	150
6:16	64
6:17	159

Ephesians

	158, 168, 290n23, 293
1:3	70
1:7–8	70
1:7	149
1:9–10	158
1:10	246
1:18–22	154
1:18	70
1:19–23	153, 236, 242, 281
1:20–23	158
1:20–21	151
1:21	241
1:22	282
2:1–23	168
2:2	33, 121n54, 241
2:4–6	281
2:8–10	202n5
2:11–22	170, 304
2:13–17	169
2:14–18	52
2:14–17	59, 308
2:16	136
2:19–22	62
2:21	52
3:8–10	242, 244
3:9–11	281
3:9–10	154, 253n44
3:10	231, 242, 245, 324
3:17–19	153
4:1–5:20	167n52
4:1–6	253
4:21	263, 276
4:25–32	150
4:26–27	149, 281
4:26	149
4:31	32
5:16	31, 172
5:23	245n25
6	191
6:1–4	254n52
6:4–10	168
6:10–20	168
6:10–19	281
6:10–18	34n53, 36, 165–67, 165n44, 170, 177, 234, 281, 283, 296
6:10–17	304
6:10	44n21
6:11–12	153
6:11	154n10, 165
6:12–18	154
6:12–13	168

6:12	33, 240
6:13	31, 161, 165, 205
6:16	154n10, 169, 213
6:17	195
6:19	31

Philippians

2:5–11	141, 234, 324
2:9–11	35, 154, 241
3:9–10	202n5, 282
2:11	246
3:10	159
3:19	205
3:20	159
4:7–9	95

Colossians

	168
1:10	153
1:13–14	149
1:13	1, 282
1:14	223
1:15–20	156
1:15–16	153
1:18–20	34n53
1:19–20	158, 246
1:20	153
1:24	212
2	324
2:8–15	148n1
2:8	150, 304
2:9–15	324
2:10–15	35
2:10	240, 242, 245n25, 282
2:13–15	157
2:14–15	235n63
2:15	148, 153, 235, 242, 245
2:18–23	150
2:20–23	304
3:1–17	150
3:15	149

1 Thessalonians

2:18	149, 149n3
3:5	149n3
5:8	165
5:15	76

2 Thessalonians

3:3	170
2:3–11	158
2:8–9	34
2:9–10	56n62
2:9	263
1:5	291

1 Timothy

	170
1:19–20	171
1:20	56n62, 58, 170
2:1–4	153
2:1–2	253n48
3:16	64
4:1–2	172
4:2	171n66
5:14–15	171
5:15	170
5:20–21	172
6:9–12	171–72

2 Timothy

	170
1:14–19	171
2:23–26	171
2:26	170
3:1–9	171
4:1–5	301
4:17–18	172

Titus

1:10–12	171
1:15	171n66
2:7–8	172
3:1–5	172
3:1	153
3:8–11	171

Hebrews

	10
2:5–9	282
2:14–16	265
2:14–15	35, 198, 282
2:14	263
2:16–17	202n6
2:17–18	200
2:18	199
3–10	200
3:12	202
4:12	195
5:11–14	202
7:23	200–201n4
7:25	200
7:27	200
8:6–9:15	201
8:8–13	65, 201
9:12	200
9:26	200
9:28	200
10:10	200
10:12–13	200, 202
10:21–23	202
11	202n5
12:1–3	202–3
12:10	54
13	203
13:12–14	203
13:15	83
13:20–21	201

James

	10, 153
1:12–15	131
1:13–16	203–4
1:13	205
2:6–7	207
3:14–16	204
3:15	205
4:7–8	204
4:7	177, 205
4:8–11	205–6
4:10	204
5:1–6	206
5:6	207
5:14–17	11n40
5:14	207

1 Peter

	10, 32, 53, 158
1:2	214
1:7	214
1:14	214
1:15–16	52
1:15	53
1:17	212
1:18	214
1:21	212
2:5	212
2:4–10	62
2:9–10	225
2:9	52
2:12–15	210–11
2:13–3:7	209
2:13–17	153, 243
2:16	211
2:21–25	209, 211, 213
2:21–24	212
2:23	212
3	32
3:6	211
3:9	76
3:9–22	211
3:9–17	212
3:9–13	208
3:9–12	210
3:13–22	211
3:18–22	212
3:18–21	212n21
3:21–22	208
3:22	35, 221, 242, 282, 154
4:5	212
4:6	212, 212n21
4:8–9	36
4:11	212
4:13	211
4:17	212
4:19	212
5:6–7	213
5:7	212

5:8	4	**Jude**	
5:8–9	205, 209, 213		10
5:10–11	213	6	34, 34n53, 57
		7–8	214
2 Peter		9	57, 214
	10	10	34
1:4–7	214–15	16	214
1:4	214	24–25	216
1:9–11	214–15		
2:1	213–14	**Revelation**	
2:6	214		9, 29, 36, 44n18,
2:10	214		51, 53, 71n33,
2:12–16	214		158, 180n14,
2:18–19	213–14		185–86, 293
3	42n14	1:1	192
3:10–14	215–16	1:2	195
3:11–13	258	1:5	192, 195
		1:9	195
1 John		1:10	184
	9, 10n35, 180,	1:13	185
	180n14	1:16	195
1:9	263	2–3	5, 186, 187n31,
2:13–14	31		285
2:15–17	178–79	2:1–7	187
2:15	180n16	2:2	34
3:7–10	180	2:7	195
3:8	179, 199, 321	2:8–11	187
3:12	31	2:11	195
3:13	180	2:12	195
3:24	71	2:12–17	187, 187n35
4:14	179	2:13	192, 195
4:17–18	265	2:17	195
5:3–5	179	2:18–29	188
5:4–5	182	2:26	195
5:18–19	31, 173, 175, 179,	3:1–6	188
	304	3:5	195
5:19	121n54, 241	3:7–13	188
		3:12	195
2 John		3:14	195
	9, 10n35, 180n14	3:14–21	188
		3:21	195
3 John	9, 10n35	4–5	65
		4:8	51–52
		4:11	268
		5:1–6:1	34
		5	193–95

Revelation (continued)

5:5	195
5:6	185
5:12–13	268
5:13	246
6:4	188n36, 305
6:9	195
7	34, 158
7:9–12	197
7:37–39	185
8:1	34
9:20–21	190
11:3	195
11:7	195
11:15	299
11:17–18	65
11:18	185
12–13	189
12:3	327
12:7–11	34, 184
12:7–10	34n53
12:9	153
12:11	195
12:12	4
12:17	195
13–20	189
13	33–34, 152–53
13:1–3	185
13:1	190
13:2–4	190
13:6	190
13:7	195
13:8	190
13:12–15	190
13:16–17	189
13:18	152n9
14:6–13	190
14:9–11	190
15:2–3	195
15:2	34, 195
15:5–16:21	190
16:2	34
16:9–11	190
16:11	190
16:13–14	191
16:16–17	191
16:19	190
17:1–19:10	190
17:1–2	190
17:3	190
17:5	191
17:6	195
17:14	34, 65, 195
17:15	190
17:16–17	27n29
18	185, 188–89
18:2	154, 191
18:9–19	190
18:10	154
19–22	35, 308
19:6–9	34
19:6	268
19:10	195
19:11–16	65, 195
19:11–12	190
19:13–21	195
19:13	191
19:15	195
19:16	196
19:19–20:4	191
19:20–21	190
19:20	191
19:21	196
20	34n53, 328
20:1–15	190
20:2	150, 184, 191, 327
20:4	195
20:7	327
20:10	196
20:14–16	196
21:1–9	190
21:1–4	62, 258
21:2	51
21:3	71
21:6	185
21:7	195
21:9–22:9	190
21:10	52
22:17	185
22:19	52
21–22	187n32, 190
21:22–26	53
21:23	196
22	196

ANCIENT DOCUMENTS INDEX

DEAD SEA SCROLLS

NAMED AND NUMBERED

Rule of the Community (1QS)

1.1–4	74n45
11	66n14

Thanksgiving Hymns (1QH)

5.20–22	66n14

WarScroll (1QM)

	25
14.9–11	119n44

Zadokite/Damascus Document (CD)

4	25
20.17–34	25

NUMBERED ONLY

4Q213a.1.i.10–18	25	8Q5	24n26
4Q491	119n44	11Q5.xix.15	25
4Q560	24n26	11Q11	24n26

RABBINIC WRITINGS

Aboth of R. Nathan

35.9–24	26n27

Baraitha Megillah

17b–18a	26n27

Mishnah Pesahim

10:6	26n27

OTHER JEWISH WORKS

A<small>QIBA</small> xi

Eighteen Benedictions

	305
10	26n27
14	26n27
17	26n27

J<small>OSEPHUS</small>

Antiquities

17.10.5	75n48
17.10.10	75n48

Jewish War

2.9.4	75n47

GRECO-ROMAN WORKS

Cicero

Pro Cluentia

6.15   58n67

Gaius

Institutes

1.63   58n67

EARLY CHRISTIAN NAMED AUTHORS

Aristides

Apology

16.6   233n57

Athenagoras   32

Athanasius   219n1

Incarnation

52.4–6   167n50, 229n44

Cyprian

Treatise

1.3   220n5

Gregory of Nyssa

156n15

Hippolytus

Apostolic Tradition

19   229n43

Commentary on Daniel

3.24.7   233n57

Ignatius

To the Trallians

6–8   220n5

Irenaeus   156n15

Against Heresies

1.13.1–4	220n5
4.34.4	229n43
5.26.2	220n5
40	220, 220n5

John Chrysostom

76n54

Homilies on Matthew

41.2   133n12

Justin Martyr

111, 219–20, 219n1, 223, 291, 291n29, 326

1 Apology

5	220, 220n3
9	220, 220n3
26	220n5
39	229n43
58	220n5

Marcellus   230

MARCION 220, 301

MINUCIUS FELIX
220, 220n4

ORIGEN
111, 219–20, 219n1, 223

Against Celsus
3.7–8	229n43
5.33	229n43
7.65	220, 220n2
8.68–75	167n50, 229n44
8.69	220, 220n2
8.73	233n57

Homily on Numbers
25.4.3	233, 233n59

Selecta in Num.
109n20

TERTULLIAN
xi, 111, 219n1

Against Judaizing Christians
3	229n43
40	220

Apology
26	220n5
32	167n50 229n44
50	184
58	220n5

Prescription against Heretics
40	220, 220n5

THEOPHILUS OF ANTIOCH
219n1

VALENTINUS
220

OTHER EARLY CHRISTIAN WORKS

Apostles' Creed
212n21

Barnabas
2.10	220n5

Gnostics 220

Didache 293

Didascalia apostolorum
9	225
16	225

Diognetus
5.5	63

Shepherd of Hermas, Mandates
9.11	205n10
11:3–4	220n5

Sourcebook 228n38

Syrian Orthodox/Armenian
Baptismal Rites
224–26, 224n24

Lenton Ritual
239, 239n11

Liturgies
225–26, 225n26

OTHER SOURCES

Muhammad   18n12

papyrus, 2nd c.   238n9

Roman coins/inscriptions
158

www.ingramcontent.com/pod-product-compliance
Lightning Source LLC
Chambersburg PA
CBHW021928290426
44108CB00012B/761